Handbook of Worldwide Postal Reform

ADVANCES IN REGULATORY ECONOMICS

Series Editors: Michael A. Crew, *CRRI Professor of Regulatory Economics and Director, Center for Research in Regulated Industries (CRRI), Rutgers, The State University of New Jersey, Newark, USA and* Paul R. Kleindorfer, *Anheuser-Busch Professor Emeritus, The Wharton School, University of Pennsylvania, USA and INSEAD, Fontainebleau, France*

Edited by Michael A. Crew and Paul R. Kleindorfer, this series aims to advance research in theory, practice and policy in the area of regulatory economics. While regulation is all-pervasive in the modern economy and touches almost every aspect of economic life, this series focuses on micro-economic issues in regulation rather than macro policies. Topics of interest include contributions in the following areas: network industries, environmental, health and safety, risk and insurance, and financial services. Regulatory economics deals with both direct instruments affecting profits and prices in these industries and governance structures in regulated industries, including self-regulation. Contributions may address specific instruments across industries as well as in-depth sector-specific studies.

Titles in the series include:

Liberalization of the Postal and Delivery Sector
Edited by Michael A. Crew and Paul R. Kleindorfer

Competition and Regulation in the Postal and Delivery Sector
Edited by Michael A. Crew and Paul R. Kleindorfer

Handbook of Worldwide Postal Reform
Edited by Michael A. Crew, Paul R. Kleindorfer and James I. Campbell Jr.

Handbook of Worldwide Postal Reform

Edited by

Michael A. Crew

Center for Research in Regulated Industries (CRRI), Rutgers, The State University of New Jersey, Newark, USA

Paul R. Kleindorfer

The Wharton School, University of Pennsylvania, USA and INSEAD, France

and

James I. Campbell Jr.

George Mason University, USA

ADVANCES IN REGULATORY ECONOMICS

Edward Elgar
Cheltenham, UK • Northampton, MA, USA

Published by
Edward Elgar Publishing Limited
The Lypiatts
15 Lansdown Road
Cheltenham
Glos GL50 2JA
UK

Edward Elgar Publishing, Inc.
William Pratt House
9 Dewey Court
Northampton
Massachusetts 01060
USA

A catalogue record for this book
is available from the British Library

Library of Congress Control Number: 2008934703

PEFC
PEFC/16-33-111
CATG-PEFC-052
www.pefc.org

ISBN 978 1 84720 957 3

Printed and bound in Great Britain by MPG Books Ltd, Bodmin, Cornwall

Contents

Contributors

Peter Andersson, Associate Professor of Economics, Linköping University, Sweden.

Avi Azuz, Senior Coordinator, Regulation – Economics and Budget Division, Ministry of Communication, Israel.

Kristin Bergum, Director of Governmental and International Affairs, Posten Norge, Oslo, Norway.

Michael D. Bradley, Professor of Economics and International Affairs, George Washington University, Washington, DC, USA.

Martin Buser, Swiss Post, Bern, Switzerland.

James I. Campbell Jr., Attorney and Adjunct Professor, School of Public Policy, George Mason University, Fairfax, VA, USA.

Philippe Claeys, European Government Sector Advisor, PricewaterhouseCoopers, Brussels, Belgium.

Jeff Colvin, Manager – Finance, United States Postal Service, Washington, DC, USA.

Michael A. Crew, CRRI Professor of Regulatory Economics and Director, Center for Research in Regulated Industries (CRRI), Rutgers Business School, Rutgers University, New Brunswick, NJ, USA.

Gonzales d'Alcantara, Senior Lecturer, University of Antwerp and Economic Expert, d'Alcantara Economic Consulting, Belgium.

Alex Kalevi Dieke, Head of Department – Postal Services and Logistics, WIK Wissenschaftliches Institut für Infrastruktur und Kommunikationsdienste, Bad Honnef, Germany.

Jean-Philippe Ducasse, Director, Postal Policy and Strategy, Pitney Bowes, Inc., Stamford, CT, USA.

Richard Eccles, Partner, Bird & Bird, London, UK.

Catherine Gallet-Rybak, Head of Unit Authorizations and Universal Service, ARCEP (Autorité de Régulation des Communications Électroniques et des Postes), Paris, France.

Juan B. Ianni, Postal Policy Expert, Nashville, USA.

Christian Jaag, Economist, Swiss Post and University of St. Gallen, Switzerland.

Luis Jimenez, Consultant, former Senior Vice President and Chief Industry Policy Officer, Pitney Bowes Inc., Stamford, CT, USA.

Paul R. Kleindorfer, Professor Emeritus, The Wharton School, University of Pennsylvania, Philadelphia, PA, USA and Research Professor, INSEAD, Fontainebleau, France.

Bert Kuypers, Partner, PricewaterhouseCoopers, Brussels, Belgium.

Shoji Maruyama, Senior Manager, Japan Post Service Co., Ltd, Tokyo, Japan.

Marc Morelli, former Director, Business Development, Pitney Bowes Inc., Stamford, CT, USA.

Cécile Moreno, ARCEP (Autorité de Régulation des Communications Électroniques et des Postes), Paris, France.

Daniel Nadal, ARCEP (Autorité de Régulation des Communications Électroniques et des Postes), Paris, France.

Antonia Niederprüm, Senior Economist, Department Postal Services and Logistics, WIK Wissenschaftliches Institut für Infrastruktur und Kommunikationsdienste, Bad Honnef, Germany.

Udi Nisan, Director General, Government Companies Authority, Ministry of Finance, Israel.

Andrei Obrea, Senior Fellow, Pitney Bowes, Inc., Shelton, CT, USA.

John C. Panzar, Professor of Economics, University of Auckland, New Zealand and Louis W. Menk Professor Emeritus, Northwestern University, USA.

Chris Paterson, Director, Diversified Specifics, Melbourne, Australia.

Mary K. Perkins, Associate Professor of Economics, Howard University, Washington, DC, USA.

Leon A. Pintsov, Pitney Bowes Fellow and Vice President, Pitney Bowes, Inc., Stamford, CT, USA.

Amelia Porges, Counsel, Sidley Austin LLP, Washington, DC and adjunct professor, Johns Hopkins School of Advanced International Studies, Baltimore, MD, USA.

V. Ranganathan, RBI Chair Professor, Indian Institute of Management, Bangalore, India.

Robert A.F. Reisner, President, Transformation Strategy Inc., Washington, DC, USA.

Eli Sagi, Emeritus Professor, Berglas School of Economics, Tel Aviv University, Israel.

Shinichi Sano, Manager, Japan Post Service Co., Ltd, Tokyo, Japan.

Joëlle Toledano, Commissioner, ARCEP (Autorité de Régulation des Communications Électroniques et des Postes) and Professor of Economics (Supelec), Paris, France.

Urs Trinkner, Economist, Swiss Post and University of Zurich, Switzerland.

Ralf Wojtek, Attorney and Partner, Heuking Kühn Lüer Wojtek, Hamburg, Germany.

Preface and acknowledgements

The origins of this book can be traced back to 1990, when the first Conference on Postal and Delivery Economics was held at Coton House, Rugby, England, July 22–25, 1990, in honor of the 150th anniversary of the Penny Post and the contributions of Sir Rowland Hill. Since then there have been 15 conferences, three workshops, and now 14 edited volumes as part of the CRRI's program on Postal and Delivery Economics. In 1990 it was unclear whether the economics of the postal sector would prove a fruitful ground for research. Indeed, few participants then, including the sponsors, Royal Mail and the International Express Carriers Conference (now the Global Express Association), could have envisaged that research in the postal and delivery sector would take off to the extent that it did, or anticipate the wave of postal reform that followed.

The present volume offers an overview of the multi-faceted international postal reform movement that has been gathering definition and force for two decades (see Chapter 1). The book aims to acquaint the reader with some of the background of postal reform and to impart a basic understanding of the nature of the postal and delivery sector and why fundamental reform has been introduced despite strong opposition. The book is also forward looking, offering insights into the future direction of reform and identifying principles that will guide forthcoming policy and regulation of the postal sector.

The editors have a long history of collaboration and an abiding interest in regulatory reform. Michael Crew and Paul Kleindorfer have worked together since 1969. Their work on the postal sector has been supported by the Postal Conferences, starting in 1990. Jim Campbell has been a regular presenter at these conferences over the years and, as the representative of the express companies, was especially important in helping to organize the first ones. His first experience with regulatory reform dates from the mid-1970s when he was a young lawyer working for Senator Edward Kennedy in a series of Senate hearings that ultimately led to deregulation of the US aviation system in 1978.

The editors owe a debt of gratitude to sponsors of the Postal Conferences, which is acknowledged elsewhere in books resulting from the conferences. However, there are some individuals without whom this book would not have been possible. First and foremost the book would not have been possible without the cooperation of the authors of this volume. Second, the contribution of Paul Richards and Roger Tabor, formerly of Royal Mail, in taking the risk in sponsoring the first conference must not be underestimated. It marked the beginning of the significant interest and research that have developed in the area. Others were of assistance along the road, including Marc Smith, of the United States Postal Service. Marc was instrumental in providing powerful encouragement to Crew and Kleindorfer to work in the area of postal economics and coauthored two papers with them.

Finally, we express our gratitude to the numerous participants in the Postal

Conferences that have shaped our own thinking over the years on postal economics and who have in the process given energy and direction to the postal reform efforts that are the focus of this volume.

Michael A. Crew, Paul R. Kleindorfer and James I. Campbell Jr.

1. Postal reform: introduction

Michael A. Crew[†]**, Paul R. Kleindorfer**[‡] **and James I. Campbell Jr.**[§]

1. INTRODUCTION AND ORIGINS OF POSTAL REFORM

Although Herodotus wrote admiringly of Persian messengers undaunted by 'either snow, or rain, or heat, or darkness of night', not the Persian Empire, or the Greek city states, or the Chinese Emperors, or the Senate and People of Rome ever developed a service that is comparable to what is today known as a 'postal service'. None provided a universal collection and delivery service for documents and parcels. Persian messengers and their successors were, government couriers to whom the citizen had no access.

The concept of a public service for the transmission of documents developed gradually with the development of Europe after the Middle Ages. In the twelfth century, inexpensive paper (as opposed to parchment) was introduced. Enterprising Venetian merchants of the fourteenth century organized private courier systems to deliver commercial documents, eventually extending their reach into the German hinterland. The Renaissance saw, after centuries of repression, the reemergence of scholarly exchanges of ideas. Monasteries and universities, notably the University of Paris, began to organize messenger systems. In the fifteenth century, the invention of a printing press with moveable type accelerated the dissemination of ideas.

The fifteenth and sixteenth centuries saw the slow emergence of nation states in France and England. Royal governments sought to ban private messenger services, especially international services, as part of the process of consolidating their authority. Postal communications thus became a government monopoly. At the same time, to sustain and facilitate commerce, government courier systems were opened to the public.

In the nineteenth century, the new technologies of the Industrial Revolution prompted reconsideration of a broad range of social institutions including the national post office. In 1840, Great Britain radically reduced and simplified postage rates and introduced the practice of prepaying postage at a uniform rate irrespective of origin and destination by means of adhesive stamps. It would be difficult to exaggerate the impact of this change in the development of modern postal systems. The British reforms were rapidly adopted in other countries. For the first time, the postal service became affordable for ordinary communications by the common man. Mail volumes exploded, paving the way for eventual development of the modern, affordable, universal postal service of today.

† Rutgers University.
‡ Wharton School and INSEAD.
§ George Mason University.

Mail service originated as a government function and has remained a government function almost universally until recently. So it was not surprising that national post offices (POs)[1] were run as government bureaucracies and not as commercial enterprises. In the last half-century some steps were taken to change the status of POs from government departments to government-owned corporations. The most notable of these changes in governance was probably the Postal Reorganization Act of 1970 (PRA) in the United States which, in creating the United States Postal Service (USPS), moved the US Post Office a step away from a government department.

At the end of the twentieth century, another wave of technological advances has transformed infrastructure industries and the way they are regulated by government. Once again, fundamental post reform is necessary. Some would suggest that this process began with the laws that changed national post offices into more independent, 'business-like' government agencies, for example, the British Post Office Act of 1969 and the US PRA of 1970. Others would point to the division of ministries for post, telephone, and telegraph (PTTs) into separate postal and telecommunications agencies, for example, the British Telecommunications Act of 1981 or the German Postreform I of 1989. However, the present wave of fundamental postal reform originated arguably in 1988, when the European Union (EU) began work on a regional postal policy and the government of New Zealand first broached the idea of repealing the post monopoly.

From these stirrings a wave of postal reform has spread across the globe. Important milestones include publication of the European Postal Green Paper (1992), publication of the Australian Industry Commission Report (1992), repeal of the Swedish postal monopoly (1993), substantial privatization of the Dutch Post Office (1994), adoption of the European Postal Directive (1997), enactment of an end date for the German postal monopoly and creation of a German regulator in Postreform III (1997), repeal of the New Zealand postal monopoly (1998), creation of a British postal regulator with authority to end the postal monopoly (2000), substantial privatization of Deutsche Post (2000), privatization of the Japanese Post Office (2005), the initial public offering (IPO) of Österreichische Post (2007) and adoption in 2008 of a Third European Postal Directive setting an end date for all postal monopolies in Europe as of 2011 for most countries and 2013 for the remaining. Asia, Latin America and others have joined this wave of postal reform, with restructuring of national POs, regulatory authorities and increasing liberalization of postal markets.

Postal reform may be considered part of a broader movement worldwide, which included privatization of network industries. The intellectual foundations of the movement might be traced to an uprising in economic thinking in the 1970s and 1980s, which argued for the greater use of market forces and greater commercial orientation rather than bureaucratic structures in major sectors of the economy. This uprising was visible in different countries at different times. With sectors such as aviation, telecommunications, and energy leading the way, governments turned to privatization, new regulatory forms, lower entry barriers, and other forms of market liberalization. The postal sector seemed immune to these currents for a long time. However, the increasing need to integrate postal operations with other means of communications and the increasing need to come to grips with electronic substitution and technology change have pushed the postal sector inexorably in the direction of commercialization and markets. Finding an appropriate confluence with these trends is the primary objective of postal reform.

This book will examine a number of aspects of postal reform including the origins of the postal monopoly and universal postal service and the relationship between the monopoly (or the reserved area) and the legal obligation to maintain universal service (the universal service obligation or USO). Such considerations are at the heart of the postal reform debate and will be a prominent and continuing theme in this book. This debate will be apparent in many chapters that follow, including the studies of individual countries or regions provided in the book. This chapter sets the scene for the book by providing, in Section 2, a sketch of reform in a number of countries and, in Section 3, some highlights of the chapters that follow.

2. POSTAL REFORM WORLDWIDE

Postal reform is taking a firm hold around the world. The driving force is undoubtedly the changes that have been occasioned by increased competition, first by the emergence of substantial private express companies in the 1980s and second, and more importantly, by the evolution of the Internet of other electronic services in the 1990s. Electronic competition, in particular, means that POs are facing declining demand for the letter mail that not only provides higher margins than, for example, newspapers and advertising mail, but has traditionally been the *raison of d'être* of the government post. So POs are facing increasing financial pressure through electronic competition. For most governments, an increasingly competitive environment clearly implies the need to allow POs to operate more efficiently and more like commercial companies as opposed to government bureaucracies. This transformation requires not only operational changes but also the freedom to price in a more commercial manner. At the same time, governments are unwilling to allow POs to follow commercial logic to the point of cutting back on politically popular services in areas of the country or for portions of the population.

Therefore, in granting commercial flexibility, governments have also found it necessary to define with precision the standards of universal postal service which must be maintained, that is, the USO. And governments, or their post offices, still have to finance the USO as traditional postal markets are being eroded. Yet, at the same time, it is generally agreed that the need to finance the USO or expand into new markets does not justify the extraction of monopoly rents from captured mailers or the use of predatory pricing against competitors. This three-way balancing among commercial flexibility, universal service, and fair competition has been a continuing theme in the postal reform area and will continue to be for the foreseeable future. We start with a brief overview of some of the major developments to highlight the approaches taken towards this issue and other issues arising from competitive entry into traditional postal markets.

The Netherlands and New Zealand were among the first of the postal services to recognize the importance of becoming more commercialized (Toime, 1991), followed closely thereafter by Sweden, which opened its markets to competition in 1993. The Netherlands and Germany embraced privatization, while New Zealand Post and Sweden Post adopted a corporate structure and have remained wholly owned by the government.

Across Europe, a major restructuring of the postal sector across all 27 member states of the EU is well underway. Shortly after the formal opening of the European internal market in 1992, the postal and logistics sector was recognized as a sector in need of reform. The Postal Directive of 1997, as amended in 2002 and 2008, is moving the EU to a full opening of the postal market to competition by January 1, 2011.[2] Full market opening means, among other things, no statutory monopoly privileges (that is, no 'reserved area') for any of the components of the postal value chain or for any postal products. Thus, competitors will be free to collect, sort, and deliver all types of documents and parcels whenever and wherever they wish. The impending market opening is transforming the European postal sector from a slow-moving government service, with a limited range of traditional products and excess employment, into a vibrant new industry. Crew and Kleindorfer (2006 and 2008) provide details of the ongoing transformation of European postal markets.

Some of the countries that are implementing wide-ranging postal reform have done so through changes in regulation and corporate structure directed at promoting commercialization of the national PO. A common approach has been to promote strong management incentives for performance through executive profit targets as, for example, in Australia, Canada, Sweden and New Zealand, where the post offices are organized as corporations, with a for-profit, commercial culture, but with the government still the sole owner. Other countries are headed to full privatization. Today (February 2008), 69 percent of equity in the postal service is privately owned in Germany and 100 percent in the Netherlands and Malta.

In addition, Post Danmark A/S recently transformed itself into a public limited company (that is, a corporation), and then began a process of privatization; 25 percent of its shares are now owned by a private investor. In 2005, Post Danmark and its investor, in turn, bought 50 percent of the Belgian Post Office (La Poste). The Austrian Post Office (Österreicherische Post AG) began the process of privatization with an IPO in 2006, in line with the changes that are occurring in Europe in communications markets as well as in parcel and express markets. The first tranche of shares in the Austrian Post Office, amounting to 49 percent of the business, were sold in an oversubscribed IPO, and shares began trading on the Vienna Exchange on May 31, 2006. The Italian Post Office (Poste Italiane) has also announced the possibility of an IPO. Japan Post is a further interesting case of privatization, which was the central issue in the Japanese parliamentary elections in 2005 (see Campbell and Porges, Chapter 21, this volume).

The above represents some highlights of the fast-moving developments in the postal arena outside the United States. To give a sense of some of the important details that have occurred, we shall briefly summarize the experiences of four countries: New Zealand and Sweden, which were early entrants to postal reform and have remained corporatized but not privatized operators; and Germany and the Netherlands, the two largest privatizers. Sweden is examined in more detail in Chapter 17 by Andersson in this volume, and aspects of the other three countries are also covered in the chapters that follow. This brief review of the experiences of these leaders in the postal reform area aims at setting out some of the main issues that are at stake in the postal reform movement.

2.1 Commercialization: New Zealand Post and Swedish Post

New Zealand Post and Sweden Post were early adopters of a commercialization approach. New Zealand Post is chartered and organized as a corporate entity and is expected to be run as a business: specifically, it is expected to give its primary shareholder, the government, a reasonable return on invested capital. It is also expected to maintain a specified minimum level of national postal services agreed with government; since April 1998 it has done so with an open market without a reserved area. Executives face performance-based executive compensation systems, modeled after the private sector with which they compete for managerial talent. Shares in the corporation are owned by the Ministry of Finance and the Ministry of State Owned Enterprises. There is virtually no sector-specific regulation of postal operators except a registration procedure and consumer-protection measures administered by the Ministry of Economic Development. The combination of corporate structure, a charter that underlines the commercial nature of their activities, proper incentives for management, and light-handed regulation have all combined to make New Zealand Post a successful business venture. Reflecting the efficiency improvements associated with commercialization, revenue per employee has more than doubled in nominal terms, while the real price of a single-piece stamp has fallen by almost a third during the 1987–2004 period.

In Sweden, the market was fully opened to competition in 1994, with Sweden Post (known as Sverige Posten AB) maintaining responsibility for the USO. The price of a single-piece stamp was increased dramatically, by 38 percent between 1993 and 1997, but subsequently moderated. In addition, Sweden Post took action to change the way it provided universal service: the number of full-service postal counters was decreased dramatically after liberalization, with extensive franchising taking place. Similarly, in high-cost rural areas, fixed counter services were replaced by rural postmen/women who delivered the mail and sold postal services. These and other activities by Sweden Post have led to significant cost savings and improved quality of service (measured by the percentage of mail meeting its delivery requirements). Faced with competition in major urban areas because of the open market, Sweden Post has undertaken significant restructuring to better align the cost, value and prices of its services with customer demand. Although fully owned by the government, Sweden Post's status and culture as a for-profit corporation and the competition it faces have made Sweden Post an oft-cited example to illustrate the benefits of corporatization and competition.

Posten turned out to be a formidable competitor, so formidable that it quickly faced antitrust action from its major competitor, CityMail, which complained of Posten's discriminatory pricing and other practices. Ultimately a settlement was reached. Interestingly, CityMail has changed ownership a number of times. It has rarely reported profits, though it did so in 2005 and may now have finally reached a stage of profitability under the ownership of Norway Post. The Swedish case raises interesting issues of the conflicts of interest created by public enterprise. Where a PO acts in a commercial manner and prices aggressively, it may be subject to antitrust action. If the PO is publicly owned, the government has a conflict of interest in enforcing antitrust actions against a company it owns.

Commercialization without privatization thus introduces inevitable anomalies. While legal institutions may provide adequate safeguards, at a minimum public ownership makes the application of competition law less straightforward than when two privately owned companies are parties to an antitrust dispute. A further difficulty with commercialization relative to privatization is that executive compensation is not related to an exogenous index of value like stock price and, thus, attempts to link compensation to performance are subject to additional problems of both measurement and legitimating. Perhaps most significantly, absence of private ownership means that public postal operators are not subject to the scrutiny and discipline of capital markets.

Table 1.1 TNT: then and now, 1989 to 2005

	1989 (=PTT Post)	2005
Total employment (full-time equivalents, average for the year)	59,300	128,307
Employment in postal operations	59,300	77,447
Employment in express and courier services	NA	50,860
Service quality D+1 letter mail	D+1: 93%	D+1: 97%
Single-piece letter mail price	€0.34	€0.39
Total postal revenues from letter mail, parcels & express services [2]	1.9	10.1
Revenues from mail[2]	NA	4.0
Revenues from express services[2]	NA	6.1

Notes

1. The employment figures here do not reflect the additional 35,007 employees who are part of the TNT Logistics Group. According to the TNT Annual Report 2005, the TNT Logistics Group is being divested in order for TNT to focus entirely on its core delivery network businesses, for both mail and parcels. Employment and revenue figures for the Logistics Group are therefore excluded from this table. Similarly, telecommunications activities were included in KPN in 1989, and these figures have also been excluded in the above table.
2. Revenues are in billions of euros. Excluded here are revenues from financial services and logistics services not directly connected to TNT's delivery network businesses. Including such revenues for 2005 would yield total operating revenues for TNT of €13.6 billion as reported in the 2005 TNT Annual Report.

Sources: PTT, Annual Report 1989 (PTT Post only); TNT, Annual Report 2005.

2.2 Privatization: The Netherlands and Germany

The Netherlands changed the structure of its post office in 1989 from a state enterprise to a private company whose stock was entirely owned by the government. As it turned out, this change was the first step towards full privatization. A close commercial relationship began to develop between the Dutch post office and TNT, an international express carrier with its origins in Australia. In 1994, the flotation of the Dutch Post as part of KPN (the combined postal and telecommunications operator) took place on the Amsterdam Stock Exchange. In 1996, KPN acquired TNT. In 1998, KPN 'demerged' into two companies, the new KPN, a telecommunications company, and TNT Post Group (TPG), a post and transportation company. In 2005, the various strands of the relevant business were regrouped and renamed as TNT. As Table 1.1 shows, TNT is now a large company with around 128,000 employees and revenues of €10.1 billion in 2005 from its postal businesses. Its success has arisen from a solid base of mail revenue upon which to build, but its more recent activity is clearly global in scope, reaching out in both the express area and in letter-mail activities in various countries. TNT has used its privatized status, and its improved knowledge of investor relations and markets, to gain an early-mover advantage in many of the growing areas of business-to-business and business-to-consumer commerce. It is now a force to be reckoned with in traditional mail, express and parcel markets, and supporting infrastructure, as well as in international trade.

The German privatization story begins with 'Postreform I' adopted in 1989. Postreform I created separate departments within the Ministry for Posts and Telecommunications for

Table 1.2 Deutsche Post: then and now, 1989 to 2005

	1989	2005
Employment figures (full-time equivalents, average of the year) Total employment	272,491[1]	347,607
Employment in postal operations	232,985	129,200
Employment in other operations	39,506[1]	218,407
Service quality D+1 and D+2 letter mail	D+1: 76% D+2: 95% [2]	D+1: >95% D+2: >99%
Single-piece letter-mail price	€0.51 [3]	€0.55
Revenue figures (€bn) Total revenue	9.3 [1]	44.6
Letter-mail revenues	NA	12.9
Postal revenues (letter mail, parcel and express services) [4]	8.2	31.2
Revenue from all other operations	1.1[1]	13.4

Notes:

1. Note: in 1989 Deutsche Post also provided telecommunications services. However, all figures given here exclude telecommunications services. The figures for 1989 do not include the 86,000 employees that Deutsche Post absorbed in 1990 from the former East German Post Office after reunification of East and West Germany. Thus, the reduction in employment in postal operations is even more pronounced than is apparent from these comparisons for the years 1989 and 2005.
2. Figures for the year 1991 (no exact measurements before that year).
3. €0.51 = 1.00 DM; price as of 1 April 1989.
4. Excluding financial services and logistics.

Sources: Deutsche Bundespost, Annual Report 1989; DPWN, Annual Report 2005.

postal services, postal banking, and telecommunications. The new Board of Directors of the postal agency, Deutsche Bundespost Postdienst (German Federal Postal Service), introduced a greater degree of private sector management and accounting practices. Further legislative and operational reforms followed, culminating in the sale of around a third of the equity in 2000 in an IPO. At the beginning of 2008, private investors own 69 percent of what is now called Deutsche Post World Net (DPWN). In consort with these changes, the reserved area was completely eliminated as of 1 January 2008.

DPWN has become a force of change in the postal market worldwide; privatization has transformed a once sleepy bureaucracy into a major multinational corporation. Maschke (2002) describes the transformation process of the German Post Office into the corporate giant DPWN over the course of the 1990s and early 2000s. The compensation structure was transformed and managers imported from other industries, the mail and parcels network were modernized within Germany, and new products (such as hybrid mail and e-commerce) were developed. DPWN now has interests not only in the traditional mail and parcels businesses, but also in express mail, logistics, banking, and more. Indeed, DPWN has grown to a company with sales of €44.6 billion in 2005 and total employment of nearly 350,000, making it one of the world's largest corporations.

The extent of the transformation is highlighted by comparing Deutsche Bundespost in 1989 and DPWN in 2005 as illustrated in Table 1.2. Total employment in postal operations was more than halved, and the 1989 figures in Table 1.2 do not even reflect the additional 86,000 employees absorbed in 1990 from the former East German Post Office. Notwithstanding the employment reductions in postal operations, total employment in the firm rose by around 25 percent over the 1989–2005 period. As traditional employment opportunities declined, new opportunities were opened up in other growing businesses in the overall enterprise. In addition, service quality improved, alleviating the concern that a profit-oriented business might skimp on quality relative to a public enterprise. The price of a single-piece stamp also fell significantly in real terms, reflecting internal restructuring and improvements in operating efficiency.

2.3 The United States: Separating Market Dominant and Competitive Products

The 2006 Postal Accountability and Enhancement Act (PAEA) enacted a number of significant changes to the Postal Reorganization Act (PRA) of 1970. Many of these changes relate to the modernization of the operational, financial, and management structures of the USPS in the light of increased competition and USPS's continuing requirement to meet its USO. In addition, the PAEA includes a number of provisions that require separate accounts and reports for USPS's competitive products, that is, those products that compete with similar products offered by commercial entities. Given the size and importance of USPS for the postal industry, the history and structure of the postal reform movement in the United States is described in several chapters in this volume, as we note in greater detail in the next section. These chapters contrast the approach taken in the US to that of the four countries above, which are clearly further along the postal reform path than the US. While the developments envisaged in the US under the PAEA do not go as far, they must still be seen in the context of major secular trends affecting postal service, particularly competition from electronic media, postal regulatory reform, and the opening up of postal markets worldwide to increased competition. USPS is clearly part of major changes that are affecting the postal sector worldwide and the PAEA is a partial reflection of this.

2.4 Commercialization as the Central Objective of International Postal Reform

Nations across the world are opening up their postal systems to commercialization and in a growing number of cases to privatization. They often had a unionized workforce before and after reform. In addition, workers in some countries enjoyed civil servant status. The combination of these two factors gave rise to wage and benefit terms that were often in excess of competitive levels, often exacerbated by the legacy costs of pensions or healthcare commitments made to earlier generations of postal workers now or soon-to-be retired. Anyone designing and implementing changes in governance and regulation for POs thus faces a number of major problems, in addition to the environmental changes encompassing electronic substitution. It is no surprise, therefore, that postal reform and commercialization of POs remains a work in progress in many countries. Nonetheless, the direction of change is clear, and there is growing evidence of the benefits from change. What is emerging from international efforts to date is that, when coupled with appropriate changes in regulation and commercial restructuring of the national PO, allowing greater competition into the market for postal services can provide an important spur to efficiency and innovation for both corporatized and privatized post offices. This spur is needed to allow POs and other stakeholders to adapt efficiently to the fundamental changes that continue to transform broader communications markets.

3. THE WAY AHEAD

The book addresses three principal topics: Economic Analysis of Reform (Part I), Transformation and Innovation (Part II), and Regional and Country Studies (Part III). The first provides some of the analytical foundations for the postal reform movement; the second examines how the postal sector is reinventing or transforming itself through organizational change and technological innovation; and the third examines some of the significant developments taking place across specific countries and regions. The coverage is intended to be illustrative rather than provide comprehensive global coverage.

The analytical foundations of the postal reform movement rest on the deregulation movement that began in the 1970s and is outlined in the survey of regulatory economics by Crew and Kleindorfer (2002). A landmark event, if not *the* landmark event in the deregulation movement, was the divestiture by AT&T of its operating companies in 1984.[3] John Panzar recognizes the importance of the AT&T case as a principal motivator of his chapter on antitrust policy and regulation (Chapter 2). The AT&T case broke new ground by reducing the considerable immunity offered by regulation to prosecution under antitrust law, or competition law as it is usually known outside the US. Panzar argues, *inter alia*, that with an increasingly commercial orientation, POs are facing challenges under antitrust law as well as under regulation. In addition, he indicates some areas where regulation and antitrust may be rivals. Indeed, as Richard Eccles notes in his chapter on legal developments in the EU, there may be instances where regulation takes on the role normally taken by antitrust. From reading Eccles and Panzar there should be little doubt that antitrust will be a powerful force in the future of POs under full market opening (FMO).

In Chapter 3, Crew and Kleindorfer address access, an area that is of serious concern to regulators and could concern competition authorities. Given the scale economies in delivery and the ubiquitous coverage by POs, specifying the terms under which the PO should provide access to its network by its competitors is currently an important issue and likely to become more so. Access continues to be a major issue in other network industries, notably, telecommunications. While Crew and Kleindorfer note the experience of other industries, their chapter primarily surveys the issues of access in the postal sector, drawing on the developing literature on the topic. In Chapter 4, Michael Bradley, Jeff Colvin, and Mary K. Perkins examine a topic that figures prominently in Crew and Kleindorfer's chapter on access, namely, the role of price-cap regulation (PCR). In postal regulation, PCR has become the dominant form of regulation. One of the major changes in US postal law introduced by the PAEA is the adoption of PCR. Bradley et al. examine the impact that PCR is likely to have on the future of USPS.

The USO has played a very prominent role in the postal reform debate. Funding and costing of the USO are addressed by John Panzar (Chapter 6) and by Kristin Bergum (Chapter 7). Panzar provides some general background to the cost of the USO and an approach to costing it. Bergum provides an interesting case study of how one country, Norway, has addressed in an innovative manner the issue of costing and funding the USO. Norway's case describes the method that is used there to determine compensation from the government for Posten Norge based upon estimates of the cost of the USO. In Chapter 5, Martin Buser, Christian Jaag and Urs Trinkner address another important aspect of the USO, namely, the effect of density of post offices on mail demand. Their chapter contains a number of new wrinkles. Of especial interest is their comparison of the impact on financial viability and the extent of the network if banking and similar services are provided at post offices. Their chapter throws new light on issues of economies of scope.

As transformation and innovation have figured prominently in the postal reform movement, it is fitting that the topic should be covered in this book. As a result of postal reform, POs have been required to reinvent or transform themselves. In addition, they have not been able to ignore the revolution that has taken place in microelectronics and fiber optics. The Internet continues to transform the way in which almost everyone does business, and POs are not immune from its impact. Chapter 8 by Crew and Kleindorfer, and Chapter 9 by Robert Reisner, examine how USPS is transforming itself. They evaluate progress and indicate where further change is needed. Crew and Kleindorfer criticize the PAEA for providing little real reform. They argue that it may have provided too little too late for USPS to avoid much more serious disruption down the road. They examine not only shortcomings in the PAEA but also the possible role of privatization in the future of USPS. On the other hand Reisner, a former Vice President for Strategic Planning at USPS, argues that USPS has achieved a considerable degree of transformation within the constraints it faces. The question is whether the transformation has been sufficient. Crew and Kleindorfer argue that it has not. Reisner leaves the question open.

The role of technological innovation in the postal industry is examined in Chapter 10 by Jean-Philippe Ducasse, Luis Jimenez and Marc Morelli and in Chapter 11 by Leon A. Pintsov and Andrei Obrea. Given their common employer, Pitney Bowes, it is not surprising that they all have a deep interest in the future of mail. Ducasse et al. examine the impact of the microelectronic revolution and the Internet on the future of mail. They see important consequences of the empowerment of mailers arising out of the technological revolution. They examine ways to sustain the demand for mail, for example, through the use of advances in database management. Pinstov and Obrea take the summary of possible innovations in mail a step further and show how the electronic and the physical can be brought together to provide many enhancements not present in traditional mail. They examine the details of what customer empowerment means. They envisage a postal world where customers themselves play a role in product design. For POs what they are proposing may be revolutionary, as it involves an entirely more proactive role by POs in working with their customers. The challenge they throw down is ostensibly daunting. However, capabilities that the electronic and Internet revolutions offer to meet the challenge appear very promising. Not only must POs reinvent themselves, but the technology is here for them to do so, in particular in the areas of improved marketing and innovative products.

While Part III, Regional and Country Studies, is inevitably the longest of the three parts, it still has, of necessity, a number of omissions. An overview of regulatory and other developments of selected POs in Asia is provided by Shoji Maruyama and Shinichi Sano (Chapter 20). Jim Campbell and Amelia Porges (Chapter 21) analyze in more detail the new postal privatization law in Japan. Chris Paterson (Chapter 22) contributes a study of Australia Post. Australia is a case where reform has been limited. Australia Post continues to benefit from a reserved area, and there appear to be no plans for radical change along the lines of the FMO in Europe. In some ways the Australian story makes a powerful case for gradual reform as opposed to radical reform. It is also a case for light-handed regulation. Australia Post is not regulated by a sector regulator but by the Australia Competition and Consumer Commission.

Postal reform in developing countries generally is the topic of Chapter 23, by Juan B. Ianni. Drawing on his experience as a postal policy analyst for the World Bank, Ianni questions the benefits of the USO for emerging economies and looks to competition to provide postal and delivery services where volumes are so low that scale and scope economies are non-existent. This view should be weighed against the approach put forth by Ansón et al. (2006), whose studies have been influential at the Universal Postal Union. India, one of the most important developing countries, is examined by V. Ranganathan (Chapter 24). India Post faces major problems driven by a stifling bureaucracy, lost opportunities, and significant subsidization. Potential for reform in India is significant, but changes to date have barely scratched the surface. Israel provides another interesting case study in a study by Avi Azuz, Udi Nisan and Eli Sagi (Chapter 25). The authors had the opportunity to influence the process of reform in Israel as all three served on the committee that recommended the reforms.

In any treatise on postal reform the star has to be the European Union, which has made the most significant changes in postal markets, including its plans for full market opening of all EU member states by 2013. The impact of the reforms in the EU has been considerable. Deutsche Post and TNT have transformed themselves from bureaucracies into major international corporations. Klaus Zumwinkel led the dramatic transformation of Deutsche Post into a world leader in courier, logistics and parcel service, comparable in many ways with the two leaders worldwide, UPS and FedEx. The transformation of the Dutch PO into a leader in the sector tells a similar story, the main difference being the size of the two companies (so far). Reflecting the important place occupied by Germany in the postal reform movement, Alex Kalevi Dieke and Ralf Wojtek (Chapter 16) provide a discussion of the government's recent adoption of a minimum wage law which applies to the postal sector only. While the relation between wages in the postal sector and those in the general economy has been debated for many years (see, for example, Wachter and Perloff, 1991), this chapter adds to this debate by examining the legal, political and economic considerations underlying the change in the German law.

Michael Crew, Gonzales d'Alcantara, Paul R. Kleindorfer, Philippe Claeys and Bert Kuypers (Chapter 13) review the likely economic impact of FMO across member states in the EU. Some are better prepared than others. Yet the legal and regulatory changes that have already taken place are considerable, as shown in Chapter 12 by Jim Campbell, Alex Dieke and Antonia Niederprüm in their review of the legal and regulatory landscape on the eve of the Third Postal Directive. In Chapter 14, Richard Eccles examines the implications of the Third Postal Directive and some of the legal principles underlying the postal policy at the EU level. Jim Campbell (Chapter 15) also provides a brief historical overview of the United States postal monopoly law; his account suggests that the need to fund the USO was not the primary driver of the monopoly law in the United States.

No discussion of postal reform would be complete without some discussion of Sweden, France, and the UK. Sweden and the UK were both early adopters of FMO. Sweden was well ahead of the rest of Europe with its repeal of postal monopoly in 1993. Peter Andersson (Chapter 17) reviews the results of the opening up of the Swedish market, including its effects on competition and consumers. France is notable in that it was initially opposed to FMO but was the leading protagonist among European POs of worksharing and access. Major changes are in store for France with FMO. Significant developments are already underway, as described in Chapter 18 by Catherine

Gallet-Rybak, Cécile Moreno, Daniel Nadal and Joëlle Toledano in their analysis of the French postal market in the wake of the Postal Law of 2005. Finally, there is the UK, where regulatory change has been considerable. The postal regulator, Postcomm, is regarded by many as the most active in the world. It brought about FMO in 2006, well ahead of the rest of Europe. In Chapter 19, Richard Eccles reviews the regulations and policies of Postcomm and their impact on the postal market.

Postal reform is a continuing story, so this book cannot hope to offer the final word. For many, the 'proof of the pudding' will be revealed by the outcome and aftermath of the liberalization in Europe, which begins for most of the EU on January 1, 2011. Others will have to wait longer, perhaps much longer, before they will be able to evaluate the benefits and costs of postal reform. This book is at least intended to prepare the reader for some of the possible outcomes that might unfold.

NOTES

1. Throughout the book the abbreviation, PO, will be used to mean national post office or postal operator. Where the term 'post office' is used, it will be to describe a postal retail outlet.
2. Full market opening is delayed for some EU countries until January 1, 2013.
3. William Kovacic, who is now Chairman of the United States Federal Trade Commission, evaluated this case, *United States v. AT&T Co*, as 'probably the most important judicial decision in the field of economic regulation in the past 20 years' (Kovacic, 2002, p. 25).

REFERENCES

Ansón, J., R. Cuadra, A. Lindares, G. Ronderos and J. Toledano (2006), 'First steps towards new postal economics models for developing countries: learning from the Latin American experience', in M.A. Crew and P.R. Kleindorfer (eds), *Liberalization of the Postal and Delivery Sector*, Cheltenham, UK and Northampton, USA: Edward Elgar, pp. 217–36.

Crew, Michael A. and Paul R. Kleindorfer (2002), 'Regulatory economics: twenty years of progress?', *Journal of Regulatory Economics*, **21** (1) January: 5–22.

Crew, Michael A. and Paul R. Kleindorfer (2006), 'Approaches to USO under entry', in Michael A. Crew and Paul R. Kleindorfer (eds), *Liberalization of the Postal and Delivery Sector*, Cheltenham, UK and Northampton, USA: Edward Elgar, pp. 1–18.

Crew, Michael A. and Paul R. Kleindorfer (2008), 'Regulation and the USO', in Michael A. Crew and Paul R. Kleindorfer (eds), *Competition and Regulation in the Postal and Delivery Sector*, Cheltenham, UK and Northampton, USA: Edward Elgar, pp. 3–22.

Kovacic, William E. (2002), 'Economic regulation and the courts 1982–2001: ten cases that made a difference', *Journal of Regulatory Economics*, **21** (1) January: 23–34.

Maschke, Walter (2002), 'Transformation at Deutsche Post World Net using the example of socially compatible workprice adjustment', in Michael A. Crew and Paul R. Kleindorfer (eds), *Postal and Delivery Services: Delivering on Competition*, Boston, MA: Kluwer Academic, pp. 303–20.

Toime, Elmar (1991), 'Competitive strategy for New Zealand Post', in Michael A. Crew and Paul R. Kleindorfer (eds), *Competition and Innovation in Postal Services*, Boston, MA: Kluwer Academic, pp. 275–82.

Wachter, Michael L. and Jeffrey M. Perloff (1991), 'A comparative analysis of wage premiums and industrial relations in the British Post Office and the United States Postal Service', in Michael A. Crew and Paul R. Kleindorfer (eds), *Competition and Innovation in Postal Services*, Boston, MA: Kluwer Academic, pp. 115–38.

PART I

Economic analysis of reform

2. Interactions between regulatory and antitrust policies in a liberalized postal sector

John C. Panzar†

1. INTRODUCTION AND SUMMARY

Liberalization has brought many changes to the postal sector. In the European Union (EU) and elsewhere, recent decades have seen the 'corporatization' of postal operators. Posts have been transformed from ministries or government departments into more commercial enterprises. While privatization has been relatively rare, posts are typically subject to economic regulation by an independent regulator. The 'full market opening' of the postal sector (scheduled for most countries in the EU for 2011) will likely bring with it additional scrutiny from competition authorities. In the US, the Postal Accountability and Enhancement Act of 2006 (PAEA) subjects the United States Postal Service (USPS) to antitrust scrutiny for the first time in its history. The liberalization experience of other vertically integrated network industries such as telecommunications and electric power have illustrated that the issues facing postal regulators and competition authorities are likely to be closely linked.

Historically, the postal sector was largely insulated from both regulatory and antitrust control. Not only was the post a state-owned enterprise (SOE), in most countries it was also an integral part of the government. For example, in the United States, the Postmaster General was a cabinet-level position, while in many European countries the post was part of a government ministry: for example, the 'Ministry of Posts and Telecommunications'. Under these circumstances, there was little if any room for regulatory or competition policy to operate: 'postal policy' *was* government policy.

This situation changed dramatically in the US with the Postal Reorganization Act of 1970 (PRA). USPS was established as a government corporation whose operational decisions were removed from the political process. Importantly, the PRA mandated that the Postal Service operate essentially without direct government subsidy: that is, its operating expenses must be recovered through rates. The PRA also created the Postal Rate Commission as a semi-independent regulatory body to approve the structure of postal rates. Thus a system of cost-plus, public-utility-style rate regulation was introduced into the postal sector. However, as continued to be the case in other network industries such as telecommunications and electric power, the USPS markets were not generally opened to competition under this new regime. In contrast, corporatization did not get seriously

† Northwestern University and the University of Auckland.

underway in Europe until the 1990s, following the issuance of the Green Paper by the European Commission.

Traditionally, antitrust (or competition) policy is an *ex post* form of government intervention. That is, the antitrust authorities monitor the actions of market participants and take corrective action *after the fact* if a violation is found as a result of a judicial proceeding. In contrast, regulatory authorities act primarily on an *ex ante* basis. They formulate policies and procedures that usually are put in place *before* the firm takes its market actions.

In the United States, this distinction began to blur with the break-up of AT&T. A major premise of the Justice Department's antitrust case was that the Federal Communications Commission (FCC) and state regulation of telecommunications was not adequate to prevent the Bell System from impeding the development of competition in the sector. The settlement of that case created a complex situation in which the telecommunications sector was, in effect, 'administered' by the federal courts as well as state and federal regulators.[1] The Telecommunications Act of 1996 did not eliminate the potential for conflict between antitrust and regulatory authorities.[2]

It seems likely that competition and regulatory authorities will also have overlapping concerns as postal liberalization continues. For the foreseeable future, incumbent posts continue to have a dominant share in many postal markets that are also open to competition. Thus, even though they are under the scrutiny of sector-specific regulatory bodies, their market actions will naturally be of concern to competition authorities as well. Under EU competition policy, the concern would be 'abuse of dominance', while in the US, the terms used might be 'exclusionary' and/or 'predatory' behavior. The purpose of this chapter is to discuss some of the economic issues that are likely to be of concern to both regulatory and antitrust authorities and identify any potential conflicts.

The structure of the postal sector differs greatly from country to country, even within the EU. However, this chapter addresses general issues involving regulatory and competition policy in the sector, rather than the details of such interactions within a particular country (Eccles, Ch. 14, this volume). Therefore, the interactions between regulatory and competition policy will be examined in the context of a hypothetical, 'typical' postal sector with certain basic market and institutional characteristics, namely:

1. The incumbent post is an SOE.
2. The incumbent post is regulated by a sector-specific, postal regulator.
3. The incumbent post is a dominant firm in at least the letters market.
4. As a dominant firm, the incumbent will be subject to the competition authorities, especially concerning charges of 'abuse of a dominant position'.
5. The incumbent's overall rate level is controlled by some form of price-cap regulation, at least for markets in which it is dominant.
6. Despite its overall dominance the incumbent post faces actual or potential competition in at least some of its markets.
7. Despite the inroads of competition, the incumbent post faces a universal service obligation (USO).

These characteristics reflect the modal situation in liberalized postal markets, although (with the possible exception of the third), none holds universally. Taken together, these characteristics naturally give rise to the policy issues that are the subject of this chapter.

The remainder of the chapter is organized as follows. Section 2 analyzes issues that arise in regard to the market for downstream access to the incumbent's delivery network. There are at least three policy interests there that may conflict. The first is that downstream access creates the possibility of a competitive market for upstream services. But, along with that comes the possibility of exclusionary behavior in that market. A second role of downstream access is to facilitate competition in the end-to-end market. Finally, access prices are part of the overall allocative efficiency of the postal rate structure. Given three possible policy targets and only one policy instrument, it is not surprising that conflicts may arise.

Section 3 revisits the long-standing question of the proper scope of operations for SOEs in competitive markets. Competitors have long argued that the only way to ensure a 'level playing field' is to prohibit incumbent firms that enjoy either *de facto* or *de jure* monopoly power in one market from participating in related competitive markets. Regulators are typically reluctant to give up the benefits of substantial economies of scope that this would require. The analysis supports the view that participation by the incumbent in related non-dominant markets is highly likely to be efficiency enhancing so long as the incumbent is motivated primarily by profit. However, if the incumbent SOE is more concerned with maximizing its sales, it may have an incentive to use its economies of scope to foreclose more efficient competitors.

Section 4 discusses a similar issue caused by economies of scope between the USO providers of basic letter and competitive services. Given the cross-subsidy embodied in the uniform rate, rivals who have substantial market shares elsewhere have little interest in competing with the incumbent in high-cost areas. However, should the incumbent begin to receive USO payments to continue providing basic delivery service in such areas, competitors could rightfully claim that they were 'excluded' by the subsidy.

Section 5 takes up another access problem that has vexed regulators and competition authorities: the terms under which competitors can deliver mail to the incumbent's PO Box (PB) addresses. Incumbent posts tend to argue that placing letters into a subscriber's PB is just a very far downstream form of access and that something like the efficient component pricing rule (ECPR) is the appropriate methodology to use. Regulatory commissions tend to argue that the appropriate standard should be cost based, arguing that the likely outcome in workably competitive postal and PB markets should be operated on a cost-based access charge. There is also concern lest the incumbent post succeed in 'making use of its dominant position' in the PB market to thwart competition in markets for postal services. It turns out that this debate ignores an important aspect of the market for PB services and postal markets generally: they are two-sided markets. As the emerging literature on this topic has indicated, simple cost-based rules rarely suffice to characterize either desirable or equilibrium characteristics of the marketplace.

Section 6 concludes.

2. DOWNSTREAM ACCESS

The ubiquitous network of the incumbent is a tempting target for competitors, entrants, and regulators. A variety of empirical studies have shown that incumbents' delivery networks exhibit significant economies of scale. Yet, they do not exhibit the substantial sunk costs that characterize the 'monopoly bottlenecks' of other network industries such as telecommunications and electric power.

From the regulatory point of view, any activity which exhibits economies of scale has the potential to be efficiently shared with competitors. It does not really matter if the productive resource is 'impossible or impractical' to reproduce. If the transactions costs from unbundling are sufficiently low, a policy of compulsory access can be used to open significant portions of the value chain to competition. This argument has little connection with the considerations associated with the typical essential facilities deliberation.

It is perhaps possible to reconcile the regulatory and antitrust views of mandated access in a postal sector in which the incumbent has a statutory delivery monopoly for at least some products. In that case, one could take the view that the illegality of replicating the incumbent's network plays the same role as technical impossibility. In such circumstances, a regulatory policy of mandated downstream access at regulated rates has been demonstrated to have a significant impact on increasing upstream competition and overall cost efficiency in the postal sector.[3] However, this harmony begins to be strained once the delivery market is fully opened to competition. In the absence of significant sunk costs, and ample direct and indirect evidence that it *is* possible for entrants to create duplicate delivery networks, it is difficult to defend a policy of mandated access on the basis of an essential facilities argument.[4]

Nonetheless, it seems likely that regulators will accede to the requests of end-to-end competitors that forced access be granted. The important question, as always, will be determining the *terms* of such access. Once such terms have been established, the competition authority – even one that had no interest in compelling access itself on essential facilities grounds – should find itself interested in the pricing of access. This is so because the spread between the access price and the retail price affects the ability of 'equally efficient' competitors to compete with the incumbent in the market for the upstream component.

In particular, such exclusion will be a problem whenever the regulatory process leads to the establishment of access prices that exceed those that would result from the application of the ECPR, that is, worksharing discounts that are *less* than the upstream costs saved by the incumbent.

2.1 'Exclusionary' Access Charges Resulting from the Introduction of Global Price-cap Regulation

To make this issue concrete, consider the potential antitrust implications of the regulatory changes mandated by the PAEA. In an attempt to improve pricing flexibility on the part of the Postal Service, the PAEA mandated that the Postal Regulatory Commission (formerly Postal Rate Commission) implement a price-cap regime to control the prices of the Postal Service's market dominant services. While the detailed structure of this price-cap regime are still evolving, in its initial application, the prices of workshared and non-workshared products were treated symmetrically under the cap.[5] The following example illustrates the possible 'exclusionary' effects of this regulatory policy change.

Consider an incumbent that provides two market-dominant services: an end-to-end service and a workshared (or 'access') service. In the case of the workshared service, competitive consolidators provide upstream, sorting functions and the incumbent provides only delivery. Assume that, initially, the incumbent was regulated to break even by cost of service regulation and the worksharing discount was set equal to the upstream unit costs of the incumbent, that is, according to the ECPR. Now suppose a price-cap regime is introduced to control the prices of the incumbent and that, as is common, the price weights are set equal to the actual market quantities in the previous period.

More formally, let $D(p)$ denote the total demand for the end-to-end service as a function of the stamp price p and let $S(\delta)$ denote the competitive supply of upstream services as a function of the worksharing discount δ. Thus, end-to-end and workshared volumes carried by the incumbent are given by $D(p) - S(\delta)$ and $S(\delta)$, respectively. Let t and c, respectively, denote the incumbent's unit costs of upstream sorting and downstream delivery and let F denote its fixed costs (from all stages). Finally, let p^0 and δ^0, respectively, denote the stamp price and worksharing discount established by the regulator before the move to price-cap regulation. Then, the initial quantities of end-to-end and workshared quantities are given by $D(p^0) - S(\delta^0)$ and $S(\delta^0)$, respectively.

Under these circumstances, the profits of the incumbent postal operator are given by:

$$\pi(p, \delta) = (p-t-c)[D(p) - S(\delta)] + (p-\delta-c)S(\delta) - F. \tag{2.1}$$

The global price-cap regulation subjects the incumbent's choice of stamp price and workshare discount to the following constraint:

$$p(D^0 - S^0) + (p-\delta)\, S^0 \leqslant p^0(D^0 - S^0) + (p^0-\delta^0)S^0 = R^0. \tag{2.2}$$

This condition requires that, when evaluated at last period's volumes, the stamp price and discount chosen by the incumbent cannot be expected to yield more than last period's revenues. When the constraint is binding, it can be solved to yield an expression relating the allowed levels of the stamp price and worksharing discount, that is,

$$p^*(\delta) = (R^0/D^0) + \delta(R^0/D^0). \tag{2.3}$$

Equation (2.3) has the intuitive interpretation that the price-cap constraint allows the incumbent to increase its stamp price *only if* it also increases its worksharing discount.

It is now possible to evaluate the incentives facing an incumbent which has been subjected to price-cap regulation in these circumstances. In order to examine the effects on incumbent profits of a small change in the worksharing discount, substitute equation (2.3) into equation (2.1) and differentiate with respect to δ to obtain:

$$\frac{d\pi[p^*(\delta), \delta]}{d\delta} = \frac{\partial \pi}{\partial p}\frac{dp^*}{d\delta} + \frac{\partial \pi}{\partial \delta} = \frac{[(p-t-c)D' + D]S^0}{D^0} + (t-\delta)S' + S. \tag{2.4}$$

Evaluating this expression at $\delta = \delta^0 = t$ and $p = p^*(t) = p^0$ yields:

$$\frac{d\pi[p^*(t), t]}{d\delta} = \frac{(p - t - c)D'(p^0)S(t)}{D(p^0)} < 0. \tag{2.5}$$

Thus, the incumbent has a profit incentive to *reduce* the worksharing discount below its initial ECPR level.

Under ECPR (avoided cost) worksharing discounts, all upstream competitors that were at least as efficient as the incumbent were active in the market. After the change in regulatory policy, the incumbent would have a profit incentive (and regulatory 'permission') to exclude some of them. Presumably, this outcome would be of concern to the competition authorities. That is, even if application of essential facility considerations does not dictate that there *must be* an upstream market for competition policy reasons, once such a market has been created by regulatory fiat, competition policy criteria would apply. Usually, such potential conflicts can be avoided through adjustments in regulatory policy, for example, in the present example, one could change the form of the price cap and/or impose the added constraint that worksharing discounts satisfy the ECPR. However, this just reinforces the point that regulatory policies may sometimes conflict with competition policy in this important area.

3. PREVENTING 'UNFAIR' COMPETITION BY STATE-OWNED ENTERPRISES

Competitors continually claim that incumbent posts 'compete unfairly.'[6] Sometimes these complaints have obvious merit, for example, the 'mail-box monopoly' of the USPS – which certainly has the effect of raising rivals' costs. More commonly, charges of cross-subsidization are thinly disguised attempts to influence the regulatory process to set higher rates for the incumbent's products that are close substitutes for those of the complaining rival. This debate will intensify following liberalization, and it has the potential to lead to conflicts between regulatory and competition policy objectives.

True, the end of the letter monopoly will also end critics' most common complaint of this kind, that is, that the incumbent uses its protected monopoly to obtain the resources to finance 'unfair' competition. Yet charges of cross-subsidization will undoubtedly continue. Therefore, price-cap regimes are typically extended to include additional provisions for a 'price floor' that prevent the incumbent from setting the price of any product below its average incremental cost. It is here that the status of the incumbent as an SOE complicates matters.

A profit-maximizing firm that has an opportunity to earn at least some profits will not price competitive products below their average incremental cost *except* as an attempt at predation. It would increase its profits by abandoning that product line altogether. Predatory pricing by a profit-maximizing firm seems unlikely in the postal sector because of the relative ease of entry into the market. This makes it very difficult for a predator to successfully recoup the losses resulting from the below-cost pricing required to drive the prey out of the market. However, work by Sappington and Sidak (2003a and 2003b) has argued that SOEs may have the incentive to engage in predatory behavior on a *continuing* basis.

This argument has serious implications for the coordination of regulatory and antitrust policies: the regulator may trust to conduct (pricing) restraints to limit cross-subsidization, while the antitrust authority may feel obliged to resort to structural measures to prevent the incumbent from 'damaging competition'. Sappington and Sidak's analysis provides the rationale for these differing policy conclusions.

From the regulatory point of view, there would seem to be little need for such 'price floors' as a tool to prevent predatory pricing. After all, the regulatory process would generally make it impossible for the incumbent to recoup its investment in below-cost pricing.[7] However, as Sappington and Sidak's analysis explains, the situation changes dramatically when the incumbent is an SOE whose goal is *not* profit maximization, but the pursuit of some other, more bureaucratic, objective. Sappington and Sidak suggest 'revenue maximization' as a way to summarize, or proxy, the goals of SOE managers who pursue careerist considerations in the absence of access to the stock option incentive schemes available in privately owned companies. Profit considerations are reflected through a (typically binding) constraint that the firm achieves at least a 'satisfactory' level of profits.[8]

Mathematically, this does not require a major change in the formulation of the usual constrained optimization problem used to model the regulated firm. However, it leads to the possibility of profound changes in the nature of the choices of the firm. Now, it is entirely possible for the firm to wish to adopt prices below marginal costs on a long-term, continuing basis, that is, *not* as a predatory device with an eye toward raising rates as soon as the prey has exited the market. For the reasons discussed below, regulatory cross-subsidy tests are ill-suited to deal with this situation.

There are potentially more serious problems as well. Because a revenue-maximizing SOE wishes to offer below-cost prices on a continuing basis, it may find it optimal to alter its strategic investment policies so as to distort the outcome of any incremental cost test to which its rates may be subject. There are many forms such distortion might take. As a very simple example, consider the following: an incumbent wishes to promote its 'X-Mail' service. However, instead of advertising that service explicitly, it decides upon an extensive 'corporate image'-type advertising campaign. While not as cost effective as a targeted campaign, such an advertising strategy has one obvious advantage: its costs are truly 'joint and common costs'. If it had done an X-Mail ad campaign, its costs would be 'product-specific fixed costs', directly attributable to that product. As such, they would increase the average incremental cost floor pertaining to X-Mail rates.

Competition authorities could be forgiven for looking for structural remedies in situations in which the incentives for anticompetitive behavior are ongoing and the regulatory safeguards in place to control it are subject to strategic manipulation. A typical proposed structural remedy is to prevent the incumbent from offering services outside its dominant market. Structural separation remedies are frequently proposed in network industries such as telecommunications and electric power. In those cases, as in the postal case, the tradeoff is the potential loss of the economies of scope enjoyed by the operator offering a wide range of products. The incumbent (and most regulators) see such economies of scope as an important factor in keeping basic service rates low, while competitors see them as the key source of the incumbent's (unfair) network advantage.

Take the following hypothetical situation. Suppose that, initially, the incumbent postal provider (the incumbent) provides a set of mail services with the resulting revenues being at least sufficient to cover the incumbent's cost of operation. Now suppose that a market emerges for a new service, 'X-Mail'. After observing the development of this market and the level of the price being charged, the management of the incumbent concludes that it is desirable to enter this market. From the public interest point of view, what criteria should be used to evaluate the desirability of the incumbent's diversification?

The answer is straightforward if it can be assumed that the incumbent maximizes its profit and that the X-Mail market is competitive. Then the incumbent would make its diversification decision based upon whether the added revenues it could earn from selling a volume of X-Mail exceeded the added, or 'incremental', cost of producing that volume. As is discussed more fully below, this incremental cost test is precisely the standard that a social planner would use in evaluating the general desirability of the incumbent's diversification into competitive markets. The reason is quite intuitive. Ultimately, the key condition for social efficiency is whether or not the volume of service sold in the marketplace is produced at the lowest possible cost. When this volume is produced by two or more firms, productive efficiency requires that the marginal costs of all active firms be equal. Competition ensures that this condition is satisfied for the incumbent's rivals. Furthermore, the greatest profits for the incumbent in a competitive market would be obtained by operating at the quantity at which its marginal cost of X-Mail also equaled the market price. Then, as long as the market price covers the average incremental costs of diversification, the participation of the incumbent in the market lowers the total costs of providing X-Mail service.

Thus, the entry of a profit-seeking incumbent into a competitive related market improves productive efficiency. More than likely, the market price will fall as a result of the additional supply of the incumbent, further benefiting the consumers of X-Mail.[9] However, the other firms providing X-Mail will *not* benefit from the incumbent's entry. Even if the X-Mail market were initially perfectly competitive, the largest firms would likely earn significant 'economic rents', that is, profits. Not surprisingly, such competitors are vehemently opposed to such market participation by incumbent postal providers.

The situation becomes even clearer if the X-Mail market is not perfectly competitive. Then, the strategic actions of a profit-seeking incumbent and/or its rivals will undoubtedly result in a lower post-entry equilibrium price for X-Mail. First, consider the case in which the incumbent enters to dominate an existing competitive domestic X-Mail market. In order to obtain market share (and earn profits), the incumbent must lower the pre-existing market price. To do this, of course, it must be more efficient than the marginal competitive producers. Equally obvious is the fact that such entry would directly benefit consumers and harm competitors. Things are more complicated if the X-Mail market is an oligopoly, simply because there is a large range of oligopoly models that might conceivably be used to analyze the situation. However, in the vast majority of cases, the end results of strategic entry by a profit-seeking firm are lower market prices and lower competitor profits.[10]

The message should be clear: diversification by a profit-seeking or socially motivated, profit-constrained incumbent results in lower prices for consumers and lower profits for its competitors. Thus it is hardly surprising that competitors routinely and vociferously oppose such diversification by the incumbent and similarly situated monopolies.

Sappington and Sidak (2003a and 2003b) argue that the situation changes when the SOE is assumed to maximize revenues rather than profits or consumers' surplus. The gist of their argument can be summarized as follows:

1. the public firm (for example, the incumbent) is interested in maximizing revenue subject to a break-even constraint;
2. pursuit of this objective may induce the public firm to enter competitive markets despite the unprofitability of such entry;
3. incremental cost tests may be ineffective in preventing such entry; because
4. the public firm may, *ex ante*, choose to employ production technologies with high common costs relative to product-specific fixed costs in order to be able to pass any incremental cost test, *ex post*.

Theoretical arguments alone cannot resolve this debate. The choice between behavioral and structural approaches to the problem of the participation of state-owned incumbents in competitive postal markets is highly dependent upon the hypothesized objectives for these SOEs. Increased attention to executive compensation for SOE managers, together with corporatization and commercialization, may result in a movement away from bureaucratic objectives to market-oriented profit objectives.[11]

4. UNIVERSAL SERVICE: A 'BURDENSOME' OBLIGATION OR AN 'UNFAIR' COMPETITIVE ADVANTAGE?

There is, as yet, no settled methodology for measuring the costs of an incumbent post's USO.[12] Indeed, there are some who argue that the ubiquity of the incumbent's network is a competitive advantage rather than a burdensome obligation. Liberalization will undoubtedly shed light on this question. However, regulatory policies designed to compensate the incumbent for its USO may well generate competition policy concerns. A simple example will serve to illustrate this point.

Consider an incumbent serving a high-cost delivery area to which it delivers letter mail (in which it is market dominant) and X-Mail, a competitive product. Assume that the fixed costs of its delivery network are 6,000; the marginal cost of a letter is 1 and the marginal cost of a unit of X-Mail is 2, given that its letter delivery network is in place. However, because of economies of scope, without its letter-mail network, the incumbent's unit cost of X-Mail would be 6. Assume also that there are 1,000 units of letter mail and 1,000 units of X-Mail addressed to the area each period and that revenues minus upstream costs are 4 per unit for both letters and X-Mail.

To illustrate the potential competition issues involved, assume that there are two types of competitors able to provide X-Mail delivery in the high-cost area. 'Newsco' is the local newspaper delivery provider. Due to economies of scope with its newspaper delivery network, it is able to deliver X-Mail at a cost of 4 per unit. The other potential source of X-Mail service are a number of competitive couriers, who are able to deliver X-Mail within the high-cost area at a cost of 5 per unit.

In the initial situation after liberalization, the incumbent continues to monopolize both services.[13] However, the incumbent earns net revenues on its high-cost operation of 5,000: 3,000 = 1,000(4–1) from letters and 2,000 = 1,000(4–2) from X-Mail. Since this falls short of its fixed costs by 1,000, there would be a profit incentive to abandon providing delivery to the high-cost area. The result of 'free exit' from the high-cost area delivery by the incumbent would be that residents would have to pick up their mail at the Post Office *and* the profitable entry of Newsco into the local delivery of X-Mail. It would earn an incremental profit of 1,000 by (slightly) undercutting the competitive couriers' unit cost of 5.

One would expect that residents would be upset at the prospect of loss of letter delivery and would complain to the postal regulator. Suppose that a USO payment of 1,000 were offered to the incumbent in return for the continued delivery of letter mail.[14] While this would please the residents of the high-cost area, it would bring howls of protest from Newsco. How would the antitrust authorities respond to the claim that 'but for' the USO subsidy, the incumbent could not successfully compete in the market for X-Mail addressed to this area?

The regulator would have two responses to any suggestion that a USO-supported incumbent be barred from delivering X-Mail: (i) It is socially efficient for the incumbent to provide X-Mail delivery to the area, given that it provides letter-mail delivery; and (ii) the USO payment would have to be raised to 3,000 if the incumbent were to be barred from X-Mail delivery.

A possible objection is that the example presumes that the incumbent will emerge as the USO provider. However, it is easy to extend the example to demonstrate that the issue cannot necessarily be resolved by introducing competition 'for the market' into the USO funding process. Suppose that the 6,000 in fixed costs associated with the local delivery network represents the incumbent's true incremental fixed costs for serving the area given that it also serves several neighboring (profitable) areas. Suppose that if, instead, one calculated the incumbent's *stand-alone* fixed costs for serving the area, the figure would be 7,500. In addition, assume that Newsco could also achieve letter-mail unit costs of 1 by incurring additional network fixed costs of 7,000.

In the hypothesized situation, Newsco would be the efficient provider of letter *and* X-Mail delivery services for *only* the high-cost area. Yet, Newsco would not be expected to 'outbid' the incumbent in any competition for the USO. Why not? The incumbent would win, not because of its absolute efficiency, but because of its economies of scope between the high-cost area and other, profitable areas that it serves.

Thus, it is not surprising that competitors view economies of scope as a threat to competition, rather than a source of efficiency.[15] However, it would appear that the only resolution to this problem would be to prohibit the incumbent from serving any non-dominant markets, regardless of the scope economies that would be forgone. As this example illustrates, there may well be a conflict from regulatory desires to exploit economies of scope in order to minimize USO payments and the desire to encourage entry.

5. PROBLEMS POSED BY 'TWO-SIDED MARKET' ISSUES IN THE POSTAL SECTOR: PO BOXES

Both senders and receivers derive value from postal service. Potentially, this makes it a 'two-sided market'. The two-sided nature of postal markets is not a major issue when services are provided by a vertically integrated monopolist. Rowland Hill's 'sender pays' innovation was primarily an attempt to reduce the transaction costs of using the post and, thereby, more effectively exploit economies of scale. However, liberalization and unbundling give rise to many novel pricing opportunities, which may cause the unraveling of the Rowland

Hill model. This promises to create serious conceptual difficulties for both regulators and competition authorities.[16] Many such two-sided market issues are likely to arise in the future. Here, the focus is on the issues raised by the market for Post Office Boxes.[17]

As noted earlier, the role of essential facilities has been a controversial feature of the process of liberalizing postal markets. Some have argued that the absence of substantial sunk costs means that there is no need for policies designed to deal with 'monopoly bottlenecks', such as those used in other network sectors such as telecommunications or electricity.[18] Others have argued that requiring incumbents to grant downstream access is essential for the development of significant competition, at least in the short to medium run. I will not try to resolve this question here. However, all parties to the debate seem to agree that entrants must be granted access to the incumbent's PB subscribers. In some jurisdictions, such access is a matter for 'commercial negotiations' between the incumbent and potential entrants. In others, the rate is set by the postal regulator directly or indirectly (should negotiations break down). However, there remains considerable debate over the appropriate pricing methodology.

Incumbent posts tend to argue that the ECPR is the appropriate methodology to use for access pricing. Regulatory commissions tend to argue that the appropriate standard should be cost based, that is, 'bill and keep' when the costs of receiving mail at a PB location are zero. The incumbent post's position is based on the claim that PBs are an integral part of its postal network and that ECPR-based pricing of network access is not anticompetitive. The regulatory position is based upon the argument that the likely outcome in workably competitive postal and PB markets would be a cost-based access charge. There is also concern lest the incumbent post succeed in 'making use of its dominant position' in the PB market to thwart competition in markets for postal services by denying access to a significant set of addressees.

It turns out that this debate ignores an important aspect of the market for PB services and postal markets generally: they are two-sided markets. As the emerging literature on this topic has indicated, simple cost-based rules rarely suffice to characterize either desirable or equilibrium characteristics of the marketplace.[19] Therefore, before it is possible to truly understand access pricing for PBs, it is necessary to understand the benchmark pricing outcomes under competition, monopoly and welfare maximization.

As usual, the market definition exercise involves determination of both relevant product or services markets and relevant geographic markets. In the present case, the product markets consist of two retail markets for postal services, one wholesale (or service component market) for postal service, and the market for PB services. The geographical market definition for all markets considered is local/regional, because it is my understanding that this is the initial business model of many postal competitors. The retail markets are those for locally originating mail addressed to street addresses (street-addressed mail) and locally originating mail addressed to PBs (PB-addressed mail). Separating these two markets greatly clarifies the analysis. The wholesale markets discussed are the complementary components 'access to PBs' and that portion of the value chain that is 'upstream' of the PB in the retail PB-addressed mail market. That is, it involves all the steps of local mail processing *except* the actual placement of the piece in the secure PB. The market for PB services involves the rental of locked facilities to subscribers (mail recipients) for a fee. It is assumed that the incumbent has a dominant position in all of these markets.

5.1 'Making Use' of PB Dominance

This breakdown helps clarify the issue at hand. Would an above-cost price for access to the incumbent's PBs adversely affect competition in any of the above mail markets? I shall analyze each, in turn.

The retail market for street-addressed mail
A local competitor provides end-to-end service in this market, entirely bypassing the incumbent's network. Nothing the incumbent does in the access market will have any direct effect on competition in this market. Nonetheless, there is an important interrelationship between the market for PB services and the associated wholesale market involving collection, sortation, and partial delivery. In order for an entrant to compete successfully in this wholesale market, it must be granted access to the incumbent's PB addresses. Similarly, the connection between this wholesale market and the retail market for street-addressed mail in the same region is also very close. It is difficult (but not impossible) to envisage an entrant competing successfully in the market for street-addressed mail without being granted access to the incumbent's PB addresses. However, as long as access is granted at some price, entrants have shown that they can limit the impact on their ability to compete in the street-addressed mail market by passing through some portion of the PB access charge by charging a high price for PB-addressed mail.

One argument is that by forcing entrants to charge different prices for street- and PB-addressed mail, the incumbent is 'raising its rivals' transaction costs'. This point may have some validity but is considered 'secondary' for present purposes.

The retail market for PB-addressed mail
As long as the incumbent has an overwhelming dominance in the market for PB *service*, its dominance in end-to-end provision of service for PB-addressed mail is largely a matter of definition. In any event, competition in this market cannot be significantly impacted by PB access pricing.

The wholesale market for PB-addressed mail
This situation is where the ECPR methodology is traditionally applied. As long as ECPR principles are followed, no equally efficient competitor will be excluded from this market by a PB access price above cost. Therefore, it seems that the ability of the incumbent to charge ECPR access prices for PB-addressed mail has the effect of limiting the inefficient bypass of its local delivery network to street-addressed mail. This does not exclude an equally efficient competitor from the delivery market for PB-addressed mail. Rather, it prevents the expansion of an arguably less-efficient competitor into that market as well.

5.2 Analysis of Alternative Counterfactual Benchmarks

The above discussion indicates that if one believes that the incumbent's PB services are an integral part of its postal network, ECPR pricing of access is not exclusionary. However, this does not necessarily resolve the issue of whether such market-dominant pricing in the PB access market can be used to affect competition in markets for postal services adversely. There are two counterfactual situations whose analysis may shed light on this issue: (i) that of a hypothetical PB monopolist (PO Box Inc.) facing a competitive market for postal services; and (ii) that of fully competitive postal services *and* PB markets.[20]

It is my understanding that, in most jurisdictions, the incumbent's initial dominant position in the PB market is *not* a violation of the law. Therefore, an alternative counterfactual benchmark to use in evaluating its access pricing policy is that of a hypothetical PB monopolist facing a workably competitive postal delivery market. This hypothetical firm is called PO Box Inc. This monopolist would have two sources of revenue: the rental fees it charged its subscribers and the revenues from any access charges it collected from postal operators. Then, the relevant theoretical issue is whether or not PO Box Inc. would choose to charge an access fee above cost to postal operators.

Assume that PO Box Inc. faces a perfectly competitive postal delivery market (in which it may or may not participate). Assume also that a large enough percentage of mail was addressed to PBs that no postal operator could remain viable if it refused to deliver to them. In that case, any access price it might charge postal operators would be passed through to mailers through an increase in the equilibrium stamp price(s). Furthermore, the price for mail addressed to PO Box Inc. would be increased by the amount of the access charge. This means that PO Box Inc. would be in a position to use its access price to extract the monopoly profits associated with a vertically integrated end-to-end PB operator! It seems clear that PO Box Inc. would have an incentive to set an access fee substantially above its cost of handling incoming mail.

Taking this as the benchmark situation, consider what happens as a result of a firm (for example, the incumbent) *lawfully* acquiring dominance in the PB market. As noted above, PBs are a two-sided market. Operators can potentially collect revenues from postal firms delivering mail as well as from subscribers. As a result of acquiring dominance in the PB market, the incumbent would find it profitable to increase *both* of these prices above cost. As long as it increased the access price in accord with ECPR principles, this would not impede equally efficient competitors in any relevant market.

Thus, the existence of a dominant provider in the PB market is unfortunate for postal operators and consumers of both postal and PB services. However, this is the result of the exercise of monopoly power, not exclusionary tactics. If the dominant PB provider is vertically integrated into the market for postal services (as is the case with the incumbent), ECPR pricing of access to PBs should prevent the exclusion of equally efficient competitors from any relevant market, but it will *not* serve to limit the dominant firm's monopoly profits from either side of the PB market.

More surprisingly, these mark-ups above cost do not necessarily disappear in fully competitive PB markets! Panzar (2006) develops a two-sided model of the postal sector in which profit-maximizing PB firms charge the same access price under monopoly and perfect competition. The effect of competition is to lower the fees paid by PB subscribers. Again, this result is familiar from the two-sided market literature. As in the case of fixed-to-mobile termination charges, a 'competitive bottleneck' results: firms charge mailers a monopoly rate and compete away the profits by offering low prices to PB customers (see Armstrong and Wright, 2004).

My analysis has revealed that the PB market exhibits many of the now classic characteristics of two-sided markets. This means that care must be taken before applying the standards of traditional competition policy when evaluating the pricing of access to this essential facility.[21] In particular, an access price well in excess of the marginal cost of access does not constitute prime facie evidence of either 'abuse of dominance', or an attempt at 'leveraging monopoly power'. Nor does it necessarily signal a lack of competition in the PB market itself.

6. CONCLUSIONS

Postal liberalization has brought many changes to the sector, especially outside the United States. In the EU and elsewhere, recent decades have seen the 'corporatization' of postal operators. While privatization has been relatively rare, posts are typically subject to economic regulation by an independent regulator. The full market opening of the postal sector (scheduled for most member states in the EU for 2011) will mostly likely bring with it additional scrutiny from competition authorities.

The liberalization experiences of other vertically integrated network industries such as telecommunications and electric power have illustrated that regulatory policy and competition policy are likely to be closely linked. This chapter has analyzed four areas in which such interactions are likely to be important:

1. *Worksharing discounts and downstream access pricing under price-cap regulation* Obviously, the issue of competitive access is of concern to both regulatory and competition authorities in any network industry with an increasing returns to scale component, such as local delivery. The lack of the need for entrants to invest in sunk facilities in the postal sector makes it unlikely that competition authorities will compel downstream access on 'essential facility' grounds. Postal regulators, on the other hand, have shown some interest in requiring downstream access to promote efficiency and/or entry. However, the combination of global price-cap regulation with unbundled access may give rise to incentives for the incumbent to exclude equally efficient upstream competitors.
2. *Competition by state-owned incumbents* Incumbent postal operators, with or without a legal monopoly, are likely to remain dominant in some monopoly markets for the foreseeable future. Such incumbents also typically participate in related, competitive markets which enjoy economies of scope with the monopoly market. Should this diversification by a dominant provider into competitive markets be encouraged or discouraged? Analysis shows that participation in such markets by a *profit-seeking* incumbent will almost certainly be beneficial, for example, it will result in lower total postal sector costs and lower any required USO payments. However, as Sappington and Sidak (2003a and 2003b) have shown, if the incumbent has expansionary objectives (for example, revenue maximization), its participation in related competitive markets may be exclusionary. Regulatory strategies to adequately control such incentives await further research.
3. *Economies of scope and the USO* The fate of universal service subsequent to liberalization is of great concern to policy makers around the world. However, a firm receiving a USO payment to provide basic service in a high-cost area is likely to enjoy economies of scope with competitive products. As a result of USO support, the

incumbent may not only be able to continue to provide delivery service in a high-cost area (which nobody else wants); its economies of scope may also allow it to continue to monopolize competitive services in the area. Such service might have been taken over by alternative providers but for the USO support received by the incumbent. Again, there is a potential conflict between the desire of regulators to minimize USO support payments and their desire to encourage competitive entry.

4. *PB access* The need for granting access to the incumbent's PBs is widely recognized. Not so widely recognized is the fact that the market for PB services is a *two-sided* market. As the emerging literature on two-sided markets has made clear, standard cost-based pricing rules can no longer automatically serve as a normative benchmark for regulatory and antitrust policy.

The purpose of this chapter has been to raise questions, not provide answers. The discussion has focused on some postal sector issues that are likely to involve both postal sector regulators and competition authorities as liberalization unfolds. Undoubtedly, other similar issues will emerge and this chapter will suggest areas in which economic research can contribute to the future postal policy debates.

NOTES

1. The literature on the break-up of the Bell System is immense. See Viscusi et al. (2005) for a list of references and a discussion of the economic aspects of the associated regulatory and antitrust issues.
2. See Crandall (2005) for an in-depth discussion of the results of the Telecommunications Act of 1996.
3. See, for example, the evidence presented in Cohen et al. (2002).
4. See Panzar (2002) and de Bijl et al. (2006) for a discussion of the pros and cons associated with mandating unbundled downstream access.
5. That is, the regime was of 'global' price cap regulation. See de Donder et al. (2006) for a discussion.
6. See, for example, Sidak and Spulber (1996).
7. Things change somewhat under price-cap regulation.
8. Sappington and Sidak's formal model assumes that the SOE maximizes a weighted sum of revenue and profits.
9. The only situation in which the incumbent's entry would *not* result in a lower market price would be the case in which the market price is completely determined by a perfectly elastic competitive supply curve. That is, when there are a large number of actual and potential suppliers willing and able to supply an unlimited quantity at the going price. This is unlikely to be the case in any real-world market, but is a useful simplifying assumption in the example below.
10. The most relevant *possible* exceptions that come to mind are cases in which the competitive market in question utilizes the network of the incumbent. For example, consider the entry of an incumbent post into retail banking. Obviously, it could easily dominate that market (and raise prices) by simply refusing to deliver the mail of its competitors. Of course, this negative outcome is not a result of diversification itself, but rather, of an anticompetitive violation of the post's common carrier obligation.
11. See Crew and Kleindorfer (2008) for a discussion of various objectives of SOEs and the potential effects of commercialization in increasing incentives for profit-oriented behavior.
12. But see Crémer et al. (2000) and Panzar (2001) for methodological suggestions.
13. By hypothesis, no one can compete with the incumbent for high-cost letter delivery under a uniform stamp price. In the example, even if it were allowed to do so, Newsco would not find it profitable to undercut the transfer price of 4 implicitly paid by the incumbent for delivery of X-Mail in the high-cost area.
14. I shall not go into detail here concerning the appropriate amount of USO funding that should be awarded in this situation. See Panzar (2001) for a discussion.
15. For example, see US Federal Trade Commission (2007).
16. There is already a voluminous literature on appropriate antitrust policies in the payment sector. See Wright (2004), Armstrong (2006), and Rochet and Tirole (2006) for more general discussions of the problems posed by two-sided markets.

17. See Panzar (2006) for a first attempt at a formal analysis.
18. See, for example, Crew and Kleindorfer (2002), Panzar (2002), and de Bijl et al. (2006).
19. See Rosson (2005) for an early review of this literature.
20. See Panzar (2006) for a formal analysis of these two counterfactuals.
21. For a discussion of the necessary caveats, see Wright (2004).

REFERENCES

Armstrong, M. (2006), 'Competition in two-sided markets', *Rand Journal of Economics*, **37**, 668–91.

Armstrong, M. and J. Wright (2004), 'Two-sided markets, competitive bottlenecks and exclusive contracts', mimeo, University College London, and National University of Singapore.

Cohen, R.H., W.W. Ferguson, J.D. Waller and S.S. Xenakis (2002), 'Impacts of using worksharing to liberalise a postal market', in G. Kulenkampff and H. Smit (eds), *Liberalisation of Postal Markets*, Bad Honnef: WIK.

Crandall, R. (2005), *Competition and Chaos: U.S. Telecommunications since the 1996 Act*, Washington, DC: Brookings Institution.

Crémer, H., A. Grimaud and J.-J. Laffont (2000), 'The cost of universal service in the postal sector', in M.A. Crew and P.R. Kleindorfer (eds), *Current Directions in Postal Reform*, Boston, MA: Kluwer Academic, pp. 47–68.

Crew, M.A. and P.R. Kleindorfer (2002), 'Balancing access and the universal service obligation', in M.A. Crew and P.R. Kleindorfer (eds), *Postal and Delivery Services: Delivering on Competition*, Boston, MA: Kluwer Academic, pp. 3–32.

Crew, M.A. and P.R. Kleindorfer (2008), 'Regulation and the USO', in M.A. Crew and P.R. Kleindorfer (eds), *Competition and Regulation in the Postal and Delivery Sector*, Cheltenham, UK and Northampton, MA, USA: Edward Elgar, pp. 3–22.

de Bijl, P., E. van Damme and P. Larouche (2006), 'Regulating access to stimulate competition in postal markets?', in M.A. Crew and P.R. Kleindorfer (eds), *Progress Toward Liberalization of the Postal and Delivery Sector*, New York: Springer, pp. 153–72.

De Donder, P., H. Cremer and P. Dudley (2006), 'A welfare analysis of price controls with end-to-end mail and access services', in M.A. Crew and P.R. Kleindorfer (eds), *Liberalization of the Postal and Delivery Sector*, Cheltenham, UK and Northampton, MA, USA: Edward Elgar, pp. 53–72.

Panzar, John C. (2001), 'Funding universal service obligations: the costs of liberalization', in M.A: Crew and P.R. Kleindorfer (eds), *Future Directions in Postal Reform*, Boston, MA: Kluwer Academic, pp. 101–16. Reprinted in this volume.

Panzar, J.C. (2002), 'Reconciling competition, downstream access, and universal service in postal markets', in M.A. Crew and P.R. Kleindorfer (eds), *Postal and Delivery Services: Delivering on Competition*, Boston, MA: Kluwer Academic, pp. 93–118.

Panzar, J.C. (2006), 'PO Box access: competition issues in a two-sided postal market', paper presented at the 4th IDEI/La Poste Conference on Regulation, Competition and Universal Service in the Postal Sector, Toulouse, March 16 and 17.

Rochet, J. and J. Tirole (2006), 'Two-sided markets: a progress report', *RAND Journal of Economics*, **35**(3), 645–67.

Roson, R. (2005), 'Two-sided markets: a tentative survey', *Review of Network Economics*, **4**(2), June, 142–60.

Sappington, D. and J. Sidak (2003a), 'Incentives for anticompetitive behavior by public enterprises', *Review of Industrial Organization*, **22**, 183–206.

Sappington, D. and J. Sidak (2003b), 'Competition law for state-owned enterprises', *Antitrust Law Journal*, **71**(2), 479–523.

Sidak, J. and D. Spulber (1996), *Protecting Competition from the U.S. Postal Monopoly*, Washington, DC: American Enterprise Institute.

US Federal Trade Commission (2007), Postal Service Study, Project No. PO71200, Declaration of J. Gregory Sidak.

Viscusi, W., J. Harrington and J. Vernon (2005), *Economics of Regulation and Antitrust*, 4th edn, Boston, MA: MIT Press.

Wright, J. (2004), 'One-sided logic in two-sided markets', *Review of Network Economics*, **3**(1), March, 42–63.

3. Pricing for postal access and worksharing*

Michael A. Crew[†] and Paul R. Kleindorfer[‡]

1. INTRODUCTION

This chapter evaluates approaches to setting access prices and worksharing discounts by postal operators (POs). POs are typically synonymous with universal service providers (USPs), so the terms are used interchangeably here. In the postal sector, the term 'worksharing' is used to describe what is known more generally in network industries as access pricing. As with other network industries, access to a postal network can occur at multiple stages, but it is usually referred to in the postal sector as either upstream or downstream access. The latter refers to access to the regional or local delivery network; for example newspaper or periodical publishers might print and address their publications and then deliver them in bundles to local post offices for final delivery. Competitors of the PO may also use downstream access provided by the PO to complete their coverage offerings for high-cost areas. All other types of access are deemed upstream access. Upstream access activities are also referred to as 'worksharing'. These include collection, consolidation, presorting, barcoding and transportation undertaken by customers or mail preparation companies in advance of tendering the mail to the PO. While there are some important differences in costing and pricing of upstream and downstream access, this chapter will treat both of them under the umbrella of access pricing, drawing distinctions as needed.

The notion of access implies that worksharing activities by customers or third parties have been undertaken, which substitute work that would otherwise have to be undertaken by the PO. Thus, mail may be delivered to a processing facility and it may, if it is barcoded, go straight to a sorting machine, saving the PO the expense of 'facing up' mail, reading the address and applying the appropriate barcode. There is considerable experience of worksharing discounts, most highly developed in the case of the United States Postal Service (USPS) and La Poste in France, but also common in many other countries. Upstream access is likely to be beneficial when there are technologies available to entrants and postal customers that are lower cost than using the existing postal technology. The lower cost arises from a number of factors. First, there is the ability of worksharing companies to use lower-cost labor. Second, these companies are driven by the profit motive and competition and may therefore achieve greater efficiencies. Third, worksharing technologies may benefit from additional economies of scale and scope in mail preparation and consolidation that would otherwise be lost if mail or parcels were simply deposited or co-mingled in the PO's general collection and mail processing system. These technologies include mailroom activities on a customer's premises to accomplish barcoding and

[†] Rutgers University.
[‡] Wharton School and INSEAD.

pre-sorting of mail. Providing incentives for the efficient adoption, use and development of these technologies is the primary objective of worksharing discounts and access pricing. These discounts are the drivers for postal customers and third parties to undertake worksharing and transportation activities, and give rise to the corresponding access products by the PO.

Pricing of access is generally recognized as an important feature of assuring the development of competition in postal markets (Crew and Kleindorfer, 2004b; de Bijl et al., 2006). Upstream access is an important catalyst for having the most efficient party (the PO, a mailer or a consolidator) undertake collection and pre-sortation activities. Downstream access in the early stages of competition provides the means of allowing an entrant to use the PO's network for some delivery zones (those for which the entrant has not yet developed full service) while bypassing the PO's network partially or completely for other zones. Thus, in considering and comparing access pricing rules across countries, it is important to note that the scope of competition within which access takes place has important implications for the role of access and for the principles that govern the structure of efficient access prices.

Consider USPS. The presence of extensive upstream access has been undertaken against a continuing presumption of a monopoly in final delivery of all mail items below a rather high weight and value threshold (the reserved area).[1] The fundamental question in this environment has been to communicate the right signals to potential access customers on the costs avoided by USPS as a result of these customers' worksharing or transportation activities. Contrast USPS with the case of Royal Mail in the United Kingdom and La Poste in France. In these countries, access products will serve as a stepping stone to full liberalization of their postal markets.[2] Full liberalization is already the case in the UK, with the removal of the reserved area in 2006, and La Poste can also expect to see its postal market fully liberalized in 2011, as dictated by the directives and laws of the European Union (EU) that will result in the opening of all EU postal markets by 2013. This is usually referred to as 'full market opening' (FMO).[3] As examined below, there are significant differences in the design of efficient pricing rules for access when bypass, namely end-to-end (E2E) competition is allowed than when a delivery monopoly (or reserved area) is maintained. In particular, under competitive entry the PO is likely to supply almost the entire market for downstream access and E2E service for high-cost areas. So the regulator needs to be concerned as to whether the terms and conditions of access undermine the PO's ability to maintain the universal service obligation (USO).

The basic economic efficiency principle underlying access pricing is that incentives should be aligned so that the lowest-cost producer for a given service, whether it is the PO or an entrant, actually provides the service. The application of this principle to accommodate particular features of the postal market, especially of the USO, adds a number of complexities. These are driven primarily by the requirement that single-piece letters are priced uniformly across the country. First-best pricing cannot be achieved because of the constraints arising from the USO. It is useful to anticipate some of the developments of this chapter by stating the various approaches to access pricing that have been proposed or implemented.

The current practice for setting access prices in many POs is the 'avoided cost approach', also called the 'retail minus' approach since it sets access rates at the price of the corresponding E2E service minus the PO's avoided cost of the upstream work performed prior to access (for example, the level of pre-sorting performed).[4] However, this approach to access is not efficient in general because it leads to uniform access and worksharing tariffs, independent of the remaining transportation and delivery costs to be undertaken by the PO in delivering mail to different areas. An alternative approach is to develop pricing signals that allow the incumbent, through publicly posted tariffs, to charge for access as a function of the ultimate destination of mail and the remaining work to be performed by the access provider/PO in further processing and delivering this mail. The approach amounts to pricing access according to its cost, marked up appropriately to make a contribution where possible to USO costs. This approach, proposed by Crew and Kleindorfer (2002b), is termed 'zonal pricing' or 'delivery-area access pricing' or DAP, which foresees charging higher access prices for downstream access where such access requires delivery to high-cost areas. The DAP approach is one of several that go under the general title of 'bottom-up' approaches, to reflect the fact that these approaches charge for access not according to the cost of work avoided by the PO, but according to the cost of work yet to be performed by the PO in delivering the mail. The DAP approach, and other bottom-up or cost-based approaches can be important in countries such as Canada and Australia with a large proportion of rural, high-cost routes as well as in other countries with significant numbers of rural delivery areas whose costs are much higher than the urban delivery areas.[5]

Avoided cost and DAP, must take into account requirements to finance the USO and the extent to which consolidators and entrants provide differentiating features to their products. This chapter also considers a 'negotiated pricing approach' whereby the PO and potential worksharing providers (WSPs) may negotiate customized contracts based on the particular features of individual WSP mailing patterns and preparation and delivery protocols. Typically, negotiated access pricing occurs against a default option that is available to all WSPs, where the default could be a DAP or an avoided cost access tariff. Negotiated pricing recognizes that there may be additional gains to trade between the PO and individual WSPs. At the same time, as we discuss below, customized arrangements present special problems for price regulation and in assuring non-discriminatory treatment of WSPs. Furthermore, many POs and regulators may not currently be prepared for the complexities arising out of negotiated access agreements.

Two additional issues that are important in setting efficient postal worksharing discounts are: (i) customer and consolidator heterogeneity and (ii) the relationship between price regulation and access. The second issue entails both a consideration of the principles that should underlie efficient access pricing but also the degree to which these are subject to *ex ante* or *ex post* approval and adjustment by the regulator.

The chapter proceeds as follows. The next two sections review the theory and practice of access pricing, including a discussion of practice in the US, France and the UK. Building on this, Section 4 addresses some specific policy questions often raised about access pricing and worksharing discounts, and specifically the comparison of retail-minus (top-down) approaches versus cost-based (bottom-up) approaches. Finally, there is a technical appendix, which summarizes some of the theory and analytics underlying recent developments in access pricing and worksharing.

2. THE ECONOMICS OF ACCESS PRICING AND WORKSHARING DISCOUNTS

This section provides a review of the economics of access pricing. The basic economic efficiency principle underlying access pricing is that incentives should be aligned so that the lowest-cost producer of a given service, whether it is the PO or a WSP, supply the service. Generally, the approach involves unbundling, and separately pricing, the various components of the postal value chain (see Figure 3.1). As shown in Figure 3.1, access can occur at various points in the (USP) network, representing worksharing activities that range from collection and consolidation activities, to various steps in mail processing, and possibly also transportation to the USP's delivery areas. For those product markets that are open to competition, WSPs can bypass the USP's network entirely, where it is profitable to do so. This is shown in the lower section of Figure 3.1, where the WSP delivers E2E parcels and other products not subject to the reserved area. The more work that is done upstream, the greater the worksharing content of the mail processed by WSPs and the less work there is for the PO to accomplish final delivery. Access pricing is the method by which potential WSPs (for example, customers of the PO, consolidators or transportation organizations) are provided incentives to undertake one or another activity in the worksharing process.

2.1 Approaches to Pricing Access and Worksharing

Several approaches have been proposed for setting access prices or worksharing discounts. To introduce basic concepts, let us consider three types of access rules,

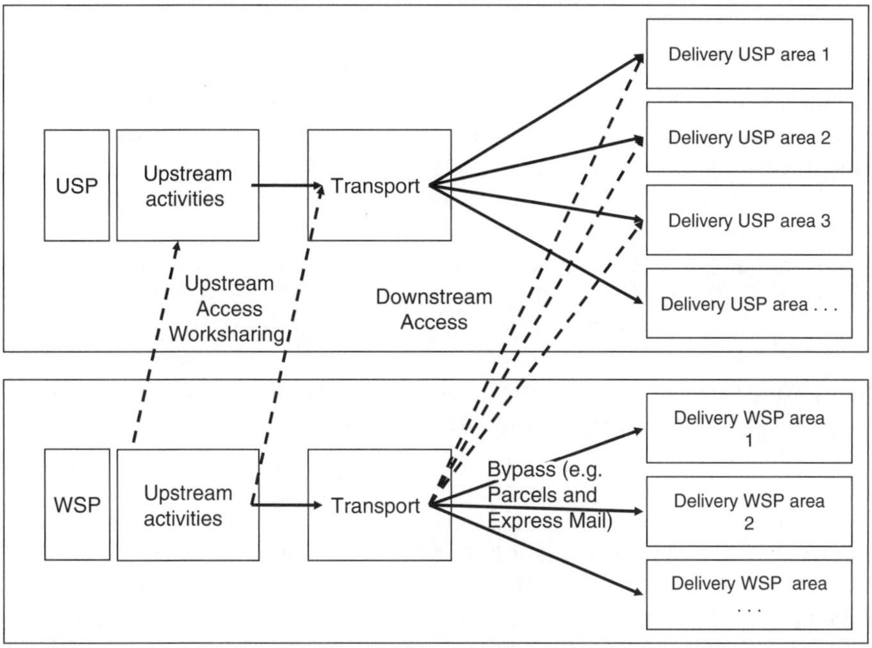

Figure 3.1 Illustrating upstream (worksharing) and downstream access

currently in use in postal markets or being discussed as possible rules to govern access pricing:[6]

- *Avoided cost pricing (ACP), a top-down approach also known as retail-minus pricing:* Charge for access according to discounts off the price for the corresponding E2E service, based on the avoided cost of bypassed activities provided by the WSP.
- *Delivery-area access pricing (DAP), a subset of cost-based or bottom-up pricing:* Charge for access not only according to the work that is bypassed, but also according to the work yet to be performed in delivering the mail to be reposted by the WSP and delivered by the PO.
- *Negotiated access pricing (NAP):* The outcome here is whatever price the PO and WSPs agree through negotiations. NAP may be subject to additional constraints on non-discriminatory treatment across WSPs, as well as floors and ceilings set by the regulator.

We first consider the arguments supporting each of the above approaches. In the process, we shall ignore issues concerned with heterogeneity of worksharing WSPs, the effects on demand of worksharing, and issues related to rebalancing of the PO's financial breakeven constraint. We return to these matters after covering the basics.

Avoided cost pricing (also known as retail-minus pricing)

The ACP approach can be summarized as follows:

Access Price under ACP = E2E Price of PO – Avoided Cost of Activities Provided by the WSP

Thus, suppose the PO's E2E price for a particular service is P and suppose that the activities involved in providing this service are upstream (at cost C_u), transportation (at cost C_t) and downstream delivery (at cost C_d), so that $P = (1 + M)(C_u + C_t + C_d)$, where M is the mark-up over cost for this service to contribute to the payment of the fixed costs of the PO's network. Then the access price under ACP for worksharing that encompasses only upstream activities (leaving transportation and delivery to the PO) would be:

$$A_u = P - C_u = (C_t + C_d) + M(C_u + C_t + C_d)$$

and for worksharing that encompasses both upstream and transportation activities (leaving only delivery to the PO) would be:

$$A_{u+t} = C_d + M(C_u + C_t + C_d)$$

Note that in both cases, the price of access for these 'partial services' maintains the full contribution margin of the E2E service. As explained in Panzar (2002), the logic for ACP is twofold: first, under ACP a WSP will provide worksharing services in competition with the PO if and only if the WSP is more efficient than the PO in doing so; second, since the same contribution margin is maintained, whether a mail item is workshared or not, the incumbent PO continues to receive the same level of contribution per unit of mail ultimately delivered to pay for fixed network expenses.

Additional complexities could be incorporated. For example, a more detailed model could be developed of the sensitivity of the PO's costs to WSP volume (including transaction costs of processing WSP orders and accounting for economies of scale at various stages), as well as various forms of fixed costs and heterogeneity across WSPs (Panzar, 2006). However, these extensions do not take away from the simple logic of ACP that the price of access is obtained by subtracting from the 'retail' (E2E) price of a service the average avoided cost of those activities undertaken by the WSP seeking access for this service. Usually, only the PO's costs are estimated in applying ACP. As we shall discuss further below, the simplicity of ACP and its relationship to static efficiency have promoted its widespread use in practice. However, this simplicity may lead to inefficiencies in liberalized markets when access prices account for the effects of bypass and the simultaneous need to finance the USO.

Delivery-area access pricing (also known as 'zonal access pricing')

DAP is part of a more general class of pricing policies, known as cost-based or bottom-up pricing. In addition to the ACP logic of recognizing the cost of workshared activities avoided, DAP also takes into account the cost of remaining activities to be performed. DAP pricing gives rise to zonally deaveraged access prices, whereas the ACP would be unaffected by the costs of remaining activities, since it is only a function of the avoided cost of workshared activities. Following Crew and Kleindorfer (2002b, 2004b), the structure of DAP may be expressed as follows:[7]

> Access Price under DAP = Minimum of {E2E Price, Cost-based Price}
>
> where 'Cost-based Price' (which will generally be delivery zone specific) is given by:
>
> Cost-based Price = Maximum of {ACP Price, Cost of Remaining Work of PO}.

The DAP rule recognizes the fact that for high-cost areas, the ACP rule would subsidize access (at least whenever the price determined by the ACP rule is less than the 'cost of remaining work to be done by the PO' in completing the delivery of the mail tendered to it by a WSP). This implies that DAP is capped at the E2E (or retail price) of the PO for the service in question, since attempting to charge more than this will give rise to the WSP using the E2E service. Under DAP, access prices depend on both the origin and destination of the mail for which access is being provided by the PO.

An example of a DAP access tariff is given in Table 3.1 (which shows tariffs for both downstream access and upstream access). In interpreting the table, assume that the PO offers only a single product ('letter mail') and that its cost structure is of the form:

$$\text{Total Cost for PO} = (C_u + C_t + C_d)V + F,$$

where V is the annual volume of mail, F are the fixed costs of the USO and C_u, C_t, and C_d are the respective marginal costs of upstream, transportation and downstream delivery activities. For simplicity, we assume that upstream cost C_u is independent of origin of

Table 3.1 Illustrating ACP and DAP access prices

Delivery zone z	Zone A	Zone B	Zone C	Zone D
PO's C_u	2	2	2	2
PO's $C_t(z)$	2	3	4	5
PO's $C_d(z)$	10	14	18	22
$P(E2E)$	20	20	20	20
$P_{ACP}(UPS, z)$	18	18	18	18
$P_{DAP}(UPS, z)$	18	18	20	20
$P_{ACP}(DEL, z)$	16	15	14	13
$P_{DAP}(DEL, z)$	16	15	18	20

Notes
$P(E2E)$ = E2E price for the full service in question with no worksharing.
$P_{ACP}(UPS, z)$ = Access price for zone z for upstream access/worksharing – ACP rule.
$P_{ACP}(DEL, z)$ = Access price for zone z for downstream access/worksharing – ACP rule.
$P_{DAP}(UPS, z)$ = Access price for zone z for upstream access/worksharing – DAP rule.
$P_{DAP}(DEL, z)$ = Access price for zone z for downstream access/worksharing – DAP rule.

the mail and that transportation cost to local post offices in different delivery zones $C_t(z)$ is irrespective of the origin of the mail and depends only on the ultimate delivery zone z. We also assume that the PO's upstream cost is independent of zone. The fixed costs F of counters and other aspects of the USO are intended to be recovered in mark-ups. In Table 3.1, zones are ranked according to delivery costs. Zone A is lowest cost and the PO can deliver mail there at a marginal cost of 10c. Transportation costs $C_t(z)$ to zone z, for this example, are also increasing in the same order as $C_d(z)$.

To illustrate, the ACP rule would calculate the access price for worksharing encompassing upstream operations as $P_{ACP}(UPS) = P(E2E) - C_u = 18$, and this would be independent of the zone to which the workshared mail was ultimately delivered by the PO. The DAP rule would determine zone-differentiated prices as shown. For example, DAP would compute the access price for upstream workshared mail destined for delivery to zone B as $P_{DAP}(UPS, \text{B}) = \text{Min}\{20, \text{Max}\ [18, 14+3]\} = 18$, while the access price for upstream workshared mail destined for delivery to zone C would be $P_{DAP}(UPS, \text{C}) = \text{Min}\ \{20, \text{Max}\ [18, 18+4]\} = 20$. Similarly, the ACP rule would calculate the access price for worksharing encompassing upstream and transportation operations to zone B as $P_{ACP}(UPS, \text{B}) = P(E2E) - C_u - C_t = 15$, which now does depend on the zone to which delivery is required, because (avoided) transportation costs depend on the final delivery zone. The corresponding DAP access price for workshared mail processed and transported to zone B for delivery would be $P_{DAP}(DEL, \text{B}) = \text{Min}\{20, \text{Max}\ [15, 14]\} = 15$.

DAP and ACP are closely related: first, by its structure DAP access prices are always at least as great as ACP prices; second, both ACP and DAP prices decrease (that is, worksharing discounts increase) as the WSP organization does additional work, unless the DAP price hits its upper limit (the price of the corresponding E2E service), in which case no further decreases are possible. As can also be seen in Table 3.1, the DAP rule is identical to the ACP rule except in high-cost areas. Note also that while averaging (uniformity) of prices might be in the interest of efficiency for single-piece rates because of transaction cost savings, there is no reason to maintain such averaging across delivery zones in pricing unbundled access.

DAP implies that a WSP would not be given any discount at all for mail destined for high-cost delivery zones. The PO loses money on each piece it delivers in the high-cost zones. By eliminating a payment to the WSP, DAP avoids stimulating demand for a service for which the PO is losing money. In this way, DAP increases efficiency. This can be seen from Table 3.1. Suppose that the PO provided a discount for downstream work-shared mail destined for delivery zone D of 2c, so that the access price was set at $P_{DAP}(DEL, \text{D}) = 18$ instead of $P_{DAP}(DEL, \text{D}) = 20$, as shown. If the access price were equal to the E2E price, the WSP would not undertake any additional work on such mail and would, in the worst case, simply redeposit it at a price of $P(E2E) = 20$ for delivery by the PO, whereas the WSP would undertake upstream worksharing activities for this mail if the access price were 18 (and if the WSP's upstream worksharing cost were less than the PO's, namely $C_u = 2$). Unit profit is the same in each case, namely:

$$\text{PO's Unit Profit } [P_{DAP}(DEL, \text{D}) = 20] = 20 - 2 - 5 - 22 = -9,$$

$$\text{PO's Unit Profit } [P_{DAP}(DEL, \text{D}) = 18] = 18 - 5 - 22 = -9.$$

The efficiency gain from the simple form of the DAP rule illustrated here does not arise without a cost. If a WSP could accomplish the upstream and transport activities at a cost less than the avoided cost of these activities for the PO, then setting the access price at the price of the E2E service will provide no incentive for the WSP to do so. Thus, the DAP rule partially ameliorates the subsidies to high-cost areas in that it does not encourage increased demand for service in these areas, but it may do so at the cost of not having the least-cost producer perform the upstream and transportation activities. To the extent that marginal cost in the high-cost areas exceeds price, the DAP rule lowers demand and increases efficiency. For example, in the case noted just above, if a WSP were able to do the upstream and transportation activities for delivery in zone D for less than the PO (for which $C_u + C_t = 7$ for zone D), then the simple DAP rule presented here would forgo these efficiency benefits in order not to further subsidize deliveries in zone D.

We shall see below that the optimal DAP rule does account for these effects and trades off the inefficiencies of subsidized delivery in high-cost areas with avoided cost of upstream activities. Note that these inefficiencies would be further exacerbated if delivery bypass were possible, since then cream-skimming would occur for low-cost urban areas, which would be captured by entrants, leaving only the higher-cost areas for the PO to serve (see Crew and Kleindorfer, 2005b). In this sense, the ACP rule may be appropriate in countries like the US where bypass is prohibited, whereas the DAP rule and zonal pricing become increasingly important when, as in the EU, the reserved area is eliminated.

Negotiated access pricing

The NAP rule calls for the PO and WSPs to negotiate freely the terms of access. Especially under conditions of increasing competition and complexity, there are transaction costs and other efficiency losses associated with having regulators or regulatory processes intervene in issues that can be better determined by negotiation, assuming that both parties to the negotiation are properly motivated.[8] As we shall describe in the next section, in some countries, notably the United Kingdom, there has been an increased interest in NAP. The primary reason for this movement is that customers have different mailing patterns, so that trying to impose a uniform access tariff by regulation can lead to inefficiency and unwillingness of the parties to enter into or execute access agreements that are not geared to cost and value.

The structure of NAP access agreements can be described as follows:

Access Price under NAP = Negotiated Outcome between PO and WSP, subject to 'default options' available to both parties.

Based upon the theoretical and experimental literature on bargaining in economics originating with Nobel Laureate John Nash in the 1950s relating to negotiated arrangements, it is clear that negotiated settlements can be expected to have several important properties. First, if the parties are properly motivated, one can expect efficient solutions to result from bargaining. Second, the bargaining power of the parties will affect the magnitude of the surplus each extracts from negotiations. Third, the default options available to the parties are important determinants of the outcome and the share of the gains to trade that each will harvest.

In the context of postal access agreements, default options can be set by the regulator. These include setting generic access tariffs that any WSP is guaranteed (these generic tariffs could be, for example, either the result of an ACP or a DAP rule). Non-discrimination clauses, which are a part of the Postal Directive in the European Union, provide further defaults for WSPs. One approach to implementation of non-discrimination is to require the PO to file any negotiated agreement with the Regulator for posting, thus making it available as a default option for any other WSP with volume or mailing patterns consistent with the agreement. Other restrictions on the bargaining process might be imposed as well by the Regulator, including floors and ceilings on access prices, and these might favor either the PO or a potential WSP.

Because of the idiosyncratic nature of negotiated settlements, and the complexity of the theory underlying bargaining, we shall not provide an in-depth review of this theory in the postal context. The motivation for negotiated contracts in the postal context is the increasing complexity of the relationships between the PO and large business mailers. For small mailers, appropriately designed generic access rates and conditions can capture most of the benefits of worksharing. However, for larger mailers, closer coordination between the PO and the mailer can uncover mutually beneficial opportunities that are often best captured through the negotiation/bargaining process.

2.2 Access/Pricing: Some Results from Theory

ACP, DAP and NAP capture the essential ingredients of pricing of access and worksharing. These rules recognize that access prices must signal three sources of scarcity and value: (i) the upstream costs avoided through worksharing; (ii) the downstream costs of work yet to be done by the access provider; and (iii) some contribution to the costs of the USO. Balancing these three elements optimally has been a focus of the theoretical literature on access pricing which we now review. The theoretical literature shows that the optimal tradeoff among these elements of access pricing must account for two essential elements: WSP heterogeneity and demand stimulation effects of access. Given the history of POs as public enterprise, the theory has generally been in the context of Ramsey pricing to generate the mark-ups over marginal cost needed to cover fixed costs and the USO.

Customer heterogeneity

The above discussion on DAP underlines the importance of delivery zone cost heterogeneity. Indeed, without the differences in delivery cost, many of the classic problems in postal economics would be much less interesting. However, delivery costs are not the only source of heterogeneity; a further concern analyzed in the postal economics literature has been with heterogeneity in customers. Crew and Kleindorfer (1991) first examined Ramsey-optimal worksharing discounts where customer heterogeneity arises not only from the obvious differences in cost that arise from the different location of customers but also from differences in a WSP's value of establishing a relationship with the PO. This value may arise from the size of WSP operations that would make it worthwhile to invest in such a relationship. Heterogeneous valuation may arise for other reasons, including not only differences in volumes of WSPs but also different mailing patterns. Intuitively, these considerations mean that large customers will be the first to engage in worksharing, assuming uniform prices across customers.

A model of customer heterogeneity and the demand for access services has been developed, and calibrated for La Poste, by Billette de Villemeur et al. (2002, 2005, 2006), and we incorporate the results of this approach in our summary of the theory of access pricing below.[9] Beyond its theoretical importance, modeling WSP heterogeneity is critical in predicting the demand for access products, which is important for the PO in both its facilities' planning and profitability analysis. In particular, under FMO and bypass, customer heterogeneity is a critical determinant of outcomes since those customers will be most attractive to entrants who have large volumes of mail destined for low-cost areas.

Demand stimulation and funding the USO

The original driver of worksharing was the cost savings to the PO from having a lower-cost WSP perform the work. Both were better off, and so too was the ultimate mailer as a result. Because the mailer is better off as a result of the WSP passing on some of the cost savings, demand is stimulated. Pearsall (2005) reviews several studies showing that worksharing in the US has had a substantial impact on demand for postal services. Intuitively, this arises from two sources. First, revealed preference suggests that WSPs will not engage in worksharing unless they save money by doing so. These savings represent effective price decreases in the resulting E2E product, with greater demand being one result. Second, the improved service quality of a customized relationship between consolidators, mailing houses and business mailers makes the resulting bundled product produced by the WSP and the PO more valuable to the mailer than would be the non-workshared E2E product of the PO, again resulting in demand stimulation. Given this, it is important to capture these demand stimulation and substitution effects between the PO's E2E product and the bundled product offered by a WSP in conjunction with the PO.

Structure of Ramsey-optimal worksharing discounts with heterogeneous WSPs

The accepted approach to efficient access pricing is derived from maximizing a weighted sum of consumer and producer surplus, subject to a break-even constraint for the PO, where the decision variables are the E2E prices for various products and their corresponding workshared products. To avoid cumbersome notation, we consider only a single product in our overview here, which may be thought of as letter mail to a fixed delivery zone. We also begin with a presumption of no bypass, that is, ultimate delivery will be undertaken by the PO itself. The value chain in the theoretical models on worksharing is typically simplified to two aggregate stages: upstream activities and downstream delivery. Worksharing consists of bypassing the upstream activities. Customers are either 'households' who never engage in worksharing, or 'firms' who may or may not use worksharing. The firms are the potential WSPs and they may be thought of as business customers, possibly using the services of consolidators and third parties to workshare their mail.[10] These WSPs are assumed to be heterogeneous, with their 'type' being represented by their unit cost 'k' of accomplishing the work associated with the upstream portion of the postal value chain. It is assumed that the PO knows the distribution of types of firms and uses this information in setting worksharing discounts.

Following Crew and Kleindorfer (1991), Laffont and Tirole (1994), Armstrong et al. (1996), Billette de Villemeur et al. (2002), Crew and Kleindorfer (2004b) and de Donder (2006), we can summarize the results of the theoretical analysis as follows. Welfare-optimal worksharing discounts for a given worksharing activity A (for example, pre-sorting, or pre-sorting plus transportation), subject to a breakeven constraint for the PO, should be set so that:

$$\text{Discount(A)} = \text{Optimal Worksharing Discount (Activity A)} = \text{Max}\,[\text{D(A)}, 0], \quad (3.1)$$

where D(A) is given by:

$$\begin{aligned}\text{D(A)} = \; & \text{R(A)} \times [\text{PO's Avoided Cost of A}] \\ & + [1 - \text{R(A)}] \times [\text{PO's Margin on Remaining Work to be Done Following A}] \\ & - [\text{Ramsey Adjustment}]. \qquad (3.2)\end{aligned}$$

In the formula for D(A), R(A) is the so-called 'displacement ratio' associated with A (defined below), [PO's Margin on Remaining Work to be Done Following A] is the price of the corresponding E2E service minus the cost of all activities in the value chain *NOT* undertaken by the WSP in performing A, and the Ramsey Adjustment is a non-negative number[11] (which is subtracted in the expression (3.1)) which increases as the fixed costs of the USO increase. This implies, as might be expected intuitively, that larger USO costs lead to lower worksharing discounts.

Note that the optimal discount will depend on the ultimate delivery zone of the workshared product since the [PO's Margin on Remaining Work to be Done Following A] will depend on this zone, and on other factors. Note also the fact that workshared discounts cannot be negative, as WSPs would then simply choose the corresponding E2E product rather than undertaking the cost of worksharing. This is the reason for the truncation of D(A) at zero in (3.1).

The 'displacement ratio' R(A) is defined as:[12]

$$\text{R(A)} = -\left[\frac{\text{Change in Demand for E2E Product as Discount(A) Changes}}{\text{Change in Demand for Work-shared Product as Discount(A) Changes}}\right]. \quad (3.3)$$

The displacement ratio captures the demand stimulation effect of worksharing at the margin. When R(A) = 1, there is no demand stimulation in that any change in worksharing activity is exactly matched by changes in the corresponding E2E service (which completes delivery for the worksharing activity). However, when R(A) < 1, then demand stimulation occurs in the sense that an increase in the discount for worksharing activity A leads to a greater increase in the demand for workshare activities performed by WSPs than the overall reduction in the demand for the corresponding E2E service (which would be reduced somewhat as some of the E2E demand at the lower discount would now be performed as workshared demand because of the higher discount). With a displacement ratio of, say, 0.8, at the margin, one of every five mail items workshared is new mail, while four of every five mail items workshared displace those of the USP. Given that workshared and E2E products are close substitutes, reasonably high displacement ratios (for example, between 0.8 and 1.0) might be expected, but no detailed empirical estimates appear to be available for postal displacement ratios.[13]

An example from our earlier Table 3.1 will illustrate the tradeoffs here. Table 3.2 reproduces the costs from Table 3.1 for zones A and D and shows the results of the optimal rule (3.1) disregarding the Ramsey term (including the Ramsey term would give rise to larger access prices/lower discounts than those shown).

Table 3.2 points to the following properties of the optimal rule. Just as for ACP and DAP, for any given delivery zone, the optimal rule determines discounts that increase (or at least do not decrease) as the amount of worksharing increases. However, the optimal rule is sensitive to the displacement ratio and the same workshared activity may

Table 3.2 Illustrating welfare-optimal access prices when bypass is negligible

	Zone A costs & prices for R(A) = 1.0	Zone A costs & prices for R(A) = 0.8	Zone D costs & prices for R(D) = 1.0	Zone D costs & prices for R(D) = 0.8
PO's C_u	2	2	2	2
PO's $C_t(z)$	2	2	5	5
PO's $C_d(z)$	10	10	22	22
$P(E2E)$	20	20	20	20
$P_{ACP}(UPS, z)$	18	18	18	18
$P_{DAP}(UPS, z)$	18	18	20	20
$P_{OPT}(UPS, z)$	18	16.8	18	19.8
$P_{ACP}(DEL, z)$	16	16	13	13
$P_{DAP}(DEL, z)$	16	16	18	20
$P_{OPT}(DEL, z)$	16	14.8	14	14.8

Notes
$P(E2E)$ = $E2E$ price for the full service in question with no worksharing
$P_{ACP}(UPS, z)$ = Access price for zone z for upstream worksharing – ACP rule.
$P_{ACP}(DEL, z)$ = Access price for zone z for downstream worksharing – ACP rule
$P_{DAP}(UPS, z)$ = Access price for zone z for upstream worksharing – DAP rule.
$P_{DAP}(DEL, z)$ = Access price for zone z for downstream worksharing – DAP rule.
$P_{OPT}(UPS, z)$ = Access price for zone z for upstream worksharing – equation (3.1)
$P_{OPT}(DEL, z)$ = Access price for zone z for downstream worksharing – equation (3.1)

receive larger or smaller discounts when moving from one zone to the next, depending on both the avoided cost of the worksharing activity and the forgone margin of remaining work left for the PO after worksharing. Note also that the optimal rule is likely to provide discounts in excess of avoided cost in the low-cost delivery areas and discounts less than avoided cost in the high-cost areas, with the sensitivity to changes across delivery zones depending on the displacement ratio. Interestingly, for this example, the optimal worksharing discount for combined pre-sorting and transportation activities is the same for zone A and zone D when we assume the same displacement ratio $R = 0.8$ for both zones. In the case of zone A, the optimal discount for downstream access is computed as:

$$\text{Discount} = (0.8 \times \text{AC}) + (0.2 \times \text{Margin}) = (0.8 \times 4) + [0.2 \times (20 - 10)] = 5.2.$$

For zone D, the corresponding discount is computed as:

$$\text{Discount} = (0.8 \times \text{AC}) + (0.2 \times \text{Margin}) = (0.8 \times 7) + [0.2 \times (20 - 22)] = 5.2.$$

This illustrates that the two effects of increased worksharing (increased avoided cost and decreased margin) work in opposite directions in determining discounts. Of course, it is also likely that the displacement ratio will increase (less substitution, namely, R(A) is close to unity) as one moves to more high-cost delivery areas, where there is likely to be less interest in worksharing to begin with. In this case, optimal discounts for high-cost areas will tend to become more like avoided cost discounts, though adjusted downwards for the reduced (and possibly negative) margin in high-cost areas, and further reduced in both low-cost and high-cost areas by the Ramsey adjustment.

All of this is in line with the dual purpose of worksharing discounts as providing both incentives for worksharing as well as providing appropriate contributions to support the fixed network costs of the USO. In particular, when worksharing activities are the front end of multiple delivery products, and when uniform pricing restricts pricing flexibility, then the simple logic of avoided cost discounts needs to be altered to capture the effect of lost margin by the PO and to avoid subsidizing downstream delivery for high-cost areas.

Impact of bypass

It is important to draw attention to the impact that bypass has on optimal access prices. Several of the papers that are the basis of the above review do, in fact, include delivery bypass as a possibility (which it is, of course, for products like express mail and parcels). General results are contained in Calzada (2006) and in Bloch and Gautier (2008), who extend the earlier results of Crew and Kleindorfer (2002b, 2004b), Panzar (2002) and Billette de Villemeur et al. (2007) to show that the introduction of bypass leads generally to a decrease in welfare-optimal access prices, essentially to avoid inefficient bypass from occurring. This is the tradeoff that is already evident in Table 3.1 and which variations of DAP are intended to combat as well (recall that DAP is intended to charge at least the cost of remaining work to be accomplished by the PO). When E2E competition is possible, then access prices must serve the dual purpose of providing incentives for efficient entry into worksharing markets as well as providing incentives for efficient bypass. Doing so while continuing to fund the USO and meet other constraints imposed by the regulator requires tradeoffs among these sometimes competing objectives. When bypass is possible, as noted earlier, special attention must be paid to access prices (such as those based on ACP) avoiding subsidy of high-cost delivery zones.

Regulation

There has been a clear evolution in the postal sector towards some form of price-cap regulation in the tradition of Littlechild (1983). This is usually referred to as either RPI minus X or CPI minus X. In the postal sector, X is typically set low or at zero. Within the context of price-cap regulation, several approaches to the regulation of access prices are possible. They are characterized by the degree of discretion left to the incumbent USP. Under a reserved area, the degree of discretion will be less than under FMO. It is important that sufficient flexibility be granted the PO/USP under FMO that customization of products to individual customer segments can be achieved without excessive intervention by the regulator. Considerations of autonomy and flexibility for the PO are more crucial when the optimal discount structure differs significantly from rules such as avoided cost that are simpler to implement and regulate.

Price-cap regulation can give considerable pricing flexibility to the PO. One example, giving close to maximum flexibility, could take the form of a regulated basket for letters, primarily the single-piece USO prices for a number of weight steps. This basket might include services such as registered mail and cash on delivery (COD). There could also be a single-piece parcels basket. All other products would then be in the competitive basket. However, given the market-dominant position of an incumbent PO, it is unlikely that this level of flexibility would be acceptable, as there would be a concern that prices and conditions of access be offered on a non-discriminatory basis to both the PO's customers of the USP as well as to third-party WSP competitors seeking access to the PO's network. So it is likely that the level of prices for worksharing and access products will continue to be regulated while the PO is market dominant. How should this be accomplished?

The approach, first proposed by Crew and Kleindorfer (1994), which may strike the appropriate balance between price control and price flexibility is to subject access products to price-cap regulation. This can be done by including a weighted average of all access products in the regulated basket along with all other regulated products to which the traditional price-cap formula applies. An alternative is that only a few products such as basic downstream access and the single-piece letter rate could be included in the price-cap formula, with then the requirement that the prices for all other access products be subject to the floor and ceiling prices of the single-piece rate and the (possibly zone-specific) applicable delivery zone rate, otherwise leaving the determination of pricing for all intermediate forms of access entirely to the discretion of the incumbent.[14] This latter regime is similar to what is described above under NAP. Both of these regimes could be further bolstered by posted generic access terms and rates available to all comers and by governing regulatory principles, for example, those embodied in the DAP regime described above.

3 EXAMPLES FROM PRACTICE IN ACCESS PRICING AND WORKSHARING[15]

As noted in de Bijl et al. (2006) and in the PricewaterhouseCoopers prospective study of market opening in the European Union (PwC, 2006), access conditions vary considerably across countries. In the UK, Royal Mail is required by its regulator (Postcomm) to provide access to any of its postal facilities (including, for example, its delivery network) by individual customers, consolidators and competitors. The terms under which access is provided are based usually on negotiated contracts between Royal Mail and parties seeking access, but Postcomm can impose a settlement in the event that the parties cannot agree. In Germany, Deutsche Post AG (DPAG) is obliged by law to offer downstream access services under terms and conditions that are largely determined by the National Regulatory Authority (BundesNetzAgentur). The Netherlands and Sweden employ NAP, largely determined by free negotiations between the USP and parties seeking access to the USP's network. From these examples, we can already see that there are significant differences across countries regarding access policies. Our review here will focus on three countries that are recognized leaders in the area of access pricing and worksharing: the United States (USPS), France (La Poste) and the UK (Royal Mail).

3.1 Worksharing and Access at USPS

USPS is a recognized pioneer in worksharing. Introduced in 1976 (Cohen et al., 2006), there were two expectations associated with having large mailers and consolidators pre-sort their mail prior to tendering it to USPS. First mail preparation, especially if done on the premises of the original customer sending the mail, could be performed at lower cost by WSPs than by USPS. Second was the expectation that, because of the increase in quality of mail preparation resulting from worksharing, the efficiency of USPS itself might improve. As explained in Cohen et al., both of these effects did occur, with some lag between the introduction of worksharing and productivity effects. The magnitude of worksharing in USPS is evident in Table 3.3, which shows that the percentage of total volumes that were workshared had grown by 2004 to nearly 73 percent across all major product groups.

The worksharing activities shown in table 3.3 resulted in some $14.4 billion in discounts or rebates to worksharing organizations, and reflect some $14.4 billion in avoided costs for the USPS. Cohen et al. estimate that these activities were undertaken at a fraction of that cost by the third parties who undertook worksharing, leading to an overall economy-wide saving of some $11 billion in 2004 alone.

In addition to these significant cost savings, there are also substantial demand effects resulting from the price decreases associated with operating a less expensive postal value chain for business customers. Pearsall (2005) estimated the demand stimulus effect of worksharing by separating out in his econometric model the secular and pricing effects of demand growth from the effects associated with various worksharing innovations. His conclusions are that over the period 1976 through 2003, postal volumes were increased by 37 percent by worksharing and postal revenues were increased by 26 percent relative to what they would have been without the worksharing innovations.

Pearsall and Cohen et al. conclude that these effects are likely the result of the synergies between mail preparation, collection and overall convenience of worksharing

Table 3.3 USPS 2004 total avoidable costs and the total value of worksharing discounts (volume and $m.)

Class of mail	Total volume	Workshared volume	Volume workshared (%)	Total USPS cost avoided ($m.)	Value of discounts ($m.)
First-class mail	97,926	50,239	51	3,466	3,440
Periodicals	9,135	8,731	96	1,485	1,396
Advertising mail	95,564	89,762	94	9,297	9,121
Package services	1,132	826	73	151	108
Other	2,349	–	–	0	0
Total	206,106	149,558	73	14,399	14,065

Source: Cohen et al. (2006).

organizations which have, in effect, brought new services to the marketplace through their specialized activities that allow their business customers to use postal products conveniently while reaping cost savings from the worksharing discounts provided by USPS.

Pricing of worksharing products in USPS is based upon avoided cost pricing (ACP) principles. Thus, workshared products in USPS are priced at the respective E2E price of the product minus the avoided cost to USPS for worksharing (that is, the cost avoided by the USPS for the work undertaken by the worksharing organization). The efficiency losses of the ACP approach are mitigated in the USPS context by the fact that no bypass (that is, no delivery competition) is allowed for other than parcels and express mail.

There are continuing questions raised as to whether the avoided costs used by USPS are too narrowly construed and reflect actual costs avoided (see, for example, Haldi and Olsen, 2004). Moreover, as noted in our review of theory above, there are questions about how to identify and pass on differences in avoided cost for mail having different quality preparation standards (Panzar, 2006). However, generally the methodology used for ACP (or retail-minus) access price implementation in USPS and the arguments underlying it are understood by those involved. The success of the USPS worksharing program over the years illustrates the effectiveness of upstream access in leveraging the incumbent PO's network and in stimulating business demand.

3.2 Worksharing and Upstream Access at La Poste[16]

Interestingly, the French national PO, La Poste, has an even longer history of worksharing than USPS, with its roots dating to significant increases in parcels and direct mail in the 1960s. This led La Poste in 1967 to seek third-party assistance for the collection, sorting and preparing of parcels, which were then tendered to La Poste for ultimate delivery. Encouraged by the additional flexibility evident in this arrangement, La Poste extended this to direct mail products in 1969, thereby encouraging major mailers to presort their mail and to undertake other activities that led to cost savings for La Poste.

During the 1970s, stimulated by a significant strike in 1973, this process led to the further development of worksharing in La Poste, and this has continued to grow to this date. Contributing to this was the elaboration of the theoretical foundations underlying the design of worksharing discounts in La Poste as reviewed earlier in this chapter (see Billette de Villemeur et al. 2002, 2006).

Several types of contract govern worksharing arrangements between La Poste and providers of worksharing services (large mailers and consolidators). The *standard* contract (*contrat produit*) is 'product based' and covers direct mail, parcels or transactions mail, specifying the general access conditions and service quality standards for the product in question and the discounts (or rebates) for various levels of worksharing. The second type of contract governing worksharing is the *technical* contract (*contrat technique*) and covers specific additional matters such as time windows to tender mail, additional refinements in sortation, and other matters for which La Poste wishes to provide incentives to mailers and consolidators because of the cost implications of these activities. Finally, a *commercial* contracts (*contrat commercial*) specifies total periodic rebates based on total volumes provided by a commercial customer. A typical example would be a 5 percent annual rebate of total mailing costs provided by La Poste to a financial institution based on the total volume of that institution tendered to La Poste for delivery. Interestingly, rebates on commercial contracts are computed on the basis of total volume ultimately delivered by La Poste, whether this is tendered directly to La Poste by the customer or comes to La Poste via a consolidator/worksharing organization that might prepare the customer's mail.

Given the product focus of worksharing contracts, the intent is to build prices on the basis of specific accounting information on costs for each product class (transactions mail, direct mail, and so on). The current methodology for pricing of workshared products at La Poste is based on avoided costs, but somewhat more flexibly than in the USPS case reported above. The intent is to capture for each product class and each technical feature for access the appropriate incentives to promote efficiency in the value chain between mail generation and receipt of the mail in a La Poste facility.

As can be seen in Tables 3.4 and 3.5, worksharing is an important feature of the French market. From Table 3.4, we see that more than 9.3 billion mail items were affected, representing some €1 billion in worksharing discounts, in 2004. For the same period, mailing houses and consolidators (some 200 in total) processed more than half of the bulk mail, including 81 percent of the direct mail and 24 percent of total transaction mail. These 200 small and medium businesses are either subsidiaries of international groups (DPWN, Belgian Post, Bertelsmann, Wegener, Quebecor) or of advertising companies or routing companies previously owned by the banking sector for their transaction mail. Worksharing discounts are identical for large mailers and consolidators.

Market studies of the French postal sector show that both markets – transaction mail consolidation and direct mail consolidation – have evolved significantly in the last 15 years. Once composed of many fragile small and medium-sized enterprises (SMEs), with unskilled employees and limited automation, these markets are now dominated by significant players, many of them subsidiaries of international groups (Gallet-Rybak et al.,ch.18, this volume).

As with USPS, the details of worksharing contracts are sufficiently complex that this area has created some tension between consolidators and La Poste. In response to this, the French postal regulator ARCEP (L' Autorité de Régulation des Communications Électroniques et des Postes) has set up a dispute resolution procedure to allow the identification of sources of tensions in worksharing arrangements and resolution of these.

Table 3.4 Workshared volumes at La Poste for 2005

2005	Type of customer	Number of items (millions of items)	%
Total direct bulk mail	Mailer	900	19
	Consolidators	3,900	81
	Total	4,800	100
Total transaction bulk mail	Mailer	3,400	76
	Consolidators	1,100	24
	Total	4,500	100
Total bulk mail*	Mailer	4,300	46
	Consolidators	5,000	54
	Total	9,300	100

Note: * The 'total bulk mail' category includes all types of mail that could be workshared, that is, which could benefit from rebates in the case of pre-sorting and handling preparations. Periodicals and magazines are not included in this table.

*Table 3.5 Workshared rebates available at La Poste**

Postal product		Prices (in €)	Maximum rebate**
D+1/2	Single-piece mail	0.53	23.7%
Transaction mail	Workshared bulk mail	0.40	
D+3/4	Single-piece mail	0.48	25.6%
Transaction mail	Workshared bulk mail	0.36	
D+7	Non-workshared bulk mail	0.35	33.5%
Direct mail	Workshared bulk mail	0.23	

Notes

* The prices for workshared products shown here correspond to the maximum degree of pre-sorting and mail preparation, which differs according to the different products considered (direct or transaction mail, different type of direct mail, etc.). This table shows the average rebate for the workshared product indicated relative to a comparable 'bundled' product. For example, for transaction mail, the bundled product benchmark (and the maximum rebate of 23.7% for D+1/2 workshared bulk mail) is the single-piece rate. For direct mail, the benchmark product is the least demanding non-workshared bulk-mail contract – in terms of volume and sorting preparation – since direct mail is a business product and there is therefore no specific private customer tariff for direct mail.

** The 'maximum rebate' indicated in the table includes the combined effects of three types of rebates available to La Poste customers: rebates related to *contrats produits* subject to volume and pre-sorting conditions (avoided costs in collecting and sorting); rebates related to *contrats techniques* subject to supplemental pre-sorting and mail preparation (avoided costs in collecting, sorting and handling of mail); and rebates related to *contrats commerciaux* subject to total (e.g., annual) volume conditions (reflecting avoided costs in the distribution segment).

As the market opens to E2E competition in 2011, there will be pressure to move from the current ACP approach to a zonal pricing approach along the lines of DAP, in order to avoid inefficient subsidies to new entrants in delivering their customers' products by La Poste to outlying, rural areas. As in the case of USPS, worksharing and upstream access represent a success story in France, promoting the leveraging of the incumbent PO's network through incentives that motivate efficient preparation of mail and parcels.

3.3 Worksharing and Access at Royal Mail

Access prices were originally agreed between the incumbent operator Royal Mail and UK Mail in February 2004. This was followed in April 2004 by similar downstream access agreements with TNT and Deutsche Post. All three companies are licensed by Postcomm (the postal regulator) to provide 'consolidation' services, where mail is collected from customers or groups of customers and is then handed to Royal Mail for final delivery. Initially agreements for access were set on a geographically averaged cost-recovery basis. This meant that licensed operators were required to present mail to Royal Mail in a form that reflected the overall letter volume of Royal Mail's business, on the basis of individual postcode areas. Should volume vary from Royal Mail's by more than 7.5 percent but less than 15 percent in any 'reference period' (each such period being approximately three months) Royal Mail had the right to levy a surcharge. If volume in any outward postcode area varied from Royal Mail's by more than 15 percent in any 'reference period' Royal Mail had the right to levy a higher surcharge, ask the customer to transfer to a zonal agreement or, if all else fails, terminate the agreement.[17]

Effective from October 2004, Royal Mail added to its set of generic agreements (described above) access contracts based on geographically de-averaged access prices. These de-averaged access contracts are negotiated freely between Royal Mail Wholesale, the access arm of Royal Mail and different operators and users, subject only to being offered on a non-discriminatory and non-preferential basis.

Once a contract is negotiated, it is published on Royal Mail Wholesale's website, so it is available to other customers if they meet the terms of the contract. If they want something different, then a new negotiation is initiated. Thus, the first contract negotiated was the one with UK Mail, and that continues to be in place. A non-uniform price contract was negotiated with a different customer later in 2004 and that is also still in place. Furthermore, there is nothing preventing a customer from having two separate access agreements, one with a uniform price based on the national distribution pattern and one with a non-uniform price, provided that they meet the terms for each contract.

Royal Mail published an explanatory note on geographically de-averaged pricing (which it calls 'non-uniform' pricing).[18] The note included the following comments:

> In calculating a non-uniform access price, two of the most important cost drivers . . . are Delivery Point Density (DPD) and Business Density (BD) . . .
>
> DPD . . . determines the average travel distance between delivery points. BD is the proportion of delivery points that are registered as businesses.

Royal Mail divides clusters of delivery points around the country into five bands, known as delivery zones, defined in terms of their major cost drivers (DPD and BD). Zone A has the lowest delivery costs and hence the lowest access price. Access prices increase from zones B–E to reflect the cost differences of delivery to points in each zone.

In 2006, 14 licensed operators competed with Royal Mail. Although the UK postal market has been fully liberalized as of January 1, 2006 (the reserved area was abolished for all postal items), Royal Mail still has a dominant position. Royal Mail accounted for

97 percent of mail volumes in the regulated area in 2004–05[19] with revenue growth over this period of 3.7 percent.

Until 2006, geographically de-averaged access prices changed from year to year on the basis of a pre-determined formula (RPI – 1 percent). The original access prices to which this clause applied were the negotiated prices; that is, this formula was incorporated directly within the negotiated access agreements itself. The initial underlying prices (to which the RPI – 1 percent per annum adjustment was applied) were roughly in line with avoided costs associated with a typical second-class[20] item of mail.

Subsequently, the 2006 regulatory review conducted by Postcomm has suggested an alternative pricing mechanism which preserves the headroom[21] between access and retail prices over the next four years (2006–10) as compared with an equivalent E2E product.[22] This is expected to filter through to access agreements as they are renegotiated.

The requirement that access price meet the minimum price difference with its corresponding E2E product is checked as part of the audit conditions for the price-cap control, but only the E2E product is directly in the price-cap formula. New access products are outside the control unless Postcomm determines that they are 'substantially similar' to an existing product and hence would be treated the same as one of the existing price-controlled access products. Hence, there is no allowed revenue calculation for access, only the requirement that access prices not violate the headroom requirement.

This arrangement of allowing considerable flexibility to Royal Mail to price its access products, subject only to non-discriminatory offering of access services to all parties and to the ceilings derived from the respective E2E products, is in line with what was described earlier as negotiated access pricing. However, there are also key elements of the DAP/bottom-up costing approach evident in the headroom requirement.

Postcomm requires that any access agreements entered into by Royal Mail arc passed to the regulator as soon as practical for review and published on its website. As a result of a recent license amendment, a grace period of one month is now required, before the arrangements can be implemented. Postcomm uses this period to assess the regulatory implications of the proposed arrangement and its competitive properties.

The process through which mark-ups are determined in setting access prices (so as to make a reasonable contribution to Royal Mail's fixed costs of running its network) is treated with some skepticism by entrants and competitors. On Royal Mail's side, there is an understandable push to have increased flexibility in setting access prices so as to cover the costs of their USO. The tensions here are normal in moving to a more competitive marketplace, and have been seen in several other sectors as well (as discussed in Armstrong, 2002, 2008). In the current period of developing competition, Postcomm have committed to preserving the 'headroom' between access and retail prices for the next four years to foster the development of competition through access. In the longer term, it is likely that the pressures of competition will force a re-examination of the role of downstream access arrangements as the most appropriate and efficient mechanism of fostering competition.

Summarizing the experience to date, access pricing in the UK is viewed as one of the important instruments employed in leading to workable competition, both upstream (through worksharing) and downstream. Growth in use of access products has been significant,[23] and is expected to continue. Indeed, given the complete abolition of the reserved area as of January 1, 2006, and the importance of access for both consolidators and E2E competitors, pricing and terms of access are expected to remain a central focus of Royal Mail and the UK regulator Postcomm.

4. IMPLICATIONS OF THE THEORY OF ACCESS PRICING FOR PRACTICE

As the previous sections have shown, the theory and practice of postal access and worksharing addresses a number of issues that vary across countries. These issues include the state of actual and desired competition in the market, the demographics and other postal cost drivers, and differences in the nature and magnitude of the USO facing the PO. As a result, policy makers and regulators have adopted different approaches and a consistent policy has yet to emerge. Among the POs there is much more agreement. Almost all POs, not surprisingly, favor less regulation of access products, arguing that such products are mostly competitive. Probably a majority would support no regulation[24] but recognize that it is infeasible at this stage in the development of the industry. In part this lack of consensus on access pricing arises from the lack of a set of underlying principles to which both sides can relate and therefore apply. Perhaps the central problem has been a failure to appreciate the fact that optimal access prices must reflect a number of potentially conflicting objectives, including signaling to WSPs the avoided cost of their activities for the PO (a signal to WSPs on cost-efficient entry), signaling the remaining cost of activities required to complete delivery of workshared products (a price signal on the cost of access), and signaling the required contribution to support the fixed cost of the PO's network (a signal on the cost and value of the USO). Before any policy conclusions can be drawn on the appropriate structure and regulation of worksharing discounts, it is in our view critical to recognize this fact that they must simultaneously address these three objectives. Let us consider the details.

4.1 Avoided Cost/Retail-minus and Bottom-up/DAP Redux

From the beginning, the theory of access pricing rested on the notion of avoided cost. The notion, best known as the efficient component pricing rule (ECPR), was that the PO should allow a discount to a competitor/WSP accessing the network equal to the costs avoided by the PO as a result of work done by the WSP. In a first-best world, discounts based upon avoided cost would have the benefit of ensuring that the lowest-cost producer did the upstream work.[25] If a WSP can do the work cheaper than the PO, then signaling this through a discount equal to the PO's avoided cost would provide the right incentives for the WSP to do the work, resulting in a cost-minimizing solution.

However, in the postal world, the existence of multiple products and uniform pricing of E2E products gives rise to problems in that a discount based on avoided cost would yield access prices that would not vary according to delivery zone. The result is that the avoided cost logic would not capture either the demand stimulation effects of worksharing or the problems of pricing distortions downstream that arise from uniform access prices (when the products provided entail different costs). This has special importance when the market is opened to competition, as emerging in the EU, since uniform access prices can trigger inefficient entry and cream-skimming. The result has been the development of 'bottom-up' approaches, such as the DAP rule, which sets worksharing discounts based in part upon the cost of the remaining work to be performed by the PO in providing access to the network and performing the final delivery function.

Note, however, from the review of theory in Section 2, that in a second-best world – the world of Ramsey pricing in postal markets – optimal discounts would almost always be less than avoided costs.[26] Such discounts should also decrease, *ceteris paribus*, as the cost of remaining work (beyond worksharing) for the PO to complete delivery increases.[27] Such discounts should also be reduced as the cost of the USO increases. The welfare-optimal rule reflects a tradeoff among these competing effects. In particular, optimal worksharing discounts could exceed avoided cost for workshared products destined for delivery in low-cost urban zones where the PO's margins are high and where demand stimulation might also be assumed to be high (relative to high-cost areas).

In practice, where retail-minus or avoided cost approaches have been formally adopted, as in USPS and La Poste, discounts above avoided cost are normally not employed, at least overtly. For example, the US Postal Rate Commission (PRC) has stated, and reinforced several times, in its Recommended Decisions that worksharing discounts should be based upon the avoided cost of USPS (Cohen et al., 2006). However, even where there is general agreement or regulatory ruling on the principle of avoided cost, there are measurement problems in estimating avoided costs of postal activities. For example, Haldi and Olson (2004) argued that the PRC had set discounts lower than avoided costs and Panzar (2006) examines further the problem of determining avoided cost discounts when mail heterogeneity is present.[28]

The second-best world is further complicated by the requirement of a USO. In a second-best world where there is a need to fund the fixed burden of the USO, setting discounts at above avoided cost may not be efficient and it is not likely to be politically feasible. It is well known that Ramsey prices can be less than marginal cost if strong complementarities are present (Crew and Kleindorfer, 1986). Price less than marginal cost is equivalent in the case of worksharing discounts being greater than avoided costs, and complementarity here is to be thought of in terms of the demand stimulation effect of worksharing on ultimate delivery (the access products provided) by the PO. However, as we have seen in our study of the structure of the welfare-optimal rules for worksharing, the demand stimulation effect of worksharing has to overcome an offsetting Ramsey adjustment term in order to give rise to discounts greater than avoided cost. If fixed network costs for maintaining the USO are high, then the demand stimulation effect would have to be exceedingly strong to justify a discount greater than avoided costs. In the absence of extensive empirical estimates of the demand stimulation effects, based upon current understanding of postal demand, this is not likely to be the case.[29]

In practice, the upper limit of discounts will not exceed the avoided cost of the incumbent PO for the worksharing activity in question. What is the lower limit? The lower limit is the avoided/marginal cost of the lowest-cost WSP, because, if the discount is set lower than this, there will be no takers. There will be no worksharing. As discussed in the Technical Appendix (3A), the role of WSP costs (and not just the PO's avoided costs) is important in setting optimal worksharing discounts, but it is also complex. This is because WSP costs enter into the optimal worksharing discounts only indirectly through the displacement ratio. If, as seems very likely, it is the largest customers that have the lowest marginal cost of worksharing, and moreover if these costs are significantly lower (because of economies of scope in mail preparation) than the corresponding avoided costs of the PO, then setting the discount at the avoided cost level will definitely capture the benefits of worksharing by WSPs with the lowest-cost potential. As Billette de Villemeur et al. (2006) have shown in their calibrated study for La Poste, there may be benefits from extending the incentives to workshare beyond these largest customers, but they show that most of these benefits can also be attained by adjusting the price of E2E services while maintaining workshared discounts at avoided cost. From empirical and theoretical work to date, therefore, it is reasonable to conclude that avoided cost should be the upper limit on worksharing discounts, pending detailed and country-specific empirical work demonstrating the benefits of going beyond the avoided cost level for some workshared products (certainly only those destined for low-cost, high-density delivery zones).

An additional element that needs to be considered in discussing the issue of avoided cost as an upper bound on worksharing discounts is the issue of X-inefficiency of the PO.[30] Even under apparent first-best conditions, with no demand stimulation from worksharing, where the optimal worksharing discount is avoided cost, there is a problem. Of concern is the high likelihood that the PO's avoided cost is inflated because of X-inefficiency or as a result of higher labor compensation paid by the PO compared to competitors. If the PO's costs are high because of X-inefficiency, the case for discounts below the PO's avoided costs is rather strong. If the PO sets discounts equal to its (inflated) avoided cost it is likely to encourage excessive entry or supernormal profits in the worksharing industry. If, as a result of competition, the PO's costs are reduced, this will subsequently require a reduction in the discount it offers. It is likely to be more efficient to set discounts closer to the long-run equilibrium, which is closer to the entrants' costs. PO's profits or contribution to the burden of the USO would be increased as well. The key problem is providing the proper incentives to the PO to respond to workshare competition and to reduce its costs.

4.2 Understanding the Structure of Optimal Access Prices

In order to provide a synthesis of the above discussion, let us consider how the three factors of avoided cost, margin on work yet to be done and USO costs interact in the structure of optimal worksharing/access prices.

Let us begin with the simplest example of upstream worksharing, in which the PO has the same avoided cost C_u of some workshared activity A, irrespective of its origin. The reader might think of this activity A as collection and pre-sorting, with delivery to a local post office for further sortation, transportation and delivery. Denote by $C_{tj} + C_{dj}$ the PO's unit cost of all work, including final delivery, following the workshared activity, where $C_{tj} + C_{dj}$ depends on the ultimate delivery zone $j = 1, \ldots, J$. We have assumed here for simplicity that $C_{tj} + C_{dj}$ depends only on the final delivery area and not on the origin of the mail; in reality, these 'costs of work yet to be done' could depend on the origin of the mail as well as other factors.

Figure 3.2 shows various quantities plotted against the delivery zone $j = 1, \ldots, J$ on the horizontal axis, where we have ordered the delivery zones in terms of increasing cost of transportation and delivery. We assume a linear increasing form for $C_{tj} + C_{dj}$. Note the constant avoided upstream cost C_u for worksharing activities and the corresponding E2E price P for the workshared product in question. The margin on work yet to be done after

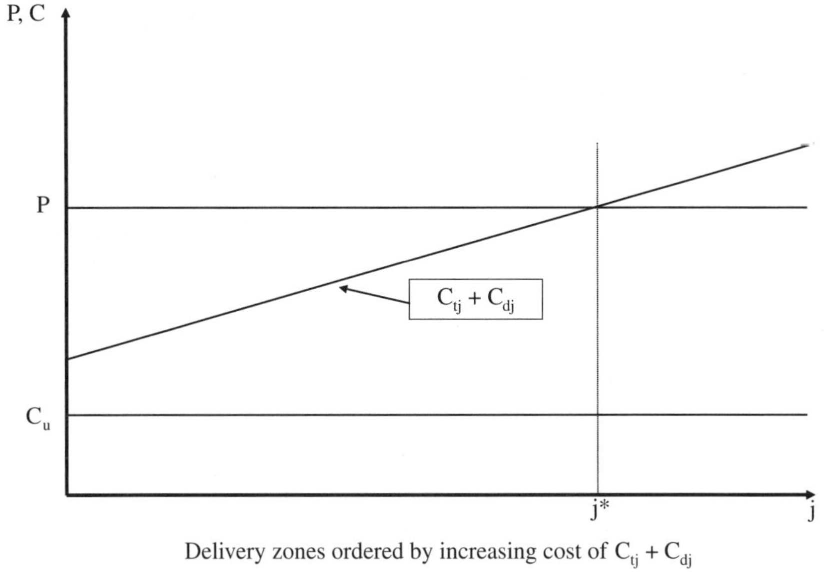

Figure 3.2 Avoided cost (C_u) and cost yet to go ($C_{tj} + C_{dj}$)

worksharing, for any zone j, is $[P - (C_{tj} + C_{dj})]$, which is decreasing as one goes from low- to high-cost zones, and we show it for this example to be negative for the very highest-cost zones (those with higher costs than j*).

From our earlier analysis (see equations (3.1) and (3.2) of Section 2), the optimal worksharing discount for mail destined for delivery in zone j has the form:

$$\text{Discount}(A, j) = \text{Maximum}\,[D(A, j), 0], \tag{3.4}$$

where:

$$D(A, j) = R(A, j)C_u + [1 - R(A, j)][P - (C_{tj} + C_{dj})] - \text{Ramsey adjustment}, \tag{3.5}$$

where R(A, j) is the displacement ratio for activity A and workshared access product j.[31] We assume for simplicity that R(A, j) is constant across delivery zones.[32] A typical result of applying the above logic to the costs and price in Figure 3.2 is given in Figure 3.3. The dashed line in Figure 3.3 is the optimal price ignoring the Ramsey adjustment, while the dotted line is the optimal price after applying the Ramsey Adjustment. In the latter case, we note that, for this example, the discount goes to zero for the highest-cost delivery zones, which would be expected when there are significant differences in delivery costs across urban and rural zones.

Now let us consider a product like downstream access. As an example, consider the situation where a WSP would use electronic means to prepare and print mail in each local delivery zone, bypassing both upstream and transportation activities, with costs C_u and C_{tj}, $j = 1, \ldots, J$. In this case, the avoided cost portion of the optimal worksharing discounts would include avoided transportation costs, and (3.4)–(3.5) would have the form:

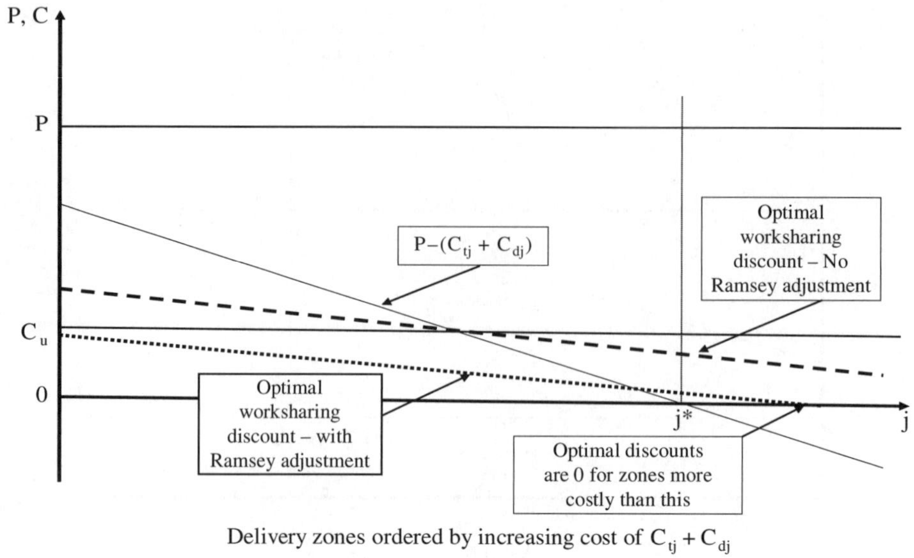

Figure 3.3 Optimal worksharing discounts with constant displacement ratio

$$\text{Discount }(A, j) = \text{Maximum }[D(A, j), 0], \tag{3.6}$$

where:

$$D(A, j) = R(A, j)(C_u + C_{tj}) + [1 - R(A, j)](P - C_{dj}) - \text{Ramsey adjustment}. \tag{3.7}$$

Now avoided costs increase with the ultimate delivery zone *j* (since they also include transportation costs avoided). We illustrate the result of using the optimal discount structure for this case in Figure 3.4, using the same cost and displacement ratio assumptions as those underlying Figure 3.3.

These figures, together, illustrate the basic tradeoffs involved in computing the optimal discount structures, which include the following general effects embodied in these examples:

1. Welfare-optimal discounts incorporate three components: (a) avoided cost; (b) margin/cost on work to be performed; and (c) USO costs, where the weights on the first two effects are determined by the displacement ratio for the workshared product in question.
2. Optimal discounts decline in going from low- to high-cost regions, and they may be zero for the highest-cost areas.
3. The Ramsey effect associated with USO decreases worksharing discounts, that is, increases access prices.
4. Discounts increase the greater the workshared activity (for example, contrast the discounts for upstream worksharing alone in (3.4) and (3.5) with the discounts for upstream plus transportation worksharing in (3.6) and (3.7)).

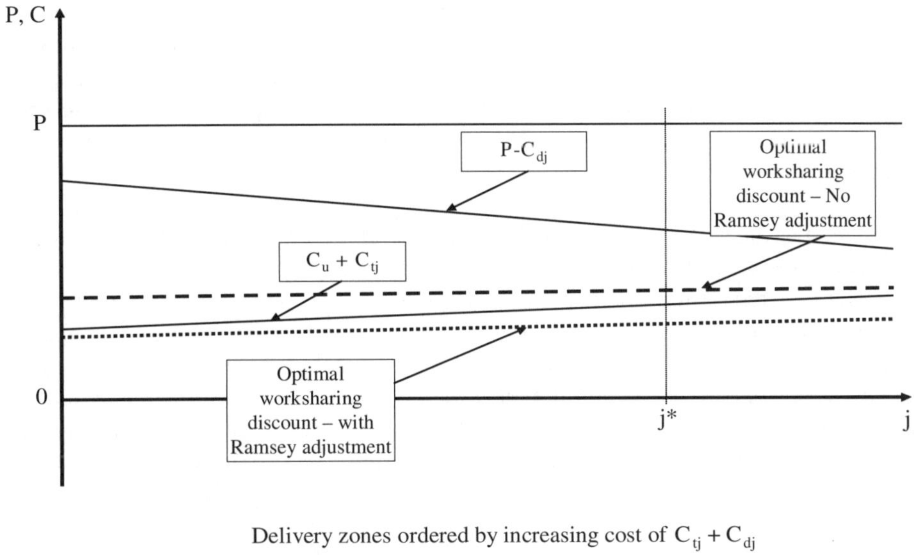

Figure 3.4 Optimal worksharing discounts for downstream access

The above examples are also intended to indicate that (after the Ramsey adjustment has been made) an upper bound of avoided cost on worksharing discounts would not impose any significant loss in welfare (as, in the cases illustrated, the optimal worksharing discounts never exceed avoided costs).

4.3 Policy Implications

The information requirements to compute this optimal rule are very demanding, in that the rule relies on both demand and cost information of a very detailed nature (including displacement ratios for each delivery zone, plus detailed cost and profit information). There seems to be no way a regulator could actually figure out how to set access charges according to the optimal rule, as it requires all kinds of information that the regulator (and even perhaps the PO) is not going to have. Thus, trying to dictate the optimal worksharing rule by regulatory fiat seems impractical and destined to lead to significant transactions costs from micro management. Given this, from a practical policy perspective, two approaches that are likely to be feasible are:

1. *Method 1* Employ a global price cap (RPI-X, with access products included in the price cap) and let the PO set workshare discounts, subject to floors and ceilings, and a non-discrimination clause that requires the PO to offer the same discounts to its own customers as to third-party WSPs. If the price caps are set in an appropriate fashion,[33] then the PO will face incentives to implement close to the optimal discount structure. (We discuss this further below.)
2. *Method 2* If the regulator wishes to specify an explicit rule that relies only on the PO's accounting information, such as avoided cost and margin on cost of work yet to

go, then the most appropriate intermediate rule would be DAP, which will result in retail-minus in the low-cost areas and something less than that in the high-cost areas. This would encourage the PO to consider both avoided cost and margin on remaining work and would make the rule responsive to both changes in avoided cost across various worksharing products as well as preventing inefficient subsidy of downstream access in high-cost areas.

We argue that the first of these approaches is likely to be superior on efficiency grounds, as it encourages an outward, value-based customer focus for the PO, rather than an inward cost focus. It would also encourage negotiated access agreements, subject to non-discrimination (so that agreements would be posted with the regulator and available to any other party who met the same volume and coverage details of the original party negotiating access). This provision would be like the posting provisions for agreements in the UK. The floors and ceilings are also easy to specify, namely avoided cost as the ceiling and a cost-based floor specified as the maximum of zero and the E2E tariff minus the average cost of final delivery for the zone for which the mail is destined. This would ensure that worksharing discounts still covered final delivery costs, unless this would give rise to an access price in excess of the corresponding E2E tariff. Usually, there will be a wide range of possible discounts between these two limits, especially for upstream workshared products. This would allow the PO discretion and opportunities to account for large-volume mailers, clean mail, special mail preparation and tendering conditions, mailing patterns such as saturation mailings or special timing of mailing, and other factors that might distinguish the costs and profits of one WSP from another. Subject to non-discrimination, the PO and WSPs should have the incentive and the opportunity to find and profit from these mutual efficiency benefits. In addition, it would require a less active stance on the part of the regulator. True, periodically, say every five years, the regulator would conduct a review on performance and might have some continuing quality monitoring. However, the burden placed on the regulator would not be such as to require micro management.

In concluding, it is important to note that this survey of possible approaches to access pricing in an age of postal reform and liberalization is a starting point for more-detailed policy prescriptions, which would need to address several specific issues. Perhaps the most important country-specific issue will be the integration of access pricing policy with the USO. In this chapter we have not focused on the details of the USO, but we and others have devoted a great deal of energy elsewhere to examining the relationship between the magnitude of USO costs and the pricing of access and worksharing.[34] The key insight arising from this literature that is explicitly represented in all of the analysis above is that the greater the scope of the USO, the larger the fixed costs that will have to be recovered from both E2E and access prices. We have seen the direct effects of the associated Ramsey adjustments to the optimal worksharing discounts. Less apparent, but no less important, are the pricing uniformity constraints of the USO, which have enormous implications for the structure of access prices. Indeed, a key implication of efficiency analysis under competition and FMO is the need to align price, cost and value of all postal products, including access. This implies, *inter alia*, the need to move toward zonal (that is, non-uniform) access prices that balance avoided cost, margin on work yet to be done, and the cost of the USO.

APPENDIX 3A OPTIMAL ACCESS PRICES AND WORKSHARING DISCOUNTS FOR POSTAL SERVICES

The theory of access pricing has been an active area of research for several years. We do not provide a survey of this literature, but rather summarize in concise fashion the main results obtained concerning the structure of optimal worksharing discounts, employing Billette de Villemeur et al. (2002), Crew and Kleindorfer (2002b), and de Donder (2006). These studies address different aspects of the problem. Billette de Villemeur et al. analyze the single-zone access problem, but they do so for heterogeneous customers (customers have different costs of undertaking worksharing activities), while Crew and Kleindorfer and de Donder analyze the case of multiple delivery zones for homogeneous customers. De Donder also considers the case where price discrimination is allowed between the direct customers of the PO and third-party WSPs. We do not consider price discrimination. The results presented draw on all three of these studies in selecting features of their models that are more general in application. This setting embodies heterogeneous customers, significant variability in transportation and delivery costs across the country, and no delivery bypass allowed.

We formulate the problem for a uniformly priced E2E product[35] ('letter mail') and for access prices to different zones $j = 1, 2, \ldots, J$ (the 'zones' can be understood not only as delivery zones, but also as general classes of worksharing products). We assume two types of customers, households and firms. Firms (but not households) have different costs for using worksharing technologies, where k represents the unit cost of worksharing for firm k. Bypass is not allowed, so that final delivery is always undertaken by the PO. Table 3A.1 shows the notation for the products, prices and costs involved.

Following the notation of Billette de Villemeur et al. (2002), let firm/WSP types (that is unit worksharing costs) k be distributed according to the pdf g(k), which we assume to be non-zero only in the interval $[\underline{k},\bar{k}]$. Given a price vector $\mathbf{P} = (P_x, P_z = P_{z1}, \ldots, P_{zJ})$ by the PO, each firm elects to workshare or not based on whether the firm's upstream preparation cost $k < P_x - P_{zj}$ (the worksharing discount offered) or not. Thus, if there are N_f firms in total who could potentially workshare, then the number of firms actually doing worksharing are those with unit worksharing costs less than the discount, that is:

$$\text{Number of Firms that Workshare at Prices } (P_x, P_{zj}) = N_f\left(\int_{\underline{k}}^{P_x - P_{zj}} g(k)\,dk\right). \quad \text{(3A.1)}$$

Assuming a known demand structure for each firm, one can then formally compute E2E demand X(P) at any price vector $\mathbf{P} = (P_x, P_z)$, which would be the sum of household demand and the demand of firms not electing to do worksharing, and workshare demand Z(P) which is the sum of the demand of firms electing to do worksharing.

The resulting Ramsey problem has the structure:

$$\text{Maximize} \quad W(P_x, P_z) = (1 + w)S_h(P_x) + S_f(P_x, P_z) + \Pi(P_x, P_z) \quad \text{(3A.2)}$$

$$\text{Subject to:} \quad \Pi(P_x, P_z) \geqslant 0, \quad \text{(3A.3)}$$

Table 3A.1 Notation for end-to-end (E2E) service and workshared (WS) service

	E2E service to zone j	WS service to zone j
Household demand	X_{hj}	NA
Firm demand	X_{fj}	Z_{fj}
Total demand	$X_j = X_{hj} + X_{fj}$	$Z = Z_{fj}$
Price of service	P_x	P_{zj}
Cost to PO of customer consuming service	$C_u + C_{dj}$	C_{dj}
Effective price for WSP(k) of consuming Service	P_x	$k + P_{zj}$

where $w \geqslant 0$ is the welfare weight on household surplus relative to firm surplus, where S_h and S_f are the surplus (excess of willingness to pay over price) for the household and firm sectors, respectively and where the PO's profits $\Pi(P_x, P_z)$ are given by:

$$\Pi(P_x, P_z) = \sum_{j=1}^{J} \{(P_x - C_u - C_{dj})[X_{hj}(P_x) + X_{fj}(P_x, P_{zj})] + (P_{zj} - C_{dj})Z_{fj}(P_x, P_{zj})\} - F, \tag{3A.4}$$

and F represents the fixed costs of the USO. Under the assumption that bypass is not allowed, the solution to (3A.1)–(3A.3) can be shown to be of the Ramsey form of optimal mark-ups for the 2*J products (one E2E and one WSP product for each of the J zones). We shall not consider the details of the optimal E2E price P_x, but rather focus on the optimal access prices P_{zj}. In general, of course, it is important to solve for both P_x and P_z simultaneously, as the solution to (3A.2)–(3A.3) is a joint solution over both prices. However, even if P_x is not set optimally, the optimal solutions for the vector of access prices P_z must solve their respective first-order conditions. These are given by:[36]

$$\frac{P_{zj} - C_{dj}}{P_{zj}} = \left(\frac{\lambda}{1+\lambda}\right)\frac{1}{\varepsilon_{zj}} - \left[\frac{P_x - (C_u + C_{dj})}{P_{zj}}\right]\frac{\partial X_j/\partial P_{zj}}{\partial Z_j/\partial P_{zj}}, j = 1, \ldots, J, \tag{3A.5}$$

where $\lambda \geqslant 0$ is the Lagrange multiplier on the profit constraint (3A.3), $\lambda/(1+\lambda)$ is the Ramsey number and where $\varepsilon_{zj} > 0$ is the absolute value of the own-price elasticity of Z_j to P_{zj} (that is, $\varepsilon_{zj} = -(\partial Z_j/\partial P_{zj})(P_{zj}/Z_j)$).

Multiplying both sides of (3A.5) by P_{zj} and subtracting the result from P_x, we readily obtain the optimal worksharing discounts δ_j for each of the worksharing products $j = 1, \ldots, J$ as:

$$P_x - P_{zj} = \delta_j = \sigma_j C_u + (1 - \sigma_j)(P_x - C_{dj}) - \left(\frac{\lambda}{1+\lambda}\right)\left(\frac{P_{zj}}{\varepsilon_{zj}}\right), \; j = 1, \ldots, J, \tag{3A.6}$$

where the so-called displacement ratio $\sigma_j \leqslant 1$ is defined as:

$$\sigma_j = -\frac{\partial X_j/\partial P_{zj}}{\partial Z_j/\partial P_{zj}}. \tag{3A.7}$$

In fact, (3A.6) needs to be further restricted to ensure that optimal worksharing discounts δ_j are non-negative (since there would be no demand for workshared products which cost more than the associated E2E product), so that optimal rule is of the form $\delta_j^* = \text{Max}[\delta_j, 0]$, with δ_j as given in (3A.6).

To interpret σ_j, consider the consequences of increasing the price P_{zj} of the workshared product j. Some firms purchasing the workshared product would now find it preferable to consume the corresponding E2E product (leading to a decrease in Z_j and a corresponding increase in X_j). Other firms would continue to consume the workshared product, but would use less of it given the higher price. In general, the decrease in Z_j would therefore be at least as great as the increase in X_j, so that $\sigma_j \leq 1$.[37] Thus, the displacement ratio σ_j represents the fraction of mail that is displaced from the PO to the WSP under worksharing and $1 - \sigma_j$ represents the fraction of 'new mail' generated by worksharing. So if $\sigma_j = 0.9$, then for every 10 pieces of mail workshared, nine of them are displaced from the PO's corresponding E2E product and one would be newly generated mail resulting from the demand stimulation effect of worksharing.

Consider the structure of (3A.6). The first two terms are a convex combination of the avoided cost of the workshared product j and the margin on the work yet to be performed. When $P_x - C_{dj} > C_u$, this convex combination is clearly greater than the PO's avoided cost C_u of the workshared product. However, when $P_x < C_u + C_{dj}$, as might well be the case for high-cost delivery areas, then this convex combination is less than the PO's avoided cost of the workshared product. The final Ramsey term further reduces the discount (assuming that the profit constraint (3A.3) is not binding so that $\lambda > 0$). In particular, for unconstrained worksharing discounts (usually referred to as first best or welfare optimal) where $\lambda = 0$, we see that (assuming the displacement ratio remains constant) the optimal discount rule implies that discounts would decrease in providing workshared products to low-cost urban areas versus high-cost rural areas. When $\lambda > 0$, assuming the likely case that demand elasticities (ε_{zj}) do not increase significantly in going from urban to rural areas, the same conclusion also applies in the breakeven-constrained (second-best) case.

Implicit in (3A.6) is the cost structure of WSPs because the distribution of worksharing costs across all potential WSPs determines, for any given discount $P_x - P_{zj}$, which firms/WSPs will workshare (at unit cost k) and which will use the PO's E2E service. However, the relationship between the WSP cost structure and optimal discounts is complex, since its effect is through the displacement ratio, which is a function of both the cost structure across potential WSPs and their interdependent demands. Understanding the implications of (3A.6) therefore requires an empirical study of both WSP demand and the distribution of unit costs, as in Billette de Villemeur et al. (2006) and De Donder et al. (2006).

As noted in Billette de Villemeur et al., the higher the weight w on household surplus, the greater the reliance on access prices to generate gross profits to support the fixed costs of the USO and the lower the corresponding E2E tariffs (that is, the lower would be P_x). We do not analyze these matters further here, as our concern is with the structure of access prices rather than with the relative profit responsibility of access products versus E2E products. Note, however, that increases in cost of access to business customers will flow through to their ultimate consumers, including households. As a result, the case for asymmetric weighting on households versus businesses is reduced.

Expanding this logic to more general upstream avoided costs, we obtain the expression noted in equation (3.1) for general workshared products. Note that the structure of the optimal rule here weights both avoided cost and the margin on work to be performed by the PO. If this margin is less than the avoided cost of the workshared product, then the workshared product should be priced below avoided cost. Certainly if this margin is sufficiently negative (as it might be for high-cost delivery areas), then no discount will be given for workshared activities, as doing so would lead to subsidization and increased demand for products already making losses. These considerations give rise to rules that are similar in structure to the DAP rule discussed in Section 2.

NOTES

* The authors acknowledge with thanks comments on earlier versions of this chapter by Joan Calzada, Axel Gautier, Frank Rodriguez, and Joëlle Toledano. The usual disclaimer applies.

1. There is also a mail box monopoly in the USA, which means that only USPS is allowed to put mail in the recipient's mail box.
2. According to the proposal for a Third Postal Directive, approved by the European Parliament in 2008, markets in most of the EU-15 member states will be open for competition in 2011, with all EU states open to competition by 2013.
3. For background and analysis of the impact of FMO see PwC (2006).
4. The avoided cost rule for access pricing also is known as the efficient component pricing rule (ECPR); see Armstrong (2002, 2008).
5. See d'Alcantara and Gautier (2008) for a discussion of the impact of route cost structures on postal pricing, including access pricing.
6. For details on these rules, see Crew and Kleindorfer (2002b); Panzar (2002); Billette de Villemeur et al. (2006).
7. For a discussion of the logic of this rule, see Crew and Kleindorfer (2002b, p. 30) and Panzar (2002, p. 114). Note that zonal pricing/DAP is sometimes confused with long-run incremental cost (LRIC) access pricing, for example, Armstrong (2002) as practiced in the telecommunications sector. In the postal sector, it is not usually appropriate to charge less than avoided cost under DAP, even if LRIC is less than avoided cost. Of course, LRIC still serves as a floor for access costs, but is not itself the proper benchmark for prices themselves. The reason is that all products, including access products, should make a contribution toward covering the fixed costs of the USO.

   As discussed below, various complexities can be added to the simple form of the DAP rule displayed here. These complexities would reflect customer heterogeneity, demand substitution effects, alternative origin-destination cost differences and mark-ups to cover the USO. We note that the DAP rule is intended to also cover the possibility of delivery bypass (that is, full E2E competition) by WSPs. Indeed, as noted in Crew and Kleindorfer (2004b), the efficiency gains from the DAP rule relative to the ACP rule are likely to be much greater when bypass is possible.
8. For example, negotiated service agreements (NSAs) in the United States are not carrier access pricing agreements, but are more similar to quantity discounts. Levy et al. (2006) argue that the transactions costs and time associated with regulation of these NSAs by the US Postal Rate Commission have resulted in very few of them actually being completed. Levy et al. point out further that there have been considerable benefits lost from NSAs that would have been achieved if they had been freely negotiated. See also Sappington and Unel (2005).
9. As will be seen in the structure of the optimal results below, optimal access pricing results for the postal sector have earlier roots in Laffont and Tirole (1994) and Armstrong et al. (1996).
10. In discussing worksharing discounts, we shall not distinguish here between direct customers of the PO and third-party providers of worksharing. In many jurisdictions, including the EU, anti-discrimination rules prohibit discriminatory treatment of these two types of WSP. In theory, however, some efficiency improvements could be obtained from price discrimination. See de Donder (2006) for a discussion.
11. Billette de Villemeur et al. (2002) show that if one solves jointly for access prices and the welfare optimal E2E price, then the resulting Ramsey adjustment term also involves the weight put on households relative

to business activities in the welfare function. The higher this weight is, the lower will be the optimal discounts, that is, the higher will be access prices paid by business customers using worksharing. An alternative way of thinking of this in the present context (where the E2E price is assumed fixed in the analysis) is that the higher the weight on household welfare is, the more profit will have to be raised from workshared products, and therefore the lower will be the corresponding worksharing discounts. See also Billette de Villemeur et al. (2006) for a discussion of fixed versus flexible E2E prices.

12. More formally, for a given worksharing activity A, let $X(p, \delta) =$ E2E demand and let $Z(p, \delta)$ be workshared demand, when E2E price is p and the worksharing discount is δ. Then the displacement ratio is defined as $\sigma_A = -(\partial X/\partial\delta)/(\partial Z/\partial\delta)$. See Appendix 3A for details.
13. De Donder et al. (2006) provide a model of price controls for Royal Mail, and they use values of 0.75 to 0.90 for the displacement ratio. This would seem to be the relevant range, implying only limited demand stimulation at the margin from worksharing and access.
14. Both of these forms of access price regulation have been discussed in the literature, and the inclusion of access prices in the price-cap formula has come to be known as 'global price-cap regulation'. For details, see Crew and Kleindorfer (1994, 2008), Laffont and Tirole (1996) and Billette de Villemeur et al. (2003).
15. This section is largely based on the authors' work in Crew and Kleindorfer (2002b, 2004b) and in the European Commission Paper (PwC, 2006), to which the reader is referred for additional details on the role of access pricing under full market opening.
16. For details on the French worksharing market, see Ambrosini and Klargaard (2006) and Gallet-Rybak et al. (ch.18, this volume).
17. The Universal Service for Bulk Mailers: A Postcomm Decision Document', 30 June 2005.
18. Access to Royal Mail's Postal Facilities, 15 October 2004.
19. Though these figures exclude document exchange mail which is not regulated and which accounts for approximately another 2 percent of addressed business mail, thus reducing Royal Mail's market share to some 95 percent.
20. The precise benchmark for computing Royal Mail's access prices is still under discussion, but Postcomm notes that the correct basis upon which underlying avoided costs, and delivery costs for zonal access tariffs, should be calculated is that of a second class mail item, since this is where access and competition primarily exist.
21. The 'headroom', is a minimum. Access prices can be lower than required by this difference but not higher.
22. The possibility is foreseen in the access regulations of reviewing the current headroom minima and changing them after two years.
23. See http://www.royalmailwholesale.com/c9_papers.cfm. As of March 2006, downstream access in the UK was at a level of approximately 32 million items per week, with 14 access contracts in operation.
24. See de Bijl et al. (2006) for the argument in favor of light-handed regulation.
25. It should be noted that economies of scale are often neglected in the discussion of avoided cost principles. In the context of postal worksharing, these are probably not critical except in delivery. Thus, absent bypass, neglecting economies of scale in access pricing is not likely to be a major concern.
26. Theoretically, Ramsey discounts might exceed avoided cost. However, as we argue below, this is extremely unlikely in the postal contexts.
27. The most important instance of this discussed is high-cost delivery zones, and hence, the development of DAP.
28. Mail heterogeneity arises for a number of reasons, having to do with volumes of mail presented and the quality of mail preparation by a WSP. In addition to these differences, there is co-mingling of mail from multiple sources at various stages of mail processing, which introduces uncertainty in the estimation of the avoided cost of a particular type of mail in these stages.
29. See de Donder, et al. (2006) and Billette de Villemeur et al. (2006) for some calibrated demand models for Royal Mail and La Poste. In their study of Royal Mail, de Donder et al. used values of 0.75 to 0.90 for the displacement ratio. This would seem to be the relevant range, implying only limited demand stimulation from worksharing/access at the margin.
30. By X-inefficiency, following Leibenstein (1966), we mean operational inefficiencies that give rise, for the outputs produced, to greater costs than the available least-cost technology would dictate. X-inefficiencies are to be expected under non-competitive conditions.
31. Recall from Section 2 that the displacement ratio is a number ≤ 1 indicating the fraction of mail, at the margin, that worksharing displaces from E2E mail as the worksharing discount changes. If all worksharing mail is just displaced mail from the E2E product, then $R(A) = 1$. If worksharing stimulates additional demand, beyond displacing mail from the E2E product, the $R(A) < 1$, where $1 - R(A)$ would then represent the fraction of worksharing mail that was 'new' mail generated by the stimulus of worksharing.
32. One might reasonably expect the displacement ratio to increase in going from the low-cost urban zones to higher-cost rural zones. Such an increase would indicate that workshared products would have less of a demand stimulation effect for rural zones than they would for urban zones. Assuming this, then (3.5) indicates that the first two terms in the untruncated discount $D(A, j)$ should become closer to avoided cost in the high-cost areas than they would under a constant displacement ratio assumption.

33. For a discussion of appropriate approaches to price-cap regulation in general, see Crew and Kleindorfer (1996). For applications to access pricing in the postal sector, see Crew and Kleindorfer (1994, 2008) and Billette de Villemeur et al. (2003).
34. See, for example, our review of this literature in Crew and Kleindorfer (2004b). For a discussion of the changes that might be expected in balancing the USO and access pricing under full market opening (FMO), see Crew and Kleindorfer (2006d).
35. When the uniformity constraint is not required, as for parcels, the problem separates into a set of single-zone cases. Each is of the form of the single-zone case analyzed in Billette de Villemeur et al. (2002), where the access price and the E2E price for each zone or origin–destination pair is determined independently, subject to the overall profit constraint, which results in a common shadow price on profits in each zone.
36. See equation (7) in Billette de Villemeur et al. (2002), (13)–(15) in Crew and Kleindorfer (2002b) and (1)–(2) in de Donder (2006). Note, however, that (7) of Billette de Villemeur et al. has a typo in that ε_x should be ε_z. In the case of de Donder, note that we do not treat customers and third parties differently, so that only equation (3.2) need be considered with $\sigma_j^{ED} = 0$. Each of these authors formulates the problem somewhat differently. This gives rise to different first-order conditions for the optimal E2E price. However, the first-order conditions for optimal access prices P_{zj} are consistent across these studies, at least for cases in which comparisons can be made. Billette de Villemeur et al. only consider a single zone and use the formulation for welfare (3A.2), while incorporating heterogeneity across firms. Crew and Kleindorfer consider two zones and equal weights in the welfare function (that is, assume $w = 0$ in (3A.2)), but they assume homogeneity across firms in terms of the cost of worksharing. De Donder considers two zones and has no separate household sector, that is, all agents are assumed to be able to make use of worksharing. There are other differences as well. The reader wishing to compare across these studies should consider the case where the additional weight on customer welfare is 0 (that is, $w = 0$ in (3A.5)).
37. The model of Billette de Villemeur et al. (2002) provides the explicit logic noted in this paragraph.

REFERENCES

Ambrosini, Xavier and Olaf Klargaard (2006), 'From theory to practice: vertical relations in the French postal market', in Crew and Kleindorfer (eds), (2006c), pp. 183–202.

Armstrong, Mark (2002), 'The theory of access pricing and interconnection', in Martin Cave, Sumit Majumdar and Ingo Vogelsang (eds), *Handbook of Telecommunications Economics*, Amsterdam North-Holland, pp. 297–384.

Armstrong, Mark (2008), 'Access pricing, bypass and universal service in the post', forthcoming, *Review of Network Economics.*

Armstrong, Mark, Chris Doyle and John Vickers (1996), 'The access pricing problem: a synthesis', *Journal of Industrial Economics*, **44**(2), June, 131–50.

Billette de Villemeur, Étienne, Helmuth Crémer and Bernard Roy (2006), 'Worksharing and pricing in the postal sector: a calibrated model', IDEI Working Paper, Institut d'Économie Industrielle, University of Toulouse, presented at the 4th Toulouse Conference on Postal Economics, March 16–17.

Billette de Villemeur, Étienne, Helmuth Crémer, Bernard Roy and Joëlle Toledano (2002), 'Pricing and worksharing discounts in the postal sector', in Crew and Kleindorfer (eds) (2002a), pp.33–48.

Billette de Villemeur, Étienne, Helmuth Crémer, Bernard Roy and Joëlle Toledano (2003), 'Optimal pricing and price-cap regulation in the postal sector', *Journal of Regulatory Economics*, **24**(1), 49–62.

Billette de Villemeur, Étienne, Helmuth Crémer, Bernard Roy and Joëlle Toledano (2005), 'Worksharing, pricing and competition in the postal sector', in Crew and Kleindorfer (eds) (2005a), pp. 139–61.

Billette de Villemeur, Étienne, Helmuth Crémer, Bernard Roy and Joëlle Toledano (2007), 'Worksharing, access and bypass: the structure of prices in the postal sector', *Journal of Regulatory Economics*, **32**(1), 67–85.

Bloch, Francis and Axel Gautier (2008), 'Access pricing and entry in the postal sector', paper presented at the 4th Conference on Postal Economics, Toulouse, March 16–17. Forthcoming in *Review of Network Economics.*

Calzada, Joan (2006), 'Worksharing and access discounts in the postal sector with asymmetric information', *Journal of Regulatory Economics*, **29**(1), 69–102.

Cohen, Robert H., William W. Ferguson, John D. Waller and Spyros S. Xenakis (2006), 'Worksharing: how much productive efficiency, at what cost and at what price? Universal Service without a Monopoly', in Crew and Kleindorfer (eds) (2006a), pp. 141–52.

Crew, Michael A. and Paul R. Kleindorfer (1986), *The Economics of Public Utility Regulation*, Cambridge, MA: MIT Press.

Crew, Michael A. and Paul R. Kleindorfer (1991), 'Peak load pricing of postal service and competition', in M.A. Crew and P.R. Kleindorfer (eds), *Competition and Innovation in Postal Services*, Boston, MA: Kluwer Academic, pp. 37–56.

Crew, Michael A. and Paul R. Kleindorfer (1994), 'Pricing, entry, service quality and innovation under a commercialized postal service', in G. Sidak (ed.), *Governing the Postal Service*, Washington DC: AEI Press, Chapter 6.

Crew, Michael A. and Paul R. Kleindorfer (1996), 'Incentive regulation in the United Kingdom and the United States: some lessons', *Journal of Regulatory Economics*, **9**(3), May, 211–25.

Crew, Michael A. and Paul R. Kleindorfer (eds) (2002a), *Postal and Delivery Services: Delivering on Competition*, Boston, MA: Kluwer Academic.

Crew, Michael A. and Paul R. Kleindorfer (2002b), 'Balancing access and the universal service obligation', in Crew and Kleindorfer, (eds) (2002a), pp. 3–32.

Crew, Michael A. and Paul R. Kleindorfer (eds) (2004a), *Competitive Transformation of the Postal and Delivery Sector*, Boston, MA: Kluwer Academic.

Crew, Michael A. and Paul R. Kleindorfer (2004b), 'Access and the USO for letters and parcels', in Crew and Kleindorfer (eds) (2004a), pp. 3–41.

Crew, Michael A. and Paul R. Kleindorfer (eds) (2005a), *Regulatory and Economic Challenges in the Postal and Delivery Sector*, Boston, MA: Kluwer Academic.

Crew, Michael A. and Paul R. Kleindorfer (2005b), 'Competition, universal service and the graveyard spiral', in Crew and Kleindorfer (2005a), pp. 1–30.

Crew, Michael A. and Paul R. Kleindorfer (eds) (2006a), *Progress toward Liberalization of the Postal and Delivery Sector*, New York: Springer.

Crew, Michael A. and Paul R. Kleindorfer (eds) (2006b), 'The welfare effects of entry and strategies for maintaining the USO in the postal sector', in Crew and Kleindorfer (eds) (2006a), pp. 3–22.

Crew, Michael A. and Paul R. Kleindorfer (2006c), *Liberalization of the Postal and Delivery Sector*, Cheltenham, UK and Northampton, MA, USA: Edward Elgar.

Crew, Michael A. and Paul R. Kleindorfer (eds) (2006d), 'Approaches to the USO under entry', in Crew and Kleindorfer (eds), (2006c), pp. 1–18.

Crew, Michael A. and Paul R. Kleindorfer (2008), 'Regulation and the USO', in Crew and Kleindorfer (eds), *Competition and Regulation in the Postal and Delivery Sector*, Cheltenham, UK and Northampton, MA,USA: Edward Elgar, pp. 3–22.

d'Alcantara, Gonzales and Axel Gautier (2005), 'National postal strategies after a full postal market opening', in Michael A. Crew and Paul R. Kleindorfer (eds), *Competition and Regulation in the Postal and Delivery Sector*, Cheltenham, UK and Northampton, MA, USA: Edward Elgar, pp. 167–86.

de Bijl, Paul, Eric van Damme and Pierre Larouche (2006), 'Regulating access to stimulate competition in postal markets', in Crew and Kleindorfer (eds) (2006a) pp. 153–72.

de Donder, Philippe (2006), 'Access pricing in the postal sector: theory and simulations', *Review of Industrial Organization*, **28**, 207–326.

de Donder, Philippe, Helmuth Crémer, Paul Dudley and Frank Rodriguez (2006), 'Pricing and welfare implications of alternative approaches to setting price controls in the postal sector', in Crew and Kleindorfer (eds) (2006a), pp. 227–47.

Haldi, John and William J. Olson (2004), 'An evaluation of USPS worksharing: postal revenues and costs from workshared activities', in Crew and Kleindorfer (eds) (2004a), pp. 185–96.

Laffont Jean-Jacques and Jean Tirole (1994), 'Access pricing and competition', *European Economic Review*, **38**, 1673–710.

Laffont Jean-Jacques and Jean Tirole (1996), 'Creating competition through interconnection: theory and practice', *Journal of Regulatory Economics*, **10**(3), November, 227–56.

Leibenstein, Harvey (1966), 'Allocative efficiency versus X-efficiency', *American Economic Review*, **56**, June, 392–415.

Levy, David M., Joy M. Leong, Lawrence G. Buc and Michael K. Plunkett (2006), 'Benefit–cost regulation of negotiated service agreements', in Crew and Kleindorfer (eds) (2006a), pp. 341–58.

Littlechild, Stephen C. (1983), *Regulation of British Telecommunications' Profitability*, London: Department of Trade and Industry.

Panzar, John C. (2002), 'Reconciling competition, downstream access, universal service in postal markets', in Crew and Kleindorfer (eds) (2002a), pp. 93–115.

Panzar, John C. (2006), 'Efficient worksharing discounts with mail heterogeneity', in Crew and Kleindorfer (eds) (2006c), pp. 121–34.

Pearsall, Edward S. (2005), 'The effects of worksharing and other product innovations on U.S. postal volumes and revenues', in Crew and Kleindorfer (eds) (2005a), pp. 213–41.

PwC (PricewaterhouseCoopers) (2006), 'The Impact on Universal Service of the Full Market Accomplishment of the Postal Internal Market in 2009', European Commission, Brussels, May, Available online at http://ec.europa.eu/internal_market/post/studies_en.htm.

Sappington, David E.M. and Burcin Unel (2005), 'Privately-negotiated input prices', *Journal of Regulatory Economics*, **27**(3), 263–80.

4. An economic model of the regulatory structure created by the Postal Accountability and Enhancement Act of 2006*

Michael D. Bradley,[†] **Jeff Colvin**[‡] **and Mary K. Perkins**[§]

1. INTRODUCTION

The enactment of the Postal Accountability and Enhancement Act (PAEA) in December 2006 substantially changed the structure of the regulations governing the United States Postal Service (USPS). USPS, like postal administrations in other industrialized countries, operates in an environment made harsher by competition from electronic alternatives to the mail – illustrated by the continual fall in First Class single-piece volumes since 2000. The reforms included in the PAEA are intended to provide the flexibility that will allow USPS to succeed in today's communications market.

Under the PAEA, USPS is allowed to accumulate reserves rather than being obliged to break even, its 'market-dominant' products are subject to price-cap regulation (PCR), whereas its 'competitive' products' prices are set by USPS. Although the PAEA includes other reforms, these changes, designed to affect pricing behavior, have very powerful implications for the economic structure in which USPS operates and in this chapter we take an initial look at the consequences of the new economic structure.

There has been important previous work in modeling regulatory regimes for different posts (Crew and Kleindorfer, 1995; Billette de Villemeur et al., 2003; Dudley et al., 2005; de Donder et al., 2006a, 2006b) with a focus on the European Union. This focus is due to the changes in the actual regulatory frameworks governing European postal administrations, changes in pricing procedures, universal service obligations, and the scope of the postal monopoly. Because important changes are now occurring in the United States, we build upon the previous work to examine some of the key elements of the new law on the US postal industry. Such an exercise is important because the PAEA, like most legislation, gives rise to some conflicting interpretations and sorting out the implied economic structure helps foster understanding of those interpretations.

A primary change is the shift from a price-setting regulatory structure in which USPS was required to break even to PCR which provides some additional pricing discretion to

† George Washington University.
‡ United States Postal Service.
§ Howard University.

USPS. The focus of our modeling effort is on the price cap and on analyzing the implications for prices, consumer demand and USPS financial performance.

It has been argued that public enterprises, lacking obvious residual claimants to net revenues, will exhibit significantly different pricing behavior from private firms under the same conditions.[1] The question of the optimal ownership structure of firms, and of the impact of ownership on the pricing behavior of the firm, is a complicated issue with a long history. In this chapter, we limit ourselves to an examination of the impact of alternative objective functions under PAEA regulation.

In Section 2 we review the key aspects of the PAEA as they relate to the regulatory structure. We then specify an economic model of the new regulatory structure and solve for the resulting equilibrium conditions. Because the analytical solutions are quite complex, it is difficult to draw useful inferences from them; to address this difficulty, we calibrate the model in Section 3 and solve numerically. We then discuss the findings of our research in Section 4.

2. MODELING THE NEW LAW

The PAEA represents a broad reconstruction of the way in which USPS is regulated; the law includes provisions relating to universal service, antitrust, service quality, compliance, supply purchasing, health and retirement benefit costs, and many other items. As the focus of this chapter is on pricing regulation, however, it will be useful to review briefly those changes with impacts upon pricing behavior.

The new law establishes two product groups, 'market dominant' and 'competitive'.[2] The rates of market-dominant products are subject to 'an annual limitation on the percentage changes . . . equal to the change in the Consumer Price Index [CPI] for all Urban Consumers'.[3] The annual limitation applies separately to the average rate of each class of mail.[4] Workshare discounts may only exceed the cost avoided as a result of the workshare activity under certain circumstances.[5] With regard to competitive products, USPS has the authority to set its own prices,[6] subject to compliance with regulations promulgated by the Postal Regulatory Commission (PRC; formerly Postal Rate Commission), (i) prohibiting the subsidization of competitive products by market-dominant products, (ii) requiring that each competitive product covers its costs attributable, and (iii) requiring that all competitive products collectively cover an appropriate share of the institutional costs of USPS. Finally, the law removes the break-even constraint that has guided pricing in the past. USPS is free to earn profits as long as it is in compliance with the various regulatory constraints.

In this chapter, we take the first steps in modeling the economic behavior of a postal service faced with the profit and pricing constraints required by the new postal law in the United States. Our main interest lies in integrating some of the most important provisions of the new law into a consistent economic structure to permit the analysis of postal pricing regulations. Toward that end, we model postal pricing behavior in the presence of both USPS and competitor products. We include both customer worksharing and delivery access provided to competitors and we calculate a numerical solution to the model to foster understanding of its implications.

Although the PAEA imposes a set of complex regulations on USPS, there are a limited number of key economic structures that fashion the regulatory environment. In this section, we build a model of the PAEA regulatory structure that embodies these key structures. As discussed above, the PAEA assigns each postal product to one of two vectors, 'market-dominant' products and 'competitive' products. The former products are covered by the legal monopoly while the latter face direct product-to-product competition. Note that these vectors are nowhere near equal in size, in either volume or revenue. For example, in 2007 about 99 percent of USPS's domestic volume and 90 percent of its domestic revenue was generated by market-dominant products.

However, the division is important for regulatory purposes. The market-dominant products are under a price cap and their prices are limited by the CPI. The price cap was initiated at the last set of prices determined under the old regulatory regime and the weights on the products in the cap are the volumes USPS handled in the last year under that regime. In contrast, USPS is free to set any price for a competitive product as long as it exceeds the product's attributable cost floor and competitive products as a group make a 'reasonable' contribution to defraying institutional costs. Finally, because the product classifications defined in the law do not distinguish among types of mail users, USPS is effectively required to charge the same price for access to its delivery network to competitors as it does to customers. Access prices are established through 'worksharing' discounts, in which mailers receive reduced rates for preparing and transporting the mail. USPS provides the same 'discounts' to customers and competitors alike.

We model these essential characteristics in the following way. First, we start by defining a product vector which will include both 'market-dominant' and competitive products. In the market-dominant group there are three products. 'Product 1' is an end-to-end product for which USPS performs both upstream activities and delivery. There is no competitive offering for this product. The second market-dominant product is a delivery-only product. However, to reflect the fact that USPS provides this service both directly to customers and indirectly through 'pre-sorters' or 'mail service providers', we model the delivery-only product in two parts. The first part, termed 'Product 3' is sold directly to customers who provide their own mail preparation and transportation. The second part, termed 'Product 4' reflects the situation in which USPS sells delivery services to a third part vendor, who then in turn provides all upstream services and sells the combined end-to-end product to the final customer.[7] The last product, termed 'Product 2' is in the 'competitive' product group and faces direct competition. It is a higher service quality, higher-cost product and can be thought of as a hybrid of expedited and package services.

We complete our specification of products by describing the offerings of competitors of USPS. The first product, Product 4, was described above. From the competitor's perspective, they obtain delivery services (at an access price) from USPS and combine that with their own upstream services. The price to the customer for Product 4 is set by the competitor. Finally, the competitor also provides an expedited/package service, 'Product 5', similar to USPS's Product 2.

On the demand side, we model the products as being imperfect substitutes and, in theory, all five products are potential substitutes for one another. With five products, this implies a very complicated menu of cross-price effects and in itself renders the resulting model intractable. However, the degree of substitutability between a 40-cent letter and a $10.00 expedited package is clearly small. Thus to increase the likelihood of tractability, we restrict the cross-price effects. We assume that the market-dominant products (1, 3, and 4) have a complete set of cross-price effects as do the competitive products (2 and 5). In addition, we assume no cross-price effects across the product vectors.

The final specification required is the determination of the objective functions for USPS and the competitors. For the competitors, we simply assume profit maximization, but it is more problematic to determine the objective function for USPS. Normally a firm under PCR is modeled as being a profit maximizer with respect to the capped products.[8] In this case, however, the regulated firm is a public entity with no obvious residual claimant. One approach to this issue is to assume that USPS maximizes profits in order to provide the maximum contribution, over time, to the federal budget. However, Crew and Kleindorfer (2008) examine alternative approaches, for example, where postal operators subjected PCR set prices to maximize revenue. They argue that in the absence of a residual claimant postal operators may be influenced by the objectives of any of several groups of economic agents, and they argue that the closer the PO comes to creating pseudo residual claimants with interests aligned with profits the closer the behavior coincides with profit maximization under PCR.

The appropriate objective function for a public enterprise under PCR is unsettled and we thus follow an approach that investigates and compares the two main approaches. One approach is to model USPS as a revenue maximizer with respect to its market-dominant products subject to a profit constraint. This is consistent with a public service motive in which USPS is attempting to provide widely available services at reasonable prices. Furthermore, it reflects the fact that USPS has a statutory monopoly over delivery of these products and can thus sustain this line of business without necessarily maximizing profits. In addition, we analyze the outcome of the PAEA structure under the more traditional approach by assuming that USPS maximizes profit with respect to the products under the cap. We then compare the results under revenue maximization to those obtained under profit maximizing to help assess the importance of this issue for the implementation of the PAEA.

With regard to competitive products, in contrast, USPS is a relatively small player in the market and is prohibited by law from cross-subsidizing those products. In addition, the PAEA specifies a profit goal for competitive products by requiring them to provide a 'contribution' (profit) to defraying USPS's institutional costs. Consequently, we model USPS as maximizing profits with respect to competitive products.

With these specifications, the maximization problem for the USPS is:[9]

$$\max_{p_1,p_2,p_3} \; p_1v_1 + p_2v_2 + p_3(v_3 + v_4) - F_2 - (c_{U2} + c_{D2})v_2,$$

subject to a minimum profit constraint (Π^*):

$$p_1v_1 + p_2v_2 + p_3(v_3 + v_4) - F_{13} - c_{U2}v_1 - c_{D1}(v_1 + v_3 + v_4) \\ - F_2 - (c_{U2} + c_{D2})v_2 = \Pi^*,$$

an attributable cost floor on the competitive product,

$$p_2v_2 \geq F_2 + (c_{U2} + c_{D2})v_{2c},$$

and a price cap (ρ):

$$\theta_1 p_1 + \theta_3 p_3 = \rho,$$

where the weights $\theta_1 + \theta_3 = 1$. All upstream and downstream marginal costs ($c_{U1}, c_{D1}, c_{U2}, c_{D2}$,) are assumed constant. In addition, the incumbent post incurs fixed costs, denoted as F_{13} for market-dominant products, and F_2 for competitive products.

The competitive sector maximizes profits with respect to Product 4 and Product 5. Because Product 4 is a market-dominant product for USPS, the competitive sector is treated as a competitive fringe. On the other hand, USPS is a relatively small player in the competitive product market, so competitors earn a positive mark-up on marginal cost for Product 5. Optimization of USPS maximand and the competitor profit function yields five first-order conditions, which can be solved for a set of seven equilibrium conditions, one for each of the five products and two for the Lagrange multipliers:

$$(1+\mu_1)\left(1+\frac{1}{\varepsilon_1}\right)p_1 + (1+\mu_1)(\sigma_{31}+\sigma_{41})p_3 = \mu_1 c_{U1} + \mu_1 c_{D1}(1+\sigma_3+\sigma_4) + \mu_2\theta_1\frac{\partial p_1}{\partial v_1}, \tag{4.1}$$

$$p_2 = \frac{C_{U2}+C_{D2}}{1+\frac{1}{\varepsilon_2}}, \tag{4.2}$$

$$(1+\mu_1)[p_1(\sigma_{13}+\delta_{13})] + p_3\left[1+\frac{1}{\varepsilon_3}+\frac{\delta_{43}}{\varepsilon_3}+(\sigma_{43}+\delta_{33}+\delta_{43})\right](1+\mu_1)$$

$$= \mu_1[c_{U1}(\sigma_{13}+\delta_{13}) + c_{D1}(\sigma_{13}+\delta_{13}+1+\delta_{33}+\sigma_{43}+\delta_{43})] + \mu_2\theta_3\frac{\partial p_3}{\partial v_3}, \tag{4.3}$$

$$p_4 = c_{U4} + p_3, \tag{4.4}$$

$$p_5 = \frac{c_{U5}c_{D5}}{1+\frac{1}{\varepsilon_5}}, \tag{4.5}$$

$$p_1v_1 + p_2v_2 + p_3(v_3+v_4) - F_{13} - c_{u2}v_1 - c_{d1}(v_1+v_3+v_4) - F_2 - (c_{u2}+c_{D2})v_2 = \Pi^*, \tag{4.6}$$

$$\theta_1 p_1 + \theta_3 p_3 = \rho. \tag{4.7}$$

Solution of this set of equations for the market-dominant prices is quite complicated and insights into the implications of the results are not obtainable analytically. Thus, numerical analysis is required to gain a full understanding of what the solutions imply. However, a review of the equilibrium conditions yields some insights into the solutions. First, as expected, own-price elasticities will play an important role in determining prices. In the range of current prices USPS faces inelastic demand for its products, particularly its end-to-end products. With inelastic demand, revenue is enhanced by *increasing* price, not decreasing it. This has implications for revenue maximization under PCR. Second, two types of cross-effects are important. First, there are standard cross-price effects between products and these are captured by the σ_{ij} terms.[10] These measure the cross-price effect relative to the direct effect. That is:

$$\sigma_{ij} = \frac{\frac{\partial v_i}{\partial p_j}}{\frac{\partial v_j}{\partial p_j}} \quad i = 1, 2, 3;\; j = 1, 2, 3;\; i \neq j.$$

An increase in the price of Product 1 influences not only the demand for Product 1 but also the demand for Product 3. This, of course affects the price of Product 3, which in turn has a feedback effect on Product 1. The σ_{ij} terms thus measure the relative impact on the volumes of the two products of an increase in the price of the *j*th product. The other type of cross-product effect reflects the structure of the postal market in which competitors buy access to USPS's delivery network and then combine this with their own upstream services to charge the final customer and end-to-end price. Because USPS is required to charge the same price for access to customers and competitors, any change in the price of Product 3 not only affects customers of Product 3 but also Product 4.[11] For example, a higher Product 3 price implies a higher access price for providers of Product 4. This implies a higher Product 4 price. But the substitutability between Product 4 and Products 1 and 3 creates an additional channel for the Product 3 price to influence the demand for the three market-dominant products. This effect is captured by the δ_{i3} terms:

$$\delta_{i3} = \frac{\left(\frac{\partial v_i}{\partial p_4}\frac{\partial p_4}{\partial p_3}\right)}{\frac{\partial v_3}{\partial p_3}}.$$

3. CALIBRATING AND SOLVING THE MODEL NUMERICALLY

The complexity of our model of the PAEA structure precludes interpretation of the prices derived as the analytical solutions to the seven equilibrium conditions. To gain insight into the implications of PCR for the economic behavior of USPS, we solve the equilibrium conditions numerically. The actual implementation of the PAEA by the PRC relied upon the last set of prices for the market-dominant product set under the prior regulatory structure. These prices were set by the PRC in the last rate case, Docket No. R2006-1,[12] before the passage of the PAEA. Our calibration is thus to those prices.

Numerical solution of the model requires an explicit specification of a utility function for postal consumers and derivation of demand equations for each of the five products. We follow de Donder (2006) in specifying a representative consumer model with quasi-linear preferences and a quadratic utility function. Thus, the demand equations are derived from maximizing the net surplus of the representative customer:

$$U(v_1, v_2, v_3, v_4, v_5) - \sum_{i=1}^{5} p_i v_i.$$

Table 4.1 USPS reported values versus model calibration results

	Price*	Volume	Elasticity
First class mail	$0.400	90.100	−0.134
Product 1 (calibrated)	$0.400	90.420	−0.130
Priority mail	$5.835	0.897	−1.023
Product 2 (calibrated)	$5.835	0.890	−1.031
Standard mail	$0.200	103.500	−0.545
Products 3 & 4 (calibrated)	$0.200	102.600	−0.551

Note: * Prices are measured by recorded average revenues per piece in 2007.

After the demand equations have been derived analytically, the next step is to calibrate them. Because we specify a functional form that permits non-constant elasticities, we must go beyond simply specifying elasticities and calibrate the set of demand equations parameters. In other words, it is not sufficient to select elasticities. Instead, we must identify values for the utility function parameters that will generate demand equations that simultaneously replicate existing elasticities (and volumes) for all products at the specified prices. We start with the prices determined in Docket No. R2006-1, and then attempt to replicate the actual volumes and elasticities reported by USPS. Table 4.1 presents the results of the exercise and shows that calculated volumes and elasticities are quite close to these USPS reported values.

For Product 1, we use USPS's First Class product as our calibration target. It is a market-dominant product that provides end-to-end service. While part of the volume of the class is workshared, the option to enter mail at the destination delivery unit ('drop-shipping) is not included. Thus, all first class mail requires some mail processing and transportation. Our calibration target for Product 2 is USPS's Priority Mail. This is the largest of USPS's competitive products in terms of both volume and revenue. The calibration target for Products 3 and 4 is USPS's standard mail. All of this mail is workshared and a large portion of it is drop-shipped to the delivery unit. While our product vector is considerably simpler than USPS's actual product vector, it represents the overwhelming majority of USPS volume and revenue. The calibrated products represent approximately 95 percent of the USPSs domestic volume and 92 percent of its domestic revenue.

The final part of the calibration exercise is the specification of the marginal costs for the products. For these we use the volume variable costs per piece for the calibration targets as calculated by USPS for 2007. These are estimates of the marginal costs for the products used as calibration targets.

Our benchmark is the last set of break-even rates established by the PRC. Using our calibrated parameters, this benchmark produces a break-even scenario, which serves as the basis for calculating the price cap. The results of this scenario are presented in Table 4.2.

Our initial analysis of the PAEA structure is to examine the revenue-maximizing market-dominant prices under the price cap along with the profit-maximizing price for the competitive product. The values for the cap and the cap weights come from the prices in the benchmark scenario.[13] The results for revenue maximization are provided in Table 4.3.

Table 4.2 Initial prices, revenues and costs for the benchmark (breakeven) rule

	Product 1	Product 2	Product 3	Product 4	Total
Price (cents)	40.00	583.50	20.00	20.00	
Volume (bn)	90.42	0.89	82.56	20.05	
Elasticity	−0.130	−1.031	−0.546	−0.551	
Revenue ($bn)	$36.17	$5.20	$16.51	$4.01	$61.89
Product cost ($bn)	$18.45	$4.02	$10.48	$2.55	$35.50
Contribution ($bn)	$17.72	$1.18	$6.03	$1.46	$26.39
Fixed cost ($bn)					$26.40
Profit ($bn)					$0.00

Table 4.3 Price cap with revenue maximization for market-dominant products

	Product 1	Product 2	Product 3	Product 4	Total
Price (cents)	43.20	800.40	16.50	16.50	
Volume (bn)	89.41	0.55	90.35	21.33	
Elasticity	−0.142	−2.29	−0.41	−0.45	
Revenue ($bn)	$38.63	$4.41	$14.90	$3.52	$61.46
Product cost ($bn)	$18.24	$2.48	$11.47	$2.71	$34.90
Contribution ($bn)	$20.39	$1.92	$3.43	$0.81	$26.55
Fixed cost ($bn)					$26.40
Profit ($bn)					$0.14

The first thing to note about the results is that the total revenue earned under the price cap is less than the revenue earned under the benchmark prices, which seems contrary to the revenue-maximization goal.[14] The apparent contradiction is resolved by recognizing that the price cap applies to just the market-dominant products. Profit maximization of the competitive product requires raising its prices and lowering its revenue. The revenue generated on the competitive product thus falls by $800 million and it is this decline that lowers total revenue relative to the benchmark. In fact, the revenue earned on market-dominant products does rise by $360 under revenue maximization but this gain is not large enough to offset the loss of revenue on the competitive product.

Nevertheless, a comparison of the results of PCR with the benchmark shows relatively little change. The change in revenue earned by the market-dominant products is relatively small because the price cap is 'tight' and market demands are inelastic. As one might expect, to increase revenue, the price of the relatively inelastic product rises as the price of the relatively elastic product fall. As a result, Product 1's price rises by 3.2 cents and Product 3's price falls by 3.5 cents. While price declines are often associated with the standard analysis of revenue maximization (setting marginal revenue equal to zero), this result obtains under the working assumption that the profit-maximizing firm would already be in the elastic range of demand. As this is not the case for USPS, it could raise revenue by raising prices, but the cap precludes it from raising both the price of Product 1 and Product 3. As shown in Figure 4.1, revenue maximization is thus found by trading off

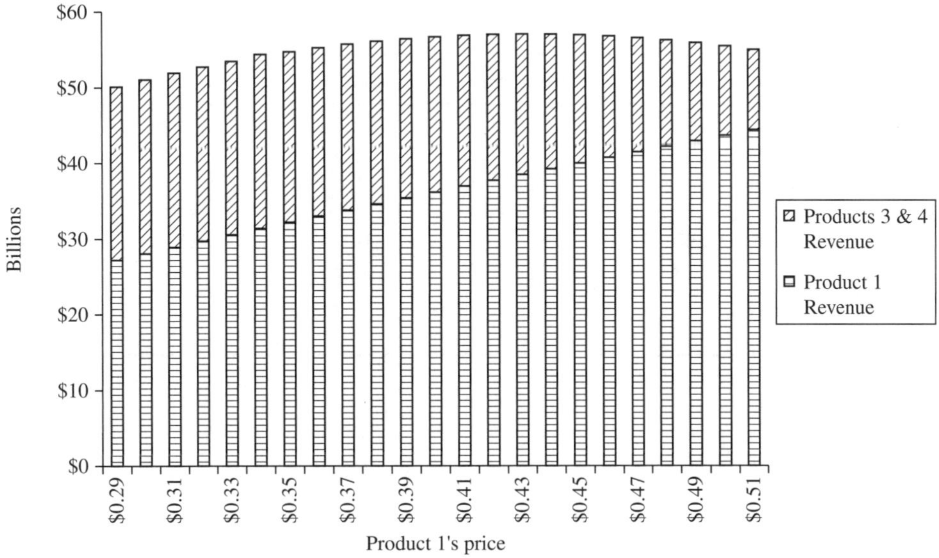

Figure 4.1 Revenue from market-dominant products

revenue gains on Product 1 with revenue losses on Product 3. As Product 1's price increases, its revenue rises but at the cost of lowering the price of Product 3 and thus reducing the revenue earned on Products 3 and 4.

We further investigate the role of the price cap by investigating an alternative maximand for USPS. We expand our analysis to include investigation of profit maximization for both the market-dominant products and the competitive product under the cap. We know that to maximize profits, USPS must substantially raise prices for its market-dominant products, but the cap precludes such an action. The profit-maximizing prices for the market-dominant products are given in Table 4.4. Note that here the price of Product 1 falls relative to the benchmark. This decline occurs because the tradeoff is now for contribution (revenue minus volume variable cost) and not just revenue.

Raising the price of Product 3 increases revenue and lowers volume. This latter effect also lowers volume variable cost, driving up total contribution, but to stay under the cap, the higher Product 3 price must be offset by a lower Product 1 price, which reduces its contribution. Because of the relative inelasticity of Product 1, the loss in contribution from lowering Product 1's price is less than the gain in contribution for increasing Product 3's price and total contribution (profit) is maximized. This is illustrated in Figure 4.2. One other result to note is the relative similarity, in terms of orders of magnitude, between the results of profit maximization in Table 4.3 and revenue maximization in Table 4.4. This occurs in part because the marginal costs of the postal products are quite low relative to prices. Thus setting marginal revenue equal to marginal cost is not that different in terms of the resulting quantities from setting marginal revenue equal to zero. In addition, the similarity of results is an implication of a relatively tight price cap.

Under the PAEA structure, a relatively tight cap is imposed on break-even prices. Our analysis of the cap shows that whether maximizing revenue or profit, USPS will be close

Table 4.4 Price cap with profit maximization

	Product 1	Product 2	Product 3	Product 4	Total
Price (cents)	38.90	800.40	21.20	21.20	
Quantity	90.77	0.55	79.88	19.60	
Elasticity	−0.126	−2.29	−0.60	−0.59	
Revenue	$35.31	$4.41	$16.94	$4.16	$60.82
Product cost	$18.52	$2.48	$10.14	$2.49	$33.63
Contribution	$16.79	$1.92	$6.79	$1.67	$27.17
Fixed cost					$26.40
Profit					$0.78

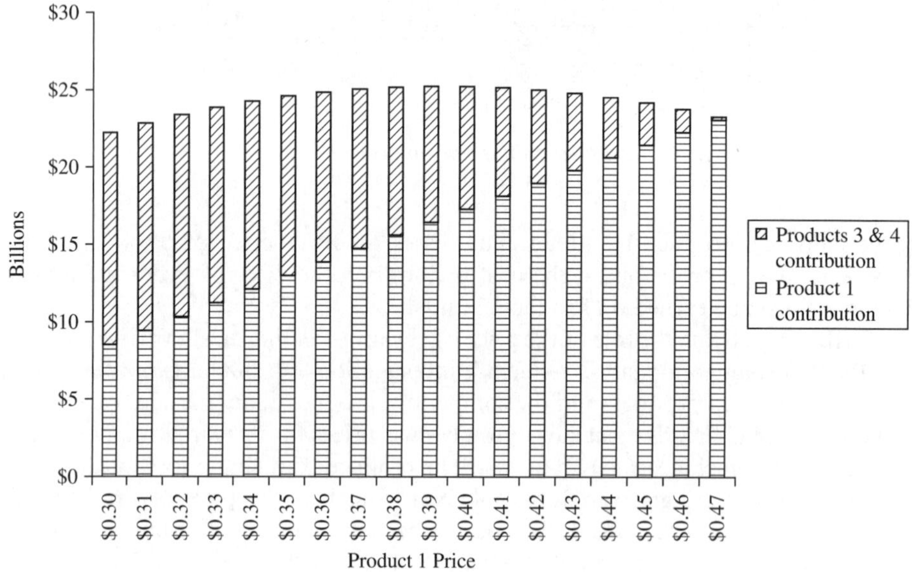

Figure 4.2 Contribution from market-dominant products

to breaking even under the cap. Thus, to become a profit-making enterprise, USPS will have to control its costs relative to growth in the cap.[15] The cap is allowed to grow at the rate of inflation as measured by the CPI. Therefore, to improve profitability, USPS will have to ensure that its costs rise at a rate that is below inflation.

To examine how USPS might fare in such a situation we simulate the model assuming 4 percent inflation but no increase in USPS costs. While this would likely be an extreme outcome in any given year, such a gap could arise from four successive years in which USPS costs grew at 1 percent less than the inflation rate.

The results of simulating an increase in the cap with no concurrent increase in costs are presented in Table 4.5, which shows the outcomes under revenue maximization and profit maximization, respectively.

Table 4.5 The impact of relaxing the price cap

Price cap with revenue maximization for market-dominant products

	Product 1	Product 2	Product 3	Product 4	Total
Price (cents)	45.30	800.40	16.70	16.70	
Quantity	88.80	0.55	89.83	21.24	
Elasticity	−0.15	−2.29	−0.42	−0.46	
Revenue	$40.23	$4.41	$15.04	$3.56	$63.24
Product cost	$18.12	$2.48	$11.41	$2.70	$34.71
Contribution	$22.11	$1.92	$3.63	$0.86	$28.52
Fixed cost					$26.40
Profit					$2.13

Price cap with profit maximization for market-dominant products

	Product 1	Product 2	Product 3	Product 4	Total
Price (cents)	41.00	800.40	21.50	21.50	
Quantity	90.16	0.55	79.35	19.52	
Elasticity	−0.13	−2.29	−0.61	−0.60	
Revenue	$36.96	$4.41	$17.03	$4.19	$62.59
Product cost	$18.39	$2.48	$10.08	$2.48	$33.43
Contribution	$18.57	$1.92	$6.95	$1.71	$29.15
Fixed cost					$26.40
Profit					$2.76

Note: Results assume a 4% increase in the cap with no increase in marginal or fixed costs.

In both cases, revenue and profit rise as USPS can raise prices without an associated increase in cost. In both cases, USPS raises the price of Product 1 by about two cents, which is consistent with Product 1's relative inelasticity. Unlike the situation under a fixed cap in which an increase in one price requires a decline in the other, an increase in the cap allows both prices to increase. When demand is inelastic, both revenue and profit rise with the price increase and the increase is steepest for the product with the most inelastic demand.

4. CONCLUSION

The PAEA represents a major restructuring of the regime under which USPS operates, one in which an effort has been made to provide USPS with the tools needed to overcome the problems arising from recent developments in the communications market, including electronic diversion and other shifts in demand against the traditional use of letter communication. The challenge USPS faces is to use these tools to succeed under current market conditions. The changes wrought by the PAEA go beyond PCR and similar issues discussed here, but we have attempted to shed light on key changes in the regulatory incentive structure with impacts on pricing behavior.

In that regard, we model certain important economic aspects of the PAEA as they apply to the regulatory apparatus governing USPS. We then calibrate the cost and demand function parameters of the model so that it replicates current USPS costs, prices, volumes and demand elasticities. The calibrated model is used to simulate the outcomes of both profit- and revenue-maximization behavior on the part of USPS.

We find that the different maximands will lead to somewhat different reactions under PCR. Revenue maximization leads to a price increase (relative to the pre-cap benchmark) for the relatively less elastic end-to-end product and a price decrease for the relatively more elastic delivery-only product. Just the opposite movement in relative prices occurs under profit maximization. However, we also find that the PAEA price-cap structure is relatively 'tight' in that it allows only modest movements in the capped prices and thus leads to similar overall outcomes under profit and revenue maximization. Although we have not, in this chapter, modeled all aspects of the PAEA – USPS offerings, for example, remain constant across the scenarios we discuss – the importance of cost control is highlighted. In particular, the analysis shows that under reasonable assumptions, controlling costs relative to inflation will be required if USPS is to earn profits.

NOTES

* The opinions expressed in this chapter are those of the authors and do not necessarily represent the views of United States Postal Service. The authors thank Kristin Bergum, David Levy, Edward Pearsall, and Frank Rodriguez for thoughtful comments on an earlier draft. The authors also thank Jose Toasa for excellent research assistance.

1. See Sappington and Sidak (2003). For an opposing view, see Bradley et al. (2004).
2. 39 U.S.C. 3642(b)(1).
3. 39 U.S.C. 3622(d)(1)(A).
4. 39 U.S.C. 3622(d)(2)(A). Within each class of mail, there are subclasses. For instance, the class of standard mail comprises the subclasses regular and enhanced carrier route.
5. 39 U.S.C. 3622(e)(3)(A).
6. 39 U.S.C. 3632.(a).
7. For analytical purposes we make the only division between end-to-end products and workshared products at delivery. In reality, the Postal Service provides gradations of access at different points in its network. Analysis of this detail is interesting but beyond the scope of this chapter.
8. For modeling purposes we have simplified the structure of the cap. Under the PAEA, USPS has separate caps for its broad classes such as first class and for standard mail. Within each of these classes there is a less workshared product with a relatively low elasticity and a more workshared product with relatively high elasticity. Rather than modeling this structure twice, we do it only once with Product 1 being the less workshared product with a lower elasticity and Product 3 being the more workshared product with a higher elasticity. Thus, any conclusions we draw about the relative prices of Products 1 and 3 under the cap can be applied to the relative pricing of the products within each of the broad classes.
9. We present the revenue-maximization case because that is less traditional. The profit-maximization case simply has the Postal Service profit function as the maximand along with the incremental cost and price-cap constraints.
10. De Donder (2006b) refers to these cross-effect terms as 'displacement ratios'.
11. This is in addition to the traditional cross-price effects captured by the sigma terms.
12. It was called the Postal Rate Commission at the time of the case.
13. The profit constraint imposes a minimum profit of zero. Revenue maximization for market-dominant products is reached just before total profit becomes zero. Note that the contribution by the market-dominant products alone is not sufficient to cover the fixed costs.
14. Not surprisingly, prices in all regulatory models, benchmark or PCR, are significantly lower than those found in the unregulated profit-maximizing outcome. The unregulated monopolist raises prices until all product demands are in the elastic region of their relative demand curves, with substantial reductions in volumes and consumer welfare. The scenario suggests that regulation has been effective at moving USPS away from the high-price–restricted-output solution generally associated with a monopoly.

15. Scenarios that include proportionate increases in the cap and cost do not lead to an appreciable increase in profits.

REFERENCES

Billete de Villemeur, É., H. Crémer, B. Roy and J. Toledano (2003), 'Optimal pricing and price-cap regulation in the postal sector', *Journal of Regulatory Economics*, **24**(1), 49–62.

Bradley, M.D. J. Colvin and M.K. Perkins (2004), 'Testing for anti-competitive behavior in public enterprises', in M.A. Crew and P.R, Kleindorfer (eds), *Competitive, Transformation of the Postal and Delivery Sector*, Boston, MA: Kluwer Academic, pp. 165–83.

Crew, M.A. and P.R. Kleindorfer (1995), 'Pricing in postal service under competitive entry', in Crew and Kleindorfer (eds), *Commercialization of Postal and Delivery Services*, Boston, MA: Kluwer Academic, pp. 3–22.

Crew, M.A. and P.R. Kleindorfer (2008), 'Regulation and the USO under entry', in Crew and Kleindorfer (eds), *Competition and Regulation in the Postal and Delivery Sector*, Cheltenham, UK and Northampton, MA, USA: Edward Elgar, pp. 117–36.

de Donder, P. (2006), 'Access pricing in the postal sector: theory and simulations', *Review of Industrial Organization*, **28**(3), 307–26.

de Donder, P., H. Crémer, P. Dudley and F. Rodriguez (2006a), 'Pricing and welfare implications of alternative approaches to setting price controls in the postal sector,' in M.A. Crew and P.R. Kleindorfer (eds), *Progress toward Liberalization of Postal and Delivery Sector*, New York: Springer; pp. 207–326.

de Donder, P., H. Crémer, P. Dudley and F. Rodriguez (2006b), 'A welfare analysis of price controls with end-to-end mail and access services', in M.A. Crew and P.R. Kleindorfer (eds), *Liberalization of the Postal and Delivery Sector*, Cheltenham, UK and Northampton, MA, USA: Edward Elgar, pp. 227–47.

Dudley, P., H. Jenkins, L. Mautino and S. Richard (2005), 'Competition and the coverage of price controls in the postal sector,' in M.A. Crew and P.R. Klcindorfer (eds), *Regulatory and Economic Challenges in the Postal and Delivery Sector*, Boston, MA: Kluwer Academic, pp. 121–38.

Sappington, D.E.M. and J. Gregory Sidak (2003), 'Incentives for anticompetitive behavior by public enterprises', *Review of Industrial Organization*, **22**, 183–206.

5. Economics of post office networks: strategic issues and the impact on mail demand*

Martin Buser,[†] Christian Jaag[‡] and Urs Trinkner[§]

1. INTRODUCTION

Postal market liberalization is a current issue in Switzerland as well as in the European Union. The reserved area has been the traditional means to finance the provision of universal postal services at uniform prices. There is, therefore, a concern that further reductions in the reserved area could undermine the ability of the incumbent postal operator to finance its universal service obligation (USO). Hence, the traditional USO has come under scrutiny in many countries. The two most important cost factors in the postal sector related to the USO are ubiquity of delivery at a uniform price and a network of post offices that is sufficient to enable accessibility to postal services for all citizens.

In our chapter, we discuss the role of the post office in the marketplace. It not only adds to the incumbent's cost, but also serves as its important and traditionally established hallmark. Hence, the optimization of the postal outlet network is of significant strategic and political importance. While some post offices may be converted into agencies, franchises and specialized counters for business customers, households beyond the reach of a postal outlet may also be served with postal products by postmen/women during their mail delivery round.

After an assessment of post office reorganization programs in selected countries in Section 2, we focus in Section 3 on Swiss Post's optimization program in recent years. The program aimed at aligning its postal network to emerging competition and changing consumer needs. Whereas a significant fraction of post offices have been closed, the remaining ones now offer a far broader range of products. Further, besides new business customer solutions in collection, a number of specialized outlets for advanced financial services have been created. These measures have seen political and regulatory counteractions which resulted in more stringent regulations. In our assessment we briefly present the effects on Swiss Post's customer satisfaction and operating costs. To identify the impact of post office closures on overall mail volumes, we use time-series techniques with quarterly data between 1980 and 2006. We find – in contrast to variables that capture the effect of the Internet – no significant effect of post office closures on overall mail volumes.

In Section 4 we identify key strategic issues of post office realignments. We conclude in Section 5 that diversifying into financial services helps to sustain a comparably larger post

† Swiss Post.
‡ Swiss Post and University of St. Gallen.
§ Swiss Post and University of Zurich.

office network. If no such option is available, agencies run by third parties seem to be the only long-term solution under competition. In either case, economies of scope play a vital role for sustaining self-financed access points for postal services.

2. REVIEW OF THE LITERATURE AND RECENT RESTRUCTURINGS IN REFERENCE COUNTRIES

2.1 Literature Review

In the recent stages of the liberalization process, the idea of universal service has become increasingly contested since the abolition of partial monopolies severely questions its financing. Crew and Kleindorfer (2006b) model the interaction of maintaining the USO and opening postal markets. They argue that a broad USO (with, for example, severe restrictions on post office restructuring) implies large mark-ups to pay for the USO. Hence, restructuring may serve not only as a cost-cutting but also as a price-cutting instrument.

The current debate is about the appropriate extent of the USO and the most efficient way to provide it, thereby making it as compatible with competition as possible. Crémer et al. (2008) assess alternative economic justifications of the USO. A USO may be used as a remedy for network externalities, and as a redistributive pricing policy. It has some aspects of a public good and serves as an instrument of regional policy. Crémer et al. argue that the largest benefits of a USO are related to the role of postal products as inputs and thus to business mail. Replacing it by other means of regional policy or redistributive channels is not an option. In that sense, it is important that postal services are universally provided at a reliably high quality. However, it does not imply that these services have to be supplied through the traditional channels in the traditional postal network.

The focus of our analysis is an exploration into whether and how a high service level can be maintained notwithstanding deep restructuring of the physical network. It is inspired by the work of Boldron et al. (2008), who analyze the accessibility of the postal network compared to other industries in France. They find that 'the presence of commercial [postal] services combined with public [postal] services creates demand for postal services' (p. 15). Moreover, they argue that the high territory presence of postal counters creates a positive externality on their immediate environment and therefore contributes to economic development. However, currently, the net cost of the high postal accessibility is borne by the universal service provider through a statutory monopoly on letters. The introduction of competition introduces the need for alternative funding or deep restructuring of the network – without damaging its social value, if possible.

Cohen et al. (2008) illustrate that many (historical) post office networks lack alignment to competitive needs. The authors show that both Italy and the United States have a disproportionate percentage of their post offices located in rural areas as compared with banks (Italy) or pharmacies (US) and argue that the distribution of post offices has a similar pattern in most postal administrations. Further, they state that 'in order to have competitive prices, incumbents will have to allocate costs based on causation, and bulk mail will pay only for the small portion of the retail network cost that it imposes' (p. 45). They conclude that under a competitive scenario, there will be 'considerable pressure to move toward a more commercial distribution of retail services, outsourcing, or both' (p. 45) because of the otherwise heavy financing burden of single-piece mail.

Our discussion embraces international experiences in post office restructuring, but focuses on the Swiss market. Thereby, it adds to previous analyses of the Swiss postal market, for example, in Dietl et al. (2005) and Jaag (2007).

2.2 Developments in (Partly) Liberalized Markets

Recent restructuring experience of postal networks varies. Networks are driven by regulatory constraints as well as by the chosen business models. We briefly present stylized cases from New Zealand, Sweden, France, Italy, Germany, and the UK.

New Zealand Post

New Zealand Post (NZ Post) started to restructure its retail network in 1988, one year ahead of a first liberalization step in 1989. It started with more than 1,200 self-operated post offices. Three years before full market opening in 1998, about 85 percent of the post offices had been shut down and the first experiences with franchised post offices were successfully completed. Nowadays, NZ Post's retail network has grown again and consists of two different kinds of access points that exploit two different kinds of economies of scope. First, postal as well as banking services are provided in 142 post offices operated by NZ Post and 181 franchised agencies. Thereby, economies of scope are exploited between postal services and Kiwibank, a subsidiary of NZ Post that was founded in 2002. Second, 672 additional sales points are available, where third parties sell selected postal services besides their core business ('shop in shop'). Again, economies of scope are exploited – here between postal services and other products such as groceries. Hence, traditional post offices that supply just postal services seem not to be an option for NZ Post. Kiwibank appears to be a story of success with more than 550,000 customers as of September 2007 and strong yearly growth in deposits (64 percent), lending (39 percent), and mortgages. Recently, mobile banking, insurance products, personal loans, and foreign currency services have been launched. Kiwibank also contributed considerably to the financial performance of NZ Post, which steadily improved its value added from NZ$2.7 million in 2002 up to NZ$28.1 million in 2007. Importantly, Kiwibank increases NZ Post Group's EBITDA (earnings before interest, taxes, depreciation and amortization) margin, that is, Kiwibank's EBITDA margin lies well over 13.1 percent.[1]

Posten AB

The realignment of Sweden's Posten AB exhibits similar patterns but also important differences. In Sweden, the market was completely liberalized in 1993. Similar to NZ Post, Posten AB quickly reduced its original network of approximately 4,000 self-run full-range post offices. In addition, it started franchising some of the remaining ones. However, in contrast to NZ Post, in 2002 Posten AB did not opt for starting a bank but chose to completely shut down its traditional post office network and to separate its postal services from financial transactions. For postal services, business centers were established for business customers whereas for small customers 'shop-in-shop' solutions were on the agenda. At the same time a new network for financial services, *Svensk Kassaservice*, was developed. The latter remained in a serious financial position despite subsequent branch closures, the opening for other financial suppliers, and government subsidies of SEK 300 million (about 40 percent of net sales!). In 2007, Posten AB submitted a closure schedule for its cashier service which suffered from steadily declining transaction volumes of about 20 percent per year.[2] Subsequently, Posten AB decided to shut down *Svensk Kassaservice* entirely.

La Poste

In 2004, La Poste, the national postal operator of France, planned to overhaul its post office branch network by earmarking 6,000 of its 17,000 offices for closure. Furthermore, La Poste intended to convert some of the remaining offices into 'sub-post offices' run by grocery stores or located in town halls. Hence, La Poste intended to move in a similar direction to NZ Post. These ideas faced stiff resistance from both labor unions and local elected officials. Under heavy political pressure, La Poste was forced to put forward an alternative reorganization plan. Thereby, La Poste changed its strategy and is now adding additional services to its offices in order to increase revenues. This strategy was made easier by the decision of the French government to allow La Poste to expand its financial services by launching a bank. These initiatives are supported with the development of new post office concepts that aim at combining different business lines such as banking, letters and parcels, and retail in a modern environment.

Poste Italiane

Poste Italiane follows a similar path to La Poste. Instead of trying to restructure the office network by closing down or outsourcing post offices, Poste Italiane focused from the beginning of its overhaul process on financial services. Starting in 2002, Poste Italiane used its 14,000 outlets to add bank accounts and loans to its product range. This strategy proved to be very successful, turning around the national incumbent into a profit-making company. Poste Italiane might be even more profitable when it is given a banking license. So far, the company still has to remarket loans from other banks.

Deutsche Post

The transformation of Deutsche Post's post office network followed two main directions that exhibit patterns similar to those of NZ Post. On the one hand, small and medium-sized post offices were transformed into agencies; on the other, larger offices were developed into bank branches. As in many other European postal organizations, the agency concept is used to replace existing post offices. With the agency concept, postal services are provided at the retail locations of existing businesses. Deutsche Post has two different types of agency in place. Either a partner (for example, a grocery store) combines the postal services with its own business or Deutsche Post provides the services with its own personnel at a partner location. The second type of agency is required in order to fulfill the regulatory obligation of maintaining 5,000 self-run branches. In 2005, Deutsche Post sold 850 of its biggest branches to its subsidiary Postbank. With this move, Postbank aims to strengthen its position in the retail financial services market. These branches are gradually transformed into bank branches by adding consulting capacities and financial services know-how. The strategy of Deutsche Post and its subsidiary Postbank is obviously either to generate higher profits by selling more high-margin products (financial services) or to cut costs by outsourcing the services to third parties (agencies).

Royal Mail

The case of Royal Mail, UK's incumbent postal organization, shows that maintaining a post office network that provides postal services without the help of high-margin financial services leads to considerable problems. Between 2001 and 2005, Royal Mail closed over 3,000 post offices, nearly 20 percent of its network. For a long time, Royal Mail post offices acted as a provider of benefit and pension payments besides the traditional letters and parcels business. The transfer of these payments to direct payments into bank accounts and the full market opening for letters and parcels at the beginning of 2006 left Royal Mail and its subsidiary, Post Office Ltd, with an increasingly unprofitable network. Although Royal Mail added additional services to its product line, this seemed not to be sufficient to maintain a post office network of this size and scope as a viable business. Royal Mail has recently put in place a new initiative which will involve a closure of up to 2,500 branches. Partially, these will be replaced by mobile post offices, hosted and partner services, and home delivery services. Despite these efforts, Royal Mail still draws on government subsidies of currently £150 million in order to keep its post office network in place. Meanwhile, an additional £1.7 billion government reorganization is on the table.

Table 5.1 provides further background for the country studies discussed above as well as for Switzerland, which we discuss in detail in Section 3.

3. THE SWISS CASE: RECENT RESTRUCTURINGS AND VOLUME EFFECTS

3.1 Main Developments and Policy Responses over the Past Decade

At the beginning of 1998, PTT, Switzerland's postal and telecommunication organization, was divided into two separate state-owned companies. The telecommunication part became Swisscom while the postal and financial services part was transformed into Swiss Post.

Between 1998 and 2001, Swiss Post made several attempts to restructure and optimize the postal network. These attempts faced political and public resistance but resulted in an optimization project that was started in 2001. Under this project, roughly 1,000 post offices were closed until 2005 (see Figure 5.1). In most cases a 'doorstep service' (postal services upon request at the doorstep of each household provided by delivery personnel) replaced the post office. During that time, Swiss Post also introduced the agency concept to its postal network. In an agency, postal services are provided through third-party contractors such as grocery stores or other existing retail businesses. Furthermore, Swiss Post started selling additional products such as stationery goods, mobile phones or lottery tickets in selected outlets. At the same time, PostFinance, Swiss Post's financial services unit, developed from a payment transactions provider into a provider of financial services by adding savings accounts, funds and mortgages (the last two backed by banks as PostFinance lacks a banking license). These products were also distributed through the post office network. Last but not least, Swiss Post steadily complemented its post office network with automated, electronic or hybrid services. Examples include ATMs, payment orders, online banking, electronic stamps, and online counters.

Table 5.1 Post office networks in selected countries as of 2006

	Regulation			Network features					
	Market opening	Selected regulatory restrictions related to post office network	Banking license	Financial transactions/ financial services	Subsidies	Number of postal access points	Thereof agencies	Thereof postal services	Thereof financial transactions/ services
France	Monopoly 50 grams*	No formal requirements Accessibility must, however, be in line with the needs of local population, taking account of demographic, economic and social changes	Yes	Yes / Yes	Yes (for *service de proximité*)	17,000	4,800	17,000	17,000
Italy	Monopoly 50 grams*	No requirements	No	Yes / Yes	Yes	13,900	0	13,900	13,900
United Kingdom	Open*	Not less than 95% of users within 5km of an access point capable of receiving the largest relevant postal packets and registered mail, and that the premises of not less than 95% of users in each postcode area are within 10km of such access points	No	Yes / Yes	Yes (for rural post offices)	14,200	13,600	14,200	14,200
Germany	Open*	Since 1.1.2008 no formal requirements	Yes	Yes / Yes	No	12,600	7,000	12,600	6,500
Sweden	Open	Accessible to everyone at a reasonable distance from their home or workplace. The density of the access	No	Yes / No	Yes (for financial transactions)	2,000	1,630	2,000	0

Table 5.1 (continued)

	Regulation					Network features			
	Market opening	Selected regulatory restrictions related to post office network	Banking license	Financial transactions/ financial services	Subsidies	Number of postal access points	Thereof agencies	Thereof postal services	Thereof financial transactions/ services
		points must take into account the needs of users Legal mandate to provide nationwide financial transaction services							
New Zealand	Open	Minimum 880 postal shops and centres (at least 240 postal outlets to be full service outlets)	Yes	Yes / Yes	No	990	850	990	320
Switzerland	Monopoly 100 grams	90% of population in 20 minutes by foot/public transport	No	Yes / Yes	No	2,469	150	2,469	2,300

Note: * VAT exemption for USO-provider/historical operator.

Table 5.2 Swiss Post network (as of 31 December 2007)

Access points for retail customers	No.
Post offices and agencies	2,469
of which, post offices with payment services	2,300
of which, post offices without payment services	12
of which, agencies with payment services	136
of which, agencies without payment services	14
of which, PostMobile stops	7
Routes with doorstep services	1,043

Importantly, these restructurings provoked political resistance. At its peak in 2004, a public vote targeted at preventing further restructurings was rejected by only a small majority of 50.2 percent of the Swiss population. In anticipation of this vote, the parliament had already amended the postal act with an 'infrastructure obligation' that obliged Swiss Post to operate a physical post office network throughout the country. That is, a new 'input regulation' was put into place, aiming at restricting Swiss Post in its attempts to close or replace post offices or agencies by other forms of access points such as doorstep service or electronic/hybrid alternatives. Currently, the regulatory authority translates this obligation into the rule that 90 percent of the population have to be able to reach a post office within 20 minutes by foot or by public transport. Where a doorstep collection service is available, the time range is extended to 30 minutes.

Despite these political developments, Swiss Post decided in 2003 that the results of the aforementioned optimization project were not sufficient to adapt the post office network to the changing consumer needs. Therefore, a new project, 'Ymago', was launched in order to further reduce the cost of the post office network while improving customer satisfaction at the same time. Several new concepts were tested in pilot studies and two of them, a new agency concept and a new way of organizing post offices, were implemented from 2007 onwards. Table 5.2 shows Swiss Post's network by the end of 2007.

Politicians reluctant to endorse those plans have already started new actions aimed at obliging Swiss Post to offer physical financial transactions (that is, in-payments and out-payments) in agencies too. Such regulations would have a strong negative effect on the profitability of agencies, as one cannot expect grocery stores to invest in expensive security installations, counter concepts and anti-money-laundering measures.

The political opposition against post office restructuring appears large in relation to its minor impact on customer satisfaction and, overall mail volumes. We discuss those issues in the following two sections.

3.2 Impact on Customer Satisfaction and Channel Costs

Swiss Post measures its customer satisfaction annually through a standardized process. Interestingly, the two major reorganization projects do not seem to have had a negative effect on customer satisfaction. Total customer satisfaction was 87 points (out of 100) for private customers in the year 2000 (before the first project), dropping slightly to 85 points in 2001. Subsequently, customer satisfaction oscillated between 86 and 85 points until 2004. After that it increased to 88 in 2005 and 89 in 2006. Despite political resistance, Swiss Post obviously managed to maintain or even increase its customer satisfaction during these times of change.

On the financial side, Swiss Post was able to reduce its channel costs (that is, operating costs of the post office network) significantly to save CHF 100 million annually with the first restructuring project and with the Ymago project, and additional savings of another CHF 50 million annually are projected after its full implementation at the end of 2008. So far the data show that the conversion of a post office into a partner agency significantly reduces the operating costs. For more details, see the econometrical analysis of Jaag et al. (2009). These restructuring initiatives of the post office network were one of several factors boosting Swiss Post's profits to CHF 837 million in 2006, up from CHF 118 million in 2000.

3.3 Impact on Overall Mail Volumes

The size of the network influences the demand for postal products. In the following, we empirically discuss the impact of postal network restructuring on mail volumes using time-series techniques with quarterly Swiss data between 1980 and 2006. We operate with an updated dataset as used by Trinkner and Grossmann (2006), with the addition of a series of postal counters. Table 5.3 gives an overview of the dataset used in our empirical assessment. For a more detailed description of the various variables, see Trinkner and Grossmann.

Although mail volumes in Switzerland have increased in the observed period, they started to decline starting from 2001 (see Figure 5.1). Apart from GDP and prices, electronic alternatives and restructurings of the postal network may have influenced mail volumes. It is difficult to ascribe volume changes to one of the last two potential sources of impact, however, as they emerged around the same time.

On the one hand, beginning with the development of the internet, the use of e-mail and online platforms increased steadily. Whereas the use of the Internet (*eUse*) exhibits an S-shaped penetration curve, e-banking platforms like the one from PostFinance (*eBank*) grow almost linearly. Similarly, digital networks such as mobile telephony or broadband (*eBand*) datastreaming emerged. Both are likely to affect mail volumes negatively as they present potential substitutes for physical mail. On the other hand, the number of post offices had already started to decrease in 1980, albeit at a low rate. Only in the late 1990s did a more pronounced decline set in. In 2001, Swiss Post started converting full post offices into agencies. Due to fewer access points and negative effects on customer loyalty, such closures could affect volumes negatively. Time-series econometric techniques offer a powerful tool to separate these two effects. More specifically, they allow us to determine whether mail volumes are shrinking due to 'e-substitution', that is, market share losses of letters due to emerging digital substitutes, or to post office closures, or both.

We first estimate the impact of the postal network and e-substitution on mail volumes by means of a static regression of the form

$$\ln(q) = \beta_0 + trend(t) + \beta_1 \ln(gdp) + \beta_2 \ln(p) + \beta_3 \ln(s) + \beta_4(eproxy) + \beta_5(office).$$

Table 5.3 The data

Time series (variables in brackets)	Data source	Compound annual growth rate p.a.	Sample period	Order of integration
Mail volumes and GDP				
Total mail volume (*q*)	Swiss Post	1.50%	1980Q1–2006Q4	I(1)
Nominal GDP (*GDP*)	SECO	3.60%	1981Q1–2006Q4	I(1)
Real GDP (*gdp*)	SECO	1.70%	1981Q1–2006Q4	I(1)
Prices				
Mail real price index (*p*)	Swiss Post	1.76%	1981Q1–2006Q4	I(1)
Substitute real price index (*s*)	BFS	−2.36%	1981Q1–2006Q4	I(1)
Consumer price index (*CPI*)	SECO	1.86%	1981Q1–2006Q4	I(1)/I(2)
Infrastructure				
No. of self-operated post offices (*s_office*)	Swiss Post	−1.37%	1980–2006	I(1)
No. of postal agencies (*agency*)	Swiss Post	35.43%	1980–2006	I(1)
Total number of post offices (*office*)	Swiss Post		1980–2006	I(1)
Substitution Proxies				
Online accounts with PostFinance (*eBank*)	Swiss Post		1998Q3–2006Q4	I(1)
% active internet users (*eUse*)	BFS		1994Q1–2006Q4	
% broadband internet access (*eBand*)	BFS		2001Q1–2006Q4	
Other				
dAB	Reflects the introduction of A- (priority) and B- (economy) class mail in 1991			
dq2, *dq3*, *dq4*	Seasonal-dummies			

Note: The data on online accounts with PostFinance are available on a monthly basis. Up to the present, they indicate a constant linear trend. Other substitution proxies are available on a yearly basis. For data quality reasons, we therefore only use the number of online accounts in our estimations.

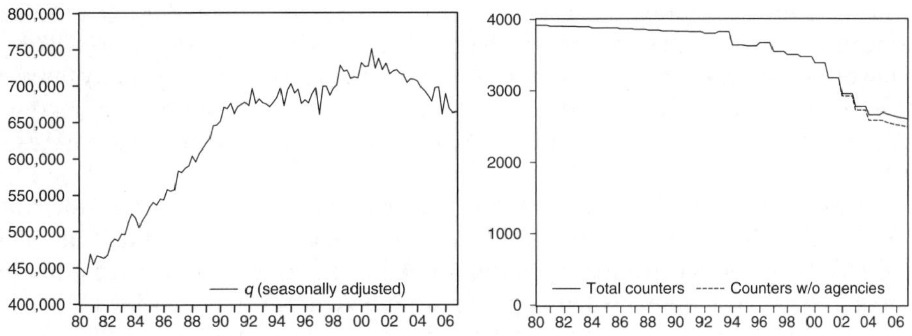

Figure 5.1 Overall mail volumes and post office development

Table 5.4 Estimation results linear regression

Variable	Model 1 (seasonal dummies) Coefficient [*t*-statistic]	Model 2 (seasonal adjustment) Coefficient [*t*-statistic]
C	8.16 [4.66]**	6.92 [4.70]**
trend	0.01 [6.48]**	0.01 [6.33]**
log(*p*)	−0.34 [−7.38]**	−0.33 [−8.24]**
log(*gdp*)	0.38 [2.29]*	0.51 [3.60]**
log(*s*)	0.05 [1.79]	0.06 [2.45]*
office	8.17e-5 [1.78]	4.17e-5 [1.00]
eBank	−1.71e-7 [−5.01]**	−1.97e-7 [−6.20]**
dAB	0.02 [1.21]	0.02 [2.01]*
dQ2	−0.03 [−4.29]**	
dQ3	−0.13 [−20.36]**	
dQ4	0.08 [11.24]**	
Adjusted R^2	0.98	0.98
Durbin–Watson	1.50	1.00

Notes: Standard errors are White heteroskedasticity-consistent; *t*-statistic in parentheses. Included observations: 104.
** significant at 99% level; * significant at 95% level.

In order to eliminate seasonal effects and possible volume effects of changes in the product structure, we include appropriate dummy variables or adjust the data seasonally. For seasonal adjustments, in Model 1, we include *dQ2*, *dQ3*, *dQ4* and consider the introduction of A- and B-Post in 1991 with *dAB*. In Model 2, we also use *dAB* but seasonally adjust *GDP* and *q*. The trend variable serves to avoid spurious regressions (which is likely given the I(1) property of most variables). However, one can assume a close relationship between economic activity, measured by *GDP*, and overall mail volumes.

We tried several specifications and combinations of the various e-proxies. The results appear quite robust. We prefer *eBank* over the other e-proxies because of better data quality. Further, the series exhibits a more direct impact on overall mail volumes as customers of e-banking solutions are usually incentivized by banks to opt for electronic bank statements. The results are also robust with regard to self-operated post offices (*s_office*) or the sum of post offices and agencies (*office*). As the latter reflects the availability for postal service better, we include it in our preferred static regression (in real terms). The regression output is given in Table 5.4. We prefer Model 1 as it exhibits better Durbin–Watson statistics.

We hence confirm older estimates on the price elasticity of mail demand with a value of −0.34/−0.33. The estimate for the GDP elasticity of demand is lower than earlier estimates. This deviation is explained by our introduction of a trend and quarterly dummies which absorb much of the explanatory power of GDP (see VEC model below). Figure 5.2 displays the actual time series for volume, the fitted series and residuals.

We also use a long-run vector error correction (VEC) model to assess the long-run equilibrium relationship between the non-stationary series of mail demand, GDP, prices, substitutes, and counter availability. The model allows us to discern between long-run

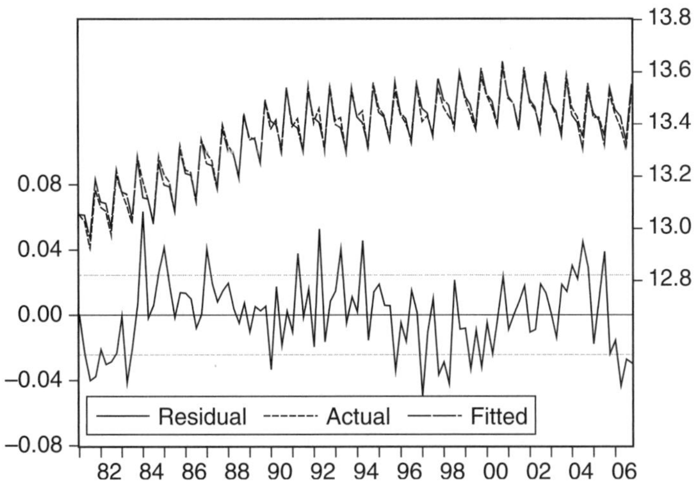

Figure 5.2 Fit and residuals of linear regression (Model 1)

equilibrium effects and short-run off-equilibrium adjustments. It assumes no constant or trend in the cointegrating equation and the vector autoregression (VAR). The estimated functional form is:[3]

$$\Delta q_t = \alpha(q_{t-1} - \beta_1 gdp_{t-1} - \beta_2 p_{t-1} - \beta_3 s_{t-1}) + \gamma_1 dAB + \gamma_2 eproxy_t + \gamma_3 office_t + \sum_L(\gamma_{4,L}\Delta q_{t-L} + \gamma_{5,L}\Delta gdp_{t-L} + \gamma_{6,L}\Delta p_{t-L} + \gamma_{7,L}\Delta s_{t-L}) + \varepsilon.$$

The first summand contains the error correction term, which is also the cointegration relationship. The Johansen cointegration test indicates that there is one cointegrating relation.[4]

Table 5.5 reports the results obtained from Johansen's two-step procedure. First, the long-run equation (error correction term) is estimated; second, the VAR is estimated, incorporating the cointegrating relation from the first step.

In this empirical model, we find that mail volume is highly correlated with GDP. The estimated coefficient of 1.19 is close to the one found by Trinkner and Grossmann (2006), which is 1.09. The price elasticity of demand is −0.42, which is also in the range usually found in the empirical literature. From his survey of studies, Robinson (2007) concludes that price elasticity measures for mail products typically range between −0.2 and −0.8.[5] The cross-elasticity with respect to substitute prices is not significantly different from zero. Note that – as in the static model – the distinction between priority and economy mail in 1991 had a (non-significant) positive impact on overall mail volumes.

We therefore find with both approaches that the decline in the number of post offices had no significant influence on mail volumes. Rather, we have to reject the null hypothesis that e-substitutes had no effect on overall mail volumes: the emergence of electronic substitutes structurally changed the pattern of mail demand in a negative way. The result on

Table 5.5 Estimation result, VEC

Variable		Coefficient	Std error	*t*-statistic
Long-run equilibrium equation				
log(*gdp*)		1.19	0.03	41.04
log(*p*)		−0.42	0.10	−4.27
log(*s*)		0.03	0.11	0.26
Short-run equation				
α		−0.12	0.05	−2.27
dAB		−0.01	0.01	−0.95
eBank		−4.87e-8	1.3e-8	−3.68
office		−8.78e-6	7.6e-6	−1.15
	t−1	*t*−2	*t*−3	*t*−4
Δlog(*q*)	−0.87 [−8.53]	−0.68 [−5.58]	−0.48 [−4.15]	0.30 [−3.08]
Δlog(*gdp*)	0.21 [0.87]	0.36 [1.58]	0.18 [0.74]	−0.33 [−1.46]
Δlog(*p*)	−0.11 [−2.52]	−0.09 [−2.16]	−0.06 [−1.33]	−0.10 [−2.44]
Δlog(*s*)	0.16 [1.94]	−0.11 [−1.37]	−0.09 [−1.12]	−0.16 [−2.07]

Notes:
t-statistic in parentheses.
Adjusted R^2: 0.53.
Johansen cointegration test (number of cointegrating relations)

H_0	Trace	Max. EV
none	40.93	26.77
at most 1 relation	14.17	10.54
at most 2 relations	3.63	3.62

All endogenous variables are Granger-causal and according to lag-exclusion Wald tests, all lags are significant.

post office closures does not come as a surprise: private customers reflect only a small fraction of total mail volumes (about 15 percent) and as a collection channel for private customers, letterboxes are a valuable and very accessible alternative to post offices.

3.4 Impact on Parcel Volumes and Financial Services

In the above section we discussed at some length the impact of post office restructuring on overall mail volumes. The reason for our empirical exercise with respect to mail volume was to explore whether resizing the post office network would induce customers to change their mailing behavior such that it may backfire in the face of competition. If there had been a large impact of post office closures on volumes, the existing network may well have been optimal in size and scope.

Similar or even more pronounced effects may be expected with respect to parcels volumes and financial services, as these are counter-intensive services as well. Empirically addressing these issues is beyond the scope of this chapter, largely for two reasons. First, the estimation is made possible by clean time series, especially with respect to mail volumes, which still have a monopoly. In the parcels and financial services markets, however, such clean time series are not available over a long enough time period. Further, volumes are affected by various other factors, such as competition (third-party networks, services, prices, and so on) which cannot be controlled for properly. Hence, an empirical assessment fails through data availability.

Second, in order to answer the initial question, a similar empirical assessment for the parcel and financial services markets is not necessary. In both of these markets, the postal network holds its ground against competing networks which can serve as a benchmark in our analysis. Recent analyses, for example, by Cohen et al. (2008) show that compared to other networks, these are often a disproportionate percentage of post offices located in rural areas, as compared with banks or pharmacies. In 2007, Swiss Post operated 2,469 post offices, offering various financial services. Compared to private banking networks in Switzerland, this is obviously an excessive number: the largest private banking network (operated by the Raiffeisen Group) consists of 1,162 offices (there are plans to reduce these to 800); the second largest (operated by cantonal banks) consists of 727 offices. Hence, considering this competitive benchmark, a reduction in self-operated post offices is not expected to affect greatly the demand in the market for financial services.

A similar argument applies to the parcels market: in Switzerland, presence in self-operated outlets does not seem to be necessary to attract customers. Private competitors do not operate retail offices themselves: these can be found in selected train stations, gas stations or stationery shops. However, all suppliers operate about 100 outlets in total, indicating that the present network of Swiss Post is probably not too small. This is in contrast to Germany, where Hermes now operates about 13,000 agencies for its parcels business.

4. KEY STRATEGIC ISSUES

In this section, we identify key strategic issues of post office realignments. The review of the literature suggests the need of such restructuring in the light of increasing competitive pressure, since historically most post office networks seem to have located a disproportionate percentage of their post offices in rural areas, which reflects the distribution of public services rather than competitive goods. However, minimal coverage regulations usually limit the possibility of commercial realignments. Hence, regulatory restrictions and (potential) political responses to optimization projects significantly determine the available options. We therefore treat such minimal coverage restrictions as given and explore the basic options available for postal incumbents in the light of the various country studies as described above (New Zealand, Sweden, France, Italy, Germany, the UK, and Switzerland). Note that minimal coverage restrictions also preclude hybrid electronic means to deliver selected services. We therefore concentrate on a feasible set of post office strategies, given a realistic amount of input-oriented regulation.

A comprehensive restructuring requires postal operators to value various issues that are interrelated. On the services side, restrictions on product offerings, cross-selling potential, credibility, and other revenue effects are important. On the cost side, channel selection, potential partners, information technology (IT) and other infrastructure in place, economies of scale and scope, outsourcing possibilities, estimated savings, existing contractual arrangements, and possible external financing mechanisms play an important role. We shall not explore these factors in detail. Rather we derive three postal network models that are sustainable in a fully competitive scenario.

The first model, the 'postal network', focuses on the efficient provision of the postal core business and requires a complete shutdown of the traditional post office network. Instead, retail customers are offered a basic range of services in agencies run by partners countrywide. Thereby, the necessary economies of scope are exploited between postal services and a standalone partner core business such as the retailing of groceries. At the same time, regulatory accessibility restrictions are met. In contrast, business customers are served in tailored business centers that exhibit the necessary economies of scale and fulfill the specific needs of large customers. If no agencies are available, the model can be complemented with doorstep services. The main example of this model is Sweden's Posten AB. The model requires a broad absence of input regulations that aim at preserving traditional post offices.

The second model, the 'universal network' basically consists of traditional, countrywide post offices whose functions are extended with payments and financial services. This requires an IT infrastructure to be put in place. In addition, the network can be opened for other complex, but standardized services such as insurance policies or community services. Thereby, remote 'universal post offices' will likely develop into regional centers for 'high-value retailing' and services that require personal identification. To meet the needs of large postal customers, the model should be complemented with selected specialized business counters and collection services. Examples include La Poste from France or Australia Post. Royal Mail in the UK seems to be developing in this direction, too. However, the model has USO costs. In remote areas, the closure of such universal post offices will most probably bring net benefits. The reason is that for a once-in-a-lifetime mortgage signing, people are prepared to drive to the next town – the network will be too dense in a commercial sense. That is, the respective cost of the USO is positive and calls for external financing (we assume a fully competitive scenario and hence no financing through a residual monopoly on light letters). The model applies to countries with high input regulations in terms of the number of non-franchised post offices and various possibilities for diversifying into 'high-value retailing'.

In the third model, the 'postal bank network', selected post offices are converted into banks that also perform postal services. To meet the regulatory coverage constraints, the network is complemented by agencies that are run by independent partners as well as doorstep services. Hence, economies of scope are exploited either with the own bank or with partners such as grocery stores. Again, the network is to be complemented with selected large customers' solutions. The model exists in the real world in the mostly deregulated postal market of New Zealand. However, it requires the postal operators to have the regulatory possibility and commercial capability to run a bank.

Table 5.6 provides an overview of the three basic strategic models. Thus, the model that postal services can opt for is essentially determined by regulatory restrictions. For the case of Switzerland, Swiss Post is currently moving towards model 3 and intends to provide a full coverage 'postal bank network' free from the need for government subsidies but still securing the nationwide provision of postal services. However, the issue, which will be discussed in parliament, is highly controversial as banks fear the postal banking license, right-wing parties fear subsidies, and left-wing parties and unions fear the conversion of post offices into agencies and its impact on employment conditions.

Table 5.6 Three stylized sustainable models of post office networks

	Postal network	Universal network	Postal bank network
Leading example	Sweden	France	New Zealand
Required authorizations		Supply of financial services / banking license	Banking license
Offered products (by incumbent)	Postal services only	Postal services Financial transactions Financial services Other	Postal services Financial transactions Banking services
Agency types	– Business centers Agencies Doorstep services	Full-range offices Postal business counters	Full-range offices Postal business counters Agencies Doorstep services
Franchising	Only agencies	No	Mixed
External financing	No	Yes	No
Ideal for incumbents . . .	. . . that are not allowed to provide financial services	. . . that can count on external financing and are limited in outsourcing possibilities	. . . that have a banking license

5. SUMMARY AND CONCLUSIONS

Post offices constitute an important part of the universal service and its cost. Whereas post offices might play a vital role for communities, local labor markets, and social cohesion, the operators providing them increasingly face competition – be it through electronic substitutes or opening postal markets. Therefore postal incumbents strive to align their networks to competitive pressure and changing consumer needs.

This chapter aimed to contribute to a better understanding of post office network optimization and to identify its key strategic issues based on sound economics.

We first examined recent realignments of postal incumbent networks in various countries in the face of upcoming or increasing competition. It turns out that none of the incumbents has left its network unchanged. In the light of the realignments, the exploitation of economies of scope of postal products with other retail products seems to be at the heart of every restructuring. In other words, operating counters with postal services alone seems not to be a viable option. We observe two kinds of complementary products: (a) counter-based financial transactions/services needing support and security; and (b) shop-based consumer goods such as in grocery stores. For the latter category, counters seem inappropriate. Hence, incumbents have either started to supplement their post offices with mainly financial products or replaced their post offices by agencies run by third parties such as grocery stores. In the latter case, some operators have complemented those agencies with mobile postal services such as collection services by the postman/woman.

Second, to understand the impact of such restructuring on volumes and profitability we assessed recent realignments of Swiss Post in more detail. Using time-series techniques we found that the considerable decline in the number of post offices in Switzerland had no significant influence on mail volumes. Rather, the recent decline in overall mail volumes is due to the rise in electronic substitutes. At the same time, Swiss Post's profitability increased steadily, (partly) due to channel cost savings in collection related to the post office restructuring, and consumer satisfaction remained high. It is important to note that the restructuring, despite being successful, faced heavy political resistance and resulted in new regulations: Swiss Post's USO was extended with a new requirement to run an area-wide physical post office network and detailed input regulations which hampered further optimization. Hence, Swiss Post's network currently in place represents only a politically constrained second-best solution.

Third, we identifed key strategic issues against this background. Given regulatory constraints present in the investigated countries, we derive three basic network strategies for fully liberalized postal markets. Depending on the respective national regulations, incumbents will opt for (i) a pure postal collection network that requires a radical realignment and in effect a complete shutdown of the traditional (counter) network, or (ii) a universal postal network where traditional post offices are complemented with high-value retailing such as financial services, or (iii) a postal bank network where a large number of post offices will be converted into third-party agencies and the rest developed into postal banks offering basic postal services as well. For the case of Switzerland, the necessary political decisions have not yet been taken, and it is unclear whether Swiss Post will end up like model (ii) or model (iii).

We conclude that diversifying into financial services helps to sustain a comparably larger and traditional post office network based on the counter concept. If no such option is available, the substitution of traditional post offices by agencies run by third parties seems to be the only long-term solution under competition. In either case, economies of scope play a vital role for sustaining self-financed access points for postal services. Hence, national regulations regarding (a) the possibility of postal operators offering financial services and (b) the accessibility of postal services and eventually counters, play a key role for both the incumbent's feasible network strategies and the degree of freedom within the chosen one. If alternative and hybrid forms of service provisions are allowed to replace physical access points, the network will more likely be fully aligned to competitive needs and exhibit a more diverse range of collection services.

NOTES

* The views expressed are those of the authors and do not necessarily reflect the opinion of the institutions with which they are affiliated.

1. New Zealand Post, Group Annual Report 2007.
2. Posten AB, Interim Report 2007.
3. It is similar to the one estimated by Harding (2005) and Trinkner and Grossmann (2006).
4. According to econometric theory, a long-run equilibrium relationship may exist for nonstationary series if they are cointegrated, that is, that a stationary linear combination of the variables is I(0). Under such conditions, a so-called (vector) error correction model (VEC) gives efficient estimates.
5. See also Fève et al. (2006) for a recent study on mail price elasticities.

REFERENCES

Boldron, François, Karen Dewulf, Denis Joram and Bernard Roy (2008), 'The accessibility of the postal retail network and the objectives of social cohesion and economic development', in Crew and Kleindorfer (eds), pp. 47–59.

Cohen, Robert, Luigi Di Paola, Renée Sheehy and Vincenzo Visco Commandini (2008), 'The distribution of post offices in Italy and the United States', in: Crew and Kleindorfer (eds), pp. 36–46.

Crémer, Helmuth, Philippe De Donder, François Boldron, Denis Joram, Bernard Roy and Olivier Vialaneix (2008), 'Social costs and benefits of the universal service obligation in the postal market', in Crew and Kleindorfer (eds), pp. 23–35.

Crew, Michael A. and Paul R. Kleindorfer (eds) (2006a), *Progress toward Liberalization of the Postal and Delivery Sector*, New York: Springer.

Crew, Michael A. and Paul R. Kleindorfer (2006b), 'Approaches to the USO under Entry', in Crew and Kleindorfer (eds) (2006a), pp. 1–18.

Crew, Michael A. and Paul R. Kleindorfer (eds) (2006c), *Liberalization of the Postal and Delivery Sector*, Cheltenham, UK and Northampton, MA, USA: Edward Elgar.

Crew, Michael A. and Paul R. Kleindorfer (eds) (2008), *Competition and Regulation in the Postal and Delivery Sector*, Cheltenham, UK and Northampton, MA, USA: Edward Elgar.

Dietl, Helmut M., Urs Trinkner and Reto Bleisch (2005), 'Liberalization and regulation of the Swiss letter market', in M.A. Crew and P.R. Kleindorfer (eds), *Regulatory and Economic Challenges in the Postal and Delivery Sector*, (eds), Boston, MA: Kluwer Academic, pp. 53–72.

Fève, Frédérique, Jean-Pierre Florens and Sophie Richard (2006), 'Microeconomic demand modelling for price elasticities', in Crew and Kleindorfer (2006c) (eds), pp. 357–68.

Harding, Matthew C. (2005), 'Mail demand models', mimeo, paper presented at the CRRI – Rutgers University's 13th Conference on Postal and Delivery Economics, Antwerp, June 4–7.

Jaag, Christian (2007), 'Liberalization of the Swiss letter market and the viability of universal service obligations', *Swiss Journal of Economics and Statistics*, **143**(3), 261–82.

Jaag, Christian, Martin Koller and Urs Trinkner (2009), 'Estimating the cost of the USO – the need for a global approach', in M.A. Crew and P.R. Kleindorfer (eds), *Progress in the Competitive Agenda in the Postal and Delivery Sector*, Cheltenham, UK and Northampton, MA, USA: Edward Elgar, forthcoming.

Robinson, Alan (2007), 'A Review of Price Elasticity Models for Postal Products', Pitney Bowes Background Paper 2007-01.

Trinkner, Urs and Martin Grossmann (2006), 'Forecasting Swiss mail demand', in Crew and Kleindorfer (eds) (2006a), pp. 267–80.

6. Funding universal service obligations*

John C. Panzar[†]

1. INTRODUCTION

One of the many challenges facing policymakers is fostering competition in postal markets while, at the same time, preserving universal service. This is a difficult undertaking, for to declare the need for a universal service *policy* is to admit that the unsubsidized competitive marketplace will fail to deliver a politically acceptable level of service at a politically acceptable price. However, competition and subsidization are like oil and water; they can be mixed only with great care.

The purpose of this chapter is to explain the underlying logical exercise one must go through when attempting to measure the cost of fulfilling any specified universal service obligation (USO). My main point is that any USO costing exercise must begin with a careful specification of an unsubsidized market scenario that would prevail in the absence of the USO. Many proposed measures of USO costs ignore this basic requirement. Or, more charitably, they implicitly assume an unsubsidized market scenario with only limited competition. Not surprisingly, the true cost of any specified USO is higher, the more competitive is the unsubsidized market scenario postulated.[1]

The remainder of the chapter is organized as follows: Section 2 presents the general principles for measuring USO costs relative to an unsubsidized market scenario. These include the need to take into account the incremental costs of subgroups of users as well as services, and the incumbent's forgone revenues. Section 3 applies these principles to a stylized postal network under several market scenarios. Section 3.1 provides the required definitions and notation to present the argument in the context of a postal network with two delivery areas, two service categories, and two cost components. Section 3.2 analyzes USO cost recovery options under a variety of unsubsidized market scenarios: regulated monopoly, unregulated monopoly, competition with and without a reserved area, and competition with unbundled downstream access. The impacts of uniform pricing requirements are also discussed. Section 3.3 discusses the possibility of auctioning off the USO. The chapter ends with a brief conclusion.

2. DEFINING THE COSTS OF THE USO

By definition, a USO mandates a flow of subsidy toward one group of users or another. In order to measure the cost of implementing any such plan, it is necessary to have in mind an alternative market outcome that would be expected to occur in the absence of any

† Northwestern University and University of Auckland.

subsidy scheme. Any rate plan involving a directed subsidy has this property. Before one can hope to measure the costs associated with subsidizing a service or a group of users, one must have some idea of the market outcome relative to which the subsidy is to be implemented.

The typical rationale for directly or indirectly subsidizing universal service is that, left to their own devices, carriers would not find it profitable to provide it. The economically correct rationale is, instead, the fact that, without a source of subsidy, there would be a significant group of customers whom it would not be economic for the firm to serve, yet for whom it is socially desirable to ensure that service be provided. The social desirability of such a subsidy can sometimes be defended on purely economic efficiency grounds. This follows from the fact that, in the presence of economies of scale, the decision to expand the postal delivery network by serving an additional delivery point confers benefits to mailers greater than the revenues received by the postal firms. Similarly, the requirement for uniform pricing of some products may be imposed under a USO. In this case also, the costs of meeting this obligation depend upon the characteristics of the unsubsidized benchmark alternative.

The cost of implementing any USO depends upon the cost of the resources used to provide the service, the prices at which the service is to be provided, *and* the subsidy mechanism through which universal service is to be obtained. This tripartite emphasis is required precisely because the market cannot be relied upon to achieve desired service levels. Therefore it is necessary to have in mind a hypothetical competitive market alternative before it is possible to determine the cost of implementing any USO.

2.1 Recognizing the Incremental Costs of the USO in Serving Groups of Customers, Not Just Services

The value of incremental cost analysis for forward-looking purposes results from the fact that, by its very nature, it helps focus the discussion on 'the right question'. That is, the incremental cost of a service measures the cost savings that would result from eliminating that service from the offerings of the firm. Alternatively, this calculation measures the costs that would be saved if all of the firm's customers were deprived of the service (or group of services) in question. But this is not the relevant counterfactual to consider when developing a methodology to measure the incremental costs of universal service. Rather, the pertinent cost savings are those that result from the fact that, without the USO, the firm no longer provides delivery to a subset of customers, or, no longer provides service to a subset of customers at a loss. Applying incremental analysis to the provision of universal service is conceptually straightforward, and completely analogous to the process used in incremental cost studies of postal services. Two customer sets must be identified: those that would and that would not receive delivery without subsidy support at the socially determined uniform basic service rate. Next, two total cost figures must be estimated: the costs of providing local delivery to all who would receive delivery under the USO and the costs of providing local delivery to the (smaller) set of subscribers who would receive delivery without it. The difference is the actual resource cost resulting from implementing the USO in question.

2.2 USO Costs are Defined with Reference to a Particular Set of Services and Rates

Having established that the costs of the universal service mandate spring from the need to serve a group of consumers whom the market process would otherwise ignore, it is clear that the said costs can only be measured with respect to a reference set of services and a benchmark set of rates for all services. Establishing a group of services to include in the definition of universal service is a recognized first step in any universal service inquiry. Obviously, one must know what functions and features are to be subsidized before it is possible to attempt to determine the cost of providing the subsidy.

2.3 Accounting for Forgone Revenues

The cost to the incumbent of implementing a USO includes not only the resource costs of providing delivery to a group of consumers who would not receive it in the absence of the USO; it also includes the reduction in net revenues, relative to the unsubsidized market scenario, experienced by the incumbent as a result of the pricing policies used to implement the USO.

These costs will vary from plan to plan. To see this, suppose those households who would not receive delivery at unsubsidized market rates could be identified and have their mail delivered at no cost to them. In this special case, the costs to the incumbent of implementing universal delivery would correspond exactly to the actual resource costs of providing universal service.

Now suppose that those mail volumes that would not be sent at unsubsidized market rates could (somehow) be identified and offered a special discounted rate low enough to bring them into the system. In this case the costs to the incumbent of implementing the USO are the actual resource costs incurred, less the revenue it collects from discounted rates.

The economic methodology outlined above for measuring the cost of USOs appears to require a great deal of data and analysis to implement: for example estimates of delivery patterns with and without the plan, as well as estimates of the unsubsidized prices that would be expected to prevail in the absence of the plan. All this is in addition to the usual incremental cost analyses. Of course, in practice, it is generally not possible to have any accurate way to identify individual mail volumes, which would be lost in unsubsidized market equilibrium. Further, subsidization to further universal service has been going on for so long that data from an unsubsidized market scenario is unavailable to the policy maker. However, because of the difficulty in targeting subsidies to individual users, universal service goals are often pursued using more broadly defined tools, such as a socially determined maximum allowable rate that is below the average incremental cost of serving some customers.

3. USO COSTS IN A STYLIZED POSTAL NETWORK

The method developed above, which measures the incumbent's cost of implementing any USO as the sum of the additional resource costs incurred and forgone revenues, is a logically correct way to determine the incremental cost of any USO. The following analysis of a stylized postal network should make these ideas concrete.

3.1 Postal Services, Costs, and the USO

The postal incumbent, firm *i*, serves two types of service areas: a low-cost delivery area *A* and a high-cost delivery area *B*. The incumbent provides two services: service 1, a core service such as basic letter service, and service 2, a premium service for which there may be competitive alternatives. The incumbent's costs are given by:

$$C^i = D^A(V_{A1}, V_{A2}) + D^B(V_{B1}, V_{B2}) + S(V_{A1} + V_{B1}, V_{A2} + V_{B2}). \qquad (6.1)$$

Separate delivery cost functions, D^A and D^B, are assumed for each type of service area, while mail processing costs, *S*, depend only upon the total volumes, V_{kj}, of each type of mail. It will greatly simplify notation and clarify the exposition if costs are assumed to be affine. That is,

$$\begin{aligned} D^k &= F^k_T + d_{k1}V_{k1} + d_{k2}V_{k2} \\ S &= F^S_T + s_1(V_{A1} + V_{B1}) + s_2(V_{A2} + V_{B2}) \\ k &= A, B \qquad T \subseteq \{1, 2\}. \end{aligned} \qquad (6.2)$$

This specification allows for the presence of economies of scale, economies of scope and product-specific fixed costs. For simplicity, demands are assumed independent across services and delivery destinations. However, each demand curve will depend upon the price of any competitive providers serving the same area. It will prove useful to define the *net contributions* obtained from each of the (four possible) conceptually distinct service offerings provided by the incumbent:

$$\begin{aligned} N_{kj}(p_{kj}) &= (p_{kj} - d_{kj} - s_j)V_{kj} \\ k &= A, B \qquad j = 1, 2. \end{aligned} \qquad (6.3)$$

In this simple framework the incumbent's USO consists of the requirement to provide delivery to the high-cost area *B*. Some might argue that the typical requirement that the incumbent provide some or all of its services at a uniform rate is also part of its USO. However, it is much clearer to incorporate this requirement and any associated costs indirectly. As noted above, uniform pricing requirements affect USO costs because, by definition, the said costs can only be measured with respect to a particular set of rates and services.

3.2 Alternative Unsubsidized Market Scenarios

Regulated monopoly

As a starting point, consider a benchmark situation in which the incumbent firm is constrained to exactly break even. Then the break-even constraint requires that the sum of the various contributions covers the fixed costs of the postal network: that is, that:

$$N_{A1}(p_{A1}) + N_{A2}(p_{A2}) + N_{B1}(p_{B1}) + N_{B2}(p_{B2}) = F^S_{12} + F^A_{12} + F^B_{12}, \qquad (6.4)$$

where F^S_{12} = fixed cost of non-delivery operation for a producer offering products 1 and 2 and $F^A_{12} + F^B_{12}$ = fixed cost of delivery in areas A and B for a producer offering products 1 and 2.

Now, rewrite this as:

$$N_{A1}(p_{A1}) + N_{A2}(p_{A2}) = [F^B_{12} - N_{B1}(p_{B1}) - N_{B2}(p_{B2})] + F^S_{12} + F^A_{12} \equiv U(p_{B1}, p_{B2}) + I^A_{12}, \tag{6.5}$$

where $U(p_{B1}, p_{B2})$represents the deficit from providing services to the high-cost areas. Thus, in the case of regulated monopoly regulation, one way of characterizing the break-even condition is that it requires that the contributions from all products and regions cover total network overhead costs. Equivalently, one could describe the situation as one in which contributions from profitable services and regions exactly equal their stand-alone overhead costs *plus* the deficits incurred providing service to high-cost areas. That is, it is logically correct to think of USO costs as another form of (what the United States Postal Service terms as) 'institutional' costs ($I^A_{12}= F^S_{12} + F^A_{12}$) that must be covered by the sum of contributions earned by the various profitable services.

Note that, as expected, the magnitude of USO costs depends upon the prices the incumbent is allowed to charge in high-cost areas. The higher those prices, the lower the costs of the USO. Another modification to the break-even condition will establish a benchmark for future reference. Let P denote any USO payment the incumbent might receive. Then, we have:

$$P + N_{A1}(p_{A1}) + N_{A2}(p_{A2}) \equiv U(p_{B1}, p_{B2}) + I^A_{12}. \tag{6.6}$$

Thus, any USO payment received by the incumbent can be viewed as just another source of contribution to be used to cover the institutional costs of the postal network.

If we adopt the additional constraint that USO payments should offset USO costs, the single break-even constraint is replaced by two conditions:

$$N_{A1}(p_{A1}) + N_{A2}(p_{A2}) = I^A_{12} \tag{6.7}$$

$$P = U(p_{B1}, p_{B2}). \tag{6.8}$$

In a self-contained monopoly system, it is neither necessary nor desirable to separate the funding responsibilities in this way. This is true for two reasons. First, the source of any USO payments may come from some form of tax on postal users. The separation is therefore merely an accounting convention, since the funds ultimately come from the gross contributions of the various profitable services. The second reason is somewhat subtler. Satisfying two constraints instead of one reduces the pricing flexibility available to the incumbent and/or its regulator. Whatever the ultimate objective, it can be pursued less effectively if the system of USO taxes and mark-ups over marginal costs are required to equate USO payments to USO costs.

However, there is a very good policy rationale for providing the incumbent with a payment of *at least* the USO costs in equation (6.5) when considering opening postal markets to competitive entry. This is required in order to ensure that the *remainder* of the system does not fail the stand-alone cost test. If such were the case, an entrant less efficient than the incumbent would anticipate making positive profit by undercutting the incumbents' existing rates. By the same token, there is an upper limit on the appropriate USO payment. This can be derived from the condition that the remainder of the system not fail the incremental cost test. In the present example, this requires that:

$$p_{A1}V_{A1} + p_{A2}V_{A2} \geq F_{12}^{A} + (d_{A1} + s_1)V_{A1} + (d_{A2} + s_2)V_{A2}, \tag{6.9}$$

or,

$$N_{A1} + N_{A2} \geq F_{12}^{A}. \tag{6.10}$$

Combined with the break-even condition (6.6), this yields:

$$P \leq U(p_{A1}, p_{A2}) + F_{12}^{S}. \tag{6.11}$$

Taken together, these conditions provide a range of universal service fund (USF) payments that are consistent with the absence of internal subsidy *and* cost recovery on the part of the incumbent:

$$U(p_{A1}, p_{A2}) \leq P \leq U(p_{A1}, p_{A2}) + F_{12}^{S}. \tag{6.12}$$

That is, the size of the admissible range of USF payments to the incumbent is given by the amount of non-delivery overhead costs of the postal network.[2]

Note that these system overhead costs are not presented as part of USO *costs*. Instead, they form part of the basis for determining the range of USF *payments* that are consistent with the unsubsidized market scenario that I have specified: that is, break-even monopoly. It is also important to note that the payment range derived above should *not* be interpreted as the difference between stand-alone USO costs and incremental USO costs. (As pointed out at the outset, a USO is not a group of services or customers for which 'costs' are defined independently of pricing policy.) Instead, the range of admissible USF payments comes about because of the possible differences between stand-alone and incremental costs for the remainder of the system and the need to ensure that that remainder neither provides nor receives a subsidy as the incumbent recovers its costs. Note that if, as is often assumed, the non-delivery portion of the network exhibits constant returns to scale, the only admissible USF payment is one equal to USO costs.

Uniform pricing and USO costs

The basic formula for determining USO costs derived in the previous subsection allows the incumbent to charge different prices for mail destined for high-cost delivery areas than for mail destined for low-cost delivery areas. This was done in order to emphasize that the rates charged in the high-cost areas play a key role in determining USO costs. But, most postal incumbents do not have the freedom to charge such non-uniform rates, especially for basic service. Therefore, it is important to examine how USO costs change with the imposition of a uniform pricing requirement. It must be pointed out, however, that posing this question requires further assumptions about the nature of the cost recovery process, even without competition.

To understand this issue, consider some thought experiments. In each case, the regulatory authority wishes to set the stage for competition by explicitly calculating USO costs:

1. *Case 1* The regulator negotiates with the incumbent a set of break-even prices satisfying equation (6.4). Let $\mathbf{p}^1 = (p^1_{A1}, p^1_{A2}, p^1_{B1}, p^1_{B2})$ denote this price vector. The USO costs associated with these prices are calculated using the identity in equation (6.5). Now assume that the regulator imposes the uniform pricing condition by requiring that the price established for mail delivered to the low-cost area must also be charged for mail destined for the high-cost area. Two things will happen. First, the incumbent will now run a deficit as a result of the lower prices. Second, measured USO costs will increase, also because of the lower prices.
2. *Case 2* In this case, the regulator negotiates with the incumbent a set of uniform rates that satisfy the break-even constraint and then calculates the USO costs using equation (6.5). Comparing the resulting level of USO costs to either of the Case 1 outcomes requires a detailed specification of the rate setting process: that is, what objective are the regulator and firm explicitly or implicitly maximizing?
3. *Case 3* The regulator and firm negotiate rates subject to equation (6.7), that the sum of contributions cover the network's non-USO institutional costs. The same prices are charged for mail delivered to the high-cost area and the USO costs associated with these prices are determined. The firm receives compensation for these costs from a USF. This example essentially treats USF payments as exogenous.
4. *Case 4* The regulator takes account of the taxation rules which generate USF funds and negotiates rates with the incumbent such that equations (6.7) and (6.8) are simultaneously satisfied with a set of uniform prices. Obviously, this requires a great degree of both forecasting ability and regulatory sophistication.

The point of going through these cases is to emphasize that USO costs are highly dependent upon ratemaking policies and procedures, even in a traditional protected monopoly environment. It is straightforward to calculate the level of USO costs associated with any *given* set of rates. However, it must be recognized that any policy change that affects postal rates will also impact on USO costs. USO costs calculated using pre-liberalization rates and volumes may not be a good approximation of USO costs in a new regime. This point will be increasingly important with respect to the various competitive scenarios discussed below.

Unregulated monopoly

The case of unregulated monopoly is the simplest setting in which to illustrate the logic behind my proposed methodology for measuring USO costs. In this scenario, it is assumed that the incumbent is not subject to any price-level regulation, but is subject to a USO that requires that it serve area *B* and provide basic service at a uniform rate. In the absence of the USO, it is assumed that the incumbent would be allowed to set any rates it wished and determine which delivery areas to serve.

To make the problem interesting, assume that the monopolist would not choose to serve area *B*, even if its prices were unconstrained. Let (p^*_1, p^*_2) denote the profit-maximizing prices for a monopoly serving only area *A*. Next, let:

$$(p_1^u, p_1^u, p_{2A}^u, p_{2B}^u) = \arg\max\{\pi^u(p_{1A}, p_{1B}, p_{2A}, p_{2B}): p_{1A} = p_{1B} = p_1\},$$

where:

$$\pi^u(p_{1A}, p_{2A}, p_{1B}, p_{2B}) = N_{A1}(p_{A1}) + N_{A2}(p_{A2}) + N_{B1}(p_{B1}) + N_{B2}(p_{B2}) - F_{12}^A - F_{12}^B - F_{12}^S \quad (6.13)$$

The cost of the USO is still given by equation (6.5):

$$U(p_{B1}^u, p_{B2}^u) = [F_{12}^B - N_{B1}(p_{B1}^u) + N_{B2}(p_{B2}^u)]. \quad (6.14)$$

However, there is also a cost associated with the *uniform pricing obligation* (UPO). This results from the fact that the optimal uniform price for service 1 will tend to be higher than that which a monopolist serving only delivery area A would choose.[3]

This leads to a lower contribution there and a lower total level of firm profits. Note that this loss of *potential* profit has no counterpart in the case of a firm subject to a break-even constraint. It is merely one of many pricing choices that result in less than maximum attainable profit.

Competition with a reserved service

Now consider the determination of USO costs and admissible USF payments when service 2 is opened to competition, while service 1 remains a service reserved for the incumbent. To keep things simple, assume that entrants do not find it profitable to serve area B and that the incumbent must charge uniform prices for both services. Without being specific about the nature of the competitive interactions between the incumbent and the entrant(s), assume that the presence of competition (and the uniform pricing requirement) results in an equilibrium service 2 price vector of (p_{2i}^R, p_{2e}^R), where the subscripts i and e refer to the incumbent and entrant, respectively. Then, given any USF payment P, the uniform price of the basic service would be determined by the condition:

$$N_{A1}(p_1^R) + N_{A2}^i(p_{2i}^R, p_{2e}^R) + N_{B1}(p_1^R) + N_{B2}(p_2^R) + P = F_{12}^A + F_{12}^B + F_{12}^S. \quad (6.15)$$

Rewrite this as:

$$[N_{A1}(p_1) + N_{A2}^i(p_{2i}^R, p_{2e}^R) - F_{12}^A] + P = [F_{12}^B - N_{B1}(p_1) - N_{B2}(p_{2i}^R)] + F_{12}^S = U + F_{12}^S. \quad (6.16)$$

Here, the function $N_{A2}^i(p_{2i}, p_{2e})$denotes the contribution received by the incumbent from service 2 in area A as a function of both firms' prices. Of course, since the entrant is assumed not to service area B the contributions from area B depend only upon the regulated price of the incumbent.

Equation (6.16) reflects the policy tradeoff between the level of USF payments and the level of the uniform basic service price in any break-even situation. For any given level of P, the uniform basic service price required for the incumbent to break even will be higher than in the absence of competition.[4]

If P is set just equal to USO costs, its lowest admissible value, then contributions in region A must cover all of the joint and common costs of the network. Alternatively, a lower basic service rate can be supported if P is increased to cover some or all of these network costs.

Competition without a reserved service

Next suppose that the incumbent must fulfill the USO without any reserved service. (Again, assume that entrants do not choose to serve area B.) Let us denote the equilibrium price vectors in area A. Then the incumbent's break-even condition is given by:

$$[N^i_{A1}(p^N_{1i}, p^N_{1e}) + N^i_{A2}(p^N_{2i}, p^N_{2e}) - F^A_{12}] + P = U(p^N_{1i}, p^N_{2i}) + F^S_{12}. \qquad (6.17)$$

Equation (6.17) *looks* similar to equation (6.16), but the situation is fundamentally different. Without a reserved service price to set, there will generally be only one value of USF payment that allows the incumbent to break even. As long as equilibrium contribution levels from area A at least cover the region-specific fixed costs, the required payment will be in the subsidy-free range. However, equation (6.17) reveals that the required USF payment will range from USO costs to USO costs plus network overhead, depending upon the severity of competition.

Competition with unbundled downstream access

As a final scenario, consider the case in which the incumbent is required to provide delivery services in area B to competitors. To keep the analysis simple, assume that there is only one (unreserved) service and that both the incumbent and the entrant must offer uniform prices. Let p_i and p_e denote the equilibrium price vector and a, the per-unit access charge. Then the incumbent's break-even condition is given by:

$$(p^*_i - d_A - s)V^i_A + (p^*_i - d_B - s)V^i_B + (a - d_B)V^e_B + P = F^A + F^B + F^S, \qquad (6.18)$$

which can be rewritten as;

$$(p^*_i - d_A - s)V^i_A - F^A + P = [F^B - (p^*_i - d_B - s)V^i_B + (a - d_B)V^e_B] + F^S = U^A + F^S \qquad (6.19)$$

In this case, there are two instruments, which can be adjusted to enable the incumbent to break even, the USF payment and the access charge. Clearly, an access charge greater than marginal (average incremental) delivery costs in the high-cost area reduces USO costs.

3.3 Auctioning Off the USO

It is sometimes proposed that an additional way of introducing competition into the postal network is to allow competition for the delivery market in high-cost areas through, say, a Demsetz auction. Even if such auctions are not actually carried out, it is thought that a careful calculation of 'efficient firm' costs of providing the said service would remove any ambiguity in the size of USF payments. Clearly, P should not exceed the amount a hypothetical efficient entrant would accept to take on the USO.

Let us examine this argument. Again, a single service example can be used to illustrate the issues. The incumbent's break-even condition is:

$$(p - d_A - s)V_A(p) - F^A + P = [F^B - (p - d_B - s)V_B(p)] + F^S = U(p) + F^S. \quad (6.20)$$

There is the usual tradeoff between a higher uniform price and a lower USF payment. Now consider the needs of a hypothetical efficient USO entrant. First, it must be recognized that area B delivery is *not*, itself, a product or service. Thus in order to determine the least amount a firm would accept to assume the USO, one must first specify the 'transfer price' t it would receive for accepting each piece of partially processed mail. Then the least USF payment the entrant would accept would be given by:

$$P^e = [F^{Be} - (t - d^e_B)V_B(p)]. \quad (6.21)$$

Now, if the entrant were equally as efficient as the incumbent, and the transfer price were equal to the stamp price less per-unit sorting costs ($t = p–s$), the resulting USF payment would be exactly equal to the initially calculated USO cost from equation (6.19). But in that case, the incumbent's break-even condition would be:

$$(p - d_A - s)V_A - F^A - F^S = 0. \quad (6.22)$$

That is, the consumers in area A would be required to cover all of the network overhead costs. Alternatively, suppose the USO entrant received nothing for each piece of mail it accepted. In that case, the minimum required payment would be:

$$P^e = F^{Be} + d_B V_B(p), \quad (6.23)$$

and the incumbent's break-even condition would be:

$$(p - d_A - s)V_A(p) + (p - s)V_B(p) - F^A - F^S = 0 \quad (6.24)$$

In contrast to equation (6.22), equation (6.24) makes it clear that customers whose mail is destined for area B make a contribution toward covering the systems' overhead costs.

This maximal level of the 'winning bid' USF payment could be either larger or smaller than the maximum admissible USF payment derived above. (To see this, suppose that non-delivery processes exhibited constant returns to scale.) However, it seems reasonable to set the transfer at least as large as unit delivery costs ($t \geq d_B$). Then, the USF payment would be no larger than the overhead costs of the high-cost area.

What accounts for the dramatic reduction in the range of possible USF payments? The simple answer is that the 'bidding' approach analyzed in this section *presumes* that the firm that assumes the USO will receive pre-processed mail at a uniform transfer rate. Thus, it is not directly responsible for any non-delivery overhead costs. In the analysis under 'Regulated monopoly', above, the stand-alone costs of delivery area B included those overhead costs. Therefore, not only does the level of the transfer price directly impact on the 'winning' USF payment, but so does the very presumption that such interterm transfers can be made.

4. CONCLUSION

By emphasizing the role of the 'unsubsidized market alternative', this chapter has developed a unifying framework for USO costing and funding. Indeed, one of the major contributions of the analysis is to make clear that there does not exist any single, generally applicable monetary measure of USO costs. The question to be addressed is *not*: 'How much will it cost the incumbent to provide specified service levels to unprofitable areas?'. Rather, the correct focus of quantification should be: 'What levels of subsidy, rates, and reserved areas will allow the incumbent to cover its costs in the competitive era?'.

NOTES

* This is reprinted with minor revisions from John C. Panzar, 'Funding universal service obligations: the costs of liberalization', in Michael A. Crew and Paul R. Kleindorfer (eds), *Future Directions in Postal Reform*, Boston, MA: Kluwer Academic, 2001, pp. 101–16, with kind permission of Springer Science and Business Media. Estimating the cost of the USO has taken on greater importance since the publication of the original study because of recent legislation on postal reform in the European Union and the United States. In the USA, the 2006 Postal Accountability and Enhancement Act requires that the cost of the USO be calculated annually. In the EU, the 2008 Third Postal Directive, opening the European postal market to full competition, requires the calculation of the cost of the USO and specifies a number of means by which this can be accomplished. This is especially important under the competitive environment enabled by the Third Postal Directive in view of concerns about cross-subsidization of competitive products and the prohibition of state aid to public enterprises under the Treaty of Rome establishing the European Community. Hearn (2008) describes the background and details of the EU Directive in this regard.

1. Attempts to quantify the costs of the USO in various countries include: Dobbs and Golay (1995); Elsenblast et al. (1995); Elsenblast and Stumpf (1995); Kowalewski and Muller (1995); Crémer et al. (1997, 2000); Stumpf (1997); Rodriguez et al. (1999); and Bradley and Colvin (2000).
2. In this example these overhead costs are constant. With more complicated cost structures this magnitude will vary with mail volumes.
3. The comparison can go either way unless some restrictions are placed upon demand elasticities. However, if the demand curves for service 1 in areas A and B are 'sufficiently similar', the higher marginal costs in the latter area will bring about this intuitive result.
4. This will be true whenever competition limits service 2 contributions to a level below that which would otherwise prevail.

REFERENCES

Bradley, Michael and Colvin, Jeffrey (2000), 'Measuring the costs of universal service for posts', in Michael A. Crew and Paul R. Kleindorfer (eds), *Current Directions in Postal Reform*, Boston, MA: Kluwer Academic, pp. 29–46.

Crémer, Helmut, De Rycke, Marc and Grimaud, Andre (1997). 'Costs and benefits of universal service obligations in the postal sector', in Michael A. Crew and Paul R. Kleindorfer (eds), *Managing Change in the Postal and Delivery Industries*, Boston, MA: Kluwer Academic, pp. 22–41.

Crémer, Helmut, Grimaud, Andre and Laffont, Jean-Jacques (2000), 'The cost of universal service in the postal sector', in Michael A. Crew and Paul R. Kleindorfer (eds), *Current Directions in Postal Reform,* Boston, MA: Kluwer Academic, pp. 47–68.

Dobbs, Ian and Golay, Jeanne (1995), 'Universal service obligation and reserved sector', in Ulrich Stumpf and W. Elsenblast (eds), *Cost of Universal Service*, Papers presented at the 3rd Konigs Winter Seminar, WIK Proceedings.

Elsenblast, W., Pieper, M. and Stumpf, Ulrich (1995), 'Estimating the universal service burden of public operators', WIK Discussion Paper No. 150, Wissenschafliches Institut für Kommunikationsidienste, Bad Honnef, Germany.

Elsenblast, W. and Stumpf, Ulrich (1995), 'The cost of universal service obligations in a competitive environment', in Ulrich Stumpf and W. Elsenblast (eds), *Cost of Universal Service*, Papers presented at the 3rd Konigswinter Seminar, WIK Proceedings.

Hearn, John (2008), 'The accounting implications of the EU's Third Postal Directive', in Michael A. Crew and Paul R. Kleindorfer (eds), *Competition and Regulation in the Postal and Delivery Sector*, Cheltenham UK and Northampton, MA, USA: Edward Elgar, pp. 338–51.

Kowalewski, K. and K. Muller (1995), 'The cost of universal service obligation – the German perspective', in Ulrich Stumpf and W. Elsenblast (eds), *Cost of Universal Service*, Papers presented at the 3rd Konigswinter Seminar, WIK Proceedings.

Panzar, John C. (2001), 'Funding universal service obligations: the costs of liberalization', in Michael A. Crew and Paul R. Kleindorfer (eds), *Future Directions in Postal Reform*, Boston, MA: Kluwer Academic, pp. 101–16.

Rodriguez, Frank, Smith, Stephen and Storer, David (1999), 'Estimating the cost of the USO in postal service', in Michael A. Crew and Paul R. Kleindorfer (eds), *Emerging Competition in Postal and Delivery Services*, Boston, MA: Kluwer Academic, pp. 195–208.

Stumpf, Ulrich (1997), 'Providing universal service in competitive postal markets', in Michael A. Crew and Paul R. Kleindorfer (eds), *Managing Change in the Postal and Delivery Industries*, Boston, MA: Kluwer Academic, pp. 288–303.

7. Calculating the net cost of the USO: a practical example from Norway*

Kristin Bergum†

1. INTRODUCTION

This chapter is first and foremost a story of practical experience in calculating the net cost of the universal service obligation (USO) in the postal sector. Although the cost of universal service has been the subject of much debate in the last decade, there are few instances in which a government and public operator have been agreed on a comprehensive method for fixing the cost of the USO and the government has compensated the postal operator as a result. The approach described in this chapter represents a pragmatic adaption of economic theory, which has been successfully employed in Norway since 2002.

Recent legislative developments on both sides of the Atlantic Ocean have given fresh urgency to addressing the practical problems presented by a calculation of the cost of universal service. On 20 February 2008, the European Union approved a new amendment to the European Postal Directive. The revised European directive will require member states to abandon the internal cross-subsidies made possible by the reserved area and calculate an explicit cost of universal service before public support can be provided. In the United States, the Postal Regulatory Commission is now beginning to implement the Postal Accountability and Enhancement Act of 2006. As part of the reforms introduced by the act, the Postal Regulatory Commission must annually prepare for Congress an estimate of the costs incurred by the US Postal Service in providing universal service.

This chapter is divided as follows. Section 2 contains a short review of the main theoretical approaches to calculating the cost of the USO. Section 3 explains the Norwegian approach and how it was developed after a failed attempt to apply a more theoretical methodology. The last section offers some conclusions on the relation between the Norwegian approach and various theoretical benchmarks and on the compatibility of the Norwegian calculations with the amended European Postal Directive.

2. THEORETICAL APPROACHES TO MEASURING THE COST OF THE USO

In the last decade, three theoretical models for defining the net cost of the USO have gained most attention: net avoided cost (NAC), entry pricing (EP) and profitability cost (PC).

† Posten Norge.

2.1 Net Avoided Cost Model

The NAC approach appears to be the most widely used model for estimating USO costs, notably in the telecommunications sector (Oxera, 2007). The NAC model was also recommended as the most appropriate model for the postal sector by National Economic Research Associates (NERA) in its report on the costing and financing of the USO in the postal sector to the European Commission (NERA, 1998). Although there are numerous possible refinements, the essence of the NAC approach consists of identifying and aggregating the losses related to loss-making portions of the present business of the universal service provider (USP).[1]

As discussed in several reports and papers, the NAC model is, however, burdened with a number of defects. First and foremost, the close-down scenario proposed as a result of the model does not represent any plausible alternative business model that could result from the abolition of the USO. Hence, the net cost as calculated by the NAC model does not represent profit forgone by the universal provider as a consequence of the obligation. The NAC model is also unrealistically static, at least in the absence of considerable adjustments and extensions. The basic model assumes that closing down one part of the business implies no consequences for other parts. For example, the approach implicitly assumes that discontinuation of delivery to one group of recipients leaves unaffected the demand for delivery to the remaining recipients. A third problem is more practical in nature. It is that the estimated cost of the USO varies with the level of aggregation of data, because the more aggregated the data, the more unprofitable portions of the business will be grouped with, that is, masked by, profitable portions of the business. This means that with relatively aggregated data, part of the unprofitable business will not be included in the calculation of total losses incurred by the unprofitable business. Hence, the more disaggregated the data used in the calculation, the higher the resulting calculated USO cost.

2.2 Entry Pricing Model

As a contribution to NERA's work on the report for the European Commission in 1998, British postal economists criticized the NAC model and launched an alternative for calculating the cost of the USO. This model, the entry pricing model, was subsequently described in several articles (see Rodriguez et al., 1999; Rodriguez and Storer, 2000). Their major objection to the NAC model was its presumption of a monopolistic environment when the question of most importance to postal policy is the cost of the USO in a competitive environment.

The EP model focuses precisely on a calculation of the losses incurred by the USP as a consequence of liberalizing a formerly monopolistic market, that is, on the decrease in profitability due to liberalization. Rodriguez and Storer (2000) provide an example using Royal Mail's costs as a basis for modeling the consequences of potential entry scenarios. As in the NAC model, the EP model presupposes a division of the postal operation into market segments or 'routes'. Whereas the NAC model aggregates the loss in the unprofitable segments, the EP model aggregates the reductions in profits following the introduction of competition, that is, it focuses on the profitable rather than the unprofitable segments. Oxera (2007) criticizes the EP model for failing to include potential losses in unprofitable segments which may result from additional price reductions in these segments as a consequence of competition. It seems, however, that such effects could be included without changing the fundamental logic of the model.

A more fundamental problem with the EP model arises from the development of entry models. At the outset, the choice of the level of market segmentation in the model, that is, the division of the USP's business into segments, changes the calculated cost of the USO so that the cost will increase proportionally with the level of detail of the available data. In addition, I would argue that it is unrealistic to suppose that entry scenarios can be developed that are sufficiently robust for use in the sort of calculations required by the model. For example, such scenarios could entail business models that differ fundamentally from the incumbent's model, such as twice-per-week delivery services or entry based on economic synergies that differ from those of the incumbent. Capturing the range of reasonable scenarios, and reflecting these in the cost of the USO, is likely to be very difficult.

In addition, the EP model presupposes that the (monopoly) profit that is lost due to liberalization matches exactly the burden (unprofitability) imposed on the incumbent due to the USO – that is, that the rate of return prior to competition is financially correct, and that the loss of profit could be defined as the cost of the USO. Even though one could presuppose a correct rate of return under the monopoly, different cost structures of various possible entrants would mean that there would be a different cost of the USO in every competition scenario. Furthermore, a correct rate of return would hardly be the case in any real monopoly situation. In addition there are, of course, the problems of possible inefficiencies. Hence, I agree with Copenhagen Economics (2008) that the EP model answers the wrong question, namely the cost (to the incumbent) of liberalization, and not the cost of the USO – and that the two are not the same thing.

2.3 Profitability Cost Model

The PC model was introduced by Crémer et al. (2000) and Panzar (2000). As developed by Crémer et al., the PC model evaluates the loss in profit caused by the USO, as opposed to 'the cost of liberalization'. That is, the model estimates the difference in the operator's profit with and without the USO, taking into account possible indirect benefits of the USO. Panzar emphasizes that any exercise to measure the cost of the USO must begin with a specification of the unsubsidized market scenario that would prevail in the absence of the USO. He goes on to describe a method of measuring the incumbent's cost of implementing the USO as the sum of the additional (long-run and forward-looking) costs incurred and the revenues forgone, as well as subtraction of additional revenue caused by additional services.

Copenhagen Economics (2008) accepts the PC model as the theoretical ideal. The challenge, however, is to calculate a plausible numerical result for the cost of the USO according to this method. Both Crémer et al. and Panzar describe calculations that include assumed effects of competition. Whereas estimating possible effects of competition would be commonplace in any business analysis, it is questionable whether assumptions about future competition can be made sufficiently robust to allow a plausible calculation of the cost of the USO, particularly if that calculation is to be used as a basis for financial compensation.

3. THE NORWEGIAN EXPERIENCE

3.1 Norway Post's USO

In Norway, the USO is determined by the Postal Directive of the European Union and the license granted Norway Post by government. Norway is a signatory to an international agreement between the European Union and certain countries that creates the European Economic Area (EEA). As an EEA member, Norway is obliged to implement the EU Postal Directive and, in particular, to comply with the Directive's minimum requirements for universal postal service. In addition, Norway Post has a license issued by the ministry that requires it to maintain a level of universal service that exceeds the requirements of the Directive in several respects.

According to Norway Post's license, the main elements of the USO are as follows: (i) each municipality must have at least one post office or contract post office offering basic postal and financial services; (ii) postal services must meet specified quality of service standards; (iii) delivery is required to all addresses six days per week; (iv) rates for universal postal services must be cost oriented, transparent and non-discriminatory; and (v) rates for reserved services must be geographically uniform throughout the nation.

Norway Post's license also states that the burden of the USO shall be offset by the surplus from the reserved area and, if the surplus from the reserved area is insufficient, by a compensation from the state. This means that it is necessary to calculate both the surplus (monopoly rent) from the reserved area and the extra cost, that is, the net burden, of the USO. Calculating the surplus of the reserved area is, if not trivial, at least feasible with conventional activity-based cost accounting. It is, however, less obvious in what respect the USO represents a burden and how the costs related to the burden should be calculated.

3.2 Norway's First USO Cost Model: Quantifying the NAC Model

The task of estimating the cost of the USO in Norway was first introduced in the early 1990s. In the first couple of years, there were several attempts to find a satisfactory model to calculate how much the government should pay Norway Post, if anything, for maintaining universal service. A basic requirement was that it was necessary to find a way of defining and calculating the burden that was satisfactory both to the purchaser, the government, and to the vendor, Norway Post. At the time, there seemed to be no general model for calculating the cost of the USO in the postal sector.

After a period of trial and error, the government decided to use a consultant to develop a model for calculating the burden of the USO. Coopers & Lybrand was selected because of its experience in developing a model for calculating the burden of the USO in the telecommunications sector in Australia. As a result of the work with Coopers & Lybrand, the government and Norway Post agreed on a model that was used to calculate the net burden of the USO from 1996 until 2001, when it was replaced by the current model. A brief review of the strengths and weaknesses of this 'first model' is useful because it helps to explain the rationale of the current approach.

Norway's first USO model was derived from the NAC approach. Its goal was to calculate the highest possible profit the firm would obtain if it ceased to offer the unprofitable services it was actually offering because of the USO. This hypothetical calculation was made using the latest available historical cost and revenue data, typically, from the previous year. Calculations were based on a long-run perspective, that is, the model sought to identify costs and revenues that would disappear in the long run if part of the business were closed down. The idea was to define the closed-down scenario that would maximize total profits, that is, where unprofitable parts of the business and network were stopped while the profitable parts were continued.

The first model was divided into three submodels: regional, activity and postbank. The regional model calculated whether more costs were avoided than income lost if a postal region was closed. The activity model was run after the region model and focused only on postal products in profitable regions. The aim of the activity model was to locate unprofitable postal flows in the profitable areas that could be closed down and thereby improve total profit. The postbank model was run after the activity model. In effect, the postbank model took into account the costs and revenues for banking products that were not physically transported as part of the postal system.

The first USO model was rather exciting to work with. It provided the possibility of simulating various scenarios and identifying revenues and costs related to many different parts of the business. The model addressed not only USO postal products (priority and economy addressed mail, and unaddressed mail) but also basic banking products and, if relevant, the effects on other products. Specific mail flows between and within regions were modeled. Three ways of distributing the mail to the addressee were considered: home delivery, collection at the post office, and collection at the sorting center. The model allowed for the possibility of sending mail by delivering to either a post office or a sorting center. In each case, revenues and costs were broken down into fixed and variable components. In our calculations, we examined which closed-down scenario would optimize the final result. Would it be more profitable to close a whole region or to maintain an 'unprofitable' region, but close certain postal flows or banking services? For each scenario, the model identified the NAC per product, per region, per mail flow, and per activity. Repeated iterations were needed to accommodate all of the possible combinations. The final result represented the net burden of the USO at Norway Post's present efficiency level.

Ultimately, this first USO model was considered unsatisfactory. On the technical side, the model demanded an overly complex set of detailed data. Collecting and vetting this information involved a great deal of work, especially when the underlying business was in a constant state of flux (during the years the model was used, the number of regions varied from 29 to 12 depending on which reorganization was applicable). Moreover, while Norway Post considered the quality of data to be satisfactory, data quality can always be questioned. Even if external auditors were added to the system, the complexity was such that it is always difficult to know whether the results can really be trusted. Another issue was the problem of potentially inefficient production. Forecasts tried to ameliorate this issue by allowing for savings from, for example, restructuring the post office network or cutting surplus staff. However, the model being so complex, it could not positively be proved that there was no inefficient production included in the calculations. Finally, government simply subtracted an arbitrary amount from the calculated net USO cost to allow for an assumed level of inefficiency. The level of detail was also a problem from another point of view: the more detailed data, the more unprofitable business could be located, and hence the higher the NAC. This, of course, is unsatisfactory when the calculations are used as a basis for an actual payment.

Yet the shortcomings of the model from a political point of view were even more fundamental. The complexity of the model made it very difficult to explain to politicians. The question of what exactly the state was paying for proved to be rather difficult to answer in a straightforward manner. This was especially true when it came to the question of whether the simulated scenarios really represented plausible alternatives. Indeed, the answer is quite obvious: it was out of the question for Norway Post to close postal services in large parts of the country. With or without the USO, Norway Post would continue to cover the whole country one way or another because that was the business it was in.

3.3 Norway's Current USO Cost Model: The Alternative Commercial Strategy

In early 2001, the Ministry of Transport and Communications and Norway Post agreed that a new USO cost model should be developed. For both parties a major goal was a simplified model, whose results would be easier to communicate and less sensitive to data, so that distrust in the calculated results could be minimized. From the outset, it was recognized that the new model should explicitly identify which services were actually paid for by the state. Preferably the new model should also provide the ministry and the appropriate parliamentary committee with useful information about the cost of the various parts of the USO. The revised model should thus provide a basis for political choice. Perhaps parts of the USO are not really worth the price? With this perspective, the task of calculating the USO cost came to be seen from a completely different angle.

The starting point for the new model was: 'What would Norway Post's business look like without the USO?' and 'What service levels would be offered for which product and why?'. Difficult to say, of course. If there were no USO, there could be no reserved area, for within a reserved area, a USO is logically implied, and without a reserved area, there would be competition in traditional mailing services. For Norway Post, the world *might* be completely different; at the extreme, the possibilities are beyond what could be calculated or even easily imagined. However, by lowering their ambitions somewhat and confining themselves to the broad aspects of a *plausible* strategy for Norway Post without a USO, it would be possible take a good step forward towards defining what can be called an 'alternative commercial strategy'. This imagined strategy level can be thought of as a continuation of Norway Post's current commercial strategies – including, for example, high quality of services (including transmission time) and closeness to the customer – adjusted for the absence of a USO. On this basis, what parts of its current universal service would Norway Post plausibly abandon if not subject to a USO? Surprisingly, perhaps, Norway Post concluded that the answer was, 'very little'.

Considering demographic and geographic facts, one might infer that the burden of the USO should be relatively heavy in a country like Norway. It has a very long coastline interrupted by deep fjords and with many populated islands. Mountains run north and south, producing a harsh winter climate in the interior. Due in part to long-standing government policies, Norway's population of only 4.5 million inhabitants is spread out in a relatively decentralized pattern. Population density is 12.3 inhabitants per square kilometer, about 60 percent of Sweden's and 40 percent that of the United States. Despite this unfavorable environment, however, it is not credible that Norway Post, as it currently envisages its business, would discontinue providing basic postal services to the entire population of Norway.

Taking into account the rise in electronic communications and other postal substitutes, Norway Post defined its alternative commercial strategy in the absence of a USO as follows. First, in the most rural areas, delivery frequency would be reduced from the current level of six deliveries per week. Fifteen percent of the households would likely receive mail five days per week, and another 5 percent would receive mail only twice a week. Second, mobile post office services would be reduced by half. Third, services to the blind would not be offered for free, and some extra services related to insured and registered mail would not be offered at all post offices. Fourth, uniform national rates would not apply to mail and parcels sent to and from Svalbard, an archipelago with about 2,200 inhabitants lying well inside the Arctic Circle far from mainland Norway. In all other respects, Norway Post concluded that it would continue the current pattern of universal service without obligation. The definition of the alternative strategy has later been somewhat modified, mainly by adding that banking services would not be offered and that the number of mobile post offices would be kept roughly the same.

It should be stressed that this alternative commercial strategy presupposes normal commercial flexibility. Norway Post must be able to adjust the level of its services and prices and to subcontract non-core activities like any other company. Restrictions on downsizing and outsourcing can hardly be defined as part of the postal USO but should rather be classified as labor politics.

Focusing on changes in overall business strategy alters the basic concept of what exactly the USO burden comprises. The burden is not primarily connected to the obligation of being universal, but rather to the obligation to be universal in a specific way. The problem of quantifying potential benefits from the USO, that is, economies of scale and scope or advantages in the marketplace stemming from the universal presence, disappears.

Using the new approach, it has become relatively simple for Norway Post and the ministry to develop an agreed calculation of the USO cost. The costs and revenues expected from the current commercial strategy with the USO must be calculated and compared to the costs and revenues that would be expected from the alternative commercial strategy. The difference is the estimated cost of the USO. In the case of Norway Post, the calculated cost of the USO came out to about 2 percent of total sales. By far the most important element in this calculation was the cost savings arising from projected reductions in delivery frequency. As with the first model, all of Norway Post's calculations are examined by an external auditor, and all calculations are transparently documented to the ministry. Since these calculations are much less complex and require a far more limited quantity of data, it is much easier for the ministry to examine all parts of the assumptions and calculations and to have confidence in its evaluation of the results.

The revised model was first used to calculate the cost of the USO in 2002. It has now been in use for six years although it has been somewhat adjusted over time. The methodology is now accepted by government as a basis for yearly payments by the state. At the request of the ministry, external consultants have checked the reasonableness of the model's results by using more mathematical and statistical techniques which have yielded similar figures.

4. CONCLUDING OBSERVATIONS

As is clear from the above description, the development of this model has not focused on finding the perfect model from a theoretical point of view. It has rather been focused on finding a pragmatic model that clarifies and facilitates political choice, that is, by clearly specifying the service obligations that constitute the USO burden and their respective costs. Indeed, a major advantage of the current model is that it states the cost of each non-commercial license requirement, and what service level would be offered without the requirement and corresponding payment.

Quite obviously, it may be argued that a basic problem with the Norwegian model is that the cost of the USO will vary with the definition of the alternative commercial strategy and that this strategy can be defined almost arbitrarily by the USP so as to increase its payments from government. In short, the approach is unreliable because it depends upon the willingness of the USP to act against its own financial self-interest. In practice, however, this seeming weakness has not been a significant problem in Norway. Norway Post's alternative commercial strategy for the purposes of the USO cost calculation cannot drift far from the other messages that it is communicating to its customers, its employees, and the various governmental authorities that act as owners and regulators of the firm. This overall strategic message is disciplined by many different considerations in which USO compensation plays only a small part. In fact, Norway Post's strategic commercial plan is rather ambitious – quality service, low prices, high productivity, and so on – and this implies a relatively low cost of the USO. Then, too, the government can always accept portions of the alternative commercial strategy in preference to making payments to Norway Post to sustain universal service. In such a case, Norway Post would be forced to implement its alternative commercial strategy or concede that it is unrealistic.

Our revised model may be categorized as most closely related to the PC method described above. This is also the view taken by Copenhagen Economics, who denote the Norwegian approach as the 'commercial method'. Like the Norwegian approach, the PC model focuses not on calculating losses due to competition but on a step-by-step analysis of each element of the USO and an evaluation of what would, plausibly, be the free, strategic choice of the incumbent if it did not face the obligation in question. Although the Norwegian approach defines USO costs in the same way as the PC model – namely, as the difference in profit with and without the USO – the actual calculations differ. Both Crémer et al. (2000) and Panzar (2000) include calculations of consequences of future competition. While we do not disagree that such an approach is theoretically satisfactory, it is hardly possible to conduct such calculations with the robustness, transparency, and simplicity demanded by practical relations with government. The step-by-step analysis proposed by Copenhagen Economics (2008) therefore represents a pragmatic alternative where the theoretical ideal is unachievable. Both our own experience and the analysis of the Danish situation conducted by Copenhagen Economics suggest that the results gained by this step-by-step approach are sufficiently reasonable and robust to be actually used in decisions about regulations of the postal market and even for reimbursement of costs, as the case may be.

As noted in the introduction, the European Union has recently adopted a Third Postal Directive which virtually requires a calculation of the USO cost. Annex 1 of the new directive provides guidelines for the necessary calculations. According to the annex, the net cost of the USO is defined as 'the difference between the net cost for a designated universal service provider of operating with the universal service obligation and the same postal service provider operating without the universal service obligation'. This seems to be identical with the cost of the USO as defined by the PC model. As for the method of calculation, the guidelines are rather general, but they underscore that all possible benefits should be included. It seems clear, however, that the Norwegian model fully meets the methodological requirements set out in the new directive.

In sum, it seems fair to suggest that the Norwegian approach represents a practical method for calculating the net cost of the USO which governments may use to define compensation to a USP. The Norwegian approach is an approximation of the PC model. However, the Norwegian approach clearly identifies the source of the burden of the USO in terms connected to the scope of services offered and the business rationale for curtailing the scope were it not for the imposition of the USO. While the Norwegian approach shares in the spirit of the theoretical benchmark of the PC model, the results obtained are more transparent to external stakeholders and regulators. Indeed, the Norwegian approach was developed by Norway Post and the ministry as a way of adapting the theoretical insights of economic analysis to the practical needs and constraints faced by governmental decision makers. Such practical realities, no less than the laws of mathematics, are conditions which must be satisfied in any real-life exercise to estimate the cost of the USO.

NOTES

* An earlier version of this chapter was presented at the 10th Conference on Postal and Delivery Economics: Postal and Delivery Services, organized by the Center for Research In Regulated Industries in June 2002 in Potsdam, Germany. Although the paper was never published, it has been cited in several documents leading up to the new European directive, including a report by the European Commission (2006). In light of this attention, the author was encouraged to prepare this more formal version. This chapter represents the views of the author alone and does not necessarily represent the views of Posten Norge.

1. See also the extended discussion of alternative approaches in Panzar (2001).

REFERENCES

Copenhagen Economics (2008), 'Measuring USO Cost – a Practical Guide to Profitability and Costs', Copenhagen, February.

Crémer, Helmuth, André Grimaud and Jean-Jacques Laffont (2000), 'The cost of universal service in the postal sector', in M.A. Crew and P.R. Kleindorfer (eds), *Current Directions in Postal Reform*, Boston, MA: Kluwer Academic, pp. 47–68.

European Commission (2006), 'Prospective Study on the Impact on Universal Service of the Full Accomplishment of the Postal Internal Market in 2009', COM(2006) 596 final (October 18, 2006), http://eur-lex.europa.eu/LexUriServ/LexUriServ.do?uri=COM:2006:0596:FIN:EN:PDF (accessed July 2008).

NERA Economic Consulting (1998), 'Costing and Financing of Universal Service Obligations in the Postal Sector in the European Union', Report for EC DG XIII.

Oxera Consulting, Ltd (2007), 'Funding Universal Service Obligations in the Postal Sector', a study prepared for La Poste, De Post-La Poste, Hellenic Post, Poste Italiane, P&T Luxembourg, Correos, Magyar Posta, Cyprus Post and Poczta Polska, http://www.oxera.com.

Panzar, John C. (2000), 'A methodology for measuring the cost of universal service obligations', *Information Economics and Policy*, **12**(3): 211–20.

Panzar, John C. (2001), 'Funding universal service obligations: the costs of liberalization', in M.A. Crew and P.R. Kleindorfer (eds), *Future Directions in Postal Reform*, Boston, MA: Kluwer Academic, pp. 101–15. Revised and reprinted in this volume.

Rodriguez, Frank, Stephen Smith and David Storer (1999), 'Estimating the cost of the universal service obligation in postal service', in M.A. Crew and P.R. Kleindorfer (eds), *Emerging Competition in Postal and Delivery Services*, Boston, MA: Kluwer Academic, pp. 195–207.

Rodriguez, Frank and David Storer (2000), 'Alternative approaches to estimating the cost of the USO in posts', *Information Economics and Policy*, **12**(3): 285–99.

PART II

Transformation and innovation

8. Reform of the United States Postal Service: an unfinished task

Michael A. Crew[†] and Paul R. Kleindorfer[‡]

1. INTRODUCTION: PROBLEMS FACING THE UNITED STATES POSTAL SERVICE

The United States Postal Service (USPS) faces substantial long-term challenges. Its traditional markets are declining, and its ability to reduce costs is limited by its organization structure. Many other countries have experienced similar problems with their postal services. Some, like Sweden and New Zealand, have attempted to address them through 'commercialization', a process of restructuring that retains ownership by the government but introduces modern corporate accounting, management and labor compensation, marketing, employment, capital investment and financial practices. Germany, the Netherlands and Austria have gone beyond commercialization, privatizing their postal system. The evidence from abroad suggests that both commercialization and privatization have tended to generate economic benefits, creating more flexible and efficient postal delivery systems and thereby typically reducing prices to large mailers (Table 8.1). The United States is now a surprising outlier among advanced countries in failing to undertake significant structural reform of its postal service. The Postal Accountability and Enhancement Act of 2006 (HR 6407) (PAEA) takes very modest steps by the standards of other countries embarking on postal reform toward commercializing USPS. Whether they will be beneficial and address the problems facing USPS is far from clear. More likely, the solution to these problems is to be found in privatization for three reasons.

First, although USPS accounts for roughly a third of federal civilian employment, there is no compelling reason why the government should supply postal services. Other network industries, such as electric utilities and telecommunications, operate efficiently with private firms subject to varying degrees of government regulation. The experience of European and other countries has demonstrated that this approach also works in the postal industry. Allowing the private sector to provide postal services would free the government to focus on those pressing national needs that cannot be addressed by private markets.

Second, a privatized postal service would be subject to the threat of bankruptcy, the discipline of the capital markets and pressure for improvement from their shareholders who, as residual claimants, would be directly affected by changes in the value of the firm. No equivalent discipline exists in a publicly owned firm, since citizens do not have the

† Rutgers University.
‡ Wharton School and INSEAD.

Table 8.1 Changes in postal prices internationally

Country	Structural reform	Changes in real prices for single-piece letter
Netherlands (1989–2005)	Privatization	Down 20%
Germany (1989–2005)	Privatization	Down 21%
Sweden (1995–2005)*	Commercialization	Up 29%
New Zealand (1987–2004)	Commercialization	Down 30%
United States (1987–2005)	No significant reform	Down 2%

Note: * Analyzing real price trends in single-piece letters is somewhat misleading. For example, this does not capture the significant price reductions in Sweden to large mailers, a trend likely to be replicated in other countries as markets are opened up. For further details on the Swedish situation, see Falkenhall and Kolmodin (2005).

Sources: TNT, Annual Report 2005; Deutsche Bundespost, Annual Report 1989; DPWN, Annual Report 2005; Deutsche Post (2006); data supplied to authors by New Zealand Post; USPS, 'Briefing for the President's Commission on the United States Postal Service', January 2003, and annual reports of USPS. As reported in Deutsche Post (2006), the real price of single-piece letters across the 21 countries of Europe surveyed between 1995 and 2005 was 29.78%.

residual claims of shareholders in a private firm. As a result, the government-owned USPS does not have as strong an incentive to innovate, or to be internally efficient and improve quality, as would a privatized firm.

Finally, based upon experience to date it is clear that USPS is likely to face continued oversight of Congress, which is its constitutional role, because USPS is part of the Executive Branch. This continuing scrutiny means that it will remain less than fully commercialized, and thus would have significantly less operational flexibility than a private firm. In short, the governance structure of USPS remains flawed and achieving commercial operations has little prospect of success. As a result, a number of decisions critical to the commercial success of USPS will not be made. For example, significant changes in USPS facilities and operations needed to meet the challenges of a rapidly evolving postal and communications market, are unlikely to be made under the current governance structure. Privatization is much more likely to achieve the economic benefits of an efficient postal system.

A government-owned post office (PO) may have been an appropriate solution when there were no alternatives to mail as a communications vehicle and when mail played a vital role in binding the nation together. The world has changed, however, and mail and parcel services are now elements of a much more complicated communications market and economy. As the backbone of transaction processing, advertising, and business-to-consumer services, postal services need to integrate with these developments. This would be better performed by a regulated privately owned company subject to the spur of competition. Moving USPS into the private sector would not only allow the government to focus its activities on more appropriate tasks, but also bring about an organization that was more responsive to customer needs. This would lead to lower prices for large customers, with ancillary benefits for their customers, more efficient postal delivery systems, market-driven changes in the location of postal mail-processing facilities, and greater product innovation.

Table 8.2 A costly status quo: projected mail volumes and fiscal health (all figures in millions)

Year	2002	2003	2007	2012	2017
Mail volume (pieces)	202,822	202,200	208,900	201,500	181,700
Operating revenue	$66,463	$68,868	$75,000	$81,000	$83,000
Operating expenses	$67,139	$64,368	$74,000	$85,500	$91,500
Net income (loss)	($676)	$4,500	$1,000	($4,500)	($8,500)
Cumulative net income (loss)	($6,036)	($1,536)	$4,250	($6,700)	($47,500)

Source: President's Commission on the United States Postal Service (2003, p. 4). Mail volume and financial projections are based on the 'Gradual Displacement Scenario', contained in 'Two Scenarios for Future Mail Volumes, 2003–2017', Greg Schmid, Institute for the Future, May 2003 (prepared for the Commission). See Table 8.3 below. Assumptions reflected in these projections include the following: operating revenues are based on rates adjusted annually at CPI (2.5%); labor-related costs are increased annually by 3.5%; non-labor costs are increased annually by 2%; and operating expenses have been adjusted to reflect volume variances.

Table 8.3 Gradual displacement of mail volumes (all figures in billions)

Year	2002	2007	2012	2017
First Class	102.4	98.7	90.5	81.0
Priority	1.0	1.1	1.2	1.3
Periodicals	9.7	9.5	9.1	8.7
Standard mail	87.2	97.1	98.2	88.1
Package service	1.1	1.1	1.1	1.2
International	0.9	0.9	0.9	0.9
Other government	0.5	0.5	0.5	0.5
Total	202.8	208.9*	201.5	181.7

Notes: *The actual total for 2007 was 212.2 billion pieces.

Source: President's Commission on the United States Postal Service (2003, p. 5).

1.1 The Market for Postal Service

There has been a concern over the prospects of USPS for a number of years, as highlighted by the Presidential Commission. Tables 8.2 and 8.3, based on the Presidential Commission Report (2003) indicate the nature of the problem, namely, stagnant or declining future demand for its services as currently configured. These tables show a median projection indicating that, if business as usual is continued for USPS, financial distress is a clear possibility. The problem can be seen from a number of different angles. Consider First Class mail, which is made up mainly of the letters addressed to households. First Class mail provided more than half of the revenue of USPS in 2005, but it has declined steadily from 1993 to 2004 (Figure 8.1). An upward blip occurred in 2005, but it is likely to be short-lived because electronic substitutes for mail will cause the long-term secular decline in First Class mail to continue. International studies also show the

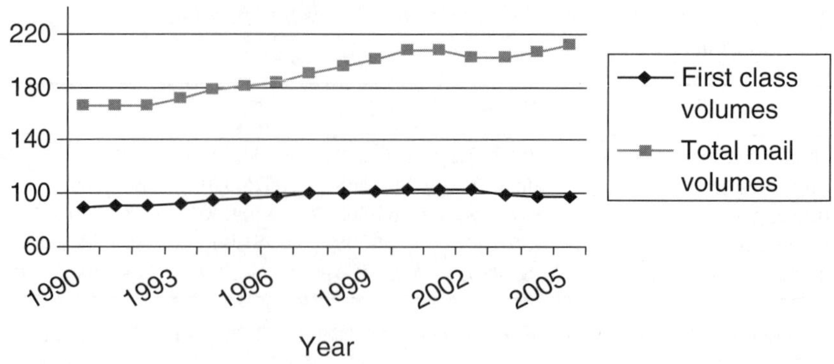

Figure 8.1 Trends in first class and total mail in United States (pieces, bn)

significant impact of electronic communications in eroding letter mail volumes and in putting pressure on PO revenues (Harding, 2006).

In recent years, the lost revenue from First Class has been made up by increases in bulk (Standard) mail, which is largely advertising mail. However, the market for advertising is very competitive, and electronic substitutes such as Internet advertising are growing fast, so the potential for significant continuing revenue growth in this area is limited. The rising intensity of electronic competition for the delivery of what used to travel by mail also means that significant increases in postal prices are not a long-term solution for stagnating sales, because higher prices will provide an even greater incentive for users of mail services to seek out electronic alternatives. Thus, the likely long-term outlook for traditional letter-mail products is inauspicious.

To understand the financial problem created for USPS as a result of stagnating demand for its traditional services, it is useful to divide the costs of mail service into two categories: variable costs (which rise and fall as the volume of mail changes) and fixed costs (which are necessary to run the mail delivery network, and thus change little or not at all as the volume of mail changes). Table 8.4, reproduced from Cohen et al. (2002), provides a breakdown of the cost structure of USPS into these two categories. For mail delivery and PO counters, fixed costs are more than half of the total cost. The universal service obligation (USO) is a major driver of these high fixed costs. Briefly, the USO is the requirement that a postal service provide ubiquitous delivery throughout the country at a uniform price. Ostensibly, and according to USPS, the cost of this obligation is increasing, since the number of addresses has been climbing by an average of over 1.5 million a year since 2001. Now, a commercially operated or privately owned enterprise would not typically view customer growth as a burden. Electric utilities with a similar obligation to serve see customer growth as a boon. Admittedly there are differences as utilities may be able to share some of the expansion costs with developers and they do receive small monthly per-customer fixed charges. Utilities see these new customers as beneficial since their consumption is higher than average. Similarly, the new addresses that USPS serves receive more than average amounts of mail and they are often supplied by new lower-cost technologies, for example, cluster boxes. The biggest difficulty seems to be USPS's inability to control and realign its costs, with the result that fixed costs continue to grow. Along with this, if it cannot stem the decline in mail volumes, and is able to reduce costs only

Table 8.4 USPS fixed/variable cost by major function (FY 1999)

Function	Fixed (%)	Variable (%)	Total cost ($bn)
Delivery*	51	49	26.2
Mail processing	6	94	22.5
Transportation	12	88	5.4
Window service	60	40	3.7
Other	80	20	10.7
Total	38	62	68.5

Note: * Delivery includes both in- and out-of-office costs.

Source: Postal Rate Commission/USPS; Cohen et al. (2002).

very gradually over time, it will find itself in an increasingly difficult financial position. We note that the costs in Table 8.4 are derived from USPS accounting records. Thus, from an economic perspective, they are likely to overstate the fixed costs of USPS. However, given the additional barriers to restructuring its operations arising from its current governance structure as a public enterprise, the difficulty of USPS in reducing its costs as a result of volume reductions is very likely at least as difficult as implied by the cost structure embodied in Table 8.4.

Exacerbating the problem facing USPS is that a process of binding arbitration applies to its labor costs, which account for approximately 80 percent of its total costs (Wachter and Perloff, 1991; Wachter et al. 2001). The arbitrator setting labor costs is not obliged to take into account postal service finances, the state of USPS revenues going forward, or any other dictates of the marketplace. The arbitration process reduces USPS's flexibility for its largest cost component. Perhaps not surprisingly, given the disconnect between productivity and wages inherent in this process, estimates suggest that post office workers receive higher pay than private sector workers who have similar qualifications and working conditions. (Wachter et al. (2001) estimate that the wage premium may be as high as 36 percent. By contrast, Sauber (2002) find no wage premium. In our view there is evidence to support a wage premium, although it may be lower than the earlier Wachter estimate.) Yet another difficulty is that USPS has promised payments in the future for healthcare benefits, but has not provided funding for those promises. These liabilities are large. Future healthcare liabilities for retirees are stated to be $55 billion in USPS Annual Report 2007. USPS is making additional payments of $5.6 billion a year through 2016 toward eliminating this liability.

This combination of declining mail volumes, growing costs to support the USO, inflexible labor practices and large unfunded liabilities has been apparent for several years. In 2002, for example, the US General Accounting Office published a report whose title summarized the situation: 'U.S. Postal Service: Deteriorating Financial Outlook Increases Need for Transformation'. The President's Commission on the United States Postal Service published a report and recommendations in 2003. The debate about how to move forward has focused on two broad approaches to postal reform, commercialization and privatization. In Section 2 we examine commercialization, the approach taken by the President's Commission and by the reforms embodied in the PAEA. While some of the Commission's proposals are not without merit, we argue in Section 3 that privatization is a preferable course. The reforms embodied in the PAEA do little to address the problems of USPS and do little to move it in the direction of commercialization. In Section 4, we discuss the mechanics of how privatization of USPS could be carried out. In Section 5, we summarize why the PAEA will likely be entirely inadequate in addressing the problems facing USPS. These arise because of a failure to take account of the experience of reform in other countries as examined in Chapter 1 and because of the conflicts and unresolved issues inherent in the PAEA. Privatization faces many barriers because of special interests that, under the current structure, are able to continue to protect their interests. Indeed, the PAEA is inadequate in addressing the problems faced by USPS primarily because it embodies a continuing protection of existing special interests under the status quo.

2. GOVERNANCE AND COMMERCIALIZATION OF THE US POSTAL SERVICE

A firm confronted with vast and disruptive change affecting its principal lines of business would typically seek to respond with flexibility and imagination to remake itself. On the cost side, the changes might include restructuring and targeted downsizing of some operations. On the revenue side, the firm might seek out product innovations and new lines of business. These accepted approaches to restructuring are not open to USPS, which faces major barriers to change under its present governance structure.

2.1 The Structure and Governance of USPS

The current structure of USPS is based on the Postal Reorganization Act (PRA) of 1970 and the PAEA. This 1970 Act abolished the United States Post Office, a government department with patronage appointments by the President, and replaced it with USPS. The entity created by the PRA was intended to be more independent of political interference, with its own Board of Governors consisting of nine members appointed by the President and confirmed by the US Senate. Governors serve for nine-year terms and are removable only for cause. The compensation paid to the Board under the PAEA remains very low compared to large private corporations: $25,000 annual retainer and $300 per day for any meetings attended. The nine governors appoint the Postmaster General, who acts as the chief executive of USPS, and the Deputy Postmaster General.

The operations of USPS are overseen by a regulatory agency, whose title was changed under the PAEA from the Postal Rate Commission (PRC) to the Postal Regulatory Commission (PRC). The former PRC differed from most regulatory commissions in that it issued 'recommended decisions', which may be overruled by a unanimous vote of the nine members of the Board of Governors. There are five commissioners, appointed by the President and confirmed by the US Senate for a six-year term. A maximum of three of the five commissioners may be members of the same party. The reformulated PRC has extensive additional authority beyond that of its predecessor, whose primary responsibilities were to review changes in postal rates and fees proposed by USPS, including the structure of classes of mail and mail services to which the rates and fees apply.

A further element of USPS governance is provided by the USPS Office of Inspector General (OIG). OIG authority was established under the Inspector General Act of 1978, which was extended to USPS OIG in 1996. USPS OIG is funded by ratepayers from postal revenues, and has a dual reporting structure to the Congress and to the Board of Governors of USPS (Williams and Sharkey, 2005). USPS OIG has a broad mandate to ensure the efficiency and integrity of USPS operations. It conducts audits of USPS financial statements, monitors the adequacy of its internal control systems, investigates allegations of fraud and mismanagement, and generally acts as an independent watchdog on USPS operations and the opportunities for improving these. The responsibilities of the USPS OIG are expected to remain effectively unchanged as a result of the 2006 Act.

2.2 The Transformation Plan of 2002 (Updated 2005)

Under its current Postmaster General, John E. Potter, the USPS financial position has improved. In 2002, Potter announced a 'Transformation Plan' (USPS, 2002) that in due course led to a reduction of USPS career employees by 14 percent and achieved by 2005 a cumulated $5 billion cost reduction on nearly $70 billion in annual sales (USPS, 2005, p. 15). The Transformation Plan also led to innovations in public–private partnerships, the most important being one with Federal Express to handle the expedited services of USPS and more of its transportation. As mentioned above, other good news for USPS arrived in the form of favorable market trends and financial reports. The decline in first class mail volumes, which had fallen steadily over the period from 1993 to 2004, was halted, in 2005 with continuing growth of 2.7 per cent in FY2006 and 1.6 percent in 2007. Moreover, as a result of changes brought about by P.L. 108-18, USPS was no longer seriously underfunded in its pension obligations as had been previously asserted (Potter, 2002). Specifically, under P.L. 108-18, USPS received a retroactive credit for $105 billion of investment earnings on past pension contributions but at the same time became responsible for the military service credit costs ($27 billion). The PAEA took this burden away from USPS, treating it the same in this respect as private companies. The P.L. 108-18 and the PAEA produced significant net benefits to USPS, placing its pension fund on a sound financial basis.

Although welcome news, these improvements have done little to address the longer-term challenges outlined previously. Rather than waiting for the organization to weaken again or even to suffer a financial crisis, and then trying to react under crisis conditions, the temporarily improved prospects of USPS can be used instead as an opportunity to bring about the significant reforms needed for USPS to regain its competitive footing for the long term.

2.3 Legislative Background to Greater Commercialization: HR 22/S662 and HR 6407

Given the challenges USPS faces in the twenty-first century competitive environment, USPS is more than ready for its first serious reform since its creation over thirty years ago. Regrettably, the 2006 Act (HR 6407) does not come close to doing the job. The PAEA changes the law in a number of ways. However, the changes move USPS at best minimally in the needed direction of increased commercialization.

The PAEA reconstituted the Postal Rate Commission as the Postal Regulatory Commission, enhancing its powers and making it independent of the Board of

Governors.[1] Price-cap regulation (PCR) replaced the previous 'cost-plus' system, which in principle represents a significant improvement. Under the previous regulatory system, USPS reported its costs, and then it was allowed to add a small contingency so that it was effectively able to break even over approximately a three-year period. A rate case was filed with the Commission whenever USPS believed its costs were likely to exceed its revenues under existing rates. This resulted in new rates, and the process continued to replicate itself approximately every three years. Under this system of postal rate regulation, USPS had weak incentives for cost economy: USPS costs are recovered through increased rates.

The PAEA introduces PCR. This system of regulation works by setting a cap on prices, rather than a mark-up on costs. As a result, USPS has incentives to reduce costs, since higher costs would not mechanically feed through to higher prices. A price cap also encourages product innovation and increased sales since price, not profits or revenue, is capped. Indeed, the experience of PCR is extensive in the US, the United Kingdom and elsewhere. In the United Kingdom throughout the 1980s, this system of regulation was adopted for the newly privatized enterprises not only among network industries such as gas, electricity, telephone and water, but also for other industries such as Britain's major airports and for its postal operator Royal Mail. Similarly, PCR has found almost universal application in the postal sector in the European Union (EU), as reviewed in WIK (2006).

Unfortunately, PCR is not a panacea for improving efficiency, even of a regulated private firm, as Littlechild (1983) noted in his original report proposing PCR for telecommunications in the UK. However, price caps are logically more obviously aligned with efficiency in a private company than they are under public ownership. The profit incentive inherent in a private ownership structure is the driver causing the firm to strive for internal efficiency, since any difference between the regulated price and its costs can be retained as profits. This profit-seeking incentive for increased efficiency is attenuated in varying degrees with public enterprise (Crew and Kleindorfer, 2008b). The PAEA is very weak in encouraging a profit orientation by USPS. True, USPS is now allowed to accumulate reserves. This may provide greater incentives for efficiency than the approach under the PRA, which passed through costs to achieve break-even. However, the mere ability to accumulate reserves inherently does not promote a profit orientation.

The previous process of arbitration to determine wages and employment conditions for USPS employees continues under the PAEA, which made some minor changes by requiring the appointment of a mediator rather than the previous fact-finding process. Although a mediator may help to achieve a solution earlier than currently, the PAEA structure does not necessarily promote a better alignment of productivity and wages, and it continues the previous situation in which the costs of labor are not under the control of USPS management. Since 80 percent of USPS costs are labor costs, removing these from the control of USPS management likely vitiates whatever incentives there may be for achieving efficiencies implied by PCR. Notwithstanding these fundamental problems that arise primarily from the continuing structure of USPS as a public enterprise, a change to PCR might at least alter the focus of the Commission and USPS toward more flexible pricing and other means of meeting customer needs rather than simply passing through costs for recovery in the next rate case.

The PAEA authorizes USPS to establish programs to provide bonuses and other rewards to officers and employees. Although these incentives may be beneficial, a key question is how they should be structured, especially since no market for corporate control exists to discipline the strategies and behavior of senior management. One possibility is to require earning at least a minimum specified rate of return on capital as a condition for incentive compensation for managers. This approach is followed by a number of commercialized post offices including Canada Post Corporation. Regrettably, not many of the lessons from other countries have been applied. The PAEA does not provide any serious incentives for management, although Section 506 does allow the Board of Governors to identify 12 'apostles', top managers, who would be allowed to earn up to 120 percent of the salary of the Vice President of the United States. This provision, arbitrary and bizarre as it is, will provide nothing by way of incentives to top management to improve efficiency.[2] Coupled with the fact that the PAEA is effectively silent on the role of profits, although it does allow USPS to retain earnings, it is difficult to see how this bonus scheme for the 12 apostles can be implemented in a meaningful manner. Add to this the noted lack of USPS management control over the major input factor to operations, labor, will surely pose additional problems in assuring efficient uses of both labor and other productive factors, including capital.

The PAEA leaves intact the process of binding arbitration that makes it difficult for USPS to control its costs. The Senate version (S662) of the Bill included language requiring the arbitrator to take into account the financial condition of USPS, but it is unclear what effect this would have on the process or outcome. However, this language is no longer present in Section 505 of the PAEA. Some attempt to address the problems of labor relations is made by requiring the appointment of a mediator rather than the current fact-finding process. Although a mediator may help to achieve a solution earlier than currently, the proposed structure would not necessarily promote a better alignment of productivity and wages.

In the end, it is not clear at all what incentives can be crafted that would promote efficiency, accountability and innovation under the PAEA. Instead, its provisions are a patchwork of non-aligned proposals that leave to the restructured PRC the task of using the imperfect tools of regulation to try to guide USPS as a public enterprise facing tough strategic problems to a soft landing.

The House version (Section 710) of the legislation did open the door just a crack to considering the possibility of privatizing USPS in the future, with a requirement for 'a two-year independent study to assess the costs, benefits, effects, and future strategies for maintaining the Postal Service as wholly part of the Executive'. Moreover, this study is explicitly required to consider and compare the results of other international experience in reforming the postal sector, which has included privatization. Section 710 of the PAEA still requires consideration and identification of 'any lessons that foreign experience may imply for each strategy identified by the research organization'. Where this will lead will almost certainly depend on whether USPS begins to experience financial difficulties in the immediate future.

2.4 Additional Steps toward Commercialization

The PAEA seems to leave open some opportunities to create improved incentives for efficiency in an organization that remains government owned. While the reserved area or monopoly on letters up to 12 ounces remains, Section 702 requires a study of universal service and the mailbox monopoly within 24 months, opening the door to increase competition in the US mail market, by curtailing the 'reserved area' and by eliminating the mailbox monopoly. Following the practice in other countries, increased competition could be introduced by defining the reserved area in terms of a weight limit, and then gradually reducing this limit. This approach has been commonly used in European countries as a way of phasing in greater competition in mail services over time, with the current weight maximum allowed limit throughout the EU being 50 grams, which is set to go to zero as of January 1, 2011 for the major POs. Reducing the reserved area would encourage commercialization by increasing the competition faced by USPS and the consequent need to change its costing systems, its pricing and its focus on customer needs.

The mailbox monopoly means that other carriers delivering items are not allowed to put them in the receptacle provided for the sole use by USPS. This rule is strictly a 'mailbox' monopoly, and does not apply to residences with mail slots (the reason is that mailboxes have a finite capacity determined by the box size, which is not the case with a slot). At least in theory, the mailbox monopoly could be lifted, but mail security considerations may limit the possibility of doing so.

3. COMMERCIALIZATION VERSUS PRIVATIZATION

The 2006 Act and the other potential steps that could be taken to commercialize USPS represent, at least in principle, if not in practice, an improvement over the status quo. Yet a strategy of commercialization would not yield as many benefits as moving USPS into the private sector, and the 2006 Act fails to provide sufficiently strong incentives for commercialization. Indeed, it offers very few incentives for commercialization.

First, the PAEA clearly leaves USPS as part of the Executive Branch, even though the services it provides are commercial and not inherently governmental. As we review below in more detail, international experience supports the proposition that regulated private firms are able to provide postal services efficiently. In the United States, other network industries such as electricity, gas and telecommunications already are mostly privately owned and subject to regulation. As the government takes on new roles in an evolving economy, it should shed those tasks that can be effectively provided by private markets.

Second, there are several reasons to believe that a private firm could deliver postal services more efficiently than a public one, although it is difficult to know for sure how much difference private ownership would make, in part because that would depend on the structure of the commercialized public firm as well as the structure of the privatized one. In particular, a private firm has shareholders who, as the residual claimants, benefit from an increase in the value of the firm and suffer when the firm declines in value and thereby exercise another form of discipline on firm behavior. No equivalent discipline exists in the publicly owned firm. These incentives, however, work with varying effectiveness, and private ownership may be subject to abuse. Similarly, a public USPS, unlike a private company, does not face the threat of bankruptcy. While it is arguable that the government would also never let such a critical private sector firm declare bankruptcy, the threat of bankruptcy facing a privatized USPS would be much stronger than the current situation.

Finally, the argument in favor of privatization rests on a judgment that the PAEA clearly stops far short of providing the full operational flexibility available to a private firm. A privatized firm would be more likely to accomplish changes in the use of high-cost buildings and land use, greater franchising of routes and post offices, composition and location of processing plants, restructuring of labor relations, better managerial accounting procedures for both profits and costs, and the introduction of new products and services.

For example, it seems somewhat implausible, given political economy constraints, that a public sector USPS would ever be able to reconfigure its sorting and delivery systems and its other operations as flexibly as a private sector USPS.[3] As another example, consider the opportunities in the introduction of new products and services associated with the huge and continuing growth in electronic commerce. Recent estimates show continued strong growth in worldwide business-to-business (B2B) and business-to-consumer (B2C) flows for various regions of the world. For example, for the B2B market, worldwide ecommerce is expected to reach $3.4 trillion in 2006 (see http://www.forbes.com/bow/b2b/main.jhtml), and B2C markets have shown continued healthy growth and profitability, especially in the United States (see http://www.forbes.com/bow/b2c/main.jhtml). Given these developments in B2B and B2C commerce, parcel post can be expected to grow significantly over the next decade (Crew and Kleindorfer, 2004b). Who will provide the logistics and delivery services for these markets? The parcel market is currently a relatively small share of USPS business; in 2005, for example, the parcel and package business in USPS yielded approximately 10 percent of its total revenue. Given concerns about a public sector firm moving into new lines of business, a privatized USPS would likely have more flexibility to move into these markets than a public sector USPS. Furthermore, success would likely require attracting or acquiring scarce managerial talent in logistics services that would be difficult for USPS to obtain in public enterprise form.

Yet another opportunity for a privatized USPS would be to take advantage of the production and marketing side of the information technology revolution. Its major competitors, like UPS and FEDEX, continue to benefit from improvements in information technology and the Internet by introducing features that enable shippers to arrange pickups, receive bills, and track and trace their packages over the Internet. While some of these innovations have made their way into USPS, it remains a labor-intensive delivery organization with very slow adoption of capital-intensive technologies. The adoption rate would, in our view, be more rapid and more efficient with a privatized firm than a commercialized one.

Given what appears to be a significant mismatch between the current configuration of USPS facilities and labor and the most efficient configurations, and given the potential for the postal market to evolve rapidly in the future and thereby require operational flexibility to respond effectively, our conclusion is that the version of commercialization embodied in the 2006 Act is not likely to produce significant improvements in efficiency and will not promote the needed adaptation of USPS to emerging market conditions. By contrast, privatization is likely to offer significant improvements.

The empirical evidence on the efficiency of commercialized public firms versus privatized ones similarly suggests that the latter are typically more efficient, although the results depend sensitively on specific market conditions. Vickers and Yarrow (1988, p. 40) conclude,

> Privately owned firms tend, on average, to be the more internally efficient when competition in product markets is effective . . . However, when market power is significant, and particularly

> when company behavior is subject to detailed regulation, there is little empirical justification for a general presumption of either type of ownership, and case-by-case evaluation of the various tradeoffs is therefore in order.

Megginson and Netter (2001, p. 380) reach a somewhat stronger conclusion: 'Research now supports the proposition that privately owned firms are more efficient and more profitable than otherwise-comparable state-owned firms'. In our view, the broader empirical evidence at least suggests a presumption that a privately owned USPS would be more efficient than a publicly owned one, which is consistent with the arguments put forward above for why a private firm would operate more efficiently. More generally, the reader should bear in mind in the present context that the efficiency at stake here goes well beyond internal production efficiency. In the context of postal and delivery services, it goes to the ability of USPS to innovate and to integrate its service offerings with the complexities of a fast-changing communications, advertising and electronic-mediated market place, not to mention the changes in logistics services resulting from e-commerce. The challenges for accomplishing this integration exceed by good measure the abilities and incentives available to a publicly owned firm. In short privatization is needed to change the culture of USPS from a government bureaucracy to a modern corporation. The bureaucratic culture of USPS is more akin to government agencies such as the Internal Revenue Service or Customs and Border Protection than a corporation. USPS needs to be allowed to be more customer oriented, especially where large mailers are concerned. There is nothing in PAEA that will bring this about. Privatization is likely to be the only feasible vehicle for bringing about the kind of change that would provide USPS with a vigorous marketing department that will unlock value by creating new services responsive to mailers' requirements and attractive relative to its competitors. In the next section, we therefore turn to our proposal for privatization.

4. THE PRIVATIZATION OPTION

Following experience in the Netherlands and Germany, we argue that privatization should be an incremental process, with USPS being sold to investors through a series of stock offerings and the government initially holding a majority of the shares. Some shares would be reserved for current employees to encourage their participation in the process, as has been the case for other utilities and post offices undertaking privatization. The intent would be to allow an orderly transition period, avoid excessive windfall gains or losses to investors and employees, and to sort out a number of critical issues and uncertainties that we discuss below. The resulting privatized firm, which we shall name the United States Postal Service, Incorporated (USPSI), would be a regulated company with a reserved area (that is, an area in which competition would be excluded) in local delivery for at least the initial period of privatization. The regulator would be a restructured Postal Regulatory Commission.

The basic ingredients of this proposal follow the path of other successful privatizations of state-owned enterprises in advanced economies (Parker and Saal, 2003). The objective is to shape expectations of stakeholders, allow a reasonable transition period of some three to five years for the privatized organization and its regulators to become accustomed to the new reality, and provide through regulation and service quality monitoring clear messages to competitors and customers that they can expect historic levels of pricing, service quality and accessibility of postal services. In particular, the scope of the USO would remain unchanged, at least initially, under privatization.

During the initial phase following privatization, local delivery (for items below a certain weight or price limit) should remain a residual and regulated monopoly to assure a stable transition to a privatized entity. However, our proposal would not affect the rights of couriers and parcel operators to deliver as currently. They would be under no obligation to use USPSI's network for any of their services.

4.1 Price-cap Regulation

In common with experience of privatization in other countries, we would envisage that USPSI would be subject to PCR for market dominant products. In contrast, a privatized firm would also control all inputs, including labor. The regulation would likely include a number of price-cap indexes for different baskets of products, because it will be important to ensure that a privatized PO is not using revenue generated from its monopoly on letter delivery to cross-subsidize and thereby unfairly and inefficiently price in competitive markets. One approach, originally introduced in Crew and Kleindorfer (1994), would be to have two regulated baskets: an 'access' basket and a 'single-piece' basket. The efficiency properties of this approach to price caps are discussed further in Laffont and Tirole (1996). Parker and Saal (2003) also offer some details on standard practices in implementing PCR. A decision would need to be made between a pure price cap, which allows the regulated firm to retain any profits it earns within the price-cap constraint, and a hybrid one, which allows the firm to retain only a percentage of the profits it makes above a specified return on its assets (Crew and Kleindorfer, 1996; Kridel et al., 1996).

The initial rate case after the announcement of privatization and before the initial public offering of the first tranche of shares would take a traditional cost of service approach based upon expected expenses, and then use that to calculate a price-cap formula. The initial rate case is likely to be highly contentious, because a privatized postal service would have every incentive to maximize its possible expenses, so that the price cap would be set high and the company could easily earn profits by reducing its inflated costs. However, by anchoring the initial rates allowed under the price cap to historical levels for the delivery sector including couriers, consumers will be protected and some sense of control of excess profits would be assured.[4] After a period of about five years, the operation of the price cap would be reviewed and adjusted to reconcile projected rates of return for the privatized entity with risk-adjusted returns for comparable private firms.

4.2 What About the Universal Service Obligation?

The USO is generally considered to be a significant cost to most postal services. However, there is continuing public support for offering what are viewed as common and necessary postal services throughout the country and subject to reasonable service quality standards and some rough notion of affordability. Given the costs that arise from the imposition of the USO on USPS, there is a reason for the use of the term 'obligation' in USO. Postal service is not the only industry with a USO. Some type of 'default service obligation' is a burden imposed by government on almost all other regulated network industries, reflecting the presumption that access to these services at reasonable prices is considered essential for every citizen.

The USO has two features: ubiquity and uniformity. Ubiquity means that it must collect and deliver to every (or almost every) address in the country. It also means ubiquitous coverage by retail outlets. POs have many more counters than a for-profit firm would have (see Cohen et al., 2008). Uniformity means that it must charge the same price irrespective of where the delivery or collection takes place. Letters (not parcels) are subject to the price uniformity requirement. All letters of the same weight carry the same postage. This rule has obvious benefits in reducing transaction costs for households and smaller mailers, and it also facilitates and reduces mail-processing costs. Service standards for both delivery and for location of post offices are also an important element of the USO. Concerning the delivery standard, First Class mail in the United States is delivered overnight within a defined area and within two or three days depending on distance and the outlying nature of the delivery point. The success in meeting the service standards is evaluated by an independent consulting company.

In the absence of a USO, USPSI would potentially not serve some residential postal customers in high-cost delivery areas, or at least not serve them with the same frequency and service quality. Unlike other network industries, it is unlikely that in postal service the competitive market has the potential to rebundle the services required for residential and other small customers to obtain fully integrated or end-to-end service. This is because traditional letter mail is an extremely low-value item, leaving little scope for competitors, in the case of single-piece letters at least, to bundle the services. In rural areas, which receive service only because of cross-subsidization from low-cost urban areas under the USO, the problem is even more severe. In effect, there would likely not be much, if any, interest by new entrants in end-to-end single-piece service for residential customers, even if the reserved area is eliminated so that they would be allowed to provide such services. However, because of potential scale economies arising from their network, a privatized USPS could handle this kind of business and receive a contribution over variable costs. Thus, even if the reserved area is significantly reduced, a privatized post office should still be required (and able) to provide single-piece end-to-end service, with service quality standards monitored as they are now. This part of the USO should continue in the privatized post office.

With respect to frequency of delivery, accessibility standards for mailboxes and other elements of the USO, some changes may become necessary including modification of the scope and funding of the USO. For more detailed discussion of the USO, and its implications for regulation, see Crew and Kleindorfer (2002b, 2006b).

4.3 Unfunded Health and Pension Costs under Privatization

Some observers may be concerned that privatization of USPS would provide a method for the organization to shirk its future unfunded health and pension obligations, perhaps through business decisions such as declaring bankruptcy. In our proposal, and in any plausible privatization scenario, this problem would be dealt with explicitly in the privatization process and not deferred. To its credit, the PAEA (TITLE VIII) has recognized the retiree healthcare responsibility and USPS is now required to set aside significant sums for healthcare. Under privatization, these liabilities would be recognized as a part of the initial public offering or other sale mechanism. The sales price would reflect the treatment of the deferred liabilities. One possibility might be for the government to take over a defined portion of the deferred liabilities to the date of privatization with USPSI beginning *de novo* as of the date of sale of the first tranche of shares. Similarly, USPSI would presumably not continue to fund the military service obligation. The new USPSI then would adopt its own benefit plans, subject to applicable regulations and statutes for the private sector.

4.4 Summing Up the Privatization Proposal

As a regulated for-profit company, a privatized post office would be organized with a corporate structure similar to that of regulated investor-owned utilities. Initially, the US government would be a majority shareholder and would be represented correspondingly on the Board of Directors, with representation and decision rights declining over time as private investors' interests grow. The privatized postal service, USPSI, would be regulated by a transformed PRC, which would have responsibilities for the implementation of an appropriately structured price-cap regulatory regime. USPSI would be subject to the same USO as is currently in place, including quality monitoring, and would offer initially the range of products currently offered by USPS.

5. BRINGING ABOUT PRIVATIZATION

The intent of privatization is to improve the efficiency of the postal sector in the US. The main way this would be achieved is freeing it from the dead hand of government, which is holding back any significant prospect of improvement. USPS, as part of the Executive Branch, is inevitably going to be subject to the oversight of Congress. Congress views USPS in a similar way that it views other departments of government that are not businesses, for example, Justice. Congress's role in overseeing USPS was somewhat reduced by the PRA and modified by the PAEA but its oversight role remains considerable and one which it is not equipped to address. It lacks the will, the ability and the resources to oversee a commercial operation.

Privatization in freeing USPS from the negative impact of congressional oversight would enable many current contradictions that exist in the 2006 Act to be resolved. Some are quite simple. Under section 204, the PAEA requires USPS to comply with section 404 (internal controls) of the Sarbanes–Oxley Act of 2002 by 2010. In this respect, it is the same as a private corporation. Without privatization, USPS would face the increased costs of Sarbanes–Oxley with no ostensible benefits. If it is seen as part of a process toward privatization, then there might be a benefit, but there is no hint that this is the case. Similarly, under section 404 USPS is now subject to antitrust law in the form of the Clayton Act, and under section 5 of the Federal Trade Commission Act relating to unfair competitive practices.[5]

Similarly, the dissonance created by making the PRC a regulatory commission similarly to industry regulators in the private sector would be resolved by privatization. The new status of the PRC is a potential source of considerable uncertainty. Arguably, the law should not have been changed to make the PRC a regulatory commission unless this was part of an announced plan for privatization. USPS is subject to effectively the same regulation as private companies, but it does not have the protection available to these legal persons. It cannot lobby in the way they can. It does not have the same right of legal redress under the takings clause of the Constitution. These kinds of issues create significant opportunities for potential problems. Indeed, they place a significant burden on the PRC, whose decisions will take on much greater importance as they may be less open to challenge from USPS than if it were privatized. If there is a silver lining here, it is that mistakes by the PRC could precipitate serious problems and these might be sufficient to generate the kind of crisis that might cause the jolt necessary to knock USPS off its current axis and on to one of privatization. By increasing the power of the PRC, the PAEA is placing great faith in the PRC's ability to address problems that Congress has not been able to address. The PRC might be able to adopt a gradualist approach and keep the system running for a number of years. However, having been asked to perform the impossible, the odds must be against this.

The PAEA changes the role of the Board of Governors. In some respects, now that it is stripped of its ultimate responsibility for the postal sector, it is closer to a board of directors of a private corporation. However, nothing has been changed to make it similar to a world class private sector board of directors, as postured in the Presidential Commission Report. Section 501 includes the following restriction: 'at least 4 of the Governors shall be chosen solely on the basis of their demonstrated ability in managing organizations or corporations (in either the public or private sector) that employ at least 50,000 employees'. How this will be achieved is not stated.

The glaring weaknesses of the PAEA and its failure to learn from experience elsewhere may be the most optimistic features of the current situation. The problems have not been addressed. One hope, and that is all it is, is that the PAEA might, by creating a new dynamic bring about an earlier realization of the problems that it has ignored by papering over the cracks that have emerged over the years with changes in postal and communication markets. For the problems to be addressed and for privatization to occur, the current stakeholders and interest groups will need to see the benefits. To the extent that the situation following the PAEA creates greater instability and even precipitates a crisis, this could turn around stakeholders' views. Three major sets of stakeholders would be affected by privatization of USPS.

The first is organized labor. USPS negotiates with a number of labor unions, who represent both full-time and part-time employees. The largest is the American Postal Workers Union (APWU), which represents 260,000 employees. Other major unions include the National Association of Letter Carriers, which represents about 222,000 active city letter carriers, and the National Postal Mail Handlers Union, which represents approximately 58,000 postal workers. These are all AFL-CIO affiliates. In addition, the National Rural Letter Carriers Association represents about 128,000 employees. Some of these union members may be concerned that a commercialized or privatized USPS would lead to lower wages and benefits and different work rules. However, the evidence reviewed above from international postal reforms shows that while commercialization/privatization would tie compensation more closely to productivity, it would do so by operational changes that increase productivity relative to current levels. Increased productivity and efficiency mean improved opportunities for employment in the long run. Moreover, providing for preferential stock options to employees in initiating the privatization process promotes a commitment to the new organization and recognition of the special status of current employees. In addition, postal workers who are retired or near-retirement may be attracted by the fact that commercialization and privatization in other countries have typically required an explicit mechanism to assure their pension and retirement health benefits. Others may be attracted to working in a dynamic firm with a better financial future than USPS.

The second affected group consists of competitors in the mail and communications industries. Under the 1970 Act these groups were able to protect their interests using rate cases, which provided an opportunity for some groups of mailers to gain at the expense of other groups. While the PAEA, in introducing PCR, apparently moves away from this previous approach, this is not guaranteed. The PRC will have to determine how it will proceed. Despite PCR, extensive hearings are not precluded. Mailers hurt by USPS freedom to set rates under the price cap might appeal to the PRC. Similarly, competitors will not favor lower prices and more flexible price arrangements for USPS and will certainly seek to use all means available to ensure higher prices and lower flexibility for products in which they compete. Going against these pressures would translate into direct benefits to households and other business consumers of mail services, and indirectly they would provide a stimulus for a more competitive and sustainable postal market. The sources of additional value in the postal markets are evident: improved operations, changes in labor practices and regulation, and unlocking some of the value in the assets of USPS, including its real estate. Moreover, some competitors will see potentially large benefits in a more competitive market for mail delivery, to the extent that they provide upstream consolidation activities that both compete with USPS as well as benefiting from more efficient downstream delivery.

The third group is large-scale mailers. Many large mailers are built on the foundations of cheap, basic mail services provided by USPS. They may perceive privatization as likely to give rise to major increases in rates, if they are not able to influence rates through the regulatory process. However, the experience (in both the postal sector and in other network industries) has indicated the contrary. In the international arena, the move to corporatization has led to prices that reflect better the cost of providing each service. The result has been that large customers have tended to benefit from deregulation and small customers have faced higher rates. This alignment of cost and value of services is a joint consequence of liberalization (that is, competition) and corporatization. Liberalization provides the pressure for improved alignment, while commercialization and privatization are the critical enabling features, as they provide a profit-oriented rationale for market segmentation, value-based pricing and the design of products to meet customer needs rather than merely responding to regulatory specifications.

An interesting evolution of this approach has been seen in both Sweden and the United Kingdom. (For Sweden, see the discussion in Jonsson and Selander (2006). For the United Kingdom, the chapter by Hill and Robinson (2006) provides background on recent developments.) Both of these countries currently offer significant discounts to large customers based on a variety of determinants, including delivery zone. Non-discrimination (similar treatment for both the PO's customers and new entrants) and other regulatory measures related to mitigating market power of the incumbent are also central to these regimes. Under the pressure of the market, and facing the rewards determined by the fundamental changes in their status as corporations, uniformity of pricing and service offerings has given way in these countries to more market-driven approaches. As commercialization and privatization initiatives grow in Europe, and as further reinforced by market opening, we expect these trends for market-based pricing and product innovation to accelerate. Rather than see this evolution as something to contravene through continuing constraints in a public enterprise setting, we see this as a natural consequence of better alignment of price, cost and value of services in competitive markets. This alignment is a necessary precondition for triggering innovation and economic efficiency.

We recognize that broader support for privatization may not currently exist. Indeed, a survey commissioned by the Presidential Commission (2003, p. 20) showed that 67 percent of consumers oppose privatization of USPS. Before deciding that a political scenario of substantial commercialization and even privatization is improbable in the United States, however, it is worth remembering that in other countries across Europe, as well as in Canada, Australia and New Zealand, the public largely accepts and supports postal reform in the direction of commercial operations. We expect that as international results continue to demonstrate the benefits of having a competitive and efficient postal sector, the US public and political process will take note. Indeed, we might go further. With the internationalization of the postal and delivery sector and with the opening of the postal market in Europe, there may be increasing pressures on the US that make it difficult to remain a monopolized island of public enterprise in a sea of competition and private ownership. Given the apparent inevitability of liberalized postal markets, it is pointless sacrificing further valuable time and opportunity waiting to restructure the ownership and governance of USPS while other countries are already reaping large benefits from postal commercialization and privatization.

The postal sector will continue to play a key but diminishing role in the communications system in the United States. The PAEA incorporates few of the lessons of other countries and, indeed, may be damaging to long-run progress by marking time while the market moves ahead. One of the implications of the PAEA would appear to be that there will be no further reform for many years. However, because of the major problems with the PAEA, this may not be the case. The pace of change in the economy has changed significantly since 1970 and the US has become a more open economy. This, together with the growing problems endemic to postal products from electronic substitution may mean that the US will be forced to reconsider, sooner rather than later, whether USPS should remain in the public sector. Moving it into the private sector would not only allow the government to focus its activities on more appropriate tasks, but also facilitate lower prices, a better orientation toward customers, a more efficient postal delivery system, and greater product innovation. Most importantly, what is needed is an agile USPS, motivated by the clarity of profits and markets, to escape from the stagnation and constraints of the traditional postal public enterprise setting and to find a sustainable confluence, through privatization, with an increasingly complex and demanding communications and logistics marketplace.

NOTES

1. Legislation was needed to bring this about as previous court rulings had indicated that the PRC was not a regulatory commission and that ultimate authority resided in the Board of Governors.

2. Under the 1970 law, USPS had authority to pay performance bonuses but did not do so. This new provision adds nothing to this prior situation, which is so much in contrast with accepted commercial practices.
3. The pious words of sec. 302 of the PAEA noting that 'the Postal Service has more facilities than it needs and the streamlining of this distribution network can pave the way for the potential consolidation of sorting facilities and the elimination of excess costs', are unlikely to give USPS any increased flexibility in closing facilities.
4. The PAEA allowed USPS to file its first rate case under the 'old rules' allowing an initialization of rates based on the most recent costs and revenue results. However, in the interests of obtaining revenue quickly USPS elected to file under the new rules, that is, the price cap formula allowed by the PAEA.
5. The PAEA provides for the Federal Trade Commission to take an increasing role in the affairs of USPS. For example, it is required under section 703 to perform a study of how state and federal laws apply differently to the competitive products of USPS from the products of private carriers.

REFERENCES

Cohen, Robert, Carla Pace, Matthew Robinson, Gennaro Scarfiglieri, Rossana Scocchera, Vincenzo Visco Comandini, John Waller and Spyros Xenakis (2002), 'A comparison of the burden of universal service in Italy and the United States', in Crew and Kleindorfer (eds) (2002a), pp. 87–106.

Cohen, Robert, Luigi di Paola, Rene Sheehy and Vincenzo Visco Comandini (2008), 'The distribution of post offices in Italy and the United States', in Crew and Kleindorfer (eds) (2008a), pp. 36–46.

Crew, Michael A. and Paul R. Kleindorfer (1994), 'Pricing, entry, service quality and innovation under a "commercialized" postal service', in J. Gregory Sidak (ed.), *Governing the Postal Service*, Washington, DC: American Enterprise Institute, pp. 150–69.

Crew, Michael A. and Paul R. Kleindorfer (eds), 'Incentive regulation in the United Kingdom and the United States', Journal of Regulatory Economics, **9**(3), May, 211–26.

Crew, Michael A. and Paul R. Kleindorfer (eds) (2002a), *Postal and Delivery Services: Delivering on Competition*, Boston, MA: Kluwer Academic.

Crew, Michael A. and Paul R. Kleindorfer (eds), (2002b), *Postal and Delivery Services: Pricing, Productivity, Regulation and Strategy*, Boston, MA: Kluwer Academic.

Crew Michael A. and Paul R. Kleindorfer (eds) (2004a), *Competitive Transformation of the Postal and Delivery Sector*, Boston, MA: Kluwer Academic.

Crew, Michael A. and Paul R. Kleindorfer (2004b), 'Access and the USO for letters and parcels', in Crew and Kleindorfer (eds) (2004a), pp. 3–42.

Crew, Michael A. and Paul Kleindorfer (eds) (2006a), *Progress toward Liberalization of the Postal and Delivery Sector*, New York: Springer.

Crew, Michael A. and Paul R. Kleindorfer (2006b), 'Approaches to the USO under entry', in Crew and Kleindorfer (eds), *Liberalization of the Postal and Delivery Sector*, Cheltenham, UK and Northampton, MA, USA: Edward Elgar, pp. 1–18.

Crew, Michael A. and Paul R. Kleindorfor (eds) (2008a), *Competition and Regulation in the Postal and Delivery Sector*, Cheltenham, UK and Northampton, MA, USA: Edward Elgar.

Crew, Michael A. and Paul R. Kleindorfer (2008b), 'Regulation and the USO under entry', in Crew and Kleindorfer (eds) (2008a), pp. 1–18.

Deutsche Post (2006), 'Letter prices in Europe', Deutsche Post AG, Corporate Regulation Management, Bonn, Germany, http://www.deutschepost.de/dpag?lang=de_EN&xmlFile=51101, accessed 6 June 2008.

Falkenhall, Björn and Anne Kolmodin (2005), 'A broad economic analysis of liberalising the postal market', Swedish Institute for Growth Policy Studies, Stockholm (August).

Harding Matthew (2006), 'A panel data study of mail demand in advanced economies', paper presented at the 14th International Conference on Postal and Delivery Economics, Bern, Switzerland, May 31–June 3.

Hill, Roger and Richard Robinson (2006), 'Establishing non-uniform access prices in the UK', in Crew and Kleindorfer (eds) (2006), pp. 123–40.

Jonsson, Per and Sten Selander (2006), 'The "real" graveyard spiral: experiences from the liberalized Swedish postal market', in Crew and Kleindorfer (eds) (2006), pp. 359–68.
Kridel, D.J., D.E.M. Sappington and D.L. Weisman (1996), 'The effects of incentive regulation in the telecommunications industry: a survey', *Journal of Regulatory Economics*, **9**(3): 269–306.
Laffont, Jean-Jacques and Jean Tirole (1996), 'Creating competition through interconnection: theory and practice', *Journal of Regulatory Economics*, **10**(3), 227–56.
Littlechild, S.C. (1983), *Regulation of British Telecommunications Profitability*, London: Department of Trade and Industry.
Megginson, W.L. and J. M. Netter (2001), 'From state to market: a survey of empirical studies of privatization', *Journal of Economic Literature*, **39**(2): 321–89.
Organisation of Economic Co-operation and Development (OECD) (2005), *OECD Communications Outlook 2005*, Paris. OECD.
Parker, David and David S. Saal (eds) (2003), *International Handbook on Privatization*, Cheltenham, UK and Northampton, MA, USA: Edward Elgar.
Potter, John E. (2002), 'Remarks of John E. Potter', Board of Governors Meeting, Washington, DC, November 5, http://www.usps.com/news/2002/press/pr 02_pmg 1105.htm, accessed 6 June 2008.
President's Commission on the United States Postal Service (2003), 'Embracing the Future: Making the Tough Choices to Preserve Universal Mail Service', http://www.treasury.gov/offices/domestic finance/usps/pdf/freport.pdf, accessed 6 June 2008.
Sauber, James W. (2002), 'U.S. Postal Service collective bargaining: is the grass greener on the other side of interest arbitration?', in Crew and Kleindorfer (eds), (2002a), pp. 243–64.
US General Accounting Office (2002), 'U.S. Postal Service: Deteriorating Financial Outlook Increases Need for Transformation', February 28, GAO-02-355, http://www.gao.gov/new.items/d02355.pdf, accessed 6 June 2008.
US Postal Service (2002), *Annual Report, 2002*, http://www.usps.com/history/anrpt02, accessed 6 June 2008
US Postal Service (2005), *Annual Report, 2005*, http://www.usps.com/history/anrpt05, accessed 6 June 2008.
US Postal Service (2007), *Annual Report, 2007*, http://www.usps.com/history/anrpt07, accessed 6 June 2008.
Vickers, John and George Yarrow (1988), *Privatization: An Economic Analysis*, Cambridge, MA: MIT Press.
Wachter, Michael L. and Jeffrey M. Perloff (1991), 'A comparative analysis of wage premiums and industrial relations in the British Post Office and the United States Postal Service', in M.A. Crew and P.R. Kleindorfer (eds), *Competition and Innovation in Postal Services*, Boston, MA: Kluwer Academic, pp. 115–38.
Wachter, Michael L., Barry T. Hirsch and James W. Gillula (2001), 'Difficulties of deregulation when wage costs are the major cost', in M.A. Crew and P.R. Kleindorfer (eds), *Future Directions in Postal Reform*, Boston, MA: Kluwer Academic, pp. 3–24.
WIK Consult GmbH (2006), 'Main developments in the postal sector (2004–2006)', Bad Honnef, http://ec.europa.eu/internal_market/post/studies_en.htm, accessed 6 June 2008.
Williams, David C. and Thomas M. Sharkey (2005), 'United States Post Office of Inspector General: developing best practices for a postal watchdog', in Crew and Kleindorfer (eds) (2005a), pp. 395–413.

9. Postal transformation: United States Postal Service builds a platform for fundamental future change

Robert A.F. Reisner†

1. BACKGROUND AND INTRODUCTION

Throughout the world, transformation[1] of the posts has become an increasingly popular and urgent theme. For example, in the US, Canada, Australia, Japan, the United Kingdom, Germany, Italy, and Switzerland, postal and mailing industry leaders are talking about transformation, though the meaning of transformation and the market contexts often differ considerably across these countries.

Indeed, there are as many definitions of transformation as there are new initiatives. Some posts have concentrated on cost reduction and productivity improvement, others on stimulating top-line growth. In some cases transformation means massive investments in letter-mail automation to permit restructuring of postal operations. In other cases, it has included an investment in new postal electronic services. In still others there have been fundamental changes in the governance structure, privatization and even the acquisition of new businesses.

This chapter explores the transformation of the United States Postal Service (USPS) to this point and the opportunities that the work to date has created for the future. The case of USPS is a useful reference point in examining the implications of global postal transformation. USPS processes 40 percent of the world's mail and it has been a model that has been followed by posts throughout the world since it has sought to transform without changing its basic public sector ownership model. In spite of a major new postal reform law, the Postal Accountability and Enhancement Act (PAEA) of 2006, USPS remains a unique governmental enterprise.[2]

One conclusion drawn in this chapter is that while USPS leadership has been successful in bringing change to the institution since the publication of the Transformation Plan of 2002, it has not 'transformed' it, at least not yet. At the same time, the leadership of USPS has advanced a number of dramatic reform proposals including the development of an Intelligent Mail Barcode, the deployment of the next generation of automation and the concept of outsourcing time definite services. Taken together these future initiatives would in fact lead to an institutional transformation by almost anyone's definition. But realizing the benefits of this vision of transformational change will take support. And without collaboration from employees, customers and policymakers, the future may be uncertain.

† President, Transformation Strategy Inc.

At this point, some may argue that this is all semantics since the CEO of the postal service has himself said that USPS has been pursuing 'transformational strategies'[3] as part of a dynamic and changing plan. Yet more than words are at stake here. A close comparison of goals and accomplishments shows that USPS is on a journey where the destination, transformation, has not yet been reached by the USPS's definitions of 2002. Being clear is necessary, especially for the new initiatives. To anticipate future challenges and to prioritize what parts of the vision of change are worth fighting for, posts need to understand what they mean by 'transforming'.

A second conclusion in this chapter is that in spite of a pattern of significant accomplishment, the major obstacles to date were not necessarily controllable by postal management. The importance of stakeholder support for transformation goals is especially important in looking to the future. USPS postal leadership is engaged in a unique journey, to transform within the framework of the traditional governmental model. If the stakeholders do not permit change to succeed then 'what is next?' will be a fair question; the debate over the answer will have proponents for the radical changes in governance and ownership that have been seen elsewhere.

The important point for postal and mailing industry leaders throughout the world is to distinguish the posts that 'are changing their character or condition'[4] from those that are not. There will be opposition to almost anything that posts seek to do to change traditional practices to survive in an increasingly competitive marketplace. What steps *must* the posts take in spite of opposition to anticipate the 'reformed' market in which competition will be more intense? Understanding meaningful strategic transformation and distinguishing it from incremental improvement is a first step. Knowing what worked and what did not, even in the case of smaller changes, will be important as well.

The balance of this chapter examines the core of the vision and some important outcomes. Section 2 discusses the situation facing many posts today and the way that the forces of competition and technology change are creating a need for transformation. Section 3 discusses the years leading to reform at USPS. Section 4 discusses the Transformation Plan and its aspirations. Section 5 reviews the results from transformation to this point and Section 6 looks to the future, to a time when the broader implications of reform may be felt.

2. PREAMBLE: THE NEED FOR TRANSFORMATION

None of this new attention to transformation should be surprising. In the Internet age, as electronic services have substituted for some traditional mail uses such as bill paying and as competitors have grown to become more serious and have shown the value-creating qualities of their increasingly sophisticated technology bases, the value of postal monopoly protection has been eroded. The former (e-transactions) drains volume although to date it has been limited. Of perhaps more consequence has been the impact of the technology-based competitors who were able to offer tracking capabilities that have actually changed the value proposition to customers.

When FedEx and UPS introduced tracking and tracing in the early 1990s, they created a bilateral, interactive communication to replace the black hole of uncertainty that surrounds traditional mailing practice. They created an expectation of performance among customers that took away some of the advantage of being the low-cost, large-scale monopolist.[5]

At the same time that value propositions changed and top-line growth dwindled, postal bottom lines were squeezed by rising costs. Economic forces that have led to cost increases have continued to squeeze the net income of postal administrations. In Asia, Europe and the US rising fuel costs, increasing labor rates, inflation in postal costs of all kinds and growth in the scope of postal networks have raised the cost of providing service. A common theme heard throughout the world is the assertion that the postal model must be transformed into a modern vigorous competitive enterprise because monopoly protections are less secure.[6]

USPS was in fact given the protection of two postal monopolies by the law that created the USPS in 1970 from the former Post Office Department.[7] The letter monopoly that makes the carriage of first class letters the exclusive province of USPS and the mail-box monopoly that does not allow anyone but USPS to deliver to the consumer's post office box, mean that the mailing industry has historically been tied to the USPS.

USPS has made a 'long term commitment'[8] to transformation in the words of the Postmaster General. In fact, consistency is one of Jack Potter's well-recognized traits. When he was first describing his plans for the Transformation Plan to his senior managers in 2001, he said that his plans were going to sound a great deal like improvements on his previous plans that he had presented to the same group – the Blueprint for Progress and Breakthrough Productivity. He added that they should not be surprised to hear this. His focus has been on continuous improvement for more than a decade.[9] If it was a good idea before, he said, he expected them to help him make it better.

3. THE ROOTS OF TRANSFORMATION

In line with Potter's consistency principle, to see the forces that shaped the Transformation Plan of 2002, it is useful to look back to the two previous Postmasters General who each sought to introduce fundamental reform at USPS.

3.1 Darth Vader Arrives at the USPS

The call for postal reform at USPS goes back to the mid-1990s. In 1992, the Board of Governors recruited an experienced top manager and change agent to become the Postmaster General. They brought in Marvin Runyon, a 40-year-old automotive executive who had been a Ford Vice President, the President of Nissan USA and the head of TVA. He quickly earned the nicknames 'Darth Vader' and 'Carvin Marvin' because of the aggressiveness with which he restructured the USPS. (He was quietly pleased with his image.) He rapidly moved to reorganize, to drop traditional functions and took out 40,000 jobs with a buyout proposal.

Regrettably, his moves fell short of their aspirations and by late 1993 (18 months after arriving) service had fallen dramatically. The job cuts were only a temporary fix and to work out of the service crisis, Runyon was forced to restructure for the second time in two years during the summer of 1994. A cadre of aggressive, iconoclastic postal managers were recruited from the ranks and brought back from retirement to save the service. The tactic succeeded even as new threats arose.

In the fall of 1994, the Republicans took over the House of Representatives and new voices were heard criticizing USPS from new angles. The new critics were more strident than past overseers and some suggested the need for privatization. Runyon decided to seize the initiative. Six years before Jack Potter took office, Postmaster General Marvin Runyon spoke at the National Press Club and called for sweeping reform of the postal service.[10]

3.2 A 'Better Version' of USPS We See Today

Marvin Runyon, the automotive engineer, did not at first put much stock in defining strategic visions. He came more from the Michael Hammer school of reinvention and quality management ('At Ford, Quality is Job One'[11]) that emphasized business process improvement. Designing for the future with process management had its limits, however. Confronted with fundamental market change, other successful leaders of transformation changed their stance. Jack Welch (GE) and Lou Gerstner (IBM), similar to Runyon, had also adopted the early position that strategy was less important than management improvement.[12] However, in both cases they ultimately recognized the significance of the changes that were introduced by the Internet age and turned to focus on defining future direction.

For Runyon this time for definition came in the fall of 1996 when he convened his management team in Norman Oklahoma. Marvin Runyon, Mike Coughlin (Deputy) and William Henderson (Chief Operating Officer) all gave speeches outlining their perspectives on long-term strategic direction taken from their independent roles in leading the USPS.[13]

When Marvin Runyon reached the critical point in his speech he outlined his vision of the long-term future: 'I see a postal service a decade from now that's a better version of the postal service that we know today'. In other words, the vision of USPS's change agent was not to change the nature of the postal service but to improve it incrementally.

3.3 The Intelligent Mailstream and the Gateway to the Household

In the spring of 1998, William Henderson, an experienced postal manager who had played a key central role in Runyon's tenure, was selected by the Board of Governors to become the 71st Postmaster General of the US. His tenure (1998–2001) came at one of the times in postal history when it would have been most difficult to have a sense of the direction of the marketplace.

In retrospect, after the crash of the dot com boom it has become accepted wisdom that the Internet visionaries of the 1990s who were designing an economy in which profit and net income was no longer the key measure of performance, were suffering from 'irrational exuberance'.[14] After the crash, after Enron, after 9–11, it seems preposterous that serious people could have argued that the degree of market change was so great that new measures for performance involving indicators of *potential* growth were more important than having revenue exceed costs. But all of this made it difficult for USPS to calculate its position in a sea of change.

At the time, the Postal Service was termed a dinosaur of the Internet age and many of Bill Henderson's initiatives sought to align USPS with the changing marketplace. In the summer of 1998, at a National Postal Forum that was convened in Washington, DC, Henderson outlined his vision for an Intelligent Mailstream in which envelopes would be able to 'talk' to the postal network and ultimately to the Internet. He embraced an alliance with new Internet players such as Amazon dot com.

Even so, when it was time to define a central strategic vision, Henderson selected 'the Mail Moment', a phrase that is still used by leaders in the postal industry around the world. At the time, the mail moment was meant to capture the strategic advantage that the posts possessed since they still controlled the Gateway to the Household and they had a unique competitive advantage at that time of day. However, over time the mail moment became a nostalgic theme that sought to justify a 'consumer preference' for paper rather than electronic communications.[15] Perhaps it should not be surprising that when a team of skilled traditional postal managers came to lead USPS in subsequent years under Jack Potter, their course would not stray far from the traditional core. After all, even the change agents and iconoclasts had, in spite of their rhetoric, focused on tradition.

4. THE USPS TRANSFORMATION PLAN

When the time came for describing a comprehensive USPS Transformation Plan (2002) the future course could have taken many different directions. The actual statement of transformation was formulated during a controversial time in which significant pressure confronted the postal service and its leadership. They were both given exceptional scrutiny and at the same time, more freedom to choose a course than at other times.

4.1 'The Ox is in the Ditch Big Time'

In the spring of 2001, Postmaster General William G. Henderson testified before the Senate Governmental Affairs Committee for the last time before his June 1 retirement when Jack Potter would become Postmaster General. The tone of the hearing was set by Comptroller General, David Walker, who testified that he had placed the transformation of USPS on the 'high risk watch list' of the General Accounting Office. Of particular concern to the postal community, the Congress and the Treasury was the financial condition of USPS.

USPS was projecting significant shortfalls (more than $2 billion) in its net income. Most certainly this would place pressure on USPS to raise rates in the near future. The process of litigating the size and character of the projected rate increase was then unfolding at the Postal Rate Commission (PRC). Under the technical provisions of the postal law, the PRC was responsible only for 'recommending' rates to the Board of Governors of the USPS. The Board had the authority to override the PRC's January proposal and it had voted to do just that. The 34-cent First Class Rate that was instituted in June of 2001 was accompanied by changes that reinstated portions of the USPS's original proposal.

Committee Chairman Fred Thompson stated his displeasure with such a violation of what he believed to be due process treatment in which independent regulators would presumably take testimony and adjudicate outcomes. Overriding the outcome of the rate case was going to be controversial, but of even greater concern to the Committee and the surrounding mailing community was the fact that the debt of USPS would soon reach its limit. The postal service was going to be seeking more money, either in higher rates or in new indebtedness. Summarizing what he had heard, Chairman Thompson declared that he understood perfectly, 'the Ox is in the Ditch, Big Time'.[16]

4.2 The USPS Transformation Plan

Almost immediately after he took office on June 1, Postmaster General Jack Potter received a letter from the four US senators who had oversight responsibility for the USPS. Senators Fred Thompson, Joe Lieberman, Thomas R. Carper and Susan Collins[17] told the new Postmaster General that they were extremely concerned with the condition of USPS and they directed him to prepare a Transformation Plan in six months.

As it turned out, other events were to intervene. The attacks of 9–11 and, just as significantly for the USPS, the mailing of Anthrax-laden letters several weeks later, disrupted plans and programs. Over time, as Postmaster General Potter included the union leadership in daily meetings following the crises, the historic events of 9–11 may have generated support for the development of a unique consensus around the Transformation Plan, which was published at the beginning of April 2002. In spite of a history of confrontational style between unions and management[18] over similar plans, the Transformation Plan of 2002 was a singularly important statement of aligned USPS intent.

The initiatives contained in the USPS Transformation Plan of 2002 (Box 9.1) illustrate the sweeping breadth of its vision. Testifying before the House six years later, Postmaster General Potter stated:

> Our *Transformation Plan* . . . was adopted in 2002, during my first year as Postmaster General. Our goal in developing the Plan was simple, to create strategies that would involve the entire organization and keep it focused on achieving steady progress in three key areas: Fostering growth by increasing the value of postal products and services to our customers; improving operational efficiency; and, enhancing our performance-based culture.'[19]

The outline of the 2002 plan shows its comprehensiveness.

BOX 9.1 THE TRANSFORMATION PLAN OF 2002

1 Foster Growth through Customer Value

1.1 Retail: Expand Access to Postal Services

- Move simple transactions out of post offices;
- Create new, low-cost retail alternatives;
- Optimize the retail network; and
- Develop new retail services that increase customer value and postal revenue.

1.2 Products and Services: Improve Value and Growth

- Use technology to enhance the value of mail;
- Design rates and mail preparation to match customer capabilities and needs;
- Position mail as a key communications medium and as a customer relationship management tool;
- Enhance package services;
- Map channel strategies around customer needs, contribution, and growth potential;
- Develop new products and services; and
- Leverage existing assets.

2 Increase Operational Efficiency

- Enhance already efficient letter processing;
- Complete automation of flats processing;
- Expand mechanization of material handling operations;
- Improve delivery efficiency:
  - Managed Service Points system improves the uniformity of daily delivery and has produced savings in street delivery operations.
  - Delivery Performance Achievement and Recognition System uses benchmarking techniques to improve and recognize good performance.
  - Rural Delivery Improvement process is designed to improve performance through enhanced training of supervisors.
  - Carrier Optimal Routing system is being tested to optimize carrier routes and travel paths using optimization algorithms. If successful, it will allow the Postal Service to structure more efficient routes and reduce vehicle costs.
- Deploy next generation package sorting equipment;
- Optimize transportation and distribution networks;
  - Surface Air Management System is a replacement system for the aging Air Contract Data Collection System and handles mail assignment to air carriers and supporting payments to the carriers.
  - Transportation Optimization Planning and Scheduling system will replace the automated dispatch generation system and will introduce a more dynamic and industry-standard route optimization engine for all transportation.
  - Surface Air Support System is a logistics information platform system that will integrate scanned data from existing postal transportation systems to ensure service performance accountability and accurate payment verification.
  - Transportation Contract Support System will support the solicitation, award, and administration of highway, air, rail, and water contracts.

- Lower costs through the use of shared FedEx capacity as opposed to dedicated capacity purchased from other providers.
- Opportunities for improved service performance.
- Simplified and centralized network management resulting from the replacement of multiple providers and networks with a single air transportation solution; and
- Improved information technology capabilities through the integration of Postal Service systems with FedEx's vast information collection infrastructure.
- Development of Network Integration and Alignment, a national effort affects $5.5 billion in transportation costs and approximately $20 billion in processing and distribution costs. As a national initiative, the NIA will model more than 500 facilities, including processing and distribution centers/facilities, bulk mail centers, Priority Mail processing centers, international service centers, air mail centers, facility annexes, and hub-and-spoke facilities. The network strategy will be developed by the fall of 2002.

- Increase retail/customer service productivity:
  - Standardization of operations to ensure optimal efficiency throughout the postal network.
  - Continued automation of mail processing operations that occur in the backroom of post offices.
- Improve performance management; and
- Manage realty assets:
  - *Postal Service properties for sale.* The sale of fee simple, leased fee, and leasehold interests (including excess land, buildings, and air rights/other developmental rights).
  - *Short-term leasing.* Leasing of excess space in postal owned buildings to the private sector (outleasing) and the General Services Administration.
  - *Developmental leasing.* The long-term leasing of excess space and development rights via a third-party developer.
  - *Developmental added value properties.* Enhancement of the value of select high-profile properties suited for commercial development, including disposition strategies.
  - *Other programs.* Tax appeals and acquisition of properties with favorable rents and purchase options.

3 Move Toward a Performance-Based Culture

- Retain and recruit quality employees;
- Develop future leaders;
- Ensure training and development;
- Create a performance-based pay system;
- Build a highly effective and motivated workforce;
- Improve labor/management relations;

- Improve workforce planning;
- Expand shared services and explore outsourcing;

4 Enabling Strategies

4.1 Enhance Financial Management
- Reduce outstanding debt;
- Improve financial reporting transparency; and
- Finance delivery network expansion on a current basis and explore alternative investments for deferred retirement liabilities.

4.2 Expand Use of Supply Chain Management

4.3 Strategically Apply Technology

Technology Strategy: Designing Enhanced Technology Infrastructure
- Enhance security across all technology;
- Upgrade the infrastructure; and
- Ensure universal computing connectivity.

4.4 Ensure Safety, Security, and Privacy of the Mail

Security Strategy 1: Prevent Use of the Mail to Defraud Consumers or Convey Dangerous Mailings;
Security Strategy 2: Reduce Theft of Mail and Other Criminal Attack of Postal Products, Services, and Assets;
Security Strategy 3: Ensure a Safe, Secure, and Drug-Free Work Environment;
Security Strategy 4: Ensure that the Postal Service Maintains its Trusted Brand and Provides Top-Rate Privacy Protection.

5 Seek Moderate Regulatory and Legislative Reforms

Reform Strategy 1: Seek the Maximum Flexibility Consistent with the Current Rate-Making Process;
Reform Strategy 2: Rationalize Retail Network Facilities;
Reform Strategy 3: Modernize Purchasing Procedures;
Reform Strategy 4: Reform Labor and Employment Provisions.

Source: USPS Transformation Plan, April 2002.

In summary, the Transformation Plan was a sweeping document that proposed initiatives throughout the sprawling US Postal Service. The impact of this plan was likely to be easier to measure in some areas than in others. Not surprisingly as the balance of this chapter shows, cost reduction became a central focus.

Initiatives aimed at top-line growth in a historically 'governmental' monopoly were not likely to take root quickly. This is not to say that USPS could not create new value for its customers. Nor does the traditional character of the parent enterprise mean that the retail and product initiatives were unworthy. The opportunities may be getting better as the postal service now has opportunities to use the pricing freedom and competitive products granted by postal reform to create new revenue. However, between new revenue creation

Table 9.1 The vision of savings: Transformation Plan savings/cost avoidance summary, March 2002

Areas of opportunity	2002	2003	2004	2005	2006	2002–06
Capital programs	267	202	290	348	359	1,464
Post Office operations (function 4)	163	189	213	274	264	1,103
Operational efficiencies (includes impacts of NIA)	313	463	259	206	320	1,561
Administrative reductions	162	140	10			312
Transportation (includes impacts of NIA)	136	81	40	48	258	561
Total	1,041	1,075	812	876	1,201	5,001

Source: Postal Service Document, President's Commission Web Site, US Treasury Department.

and cost reduction, there is little surprise that the first initiatives to yield results for USPS would be those that focused on cutting costs and enhancing productivity.

Furthermore, many of the initiatives involving culture change and infrastructure support, however important, were also likely to be difficult to measure.

4.3 The President's Commission

Not that the cost side was easy. The breadth of the Transformation Plan made it difficult to see the future sources of the savings that of $1 billion per year that USPS was committed to achieve. A Presidential Commission on USPS was convened in January 2003 and was given six months to report to Congress. The Commission, the testimony that it received and its interaction with the Postal Service, led to the development of the Commission's Report, 'Embracing the Future, Making the Tough Choices to Preserve Universal Mail Service'.[20]

In May 1973 the Commission, seeking to demonstrate that there were savings to be found in 'standardization' of mail services, engaged USPS in an intense discussion of the potential source for savings. A letter that Chief Financial Officer (CFO) Richard Strasser wrote to Commission Chairman James A. Johnson on May 8, 2003 offers a perspective on the potential source of savings.

In his 2003 cover letter enclosing the outlook, Strasser stated: 'I would like to note that the savings discussed [in 2002] in the *Transformation Plan* were commitment targets of cost reductions in certain areas over a five-year period, rather than a compilation of specific, identified savings on a detailed line-item basis'.[21] He went on to state: 'this included the then unidentified Network Integration and Alignment (NIA) strategies. 'Savings and cost avoidances as a result of the NIA strategies will improve operational efficiencies and reduce transportation costs and are included in those two categories'.[22]

What is important to note is the significance of the NIA (network) strategy within the broader vision of postal transformation. In Strasser's May 8, 2003 letter, it is apparent (see Table 9.1) that 40 percent of the savings estimates were influenced by the savings expected to come from NIA and the three other areas of projected savings (facilities, post office operations and administrative reductions) would all have been expected to include impacts from NIA as well. The important point, six years later, is not that savings were not achieved.

In fact, USPS has been able to achieve more than a billion dollars a year in savings, but not from NIA. This has been one of the frustrations of the transformation effort, a continuous source of friction with various postal stakeholders. The results of USPS transformation were reported each year in status reports, the Annual Report and the Annual Performance Report contained in the Comprehensive Statement of Postal Operations, an annual publication of the USPS. The cost savings have been achieved each year so far, even without a new network.

The conclusion of this exchange was important. When the CFO was pressed to outline his aspiration for the savings to be attained by the USPS, he pointed to network integration and alignment as being involved with at least half of it. That the balance of the story showed that the savings were attained without implanting NIA does not make it any less notable that the goal was reached. However, it highlights the significance of the role that the stakeholders who 'pushed back' on the plans for NIA have played in granting USPS the ability to reach transformational goals.

5. TRANSFORMATIONAL RESULTS

As noted above, the ability to cut costs and improve productivity may offer a more concrete measure of results than seeking to measure the effect of cultural change that has taken place to this point. In spite of the challenge in identifying concrete measures of the effect of the Transformation Plan, there are a number of measures that offer important public, objective, fact-based metrics. First, it is possible to use annual report data to gain some perspective on USPS then (2003) and now (2007) (Table 9.2). Using data from the Annual Performance Report that is published in the *Annual Comprehensive Statement on Postal Operations*, it is possible to evaluate the important dimensions of productivity improvement and service performance. These broad measures offer some perspective on the direction of change (positive) and on its scope (perhaps more incremental, rather than structural and fundamental).

Before looking at the results reported in the Annual Performance Reports, it is useful to see the overview of the changes that have taken place since the publication of the Transformation Plan in 2002.

An overview of the changes shows that revenue has grown by $5 billion as a result of rising mail volume of more than 10 billion pieces (and some price increases). USPS is processing more pieces and carrying more weight while its employee base has declined by 41,000 employees or around 5 percent. The result is that postal productivity has increased (Table 9.3).

The postal service measures its productivity using a measure known as total factor productivity (TFP). TFP compares postal outputs such as weighted mail volume and the extent of the delivery network with inputs such as capital, labor and materials used to produce the inputs. The concept behind TFP is that measuring all of the inputs will correct for the substitution of capital (or automation) for labor.[23]

Many long-time postal observers would note that until the present management team began to reduce the size of the postal workforce, it was generally believed that there might be some possibility for reducing the size of the postal service (though it was not easy) but that these reductions could not be made without sacrifices in performance and customer satisfaction. Potter's tenure has changed that.

Table 9.2 USPS then and now

Measure of USPS activity	2003	2007	Notes
Revenue	65,700.6	71,056.7	Revenue increased by $5 billion dollars
Volume (pieces)	202,184.7	212,234.0	Volume has increased by 10 billion pieces
Weight	24,851.9	25,643.2	Weight has increased by almost 800 m. lbs
Total employees	826,955	785,929	Total employees have decreased by 41 K
Total career	729,035	684,762	Career have decreased by 44 K
Total non-career	97,920	101,167	Non-career have increased by 3 K
Pieces per employee	24 K/year	27K/year	Productivity has improved
Delivery points	141,361,276	147,992,522	There are 8.6 million new delivery points

Source: USPS Annual Report, 2007.

Table 9.3 Productivity improvement

	2003	2004	2005	2006	2007
TFP measure	1.8	2.4	1.1	0.4	1.7
Cumulative	1.8	4.2	5.3	5.7	7.4

There are a number of different specific performance metrics that could be used to illustrate the overall performance of USPS in the years following the publication of the Transformation Plan. The ability to perform on plan (consistently at 100 percent) or rising customer and employee satisfaction would all have been measures that might have provided other insight into the achievements of the Transformation Plan. Each has consistently improved in the past six years in spite of a history over the past 35 years of having each of these measures periodically spiral out of control. Table 9.4 presents the core measure of on-time delivery.

In 1997 the Postal Service Board of Governors met in St. Louis and sought to understand service performance. One of the long-time executives, who had proven his ability to manage one of the most challenging parts of the country, New York, presented area results to the Board to illustrate the challenge of performance measurement. He explained that there would be a need to make an exception for some parts of the country because it was not possible to reach the same service standard in New York. However, the experience of the management team in the past five years has demonstrated that this is not the case. Consistent performance improvement was achieved in spite of tradition.

Table 9.4 Postal performance

	2003 Actual	2007 Plan	2007 Actual	Notes
Overnight	95	95	95.6	+ 0.6
2 day	91	92	92.6	+ 1.6
3 day	90	90	90.3	+ 0.3

Now there will be a new challenge. The PAEA will require that the measurement system will change and expand dramatically. The EXFC (External First Class) Measure today tests a panel of 463 three digit zip codes selected for volume and geographic density. These areas represent 90 percent of the originating First Class Mail and 80 percent of destinating First Class Mail. The current EXFC assessment also excludes periods when individuals would be unable to control performance because they are given a bonus incentive known as the National Performance Assessment (NPA). The exclusionary periods include December when air traffic capacity is significantly reduced.[24]

In the future, USPS will be required to significantly expand not only its performance measurement system to all zip codes but also the coverage to include all products. While the competitive products will not be included in the performance measurement system, First Class Mail, Single-Piece First Class Mail International, Standard Mail, Periodicals and Package services and special services will be included. For the performance measurement system, one of the most significant changes will involve resolving issues associated with the chain of custody known as 'start the clock' data. A chronic question of performance measurement has been 'when did the mail actually enter the system?'. Custody must be transferred from commercial mailers to the postal service when mail enters.

The solution that USPS has proposed will involve one of the most significant technology changes since the beginning of automation in the 1980s or even the introduction of the zip code in the 1960s. The introduction of intelligent mail will offer the postal service a piece count of all mail, 'a primary service performance measurement tool to complement EXFC. The mail with electronic documentation and intelligent mail barcodes will be tracked continuously through the operating system'.[25] by means of an Intelligent Mail Barcode (IMB). By adding this IMB data to the survey data in EXFC, a hybrid measurement system will be created.

One of the reasons for using a hybrid system is practical. The system that is used to 'seed' the mail is expensive. To measure the performance in every zip code rather than a selected panel of zip codes and to expand the measurement of performance to all of the products that will be required by the new law would require an exceptionally large survey to achieve sample sizes that were adequate for statistical purposes. Using the IMB would allow a count to be done without having to invest in such a large third party measurement system.

The problem is that the IMB system is expensive too, but the cost is partially carried by the mailers. As a result, when it was proposed, the costs and technological challenges stimulated more than a thousand comments to be submitted to USPS to protest about various aspects of the IMB. Doubters speculated that it would not be possible to implement such a controversial system. In fact, it is because of the importance of the IMB to fulfilling the obligations that USPS incurred under the PAEA that there would appear to be a high likelihood that this initiative will go forward, in spite of opposition. However, even this is not a guarantee, and here is where a transformational perspective may be particularly important.

In conclusion, it is fair to ask, 'How are the results of postal transformation – any post's transformation – to be measured?' Six years after the first Transformation Plan, cost cutting remains a more tested route for creating value than revenue generation. In his appearance before the House of Representatives on February 28, 2008, Postmaster General Potter noted that in the first quarter of the 2008 Fiscal Year, the USPS's revenue fell by 3 percent causing the service to fall below plan. Whether this volume decline is an early indicator of the nation's economic health is yet to be seen. However, Potter noted that to anticipate the balance of the year and put USPS back on plan, the management team had identified a billion dollars of cost savings in addition to the billion dollars of cost savings that was built into the initial plan.

In sum, what these results show is the degree to which the stakeholders and their support (or lack of it) play a key role in permitting the visionary elements of transformation to be implemented. The postal services of the world are highly interconnected institutions, even more than large corporations, they depend upon the support of their customers, suppliers, employees and the public to initiate change.

6. THE TRANSFORMATIONAL BASE AND THE FUTURE

From the preceding discussion, it is clear in broad strokes that the 2002 Transformation Plan was an exceptionally wide-ranging document that described new initiatives that spanned the USPS. The conclusions that might be drawn on the basis of 2007 data indicate that USPS has changed in ways that long-time observers would not have thought possible when the transformation journey began. There has been consistency, productivity improvement and, most significantly, a reduction in size without losing customer satisfaction or service performance, at least as measured by EXFC.

This final point is particularly significant in an age where the traditional threat of long-term volume decline is now becoming a reality. For USPS to be able to reduce its size (where labor costs still represent 80 percent of postal costs), and to operate consistently without sacrificing performance scores or losing customer satisfaction, will be essential in a declining marketplace. But even this achievement might not be enough.

USPS management team has proposed a series of initiatives that would arguably lead to a USPS that was fundamentally different in the role that it would be able to play in the future economy. Whether past change was great or small, three initiatives illustrate the transformational potential of what has been proposed: the introduction of the IMB, deployment of flat sequencing sorter automation for flats (for example, magazines and catalogues), and the outsourcing of a time definite network.[26] In oversight hearings before the House of Representatives on February 28, 2008, Postmaster General Potter stated:

> The new [IMB] barcode will become mandatory in 2009 for mailers who take advantage of automation prices. It will allow us to combine a system that physically measures a limited, but statistically valid, sampling of our daily mailstream with one that passively measures an exponentially greater volume.

> The mail-flow data that we collect will be the basis for a wide range of reports that customers can obtain and that can also serve as important diagnostic tools for the postal service.[27]

Potter was reported in the trade press to have stated in answer to questions that USPS was going to issue a request for proposals to outsource the BMC (Bulk Mail Center) network.[28] He also noted that the deployment of the FSS (flat sorting) machines continues and the first machine was placed in the Dulles facility to permit testing with live mail during the spring of 2008.

These initiatives promise substantial change in handling all of the product lines of USPS. More importantly, they represent a fundamental conceptual leap forward from a top-heavy, labor-intensive, inert network toward a new integrated logistics operation in which letters and flats and packages can be traced through the entire supply chain.

To take the IMB as a single important illustration, once the customer places an IMB on a letter and commits to a nesting methodology that allows individual letters within trays and on pallets to be identified at the individual piece level, a boundariless network of public and private logistics could be built. Today, customers complain that the creation of a mailpiece such as a catalogue is a highly interactive, precise networked activity in which the mailer is able to identify the status of a project with precision. However, when the mailpiece enters the mailstream, it enters a black hole, they complain, in which the customer has little idea where the project is in the process. The ability to identify the location of mailpieces allows customers to redirect them (for example, the UPS television advertisement of UPS Delivery Intercept[29]). Data on location allow USPS to create performance metrics to identify problems and to continuously improve service. Flow-through data allow managers to 'disintermediate' and bypass weak links in the supply chain. Control over logistical flows means that buyers can source strategically by consolidating volume, opening access points, pricing bottlenecks differently and, in general, creating joint process solutions that allow the shipper and the carrier to collaborate to improve service.

In short, what Potter's management team has proposed is a fundamental change in the character of a government monopoly that used to spend much of its time engaged in contentious ligation-style conflict with its customers. Instead, the barcode would permit the creation of a new collaborative infrastructure to permit collaboration in ways that are yet to be imagined. To change from a public enterprise monopoly to partner–collaborator would indeed be a change of enormous transformative value to the economy and would potentially change the role of the mail in an electronic age.

In fact, looking forward, many futurists anticipate a world of radio frequency identification and nano-technology in which barcodes are replaced with new technologies that enhance the capacity of the collaborative networks described here. We are at the beginning in terms of materials handling and logistics capabilities. The IMB may be one critical enabling step.

FSS implementation completes the automation and materials handling capacity of USPS. With this final step, USPS will be able to address the final productivity frontier. Improvements in productivity (shown in the TFP numbers above) have been achieved largely by taking out 'upstream' work hours. Downstream at the carrier stations, there is still a need for human beings to sort flat mail, and the delivery portion of the postal network has remained generally unchanged. Undertaking outsourcing of the bulk-mail centers would add still another management capability that reaches beyond the boundaries of the USPS. Tying the 'last mile' to a modern, flexible logistics network will make it possible to find the space to automate flats within the current structure and to lower the handling costs for one of the most costly services, network parcels.

The reason for making the distinction between incremental change and the introduction of these fundamental transformative initiatives is that none of the three described here, is a given. No sooner had the imperatives of the IMB been described than the customers began to resist implementation. To the extent that the resistance could be mitigated by the management team, Jack Potter made adjustments. Yet customers may yet resist the barcode's costs and complexity. As soon as the IMB was announced, some privacy advocates raised the concern that it might represent a new government intrusion. Unions resist network realignment and outsourcing the BMCs. Competitors argue that USPS should be handicapped to level the playing field.

In the end, it is plain that transformation to an institution that can realize the revolutionary potential for the mail communications channel in the Internet age will depend on the collaboration of the stakeholders as much as the vision of postal leaders. The past six years have demonstrated the importance of the insight that in the future, transformation of the posts will be a community enterprise.

NOTES

1. Merriam-Webster's On-Line Dictionary 2008 defines transformation as the act of transforming; 'to transform is to change in form or structure', to 'change the outward appearance'; and 'to change in character or composition'; a 'major change in form or function'.
2. The Postal Service is an 'independent establishment of the executive branch of the Government of the United States' established by the Postal Reorganization Act of 1970. (See Public Law 91–375, August 12, 1970, 84 Stat. 719; 39 U.S.C. S 201.)
3. Cover letter of the CEO and Postmaster General and the chairman of the Board of Governors to the Strategic Transformation Plan of 2007–2010 (hereafter 'STP 2007').
4. Merriam-Webster's On-Line Dictionary 2008 Dictionary defines transforming in this manner (See note 1, above).
5. Postmaster General Jack Potter stated in House oversight hearings in March 2007 that 'My position is . . . an acknowledgement that the dynamics of the 21st century communications market have altered – forever – the basic assumptions of postal economics in a monopoly environment. The traditional postal monopoly, while it still exists as a matter of theory and law, particularly for what the new statute terms our "market-dominant products," does not exist in actual practice'.
6. Some postal observers of considerable experience will still argue today that the core monopoly protections are essentially secure. They point out that express mail and priority mail competition from the express carriers is marginal compared with the $37 billion in revenue from 98 billion pieces of mail and $20 billion of revenue from 102 billion pieces of standard mail (USPS Annual Report of 2006). Some point to the fact that competition from electronic services has had only a limited impact. But there is abundant evidence (for example, in the record of the Postal Regulatory Commission's 2007 hearings on service standards) that choice and the value-adding qualities of tracking and tracing technology have raised customer expectations. For the USPS, even a marginal loss of volume can be difficult to manage because of the size of the institution, the degree of regulatory oversight and other factors that limit management freedom to cut costs.
7. Title 39, USC.
8. 'STP 2007' cover letter.
9. Paraphrase of Jack Potter speaking to the Officers in July 2001. The Blueprint for Progress was a broad operating improvement plan presented to the Board of Governors by Potter in January 2000 and then implemented. Breakthrough Productivity was the long-term productivity improvement plan deployed in 2001.
10. Speech by Postmaster General Marvin Runyon at the National Press Club, Washington, DC January 1995.
11. Michael Hammer and James Champy, *Reengineering the Corporation: A Manifesto for a Business Revolution*, New York, Harpers Business, 1993. The Ford advertising slogan fit with the fundamental precepts of the quality managers.

12. See Jack Welch, *Jack: Straight from the Gut*, New York: Cahners Business Press, 2001 and Louis V. Gerstner, *Who Says Elephants Can't Dance? Leading a Great Enterprise through Dramatic Change*, New York: Collins, 2002.
13. See 'Wisdom in the Winds', USPS pamphlet, October 1996.
14. Quote from a Speech by Federal Reserve Board Chairman Allen Greenspan at the American Enterprise Institute, December 1996
15. The most prolific source of such theories and 'mail moment' research is to be found at Pitney Bowes Insight dot com.
16. *The Financial Outlook of the U.S. Postal Service*, Hearing before the Committee on Governmental Affairs, United States Senate, 107th Cong. 1st Sess. (May 15, 2001) at 18.
17. See the Appendix to the April 2002 Transformation Plan of the USPS.
18. In 1998, American Postal Workers Union President, Mo Biller, stated 'I am not going to look at your Strategic Plan. You are going to have to look at mine'.
19. Testimony of Postmaster General John E. Potter before the Subcommittee On Federal Workforce, Postal Service, And The District Of Columbia Of The Committee On Oversight And Government Reform United States House Of Representatives, Washington, DC, April 17, 2007.
20. Report of the President's Commission on the USPS, 'Embracing the Future, Making the Tough Choices to Preserve Universal Mail Service', July 2003.
21. Letter from Richard Strasser, 'Postal Service Document'. President's Commission Web Site. US Treasury Department.
22. Ibid.
23. 'Mail varies by size, shape, weight, preparation levels and transportation mode. Inputs include all labor capital and materials used. Capital includes buildings, land and equipment. Materials include utilities, supplies, materials and other non-personal items', Comprehensive Statement of Postal Operations, 2007, p. 51.
24. Ibid.
25. Ibid.
26. To these three initiatives there are others that might be added such as seamless acceptance of mail, FAST scheduling of transportation, surface visibility. But the three initiatives outlined above connect with first class mail, flats and parcels and have conceptual symmetry in introducing change across the entire service.
27. Testimony of Postmaster General Potter, February 28, 2008. Statement of the Postmaster General before the House oversight hearings as reported by Postcom.org.
28. Reported by www.Postcom.org, February 29, 2008.
29. Delivery Intercept is described in the Whiteboard section of the UPS website.

10. Technological innovation and postal reform

Jean-Philippe Ducasse,[†] Luis Jimenez[‡] and Marc Morelli[‡]

1. INTRODUCTION

In this chapter we look at the ways in which advanced technology can affect the future of the postal sector. The progress of technology implementation among postal operators (POs) has been reported on various occasions in the last two decades. Jimenez (1988) identified the factors that influence the use of technology by POs. Two articles separated by a decade reviewed the progress of mail-processing technology by POs (Jimenez and Garcia, 1996; Jimenez and Morelli, 2006). Other interim reports developed a prognosis for the evolution of postal technologies over the next 10 years (Jimenez, 2002, 2004a and b Poga, 2003). In this chapter we look at the future more broadly.

In the future, POs can expect to face increasing pressures from more sophisticated and empowered customers. An array of Internet-based changes will reshape operations and sales. These trends will certainly have significant implications for both the technologies that POs select to support internal operations and the relations between POs and their customers and suppliers. The background to these trends and the challenges they imply for postal service providers are the focus of this chapter.

The role of new technologies will also be affected by the interplay between innovation and postal reform. One of the principles underpinning postal liberalization in Europe is that competition promotes innovation, leads to better services, and helps to reduce costs. Liberalization should provide stronger incentives for incumbent operators to meet user needs and avail themselves of innovative technologies. Sector-specific regulation also influences the scope and type of technological developments. For instance, the entry strategies of upstream competitors may be shaped by regulatory decisions regarding the conditions and price of access to the incumbent's network. Such decisions may also affect the potential market for equipment such as sorting machines. Changes in the incumbent's legal status – another component of many reforms – also impact on technological trends. A corporatized PO enjoying commercial freedoms will be able to access new technologies through joint ventures with technology partners. A privatized post will prioritize its investments in new technologies under the influence of profitability targets set by the market, while a state-owned PO will probably have less stringent return on investment targets.

† Pitney Bowes Inc.
‡ Formerly of Pitney Bowes Inc.

Section 2 briefly reviews the impact that communications technology has had on mail volumes. Section 3 identifies those technologies that can improve the value and effectiveness of mail from the sender's point of view. Section 4 focuses on technological developments that are enabling recipients to have greater control over the mailstream. Section 5 summarizes recent and future developments of technology inside the postal value chain. Section 6 reviews the impacts of recent sector-specific regulation on technology trends discussed in previous sections. Each section draws brief implications for the interplay between postal reform and technology implementation in the POs, and Section 7 summarizes our conclusions.

2. MAIL DEMAND AND TECHNOLOGICAL TRENDS

Research has conclusively shown that the availability of new communications options has not been sufficient to eliminate more traditional methods such as mail. Instead, a substantial body of research has shown that mail coexists with the Internet. (Mail volume trends are covered in Jimenez, 2005, 2006a, and 2006b.)

Mail volumes have not sharply declined as was so often anticipated by so many. Rather, in industrialized countries (ICs), mail has entered into what we call a slow erosion/low growth (SELG) scenario.[1] We expect total mail volumes to grow or decline by 1 to 2 percent per year in most ICs. In particular, transaction and correspondence mail is generally declining at 1 to 2 percent annually, while direct mail continues to grow, typically keeping pace with GDP. Some 15 years have passed since the debut of the Internet and the first browser. In the meantime, direct mail expenditures as a fraction of total 'advertising spend' have increased both in the US and in Europe (Jimenez, 2006b).

Highly valued transactions to consumers, such as bills and statements, present a mixed picture: they are growing in the US at 3 percent but declining annually at 1.2 percent in Europe (Fu, 2007). We observe a persisting preference by consumers to want to view statements online and then resort to the comfort and affordances of paper copies when it comes to downloading or archiving them. Most recipients still decline to completely suppress paper statements, even when charged for delivery by their financial institutions.

Studies in the US, Belgium and Denmark have reaffirmed the value of mail, concluding that there is a definite 'mail moment' (Jimenez, 2006a, b). Consumers uniquely value the experience and impact of receiving a relevant mail piece over many other forms of communication. The research also shows that consumers respond better to a 'multichannel' approach, whereby a mailer uses a combination of traditional and technology-enhanced media channels for both new customer acquisition and cross-selling to existing customers. Further, these studies show a measurable 'lift' in customer response to marketing campaigns that combine multiple channels.

Most interesting is work that shows that Internet users receive more mail than non-Internet users, a conclusion that has been reached independently in the US, the UK, and Ireland (Jimenez, 2006 a, b). Less intuitive perhaps is US research that indicates that the amount of mail a person receives depends on his or her life-stage and earning power, rather than on generational affiliation or technological adroitness (Diakova et al., 2006; Jimenez et al., 2006).

Recent projections by a leading US market-research company claim that e-mail traffic will begin to decline as this medium loses effectiveness (IDC, 2007). Meanwhile, the Internet has created new forms of mail – such as DVDs, digital photos and mail-order pharmaceuticals – which amounted to over 1.4 billion new mail pieces in the US in 2006 (Jimenez, 2006a, b). Thus, overall, the Internet now seems to be having some positive effects on what we believe is a stable mail volume base.

There is a growing consensus that, although mail volumes may slowly erode, the bulk of mail will be here to stay for many years (Nader and Lintell, 2008). Stable and healthy mail volumes will, however, be increasingly dependent on mail being valuable, relevant and affordable. Technological applications, such as those outlined in the rest of this chapter, will play a role in maintaining the value proposition for mail. Additionally, postal reform offers the opportunity to ensure that regulations and institutional frameworks in place enable all parties to take advantage of technology.

We shall begin a tour of three areas of technology application: how senders can use technology to create more valuable mail pieces; how recipients can interact better with the post; and how the processing network must evolve.

3. MAILER-DRIVEN INNOVATIONS WILL ADD VALUE TO MAIL

Several recent reports have identified a host of emerging uses of technologies and techniques that are being used to create mail pieces (Pitney Bowes, 2005; Jimenez, 2007a–d). Technologies of interest include: data mining, variable print-on-demand, mobile technology, digital photography and geocoding, to name a few. New technologies for promoting open innovation in the postal value chain are being developed (Pintsov and Obrea, ch.11, this volume). Techniques that are spurring new mail growth include finer targeting, mail piece personalization (that is, adding text and data that are particular to an individual), and customization (that is, designing and engineering the mail piece for each individual, such as with customized art and 'onserts').[2] Below we give some examples of the use of these technologies to create valuable mail pieces.

3.1 Database Marketing

Database marketing, or targeting with customer databases, has been widely practiced for more than two decades. Coupling this method with new, more sophisticated and diverse databases and with greater use of personalization allows mailers to leverage the power of targeting like never before to improve customer relationships and generate repeat business. For example, a mortgage company mailed sequentially a three-part series of highly personalized communications consisting of two postcards and a promotional letter as a follow-up to phone inquiries. They achieved 11 times the normal response rate and garnered US$7million from the first mailing.

3.2 Customization

Customization is key to increasing business turnover, and the power of Internet self-service to create more targeted mail pieces is undeniable. A US college has stopped publishing 'one-size-fits-all' school catalogs for its diverse base of applicants. Prospective students go online and design their own catalog, selecting specific information on courses, sports, extra-curricular activities – and even tips on area amenities, such as restaurants, bars and theaters. In another case study, a phone company sent customized calendars with the individual customer's name worked into the images in each page. No two calendars were alike. A market research survey estimates that personalized print improves response and read rates by an average of 21 percent.

Financial and health services companies are now tailoring their periodic statements, such as for pension and insurance benefits, to preempt the most likely questions that each individual may have. These new statements, often backed up by e-mail alerts, direct the recipients to personalized self-service websites and provide customized offers and promotions. These new applications transform the traditional 'ritual' of viewing a paper statement into an 'experience' that allows the recipient to consider a promotion or new information. These novel applications are being called 'transpromotional documents'. 'Transpromo' applications have been shown to lift traditional response rates from a few percent to the 20 to 25 percent range (Lintell et al., 2008). In one case study, a French telecommunications company redesigned its monthly statement to offer customized graphs of phone usage patterns and five alternative calling plans. The results were dramatic: the personalized statements drew five times the response rate while cost per response was cut by 75 percent.

3.3 Geocoding

An exciting new development is the application of 'geocoding', or location intelligence, to create new mail pieces. This technique relies on satellite data to tie in the physical characteristics of an address to marketing data. Physical characteristics obtainable from satellite data include precise GPS positioning of a home and geographical characteristics (elevation, flood area, and so on), allowing for unique marketing opportunities. For example, a company sent a postcard that showed each recipient's exact path to a nearby store that was selling a new set of hiking boots, making the shoes among the highest-selling in America in just one week. In another example, a New Zealand company promoting ride-on lawn mowers used satellite data to identify homes with sufficient acreage to promote their expensive product. This highly targeted approach saw 35 percent of recipients take a test ride on the lawn mower and 25 percent of trials resulted in purchases of a product costing upwards of US$1,000.

3.4 Variable Printing

Variable printing on demand (VPOD) in color is truly taking off. While black and white copies are growing at 7 percent in the US, color copies are growing at 19 percent (Infotrends, 2005). Using VPOD, mailers can vary images mail piece by mail piece and produce all the different documents during a single continuous print run without the traditional setup needed between images with static print. As costs per color impression continue to decline, mailers will increasingly develop campaigns based on more targeted, personalized, and customized mail pieces for greater impact and response. To show the power of VPOD, a furniture store used real-time digital images shot by a sales associate while the customer browsed in the display store. Within 72 hours they sent out a customized brochure with the customer's preferred selections. This approach achieved a 10 percent increase in return visits and an increase of 40 percent in dollar sales from those customers. In another example, a university solicited donations with 22 versions of personalized letters and 24 versions of 'buck slip inserts' for last-minute promotions, achieving an increase of 80 percent in donors and 30 percent in donations, while cutting mail volume and expense by 50 percent.

3.5 Leveraging Mail through the Internet

The ability to direct customers to the Internet is a proven way to leverage mail. For example, a distance-learning service personalized its promotional postcard and added a customized URL (uniform resource locator) for each recipient. Now when they go online, customers find targeted web pages for course offerings tailored to their individual educational needs. Response rates increased to more than 10 percent, or five times larger than prior experience; click-through rates reached 57 percent and order conversion topped 30 percent. In addition to using direct mail to drive Internet responses, the Internet also helps to increase the volume of mail. Small mailers can go online and develop fully integrated mailing campaigns. In these services the mailer gets advice, via easy-to-navigate sections, through the entire process of planning a campaign, designing the creative, preparing the mail piece, targeting the distribution, and submitting it for printing and mailing.

In another development, new imaging and two-dimensional coding technologies allow consumers to scan special marks on physical products with their mobile phones and later receive promotional material a few short days after they have left the store.

Marketing applications are increasingly becoming more media intensive, but it takes time to download media-rich web pages, even with high-speed Internet. Response rates increase dramatically when retailers make it easier for customers to browse through offerings on their computers. Users find it much more convenient to receive in the mail a DVD containing a complete database or promotion with pre-programmed navigation than to go to the Internet and download graphic-intensive images.

3.6 Multi-channel Marketing

In 'multi-channel' marketing, mailers avail themselves of several channels for a promotion – such as TV advertising backed up by direct mail. In what is called 'blended channel' marketing, the two channels are combined in the same promotion, such as a geocoded postcard, or a text message sent to the recipient simultaneously to the delivery of a mail-order package in an automated package-delivery station. In short, the convergence of mail with the new technologies is creating new value for senders of mail.

The above technology developments can, of course, be combined into a single mail piece to make the mail more valuable and appealing. Mailers, POs and solutions providers can work together to effect these improvements to the value of mail. Most significantly, postal reform must provide pricing flexibility to enable all parties to take advantage of these developments. For example, pricing mechanisms could provide incentives to stimulate the creation of more mail pieces with higher customer response rates.

4. TECHNOLOGY WILL GIVE RECIPIENTS CONTROL OVER THEIR MAIL PIECES

4.1 Background

Until the mid-nineteenth century, postal services were paid by recipients who, of course, could refuse payment for unwanted items. Many did. When payment switched to the sender and postmen/women could concentrate on delivery, not on collecting payment, carrier productivity increased eightfold (Burke, 1997). Since the introduction of the 'sender-pays-all' model, recipients have had little or no control over the quantity, quality or content of the mail pieces or the timing of their delivery. New strategic thinking is beginning to recognize that technology can help recipients to have greater control over the mail delivered to them and make mail more valuable and efficient. Minah (2006) researched recipient-based services offered by various POs and summarized available and emerging applications. Here we highlight some of the new services that are being facilitated by technology.

4.2 Digital Conversion

Traditionally, incoming mail into a business was sent to a processing department where it was sorted and distributed. At some point, essential but selective information from the incoming document was entered into a company's internal computer systems. Today, digital conversion and archiving allow physical mail pieces to be scanned at the first point of receipt inside a business. The mail piece is then delivered electronically to the intended recipient. Digital copies are archived for future reference. This is a burgeoning application in businesses as they increasingly optimize the handling of incoming mail. At the highest level of application of digital conversion, the documents are merged directly into the database accessible to a 'case worker' such as, for example, a customer service representative at a credit card company who handles customer calls and disputes. This saves times, increases accuracy and, most importantly, allows the clerk to see an exact copy of the complete document that a customer has sent in, rather than only selected transactional data extracted from it.

4.3 Mail Redirection

Mail redirection is also a fast-growing application. Recipients who have moved temporarily or permanently can now submit changes of address online, and this data can be increasingly moved upstream into the postal processing chain to allow for real-time redirection. With current technology, an optical character recognition sorter can consult a database, immediately determine that the intended recipient has moved, and sort the mail piece to the new destination. Previously, mail pieces would usually travel to the final destination where the postman/woman would notice the customer had moved and would mark the envelope with the new address for rerouting through the entire system. Technology now allows for temporary moves, and recipients can choose a variety of forwarding services, priced differently depending on their urgency. Further, combining the prior application of digital conversion with mail redirection, some providers will scan the physical mail on behalf of the recipient, send the electronic facsimile to the recipient on a website, and optionally forward also the physical mail piece in addition.

4.4 Notification Services

Notification services have become easier to use, benefiting from text messaging and e-mail. Some POs will send the recipient a coded message instructing him or her that a parcel is waiting at the post office or at an automated package station for retrieval. Very importantly, prior notification saves addressees an unnecessary trip to the post office when the PO Box is empty. This same service can be used to notify the sender if an urgent item was not delivered due to an incorrect address, without the sender needing to wait for the mail piece to be returned.

Notification services can be combined with mailer redirection to create a dynamic series of delivery addresses that allow a recipient to receive mail at predetermined stops during a multiple city tour throughout a country. For example, this is important for vacationers waiting for urgent documents, or for professionals with high mobility.

4.5 Recipient Subscription Services

Recipient subscription services are now beginning to emerge, whereby recipients pay extra for non-standard features. These can include special delivery times (for example, earlier or later than usual hours, redirection of home mail to the office some days a week, or separate bills from marketing material at delivery). In the past 10 years several POs have implemented software aimed at building and optimizing mail delivery routes. These products are based on a geographic database, and take into account the details of the street network (such as one-way streets, traffic restrictions, and commercial speeds), labor regulations (such as workday duration), and mail volumes. Moving forward, more sophisticated software will allow POs to dynamically reschedule their delivery workforce to meet increasingly variable demands for service. The market for these technologies will depend not only on the interest of senders and recipients in 'tailor-made' delivery features, but also on postal unions' attitude towards potentially disruptive innovation.

4.6 Consumer Preference Databases

Consumer preference databases, or so-called 'opt-in' and 'opt-out' lists, are beginning to proliferate in an attempt to reduce mail clutter and increase relevance. According to the Federation of European Direct and Interactive Marketing, FEDMA, 35 countries worldwide have so far implemented mail preference services (FEDMA, 2007). Online self-service allows recipients to conveniently specify these preferences. A sender can check the preferences of each individual recipient and 'clean' its mass mailing list for maximum relevance. More targeted pieces that result from the use of consumer preference databases have more value for both the sender and the recipient.

4.7 Life Event Services

Life event services refer to the use of databases by mailers to determine when best to advertise goods and services depending on significant events occurring in each recipient's life. Recipients can create databases of 'friends and family' and a list of life events and authorize their release to marketers, who also promote gifts to the recipient at key events, such as birthdays and anniversaries, and promote directly to the recipient, with items such as party goods. These databases can help reduce mail clutter by making each mail piece highly relevant to the recipient.

In short, these new services provide for greater recipient control over the mail received. Postal reform can influence the deployment of these new recipient services in two ways. To the extent that the universal service obligation (USO) is redefined, this process can open or close opportunities for new services to fill or complement any gaps created by that redefinition. Allowing the post to price flexibly and dynamically for extra services requested by recipients can stimulate a richer variety of product innovations.

5. THE CHANGING ROLE OF TECHNOLOGY IN COMPETITIVE POSTAL ENVIRONMENTS

5.1 Background

Over the past 30 to 40 years, the operational priorities of POs have changed. POs worldwide established firm footholds across their respective countries, fulfilling the obligations to deliver mail to each household five or six days a week. They gradually moved from market coverage to volume handling and quality objectives. In successive waves of postal mechanization, many large operators began the process of supplementing or replacing labor with more and more complex tools.

This wave of fully automated systems culminated in the 1990s. Market leaders across the world developed and deployed 'lights out' solutions designed to gradually achieve greater degrees of letter–flat–parcel sortation, item reading, encoding and tracking, as well as data management and delivery optimization. Many smaller POs have not been able to keep up with the larger ones, due to the need for massive investments, but most are looking to eventually implement the same solutions.

The transition from coverage to volume, and eventually speed has created networks that are often ill-conceived for the needs of postal customers in the twenty-first century. Technology trends have been dictated specifically by USOs. The advent of competition – whether from alternative channels or from new POs – changes the role of technology. The ability to cover an entire country and all the addresses within it, the capacity to handle any volume and type of mail, and the necessity to provide certain delivery standards are becoming less critical than the ability to respond to the widening spectrum of customer needs.

Using the example of the carrier and logistics industry, it is abundantly clear that most leading companies are defined by the quality of service they provide to their customers.

Competitive pressures have finally prompted the POs to put their customers at the forefront of their future strategies.

Let us attempt to envisage the technology impact of such changes.

5.2 First Mile

Customer perception of retail counters and post offices are the emblems of most postal problems. One of the most complained about issues in any country is waiting time and customer experience. In the case of waiting time, POs have already deployed solutions to alleviate the human factor. Automated kiosks and vending machines as well as terminals are sprouting all over the world. Interestingly enough these technologies are not new and have been used with varying degrees of success for the past 10 to 15 years.

One of the least understood elements of automated first-mile services is the need to develop solutions that are intuitive enough for anyone to understand and use without postal personnel on stand-by to help. Most of the time, these solutions are not user friendly. The appearances of avatars[3] and artificial intelligence coupled with better ergonomics have yet to be fully exploited in postal environments.

Another problem is that the entire lifecycle of the solution is not always taken into account. As a result, maintenance and servicing are still too complex and time consuming. Many of the solutions still require dedicated land lines and are unable to operate in dual modes (stand-alone versus always connected). The advent of Wi-Fi and wireless connectivity requirements adds another layer of complexity, and another challenge for suppliers of kiosks and vending machines to take up.

5.3 Mail Preparation

One of the hardest processes in mail sortation is the first step after collection of all mailstreams into the postal network. This step involves a combination of separating mail by its class, type, size, level of service, and destination. POs have dedicated large investments to develop complex technology to successively process all the mail into discrete batches that can be sorted by automated machines.

Missing from these considerations are the actual needs of customers of all sizes. Large mailers' mail, although it bypasses some of the upstream processes, still runs through the same machines as the mail of smaller mailers. Sorting mail by class forces POs to separate and hold 'lower-class' mail, even in advanced networks, at the cost of precious real estate and square footage. Similarly, direct and promotional mail usually receives the traditional heavy treatment (facing, cancellation, and so on) at the cost of dulling and damaging the face of the envelope, thus undoing some of the value of the mail.

Finally, the notion that centralized mail facilities should process all types of mail goes against the notion of improved customer services. The services and attributes of mail streams (first class, standard mail, parcels, priority, and so on) vary significantly. Most POs have adopted a 'one-size-fits-all' approach to the sorting of mail as part of their optimization strategies. However, dock operations (whether inbound or outbound) are still a time-consuming manual process and time-sensitive mail is often penalized. Some thought is currently being given to creating mail-specific sortation centers, to allow for time-sensitive mail not to be processed in a mixed mail environment.

5.4 Mail Sortation

Mail sortation, whether for letters, flats, or parcels has not fundamentally changed in the past three decades. POs have focused exclusively on fielding faster and more format flexible machines capable of processing, reading, and encoding most of the mail. Yet POs are still using peak processing designs in sizing their sortation pools, which means that most equipment sits idle for more than two-thirds of the day. Current systems still reject between 10 and 30 percent of all mailstreams, forcing POs to partially revert to manual sorting processes. This 'rest mail' issue has been the subject of many attempts at developing new solutions. While reading and decoding technology will eventually reach a plateau read-rate of about 90–95 percent for all mailstreams, the nature of certain items, such as direct mailings, will always prevent full automation.

As mail volumes and mixes evolve, so will the technology to sort them. With addressed advertising mail and parcels becoming more predominant in the future, a need for different sorters is arising. No longer should POs strictly focus on traditional letter and flat sorters. Future technology will gradually shift toward all-purpose conveyance solutions (similar to current carrier systems) with the capability to process and decode all mail types. Already technology providers are fielding advanced concepts that are moving away from pinch-belts and friction feeding and toward tilt-trays and shoe sorters.

Likewise, the old islands of automation (individual un-connected sorters) will disappear to be replaced by continuous processing solutions from reception to dispatch. POs need to step away from discrete event processing to create natural mail flows. This will require both new sorters and new containerization solutions. The requirements of advanced robotics for tasks such as loading and unloading will necessitate wider and standardized acceptance of rigid containers.

Many POs will not need to further improve delivery speed, allowing them to shift the focus to other critical components of quality. POs will eventually procure 'cleaner' sortation technology. One can envisage how 'jam-free' sorters would do less damage to mail pieces, as well as new conveyance systems less reliant upon belts, thus reducing paper pollution and dust.

In the future, we can also expect many POs to use appropriate pricing structures to encourage digital sorting, that is printing and sequenced presorting of mail by large mailers or third parties according to delivery areas. Capgemini (2007) expects 'splitting centers', specialized in optimal handling of containers and bundles of pre-sorted mail, to form the backbone of future sorting processes. In this scenario, the role of traditional sorting of mail would be limited to the handling of unsorted mail from small mailers.

5.5 Distribution

POs, like all logistics providers, have a great impact on the environment due to their extensive transportation needs. While less and less domestic mail relies upon air networks, road haulage and intra-network distribution still necessitate greater degrees of optimization and rationalization.

Again, the example of the carrier operators could guide POs into the future. While most customers are knowledgeable with United Parcel Service (UPS) tracking technology, few realize that the solution was initially developed as an operations management tool to improve and optimize internal processes.

POs are gradually installing the data capture and information technology (IT) architecture required to perform such tasks, but the typical mail volumes of most POs make the investments daunting. As POs evolve into more customer- and environmentally friendly organizations, they will need to rely more heavily on advanced modeling, simulation, optimization, and decision support tools.

The tracking tool by itself has limited functionality. With added data intelligence, POs could gradually improve not only their networks but also make better use of their facilities. Visibility into all levels of operations, from machine-level through to network-wide real-time management, will lead the POs to greater efficiencies, improve customer experience, and facilitate the interchange of data between mailers, third parties – for example, mailing houses and other upstream operators – and the PO. Finally, with predictive modeling, postal executives will be able to better forecast utilization and optimize delivery times by streamlining current batch processes.

This level of control could be the source of many future services, for example, recipient-based services. These enabling technologies will allow POs to increasingly offer more choices such as specific delivery dates for certain mail types, or actual delivery time windows, or dynamic addressing for certain businesses.

5.6 Last Mile

The delivery process typically accounts for up to 50 percent of all postal operating costs, mostly because of its huge reliance on the human factor to reach every address. As with other postal processes, most POs have attempted to save labor costs. The most common approach has been the attempt to rationalize upstream processes to save on 'in-office' time and allow delivery personnel to cover more routes each day.

In most cases, this practice has created new streams of pre-processed mail being shipped to the last-mile post offices 'ready to deliver'. This approach fails to consider that multiple bundles of mail still need to be reconciled before initiating delivery route. Last-mile personnel in many European and North American POs are now faced with a mix of machine-sorted letter bundles and machine-sorted flat bundles, as well as parcels and unsorted letters and flats still requiring some 'in-office' processing.

While a small number of large industrialized POs have fielded new enhanced flats sorters, only one, the US Postal Service, has tried to automate the co-mingling process before shipping the mail to the post offices. This effort has proved so far incomplete, and the Postal Service is rather trying to route-sequence its letter and flat streams separately. While there is potential for vendors to develop the ultimate sorter in the future, investments and associated costs will limit this solution to a very small number of POs worldwide.

One last factor not to be overlooked in any technology roadmap is the human element. POs and delivery companies, specifically in industrialized countries, have invested heavily in trying to reduce the size of their labor pool; however employee skills, more than technology, are the ultimate competitive differentiator. Even UPS, which has historically spent some US$1 billion a year on IT systems, is still heavily reliant upon its human assets. Except for the ubiquitous conveyance and distribution technology, UPS personnel do most of the package handling, scanning, sorting, and truck loading. Technology is seen as an added value, not a core strength.

Ultimately, customer needs and competition shape the use of technology by the POs, forcing them to strike difficult balances between conflicting objectives: rationalize operations in order to decrease costs but optimize operations that support an increased range of products aimed at different customer segments; train and empower the labor force but at the same time decrease labor costs and consider outsourcing non-core activities or increasingly hiring part-time or lower-paid workers.

6. RECENT IMPACTS OF SECTOR REGULATION ON INNOVATION

Looking back on the implementation of new postal regulatory frameworks in industrialized economies, we can identify several examples of sector-specific regulation that have directly impacted on the pace of innovation: regulation of quality, technical standardization, and accounting requirements.

6.1 Regulation of the Incumbent's Service Quality

The more stringent the quality of service objectives are, the more pressure there is on the POs to innovate in terms of processes, equipment and software to meet mandated quality targets.

The most conspicuous example of innovation spearheaded by quality regulations is the dramatic improvement of cross-border quality of service across the European Union (EU) since the mid-1990s (Figure 10.1). Coordinated by the International Postal Corporation, joint efforts from the POs started at the same time as the political debate over postal liberalization in Europe in the early 1990s. The 1997 Directive objective required POs to deliver 85 percent of cross-border intra-EU mail within three days of posting. Additional requirements stemming from the REIMS terminal dues agreement also put more pressure on POs to improve the processing of their cross-border mail flows. The percentage of mail delivered within three days of posting grew from 69 percent in 1994 to 95 percent in 2006. Process improvements included the adoption of tracking technologies for international dispatches, the streamlining of operations (sorting, traying, transporting), and the rationalization of accounting processes.

Simultaneously additional requirements set by the directive that quality for cross-border and domestic services be measured by reliable, independent means also created a new market for RFID cards[4] and related IT equipment and software across the EU.

In the future, while quality targets protect mailers and recipients, regulators will need to make sure that the controls in place do not stifle product innovation. In several countries, some or all domestic bulk-mail products have already been removed from the universal service, thus letting market forces determine which optimal quality attributes (beyond speed and reliability) business mailers want and how much they want to pay for them. This trend should accelerate in the next few years.

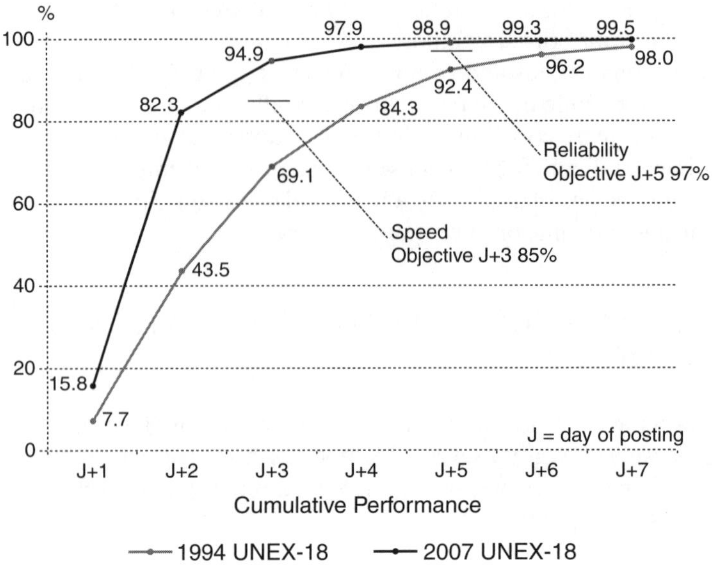

Source: ipc.be.

Figure 10.1 Intra-EU quality of service results for cross-border mail, 1994–2007 (percentage of mail items delivered within three days and five days of posting)

6.2 Regulation of Standards

The development of interoperability among postal networks has been a cornerstone of the development of a single market for postal services across the EU. In 1997, the First Postal Directive entrusted the European Committee for Standardization (CEN) with the responsibility for developing interoperability standards. The European Commission has over the years issued other 'standardization mandates' refining the scope of CEN work. The Universal Postal Union, working closely with CEN, has also driven the effort to develop worldwide standards.

Addressing standards, for instance, allow mailers and POs worldwide to determine whether an address is properly formatted based on address rules for each country of destination. It is this sort of technical standard that provides the basis for growth in the sector and the development of new products and applications for POs and customers alike (Critelli, 2004).

6.3 Cost Accounting Requirements

Legal or regulatory requirements to set up transparent cost accounting systems are another key component of regulatory frameworks. Cost accounting systems are needed for the regulator to verify that prices are geared to costs, or that the incumbent does not abuse its dominant position. In the EU, POs, building on the requirements set out in Article 14 of the Postal Directive[5] have revamped and further computerized their internal accounting systems and processes.

Accurate cost accounting systems are also key to the assessment of investment, operating changes and product policy decisions. For instance, they allow POs to measure the cost of their different channels, and therefore assess the value of alternative solutions they may consider implementing (for example, better measure the cost savings generated by alternative evidencing methods versus stamps, postal kiosks versus manned counters, handheld terminals versus paper-based forms).

7. CONCLUSION

Recitals 7 and 14 of the Third EU Postal Directive (2008/6/EC) summarize the background to our chapter:

> [Postal markets] have undergone dramatic changes in recent years, a development that has been driven by technological advancements and increased competition resulting from deregulation . . . There are a number of drivers of change within the postal sector, notably demand and changing user needs, organizational change, automation and the introduction of new technologies, substitution by electronic means of communication and the opening of the market. (Official Journal of the European Union, 2008)

Against this backdrop, we have argued that technology applications play a key role in maintaining the value proposition of mail. Some of these technologies are mailer driven, others, such as recipient-based services, give users greater control over the mail they receive. In parallel, technological advances in the value chain, such as predictive modeling or continuous collection-to-dispatch processing solutions, will increasingly allow POs to further improve their efficiency, and offer more choices to users.

Most of these changes would not have been possible if regulatory frameworks had not changed. Mandated quality objectives or cost accounting requirements have started to affect the pace of technological change in the POs. In the future, decisions regarding price controls, access, and universal service will increasingly shape the appetite of the POs – and their competitors – for technological change. In competitive environments, for instance, POs will be given increased flexibility to implement value-based pricing, that is, prices based on how customers perceive the 'inherent value' of a postal product. Value-based pricing can promote the adoption of innovation by the POs, but can also, in some cases, encourage mailers to switch to alternative media, therefore stifling further innovation. This would be the case if, for instance, a PO set the price of direct mail in relation to the return on investment earned by the mailer from his/her use of this medium.

Labor regulations, in the shape of national labor laws or sector-specific collective bargaining agreements, may lead entrants to favor product differentiation and introduce added-value products versus engage in pure price competition with the incumbent. In addition, strong regulations increasing the PO's labor costs and decreasing labor flexibility may reduce the incentive for the PO to outsource non-core activities. Burdensome or ill-defined 'one-size-fits-all' USOs of the past constrained product and process innovations. Reduced USOs, as regards the first or last mile, could also help channel the PO's resources towards more innovative services, for instance, recipient-based services.

Finally, it is still unclear whether 'unbundling' the PO's value chain – separating from an operational or financial standpoint 'upstream' from last-mile activities – would promote technical innovation (as it did in the telecommunications industry in the US in the wake of the Carterfone ruling of 1968 and the AT&T breakup in 1982/84) or would hinder it. At first glance, it would definitely promote technologies allowing for the seamless interconnection of networks and the interchange of data between all players involved.

Posts in the twenty-first century will need to rethink their core focus: the end customer. If customers perceive the value of mail, it will remain a relevant communication tool and business mailers will keep on generating new mailstreams. Stable regulatory models serving in each country the interests of senders and recipients will help POs innovate and make mail a more targeted, effective and environmentally friendly medium.

NOTES

1. The 'SELG scenario' term was coined in Jimenez (2003).
2. While an 'insert' is a separate piece of promotional material added inside the envelope, an 'onsert' consists of a promotion printed directly on the mail piece, for example, in the body of a bill or statement.
3. An avatar is a computer user's representation of him- or herself, for instance in the form of a two-dimensional icon (picture) used by a company as a way of interacting with consumers and guiding users around a website or kiosk screen.
4. Radio Frequency Identification: a method of identifying unique items using radio waves. Typically, a reader communicates with microchips (or RFID tag) contained in test letters, which hold digital information that uniquely identifies each letter. Readers are installed at key points along the mail-processing pipeline, allowing a precise, neutral measurement of processing times.
5. This article mandates universal service providers to 'keep separate accounts within their internal accounting systems at least for each of the services within the reserved sector on the one hand and for the non-reserved services on the other'.

REFERENCES

Most of the Pitney Bowes papers and presentations can be found at www.postinsight.com.

Burke, J. (1997), *The Pinball Effect: How Renaissance Water Gardens Made the Carburettor Possible and Other Journeys Through Knowledge*, Boston, MA: Little, Brown.

Capgemini (2007), 'European Postal Perspective, Facing the Challenge from Low Cost Posts', Paris, November.

Critelli, M. (2004), 'New partnerships and new practices for an efficient world postal sector', unpublished speech to the World Postal Strategy Forum, Universal Postal Union (UPU) Congress, September 17.

Diakova, E., C. Szeto and L. Jimenez (2006), Generational analysis of mail users', in M.A. Crew and P.R. Kleindorfer (eds), *Progress Toward Liberalization of the Postal and Delivery Sector*, New York: Springer, pp. 281–300.

FEDMA (2007), 'The Global Guide to Preference Services and Robinson Lists 2007', Federation of European Direct and Interactive Marketing, Brussels.

Fu, A. (2007), 'Bills, Statements and Payments – Paper and Electronic Delivery', Pitney Bowes 'Future of Mail' paper published in www.PostInsight.com, August.

IDC (2007), 'Worldwide Email Usage 2007–2011 Forecast: Resurgence of Spam Takes Its Toll', Framingham, MA, USA.

Infotrends CAP Ventures (2005), 'The Evolving U.S. Digital Color on Demand Printing Opportunity', Weymouth, MA, USA, April.

Jimenez, L. (1988), 'Forces that influence use of technology in postal systems', Arthur D. Little, paper presented at Advanced Technology Conference, Washington, DC, May.

Jimenez, L. (2002), 'Influence of new technologies on the postal network over the next ten years', Arthur D. Little, paper presented at Universal Postal Union (UPU) Future Post Strategy Conference, Geneva, Switzerland, October.

Jimenez, L. (2003), 'Evolution of mail, lower growth, bigger challenges', presentation at Pochtovaya Troika 2003, St. Petersburg, Russia, June.
Jimenez, L. (2004a), 'Emerging postal technologies', presentation to the UK's Postal Services Commission, Stamford, CT, February.
Jimenez, L. (2004b), 'Key trends in mail and document management', presentation at Morgan Stanley's Corporate Services Offsite, White Plains, NY, October.
Jimenez, L. (2005), 'Allied forces, mail has a future in a multi-channel world', in *Postal Technology International*, UKIP Media and Events, September, p. 46.
Jimenez, L. (2006a), 'The value of mail in a multi-channel world', paper presented at National Postal Forum, Orlando, April 4.
Jimenez, L. (2006b), 'The new mailstream, from substitution to convergence', keynote speech at PostExpo 2006, Amsterdam, October 10.
Jimenez, L. (2007a), 'Adding value to mail through innovation and convergence', paper presented at European Postal Services Conference, Institute of Economic Affairs, Lisbon, March 21.
Jimenez, L. (2007b), 'The changing mailing industry, dealing with convergence', paper presented at Global Envelope Alliance Conference, Berlin, June 4.
Jimenez, L. (2007c), 'Bringing together electronics and mail', Guest Column in *Postal Technology International*, UKIP Media and Events, March, p. 16.
Jimenez, L. (2007d), 'Can the Internet help mail grow?', paper presented at World Mail & Express, London, May 23.
Jimenez, L. and G. Garcia (1996), 'Is postal automation working?', in *Postal Technology International*, UKIP Media and Events pp. 90–95.
Jimenez, L. and M. Morelli (2006), 'Postal technology – today and tomorrow', in *Postal Technology International*, UKIP Media and Events, April, p. 50.
Jimenez, L., A. Owsiany and C. Szeto (2006), 'Scenarios of mail receipt patterns across generations', in M.A. Crew and P.R. Kleindorfer (eds), *Liberalization of the Postal and Delivery Sector*, Cheltenham, UK and Northampton, MA, USA: Edward Elgar, pp. 293–306.
Lintell, M., B. Tisdahl and L. Jimenez (2008), 'Transpromotional documents, an emerging innovation', paper presented at the 13th Pitney Bowes Leadership Roundtable, Whistler, BC, Canada, February.
Minah, E. (2006), 'Household recipient-based services', Pitney Bowes internal study.
Nader, F. and M. Lintell (2008), 'Mail Trends Update', Pitney Bowes research report.
Official Journal of the European Union (2008), Directive 2008/6/EC of the European Parliament and of the Council of 20 February 2008 amending Directive 97/67/EC with regard to the full accomplishment of the internal market of Community postal services, 27 February.
Pitney Bowes (2005), 'Growing the Mailstream: Case Examples from Around the World', Cooperative Research Study, December.
Poga, C. (2003), 'Technology Implementation in Selected Postal Administrations', Pitney Bowes report, December.

11. Postal reform and product innovation*

Leon A. Pintsov[†] and Andrei Obrea[†]

The multitude is more constant and wiser than the monarch.

(Niccolò Machiavelli, 'Discours', 1517)

1. INTRODUCTION

The postal sector is now facing the most challenging period in its history. On the one hand, up to now the postal sector in its letter-mail market has not faced competition as a result of the historic reserved areas and, in the case of the United States, the letterbox monopoly. On the other hand it is confronting formidable competition from outside of its traditional boundaries (this type of competition is frequently referred to as 'electronic substitution'). The main intent of the postal regulatory reform is to unlock the benefits of competition in the letter-mail market. These benefits have been extensively discussed with the main focus mostly on cost reduction and increasing service reliability. However, these benefits, even if achieved, would still seem to offer a rather modest response to the challenges facing the sector. Furthermore, since electronic substitution extends competition well beyond the bounds of the traditional postal sector, sector-specific regulatory instruments are limited in their ability to deal with this challenge.

This chapter addresses these challenges by offering a constructive solution to one of the basic imperatives of postal reform, the need to facilitate radical changes in the capabilities of postal service providers to undertake product innovation. The solution is based on far more extensive use of e-commerce technology than is currently being practiced. There are evident complementarities between many elements of e-commerce and much needed new postal products. The key is to put a platform in place that is sufficiently flexible to allow postal customers themselves to enlarge the scope and actively engage in product innovation. This is in the spirit of 'We are smarter than me!' (Libert and Spector, 2007) and the open (network-centric) innovation movement (Nambisan and Sawhney, 2007) and other recent treatises that have made plain that the locus of marketing and product design must encompass and leverage customers' knowledge rather than simply 'marketing existing products to them'. Business as usual in terms of marketing and product innovation is likely to be a failing strategy given the increasing integration among the Internet, the Web and business customers. Under these circumstances, including the climate of the postal reform, we argue that there is a huge need to transform the boundaries of postal operators from opaque curtains concealing a nineteenth-century product innovation process and technology, to a system of open innovation that has the ability to capture customer needs and desires and rapidly transform them into value-added products that can be profitably mar-

† Pitney Bowes, Inc.

keted and delivered to these customers. We focus here on traditional postal operators (POs), but many of the arguments as well as the technology platform presented in the chapter apply as well to other carriers and postal service providers. 'Postal products' are referred to simply as 'products'. Every mail item in the postal distribution network is associated with a single product and when we say 'mail item being served', we mean this product. While our technology platform is fully applicable to all categories of mail items, from postcards to parcels and packages, in this chapter we are mostly concerned with its implications for the letter mail because it is the main target of postal reform.

The chapter proceeds as follows. In Section 2, we describe postal product design and innovation as it is practiced today and its major shortcomings. In Section 3 we discuss a customer interface platform that effectively leverages the trends of e-commerce and Internet-enabled communications in the postal sector. We propose a new integrated product innovation and consumption framework that arguably has the required properties to adapt to and profit from e-commerce trends by promoting rapid product customization. We refer to this framework as 'e-postal commerce' defined as a set of activities aimed at product innovation (design), marketing and consumption. The product design aspect of e-postal commerce is shaped by the new and increasingly popular paradigm of open (network-centric) innovation. Section 4 provides a technical description of the major component and enabler of our framework, namely the Extensible Postal Product Model and Language (EPPML). The power and flexibility of EPPML is illustrated by an example of a new product customized for a specific application (damaged mail). In Section 5 we sketch the process of designing and using products in the EPPML-enabled open innovation environment. The main purpose of this section is to give a reader the flavor of e-postal commerce from a system viewpoint. In Section 6 we examine numerous advantages of the proposed framework for various aspects of mail communications as well as the challenges facing POs in adopting this framework. We conclude by summarizing the most salient benefits of e-postal commerce (as a system) and EPPML (as a tool) for postal operators facing formidable challenges as a result of postal reform and widespread adoption of electronic communications.

2. PRODUCT INNOVATION TODAY

In this section we describe the current approach to product design and innovation practiced by the majority of POs and the tensions affecting this approach, both those driven by competition and complementarities with electronic media as well as those launched or reinforced by the impact of the postal reform. We are concerned mostly with business mail and mailers since their communication needs and desires are more intricate than similar needs of the households and individual users. However, our approach and underlying technology works equally well for all categories of mailers, and when we refer to mail recipients we usually mean households and businesses alike.

The notion of the postal product is a complex one. We first readily observe that unlike common products (food, clothing, books), that are bought and consumed every day, postal product consumption requires closer cooperation between producers (POs) and consumers (mailers and recipients). This cooperation frequently involves a degree of sophistication on the part of the mail producers, specifically in meeting various access requirements imposed by POs. For example, a mail unit that requires tracking through the postal network must have an identifier, real or virtual. The real identifier must be printed or otherwise attached to the mail unit being tracked and must meet stringent postal requirements with regard to its data content, representation and placement. It is a responsibility of the mail item producer to make it compliant with postal requirements. For this reason we view the postal product consumption as a result of (frequently complex) interactions between mailer and PO.

Our second observation concerns the evolution of products, which has occurred over many years. Traditional products were first and second class mail as well as basic parcel services. These products commonly meant an obligation on the part of the PO to take a mail item at an induction point and deliver it to its destination point within a pre-specified period of time. Responsibilities of mailers, who for the most part were viewed as paying customers, included creation of the mail item containing legible indication of the destination address and deposit of the mail item into the postal network. These original products, first introduced in the industrial world in the mid-nineteenth century, are still with us. They were later complemented by additional 'value-added services' such as certified and registered mail, mail with tracking and tracing capabilities, mail with confirmation of delivery, express mail and the like. These value-added services and their features evolved as a response of POs to the growing needs of mailers and were viewed as incremental features built on the top of the 'basic' first or second class services. In some instances to accommodate delivery of new products, POs were forced to change (as is the case with the track-and-trace mail) or completely bypass (as is the case with registered mail) the mainstream processing flow and equipment. The process was slow and expensive and introduction of new products was clearly painful. The speed of product introduction was also aggravated by the regulatory environment whereby new products were to be approved via often protracted and complex regulatory processes (for example, 'rate cases' in the USA). The traditional process of product design and approval is also with us today (a recent example being the eight-year cycle of the 'intelligent mail' product in the USA – see, for example, USPS, 2002 and 2007).

Product innovation has not been the only slow process in product development, adoption and use. Once new products were introduced, their penetration was also slow due to multiple difficulties associated with increasingly complex access requirements facing potential users. While the situation is significantly better with the innovation of parcel products (attributed by many to forces of competition), there are still many untapped opportunities in this area as well.

In short, the process of product innovation has remained essentially unchanged for decades while mailers' and recipients' communication needs evolved significantly as a result of the development of new technologies (e-commerce) and the advent of ubiquitous networked computing as well as a general evolution of business and economy. The deficiency of traditional product innovation is illustrated by first class mail, which is already declining in volume because of electronic substitution. It is not difficult to see why basic information communication products such as first and second class mail are good targets for electronic substitution. These products are fundamentally unable to compete with electronic delivery of personalized information on the basis of cost and speed. While electronic delivery of information is not entirely free of defects, its ability to adapt and its speed of adaptation is much better than what is currently being offered by traditional

postal product innovation and development. On the other hand, there are complementarities between mail and electronic communications. For example, many POs are offering, or contemplating offering, 'electronic proof of delivery' (for example, Royal Mail), electronic track and trace (United States Postal Service: USPS, TNT) or 'redirections online', (Royal Mail). Importantly, these examples suggest that mail is increasingly being viewed as a collection of communication products, each of which has both physical and electronic aspects (the so-called 'data services') that are integrated into a single product.

In part driven by a changing role of mail in the modern economy and society, European and North American governments embarked on a course of postal reform. The reforms envisaged were intended to unlock the benefits of competition. These include potential benefits such as reduction in costs (resulting in lower prices for users) and improvements in service quality. These outcomes of postal reform are well studied and hardly need any additional discussion (Crew and Kleindorfer, 1992).

Of interest here is the further expectation that the opening of the postal sector to competitive pressures would result in significant product innovation (some regulators even allow essential pricing flexibility for new products – for example, Postcomm in UK and BNetzA in Germany). However, these expectations have yet to materialize. Available data concerning introduction and usage of new products are sketchy. For example, volume of delivery receipt services (a relatively new group of services offered by USPS) exhibit a growth from approximately 400,000 to over 1,100,000 pieces from 2001 to 2007 generating over $660,000 in revenue (Revenue, Pieces and Weight (RPW), USPS Reports 2001–2007). Another example of a new product that has recently been introduced by USPS is a premium forwarding service (PFS), allowing US mail recipients who temporarily relocate to another US address to have their mail forwarded for up to a year. In little over two years since PFS introduction in 2005, it has attracted approximately 300,000 customers and generated over $25 million in revenue. However, in both cases the total number of pieces, customers and associated revenues are miniscule in the context of the world's largest postal operator. These examples indicate on the one hand a growing interest and demand for new services, while on the other, difficulties of defining such services and of providing easy and convenient access to them. The latter observation concerning difficulties of selecting and accessing products is also confirmed by the USPS's new program designed to help small and medium-sized business owners and customers select the best products and services for their needs. In this program, USPS retail associates are trained to interact more personally with customers, identify their mailing needs and provide the best possible service.

Thus, available information unambiguously indicates that postal product innovation is (a) almost invisible in most POs, (b) absolutely necessary in order for mail products to keep pace with the Internet age and (c) a ripe target for significant investments in the context of a new competitive environment ushered in by postal reform. We contend that the method and the process of new product design, marketing, delivery and consumption as it is commonly practiced today by many POs and their customers is obsolete and serves as a major impediment to a more effective employment of mail.

3. PRODUCT INNOVATION AND E-POSTAL COMMERCE

In this section we consider the problem of product innovation from a different perspective. Our approach is derived from two sources. First, the development and technical evolution of e-commerce, and the role of standards such as HTML (hypertext markup language), offer valuable insights. Specifically, the HTML standard enabled information capture, presentation and sharing common to all e-commerce services and resulted in a rapid and broad adoption of these services. Second, the concept of open source innovation (or 'network-centric innovation', following Nambisan and Sawhney, 2007) allows all interested parties (for example, users, independent developers, inventors, academic researchers and so on) to participate in the innovation process. A combination of insights from these developments suggests a new approach to product definition and innovation.

More precisely, we view product innovation as an information-gathering and processing activity. This activity is focused on determining what attributes of postal products are of value to various groups of customers and on translating this knowledge into profitable products. In the process, several questions arise. Who should orchestrate this activity and what sources of information should be considered? How in practice should these sources be tapped and how should such information be processed in order to arrive at new products that can be quickly and profitably developed and marketed? These are fundamental questions that should be answered with clarity and precision.

There are many possible configurations of actors, controls and governance structures for network-centric innovation. Given the centrality of the traditional PO and the universal service obligation (USO) in mail networks, however, it seems clear that national POs will be the focal point for such innovation for the foreseeable future. Thus, after analyzing various models of open innovation, the 'orchestra model' of Nambisan and Sawhney (2007) seems the most suitable governance model at least at the present (and early) stage in the evolution of product innovation toward open models (Figure 11.1). In this model the innovation space is the space of postal products. Mailers, large and small, and recipients generate new product concepts and communicate them to the network leader (PO) using the common platform defined and controlled by the PO. Competitors also have access to the same common platform to innovate their products in communication with mailers and recipients.

Thus, in the case of e-postal commerce the PO acts as the conductor, or prime mover, of innovation. In the spirit of open innovation, this does not preclude, as already mentioned, other postal service providers and mailers from developing or cooperating in the design of new products. It simply recognizes the key role that the PO, as universal service provider, will continue to play for the near future.

The product innovation process may be viewed as a collection of information gathering and processing activities. The outcome of these activities, the product itself, can therefore also be viewed as an informational object. It is a natural requirement to make this informational object (product) processable by computers while preserving its familiar human interpretation. This requirement is due on the one hand to complementarities with e-commerce, including its associated pervasive computerization of communications, and the fact that the vast majority of mail is created and processed either directly under the control of or significantly assisted by computers. On the other hand, in the context of this chapter, mail communications are components of business applications (for example,

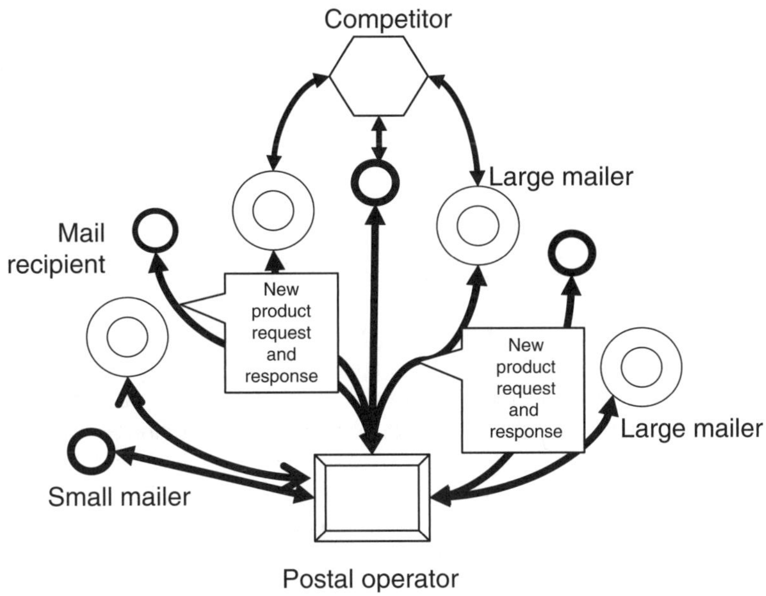

Figure 11.1 The orchestra model of product innovation

accounts payable, customer relations management, investor relations and the like). These business applications are controlled by human owners who are the primary source of information for product innovation. These human owners (mail users) need a convenient and easy-to-use mechanism to express their mailing needs, desires and concerns. The major functions of the conductor in the innovation orchestra model is (a) to enable diverse and globally dispersed (mail) users to converse using the same vocabulary, (b) to gain knowledge from information received from them and (c) to integrate that knowledge with internally developed information to design and deliver final products. In this framework, one of the major enablers is a common vocabulary powerful enough to express the wishes of users and POs and formal enough to be understood by computers. We describe the essence of such a 'vocabulary' in detail below.

Turning now to the consumption (use) of new products, it is useful to view this as the collection of information and physical processing activities associated with mail item production, induction, processing, transportation and delivery. In the developed world, physical activities sufficient for the consumption of new products are primarily computer driven. The sources of the information that are critical for the product use are constraints imposed on the mail item production, induction, processing, transportation and delivery due to restrictions of processes, materials and equipment involved. In order for the orchestrated innovation process to work, these constraints must also be expressible using a common vocabulary.

Finally, in a regulated postal market the regulatory process could also be viewed as a source of product development conditions and constraints and regulators likewise need a common vocabulary to express these. While it is a subject of separate research, we claim that regulatory conditions and constraints are expressible using the same common vocabulary that can be used for representation of users and POs' preferences and constraints. Thus, the unfulfilled need for a common and formal vocabulary emerges as a fundamental enabler of the open product innovation process. In the next section we describe such a vocabulary. Thereafter, we sketch an integrated framework (platform) that makes use of this vocabulary in providing backbone infrastructure and enables product innovation process in e-postal commerce.

4. EXTENSIBLE POSTAL PRODUCT MODEL AND LANGUAGE

A postal product as an informational object can be defined by a formal structure consisting of elements organized as an extensible collection of measurable attributes and their relations. It is convenient to group these attributes and their relations into four categories, namely physical attributes, informational attributes, rules and access requirements.

Physical attributes define the physical parameters of the mail item(s) and the postal network subject to a given product. *Informational attributes* define data to be supplied to the product users (for example, mail items, senders and recipients). These attributes are described in terms of the information that is or could be made available to the PO as a result of its operational or other information-gathering activities related to delivery of the product and its associated mail item. The *rules* define a broad variety of physical, informational and financial activities that the PO would undertake *vis-à-vis* the mail item being served. These activities depend on the conditions that are requested by users (and allowed by the delivering PO(s)) and expressed as relations between physical and informational attributes. The *access requirements* are also specified in terms of conditions imposed on (a) the mail item itself, (b) the information that is required to be collected by the user and electronically communicated to the PO, (c) accounting evidencing and payment instructions including volume or other discounting conditions, (d) packaging and containerization instructions and, (e) the product validity period. There could be other conditions as well, for example, emanating from regulatory requirements (see below).

The best-known example of conditions imposed on the mail item is the so-called 'make up', rules defining data elements that should be present (visible) on the mail item. These data elements are, for example, the destination address block, the product indicator and the postage evidencing data. The rules also control how the data elements should be encoded (for example, via a bar code) and where on the mail item they should be located (for example, two inches from the right edge of the envelope).

A typical example of the electronic information requirement is the statement of mailing submission (also known as the manifest) that describes information pertaining to the entire collection of mail items (CEN/TS 15523, 2006; Pintsov and Obrea, 2008). Other access requirements are self-explanatory. Note that the boundaries between physical attributes and access requirements for the mail item itself are not clear cut. Both can be interpreted as constraints imposed by the PO. We have chosen to consider them as separate categories because of the different amount of control and user sophistication that are required to satisfy them.

The four categories of product attributes and their relations are presented and exemplified in Tables 11.1–4. Table 11.1 describes attributes that are related to the

Table 11.1 Physical attributes

Attribute	Description	Value (example)
Mail item dimensions	Length × width × height	(10–20)″ × (5–9)″ × (0–8)″
Mail item volume	Volumetric measure of allowed mail items	(0–1,000) cubic inches
Characteristics of mail item cover material	Allowed type and parameters of cover material	Any except metal foil
Mail item content	Restrictions on the content of the mail item	No explosives or liquids
Geography of induction	Geographical area where mail item can be inducted (described in terms of a set of postal codes, geocodes or conventional addresses)	USPS zip codes 0600-06999
Geography of delivery	Geographical area where mail item can be delivered (described in terms of a set of postal codes, geocodes or conventional addresses)	USPS zip codes 90000-99999
Priority and routing information	Description of preferred routes (when allowed) expressed in terms of location codes for desirable or undesirable postal facilities	Processing facilities identified by the USPS zip codes 701 to 710 should be avoided
Timing and frequency of collection	Description of when and how frequent mail items can be collected from senders	Every Monday from 9:00 am until 17:00 pm
Timing and frequency of delivery	Description of when and how frequent mail items can be delivered to recipients	Daily except Sundays, once a day in the afternoon

physicality of the mail item and its induction, processing, transportation and delivery operations and exemplifies acceptable ranges for the values of these attributes.

The attributes in Table 11.1 define characteristics of the physical movement of mail items through the postal distribution network. They are quite conventional with the exception, perhaps, of the seventh element 'priority and routing information'. There are well-known instances when mailers would want their mail items to avoid certain postal facilities, for example, when such facilities are contaminated or known for a somewhat more frequent disappearance of mail items. The seventh element in the table allows a mailer to request avoidance of some postal facilities as an exception.

Table 11.2 exemplifies *information* attributes that describe data relevant to the use of mail by the mail senders and recipients. The attributes in Table 11.2 define 'data services' associated with physical movement and processing of mail items. Some are well known and popular, for example, tracking information defined as a special case of event information (CEN/TR 15524, 2006). Some others are either new or barely used. For instance, the third attribute 'information describing objects linked to the mail item' can be used to report certain information that is valuable but inaccessible to the mail sender. If the mail

Table 11.2 Information attributes

Attribute	Description	Value (example)
Event information for the mail item that is being served by the product	Information about events that occurred during mail item processing described in terms of date and location of its occurrence and the nature of the event (significant changes in the values of selected measurable attributes)	Tracking information, delivery confirmation, the mail item defects detected as a result of a scanning event
Event information for mail item(s) linked to the mail item being served	Information about events occurred to other mail item(s) linked to the mail item that is being served	Business reply mail tracking information
Information describing objects linked to the mail item that is being served	Information about objects that are referenced or linked to the mail item that is being served and expressed in a standardized or free format	Characteristics of a building (e.g., residential or office) attached to the delivery mail box identified by the mail item destination address
Information describing mail usage patterns of the recipient or the mailer of the mail item	Information related to the use of mail by the mailer or the recipient	Statistics related to mail sent or received by the sender or the addressee of the mail item

Table 11.3 Example of a rule

Rule	Description	Example
If the mail item is damaged during postal processing, transportation or delivery, redirect the mail item to another pre-specified address	The rule is a description of actions to be taken by the post when the physical and the information attributes associated with the mail item that is being served satisfy predetermined conditions. This also includes remedies for exceptional situations when the product could not be delivered as specified	*If* the weight of the mail item is less than its original weight by 10% or more (as measured at induction) *then* deliver the mail item to the address different from the original delivery address

item containing advertising materials aimed at residential properties is unknowingly addressed by the mailer to an office building, the PO can uncover and relate this fact back to the mail sender.

Table 11.3 exemplifies a *rule* that redirects the mail item whenever it is damaged. Rules allow one to express conditions of almost unlimited complexity. At this point it is hard to

Table 11.4 Access requirements

Elements	Description	Value (example)
Mail item make-up	Data elements that must be present on the mail item in terms of the data content, data format and data placement	Address block must be at least 2″ from the edge of mail envelope; intelligent mail barcode must be in the first line of the address block and must have 13 digits encoded in the four state bar code
Statement of the mailing submission	Electronic data that must accompany mail item(s) including data format and communication protocol	Statement of mailing submission must satisfy requirements of the XML schema defined in CEN Standard 15523
Containerization	Containerization and container labeling requirements	Mail items must be presented in trays labeled according to the XML schema SP 123
Payment	Payment requirements in terms of its timing, method and discount qualifications	Payment for the mail item must be made prior to its induction via electronic transfer into the account ABI 577546899. For mailing of more than 1,000 items there is 10% discount
Product type	Describes restriction on the use of the product by mailers when social products are allowed strictly for social mailers and social communication purposes	Social
Product validity period	Beginning and ending dates when the product is available	From May 14, 2008 to August 5, 2008

constructively describe many different (and creative) ways of using rules in product descriptions. The most important examples involve exceptional situations which are not that infrequent in practice. We expect that in the context of open innovation process rules will be employed in many unexpected ways.

Table 11.4 describes the product *access requirements* that are defined as conditions for product use that must be satisfied by mail producers, mail recipients or both and the product validity period. The access requirements can also be used to enforce regulatory constraints. For example, one of the most effective ways of designing the USO in the open market is to partition mailstream into business and social mail (Crew and Kleindorfer, 2006; (Pintsov et al., 2006). Such partitioning would require a clear segregation of mail intended for commercial purposes from all other mail. Our approach to product definition easily and naturally lends itself to the separation of business and social postal products

and allows for a cost-effective enforcement of such separation. Specifically, each product description could contain the mail type indicator as an attribute whose value would be set to 'social' or 'business', depending on whether the PO would allow the product to be used only for social communications or without restrictions respectively (see fifth element in Table 11.4).

The list of attributes, elements and relations in Tables 11.1–4 is not exhaustive and is merely meant to signify the method of identifying useful attributes rather than the attributes *per se*. The list can be extended or reduced, for example, depending on the outcome of the open product innovation process. Product attributes (whether these are desired by mailers or recipients) may be subject to further restrictions to ensure compliance with relevant data privacy regulations and constraints. The characteristics of a usable product descriptor language exemplified in Tables 11.1–4 are relatively straightforward to incorporate into a formal, computer-based language. Indeed, the formal representation of attributes and elements in the tables that is suitable for computer processing can be made using an XML schema, which is a widely used mechanism to define syntax for XML documents (files) and which can readily express constraints on their structure and content. Thus, postal products can be represented formally as XML documents processable by computers. The same products, of course, have another more familiar representation in the extended plain language description of these used by the human participants in mail communications. The XML-based framework enables the product description to be transformed from its computer representation to its human representation and vice versa with the help of computer software.

Thus, the XML schema that is designed for the product description can serve as a common language of the open innovation process. In this context it is known under the name 'Extensible Postal Product Model and Language' (EPPML), emphasizing its openness for extensions and interpretation by computers (UPU P28 EPPML draft standard 2008[1]). The EPPML is drafted as a dynamic standard adaptable to emerging requirements for new products and new data exchanges.

We shall now proceed with an illustration. Consider a business mailer that receives merchandise from a supplier in China and then sells it via mail order and ships it using a postal service provider. We assume that the postal service provider for this example is a PO. The mailer notices that as a result of multiple handlings the merchandise (a mail item) sometimes arrives damaged, generating undesirable and costly returns processing and multiple unnecessary communications with the intended recipients. The mailer therefore is interested in having the PO detect and segregate damaged mail items before delivery to the recipients, redirecting damaged items to the mailer's repair facility. The mailer further wishes that the PO, upon detection of the damaged mail item, would notify the recipient and the merchant's repair facility using e-mail. Finally, if the damage noted is the result of improper handling by the PO, the mailer may wish in some instances to receive agreed-upon monetary compensation from the PO. The friendly PO discovers that this mailer's needs are not uncommon and offers a new product intended to meet the requirements of an entire segment of mailers with similar needs.

In detecting damaged mail items, one might use formal sensory indicators that could be either emitted signals from a radio frequency identification (RFID) chip in the item, pre-programmed to indicate certain types of damage, or changes in physical dimensions or conditions of the mail item. For example, the following occurrences might be used as

indicators that a mail item is damaged: (a) 10 percent or larger change in the weight of the mail item, or (b) 13 percent or larger change in any dimension of the mail item (height, length, or width). Finally, of course, damage can be detected by human operators via visual observation indicating that the mail item appears damaged (punched, defaced, and so on). In each case, the damage causes a detectable change in the value of one or more attributes of the mail item. The attributes of the mail item that change their value as a result of the handling damage are weight, height, length, width, and damaged (the last attribute takes two values, true or false). As long as these attributes indicating 'damage condition' can be stated formally, they can be implemented by production rules that are easily programmed in EPPML. Thus, 'damage events' are detectable if significant changes occur in any of the aforementioned mail item attributes. The occurrence of the damage events can be computed by comparing observations and expectations taken at different moments in time (CEN/TR 15524, 2006). The main portion of the rule description is the event trigger function that detects the occurrence of the event and the list of actions to be undertaken after the event has occurred and has been detected. While we have focused on 'damage events' in this example, it should be clear that other events of relevance to the mailer or the recipient could also be programmed in the same manner.

We now turn our attention to access requirements. In order to deliver the new 'damage reporting product' described above, the PO would need the alternative address (that is, the address of the mailer's repair facility), the desired amount of the compensation (within the limits set up by the PO) and e-mail addresses of the mailer and the recipient. These elements must be provided by the mailer in or out of bound (that is, directly on the mail item or electronically).

A portion of the EPPML description of the new damage reporting product is shown in Figure 11.2, where *t0* denotes the original mailing (induction) time and *t1* some later time at which a damage condition is detected. The shaded area represents attributes and rules structured in accordance with the EPPML syntax while oval frames on the right-hand side contain values of the attributes. We do not include the explicit description of the access requirements in the figure due to space limitations and because creating such a description is straightforward. The information presented in Figure 11.2 conforms to EPPML order and is automatically processable by computers without human involvement.

The above example is intended to convey two basic thoughts. First, an open innovation model for postal products requires a platform and formal language for defining these products. In the terminology of product innovation (for example, Kogut and Zander, 1992), this platform and language make the definition of new products 'codifiable'. This means that the product can be communicated in a clear and transparent manner between customers and postal service providers and their computers. The second thought conveyed by the example is that designing a platform to ensure open innovation is achievable for a broad array of postal products. Indeed, the prototype EPPML-based platform already exists and can be implemented and supported readily as POs integrate their own operations with Internet-based capabilities for operations and sales. Thus, the approach here is a viable method for creating descriptions of a broad variety of products that are suitable for both human and computer processing, providing thereby a common language that is a prerequisite for the open product innovation.

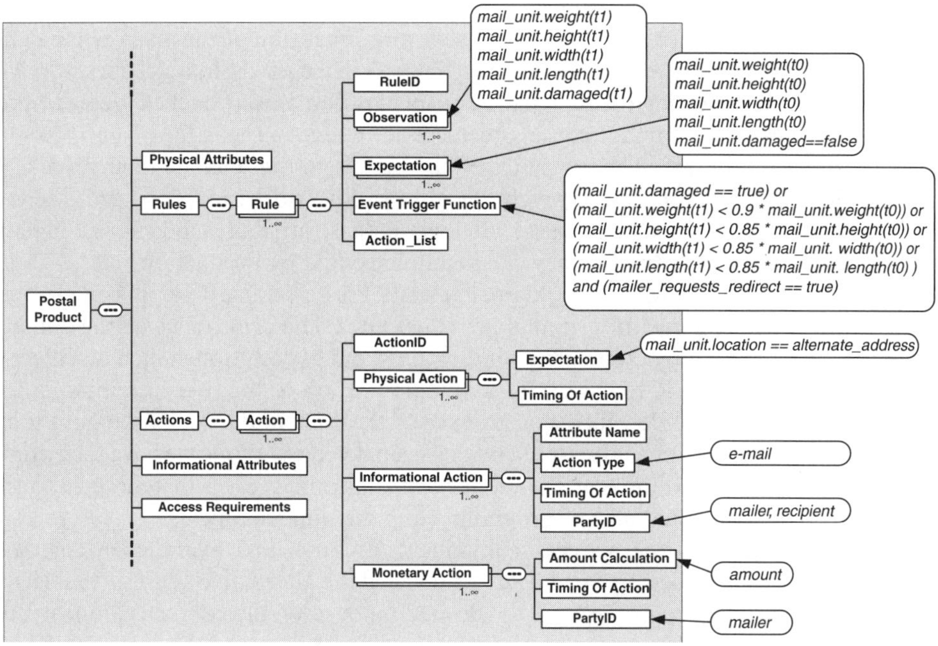

Figure 11.2 Damage reporting postal product as an EPPML document

5. DESIGNING AND USING PRODUCTS IN THE EPPML-ENABLED OPEN INNOVATION ENVIRONMENT

In this section we first give a brief description of the EPPML-enabled postal product development process (Figure 11.3). In our model the product development process consists of multi-round exchanges of information between mailers and recipients on the one hand and the PO (or other postal service providers) on the other. The process starts with the mailers' communication needs, desires and suggestions expressed in a non-technical way (for example, by using familiar terms and requiring minimal or no technical knowledge of the postal network, process or equipment). The mailers' needs are defined by the human owner of business applications that have a significant communication component, for example the CRM (Customer Relationship Management). The owner is prompted by a computer to enter his/her wishes into a computing environment where they are automatically translated into an EPPML document structured in accordance with the EPPML standard (UPU P28, 2008). The resulting document (an application for a new product) is communicated via the Internet directly into the postal product development environment where it is automatically processed. It can then be converted into a familiar human representation (in the case when there is a requirement for human review and supervision). Mail recipients could submit their wishes and suggestions in a similar way. Upon automatic (or supervised) processing of mailers' and recipients' wishes, the postal product development environment computes an EPPML document containing a full description of a candidate product or products except possibly the product access requirements. This

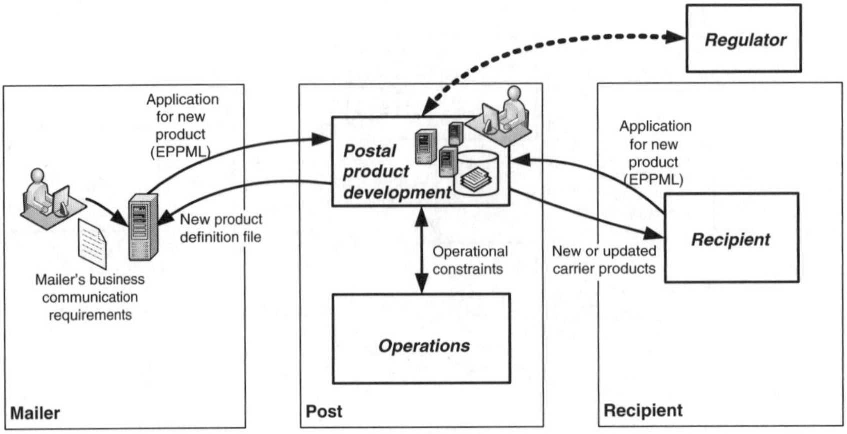

Figure 11.3 Postal product development

description of the candidate product is then forwarded to postal operations, where it is processed by a computer (again automatically or in a supervised manner) in order to determine the candidate product's feasibility and its access requirements. The candidate product is modified if the original candidate is not feasible. After the operationally feasible product has been created, its description (as an EPPML document) is sent back to the product development environment where its cost will be estimated in accordance with the established PO accounting rules. In a regulated setting where products must be approved, the feasible product candidate is negotiated with a regulator, also by using computer assisted processing enabled by the EPPML (O'Brien et al., 2008). If the candidate product is operationally, economically and regulatorily feasible, it is then made available to mailers and recipients, for example, via a postal website (postal data center). In practice this means that an EPPML document containing a full description of the product, including its access requirements (product definition file), can be downloaded into the mailer's operations via the Internet by any suitable computer or a mail assembly and finishing system controllable by a computer.

We now turn to the process of postal product consumption (Figure 11.4), which starts with the downloading of the EPPML-formatted product definition files into the mailer's operations (for example, mail assembly and finishing). Products for downloading are selected using criteria defined by the communication owner. After choosing the best-available product, the mail assembly and finishing system verifies that the product access requirements can be successfully met using the product definition file and generates (automatically or with an operator's assistance) the mail item(s) and all the associated mailing and payment information. Then the mail item is inducted and the mailing information is transferred into postal operations for processing and delivery. Requests for data captured during sorting, transportation and delivery and the resulting information (operational data) are exchanged between the operations and the data center. If the selected product requires delivery of the information to mail users (for example, tracking or confirmation of delivery) the data center transfers this information on completion of the corresponding operation. This information is known as 'customer-directed

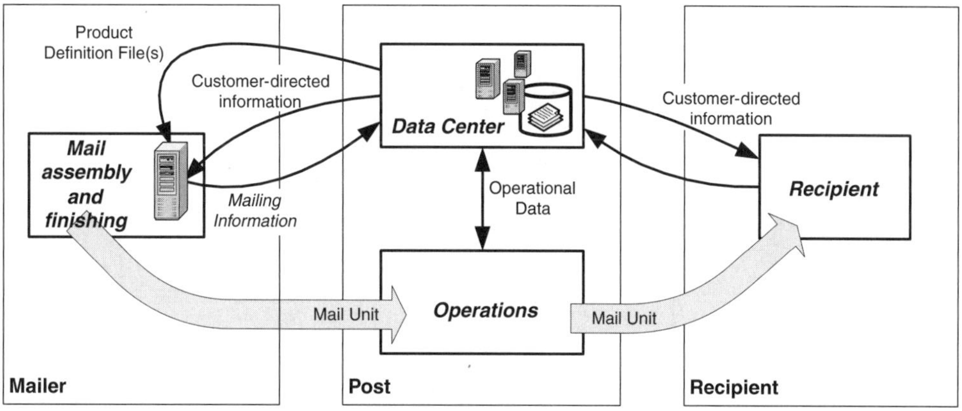

Figure 11.4 Postal product consumption

information', and it is described in detail in the European Standard CEN/TR 15524 (2006). Independently from the mailer the recipient is also enabled to request products related to the mail item via direct communication with the data center.

6. IMPLICATIONS AND CHALLENGES

The proposed EPPML-enabled product development, distribution and consumption processes present a number of benefits. Starting with the end users, the EPPML allows the establishment of an effective communication channel for POs and other postal service providers whereby mailers and recipients have a voice in product design, thus creating a modern marketplace for postal products. The access to new products is automated, avoiding common (and multiple) mail defects that hamper the use and increase the cost of current and future postal products. Postal operations benefit from the information-rich and integrated mailer–post–recipient system due to the reduction of mail item defects arising from incomplete or misinterpreted access requirements. Network and operations planning can achieve dynamic capacity management, network rationalization and process optimization, all benefiting from the availability of up-to-date computerized information from mailers and recipients. The proposed adaptive development model also opens unprecedented opportunities for definition and delivery of demand-driven products. POs will be able to create virtual private communication channels to their customers resulting in customized products and pricing, branding opportunities, simplified contract management and information privacy and integrity. Our approach allows for a much more effective technical cooperation between POs, offering perfect occasion for defining new cross-border mail products, especially cross-border mail that requires data services. In short, EPPML-enabled mail offers an opportunity to make positive and in some instances revolutionary changes in most of the critical PO functions. It is in one sense an expected elaboration of the Internet economy into the domain of e-postal commerce. On the other hand, under postal reform movements worldwide, open innovation may be viewed as a requirement for POs and other postal service providers

to achieve the necessary integration between communications, delivery functions and the e-economy.

Our approach is not without significant challenges, most notably a change to a culture of radical and open innovation that POs would be required to adopt. Although the technology underlying our approach has major benefits even in the more traditional setting of product design via personal interactions with postal customers, focus groups and the like, the effectiveness of this new technology will be greatly diminished in the absence of open innovation. Another significant impediment is the rigidity of postal operations and their supporting IT infrastructure that has been optimized over a period of many years for the cost-effective delivery of simple, high-volume products (for example, first class mail). Also, in a regulated postal environment our approach (requiring maximum flexibility and speed in approval of new products) would potentially collide with many existing regulatory processes. Undoubtedly, effective adoption of the open product innovation suggested here will require significant changes in the regulatory environment. However, despite these formidable challenges, the need for a change in the postal sector is so great and the promise of open innovation is so abundant that POs, carriers and regulators around the world need to begin planning for its implementation soon. The approach suggested here provides a starting point for this implementation.

7. CONCLUSION

We proposed an integrated customer–post framework (e-postal commerce) based on a common product description language (EPPML) that offers unprecedented opportunities in postal product innovation. We argued that e-postal commerce has the adaptive properties conducive to rapid product customization and deployment and the ability to enable quick and convenient access to new products on the part of end users (mail senders and recipients). These new products will be driven by the well- and broadly understood customer needs enabling integration of mail with critical business applications. Equally important, we expect that future developments in the postal infrastructure will be driven by the EPPML product description language. Thus, this language will become a major tool in restructuring mail as a communication media. Then the market opening ushered in by postal reform and the innovation technology proposed here will result in the transformation of the postal market into an economically efficient marketplace. A broad variety and a large quantity of products will be bought and sold and competitive forces will be working to the advantage of mail users.

We have very few doubts about the technical feasibility of our approach and we also believe that we have presented convincing evidence of that. We intend our proposal to open a new era, the era of e-postal commerce, that will be firmly rooted in twenty-first century communication and information processing technologies, and that will actively involve communities of users and suppliers in the design and delivery of postal products. The ultimate aim is to ensure that mail continues to find its proper and prosperous place in the plethora of modern business and communication tools.

NOTES

* This chapter expresses personal views of the authors that do not necessarily represent the views of their employer Pitney Bowes, Inc. We gratefully acknowledge Jim Euchner for his support, insights and unwavering commitment to innovation at Pitney Bowes.

1. Our product innovation approach strongly depends on standardization and interoperability between POs for its widespread adoption and implementation. Indeed multiple product definition languages and supporting access requirements and event definition specifications (if adopted by different POs) would create havoc and confusion. Recognizing this fact, both the UPU Standards Board and the European Standardization Organization responsible for postal standards CEN TC 331 unanimously approved development of the EPPML product definition language standard. Its supporting standards CEN/TS 15523-2006 and CEN/TR 15524-2006 have already been issued in Europe in 2006.

REFERENCES

CEN/TS 15523 (2006), Postal Service – Statement of Mailing Submission.

CEN/TR 15524 (2006), Postal Service – Customer-directed information.

Crew, M.A. and P.R. Kleindorfer (1992), *The Economics of Postal Service*, Boston, MA: Kluwer Academic.

Crew, M.A. and P.R. Kleindorfer (2006), 'Approaches to USO under entry', in Crew and Kleindorfer (eds), *Liberalization of the Postal and Delivery Sector*, Cheltenham, UK and Northampton, MA, USA: Edward Elgar, pp. 1–18.

Kogut, B. and U. Zander (1992), 'Knowledge of the firm, combinative capabilities, and the replication of technology', *Organization Science*, **3**(3), August, 383–97.

Libert, B. and J. Spector (2007), *We Are Smarter Than Me: How to Unleash the Power of Crowds in Your Business*, Philadelphia, PA: Wharton School Publishing.

Nambisan, S. and M. Sawhney (2007), *The Global Brain: Your Roadmap for Innovating Faster and Smarter in a Networked World*, Philadelphia, PA: Wharton School Publishing.

O'Brien, L., L. Pintsov and A. Obrea (2008), 'Cost analysis and pricing of innovative postal products', Abstract for 16th Conference on Postal and Delivery Economics, Albufeira, Algarve, Portugal, 28–31 May.

Pintsov, L.A. and A. Obrea (2008), 'Data requirements for cost accounting in the mail communication system', in M.A. Crew and P.R. Kleindorfer (eds), *Competition and Regulation in the Postal and Delivery Sector*, Cheltenham, UK and Northampton, MA, USA: Edward Elgar, pp. 370–84.

Pintsov, L.A., A. Obrea and T. Biasi (2006), 'Partitioning the mailstream – analysis of an innovative approach to USO', in M.A. Crew and P.R. Kleindorfer (eds), *Liberalization of the Postal and Delivery Sector*, Cheltenham, UK and Northampton, MA, USA: Edward Elgar, pp. 19–35.

Revenue, Pieces and Weight (RPW), USPS Reports 2001–2007, http://www.usps.com/financials/rpw/welcome.htm'. accessed February 2008.

United States Postal Service (USPS) (2002), http://www.usps.com/strategicdirection/fall2002/PromoteDevelopment.htm', accessed February 2008.

United States Postal Service (USPS) (2007), http://www.usps.com/mailpro/2007/janfeb/page11.htm',accessed February 2008.

UPU P28 (2008) EPPML draft standard, Universal Postal Union, Bern.

PART III

Regional and country studies

12. National postal policies in Europe on the eve of the Third Directive

James I. Campbell Jr.,[†] Alex Kalevi Dieke[‡] and Antonia Niederprüm[‡]

1. INTRODUCTION

This chapter offers a snapshot of the national postal laws of Europe as they stood in mid-2006. By this time all of the then 25 member states of the European Union (EU) – even the 10 countries from eastern and southern Europe who joined in early 2004 – had had a minimum of several years to implement the Postal Directive of 1997 as amended in 2002.[1] In 2006, the first draft of a third directive on postal services was still over the horizon.[2] A look back at the state of play in mid-2006 offers both an opportunity to evaluate how earlier reforms turned out in fact and a glimpse into what may be expected in the wake of the recent amendment to the Postal Directive to accomplish 'full market opening'.[3]

In the EU, a 'directive' is a framework law adopted at EU level institutions. To give effect to a directive, member states must adopt national laws that implement the directive. National laws may implement a directive in different ways and in some cases may fail to implement a directive fully. A directive, therefore, leaves room for substantial variation in national postal policies.

A survey of postal practices among member states of the EU, prepared for the European Commission by the authors, revealed a persistent diversity of national postal traditions within the framework of reforming and harmonizing demands set down in the Postal Directive. Of course, these national variations were shaped in part by different appetites for the liberalizing course set by the Postal Directive. But national variations also showed the value of multiple solutions to the same basic task, implementation of the Directive. In several cases, member states developed innovative approaches that advanced the art of postal regulation and thus helped to lay the foundation for the most recent directive.

Section 2 provides an overview of postal reform in Europe. Section 3 summarizes how different member states have chosen to implement the specific commands of the Postal Directive. In organization, it follows the sequence of topics in the Directive. Section 4 offers a few final observations.

† George Mason University.
‡ WIK Wissenschaftliches Institut für Infrastruktur und Kommunikationsdienste.

2. OVERVIEW OF POSTAL REFORM IN THE EU

Spurred by the Postal Directive, as well as by shifting commercial and technological circumstances, national postal laws in the EU member states evolved rapidly and substantially after 1997. In 1997, the average postal law was about 13 years old. By mid-2006, national postal laws averaged less than three years since enactment or major revision. Every member state has amended or replaced its postal law since 1997; some two or three times.

The Postal Directive imposes a range of obligations on member states. To discharge these obligations, governments must act, but they have different ways of doing so. Legislation is the most cumbersome process, reserved for the most politically sensitive issues. Entrusting a decision to the cabinet or a ministry is appropriate for less-sensitive but still fundamentally political issues. Delegation of authority to an independent regulator provides a more economically objective decision. The most economically objective method of decision, however, is the impersonal competitive market. How a member state chooses to allocate authority among these four decision-making procedures indicates the extent to which its postal policy is to be determined by political or economic criteria.

In mid-2006, most member states determined most questions of policy by legislation even though the answers may turn on technical issues better resolved by experts. For example, to decide the appropriate frequency of postal service requires the decision maker to balance the cost of service against the needs of society. In most member states, frequency of service is determined by legislation, although there are exceptions (for example, Germany, France and the Netherlands). Similarly, to determine the economically correct scope of the reserved area – no larger than necessary to ensure maintenance of the universal service (Postal Directive, Article 7(1)) – requires a sophisticated analysis of detailed accounting data, yet in all but two member states, the scope of the reserved area is determined by legislators, not economic experts. On the other hand, some policy issues are typically delegated to government. For example, quality of service standards is more usually committed to the Council, the ministry charged with administration of postal policy, or the national regulatory authority (NRA). Among member states that delegate basic policy questions to government agencies, Italy, Malta, and the Netherlands rely substantially upon a ministry whereas Denmark, Slovakia, and the United Kingdom vest substantial authority in the NRA.

The task of administering postal policy – that is, applying general rules to specific facts – is commonly delegated by parliament to a ministry or to an NRA. Sixteen member states rely exclusively on the NRA or the national competition authority (NCA) for all administrative functions. It is departures from this rule that are noteworthy. In this respect, Austria, Spain, and Italy – and to a lesser extent the Netherlands – stand out for their reliance on a ministry. At the other end of the spectrum, it is interesting to note that Denmark, the Netherlands, and Slovenia vest some administrative functions required by the Directive in the NCA rather than the NRA. Use of the NCA rather than the NRA implies that government is treating the postal sector more like other sectors of the economy and less as a special sector requiring special rules.

Article 4 of the Postal Directive requires member states to designate one or more postal operators as universal service provider (USP). While each member state has designated the 'public postal operator' – that is, a postal operator that is owned in whole or in part

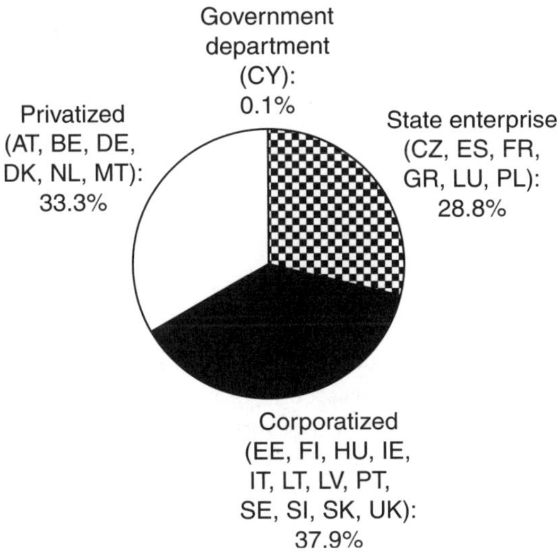

Figure 12.1 EU domestic-letter-post volume by ownership of USP, 2004

by government – as the USP, direct governmental involvement in the operation of USPs is declining. In each member state, the public postal operator was originally organized as a government department administered by a political appointee. In the last quarter of the twentieth century, many public postal operators were converted into state enterprises or at least agencies with a high degree of commercial freedom and flexibility. More recently, many public postal operators have been 'corporatized', that is, reorganized as a public limited company operating under the company law applicable to private corporations. In principle, a postal corporation, like a private corporation, is administered by a board of directors that provides independence from owners. Some governments have withdrawn further from operation of the public postal operator by selling a portion of the ownership of the corporatized public postal operator to the public or to strategic partners.

Even in the two years prior to 2006, corporatization and privatization have advanced in the EU postal sector (Figure 12.1). Latvia, Lithuania, and Slovakia have corporatized their public postal operators, and Poland has announced plans for doing so. The German government has become a minority shareholder of Deutsche Post, reducing its holding from 63 to 42 percent. The Dutch government has lowered its stake in TNT from 35 to 10 percent and plans to sell all remaining shares.[4] In June 2005, the Danish government sold 22 percent of its public postal operator to a British investment group, CVC Capital Partners and 3 percent was reserved for employee incentives. In November 2005, CVC and Post Denmark bought 50 percent (less one share) of the Belgian public postal operator. Austria sold 49 percent of Österreichische Post AG in May 2006. Italy and Poland have also announced intentions to privatize their posts in the future.

In sum, European governments are rapidly withdrawing from direct political control of the postal sector. Governmental decision making is being turned over to less political, more technically oriented bodies. Public postal operators are being reorganized as corporate entities established under the same company law applicable to private companies. The 18 corporatized public postal operators collectively account for approximately

71 percent of the EU letter post. Eight public postal operators are partially privatized, accounting for about one-third of the EU letter post.

3. IMPLEMENTING THE SPECIFIC REQUIREMENTS OF THE DIRECTIVE

3.1 Universal Service Obligation

Article 3 of the Postal Directive declares that 'each Member State shall adopt the measures necessary to ensure that the universal service includes the following minimum facilities': (i) conveyance of postal items weighing up to 2 kilograms and (ii) conveyance of postal packages weighing up to 10 kilograms (or 20 kilograms at the discretion of the member state). 'Postal items' include all types of addressed items, including items of correspondence, books, catalogues, newspapers, periodicals, and postal packages. 'Postal packages' is undefined but seems to refer only to addressed boxes of merchandise.

In mid-2006, all member states established a universal service whose scope includes delivery of letters and parcels, although only about half ensure universal service for newspapers and periodicals. Moreover, as member states contemplate further liberalization, they are reconsidering whether universal service should include *all* letters and parcels or only *single-piece* letters and parcels. The leader in this trend is the Netherlands, where universal service includes only letters covered by the reserved area and non-reserved items carried at the single-piece tariff (Netherlands, Ministry of Economic Affairs, 2004). Although the public postal operator in the Netherlands is no longer obliged by law to deliver bulk mail outside the reserved area, it continues to do so, but contracts for delivery are subject to normal commercial negotiation. Similarly, in the United Kingdom, the NRA, Postcomm, has concluded that most bulk mail should be considered outside the universal service with the exception of two 'entry-level' bulk-mail services accounting for about one-quarter of total bulk mail (UK, Postcomm, 2005a). Ireland (Ireland, ComReg, 2005) likewise appears to be moving towards exclusion of bulk mail from the universal service.

Article 3 further requires member states to ensure adequate *access* to the public postal network. Access includes street mail boxes and postal outlets such as 'post offices' operated by USP employees and 'postal agencies' operated by contractors. Postal access arrangements vary widely among member states. In most, the USP is free to convert a post office into a postal agency without regulatory approval, a minimum number of post offices may be required (for example, 5,000 in Germany). Some member states directly subsidize the operation of post offices (for example, Sweden, and the United Kingdom).

Another key element of universal service is *delivery frequency*. Article 3 requires member states to ensure at least one delivery each working day, not less than five days a week, at all points in the national territory save in extraordinary circumstances. In only three member states does the USP fail to deliver letter-post items five days per week to more than 1 percent of the population (Spain, Greece, and Hungary). Universal delivery for parcels is less assured, however. In eight member states, USPs charge the addressee for delivery of parcels; in two, parcel delivery is unavailable. In Scandinavia, for example, it has long been the custom for addressees to collect their parcels at the nearest post office.

3.2 Reserved Area

Article 7 of the Postal Directive limits the scope of services which member states may reserve for the USP. As amended in 2002, Article 7(1) declares that, as of January 1, 2006, the reserved area may include carriage of items of domestic and incoming cross-border correspondence only if two conditions are met: (i) each item weighs less than 50 grams, and (ii) the transportation charge for each item is less than two and a half times the USP's public tariff for carriage of an item in the lowest weight step of the fastest standard category of service.[5] An item which weighs more or is transported for a higher fee is outside the reserved area and may be carried by a private company. Moreover, even within these weight and price limits, postal services for domestic and incoming cross-border correspondence may be reserved only 'to the extent necessary to ensure the maintenance of universal service'. As of mid-2006, four member states had no reserved area: Estonia, Finland, Sweden, and the United Kingdom.

Article 7 goes on to provide that the reserved area may be extended in two respects. First, the reserved area may include *direct mail* falling within the same price and weight limits but again, only 'to the extent necessary to ensure the maintenance of universal service'. Second, the reserved area may include *outgoing cross-border mail* falling within the same price and weight limits but only 'to the extent necessary to ensure the maintenance of universal service, for example, when certain sectors of postal activity have already been liberalized or because of the specific characteristics peculiar to the postal services in a member state'. As of mid-2006, 14 member states declared a reservation over direct mail while 11 declared a reservation over outgoing cross-border mail (eight member states reserved both).

In practice, the legal status of direct mail is often muddled. In several member states, the precise definition of 'direct mail' has caused confusion, including in Austria, the Czech Republic, Germany, Spain, Italy, Latvia, the Netherlands, and Slovenia. Modern computers and printing technology have blurred the distinction between printed matter and individualized correspondence. Direct mail has traditionally been thought of as printed advertising matter, that is, identical items produced in large quantities by a mechanical process. Today, however, advertising items can be individualized by inserting, for example, the name of the addressee or a reference to his or her last purchase. The Directive seems to extend the concept of 'direct mail' to include advertising items that are individualized in this manner if 'the nature of the message' is the same in all items, yet this line is plainly difficult to draw. Among member states that have faced this issue, the Netherlands, Germany, and Austria have taken a simple but restrictive approach. In the Netherlands, direct mail includes only wholly printed matter, and in Austria and Germany, items of direct mail can differ only in a few specified elements. NRAs in Spain and Italy, on the other hand, interpret direct mail to include items whose body is 'essentially identical'. Other NRAs are frankly uncertain.

Article 7's repeated declaration that a reservation may be introduced only 'to the extent necessary to ensure the maintenance of universal service' implies a duty to adjust the reserved area to the economic requirements of universal service. This 'principle of proportionality' has been more honored in the breach than in the observance. At least two member states, Sweden and the United Kingdom, have concluded economic analyses showing that no reserved area is needed to maintain universal service, and they have

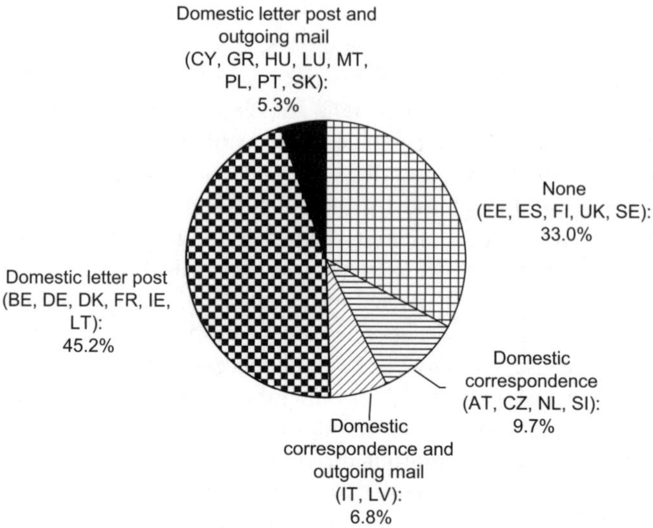

Figure 12.2 EU domestic letter-post volume by level of reservation, 2006

accordingly repealed the reserved area. Three member states – Belgium, Spain, and Portugal – report that they have completed economic analyses showing the extent of the reserved area required to maintain a specific definition of universal service but offered no documentation of these analyses.

Overall, the level of reservation of letter-post mail in 2006 may be summarized as follows (see Figure 12.2).[6] Five member states are substantially liberalized. This total includes Spain where the postal reservation has never included intra-city postal service, the largest part of a modern postal system, and private operators have captured a higher percentage of the letter-post market than in any other member state. Collectively, these five countries comprise about 33 percent of the EU letter post. Three other member states have indicated a firm intention to eliminate the reserved area in the near future: Germany, Netherlands, and Slovenia.[7] They represent roughly another third of the EU letter-post market. As a practical matter, then, the major part of the Community, measured by the volume of letter post affected, has swung in favor of liberalization, rather than reservation, as the best strategy for ensuring an efficient universal service.

3.3 Special Legal Treatment of USPs

Value-added tax

In most member states, the USP legal protections are not confined to the reserved area. Of these, exemption from value-added tax (VAT) is probably the most important. Application of VAT to the services of the USP varies among member states. Three states (Finland, Sweden, and Slovenia) do not exempt any postal services from VAT; two (Spain and Latvia) exempt only reserved services from VAT. The majority rule is to exempt from VAT either all universal services or all postal services provided by the USP. As a result, only five member states apply VAT equally to all postal operators either because there is no VAT or because VAT is limited to the reserved area. The result is to distort competition. In 2003, the Commission proposed modernization of the VAT exemption for postal services (European Commission, 2003), but this proposal remains blocked by politics. More recently, the Commission sent the United Kingdom, Germany, and Sweden formal requests for information on the application of VAT to postal services (European Commission, 2006). This investigation is ongoing.

Customs laws

Customs laws are a visible source of special legal treatment. Equal application of customs procedures to all postal operators is a necessary precondition for an undistorted postal services market. Yet documents and parcels transported by public postal operators have traditionally been afforded different customs treatment from those transported by private operators. The Universal Postal Convention (2004) provides simplified customs documentation for use by public postal operators and limitations on their liability under customs laws. The Convention does not, however, expressly limit these privileges to public postal operators, nor does it make clear to what extent such customs privileges must be accorded to the commercial shipments of public postal operators.[8] Meanwhile, when it comes to private express operators, most national customs authorities provide special expedited customs treatment, although these services come at a price. Private carriers must invest heavily in preparing reliable customs documentation for customs officials in an appropriate electronic format and may bear additional costs for dedicated customs facilities. Despite differences in customs treatement, few NRAs could explain their government's policies; many were unaware of basic facts. In general, it appears fair to say that special customs rules for public postal operators have so far received little attention from regulatory authorities.

Access to resources of the public postal network

In contrast, differential access to USP's public postal network has received substantial attention from NRAs. The Postal Directive defines the 'public postal network' as

> [T]he system of organization and resources of all kinds used by the universal service provider(s) for the purposes in particular of the clearance of postal items covered by a universal service obligation from access points throughout the territory; the routing and handling of those items from the postal network access point to the distribution centre; [and the] distribution to the addresses shown on items.

The public postal network is thus a vast network of physical and informational resources built at public expense. As postal service markets become more competitive, some private operators and their customers have sought access to portions of the public postal network without paying for use of the entire system. Member states have adopted different policies in respect to different sorts of access.

An especially important and controversial issue is downstream access. Suppose a competitive postal operator or a large mailer would like to purchase only downstream services without collection and transportation. Can the NRA require the USP to provide unbundled downstream services at a price geared to cost? Seven member states have granted the NRA authority to require downstream access to the public postal network under appropriate circumstances. Several NRAs have used this authority to encourage or compel downstream access, at least where the USP has granted access to someone.

Another type of downstream issue is access to post office boxes, that is, boxes located in an office of the public postal operators. In five member states, the NRA may require the public postal operator to give access to post office boxes to private operators, and at least two regulators (in Germany and Sweden) used this authority.

The address database – that is, lists of valid physical addresses and address changes – comprises a less intangible, but very significant element of the public postal network. Incorrect addressing is a basic problem for all postal operators. In each member state, the USP has the most extensive and up-to-date address database because of its position as the official, and historically the exclusive, provider of universal services. Competition in the postal services market will be inhibited if the USP is able to retain exclusive use of this element of the public postal network. Moreover, from a social standpoint, it may be considered wasteful to increase the number of unsuccessful delivery attempts by denying other postal operators access to a database of valid addresses. For such reasons, five member states (including Germany, France, and the United Kingdom) have authorized the NRA to require the USP to give access to the address database. In Sweden, Sweden Post and the second largest postal operator, CityMail, have established a jointly owned corporation to maintain a national address database.

Services for misaddressed and misdelivered mail constitute another feature of the public postal network which a private operator might need to make use of. Like the USP, private operators deliver mail that is incorrectly addressed by the sender or simply delivered to the wrong address by the operator. Recipients of misaddressed mail often give it to the USP, but the USP may be unwilling to take care of misaddressed and misdelivered mail for its competitor, even for a reasonable fee. In eight member states, the NRA is empowered to define common operational procedures to deal with such mail. In three, USPs and private operators have voluntarily developed contractual arrangements to ensure return of misaddressed mail. In the United Kingdom, in particular, Postcomm has pioneered development of a broad new regulatory framework intended to provide for a level playing field and cooperation among postal operators in a liberalized environment. Two codes of practice which must be agreed by all postal operators are designed to protect the integrity of mail and promote common operational procedures. The operational code addresses matters such as marking of postal items so the addressee can identify the carrier or carriers, return of misdirected mail, and customer inquiries (UK, Postcomm, 2005b, 2005c, 2005d).

3.4 Authorization of Postal Operators

Article 9 of the Postal Directive establishes rules for the authorization of postal operators. For non-reserved services within the scope of the universal service, member states may introduce 'authorization procedures, including individual licences, to the extent necessary in order to guarantee compliance with the essential requirements and to safeguard the universal service'. There are for two types of authorization: a general authorization and an individual license. The essential difference is that an individual license requires the operator to obtain specific approval from regulatory authorities before starting operations whereas a general authorization does not. The Directive thus offers several options

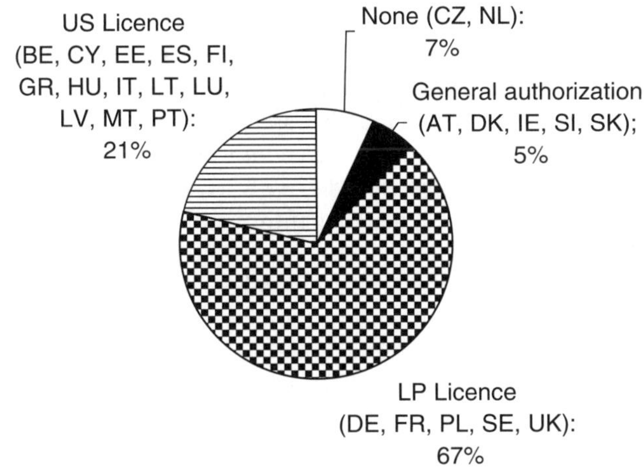

Figure 12.3 EU domestic letter-post volume by type of authorization, 2004

for authorization of postal operators within the universal service area as one or both types of authorizations are introduced for some or all universal services.

As illustrated in Figure 12.3, two main approaches to authorization have emerged: either (i) subject all universal services (US) to authorization or (ii) use authorization procedures to replace (some or all) of the formerly reserved letter-post (LP) services. A majority of member states have opted for the former, that is, regulate entry into all universal services. In most cases, this would seem to represent an increase in the scope of regulation since unreserved universal services were generally not subject to authorization procedures prior to the Postal Directive. The second approach has been adopted by a substantial minority of member states. Five states require licenses for some or all letter-post services within the universal service area, including France, Germany, and the United Kingdom. In Germany, a license is required for carriage of letter-post items weighing not more than 1,000 grams. In the United Kingdom, a license is required for carriage of letters weighing less than 350 grams and charged a fee less than £1.00 (€1.45). In France, the new postal legislation limits authorizations to services for the carriage of items of correspondence (including addressed direct mail). In five member states, only the unrestrictive general authorization has been introduced, and in two others (including the Netherlands) there are no authorization procedures. Altogether, these three relatively more liberal alternatives to the licensing of all universal services account for more than three-quarters of the EU letter post.

Another significant difference among member states is the degree to which conditions are attached to authorizations. According to the Directive, authorization procedures should be employed only 'to the extent necessary in order to guarantee compliance with the essential requirements and to safeguard the universal service'. 'Essential requirements' refers to public interest objectives of a non-economic nature such as controlling transport of dangerous goods or protection of data (Postal Directive Articles 2, 9(2)). Conditions to safeguard the universal service may include one or more of four types of obligations: universal service obligations 'where appropriate'; requirements concerning quality, availability and performance 'if necessary'; respect for the reserved area; and liability for contributions to a universal service fund. Other conditions appear inconsistent with the Directive, yet they are not uncommon. Examples include obligations to meet minimal capital requirements, give financial guarantees, or demonstrate technical or operational competence. Eleven member states, accounting for almost three-quarters of the Community market, have introduced conditions which arguably exceed the scope of what is envisioned by the Directive.

A more fundamental question is whether authorization procedures inhibit competition. The best objective test of whether an authorization regime acts as a barrier to entry into the universal service area appears to be the number of authorizations granted, although such numbers must be interpreted with caution. Where a member state requires an individual license to provide universal service but has authorized no postal operator or only one postal operator in addition to the USP, it seems reasonable to surmise that the procedures and conditions associated with such licenses may in fact constitute a significant barrier to entry. By these standards, authorization procedures appear to constitute a barrier to entry in at least six member states.

A final requirement of the Directive is that authorization procedures must be 'transparent, nondiscriminatory, proportionate and based on objective criteria' (Postal Directive Article 9(3)). In fact, however, in many member states the authorization system does not apply equally to the USP and other postal operators, often because the USP is authorized by statute whereas other postal operators are not.

To summarize, what emerges is a mixed picture with respect to authorization. In about 12 percent of the EU (measured by letter-post volume), no or minimal authorization procedures have been introduced. In 67 percent of the Community, authorization procedures have been introduced for the carriage of letter-post items, essentially replacing the reserved area with a more light-handed but still significant control. In 13 member states, comprising 21 percent of the Community letter post, authorization procedures have been introduced for the entire universal service area. Introduction of universal service licenses may have the effect of inhibiting competition especially in several member states, perhaps 5 percent of the sector, where no authorizations for competing postal operators have been granted in fact. Where authorization procedures have been introduced, it appears that in the majority of member states the authorizations include obligations that exceed what is envisioned by the Directive. In about half the member states, authorization procedures have been applied in a less than wholly non-discriminatory manner in respect to the USP and other postal operators.

For postal services *outside* the universal service area, the Postal Directive permits only general authorizations, not individual licenses. Nine member states representing almost 80 percent of the Community do not require any authorization for services outside the universal service area. Thirteen member states, however, require a general authorization, and three small member states appear to require individual licenses, the Directive notwithstanding. Several member states condition authorization on respect for the reserved area, a condition seemingly in excess of what the Directive permits. Overall, however, the reality seems to be that there is little practical control on services outside the universal service area.

Under Article 9, a theoretically important function of authorization procedures is to allow creation of a 'compensation fund' or universal service fund. Postal operators within the universal service area can be required by their licenses to contribute to such a fund if the universal service obligation constitutes 'an unfair financial burden' for the USP (Postal Directive Article 9(4)). Money from the fund may be used to support the USP despite the fact that the USP is presumably already sufficiently compensated by the reserved area. Despite Article 9's exceedingly unclear instructions, nine member states have provided for a universal service fund in their laws. Only Italy, however, has actually created a compensation fund, and the sums collected make no significant contribution to sustaining universal service. (However, it should be noted the USP does not contribute to this fund and the Italian fund was never intended to be the primary means of funding universal service).

3.5 Regulation of Postage Rates

Article 12 of the Postal Directive establishes the guidelines for regulating the prices of universal postal services. It provides that 'for each of the services forming part of the provision of the universal service' prices must be 'geared to costs', 'transparent and non-discriminatory', and 'affordable'. These few words imply a broad range of price controls.

In the first place, the Directive requires regulation of *each* service forming part of the universal service. While most member states subscribe to this standard in principle, five explicitly limit rate regulation to reserved services or to market-dominant services (notably, Germany). Moreover, as discussed below, the actual extent of regulatory control over individual agreements and special tariffs is open to question in many member states.

To regulate prices, NRAs must adopt a standard to determine which prices are too high or too low. Most NRAs regulate prices by looking to past or projected costs of the USP. Four NRAs (including Germany) purportedly refer to the costs of an efficient postal operator, in principle a far tougher standard. Alternatively, three NRAs appear to rely upon price or cost indexes (including the Netherlands) rather than the actual costs of the USP.

To ensure that the price of 'each of the services prices' is geared to costs, it appears necessary for the NRA to determine the cost to be incurred and the revenue to be earned from each class of service. These calculations depend in turn on the expected volume of mail in each class of service. In addition, a vigilant regulator might require the USP to reduce its unit costs over time, that is, improve its productivity. The ability of EU regulation to deal with such issues is open to question, however. Only two NRAs (Portugal, and the United Kingdom) appear to address all three topics in the course of rate regulation. Only a handful can determine both the costs and revenues of each postal product. Yet, without such knowledge, it is unclear how the NRA can ensure that prices of each of the services forming part of the universal service are 'geared to costs'.

As a limited exception to the principle of cost-based pricing, Article 12 allows a member state to require 'uniform tariffs', that is, postage rates that apply uniformly throughout the national territory. About half of the member states require uniform pricing for all universal services, but they represent only about 17 percent of the EU letter-post market. The largest and most progressive member states are moving towards limiting the uniform tariff requirement. Sweden applies the uniform tariff rule to single items of addressed mail. The Netherlands limits the uniform tariff rule by limiting the concept of universal service to postal items tendered at retail postal offices and reserved services. Similarly, the NRA in the United Kingdom has recently concluded that three-quarters of bulk-mail products should be considered non-universal services and therefore are outside the scope of the uniform tariff requirement (UK, Postcomm, 2005a). Finland and Germany limit the uniform tariff rule to non-bulk correspondence. Two member states (including France) apply the uniform tariff rule only to reserved services, and three have no legal requirement to maintain uniform tariffs (including Ireland and Italy).

The costs and benefits of uniform tariffs appear to be largely beyond the capacity of NRAs to quantify. The economic effect of the uniform tariff is to promote a geographic averaging of prices. Mail destined for areas where the cost of delivery is high is charged somewhat more than cost, while mail destined for areas where the cost of delivery is low is charged somewhat less than cost. The need to sustain uniform tariffs is often said to be the primary justification for the reserved area. Without the reserved area, the argument goes, cream-skimmers would serve the inexpensive delivery areas, and the USP would either have to de-average rates or confine itself to the money-losing routes. The force of this argument depends on a number of factors including the magnitude of the unit cost differential between high- and low-cost delivery areas and the distribution of these cost differentials. Therefore, in order to evaluate the costs and benefits of the uniform tariff, it is necessary for NRAs to have reliable data on the variation in delivery costs among different parts of the country. No NRA, however, has conducted an analysis of the variation in delivery costs. None could estimate the cost of delivery in high- and low-cost areas compared to the norm.

Article 12 also provides that 'for each of the services forming part of the provision of the universal service', prices must be 'transparent and non-discriminatory'. To ensure non-discrimination, it appears necessary for the NRA to determine that differences in prices charged to different mailers are justified by differences in costs or other appropriate considerations. Prevention of price discrimination requires much the same analysis as assurance that prices are geared to costs. Transparency implies that the prices of each universal service should be available to the public. Most but not all member states seek to ensure that rates for each universal service are transparent and non-discriminatory. Some (for example, Germany) extend price controls only to market-dominant services; others limit price regulation to reserved services (Spain) or single-piece services (France).

Article 12 further provides that prices must be 'affordable' for each of the services forming part of the provision of the universal service. There seems to be no clear idea among NRAs as to how to implement this requirement. Only a few NRAs can estimate how much the average non-business mailer spends on postage annually. Estimates range from €84 per year (Czech Republic) to €2.40 (Portugal). Judging from the estimates of several large member states, the average for the EU appears to be about 25 to 30 euros.

Article 12 leaves to member states the procedures for price regulation, that is, whether by explicit approval of proposed rates, by establishment of price caps (that is, limits below which prices can be revised at the discretion of the operator), or by review of rates by the NRA after they have been implemented. Explicit approval of proposed rates is relied upon exclusively by 11 member states. Three states combine explicit approval of proposed rates for reserved services with price-cap regulation of other universal services (including France and Spain). Four combine explicit approval of proposed rates for some services with post-implementation regulation of rates for other services. In Ireland, Luxembourg, and Portugal, explicit approval of proposed rates is required for changes in the prices of reserved services, and review of rates for other universal services is available after the rates have been implemented. Four member states appear to rely exclusively on price caps (including the Netherlands). Two provide price-cap regulation and review of rates after they have been implemented. In the United Kingdom, the market-dominant rates of Royal Mail are subject to price caps, while competitive rates are subject to review after implementation. Within the market-dominant category, the UK regulator has defined two baskets of products so that, overall, captive single-piece mail is regulated more strictly than 'non-captive' bulk business mail (UK, Postcomm, 2005e, 2006). In Sweden, price caps are employed only for single items delivered overnight; other universal service rates may be challenged only after they are in effect. Where a price cap is used, all member states make use of a general price or consumer price index except the Netherlands, which uses a cost index based on wages. Three NRAs use an 'X' factor to adjust the price index: the United Kingdom uses −1 percent; Belgium, +2.5 percent; and Germany, −1.8 percent.

What appears most remarkable about this picture is the widespread use of combinations of regulatory methods. Fifty percent of the Community universal service is subject to dual price control regimes with the stricter regulation being employed for services which are most politically sensitive (for example, non-bulk correspondence) or most amenable to abuse (for example, reserved services). For the most part, dual control regimes have been pioneered by the larger member states and by Ireland and Portugal.

Article 12 provides that 'the application of a uniform tariff does not exclude the right of the universal service provider(s) to conclude *individual agreements* on prices with customers' (emphasis added). At least half of EU USPs, about two-thirds of the EU letter-post market, employ individual agreements or are planning to do so. Although individual agreements appear to be subject to the general requirements of universal service tariffs – cost based, transparent, and non-discriminatory – few NRAs seem able to verify compliance or several concede non-compliance. Few NRAs can even estimate the percentage of mail affected by individual agreements. Estimates from three NRAs range from a remarkable 40 to 80 percent, although it is unclear whether NRAs are drawing a clear distinction between individual agreements and 'special tariffs'.

According to Article 12, 'special or individualized tariffs' – meaning discounts for large mailers or consolidators – are permitted but must generally conform to the same principles as other universal service tariffs. Special tariffs appear to be an important factor in the Community's universal service. Although data are incomplete, special tariffs appear to account for 40 to 90 percent of all correspondence in the large member states, but discounts seem to be 10 percent or less in most cases. Special tariffs are applied to nearly 100 percent of direct mail and to 50 to 80 percent of parcels. NRAs declare that in most cases special tariffs are transparent and open to consolidators and private operators.

NRAs appear to find it difficult to apply Article 12's standards to special tariffs. Article 12 specifically provides that special tariffs should 'take account of the avoided costs, as compared to the standard service' and 'shall apply equally both as between different third parties and as between third parties and universal service providers supplying equivalent services'. Moreover, special tariffs must be made available to 'private customers who post under similar conditions'. Only 11 NRAs seem to have complete data on special tariffs, and of these, only four (including Germany, Portugal, and the United Kingdom) have adequate information to calculate the 'avoided costs' which must be taken into account in the regulation of special tariffs. Even these few NRAs diverge on the proper interpretation of the term 'avoided costs'. Some NRAs (including Germany) consider it refers to the full retail price minus the direct costs saved by virtue of the downstream access. On the other hand, the UK's Postcomm has interpreted 'avoided costs' to refer to the end-to-end cost minus the direct costs saved (UK, Postcomm, 2004, para. 2.30), and the Irish regulator appears to agree in principle.

Another indicator of the uncertain vigor of price regulation is the low number of formal rate investigations. It appears that only 14 NRAs have ever conducted a rate investigation up to 2005, and a few of these seem to be a formality. Although there does not exist a standard concept of 'rate case' among EU NRAs, it appears that relatively few NRAs have conducted substantial and objective economic analyses of the rates charged for universal services.

Article 13 of the Postal Directive deals with a special type of rates, 'terminal dues', that is, the rates a public postal operator charges for delivery of inbound cross-border mail. Article 13 requires member states to 'encourage' USPs to adopt terminal dues agreements that respect principles similar to those in effect for domestic mail. Specifically, terminal dues 'shall be fixed in relation to the costs' of handling and delivery and shall be transparent and non-discriminatory. Article 13 also adds that for cross-border mail 'remuneration shall be related to the quality of service achieved'. In practice, it appears that only three NRAs (including Ireland and Portugal) have reviewed terminal dues practices by their USPs.

3.6 Regulating the Accounts of USPs

Article 14 establishes standards for regulating the accounts of universal service providers. The first step is separation of accounts. Article 14 requires three levels of separation. The first is between the accounts for all universal services, on the one hand, and the accounts for all non-universal services, on the other. All USPs reportedly provide this top-level separation. The second level of separation is between all reserved universal services, on the one hand, and all non-reserved universal services, on the other. The third level of separation requires separate accounts for *each* of the reserved services. With two prominent exceptions, all member states with a reserved area require these further separations as well. The exceptions are France and the Netherlands, which require separate accounts for reserved and non-reserved collectively, but do not require separate accounts for each reserved service.

For the NRA to ensure compliance with Article 14, it seems necessary for the USP to report appropriate data on a regular basis. Almost all member states require the USP to submit periodic accounts to the NRA. In Austria and Germany, however, the USP provides such information to the NRA only when it is time to adjust rates or rate caps, that is, every few years. In Finland, the NRA merely reserves the right to request such information. In Latvia, the USP is required to give the NRA volume data but not to provide cost and revenue accounts. In some new member states, the first reports were only submitted in 2006 or 2007.

The number of distinct reserved services reflected in the accounts may offer insight into the level of accounting sophistication, although allowance must be made for the size of the reserved area and the complexity of the postal system. In some member states, the USP's accounts reflect a large number of separate products and hence very fine accounting distinctions. These states include Belgium (115 reserved products), Spain (14), Greece (14), Luxembourg (31), Portugal (16), Slovakia (12), and the United Kingdom (32). In other member states, the division of accounts is less elaborate. Ireland, Malta, Poland, and Slovenia report between five and seven reserved products. The Czech Republic, Denmark, France, Hungary report two reserved products. NRAs in some large member states (including Germany, Italy, and the Netherlands) appear unable, or unwilling, to specify the number of reserved products.[9]

The obligations of Article 12 serve by implication to extend the accounting separation required by Article 14. To ensure that each universal service is geared to cost, non-discriminatory, and free of cross-subsidy, it appears logically necessary for the NRA to review cost and revenue data for each non-reserved universal service, not merely for all non-reserved universal services collectively. Despite the implications of Article 12, however, seven member states (including Germany, France, and the Netherlands), representing 54 percent of the EU letter post, do not require the USP to maintain separate accounts for each non-reserved universal service. On the other hand, 16 member states do oblige the USP to maintain such accounts and to submit them to the NRA.[10]

An obligation to maintain separate accounts presents particular questions when it comes to accounting for individual agreements and special tariffs. As described above, individual agreements and special tariffs account for 40 to 80 percent or more of the letter post in some member states. According to Article 12, the NRA is required to ensure the cost-based, non-discriminatory, and unsubsidized quality of these tariffs no less than for other universal services. Only the Irish NRA, however, requires the USP to maintain separate accounts for each individual agreement. And only five NRAs (excluding the largest states but including Ireland and Portugal) require the USP to maintain separate accounts for the upstream and downstream portions of services that are subject to special tariffs. Without such detailed accounts, it is unclear how the NRA can ensure that individual agreements and special tariffs meet the pricing standards set by Article 12. For example, how can the NRA be confident that special tariffs 'take account of the avoided costs, as compared to the standard service' if the NRA does not know what upstream costs are avoided and what downstream costs remain?

The overall status of accounting separation may be summarized as follows. The great majority of member states require separate product accounts for all universal services. These states, however, account for only about 50 percent of the Community letter post. A significant number of states, including some of the largest and most progressive, require separate product accounts only for reserved services only (including Germany) or, indeed, for no universal services (France and the Netherlands).

Separation of accounts is meaningless unless costs are allocated correctly to each account. Article 14(3) sets out principles for the allocation of costs as follows:

> (a) costs which can be directly assigned to a particular service shall be so assigned;
> (b) common costs, that is costs which cannot be directly assigned to a particular service, shall be allocated as follows:
>
> (i) whenever possible, common costs shall be allocated on the basis of direct analysis of the origin of the costs themselves;
> (ii) when direct analysis is not possible, common cost categories shall be allocated on the basis of an indirect linkage to another cost category or group of cost categories for which a direct assignment or allocation is possible; the indirect linkage shall be based on comparable cost structures;

(iii) when neither direct nor indirect measures of cost allocation can be found, the cost category shall be allocated on the basis of a general allocator computed by using the ratio of all expenses directly or indirectly assigned or allocated, on the one hand, to each of the reserved services and, on the other hand, to the other services.

In brief, paragraphs (a), (b)(i), and (b)(ii) require the assignment of costs to each particular service so far as it is possible to do so by direct or indirect means. Paragraph (b)(iii) requires the allocation of the unassignable common or 'overhead' costs to each particular service based on the proportion of assigned costs.

How strictly do EU NRAs oversee cost allocation? In 2006, a bare majority of NRAs (including Germany, France, and Spain) affirmed that they have approved the costing system of the USP; they accounted for 56 percent of the EU letter post. Looking more closely, however, it is apparent that paragraph (b)(iii) poses a critical test for the NRA's command of cost allocation, namely, can the NRA determine what percentage of costs of the USP are unassignable and therefore allocated pursuant to paragraph (b)(iii)? The answer would seem to be an automatic result of any well-developed cost allocation system, yet only seven NRAs declared that they can determine the level of unassignable costs (including Belgium, Germany, France, and Portugal). And among these seven NRAs, three declined to report the actual level of unassignable costs in the 2006 survey and the others quoted figures of 5 to 7 percent of total costs. Such low levels of unallocatable costs may be contrasted with regulatory experience in the United States where, after three decades of intensive litigation and sophisticated accounting practices, the NRA has been forced to accept that about 46 percent of all costs cannot be reliably and causally assigned to a particular postal product. Not only does the American experience raise questions about the reliability of the cost allocation in the EU, some of the most active EU NRAs – including those of Ireland, Sweden, and the United Kingdom – have expressed concerns and are investigating the validity of the cost allocation systems used by their USPs.

A final issue presented by cost allocation is the quality of the data to be allocated. Data quality depends on complex statistical issues such as the size and reliability of sampling techniques. Only nine NRAs have so far investigated the quality of data used in the costing systems of the USPs, and only six of these have reviewed and approved both the costing system of the USP and the data quality (the largest country being Belgium).

Article 14(5) goes on to require independent verification and public certification of the correctness of regulatory accounts: 'National regulatory authorities shall ensure that compliance with one of the cost accounting systems described in paragraphs 3 or 4 is verified by a competent body which is independent of the universal service provider. Member States shall ensure that a statement concerning compliance is published periodically'. While almost all member states require review of the accounts of the USP by an independent auditor, in many (including France and the United Kingdom) the auditor is retained by the USP so its independence may be reasonably questioned. Since these states collectively represent 45 percent of the Community letter post, the possible lack of independence of the auditing body is not an insignificant issue. Moreover, 13 NRAs, representing almost two-thirds of the EU letter post, report that they have never published the statement of compliance required by the Postal Directive.

The Directive does not require publication of a summary of the regulatory accounts of the USP. Nonetheless, such information could enable interested parties to evaluate better the efficiency of different services (both relative to one another and to the services of other USPs) and the potential for unfair discrimination. For example, by comparing such information year to year, interested parties could assess improvements and changes in the universal service over time. Despite lack of direction from the Directive, six NRAs declared that they do publish a summary of regulatory accounts.

Article 15 of the Postal Directive supplements Article 14 by requiring publication of periodic financial reports by the USP. The USP's financial accounts must be reviewed by an independent auditor, and they must be published in accordance with the Community and national legislation applicable to commercial undertakings. Virtually all member states comply with this provision.

3.7 Monitoring the Quality of Universal Service

Article 16 of the Postal Directive requires member states to 'ensure that quality-of-service standards are set and published in relation to universal service in order to guarantee a postal service of good quality. Quality standards shall focus, in particular, on routing times and on the regularity and reliability of services'. The Directive, it may be noted, does not require a member state to set a quality of service standard for *each* universal service. The Directive itself establishes quality of service standards for cross-border postal services but addresses only the routing time for 'postal items of the fastest standard category'.

As of mid-2006, routing time targets have been established in all member states, but their scope varies widely. Single-piece postal items of the fastest standard category are subject to quality of service standards in all cases, but bulk mailings are excluded in Belgium, the Netherlands (outside the reserved area), Spain, and Slovakia. Perhaps the most elaborate set of quality of service standards is found in the United Kingdom: routing time requirements are set for 15 services including non-bulk parcels. With the end of the reserved area on January 1, 2006, the British NRA, Postcomm, has reduced the number of (domestic) transit time targets to seven (UK, Postcomm, 2006). Quality of service standards are not established for non-priority postal services in three of the 12 member states where they are offered. Quality of service targets are not set for newspapers and magazines in the majority of member states which include periodicals in the universal service. Similarly, fewer than half of the states have established quality of service standards for parcel services.

Where standards are established, the target is usually high. More than half of the member states require that 90 percent of postal items in the 'fastest standard category' of service must be delivered by the day after posting. The lowest target is 80 percent, used in Germany and Latvia. Spain is the only member state that declines to set a delivery completion target for the day after posting; instead, it refers to the percentage of deliveries that must be completed by the third day after posting. Between 2003 and 2005, most member states either kept routing time standards unchanged or tightened them slightly. However, it appears significant that Denmark and Finland have recently reduced quality of service targets. Denmark has backed off from its very high standard for next-day delivery, from 97 to 93 percent of items. In Finland, there was a steeper reduction, from 95 to 85 percent. The reason is that in rural areas the Finnish USP has begun to deliver newspapers and letters together in the early morning, and due to early delivery, mail processing is incomplete for a significant percentage of letters collected the previous day.

In almost all member states, the routing time to which quality of service standards refer begins with the time of collection by the USP, not the time of posting. This is the measure codified by the European Committee for Standardization (CEN). Only Germany has adopted a different standard. German postal legislation requires transit time measurement from the viewpoint of the mailer, that is, by starting the clock with the posting of the letter at the street letterbox or postal outlet. As a result, in Germany, service performance as measured by the NRA is about 8 to 9 percent lower than the CEN-based results reported by Deutsche Post.

With minor exceptions, service performance actually achieved by the USP is published annually by the NRA or the USP. Recently, there has been some tendency to extend transparency to other postal operators. Belgium requires licensees other than the USP to implement a quality measurement. In Portugal and the United Kingdom, licensees must report to the regulator on the routing time performance of their postal services.

3.8 Users' Complaints and Redress Procedures

Article 19 of the Postal Directive requires member states to ensure that 'transparent, simple and inexpensive procedures are drawn up for dealing with users' complaints, particularly in cases of theft, damage or non-compliance with service quality requirements'. All member states impose such user-protection procedures on their USPs. Fifteen states apply the same requirements to other postal operators, but most of the large ones (including Italy, France, the Netherlands, Spain, and the United Kingdom) have not done so. Article 19 goes on to say that member states should define 'procedures for determining where responsibility lies in cases where more than one operator is involved'. Only Germany and Greece, however, explicitly addressed such multi-operator situations in their user-protection legislation. In the United Kingdom, the NRA, Postcomm, has recently established a common operational procedures code to manage inter-operator issues expected to occur in a multi-operator market. The code addresses such subjects as mail identification, reposted, misposted, and misdirected mail as well as misdirected customer service enquiries.

Article 19 further requires member states to provide a procedure for appeal to a 'competent national authority . . . where users' complaints to the universal service provider have not been satisfactorily resolved'. Most states have designated the NRA as the appropriate appellate authority for users' complaints, but some have nominated an ombudsman (for example, France), consumer protection agency (for example, Sweden), or specialized postal users' group (the United Kingdom). In almost all cases, the same agency is also authorized to review users' complaints against other postal operators. Six member states (including Denmark, Italy, and the Netherlands) have so far not designated an appellate body for users' complaints.

Finally, Article 19 requires member states to ensure that USPs publish the number of complaints and the manner in which they have been dealt with. In about one-third of member states, however, governments have failed to take the necessary steps.

3.9 National Regulatory Authorities

Article 22 of the Postal Directive requires member states to 'designate one or more national regulatory authorities for the postal sector that are legally separate from and operationally independent of the postal operators'. Article 22 goes on to declare that NRAs 'shall have as a particular task ensuring compliance with the obligations arising from this Directive and shall, where appropriate, establish controls and specific procedures to ensure that the reserved services are respected'.

All member states have designated NRAs, and in almost all cases the NRA is a multisector regulator. The only purely postal NRAs are those of Austria, Slovakia, Spain, and the United Kingdom. The remaining NRAs regulate electronic communications services as well as postal services with the exception of the Danish regulator, whose focus is road transport. Three postal NRAs (including Germany) have jurisdiction over the energy and gas sectors as well.

Overall, in 2005 member states spent more than €37 million and employed more than 300 persons in the regulation of postal services, roughly five or six times the operating budget of the Postal Rate Commission in the United States, a far larger postal market. The resources of postal NRAs vary enormously not only between large and small member states but also between national postal systems of relatively similar size. Some NRAs appear to lack the resources needed to implement the objectives of the Postal Directive. More generally, since the Postal Directive assigns the same regulatory tasks to small member states as well as large, the amount of resources needed in small states does not decline in the same proportion as the volume of letter post. As a result, small and very small member states employ about 28 percent of EU regulatory personnel to regulate about 4 percent of the Community market. It appears that regulatory resources could be employed more efficiently.

Article 22 requires that NRAs be 'legally separate from and operationally independent of the postal operators'. In one competition law case involving France's failure to oversee competition in the upstream market, the Commission held that Article 22 requires member states to ensure 'thanks to a proper separation of duties, that the tasks of economic and financial monitoring, on the one hand, and of supervision of [the USP], on the other, are carried out completely independently one of the other'.[11] Independence of the NRA from the postal operator depends on many factors. Ideally, the head of an independent NRA should not be appointed by a minister who is also directly responsible for the success of the USP. Indeed, if the state has an ownership interest in the USP, then a regulator with quasi-judicial independence from the government is to be preferred over a regulator located within a ministry since different ministries necessarily influence each other. Nor should the minister responsible for the USP hold the purse strings of the NRA or exercise appeal authority over decisions of the NRA. The head of an independent NRA, or the members of the committee that serves as the head, should hold office for a fixed term of several years and enjoy legal protection against dismissal. All things being equal, it seems likely that an NRA headed by a multi-member committee will, like a court composed of several judges, be more stable and independent than a single chief regulator.

By these standards, it appears that there are some causes for concern in the practices of the member states. In at least three (Austria, Spain, and Italy), the NRA appears to be simply an office within a ministry rather than an agency with genuine institutional independence. In two, the heads of the NRA and the USP are appointed by the postal minister (Ireland and the United Kingdom). In eight, there is only a single postal regulator rather than a multi-member board. In four, the head of the NRA has no fixed term of office, and in several others the term of office is fairly short (three years or less). In five (including Germany, Italy, and the Netherlands), the heads of the NRA appear to have no statutory protection against dismissal. In several states, the NRA is admittedly subject to policy guidance by the government. In eight, the budget of the NRA must be approved by a ministry. In Spain, the only appeal from the decision of the NRA is to the postal minister. Perhaps none of these features is sufficient standing alone to cast doubt on the independence of the NRA, and it is also true that the negative (or positive) effects of organizational arrangements may be outweighed by still more intangible political traditions. Nonetheless, there remain several features of the institutional arrangements for NRAs that could raise doubts about independence in the mind of a reasonable observer.

4. FINAL OBSERVATIONS

This chapter has necessarily focused on differences in the manner in which member states of the EU have implemented, or in some cases partially failed to implement, the reform principles of the Postal Directive. These variations reflect the continuing diversity in postal, and governmental, traditions among the member states. They should not, however, obscure the tremendous collective progress made by the EU as a whole in the few short years between February 1999, when the Postal Directive of 1997 became effective, and mid-2006, the period to which this chapter refers. In each member state, the national post office has been an important public institution for more than two centuries. By mid-2006, the EU had laid a solid foundation for adapting these centuries-old public institutions into commercial entities and governmental agencies suited to the quite different needs of the twenty-first century.

NOTES

1. Directive 1997/67/EC of the European Parliament and of the Council of 15 December 1997 on common rules for the development of the internal market of Community postal services and the improvement of quality of service, OJ L 15, 21 Feb. 1998, p. 14; as amended by Directive 2002/39/EC of the European Parliament and of the Council of 10 June 2002 amending Directive 97/67/EC with regard to further opening to competition of Community postal services, OJ L 176, 5 Jul. 2002, p. 21.
2. The first draft of the Third Postal Directive, a second amendment to the Postal Directive of 1997, was proposed by the European Commission in October 2006 and ultimately agreed in February 2008. Directive 2008/6/EC of the European Parliament and of the Council of 20 February 2008 amending Directive 97/67/EC with regard to the full accomplishment of the internal market of Community postal services, OJ L 52, 27 Feb. 2008, p. 3.
3. This chapter summarizes, and in some cases updates, regulatory portions of a report prepared for the European Commission by the same authors in 2006 (WIK-Consult, 2006). In mid-2006, the European Union consisted of 25 member states. Fifteen had been members since 1995 or earlier: Austria (AT), Belgium (BE), Denmark (DK), Finland (FI), France (FR), Germany (DE), Greece (GR), Ireland (IE), Italy (IT), Luxembourg (LU), the Netherlands (NL), Portugal (PT), Spain (ES), Sweden (SE), and the United Kingdom (UK). Ten countries joined on May 1, 2004: Cyprus (CY), the Czech Republic (CZ), Estonia (EE), Hungary (HU), Latvia (LV), Lithuania (LT), Malta (MT), Poland (PO), Slovakia (SK), and Slovenia (SI). These states had had several years to prepare their postal laws during the lengthy entry process into the EU. In this chapter, the phrase 'all EU member states' refers to these 25 states. After this report was completed, on January 1, 2007, Bulgaria (BG) and Romania (RO) joined the EU.
4. As of February 2008, the German government's ownership of Deutsche Post had fallen to 31 percent. The Dutch government sold its last TNT shares in November 2006.

5. Whether or not the Directive's rule limiting the reserved area to postal services priced less than 2.5 times the basic stamp rate refers to the postage charge before or after application of VAT, if any, is a matter of uncertainty among member states.
6. Figure 12.2 states the share of EU letter post volume in member states with different levels of reservation. These 'levels of reservation' (for example, 'none' or 'domestic correspondence') relate to the legal situation of 2006. Volume information used to weigh the relative importance of member states relates to 2004.
7. In late 2007, the Netherlands postponed its planned repeal of its reserved area as of January 1, 2008, due to German adoption of a labor law that imposes minimum wage rules on private operators, thus undercutting the ability of TNT to compete against Deutsche Post in Germany. As of February 2008, this German law is a continuing matter of dispute. Slovenia has not moved to repeal its reserved area.
8. See Universal Postal Convention (2004), Article 18, and Regulation RL 152.
9. These regulators are unable to provide details about the USP's account because they lack clear legal competence to review the regulatory accounts and/or determine rules for these accounts.
10. In Spring 2007 the French NRA, ARCEP, decided on the format of regulatory accounts to be provided by La Poste (France, ARCEP, 2007). In contrast to past practice (before establishing an independent NRA) ARCEP now requires very detailed operational and financial information on product classes (that is, first and second class broken down to reserved and non-reserved services and to the elements of the postal pipeline).
11. Commission Decision 2002/344/EC of 23 October 2001 on the lack of exhaustive and independent scrutiny of the scales of charges and technical conditions applied by La Poste to mail preparation firms for access to its reserved services, OJ L 120, 7 May 2002, p. 19, paragraph 29.

REFERENCES

European Commission (2003), 'Proposal for a Council Directive Amending Directive 77/388/EEC as Regards Value Added Tax On Services Provided In The Postal Sector', COM(2003) 234.

European Commission (2006), 'VAT/ Postal services – Commission launches infringement proceedings against Germany, the United Kingdom and Sweden', IP/06/484, 10 April.

France, ARCEP, L'Autorité de Régulation des Communications Électroniques et des Postes (2007), 'Décision n° 2007-0443 de l'ARCEP en date du 15 mai 2007 relative aux spécifications des systèmes de comptabilisation, en application de l'article L. 5-2, 6° du code des postes et des communications électroniques'.

Ireland, Comreg (2005), 'Universal Postal Service – A Working Definition (Response To Consultation)'.

Netherlands, Ministry of Economic Affairs (2004), 'Postal Services Policy Memorandum' (English version).

United Kingdom, Postcomm (2004), 'Promoting Effective Competition In UK Postal Services Through Downstream Access'.

United Kingdom, Postcomm (2005a), 'Decision Document: The UK's Universal Postal Service'.

United Kingdom, Postcomm (2005b), 'Licences under the Postal Services Act 2000: Licensing framework in a fully open market'.

United Kingdom, Postcomm (2005c), 'Protecting the integrity of mail – A Code of Practice'.

United Kingdom, Postcomm (2005d), 'Postal Code Of Practice For Common Operational Procedures'.

United Kingdom, Postcomm (2005e), 'Royal Mail Price and Service Quality Review: Final Proposals for Consultation'.

United Kingdom, Postcomm (2006), 'Royal Mail's Price and Service Quality Review 2006–2010: Licence Modifications'.

WIK-Consult (2006), 'Main Developments in the European Postal Sector (2004–2006)', WIK-Consult, Bad Honnef, Germany, May.

13. Economic factors underlying postal reform in the European Union*

Michael A. Crew,[†] Gonzales d'Alcantara,[‡] Paul R. Kleindorfer,[§] Philippe Claeys[¶] and Bert Kuypers[¶]

1. INTRODUCTION

The European Union (EU) has undoubtedly been the trendsetter in the postal reform area. Starting in the early 1990s, driven by the vision of a unified internal postal market, the EU and its executive arm, the European Commission (EC), set out on a course of change toward fully competitive postal markets. This process saw its culmination in the Third Postal Directive, which was formally approved by the European Parliament and Council on February 20, 2008, and which established for most EU member states the date of January 1, 2011 as the date of 'full market opening' (FMO), with all EU member states required to abolish their reserved area by January 1, 2013 at the latest. This provision of the European Directive constitutes, in fact, the 'last mile' of the long journey the EU has been undertaking in creating a liberalized internal market for postal services. This chapter reviews some of the major issues that surfaced in developing the Third Postal Directive. The centerpiece of these issues concerned the sustainability of the postal universal service obligation (USO) in each member state and the potential impact of FMO on the future provision of universal service.

Several studies were undertaken for the EC leading up to the Third Postal Directive, including ECORYS (2005), WIK (2004, 2005, 2006) and PricewaterhouseCoopers (PwC, 2006). PwC (2006) examined two key questions associated with opening the postal market: (i) Could FMO be accomplished without undermining the financial viability of the national postal operator (PO), which is the current universal service provider (USP) in all member states? (ii) What factors in postal markets would be important determinants of the outcome of FMO?

The USO has been a dominant feature of postal service for many years. Its origins can be traced back to 1840 with the implementation of the reforms of Rowland Hill in the form of the Penny Post in the United Kingdom. Prepayment by means of a stamp was a significant innovation in 1840. For the price of a stamp, delivery anywhere in the country was provided. Thus, the twin notions of ubiquitous delivery and uniform price inherent in the USO evolved, and these have remained the essence of the USO ever since.

† Rutgers University.
‡ University of Antwerp and d'Alcantara Economic Consulting.
§ Wharton School and INSEAD.
¶ PricewaterhouseCoopers.

The USO has traditionally been maintained by restricting entry to the postal market by means of a 'reserved area' (RA). The RA was traditionally defined in terms of weight or value thresholds. The prohibition of entry into the RA prevents entrants from cream-skimming by entering the low-cost markets and undercutting the PO. On the other hand, prohibiting entry leads to a weakening stimulus for innovation and optimizing customer value. So, there has been continuing pressure in the postal sector and in other previously monopolized businesses (for example, energy and telecommunications) to liberalize the sector.

In the European postal sector, the debate on increased competition has focused primarily on the desire to establish an internal European market and on integrating postal services with other communications markets. Other forms of communication have seen great technological advances (telecom, mobile telecom and the Internet) and these often have important implications for changes in postal products as well. The emerging substitutes have gradually increased the competitive pressure on letters and have resulted in a decline of overall mail demand in many countries, as several country studies in this volume have noted.

Other central factors driving postal reform and liberalization in Europe have included shifting consumption patterns, at the level of corporations as well as households and small and medium-sized businesses. These shifts have resulted in an increased need for refined market and product segmentation with corresponding pricing policies and service performance. Improved and new technologies allow the POs, but also other actors in the postal market such as large mailers and consolidators, to increase the efficiency of their logistics processes, leading to higher flexibility, more capacity to treat large volumes, and improved performance at lower costs. In addition to these economic and market factors, increasing budgetary restrictions have made national governments less willing to finance the deficits of public service organizations, including POs. Thus, increasingly, policy makers are feeling the need to review (and perhaps adapt) the principles of the postal market model to allow POs to be self-sustaining.

Given these complexities of interacting markets, changing consumer demands, and the financial and social importance of the postal sector, it is not surprising that market-based solutions, that is, liberalization, became the focus of attention for postal reform in Europe. At the same time, it has been recognized that if there is not a reasonable balance between the burdens placed on the PO and its USO, competition could have deleterious effects of inefficient cream-skimming and even financial insolvency of the PO. Given the importance of the sector in Europe,[1] the key challenge in moving the liberalization agenda forward is to garner the benefits of competition while controlling the risks.

This is one of three chapters that address regulatory reform in the EU. This chapter focuses on the economic issues underlying the liberalization in Europe and the factors that have come to be recognized as determining the prospects for competition in the EU postal sector and the ability of incumbent POs to continue to provide universal service at historical levels after market opening. Campbell, Dieke and Niederprüm (Chapter 12) describe reforms in the postal laws of the EU member states that were accomplished in the wake of the original Postal Directive of 1997 and the second, amendatory directive of 2002. Eccles (Chapter 14) reviews the legal requirements flowing from the recently adopted Third Postal Directive.

The chapter proceeds as follows. Section 2 examines the factors in postal markets that are likely to impact on the outcomes of FMO in the EU, including the outcome on the financial condition of the PO, the market share of entrants, and the nature and extent of entry under FMO. Section 3 describes efficiency and restructuring initiatives underway at national POs, and also provides summary findings on the readiness of each of the 30 countries studied in PwC (2006) for market opening as prescribed by the Third Postal Directive. Section 4 concludes.

2. THE POSTAL SECTOR IN THE EUROPEAN UNION

PwC (2006) undertook a detailed study of the potential impact of FMO on the USO in the 27 member states of the EU as well as three additional countries (Iceland, Norway and Lichtenstein). We shall use the framework developed in the PwC study to organize our discussion here.

2.1 Themes, Drivers and Diversity across the EU

In understanding the impact of FMO in different countries of the EU, four themes are central: (i) the postal market characteristics in each country; (ii) the structure and efficiency of the incumbent PO/USP; (iii) the scope of the USO in the country; and (iv) the nature of regulatory regimes imposed. These four interdependent themes are summarized in Figure 13.1, together with potential impacts that could arise from the introduction of FMO.

As shown in Figure 13.1, the economic outcomes at stake were, chiefly, the viability of the USP (and potential financing needs to support the USO), the effects on consumers as measured by price levels and the maintenance of the USO, and employment effects in the postal sector. In addition, the question of whether workable competition could be established in and across various national postal markets in the EU remains of central interest in the liberalization and postal reform debate. To inform this debate, a model-based analysis was undertaken in PwC (2006). The model employed was a variant of the model described in d'Alcantara and Amerlynck (2006), and we shall follow here the same approach in discussing the predicted impacts of FMO in the EU. The general structure of the analysis is depicted in Figure 13.2.

For each of the 30 countries studied, the postal market itself was first characterized in terms of scale, urbanization and other drivers of supply and demand discussed in greater detail below. The d'Alcantara and Amerlynck model was then used to simulate the predicted consequences of FMO under various scenarios on the scope of the USO, the efficiency of the USP, and tariff structures. The results in terms of market shares and profitability for the incumbent USP and entrants were then computed (and adjusted in consultation with various stakeholders in each of the 30 countries). We shall summarize the results of this study by considering only three representative postal markets, which were constructed using the range of parameters for demand and supply conditions present in EU member states. These three representative countries were created by choosing parameters for the national markets that represent low, average and high FMO impact countries (LoC – Low FMO impact Country, AvC – Average FMO impact Country and

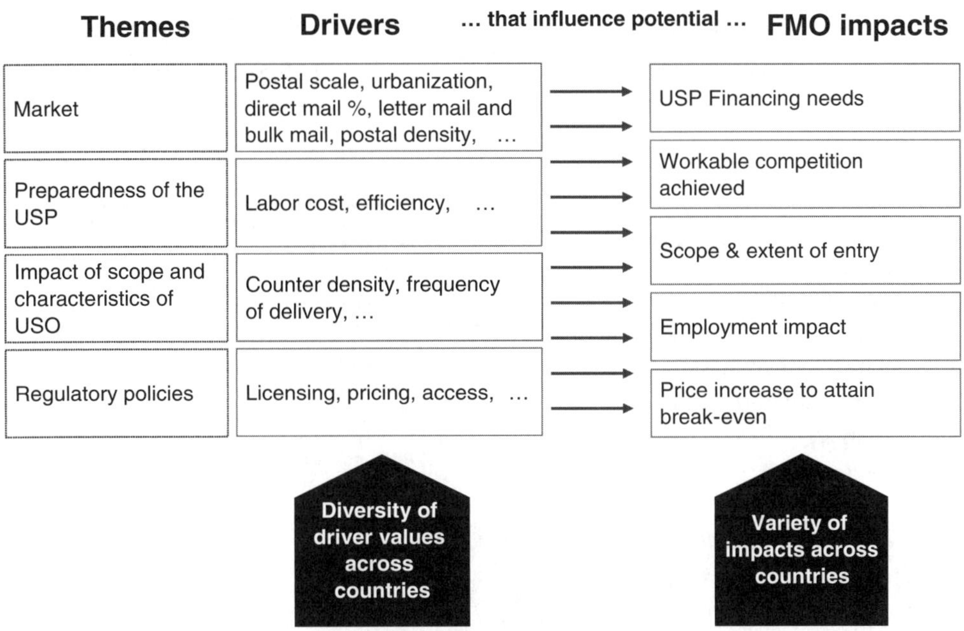

Figure 13.1 Themes, drivers and potential impacts of liberalization in the EU

HiC – High FMO impact Country). These countries represent a set of postal market conditions where FMO would have very little predicted impact on either the USP or the market, the LoC case, or would have moderate or important predicted impacts, the AvC and HiC cases.

The market structures and key parameters defining the three representative countries are characterized by the parameters in Table 13.1.

Concerning demand responsiveness, these variables are likely to be important in determining the effects of FMO on the USP and on the viability of entrants. In the results reported here, own price elasticity of market demand was assumed to be −0.2 for household demand and −0.6 for business demand for all three representative countries, a midrange for these elasticities based on a variety of studies reviewed in Robinson (2007).

Two additional parameters are used to describe shifting elasticities between the incumbent and the entrants.[2] First is the *loyalty parameter* describing the percent discount that entrants must offer in order to begin attracting business away from the incumbent USP. Second is the *cross-price elasticity* between entrant and incumbent demand, once the loyalty factor has been exceeded, which is the percent increase in demand for an entrant's product for each percentage increase in the price of the incumbent's product (beyond the initial loyalty discount). The loyalty and shifting elasticities used are shown in Table 13.2. The medium case corresponds to comparative studies from the literature (for example, Robinson, 2007). The same baseline elasticities were used for all three representative countries (corresponding to the medium case in Table 13.2). B refers to business and government sector mailers. C refers to households and small and medium-sized enterprise mailers.

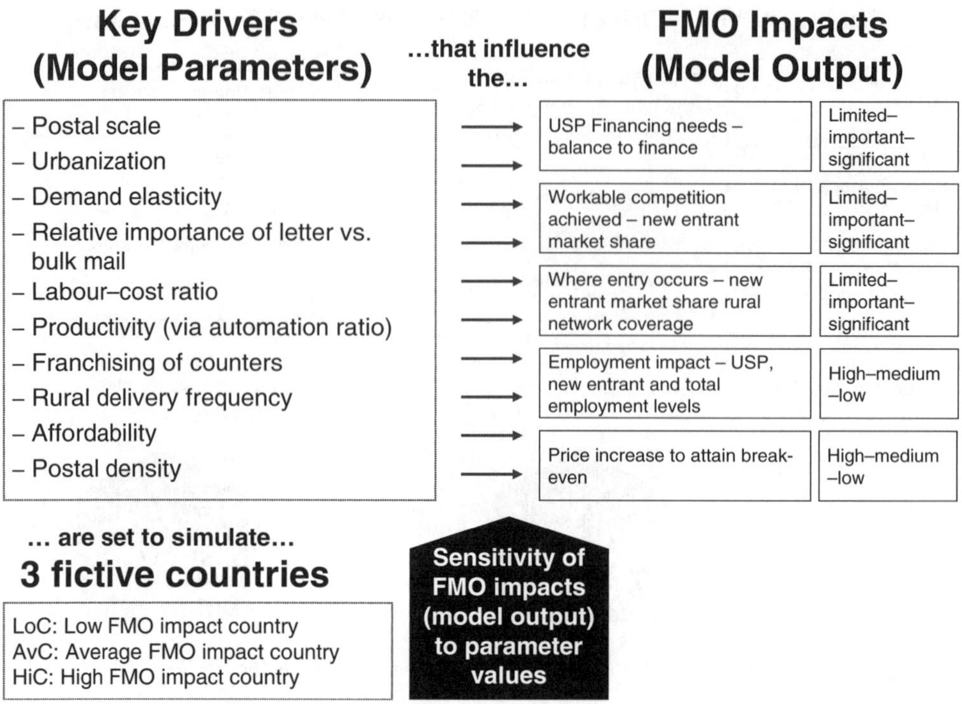

Figure 13.2 Sensitivity of model output to single parameter value modification

Note that while it is possible to vary one factor at a time in the sensitivity analysis, the final impact of introducing FMO in a market will be largely linked to the *combined impact* of various factors. The point here is that the situation facing any specific country may embody both positive as well as negative factors – for instance, a USP may have significantly higher labor costs relative to entrants, but may also operate in a market with a scale factor that makes defending the market against entry relatively easy. We shall note a few of these interactions below. The simultaneous presence of positive and negative factors implies that considerable care must be exercised in drawing conclusions on the impact of FMO on the basis of single-factor sensitivity analysis.

2.2 Representative Results of Simulation Studies of EU Markets

The intrinsic characteristics of the market are among the main factors that will determine the impact of introducing FMO. Some of these characteristics may have very significant impacts, differing from country to country, while others have a more progressive impact, more balanced from one country to the other. For example, high mail volumes per capita, potential for growth in direct mail volumes, a high degree of urbanization and population density may allow entrants to secure sufficiently high volumes to build a sustainable business case. On the other hand, some of these factors may also moderate the impact that FMO will have on the USO since they mitigate the cost burden associated with providing the USO. We review here only a few of the major factors listed in Table 13.1.

*Table 13.1 Definition of representative countries: LoC, AvC and HiC**

Name	Definition	LoC	AvC	HiC
Scale	Mail items per person per year	500	200	10
Urbanization rate (one element of postal density) (%)	Percentage of population in urban area (UN standard)	45	70	95
Labor–cost ratio (%)	Ratio of freelancer vs. employee FTE cost (Eurostat)	90	75	60
Shifting elasticity at given loyalty	Variation of 1% of volume associated with a 1% variation of price	Medium	Medium	Medium
Automation % in sorting	Percentage of mail item automatically processed	90	50	10
Automation % in sequencing	Percentage of mail item automatically processed	75	25	10
Flexible USP workforce in collection (%)	Percentage of freelancer FTE hired by USP in activity	0	0	0
Flexible USP workforce in sorting (%)	Percentage of freelancer FTE hired by USP in activity	26	6	0
Flexible USP workforce in transport (%)	Percentage of freelancer FTE hired by USP in activity	57	10	0
Flexible USP workforce in delivery (%)	Percentage of freelancer FTE hired by USP in activity	29	8	0
Franchised counters (%)	Percentage of counters franchised	46	28	0

Note: * Certain other characteristics were assumed as part of the definition of all the three representative USPs and countries. See PwC (2006, p. 38) for details. For example, USO counters costs were assumed to represent half of the total counter costs, with the latter set at 15% of total costs of the USP, franchised counter costs were assumed to equal 40% of non-franchised counter costs, and the USO was assumed to specify one collection box per 10 square kilometers and 1 counter per 5,000 inhabitants.

Postal scale factor (mail items delivered per inhabitant)

Considering that the primary costs incurred by a postal operator are in the delivery process and that those costs are often considered to be essentially fixed costs, it follows that the higher the mail scale, the lower the unit cost of delivery will be. Consequently, entrants – even if more efficient or generally benefiting from lower labor costs than the incumbent – will be confronted with a USP that benefits from these economies of scale and will have difficulties matching the unit costs achieved by the incumbent operator. On the other hand, since the USP has the obligation to deliver every day everywhere on the territory, it follows it has a fixed cost which the entrants does not.

For this reason, most of the entrants use a different business model, delivering at a lower frequency bulk mail that is pre-sorted by the mailer itself, enabling them to avoid investing in expensive sorting centers. Next to this phenomenon, in a high mail scale market, market share lost by the USP to entrants increases the USP's unit cost of delivery but to a lesser extent than in a low mail scale market.

Table 13.2 Definition of cross-price (shifting) elasticities

	(Actual) Shifting elasticity		Loyalty	
	B-originating	C-originating	B-originating	C-originating
Low	−0.75	−0.5	0%	30%
Medium	−1.0	−0.7	0%	20%
High	−1.25	−0.9	0%	10%

The relation between the postal unit cost of an operator and the postal scale is inherent to the postal process itself. Indeed, the technical coefficients and hence the fixed costs are related to the postal delivery tour that the postman / woman makes to reach households, small businesses, large companies and so on. The fixed costs relating to this delivery process are spread over the mail items volumes, which are dependent on the postal scale. In the case of a high postal scale environment, low unit costs provide an initial advantage to the historic operator relative to entrants.

Mail scale across countries in the EU vary widely from 14 (Bulgaria) to 489 (Luxembourg) mail items per inhabitant with an average of 195 and a median of 137.

Figure 13.3 shows that 37 percent of the countries show low mail scales (below 100 items per inhabitant per year) and 26 percent operate in a market that presents high postal scales (300 and more). Low postal scales (less that 150) is a characteristic of the market that may affect countries such as Italy, Greece, Spain, Latvia, Lithuania, Malta, Cyprus, Ireland, Romania and Bulgaria. In these countries, mail is often associated with administrative issues: in Italy, for example, 16 percent of the letter mail volume is registered mail. On the other hand, the (relatively) high mail scale countries (mail scale higher than 300) include the Nordic countries, Estonia, the United Kingdom, France, Germany, Belgium, the Netherlands, and Luxembourg, which present a more attractive market for entrants and hence are more prone to attract entrants.

Figure 13.4 indicates, as expected, the critical importance of scale on the ability of the USP to support its USO under entry. The simulations underlying the figure assume that a constant pricing constraint is imposed on the USP under entry, with the vertical axis being the loss sustained relative to pre-FMO operations by the USP under this constant-price scenario, which must then be financed either through price increases, efficiency gains or subsidies. One can see that the impact of FMO on the USP balance to be financed depends on scale. The balance to finance is measured by the coverage of the revenues linked to USO products of the costs associated with USO provision. In order to compare results across different countries, the balance to finance is normalized by using the total postal revenues. The (normalized) balance to finance equals the difference between the USP's revenues and costs associated with the USO divided by total postal revenues. We show only ordinal values: limited, important and significant. Countries with small postal scale will probably require counterbalancing drivers against financing problems for the USP, whereas countries with large postal scale will experience fewer difficulties with USP financing. In the AvC representative country for example, where impacts of FMO are average for the EU, the need to finance the USP decreases from important to only limited when scale increases from 10 to 200.

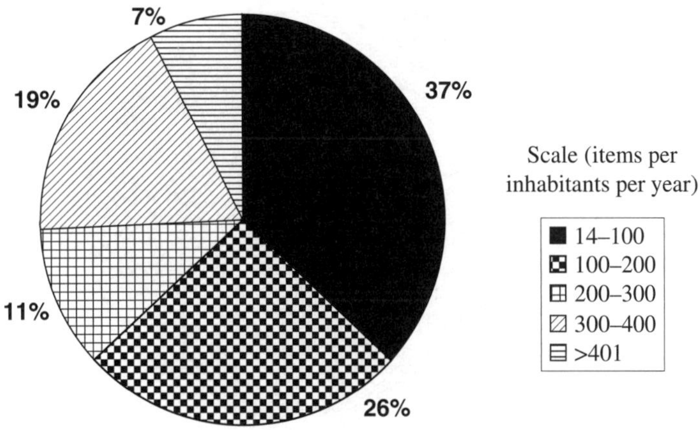

Figure 13.3 Variation in postal scale across member states

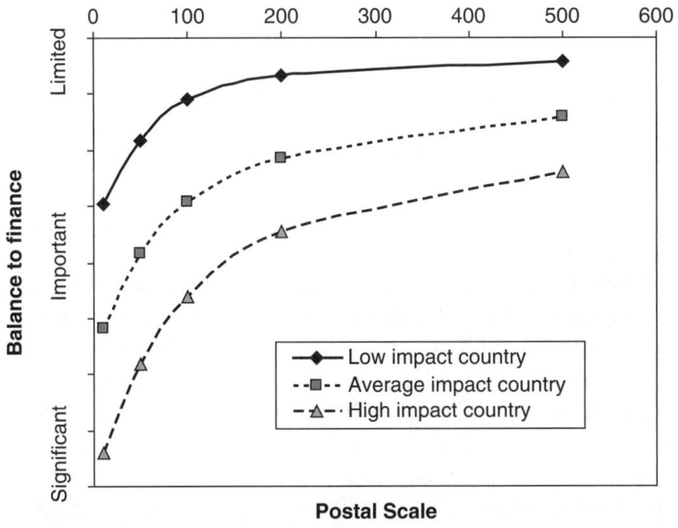

Figure 13.4 Sensitivity to postal scale of the balance to finance for the USP

Clearly, low postal scale represents a risk for the USP. However, low postal scale by itself may also be a deterrent for entrants, given the fixed costs in delivery. Thus, in terms of the impact of FMO, the impact of postal scale will be interdependent with population density and urbanization rate, factors we now examine.

Population density and urbanization rate

Price uniformity imposed on a USP as part of its USO implies that entrants will focus on less costly destinations, namely urban routes. Furthermore, urban routes are used to generate a margin to finance deliveries on rural routes. Consequently, in markets with an important proportion of rural routes, losing even a limited market share in the urban area

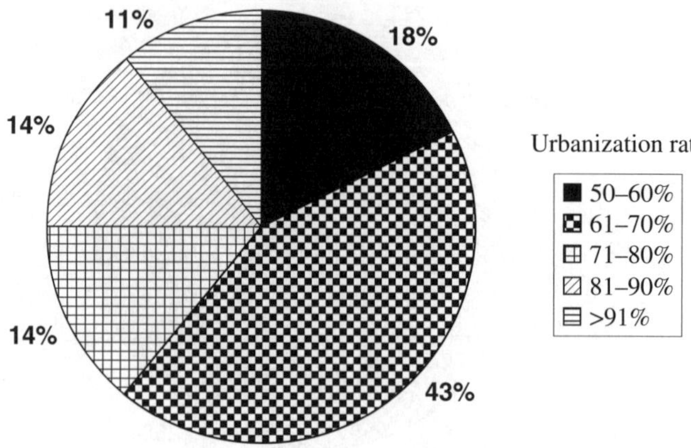

Figure 13.5 *Distribution of EU countries in terms of urbanization ratio*

implies[3] that a significant part of the de facto subsidy available to fund the rural area will be lost. Figure 13.5 shows urbanization rates across the EU.[4]

Belgium, Luxembourg, the United Kingdom, Denmark, Germany, the Netherlands and Malta are among the most urbanized countries (>80%) whereas Ireland, Finland, Portugal, Romania, Lithuania and Greece are among the least urbanized (>65%). Figure 13.6 illustrates in a matrix both postal scale and urbanization measurements (expressed as postal items per inhabitants and the urbanization rate as estimated by the United Nations) and shows 4 clusters of countries constructed according to these 2 fundamental drivers of the impacts of FMO.

The division of the clusters is based on the average values of the drivers, that is to say that in Figure 13.6, countries such as Belgium, Denmark, France, Germany, Luxembourg, Norway, Sweden and the United Kingdom all show higher than average urbanization rates and scale. In contrast, Greece, Ireland, Latvia, Lithuania, Poland, Portugal and Romania – among others – are characterized by values below average for both drivers.

According to the rationale outlined above, the impacts of FMO would be mitigated for countries in quadrant II as (i) their high postal scale allows them to drive their unit costs down making them more competitive and (ii) their high urbanization rate puts the USPs less at risk as they tend to have less expensive rural routes to support. This conclusion may be counterbalanced by the attractiveness for entrants of such high urbanization and high postal scale environments and must be considered mainly in conjunction with the efficiency level of the USP. Many other factors are also at play here, including the ratio of bulk-mail volumes (Transaction Mail + Direct Mail),[5] demand elasticities and customer loyalty in various market segments, the efficiency of the USP, and the relative cost of labor for the USP versus entrants. We consider here only USP efficiency and labor cost issues.

Labor costs and labor productivity in the EU

The USP preparedness drivers which interact with the FMO impact indicators (outcomes) fall into three categories, namely: the commercial freedom and pricing flexibility allowed the operator, the efficiency levels attained or expected to be attained in the medium term, and finally the labor-related conditions including eventual social liabilities,

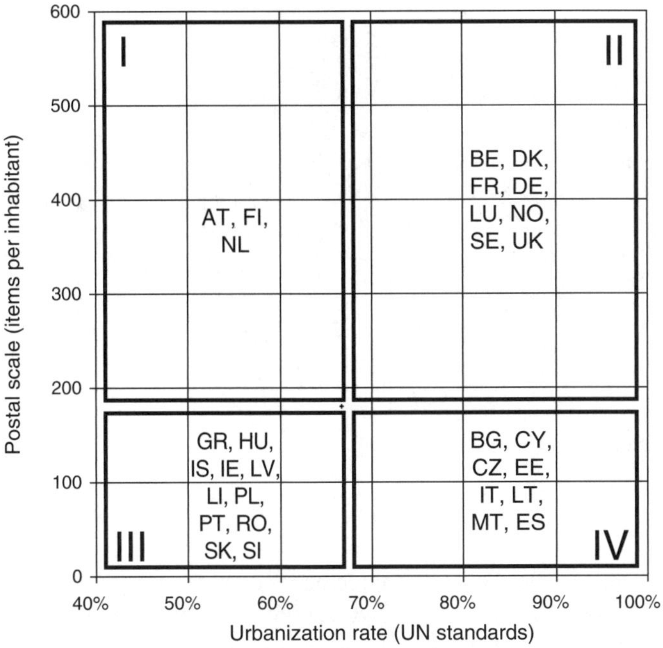

Note: For a key to country abbreviations see Figure 13.19.

Figure 13.6 Postal scale and urbanization rate

resulting from the historical status of the USPs as state-owned enterprises. These three dimensions are related to the overall USP capacity to operate in an efficient manner and the flexibility to respond to competitive threats.

In general, it can be assumed that an operator presenting overall high levels of efficiency is more likely to take advantage of new (or increased) competition following FMO, innovating in new products and services. In a context of high efficiency, the optimized cost structure and processes in place will translate to relatively lower unit costs that will make it more challenging for the entrant to align to the highly efficient operator.

Indeed, entrants will most probably follow a low-cost strategy, competing on price in order to capture sufficient market share necessary to absorb its fixed costs. This commercial strategy will only be possible – in terms of preservation of margins – if the entrant can operate in a highly efficient manner, actually more efficiently than the USP. It already can be observed that most of the entrants follow a different business model, allowing them to offer competitive prices, but also time-definite services, corresponding to clients' expectations. They focus on delivery, part of the sorting being done by the mailer itself, without requesting daily frequency of delivery.

The efficiency levels attained are strongly correlated to the ability of the management to engage in improvement exercises or restructuring without political influence. Commercial freedom allowed to the USP, performance accountability of the USP management and the USP capacity to undertake efficiency improvements are the critical factors. The same goes for the labor conditions which are also a constraint originating in

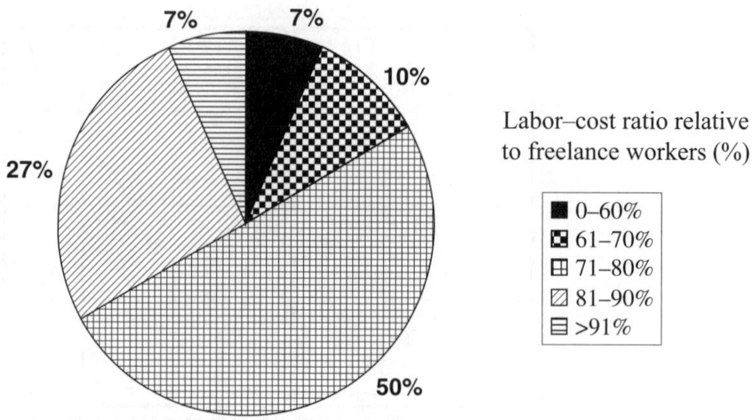

Source: PwC (2006).

Figure 13.7 Distribution of countries across labor–cost ratio ranges

general from specific collective labor agreements or more simply from the special status (mostly) of USP postal workers. The PwC (2006) study examined the issue of labor cost differences by considering the sensitivity of key outcomes to the labor–cost ratio, defined as the relative cost of the freelance workforce (the assumed source of labor for entrants) relative to the average USP labor cost. Figure 13.7, from PwC (2006), summarizes the diversity of the labor–cost ratio across EU countries.

In some countries, such as Poland, the labor–cost ratio is higher than 1, in other words the freelance labor costs are higher than for the USP. This atypical situation will make it difficult for entrants to compete, and will also not be particularly encouraging to the USP to realize efficiency gains in labor. By contrast, in two-thirds of the countries the entrants potentially benefit from favorable labor–cost ratios of 80 percent or less, that is the cost of freelance labor at a cost of 80 percent or less than that of the USP. This cost differential is most advantageous to the entrants in countries such as Sweden (74 percent), Norway (75 percent), Italy (72 percent), Greece (69 percent), France (73 percent) and Belgium (68 percent).

Figure 13.8 shows the results on market share of entrants and on the deficit of the USP under constant prices for the three representative countries of Table 13.1 as the labor–cost ratio varies. As expected, there is a high sensitivity of these outcomes to the labor–cost ratio. A low ratio allows the entrant easy market penetration. On the other hand, if the labor–cost differential is negligible, so is market penetration by entrants. Of course, the prevailing cost disadvantages for the USP in the labor market can be countered by allowing pricing flexibility in the USP, or by imposing the same collective labor conventions on entrants as obtained for the USP.[6]

A higher value of the labor–cost ratio unsurprisingly reduces the competitive advantage of entrants relative to the USP. Nevertheless, above some level (80 percent in this model) even in the HiC environment, a significant drop of the competitive advantage of the entrant leads to very limited market share for entrants. The reason for this is the combination of high population density, high urbanization rate, and low postal scale in the HiC environment. Interestingly, entrants can only exploit such a market if they have an

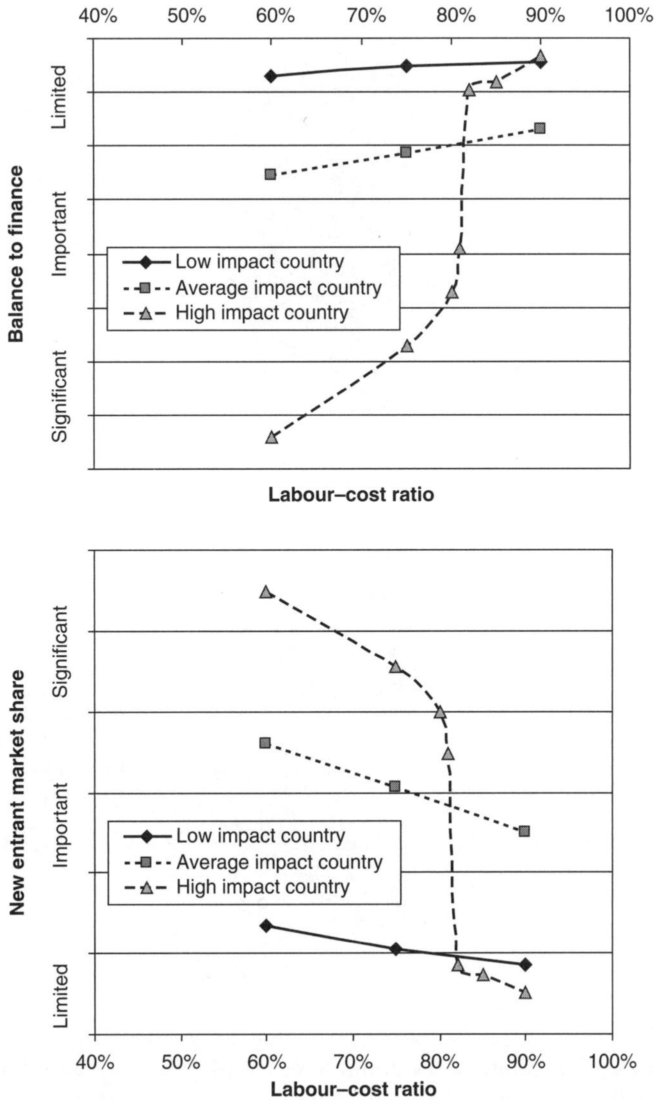

Figure 13.8 *Sensitivity of the balance to finance and of the entrant's market share to the labor–cost ratio (cost of freelancers relative to that of the USP)*

advantage in labor costs. The nonlinear relation between the unit cost and the postal scale is evident in Figure 13.8 and shows that several factors can interact in postal markets to determine outcomes.

Two important additional indicators of labor costs are the percentage of civil servants working for the USP and labor productivity, the latter of which was measured in PwC (2006) as the total number of mail items per year processed per USP FTE (full-time equivalent) staff allocated to USO. Labor productivity does not take into account country

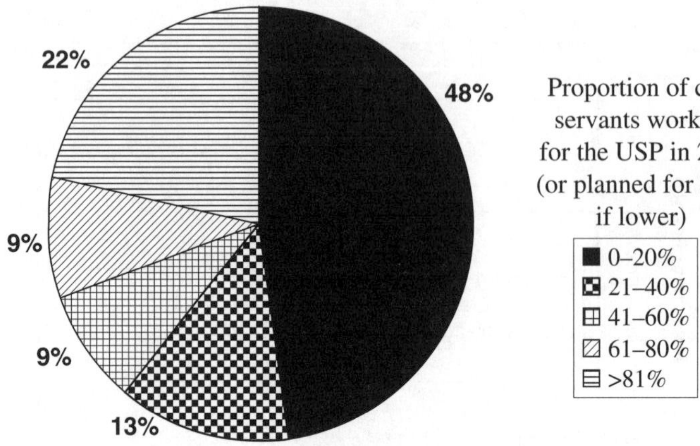

Figure 13.9 Distribution of civil servant ratios across EU countries

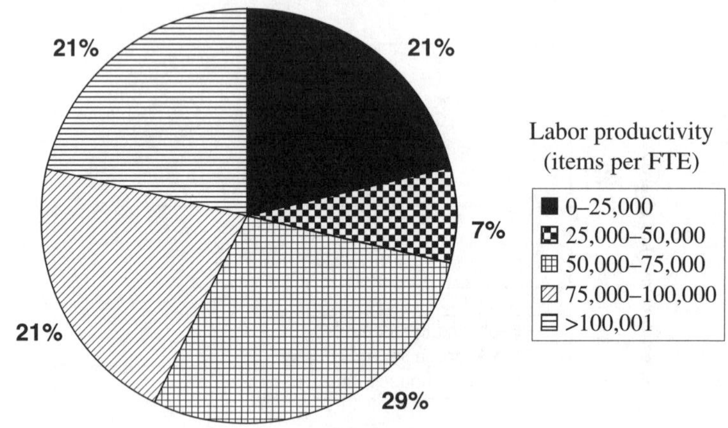

Figure 13.10 Distribution of countries across labor productivity ranges (measured as postal items per FTE)

specificities such as, for example, the country geography and population density, postal scale, ratio of bulk mail relative to total volumes, and many other factors which could affect this rather simple measure. Figures 13.9 and 13.10 below present results for civil servants employed at USPs and labor productivity ratios across EU member states in 2006.

The impact of the USO

Defining the scope of the USO remains one of the most complex questions when assessing the impact of the FMO. The USO defines the rights of postal users to benefit from postal services in a context where postal traffic still constitutes an essential channel of communication. Originally, the main objectives when defining USO were to ensure provision of postal services at a predefined quality level, accessible to all throughout a country or region on a permanent, transparent and non-discriminatory basis, under the control of an independent authority and at an affordable price.

For the last 20 years, the European Commission has worked on the regulatory framework of the postal sector with a view to the full accomplishment of the internal market for postal services. The first stage of the development of the European postal policy was the Green Paper published in 1992. The First Postal Directive (97/67/EC) that followed in 1997 outlined the basis of the universal postal services. This Directive was amended in 2002 by the Second Postal Directive (2002/39/EC). Neither the Second nor the just approved Third Postal Directive of (2008/06/EC) brought any modifications to the scope or characteristics of the universal postal services, except regarding the progressive reduction of the reserved area, which will be completely eliminated in all EU member states by 2013.

The latitude allowed by the Directive concerning the upward weight limit for parcels allows countries to set up limits on their internal market that differ from other countries. However, the upper weight limit among all countries for inbound cross-border mail should be equal to 20 kg, as part of the Universal Postal Union (UPU) obligation of acceptance for inbound cross-border postal items. The specific case of newspapers and periodicals delivery is worth mentioning. The inclusion or not in the USO product scope varies widely from country to country. Indeed, countries such as France, Italy, Finland, Germany and Denmark, have included newspapers and periodicals in the scope of the USO and in some cases, an important state subsidy is foreseen to cover the associated costs (as is the case in France, Italy and Belgium).[7]

Delivery frequency is a sensitive aspect of the USO in the EU. Most of the USO-related literature focuses on the delivery dimension of access to the postal services (receiving) although it includes both receiving and sending mail. One of the reasons provided to justify this focus is that delivery constitutes a large part of POs' costs. Although the minimum required by the Directive is one delivery per working day (equivalent to five deliveries per week), the national regulations of a large number of countries (37 percent of EU member states) impose on their operators six deliveries per week. Also some exceptions are allowed, such as lower frequency of delivery to outlying islands in Finland, Greece and Norway.

Maintaining or increasing the current delivery frequency level would increase the likelihood that the costs of the USO will not be fully covered financially (USPs balance to finance). Measurement of the USO burden remains an active area of interest in the EU, especially considering prohibitions against state aid under European competition law.[8] The PwC (2006) study and several others (for example, see d'Alcantara and Gautier, 2008) have underlined the fact that the main costs generated by the USO are due to the combination of pricing uniformity and the costs associated with delivery frequency. For example, as pointed out in the PwC study, a reduction in delivery frequency from six to three per week in rural areas would significantly reduce the balance to be financed for each type of countries (LoC, AvC, HiC) as it will reduce high costs generated in rural areas. In the case of the incumbent USPs, this would help to counterbalance the loss of market share to entrants in urban areas.

While less important than delivery frequency, another driver of the cost of the USO is the accessibility requirement to counter services, typically defined in terms of distance to classical access points (public letter boxes and traditional post offices). The definition of the postal counter access standards differs from one country to the other. However, the frequency of collection and delivery, the post office geographical accessibility (minimum

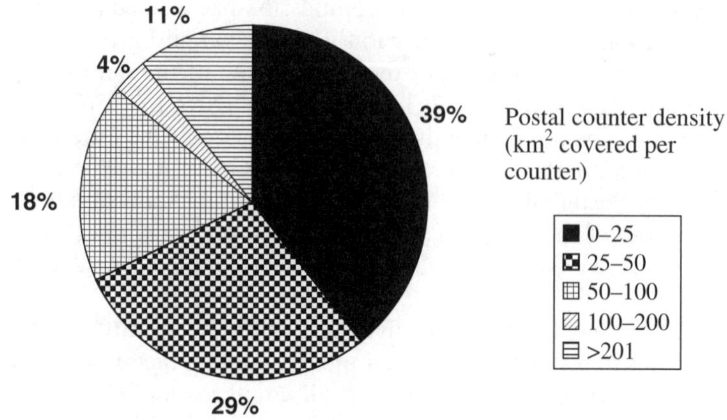

Figure 13.11 Distribution of countries across ranges of postal counter densities (geographic)

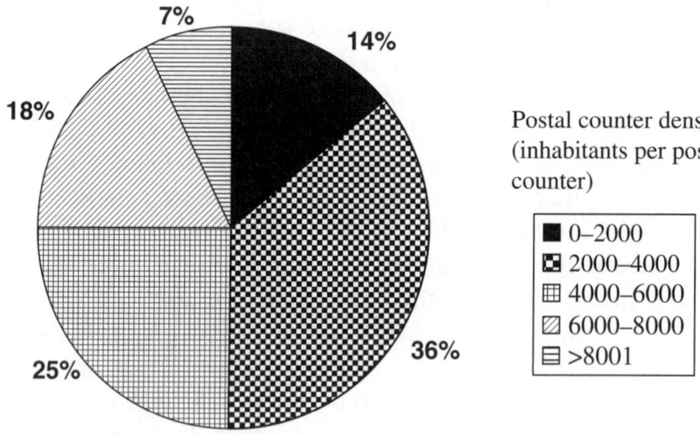

Figure 13.12 Distribution of countries across ranges of postal counter densities (inhabitants)

postal network density, franchising operation level and so on) and time accessibility (opening hours) seem to be the critical characteristics when assessing the scope of the USO. The 2006 situation in the EU relative to counter services is summarized in Figures 13.11 and 13.12. For additional details, see Cohen et al. (2008) and Buser et al. (Ch.5, this volume).

A final matter of obvious importance in considering postal reform is pricing. As discussed in Crew and Kleindorfer (2008b) and Campbell et al. (Ch.12, this volume), price regulation in the EU has generally been implemented via price caps. However, price caps are implemented in different ways, and the scope of price uniformity and the structure of access and worksharing prices varies considerably. Movement towards zonal pricing and other aspects of aligning price and underlying are expected under FMO. Similarly, given competitive pressures, one can expect that the price of bulk mail will decrease relative to

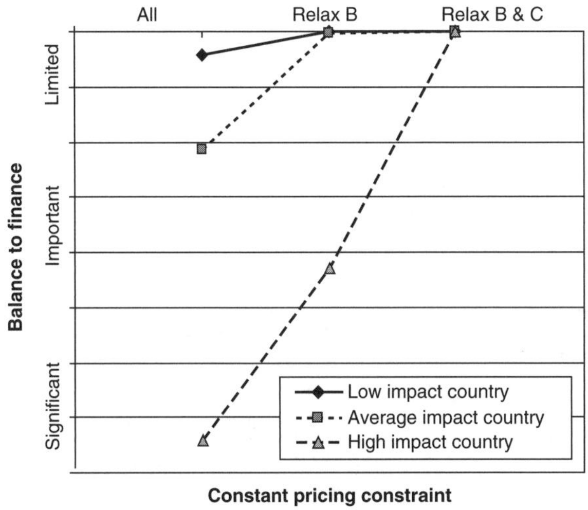

Note: B = business mailers mainly bulk; C = household mailers mainly single piece.

Figure 13.13 Sensitivity of the USP balance to finance a relaxation of the fixed price constraints

the less elastic single-piece mail. As of January 2008, EU average prices for a 20-gram letter averaged \$0.84 with a standard deviation of \$0.22,[9] though variation is considerably higher if these are adjusted for purchasing power parity (DPAG, 2006).

Constraints on uniformity of prices (for example, prohibiting zonal pricing) for bulk mail and constraints on price levels for single-piece letters can have significant impacts on the ability of incumbent USPs in the EU to finance their USO from their own earnings. Such uniformity is not required by the Postal Directives and can be expected to be under pressure as liberalization unfolds. To see the effects of pricing restrictions, consider Figures 13.13 and 13.14 for the three representative countries of interest here. These figures show the consequences of relaxing pricing uniformity and levels on bulk (B) mail, together with relaxation of constant price levels for single-piece (C) mail. Allowing pricing flexibility for the business segment (B) in the market would have different impacts depending on the group of countries discussed, growing from LoC to HiC clusters. Only small adjustments in price levels are required to achieve break-even operations for LoC countries and AvC countries. On the other hand, for HiC countries, significant price increases for both bulk mail and single-piece mail market segments are likely to be required to achieve break-even operations, given current levels of the USO. Note that allowing pricing flexibility in both markets allows the USP to maintain higher market shares, as relying on both bulk prices and single-piece prices obviously provides greater commercial flexibility to support the USO and to respond to competitive threats segment by segment.

As expected from theory (for example, Crew and Kleindorfer, 2006b), relaxing the uniformity constraint is important for bulk mail, thereby making access prices and work-sharing discounts sensitive to delivery costs (see also Crew and Kleindorfer, Ch.3, this volume). Uniformity is expected to continue for single-piece mail in EU member states.

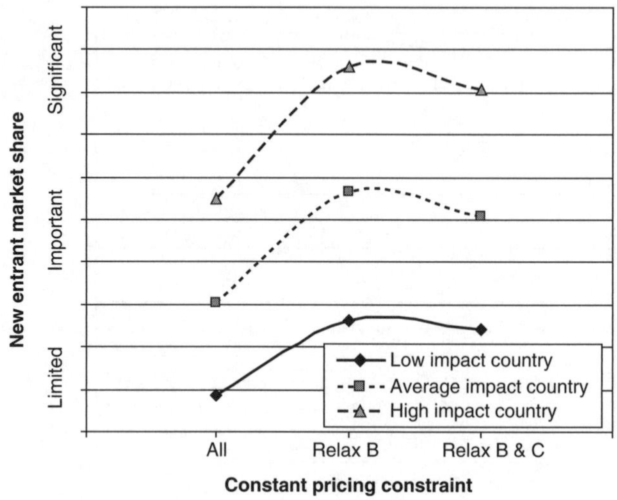

Note: B = business mailers mainly bulk; C = Household mailers mainly single piece.

Figure 13.14 Sensitivity of the entrant's market share to a relaxation of the constant pricing constraint

As a final matter of interest concerning the USO, practically all the countries have standards of quality that are based on the intra-community cross-border quality standards. In some case, incumbents have some difficulties to respect the standards incorporated in each member state's regulation. It is also the responsibility of each member state to arrange independent monitoring of universal service quality standards and for the publication of the results.

Competitors and entrants

In several countries, competition has already been present for some time on different segments of the postal market. The main segments of the postal market that have attracted the interest of the competition include the newspapers and press delivery, the bulk mail in general (above RA limits and the direct mail in countries where it is not RA), the date certain delivery products, and of course the non-addressed mail (although this is not perceived as being part of the postal market).

Entry strategies differ widely from country to country. The origin of the development of the competition ranges from the logistics business that diversified into the mail business (for example, BD in Belgium) to the pure entrant (for example, Sandd in the Netherlands) or to the development from a newspaper distribution base (for example, Adrexo in France). In a context of overall decreasing mail volumes and slightly increasing direct mail volumes (depending on the market of course), the existing market players rely for their development on the growth of direct mail as an advertisement medium and on the capture of market share from the incumbent. Some competitors claim that they could still thrive in a zero growth market by simply gaining market share from the USP.

The typical market for the competitors is the bulk mail (pre-sorted or not) delivered in the urban zones or intercity. Of course un-addressed mail remains well represented among competitors, as it is not a part of the reserved area of USPs even now, and represents much lower delivery and setup costs for an operator. Similarly, newspaper distribution has seen considerable growth in competitor services and independent providers.

Some characteristics of the USO such as five- or six-day delivery frequency are not considered by most competitors as essential to the postal service. Indeed, these operators typically operate on two- or three-day delivery frequencies, and put more emphasis on date-definite delivery rather than on fixed frequency. This alternative product feature allows their customers to better target their audiences (for example, mail delivered on the last day of the week to ensure attention during the weekend) and to better plan within their organizations (for example, customer services availability in the mail order business).

Most entrants/competitors also differentiate themselves from the incumbent postal operators by proposing more attractive pricing, but using advanced address databases. On the side of the customers, PwC (2006) reports that the vast majority of large mailer customers interviewed are looking forward to the opening of the postal market as they are all convinced that FMO will induce a decrease in prices and an improvement in quality.

Regulatory policies

PwC (2006) lists a number of common concerns by competitors and other stakeholders about barriers to entry, and these concerns are currently active issues for postal regulators in the EU. These include the pricing practices of the incumbent operator (for example, for access services); VAT exemption of POs; access to addresses database (change of address, re-expedition, PO box access); letterbox access (digital codes or keys); non-transparent standards (sorting, addressing); and constraining licensing schemes. For details on one regulator's approach to these matters, see the French case described in Gallet-Rybak et al. (Ch.18, this voulme). Figure 13.15 summarizes the basic arguments raised by EU competitors to date, as reviewed in the PwC study.

Summary of EU postal market conditions relative to FMO

Summarizing, the predicted impact of introducing FMO in the EU has been studied here in three representative countries, with postal market parameters defined in Table 13.1. The key parameters differentiating these postal markets in terms of the impact of FMO on the USP and on the USO are: postal scale, labor–cost ratio, and urbanization rate.

- *Impact of postal scale* The impact of postal scale for the most sensitive countries (HiV), exhibiting scales of 10–20 letters per inhabitant per annum, is very significant, while the impact of the same driver is much less important at average to high postal scale.
- *Impact of labor–cost ratio and postal density (urbanization rate)* Both of these parameters imply significant sensitivity in moving from HiCs to AvCs and from AvCs to LoCs. Furthermore, the 'cumulative' effect associated with reducing the labor–cost ratio from HiCs to LoCs (that is, from Table 13.1 in going from a ratio of 60 percent to 90 percent) reduces significantly the USP market share loss as well as its balance to finance. In other words, one can consider that USPs characterized by an unfavorable high urbanization rate and a high labor–cost ratio would actually not be significantly worse off than a USP benefiting from a favorable urbanization rate and an unfavorably low labor–cost ratio. It is the combined effect of

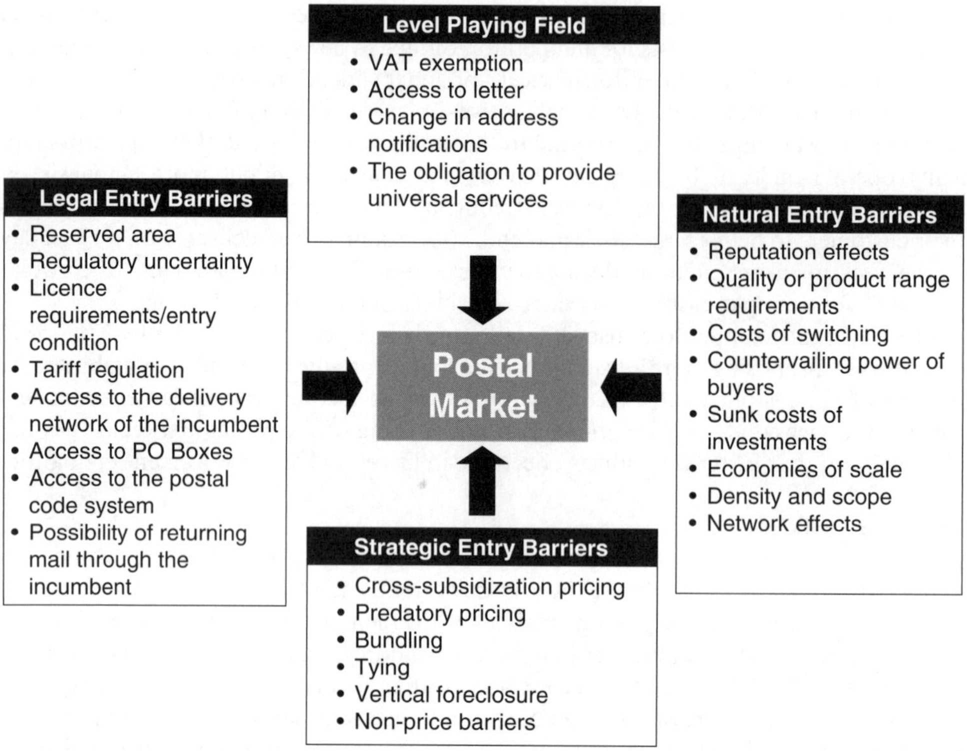

Figure 13.15 Regulatory policies and barriers to entry

unfavorable labor costs relative to the competition and high urbanization levels that encourages competitive entry that is difficult for the USP to counter.

A further key factor affecting the outcomes of market opening is, of course, the efficiency of the USP. Some of the drivers of efficiency are noted above. We now consider the wave of restructuring activity that has already been launched in EU POs in anticipation of the competition enabled by the Third Postal Directive.

3. EFFICIENCY AND RESTRUCTURING ACTIVITIES OF USPs IN THE EU

Following the gradual introduction of competition in the European postal sector, USPs have introduced various restructuring programs with a view to improving their efficiency, retaining their share of the postal markets and developing activities in new markets such as the financial and logistic sectors. Initially, two main groups of countries could be distinguished: proactive USPs, often initiating reforms in advance of the European agenda, and reactive USPs, which implemented reforms as challenges arose. In the first category are countries such as Sweden, the United Kingdom, the Netherlands and Germany. These

Table 13.3 Efficiency measures observed in various USPs in the EU

Efficiency measures	Potential expected effect
Sorting automation and/or rationalization of transport and sorting networks	Increase in productivity
Centralized sorting centers	Increase in productivity and cost reduction
Counter franchising	Reduction of fixed cost base but still a variable cost in most cases
Diversification of products and services at counters	Increase in revenue and loyalty
Modernizing and automating the counter network	Decrease in costs and increase in quality of service
Postal counter front-office automation (front office IT)	Increase in productivity and quality of service
Replacement of counters with mobile counters	Reduction of fixed cost
Counter density reduction	Reduction of fixed cost base
Reduction of mail boxes	Reduction of fixed cost base
Redeployment of mail boxes	Reduction of fixed cost
Walk sequencing and/or walk routes optimization	Increase in productivity
Increase in the motorized delivery in order to increase delivery speed	Increase in productivity and quality of service
Management and staff incentives	Increase in productivity
Outsourcing of transportation activities	Cost reduction
Contractual workforce, replacing civil servants contracts	
Hiring self-employed, or part-time workforce	Cost reduction and flexibility
Cost accounting implementation	Improvement of management decision
Management information systems implementations	Improvement of management decision
Reduction of central /regional overheads	Reduction of fixed costs and improved management accountability

may be the leaders, but nearly every PO in the EU has begun the process of restructuring, in many instances imitating initiatives set in motion by proactive POs. Introducing restructuring programs is not straightforward as such programs often confront opposing forces representing stakeholders for whom change is perceived as difficult or not in their interest. Restructuring initiatives have occurred on two dimensions: (i) reducing the level of costs while maintaining the required level of outputs and maintaining or increasing the level of output quality; and (ii) increasing the level of revenues, while maintaining the level of costs, primarily through diversification of product lines to leverage economies of scope in the USP network. We treat each of these activities separately.

3.1 Efficiency Initiatives of the USP

Efficiency initiatives of European USPs have included those listed in Table 13.3.[10]

Significant diversity is observable throughout EU POs in terms of the specifics of their efficiency initiatives. For example, (further) automation of the sorting process in countries

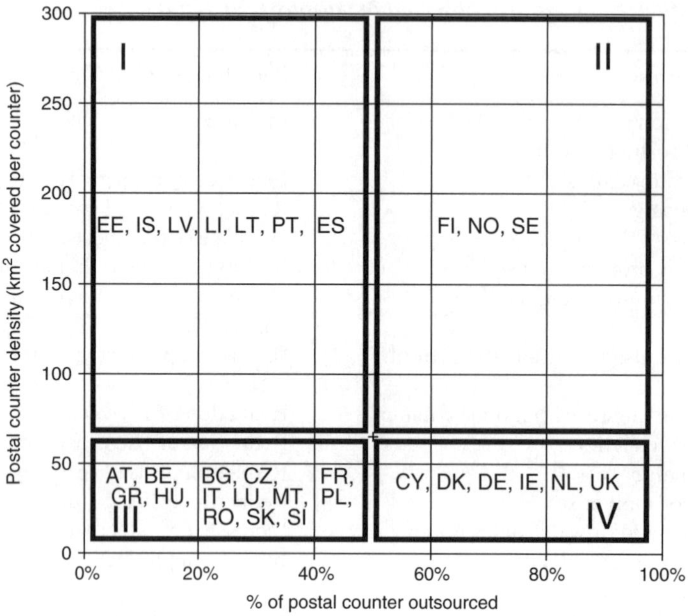

Note: For a key to country abbreviations see figure 13.19.

Source: PwC (2006).

Figure 13.16 Postal counters outsourced and postal counter density

where labor costs are relatively low (Poland, Hungary, and the Czech Republic) is not always economically sound because the return on investment remains negative due to the relatively high cost of implementation and sorting and sequencing activities may not yet be possible due to market organization (deliveries, post codes and so on). Some initiatives are driven directly by the USP whereas in other cases the postal regulator triggers efficiency improvement initiatives. For example, the Danish competition authority has encouraged Post Denmark to further outsource its post offices.

The Italian case is a good example of some of the restructuring initiatives undertaken by USPs in the EU in anticipation of FMO. Over the past 10 years, Poste Italiane has radically improved its efficiency and the overall quality of its services. Among its several initiatives, one can note: the redesign of the overall delivery processes, the ongoing reduction in the number of sorting centers, and the outsourcing of the delivery of both parcels and registered mail; all leading to an overall employment reduction from 220,000 to 150,000. This led (in 2002–04) to the first profits in 50 years and comfortable EBIT (earnings before interest and taxes) margins, demonstrating that the efficiency improvement efforts of the last decade are bearing fruit.

As one of several efficiency measures from Table 13.3, consider the level of outsourced (or franchised) postal counters. The higher the proportion of outsourced postal counters the lower the fixed costs borne by the USP, with favorable consequences in reducing mark-ups to cover these costs, as well as the opportunity for cream-skimming by entrants in low-cost areas resulting from these mark-ups.[11] Figure 13.16 from PwC (2006) shows the diversity of outsourced postal counter activity in the EU, along with postal counter density (on the vertical axis).

However, the figure does not take into account other ways that some USPs have undertaken to reduce the fixed costs of their counter network. For example, Italy has succeeded in having most of these paid for by the development of their financial services, while France maintains counters in remote areas, in part, through direct governmental subsidies.

3.2 Diversification Activities

To increase revenues, building on their existing network, EU POs have often diversified their operations, developing financial services or international logistic activities. To reduce their level of costs, POs have embarked on traditional restructuring programs aimed at increasing organizational efficiency through the introduction of more adaptive and flexible structures and increasing organizational effectiveness through the introduction of quality measurements and improvements programs. In doing so, the most proactive POs have to date managed to achieve considerable success.

In seeking to increase their profitability, POs in the EU have naturally considered reducing costs and hence potentially rationalizing their networks, for example, by increased franchising of counter services. This rationalization can, in some cases, lead to a network coverage reduction or to the perception by the public at large of a reduction in network coverage. However, even if justifiable, network rationalization is often confronted by resistance, individual interests being always difficult to balance with the public interest. Furthermore, network coverage is often associated with the terms of the USO and can therefore only be implemented to a limited extent. Consequently, even when network rationalization is necessary and has demonstrable benefits in improving the financial standing of USPs, it has not been viewed as the primary strategy for restructuring in the EU.

Rather, many USPs have attempted to increase revenues by diversifying their portfolio of activities to exploit their key strength: a ubiquitous presence in terms of counters and delivery. Diversification allows USPs to increase revenues with relatively small increases in their costs. The usual approach is through the development of new products belonging to the 'traditional' postal market as well as through the introduction of new products such as financial services, administrative support and travel services. Several postal operators, such as TNT and DPWN, have successfully managed to diversify in logistics and transport activities through the acquisition of worldwide logistic operators. Others, such as La Poste (FR), have developed their own internal logistic activities.

Diversification into financial services has been one of the most important diversifications that has been implemented by POs and it was also probably the most obvious to exploit since it allows the PO to leverage on their brand, customer base, network of counters, and existing experience in terms of support to or management of transactions between public authorities and citizens (tax bill payments and social benefit distribution). Figure 13.17 shows the relative importance of financial services in the total services for a selected number of postal operators that have diversified their activities to financial activities.

This figure clearly indicates the importance of financial services in the POs, this diversification being therefore a key means for them to spread their fixed network costs

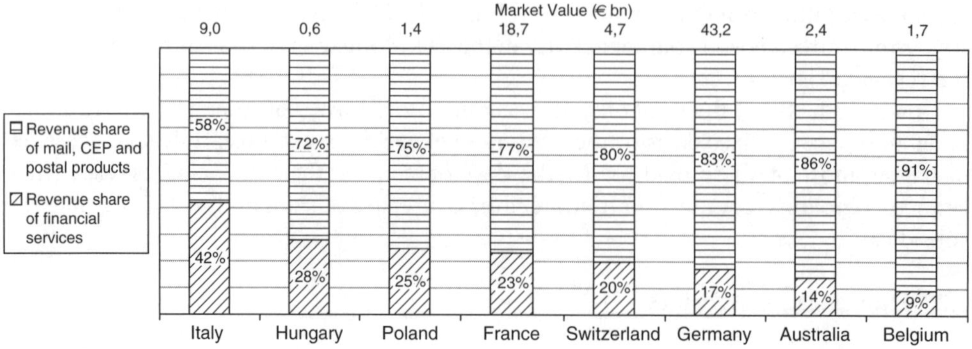

Source: La Poste/De Poste, presented at the Vienna Postal Conference, March 20–21 2006.

Figure 13.17 Share of total revenues of POs derived from financial services

over a broader range of activities, thereby reducing the burden associated with their USO coverage.

Such diversification has taken several forms, depending on the financial resources of the POs and on market conditions. The most common are briefly described below:

- *Development of fully or majority owned bank* Directly owned banks are developed as separate entities of POs. They are in possession of their own banking licenses and have concluded an agreement for using the distribution network of the PO, generally through an internal transfer fee payment. DPWN and Deutsche Postbank, as well as La Poste and La Banque Postale are typical examples of such diversification.
- *Development of banking joint venture* Another possibility is to establish a joint venture with pre-existing banks. In Belgium, Fortis provides management services, back office and asset management services of financial product to a joint venture with La Poste/De Post. The joint venture pays a fee to La Poste/De Post for the utilization of its postal network. This case is similar to the previous one, with the exception that risks are shared between the POs and existing banks. This option is generally privileged in highly developed banking markets such as Belgium. Similar arrangements are implemented between the UK Post Office and Bank of Ireland and An Post and Fortis.
- *Integration of financial services* Integrators are POs who distribute financial products under 'white label' or co-branding from different financial services providers. In such cases, the POs control the product offers, are in charge of marketing and manage the clients' database. Poste Italiane can be considered as an integrator. Its Banco Posta operates as a business unit without a banking license, and is nonetheless the largest banking retail network in Italy. Similar arrangements are implemented for instance by Swiss Post.
- *Distributor of financial services* POs can also simply conclude distribution agreements with one partner. In this case they often distribute an entire family of financial products, the partner controlling often the product offer and the product marketing. The responsibility of the PO is therefore very much limited to the dis-

tribution of the financial products. Such arrangements are for instance in force between Correos Spain and Deutsche Bank, or between Posten Norge and DnB.

- *Shared network* Another form of diversification/association, more symmetric and that exemplifies the value of a network of branches, can finally be listed. In this case, both the PO and a bank own a network in the form of a joint venture. Each partner pays fees based on volumes of sales associated to each partner. TNT and ING provide an example of such a shared network model.

Diversification can also apply to other products besides financial products. In the United Kingdom, for instance, post offices are no longer 'simple' post offices but service centers, postal services being part of a broader portfolio of services that are offered to customers. This diversification was implemented through a large franchising initiative which had already begun in 1989. Services that are commonly provided in post offices include: postal services, travel services (passport support services, social support services, travel insurance, exchange office and so on), licenses (driving, television and fishing licenses and so on), telecom services (phone cards and prepaid cards for mobile phones) as well as financial services.

4. SUMMARY AND CONCLUDING COMMENTS ON POSTAL REFORM IN EU MEMBER STATES

4.1 Readiness of Member States for FMO

Considering both the market conditions analyzed in Section 2 and the state of the USP analyzed in Section 3, as well as the independence and experience of national regulatory institutions, one might pose the question as to the overall readiness of EU member states to profit from FMO. To provide some sense of this, and the variation in the challenges in introducing FMO across the EU, a scorecard of readiness for FMO was constructed for each of the 30 countries studied in PwC (2006). This scorecard considered four dimensions illustrative of the country readiness to adopt FMO:

1. postal market characteristics favorable to efficiency gains and to the establishment of workable competition under FMO;
2. current status and market orientation of postal regulatory institutions;
3. USP preparedness and adaptability for FMO; and
4. market alignment of the USO.

Several indicators were used to evaluate the state of the postal market and the USP in each country on each of these dimensions. Scores on these dimensions were combined using a geometric average of the four dimensions, normalized so that the average value was 100. Figures 13.18 and 13.19 show the results of this exercise.

4.2 Conclusions on Postal Reform in the EU

Several lessons can be drawn from the studies and analysis undertaken to inform the postal reform and liberalization initiatives in the EU. First, assessing the impact of FMO in postal markets is a complex exercise because of the number of interacting factors that

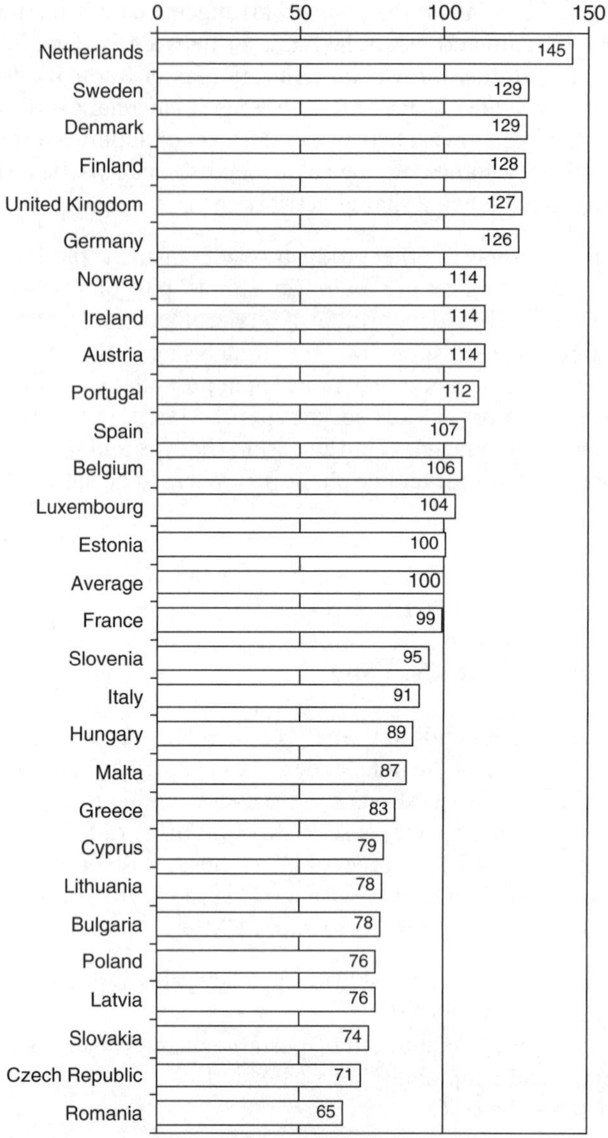

Figure 13.18 Overall FMO 'Readiness Index' for each country

need to be taken into account to predict market outcomes, and the variability of these factors across countries.

Figure 13.20 shows the main forces centered on the USO and FMO in the EU. At the top are the key forces associated with market opening. At the heart of the ensuing competition are customer communication needs, which can be met by both traditional postal products as well as from substitutes. A second critical area of importance is the current national PO, which also acts in all member states as the current USP. What happens to

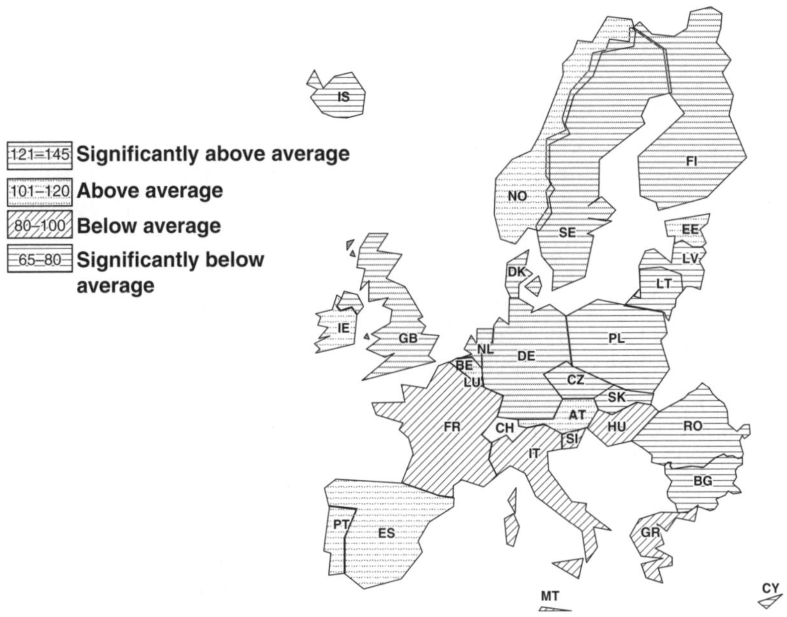

Figure 13.19 Comparative assessment of European postal markets and USPs

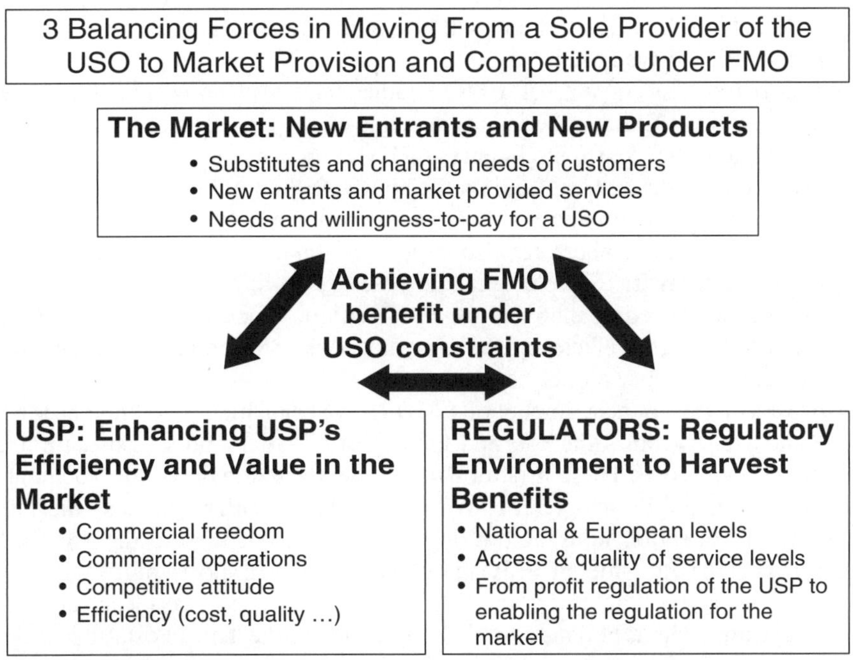

Figure 13.20 USO, USP and interacting market forces under FMO

these POs is not just an abstract matter to be calculated on a spreadsheet. These POs embody broad historical mandates that have served their public well over a long period. A key concern in the EU policy debate has been to ensure that these POs have the opportunity and the motivation to remain viable and to prosper in the new market environment.

The third key set of actors and balancing forces in the figure are regulators (both at national and EU levels). Their policies will be important in determining the nature of the interaction between entrants, the USP and customers, and they will structure the incentives and the means by which participants in these markets interact and the cash flows that they pay or receive.

The key question addressed in the debates beginning with the Postal Green Paper in 1992 and continuing through the Third Postal Directive in 2008 has been how to structure the interactions among these three main forces in the new era of FMO so as to ensure that the USO, adapted to market conditions, can continue to be guaranteed and financed to all citizens in every member state. The findings of various studies reviewed in this chapter addressing this question have identified several general conclusions.

First and foremost, by increasing competition, FMO embodies considerable advantages as a source of discipline and innovation for USPs and as a source of new value for customers in European postal markets. The impacts of FMO can be expected to be threefold. First, there will be natural alignment of price, value and cost of postal products and significant pressures wherever there is misalignment in these attributes. USO products will also face these pressures and there will be limits on regulators' ability to resist these pressures, which arise from competitive entry, without adversely affecting the financial viability of USPs. Second, there will be great pressures on national POs as USPs to become more commercial and market oriented, and to restructure their own products and processes to achieve this. Third, there will be changes for postal customers, with greater attention to market-driven needs.

In considering these impacts of FMO, studies have also noted that there are large differences across the EU member states in terms of the current status of their markets and their USP and the likely consequences of FMO on consumer well-being, on the sustainability of the historical USO, and on the ability of the USP to sustain FMO without external support, specific financial compensation or restrictions on the speed and scope of introduction of FMO. There are also large commonalities across member states, and these include the necessity to implement a sensible new regulatory model compatible with FMO, and not anchored in the past pre-FMO vision, which focused on a single USP rather than on the overall efficiency of the postal market. Several important characteristics of this new regulatory model were noted.

Key drivers of the financial impact of FMO on USPs include cost differences between the USP and likely entrants, the level and stability of USP demand, and structural factors that underlie postal costs. These structural factors are related to the country demographic, urbanistic and geographic characteristics, as these interact with postal demand. There are also key internal or endogenous factors, driven by the preparedness of the USP for FMO, which will affect the outcomes of FMO in significant ways. In short, some USPs are better prepared to face FMO than others and this was one of the key areas of debate leading to the two-stage implementation dates of 2011 and 2013 in the Third Postal Directive.

There are complex interactions among cost, demand and structural factors in terms of their impact on key outcomes of interest, including financial consequences and requirements for the USP, price changes for various market segments likely to follow FMO, and the possibility that workable competition will follow FMO for particular member states and, more broadly, across the EU.

USPs and national regulatory agencies in different member states are at various levels of preparedness for FMO. Some began preparing for FMO more than a decade ago. Some have still barely begun. There are, nonetheless, some generally applicable principles related to pricing and access regulation that can be recommended across member states that will allow a smoother and more efficient confluence with FMO. These include the pricing flexibility and incentives associated with price-cap regulation and the efficiency benefits of cost-based and negotiated-access pricing.

The impact of FMO is likely to be that both competitors and incumbent national POs will begin to understand better the true quality preferences of customers of various sizes, the cost and profit consequences of alternative methods of serving these, and there will be a better alignment over time between the costs of providing services, including those understood to be a part of the USO, and the prices paid for them. This implies that to the extent that some customers are currently receiving some services at a subsidized level as part of the USO, there will be continuing tensions to either increase these prices or decrease the costs and scope of those elements of the USO until the alignment of prices and costs is achieved. Regulatory policy clearly plays an important supportive role in this process.

The approach taken at the EU level to ensure FMO has also focused on establishing a level playing field for all participants in the market. Level playing field arguments will play an important role in ensuring that entry which does occur is efficient. These arguments include abolition of the VAT exemption for all providers in the postal market, pricing flexibility for incumbents, as well as transparent and non-discriminatory access conditions to leverage the incumbent PO's network. Much remains to be done to implement the letter and the spirit of the Third Postal Directive, but it is very clear that liberalization of markets and commercialization of POs have both entered irreversible paths in Europe.

NOTES

* This chapter relies significantly on the earlier PricewaterhouseCoopers study PwC (2006), in which all of the authors participated. This study, commissioned by the European Commission, was a prospective study on the sustainability of the postal universal service in each member state and on how competition would impact the future provision of this universal service in a fully liberalized market.

1. National POs of the 27 member states of the EU accounted for total sales of well over $125 billion and employment of over 1.1 million people, with much larger aggregate sales and employment if one includes worksharing/mail preparation organizations, newspaper distribution and the logistics sector. For details, see http://ec.europa.eu/internal_market/post/facts_en.htm.
2. For details on the demand specification used, see d'Alcantara and Amerlynck (2006).
3. More generally, as analyzed by d'Alcantara and Gautier (2008), the cost structure of routes, driven by urbanization rate, scale and other factors, has come to be recognized as a critical driver of market share losses to entrants and the sustainability of the USO by the incumbent USP under competition.
4. In the absence of reliable and comparable postal data we used the percentage of urban population following United Nations, Department of Economic and Social Affairs, Population Division, Urban and Rural Areas. See http://www.un.org/esa/population/publications/wup 2003/2003Urban_Rural.pdf.
5. Concerning bulk-mail volumes, for example, this is heavily triggered by the ratio of direct mail to total mail: in Italy for example a small proportion of mail – that is 19 percent – is composed of direct mail whereas in Germany the same proportion reaches 62 percent.

6. As is the case, for example, in Switzerland, and as has been proposed in Germany. See Dieke and Wojtek (Ch.16, this volume) for a discussion of such sector-wide constraints.
7. See Ambrosini et al. (2006) for a comparative discussion of the scope of the USO.
8. See Bergum (Ch. 7, this volume) and Panzar (Ch. 6, this volume) for a discussion of approaches to measurement of the cost of the USO. See Eccles (Ch. 14, this volume) and Panzar (Ch. 2, this volume) for a discussion of the issues competition law and their interaction with the cost of the USO.
9. See http://www.psc.gov.uk/postcomm/live/about-the-mail-market/international-market-reviews/european-comparisons--letter-prices/2008_01_stamp_price_comparison_by_country.pdf .
10. See Felisberto (2008) for a discussion of the impact of anticipated liberalization on the speed of adoption of various of these efficiency measures in EU POs.
11. Of course, there are revenue and quality benefits as well as cost effects from increased counter density. See Chapter 5, this volume for an analysis.

REFERENCES

Ambrosini, Xavier, François Boldron and Bernard Roy (2006), 'Universal service obligations in the postal sector: economic learnings from cross-country comparisons', in Crew and Kleindorfer (eds) (2006a), pp. 27–37.

Cohen, Robert H., Luigi de Paola, Renée Sheehy and Vincenzo Visco Comandini (2008),'The distribution of post offices in Italy and the United States', in Crew and Kleindorfer (eds) (2008a), pp. 36–46.

Crew, Michael A. and Paul R. Kleindorfer (eds) (2006a), *Progress toward Liberalization of the Postal and Delivery Sector*, New York: Springer.

Crew, Michael A. and Paul R. Kleindorfer (2006b), 'Approaches to the USO under entry', in M.A. Crew and P.R. Kleindorfer (eds), *Liberalization of the Postal and Delivery Sector*, Cheltenham, UK and Northampton, MA, USA: Edward Elgar, pp. 1–18.

Crew, Michael A. and Paul R. Kleindorfer (eds) (2008a), *Competition and Regulation in the Postal and Delivery Sector*, Cheltenham, UK and Northampton, MA, USA: Edward Elgar.

Crew, Michael A. and Paul R. Kleindorfer (2008b), 'Regulation and the USO', in Crew and Kleindorfer (eds) (2008a), pp. 3–22.

d'Alcantara, Gonzales and Bernard Amerlynck (2006), 'Profitability of the universal service postal provider under entry with economies of scale in collection and delivery', in Crew and Kleindorfer (eds) (2006a), pp. 39–57.

d'Alcantara, Gonzales and Alex Gautier (2008), 'Route cost structure and the USO', in Crew and Kleindorfer (eds) (2008a), pp. 67–86.

Deutsche Post AG (DPAG) (2006), Deutsche Post, 'Letter Prices in Europe', Bonn, January.

ECORYS (2005), Nick van der Lijn, Arno Meijer, Patrick de Bas, Bjorn Volkerink and Hans Kok, 'Development of Competition in the European Postal Sector', MARKT/2004/03/C, Final Study, Rotterdam, July.

Felisberto, C. (2008), 'Evidence on the effect of liberalisation and competition on innovation in the postal sector', CDM Working Papers, École Polytechnique Fédérale de Lausanne.

PricewaterhouseCoopers (PwC) (2006), 'The impact on universal service of the full market accomplishment of the postal internal market in 2009', European Commission, Brussels, May, http://ec.europa.eu/internal_market/post/studies_en.htm, accessed 8 June.

Robinson, Alan (2007), 'A review of price elasticity models for postal products', Background Paper No 2007-01, Pitney Bowes Future of Mail Project, http://www.postinsight.pb.com/files/Price_Elasticity_final.pdf, accessed 8 June 2008.

WIK (2004), James I. Campbell, Jr., Alex Kalevi Dieke, Antonia Niederprüm and Sonja Schölermann, 'Main Developments in the European Postal Sector', WIK-Consult, Bad Honnef, Germany, July.

WIK (2005), James I. Campbell, Jr., Alex Kalevi Dieke and Antonia Niederprüm, 'The Evolution of the Regulatory Model for European Postal Services', WIK-Consult, Bad Honnef, Germany, July.

WIK (2006), James I. Campbell, Jr., Alex Kalevi Dieke, Antonia Niederprüm, Mark Oelmann and Sonja Schölermann, 'Main Developments in the European Postal Sector (2004–2006)', WIK-Consult, Bad Honnef, Germany, May.

14. EU law on postal services*

Richard Eccles[†]

1. INTRODUCTION

The European Union has imposed specific legislation on the member states in the postal services sector since 1997, when the Postal Directive, Directive 97/67/EC on the internal market of Community postal services was adopted.[1] This Directive was the first stage in requiring member states to ensure minimum standards of universal service and in bringing about a 'gradual and controlled' liberalization of the postal services sector. The 1997 Postal Directive was based on the premise that postal services should be reserved to the universal service provider only to the extent necessary to ensure the continued provision of the universal service. At the same time, Directive 97/67/EC required member states to ensure cost-reflective pricing of the universal service and imposed specific requirements on cost-accounting by postal operators so as to enable prevention of cross-subsidization between reserved and non-reserved services (or between the universal service area and other services). The step-by-step opening of European markets for postal services by means of controlled reductions of the reservable area was continued by Directive 2002/39/EC ('the 2002 Directive') and is being completed by the entry into force of Directive 2008/6/EC (the '2008 Directive')[2] on 27 February 2008. This requires the member states to achieve full liberalization of the postal sector by 31 December 2010, albeit that some member states are exceptionally granted a longer period, until 31 December 2012.

At the time of writing, shortly after the entry into force of the 2008 Directive, it is necessary to assess the EC law[3] position in two stages, because member states are not required to transpose the requirements of the 2008 Directive into national law until the end of 2010, and some member states have until the end of 2012 to implement the full liberalization requirements of the 2008 Directive. Meanwhile, member states are already required under EC law to have implemented the Postal Directive as amended by the 2002 Directive into national law, so it is necessary to assess both the present position following the 2002 Directive and also the position looking forward under the 2008 Directive.

It is also important to bear in mind that EU directives, being addressed to member states, primarily impose obligations on states and not on individuals, companies, or undertakings. Member states are required to implement the provisions of a directive into national law by the date specified in the directive. Where the member state has failed properly to implement such provisions by the required date, those provisions of a directive which are unconditional and sufficiently precise can be given direct effect and enforced

† Bird & Bird, London.

directly against the member state authorities by individuals and companies.[4] Hence it is possible, depending on the facts and circumstances of the particular case, that a postal operator or other affected persons could take action to enforce those provisions of the Postal Directive which are unconditional and sufficiently precise against a member state, which has failed properly to implement such provisions into national law by the required date. By contrast, member state authorities cannot normally enforce the provisions of a directive against companies or individuals where those provisions have not properly first been implemented into national law.

This chapter is structured as follows. Section 2 explains the phased approach towards full liberalization of the postal sector under the EU Postal Directive as amended by the 2002 and 2008 Directives. Section 3 discusses the EC Treaty provisions on the grant of special or exclusive rights by a member state to undertakings and the relevant leading cases. Section 4 explains the scope of the universal service obligation under the Postal Directive. Section 5 reviews the key provisions of the 2008 Directive which are introduced in connection with and as a result of full liberalization and assesses the European Commission's underlying policy objectives when proposing the 2008 Directive. Section 6 explains the provisions of the Postal Directive concerning national regulatory authorities and the need for structural separation of regulatory and universal service operations. Section 7 analyzes the provisions of the Postal Directive concerning cross-subsidization and accounting separation, and explains the principles of EC competition law in relation to cross-subsidization. Section 8 draws some conclusions on the appropriate interpretation of the 2008 Directive and on the need for increased flexibility for incumbent universal service providers in their pricing and commercial strategies. Section 9 concludes.

2. GRADUAL AND CONTROLLED LIBERALIZATION

Directive 97/67/EC required the EU member states to impose obligations on the provider of the universal service and to reduce the reservable area (the statutory monopoly for the incumbent universal service provider) to items of domestic and incoming cross-border correspondence. This was defined by means of a weight limit of 300 grams and a price limit of not more than five times the tariff for an item of correspondence in the first weight step of the fastest category. Thus, a member state was not permitted to reserve *either* the transportation and delivery of items weighing more than 300 grams *or* transportation and delivery services for which the rate charged exceeded five times the basic letter tariff.

In July 2002, Directive 97/67/EC was amended by the 2002 Directive, which provided for two further steps in the liberalization process. Article 7(1), as amended, provided that the member states should have reduced the weight limit for reservable services to 100 grams and the price limit to a price of not more than three times the tariff for an item of correspondence in the first weight step of the fastest category by 1 January 2003. It further reduced the combined thresholds for the reservable area to 50 grams and two and a half times such tariff as from 1 January 2006. However, such services could only be reserved to the extent necessary to ensure the maintenance of the universal service. Furthermore, all outgoing cross-border mail was required to be open to competition from 1 January 2003 (that is, an additional 3 percent market opening to competition), although exceptions are possible where these are necessary to maintain the universal service, for example, where revenue from cross-border mail is necessary to finance the domestic universal service or the national postal service in a given member state has particular characteristics.

With respect to the provision of non-reserved services, the Postal Directive allows member states to grant a general authorization, without any individual approval being required before starting the activity, or to impose individual license requirements. Some countries require a license of some form, although some only for certain letter post services (for example, the UK, Germany and Sweden) and others for all universal services (for example, Belgium and Italy).

Like Directive 97/67/EC, the 2002 Directive stipulated that the reservable area relates to 'items of correspondence' (which includes any communications in written form on any kind of physical medium to be conveyed and delivered at the address indicated by the sender on the item itself or on its wrapping, with the exception of books, catalogues newspapers and periodicals). However, under the Second Postal Directive, as under the original directive, Article 7(1) provided that 'to the extent necessary to ensure the provision of universal service, direct mail may continue to be reserved within the same weight and price limits'. Although this means that member states may still include direct mail (which in practice constitutes the bulk of business-to-business (B2B) and business-to-consumer (B2C) mail volumes) in the reserved area until 31 December 2010, it puts a burden on the authorities to be able to justify that it is necessary to ensure the provision of the universal service. In any event, under the 2008 Directive, any reserved area must be abolished in respect of all postal services by 31 December 2010, except for Greece, Luxembourg and nine of the 12 member states which acceded to the EU in 2004 and 2007, which are required to achieve full liberalization in accordance with the Directive by 31 December 2012.[5]

The 2008 Directive also provides that during the period from 1 January 2011 to 31 December 2012, member states which have abolished their reserved areas may refuse to authorize postal operators which are granted a reserved area in another member state to provide postal services which are within the scope of both the universal service and the abolished reserved area.[6]

3. EC LAW ON THE GRANT OF SPECIAL OR EXCLUSIVE RIGHTS

Up until the required implementation date of the 2008 Directive, the provisions of the Postal Directive on the grant of exclusive or reserved area rights by a member state to a universal service provider have, in effect, implemented for the postal sector the provisions of Article 86 of the EC Treaty on the grant of special or exclusive rights by a member state.

Article 86(1) EC applies in the case of undertakings granted special or exclusive rights by the state and requires member states not to enact or maintain in force any measure contrary to the EC Treaty, and in particular the competition rules of the Treaty, in relation to such undertakings. Article 86(2) limits the application of the rules of the EC Treaty, and in particular of the competition rules in relation to undertakings entrusted with the provision of services of general economic interest, so that those rules only apply in so far as they do not obstruct the performance, in law or in fact, of the particular tasks assigned to them.

The grant or maintenance of exclusive rights is only justified under the Postal Directive in so far as they are necessary for the provision of the universal service. This is based on the ruling of the European Court of Justice (ECJ) in the landmark *Paul Corbeau* case[7] that exclusive rights in favor of a universal service provider are not justified under Article 86 as regards specific services, if the services are dissociable from the universal service itself (the service of general interest) and meet certain other criteria. These further criteria are that the services meet special needs of customers, call for certain additional services not offered by the traditional postal service, and can be performed without compromising the economic equilibrium of the service of general economic interest. Express mail services are an example where the specific dissociable services do not, taking into account their nature and the conditions in which they are offered, affect the economic equilibrium of the universal service provider.[8]

The Corbeau test was restated by the ECJ in May 2001 in its judgment of *TNT Traco SpA and Poste Italiane SpA*.[9] The ECJ held that the imposition by a universal service provider of postal dues (based on universal service postage prices) on the provision by independent operators of express postal services could only be justified with reference to Article 86(2) if the maintenance of such rights was necessary for the universal service provider to be able to perform its public service tasks or to perform them under *economically acceptable and financially stable conditions*. Further, the ECJ concluded that compatibility with Articles 82 and 86 meant that the proceeds from the postal dues may not exceed the amount of the losses incurred in the operation of the universal service by the universal service provider, that the universal service provider must also be required to pay the same dues when itself providing an express mail service not forming part of the universal service, and that none of the costs of that service may be subsidized from the universal service.

The Commission set out guidelines in its Postal Services Notice,[10] including a restatement of a key principle of much of the case law under Article 86 EC, that where the member state grants exclusive rights to an operator for services and that operator does not in fact provide such services so to satisfy the needs of customers to an acceptable level, the grant of such exclusive right by the member state induces the operator in question (by the simple exercise of such right) to limit the supply of the relevant service.[11] This is due to the legal impossibility of competition by other entities as the result of the exclusivity.[12]

In essence, Directive 97/67 and the European Commission's Postal Services Notice require universal service providers, particularly within the field of the reserved activities, to provide services satisfying the needs of customers to the same extent as competitive economic operators would have done. This includes providing an efficient service which takes into account technical developments. The Commission is concerned (paragraph 2.7 of the Postal Services Notice) that postal operators granted special or exclusive rights may let the quality of service decline and omit to take necessary steps to improve service quality.

4. THE UNIVERSAL SERVICE OBLIGATION

The Postal Directive imposes significant universal service obligations in Articles 3 and 5. Member states are to ensure that users enjoy the right to a universal service involving the permanent provision of a postal service of specified quality at all points in their territory at affordable prices for all users. This means that universal service providers are to guarantee, as a minimum, one clearance and one delivery to the home or premises of every natural or legal person, every working day and not less than five days a week (Article 3(3)). The Postal Directive requires all member states to ensure that the universal service includes, as a minimum, the following: first, the clearance, sorting, transport and distribution of postal items of up to 2 kilograms; second, the clearance, sorting, transport and distribution of postal packages of up to 10 kilograms (with an option to increase this to 20 kilograms); third, the delivery of postal packages received from other member states weighing up to 20 kilograms; and fourth, services for registered items and insured items.

The Postal Directive requires member states to ensure that the universal service provision complies with the 'essential requirements', that is, the need for confidentiality of correspondence, security of the network as regards the transport of dangerous goods and, where justified, data protection, environmental protection and regional planning (Article 5(1)). The Postal Directive requires the universal service to be made available without discrimination, to be provided on an uninterrupted basis, and to evolve in response to the technical, economic and social environment and the needs of users.

The Postal Directive contains various provisions concerning pricing and accounting for the universal service[13] and specifically in respect of the reservable services. Member states must ensure that, as regards the universal service, prices are affordable such that all users have access to the services at prices that are geared to costs (this requirement is amended under the 2008 Directive to require that prices be cost orientated), and on transparent and non-discriminatory terms. The universal service must be an identical service to users under comparable conditions. Member states may impose an obligation on the universal service provider to set a uniform tariff. However, the application of a uniform tariff must not exclude the right of the universal service provider to conclude individual agreements on prices with customers (that is, in practice lower prices, for example for bulk mail, under transparent and non-discriminatory conditions). The 2008 Directive requires the future scope of any uniform tariff obligation imposed by member states to be limited to single-piece items of mail.[14]

The need to safeguard the universal service is both a fundamental objective and a source of limitations on licenses granted to other operators. Moreover, under the Postal Directive, the need to safeguard the universal service is a precondition for maintaining the grant of any reserved area to the incumbent universal service provider up to the required implementation date of the 2008 Directive (31 December 2010 for most member sates and 31 December 2012 for the others). There has been no clear definition at EU level of which postal services are included within the universal service and which are not. However, it is fundamental to Directive 97/67 that services which can be reserved, namely the clearance, sorting, transport and delivery of items of domestic correspondence (within the price band mentioned above), may only be reserved 'to the extent necessary to ensure the maintenance of universal service'.

5. FULL LIBERALIZATION UNDER THE 2008 DIRECTIVE

As already explained, the 2008 Directive requires the majority of member states to achieve full liberalization of the postal services sector by 31 December 2010 (and the remainder by 31 December 2012) by abolishing any exclusive or special rights for the establishment and provision of postal services. The Directive contains a number of consequential and related amendments following from the removal of the reserved sector, as follows:

1. The obligation to ensure that prices for universal services are cost reflective, so as to stimulate efficiency gains, is strengthened by replacing the obligation to ensure that prices are geared to costs, by an obligation to ensure that prices are costs orientated. This is understood to require a closer alignment of prices and costs of the universal service, than under the 'geared to costs' obligation. However, (as explained above) member states' rights to impose a uniform tariff obligation in respect of the provision of the universal service is now to be limited to single-piece mail; as a result, the uniform tariff obligation cannot in future apply to bulk-mail services.
2. Further, the amended Article 12 requires that universal service prices give incentives for an efficient universal provision. This implies additional flexibility for the universal service provider notwithstanding the cost-orientation requirement.
3. The prohibition on cross-subsidization of universal services outside the reserved sector out of revenue from services in the reserved sector, under Directive 97/67 as amended by the 2002 Directive, is now deleted following the abolition of the reserved sector.
4. The abolition of the prohibition on member states granting or maintaining in force any exclusive or special rights for the provision of postal services, that is, the abolition of the reservable area, gives rise to a need for new means of ensuring the financing of the universal service. The new Article 7 introduced by the 2008 Directive allows member states to finance the provision of universal services by one or more of three specified means: first, by procuring such services in accordance with the EC public procurement rules;[15] second, where the universal service obligation entails a net cost[16] and represents an unfair financial burden on the universal service provider, through the introduction of a mechanism to compensate the universal service provider from public funds or through a mechanism for the sharing of the net cost of the universal service obligation between service providers (and/or users).[17] In the latter case, member states can establish a compensation fund which may be funded by service providers and/or users' fees and which is administered by a body independent of the universal service provider itself.[18] In all cases, member states must ensure that the principles of transparency, non-discrimination, and proportionality are respected when establishing any sort of compensation fund and when fixing the level of any such financial contribution. Any decisions concerning such compensation mechanisms or cost-sharing mechanisms must be based on objective and verifiable criteria and be made public.[19] These provisions represent a broadening of the original provisions of Directive 97/67 allowing the establishment of a compensation fund to compensate the universal service providers.[20]
5. An express requirement was introduced to the effect that member states that retain ownership or control of postal operators shall ensure effective structural separation

of the regulatory functions from activities associated with ownership or control. This follows from the European Commission's condemnation of France for failure to ensure separation of regulatory and operational activities in relation to La Poste (Article 22(1)).[21]

6. Further the 2008 Directive inserts a new Article 11(a) requiring member states to ensure the availability of transparent and non-discriminatory access to the following facilities which are ancillary or related to postal infrastructure or services: the post-code system, address databases, post office boxes, collection and delivery boxes, information on change of address, redirection services and return to sender services. However, recital 22 of the 2008 Directive makes clear that this access right applies to postal operators providing similar services to the universal service, and the Commission's Explanatory Memorandum (which accompanied the proposal for the 2008 Directive) stated that the requirement on member states is limited to that of adopting an informed decision on the need and extent for regulation, the choice of regulatory instrument, and any eventual compensation that might be required.

The background to and underlying policy objectives and purposes of the 2008 Directive are indicated in two European Commission documents which accompanied the proposal for the 2008 Directive: the Commission's Explanatory Memorandum, and a Report from the Commission to the European Council and Parliament[22] which was supported by a Commission Staff Working Document.[23] The Explanatory Memorandum emphasizes the need to provide sufficient freedom to universal service providers to adapt to competition while ensuring adequate monitoring of the conduct of the likely dominant operator to safeguard effective competition. In particular, the Explanatory Memorandum stated that: 'the mandatory provision of uniform tariffs in a fully competitive environment may lead to increasing costs for and risks to the viability of certain services, as the universal service provider will risk losing profitable business in those areas subject to competitive pressure' (section 3.2.2, second paragraph). The Explanatory Memorandum went on to state that member states should limit regulatory intervention to ensure the financially viable provision of the universal service and should allow universal service providers the necessary flexibility to react to competition, so as to limit any risks to the financial equilibrium of the universal service (section 3.2.2, third paragraph).

The Commission's Report to the Council and Parliament emphasized the importance of postal services and infrastructure as an input into many key sectors such as e-commerce, publishing, mail-order retailing, insurance, banking and advertising, but also emphasized that there are a number of drivers for change within the postal sector. The five most important of these were stated to be: changing customer demand, organizational change, market opening, automation/new technologies and electronic substitution.

The Commission's Report highlighted various trends including the fact that the postal services sector is increasingly focused on the B2C segment of, in particular, letter post. Over 87.5 percent of letter-post items (EU wide) are sent by businesses and 62 percent of volume (up from 60.5 percent in 2004) are B2C letters. The growth rates of direct mail (addressed and unaddressed) are substantially higher than those for traditional letter mail. The Report stated that developments in the wider communications market were resulting in a number of new products and services based around, for example, home shopping and hybrid mail, such as the digital transmission of an electronic document for remote printing and mailing. The Report added that the postal sector needs to follow the pace of change in the wider communications market and that the Postal Directive needs to continue to reflect these changes. Most importantly, the Commission's Report states that 'competition is not an end in itself'. Rather, competition is stated to be 'a means to promote innovation, investment and consumer welfare'.

With regard to the new rules in relation to the reserved area, the Commission Staff Working Document (paragraph 3.2) reviewed the progress to date and reported that at present all member states have limited their reserved areas in accordance with the Postal Directive. The reserved area is the largest barrier to the completion of the internal market as the provision of letters up to 50 grams (that accounts for the majority of all postal items) may still be monopolized. Finland, Germany, Sweden and the United Kingdom have already abolished the reserved area. Several other member states have opened up the market for direct mail.

6. NATIONAL REGULATORY AUTHORITIES

Each member state is required under Directive 97/67 (as amended by the 2002 Directive) to designate one or more national regulatory authorities for the postal sector that is legally separate from and operationally independent of postal operators. Such authorities are to be entrusted with the task of ensuring compliance with the obligations arising under the Postal Directive. They may also (but not necessarily) be charged with ensuring compliance with competition rules in the postal sector.

The Commission's Report to the European Council and Parliament[24] stressed the particular importance and role of national regulatory authorities (NRAs) and the need for them to become more active in reviewing the separation of accounts, cost allocation, and monitoring prices of universal services by conducting investigations into the major areas of tariff policy, including special tariffs, terminal dues, and cross-subsidies. In this context, the collection of information, including financial information, is of particular importance.

The 2008 Directive requires member states to establish an independent body to whom service providers may appeal any decision of a national regulatory authority.[25] The 2008 Directive adds the further requirement[26] that member states that retain ownership or control of postal service providers must ensure effective structural separation of the regulatory functions from activities associated with ownership or control.

The importance of structural separation of the regulatory and universal service operations at national level was emphasized in the European Commission's decision in the application of Article 86(1) combined with Article 82 concerning La Poste of France (above) 'on the lack of exhaustive and independent scrutiny of the scales of charges and technical conditions applied by La Poste to mail preparation firms for access to its reserved services'. The Commission decided, following the reasoning of the ECJ in *GB-Inno-BM*,[27] that the French government had allowed a situation to persist in which the public undertaking, La Poste, was faced with a risk of conflict of interest as the monopoly provider of basic postal services, in relation to determining the terms of access to its reserved services and especially its postal network, because of its activities as a competitor on the upstream market for mail preparation services. In such circumstances, it was the responsibility of the state to ensure an effective monitoring system so as to re-establish effective competition on the upstream market by ensuring that the drawing up of technical specifications and the monitoring of their application would be carried out by a body which is independent of La Poste. French legislation gave La Poste the power to set its own technical and financial conditions for access by mail preparing firms to its network, including for example, conditions as to volume and standard presentation of the mail produced. These conditions were subject to only partial scrutiny by the relevant French public authority, which was not sufficiently independent and neutral in relation to La Poste. This European Commission decision was subsequently followed by a similar decision of the Commission under Article 86 EC against a provision of the German Postal Act, in October 2004.[28]

7. OBLIGATIONS AGAINST CROSS-SUBSIDIZATION

Article 86(1) of the EC Treaty, in conjunction with Article 82 EC (which prohibits abuses of a dominant market position), will apply to the use without objective justification of a dominant position in a reserved market to obtain market power on a related or neighboring market. Accordingly, Directive 97/67 (as amended by the 2002 Directive) contains very specific provisions against cross-subsidization between reserved and non-reserved services. Subsidizing activities open to competition by allocating their costs to reserved services is regarded as likely to distort competition in breach of Article 82 EC, being an abuse of the incumbent operator's dominant position in the reserved market. Moreover, users of the reserved services would, as a result of the cross-subsidization, have to bear costs which are unrelated to the provision of those services.

Accordingly, Article 12 of Directive 97/67 as amended by the 2002 Directive expressly prohibited cross-subsidization of universal services outside the reserved sector out of revenues from services within the reserved sector (except only to the extent to which it could be shown to be strictly necessary to fulfill specific universal service obligations in the competitive area).[29] However, based on the abolition and prohibition of reservable area, this prohibition on cross-subsidization is deleted by the 2008 Directive. Nonetheless, the Postal Directive maintains a set of requirements on cost accounting by universal service providers, thus providing a basis for the application of competition law to cross-subsidization by incumbent universal service providers.[30]

Universal service providers are required to operate internal accounting systems on the basis of consistently applied and objectively justifiable cost accounting principles.[31] Under the 2002 Directive, these accounting systems must allocate costs in accordance with specified principles as follows: first, universal service providers must keep separate accounts within their internal accounting systems at least for each of the services within the reserved sector on the one hand and for the non-reserved services on the other (Article 14(2))[32]; second, such accounts kept by universal services providers for non-reserved services must distinguish between services which are part of the universal service and other services (Article 14(2)).

Under the 2008 Directive, following the abolition of the reservable area, the above requirements for separate accounting in relation to reserved area and non-reserved area activities are replaced by a single requirement on universal service providers (in the new Article 14(2)) to keep separate accounts distinguishing between services which are part of the universal service and those which are not. As regards methods of cost allocation for accounting purposes, Directive 97/67 continues to provide the following:

1. Costs which can be directly assigned to a particular service must be so assigned (Article 14(3)(a)).
2. Common costs which cannot be directly assigned to a particular service should, where possible, be allocated on the basis of direct analysis of the origin of the costs themselves and, if this is not possible, common cost categories should be allocated on the basis of an indirect linkage (based on comparable cost structures) to another cost category for which a direct allocation is possible (Article 14(3)(b)(i) and (ii)).
3. Where the above direct or indirect means of cost allocation cannot be applied, the cost category should be allocated on the basis of a general allocator based on the ratio of all expenses directly or indirectly allocated to the relevant services (Article 14(3)(b)(iii)).

The Postal Services Notice further states that the price of competitive services offered by an incumbent universal service provider should, because of the difficulty of allocating common costs, in principle, be at least equal to the average total cost of production, that is, they should cover the direct costs plus an appropriate proportion of the common and overhead costs of the operator (objective criteria such as volumes, time or labor usage or intensity of usage, being used to determine the appropriate proportion) (paragraph 3.4).

The Commission is well aware that cross-subsidizations can occur through incumbent operators which run a universal postal network practicing price and service discrimination, as between customers or classes of customers, as a result of the significant overheads which cannot be fully and precisely assigned to any one service in particular. The provisions of the Postal Directive (and the related statements in the Postal Services Notice) are therefore important measures to determine how accounts should be prepared in order to identify whether any cross-subsidization is taking place.

The objective set by the sixth indent of Article 12 of the Directive has been that cross-subsidization of universal services outside the reserved sector using revenues from services in the reserved sector should be prohibited except to the extent that it is shown to be strictly necessary in order to fulfill specific universal service obligations imposed in the competitive area.

The removal by the 2008 Directive of the prohibition on cross-subsidies is an appropriate deregulatory measure by way of partial quid pro quo for full liberalization. This move is also consistent with the judgment of the European Court of First Instance in *UPS Europe v Commission*,[33] which ruled that the alleged use by Deutsche Post of profits from the reserved sector to finance acquisitions of interests in undertakings was not abusive *per se* but could infringe Article 82 if such cross-subsidies were closely linked to abusive behavior such as predatory pricing, excessive pricing, or price discrimination.

The EC competition law approach to cross-subsidization has in any event allowed cross-subsidization from monopoly areas to competitive areas within the universal service to the extent necessary to ensure that the universal service is provided in conditions of financial equilibrium, without giving rise to unfair pricing (for example, predatory pricing in the competitive area of activities). In its decision concerning *State Aid for Deutsche Post AG*,[34] the European Commission observed (in its preliminary notice inviting comments) that revenues from reserved services, in particular the letter-post monopoly, can be used to finance a parcel service within the universal service to the extent that this allows the postal operator to provide universal parcel services under financially balanced conditions and provided that the universal parcel service costs are not over-compensated.

By contrast, cross-subsidization cannot be allowed where it directly results in abusive pricing practices in the competitive area of activities. However, the abuse can be said to exist in the resulting unfair prices in the competitive area, rather than in the cross-subsidy itself. The main examples of the European Commission's intervention against the result of such cross-subsidy are two cases against Deutsche Post. In the above *State Aid* case, the Commission found that the cross-subsidy carried out by Deutsche Post (involving €552 million received from the state to finance its public service mission) was used to finance predatory pricing in the parcel sector between 1994 and 1998.

In its Article 82 decision of 20 March 2001 against *Deutsche Post*, for abuse of dominant position in the German mail-order parcel delivery market,[35] the Commission laid down a rule for measuring cross-subsidies between reserved area and competitive activities in the postal sector to determine whether predatory prices result in the competitive area: the prices for the competitive businesses must cover at least the incremental costs incurred in the competitive activities (the costs that would be avoided if such activities were discontinued), in this case a mail-order parcels service. These incremental costs comprised the additional costs incurred solely as a result of providing the service. It was necessary to distinguish common fixed costs, which were not incurred solely as a result of such service, but the Commission did include an appropriate proportion of common variable costs that were attributable to the mail-order parcels service. For this purpose, the Commission assessed the attributable costs and determined whether or not they would be saved if the mail-order parcel service were discontinued by reference to each of the following activities: collection, sorting, long distance transport, regional and local transport, and delivery. Deutsche Post was found not to have covered the incremental costs of its mail-order parcels delivery service over a period of five years (from 1990 to 1995). This, the Commission concluded, prevented competition by deterring entry by other competitors generally; the Commission did not identify a particular competitor that was targeted. Deutsche Post's prices resulted from fidelity rebates; the Commission found that from 1974 until October 2000, Deutsche Post gave substantial discounts to its large mail-order customers in return for all or a sizeable proportion of their mail-order parcel business. Deutsche Post was required to transfer its non-reserved business parcel services business to a separate new company, and to ensure that any inputs from the reserved sector business would be at market prices, and that all inputs that it supplies to the new company would also be supplied to competitors at the same prices and conditions.

As regards the substantive rules on predatory pricing, the European Court of First Instance (ECFI) confirmed the existing case law, albeit in a 'new economy' sector (Internet access services), in its judgment of 30 January 2007 in *France Telecom S.A., formerly Wanadoo Interactive S.A. v Commission*.[36] This is that, essentially, a strategy of predation will be presumed where the dominant undertaking fails to recover its variable costs, whilst the existence of a plan to eliminate competition must be proved where it covers variable costs but its prices are below average total costs. The intention to eliminate competition must be established on the basis of sound and consistent evidence, by reference to the *Tetra Pak* case.[37] The Commission established that Wanadoo had a dominant position and was unable to cover its variable costs prior to August 2001 and was unable to recover its full costs between that date and October 2002, for which period the Commission had provided solid and consistent evidence of a plan of predation by Wanadoo. The ECFI also confirmed the Commission's statement that it is not necessary to prove recoupment of losses as a precondition to making a finding of predatory pricing.

Therefore, excessive pricing or predatory pricing by dominant postal operators, and also discriminatory pricing which clearly has a material adverse effect on competition, may be prohibited by EC competition law, whether or not such conduct results from cross-subsidization. However, cross-subsidies in themselves should not be treated as being contrary to the competition rules even if carried out by a dominant postal operator, by reference not only to the 2008 Directive but rather by reference to the ECJ's decision in *UPS Europe v Commission*.

While the abolition of the reserved sector under the 2008 Directive results in the removal of the current regulatory restriction on cross-subsidies, the retention of the (modified) rules requiring transparency of accounts and cost allocation under Article 14 of the Directive will provide a regulatory platform for observing for purposes of the general competition rules, where cross-subsidies may take place as between the universal service and non-universal service activities. In so far as the universal service area may equate in practice to the market or markets in which the postal services operator is in a dominant position, regulatory obligations may serve to enable national authorities, including competition authorities, to identify where cross-subsidies from a dominant to a competitive area of activity are taking place, in order to be able to take action where this results in unfair or anti-competitive pricing in the competitive area.

8. DOWNSTREAM ACCESS TO POSTAL NETWORKS

Article 11 of the Postal Directive required the European Parliament and Council to adopt further harmonization measures (based on a proposal to be adopted by the Commission) to ensure that users and the universal services provider(s) have access to the public postal network under transparent and non-discriminatory conditions. The 2008 Directive has revised this requirement so that such harmonization measures shall ensure that new users and postal service providers are afforded such network access. However, no such harmonization measures have yet been proposed by the Commission.

The postal services network is defined in Directive 97/67 as being the universal service provider's system for providing the universal service, comprising its system for clearing postal items from access points (physical facilities including letterboxes, where postal items can be deposited with the universal services provider) throughout the territory, the routing and handling of those items from network access points to the distribution centre, and subsequent distribution to the addressee (Article 2(2)). The Commission stated in the Postal Services Notice that member states and universal service providers should ensure that intermediaries, including operators from other member states, can choose from among available access points to the public postal network and obtain access within a reasonable period and at prices based on costs which take into account the actual services required (paragraph 8.6(b)(vii)).

The Postal Directive (as amended by the 2002 Directive) requires that 'whenever universal service providers apply special tariffs, for example, services for businesses, bulk mailers or consolidators of mail from different customers, they shall apply the principles of transparency and non-discrimination with regard both to the tariffs and to the associated conditions'.[38] The same provision requires that the tariffs 'shall apply equally both as between different third parties and as between third parties and the universal service providers supplying equivalent services'. These requirements together ensure that where universal service providers offer discounts or other special terms to bulk-mail customers involving direct access to the postal network, the same or equivalent terms must also be offered to competing postal operators or consolidators.

Further, the later part of this provision in Article 12 appears to presume an operational separation of the upstream and downstream parts of a postal operator's postal conveyance operations, yet the Postal Directive does not require any such operational separation and most postal operators are single vertically integrated entities. The Postal Directive does not impose a requirement to grant access to postal networks as such, as opposed to requiring non-discriminatory terms to be made available to different types of users (including direct customers and other postal operators). Further, in view of the comprehensive nature of the non-discrimination obligation imposed on universal service providers, the minimum obligation required to be laid down by member states pursuant to the Postal Directive is an obligation on the postal network operator to grant equivalent terms of access to bulk mail customers dealing directly with the universal service provider and competing postal operators or consolidators who collect mail from their customers in order to make use of downstream access to the universal service provider's postal network.

This issue was raised in a European Commission investigation concerning Deutsche Post AG and the German Postal Law. The European Commission announced in 2004 details of a decision finding that the German Postal Law was contrary to EC competition law in that it induced Deutsche Post AG to abuse its dominant position by discriminating against commercial mail preparation firms, by denying them discounts off the normal postal tariffs that were granted to direct bulk mailer customers in otherwise equivalent circumstances.[39] The European Commission concluded that the relevant provision, which prevented commercial mail preparation firms from earning discounts for handing over pre-sorted letter post at Deutsche Post's sorting offices, were discriminatory against such mail preparation firms. Individual large users (senders) were allowed to feed self-prepared mail directly into sorting offices and received volume-related discounts, while postal consolidators or intermediaries were prevented from obtaining comparable discounts for mail preparation. For this reason, the German Postal Law was found to infringe Article 86(1) combined with Article 82 of the EC Treaty and not to be justified on the basis of Article 86(2). The Commission depended in part on its conclusion that mail preparation services (including pre-sorting of mail and its transportation from the mailer's premises to the access point to Deutsche Post's network) did not fall within the reserved area, and that the provision of mail preparation services was, therefore, subject to the EC competition rules. In any event, Article 12 of the Postal Directive as amended by the 2002 Directive, clearly requires equivalent terms of access between bulk mailer customers and mail consolidators, notwithstanding the reserved area which continues to exist until 31 December 2010 for most member states (and 31 December 2012 for the others).

Article 12 of the Postal Directive as amended by the 2002 Directive further stipulates that where access to the universal service provider's postal network is granted under special tariffs to direct customers or other postal operators, the tariffs must 'take account of the avoided costs, as compared to the standard service covering the complete range of features offered for the clearance, transport, sorting and delivery of individual postal items'.[40] This supports the use of 'retail-minus' principle as opposed to the 'cost-plus' principle of pricing for downstream network access. The retail-minus principle involves charging the normal final price for full processing and delivery by the universal service provider, minus the costs of the upstream operations which the party seeking access saves the incumbent universal service provider. This is in contrast to the position in some other regulated network industries, where the granting of network access based on a cost-plus pricing formula is mandatory. The retail-minus or 'avoided costs' approach under the Postal Directives reflects the fact that there is no fundamental requirement under the Postal Directive to grant access to a postal network as such. As a result, controls on access pricing are to be based on a retail-minus obligation by reference to the avoided costs of the upstream collection and sorting operations.

The 2008 Directive has moved this requirement (that any such special tariffs should take account of the 'avoided costs as compared to the standard service covering the complete range of features'), from Article 12 to recital 39. This appears to change the status of this 'avoided costs' pricing principle from a substantive provision of the Postal Directive to a point of interpretative guidance in the recital. However, it is important to note the context of this statement within recital 39, which states: 'For the provision of services for all users, including businesses, bulk mailers and consolidators of mail from different users, universal service providers *may enjoy more price flexibility* in line with the cost-orientation principle'. (emphasis added). Therefore, the avoided costs principle in relation to special tariffs for services involving network access continues to apply under the 2008 Directive, but by virtue of a recital that is wider in scope. This is by way of the principle of purposive interpretation of the cost-orientation requirement which is also contained in Article 12 of the amended Postal Directive. Although the provision of downstream network access to consolidators or other postal operators would not itself normally be regarded as part of the universal service, universal service providers granting such access are required to do so on terms which are non-discriminatory as compared with the terms on which network access is granted to direct customers, for whom the prices must be cost orientated.

9. CONCLUSIONS

The EU Postal Directive has laid down minimum requirements concerning the extent and speed of liberalization and concerning the minimum scope and coverage of the universal service obligations. Following the entry into force of the 2008 Directive, full liberalization of the postal services sector across the EU is in sight, with most member states being required to achieve full liberalization by the end of 2010 and the remainder by the end of 2012. At present only Finland, Germany, Sweden, and the UK have fully liberalized their postal sectors.

Meanwhile, the pricing obligations contained in Article 12 of the Postal Directive are specific mandatory obligations on the member states and should therefore be treated as binding on the national regulatory authorities, as regards the level of prices for retail services within the universal service, especially considering the accounting requirements in Article 14 of the Directive. On this basis, any retail price controls within the universal service should (at least on a purposive interpretation) reflect the fully allocated costs of service provision.

Further, the Directive has indirectly controlled the prices of downstream network access services by virtue of the controls on the universal service prices together with the non-discrimination requirements as regards terms offered by a universal service provider to bulk mailers seeking direct downstream access and those offered to consolidators of mail or other postal operators also seeking downstream access. As shown by the European Commission's competition law decision against Deutsche Post AG and the German Postal Law under Article 86 EC, a service to bulk mailers of accepting pre-sorted mail on a worksharing, discounted basis is in essence an equivalent service to granting downstream access to the universal service provider's postal network. The requirement for non-discrimination as between direct access users and postal operators seeking downstream access has the same practical effects as requiring outright the grant of downstream access, for any universal service provider that grants special tariffs or discounts to bulk mailers seeking downstream access to the network.

This also demonstrates the unique nature of a postal network, in contrast to networks used in many other regulated utilities, where the network is more dissociable from the provision of services using that network. By contrast, postal service provision is, in principle, an integrated continuum beginning with collection and sortation through to regional and local delivery. It is in this context that the Postal Directive requires the avoided costs to be taken into account in setting tariffs for downstream access to bulk mail users and hence also (through the non-discrimination requirement) to competing postal operators.

The interpretation of the Postal Directive should follow the EU law principles of purposive interpretation of EU directives and of proportionality, which are clearly laid down in the case law of the ECJ. On this basis, the Postal Directive, including its provisions on pricing, must be interpreted in the practical context and by reference to the primary obligation of ensuring the (long-term) provision of the universal service.

The removal of the reserved sector as a result of the 2008 Directive and the consequential amendments also contained in the 2008 Directive will expand the scope for using competition law in the postal sector. The European Commission has already achieved a significant degree of liberalization through the use of EC competition law in its decision making, in particular, under Article 82 EC.

However, the Commission's report to the European Council and the European Parliament makes the important point that the promotion of competition is not an end to itself. Various provisions in or in connection with the 2008 Directive emphasize the need to safeguard the fulfillment of the primary objective of ensuring universal service provision under economically stable conditions. The requirement under the 2008 Directive to limit the applicability of the uniform tariff to single-piece tariff items (which are mostly used by consumers and small business enterprises) supports an important principle, that of allowing incumbent universal service providers to respond to competition by adjusting their tariffs so as to avoid loss of profitable business to competitors through 'cream-skimming'. Cream-skimming occurs as a result of an obligation to offer all services (even in areas in which delivery is comparatively inexpensive) under the constraints of a uniform tariff. This conclusion is reinforced by the European Commission's Explanatory Memorandum which accompanied the proposals for the 2008 Directive. The Explanatory Memorandum stated that member states should limit regulatory intervention to ensure the financially viable provision of universal service and to allow universal service providers the necessary flexibility to react to competition. On this basis, the arrival of full liberalization of the postal sector should be accompanied by increased freedom for incumbent universal service providers in setting their prices and commercial strategies.

NOTES

* This chapter includes extracts from Richard Eccles and Pauline Kuipers, 'Postal services regulation in Europe', in Michael A. Crew and Paul R. Kleindorfer (eds), *Progress Toward Liberalization of the Postal and Delivery Sector*, Dordrecht: Springer, 2006. Reprinted with kind permission of Springer Science and Business Media.

1. OJ (1984) L15/14, which required implementation into the member states' national laws by February 1999.
2. OJ (2008) L 52/3.
3. The European Union is created by several treaties agreed among the member states. Rules on competition are included in the Treaty Establishing the European Community, as amended. In this chapter, references to the 'EC Treaty' and 'EC law' refer to this treaty and the law derived from it. See OJ (2006) C 321 E/1, for a consolidated version of the Treaty on European Union and of the Treaty establishing the European Community.
4. See, for example, Case 8/81 *Becker v Finanzamt Munster – Innenstadt* (1982) (ECR 53) and Case 152/84 *Marshall v Southampton & South West Hampshire Area Health Authority* (1986) ECR 723.
5. The member states which, by derogation to the liberalization obligations of Directive 2008/6, may postpone the implementation of the Directive until 31 December 2012 in order to continue to reserve services to the universal service provider, are the following: the Czech Republic, Greece, Cyprus, Latvia, Lithuania, Luxembourg, Hungary, Malta, Poland, Romania and Slovakia: Article 3 of Directive 2008/6/EC.
6. Article 3(3) of Directive 2008/6/EC.
7. Case C-320/91, ECR (1993) I-2533.
8. The European Commission similarly drew a distinction regarding Spanish legislation, between basic letter services and international express services: Commission Decision 90/456/EEC, OJ (1990) L233/19.
9. Case C-340/99, ECR (2001) I-4109.
10. OJ (1998) C39/2.
11. Paragraph 2.7.
12. This was a feature of the judgment of the European Court of Justice in the *Port of Genoa* case (*Merci Convenzionali porto di Genova SpA v Siderurgica Gabrielli SpA* (Case C-179/90, [1991] ECR I 5889, at paragraph 17. In this case the courts found that the undertakings enjoying exclusive rights to organize dock work for third parties, were, as a result induced *inter alia* refuse to have recourse to modern technology, thereby causing increased costs and delays in the operation (at paragraph 19 of the judgment).
13. Articles 12–15.
14. Article 12 (second indent); the 2008 Directive also allows a uniform tariff obligation to be imposed in respect of *other postal items* which, by reference to recital 38 (of the 2008 Directive), would include newspapers and books, so as to protect the general public interests of access to culture, freedom of the press or regional and social cohesion.
15. Directive 2004/117/EC coordinating the procurement procedures of entities operating in the water, energy, transport and postal services sectors, covers public procurement in the postal services sector and *inter alia* allows competitive dialogue or negotiated procedures (subject to the specified criteria) with or without publication of a contract notice.
16. Calculated in accordance with Annex I.
17. Article 7(3)(a) and (b).
18. Article 7(4).
19. Article 7(5).
20. Recital 26 further provides that member states may use other means of financing the universal service, such as deciding, where and if necessary, that the profits accruing from other activities of the universal service provider outside the scope of the universal service are to be assigned, in whole or in part, to the financing of the net costs of the universal service. This recital can be treated as clarifying the new Article 7(1) intro-

duced by the 2008 Directive. However, it is an enabling provision rather than an obligation on the member states and is expressly subject to a requirement that any such assignment of profits from other activities must be in line with the EC Treaty. Therefore there is considerable uncertainty in the scope of any such right of member state authorities to take into account profits from a universal service provider's other activities in the financing of the universal service.

21. Decision of 23 October 2001, OJ (2002) L120/19.
22. Report from the Commission to the European Parliament and the Council on the application of the Postal Directive (Directive 97/67/EC as amended by Directive 2002/39/EC) COM (2006) 595 final. http://ec.europa.eu/comm/competition/antitrust/art82/hearing.html.
23. The Commission Staff Working Document 18.10.2006 is the latest report and provides a comprehensive assessment of the Postal Directive in member states, the application of key elements of the Directive as well as detailed market trends (including economic, technical, social, employment and quality of services aspects).
24. See Section 5, above.
25. Article 22(3).
26. Article 22(1).
27. Case C-18/88, *GB-Inno-BM* (1991) ECR I-5941.
28. See Section 8, below.
29. Article 12, 6th indent.
30. Article 13 of Directive 97/67 also requires that universal service providers' terminal dues, that is, charges for distribution of incoming cross-border mail from another member state (or from a third country), are transparent and non-discriminatory, based on the costs of processing and delivery, and comprise remuneration levels related to the quality of service achieved.
31. Article 14(3).
32. The Postal Services Notice stated that services made up of elements falling within the reserved and competitive services should also distinguish between the costs of each element (paragraph 8.6(b)(vi)).
33. Case T-175/99, *UPS Europe v Commission*, judgment of 20.03.2002.
34. Commission Decision of 19 June 2002 on measures implemented by the Federal Republic of Germany for Deutsche Post AG, OJ (2002) L247/27.
35. Case COMP/35141, *Deutsche Post AG*, OJ (2001) L125/27.
36. Case T-340/03, judgment of 30 January 2007.
37. Case T-83/91 *Tetra Pak v Commission*.
38. Article 12, fifth indent.
39. European Commission press release IP/O4/1254, 20 October 2004. The decision is not yet published but the draft is available on the Commission's website: http://europa.eu.int/comm/competition/antitrust/cases/decisions/38745/en.pdf.
40. Article 12, fifth indent.

15. A brief history of the United States postal monopoly law

James I. Campbell Jr.†

1. INTRODUCTION

The history of the postal monopoly law of the United States is a vast and remarkable story. The postal monopoly law is among the most ancient of legislative texts to be found in US statute books. Current law replicates the words of a proclamation by King Charles I of England in 1635, yet Congress was tinkering with the postal monopoly as recently as 2006. Despite the enormous economic and cultural significance of the national post office and long-running disputes about the scope of its monopoly, there exists no complete published account of the history and derivation of the monopoly.[1] This absence should soon be corrected by a comprehensive history which the Postal Regulatory Commission is preparing for submission to Congress and the President in December 2008.[2] While no short essay can give a full account of the postal monopoly, this chapter offers an introduction by summarizing the succession of legal instruments setting out the terms of the monopoly.

Today, the postal monopoly in the United States is created by sections 1693 to 1699 of the federal criminal law, Title 18, of the United States Code.[3] In brief, these laws make it a crime for anyone other than the United States Postal Service (USPS) to set up a collection and delivery service for the regular transmission of 'letters', although there are several exceptions to this rule. Criminal prohibitions are supplemented by sections 601 to 606 of the postal law, Title 39 of the United States Code.[4] In particular, section 601 creates important additional exceptions to the monopoly. These 13 statutory provisions are often referred to collectively as the 'private express statutes', although, as we shall see, only some of them deal with private expresses. In addition to the statutes, the Postal Service has issued lengthy regulations to implement the statutory monopoly.[5]

This chapter focuses on a few of the main threads of the postal monopoly story and some of the important links in the chain of laws stretching from its origin in 1635 to the present day. Section 2 begins with a review of the origin of the postal monopoly in English law. Section 3 describes how English precedents were reflected and modified in early American laws and then extended to private expresses and other aspects of postal service until codification in the postal act of 1872. Despite stylistic revisions during reenactments and minor amendments, the code of 1872 is essentially the current statute. Section 4 summarizes the development of the administrative interpretation of the monopoly statutes by

† George Mason University.

the Attorney General, the Post Office Department, and the Postal Service over the next century, a process that culminated in the postal monopoly regulations of 1974. Section 5 points out the still incompletely realized implications of the Postal Accountability and Enhancement Act of 2006. Section 6 offers concluding observations.

2. ENGLISH PRECEDENTS, 1635–1775

The postal monopoly predates establishment of the Postal Service. Indeed, the Postal Service is only the most recent of five governmental post offices serving the territory of what is now the United States. The Postal Service was established in 1971 as an independent governmental agency to place the national post office on a more business-like basis, free from undue political influence.[6] The predecessor of the Postal Service was the Post Office Department, established in 1792 as the office of the Postmaster General. The Post Office Department, in turn, succeeded the Continental Post Office, founded by the Second Continental Congress in 1775, when the mounting revolution rendered the British Post Office unusable. The British Post Office had provided postal services between America and England and among the several colonies since 1707. Extension of the British postal service to America supplanted a rudimentary postal service organized under a 'patent' (an exclusive license) issued by the English crown in 1692 to a court favorite named Thomas Neale. Prior to Neale's post office, there was no regular postal service in the American colonies despite several attempts by authorities in New York and Boston.

From the Neale Post Office to the Postal Service, the governmental post office in America has been protected by variations of the *same* postal monopoly law. All prohibited private competition in the transmission of 'letters and packets'. These laws were, in turn, derived from still earlier English laws that first established the postal monopoly in England. To understand the American postal monopoly law, therefore, it is necessary to begin with a brief review of English antecedents.

The English postal monopoly was born amidst the seventeenth-century struggle between the King and Parliament. At this time the growing class of merchants, Protestant in faith and sternly rational in outlook, dominated Parliament. They resented the aristocratic ways of the Stuart kings, who were not only born in Scotland but also openly tolerant of Catholics. The second Stuart king, Charles I, refused to convene Parliament after 1629 because of continual parliamentary demands for restrictions on his royal prerogatives. To obtain money to operate the government, Charles I resorted to creative financing – forced loans, taxes unauthorized by Parliament, and a revival of commercial monopolies banned by Parliament during his father's reign.

Although English kings had maintained a royal post for official correspondence since 1516, letters of the public were not admitted. Merchants operated their own commercial posts. On July 31, 1635, Charles ordered the master of posts, Thomas Witherings, to open the royal post to private correspondence and forbade private postal services to and from Scotland, then threatening rebellion. The prohibitory provision stated:

> *noe other messenger or messengers foote post or foot posts shall take upp carry receive or deliver any lr̄e or lr̄es* [letter or letters] whatsoever other then the messengers appoynted by the saide Thomas Witherings to any such place or places as the saide Thomas Witherings shall settle the

> conveyance aforesaide Except comon knowne carriers or a pticuler messenger to be sent of purpose with a lre by any man for his owne occasions or a lre by a freind . . .[7]

The monopoly of Charles I thus prohibited private carriage of a 'letter or letters'. Charles's proclamation also used the term 'packet'. It set out postage rates for the carriage of a letter based on distance and noted 'if twoe three fower or five lres in one packett or more then to pay according to the bignes of the saide packett'. It seems that a *letter* referred to a single sheet of paper and a *packet* to a bundle of letters. Because of the turbulent condition of society, the public postal service of Charles I lasted only two years; in 1637, he again closed the royal post to private letters.

Parliament, led by Oliver Cromwell, rebelled, and beheaded Charles I in 1649. There was prolonged debate about the future of the post office and advantages of competition, but in 1654 Cromwell appointed John Manley as postmaster and prohibited private carriage. Cromwell's motive was apparently one of security for the unstable government. Manley was instructed to keep careful track of all letters and unfamiliar post riders. Cromwell's death in 1658 led to a period of disorder, followed by the return of Charles II, son of the late king.

In 1660, Charles II was restored to the English crown, and Parliament approved a new postal law. The act of 1660 reenacted the postal monopoly in terms similar to the proclamation of 1635. It read in pertinent part:

> *no other Person or Persons whatsoever, shall from time to time have the receiving, taking up, ordering, dispatching, sending Post or with speed, and delivering of all Letters and Pacquets* whatsoever, which shall from time to time be sent to and from all and every the parts and places of England, Scotland, and Ireland, and other his Majesties Dominions, and to and from all and every the Kingdoms and Countries beyond the seas, where he shall settle or cause to be setled posts or running Messengers for that purpose . . .[8]

The postal act of 1660 gave the British Post Office its permanent charter. It also introduced the postal monopoly into English law on permanent basis, where it remained a fixture until it was effectively repealed by the Postal Services Act 2000. Put simply, the main purposes of the monopoly were to enable the king to enrich his friends and spy on his enemies. At the same time, however, many recognized that a public post would be a boon to society.[9]

In the American colonies, the New York legislature confirmed Neale's 1692 patent by repeating, word for word, the language of the 1660 British postal act; it forbade the 'receiving, taking up, ordering, dispatching, sending post or with speed and delivery of all letters and pacquets whatsoever'.[10] Massachusetts similarly confirmed Neale's monopoly but only on condition that the service was efficient. Pennsylvania, Connecticut, and New Hampshire agreed as well. Thus, the first postal monopoly law in America was, in essence, the English postal monopoly of 1660. Maryland and Virginia refused to recognize Neale's patent, and the Neale Post Office was limited to the northeastern colonies.[11] Service provided by the Neale Post Office was poor, and it was a commercial failure.

In 1707, the British Post Office replaced the Neale Post Office. Government purchased Neale's patent and turned over its management to the British Post Office. In 1711, during the reign of Queen Anne, Parliament enacted a new postal law, replacing the postal act of 1660. The 1711 law extended the British Post Office's operations to Scotland and the

American colonies. It also reenacted the postal monopoly of 1660 in similar terms: 'no other Person or Persons whatsoever, shall, from time to time, and at all Times, have the receiving, taking up, ordering, dispatching, sending Post, or with Speed, carrying and delivering of all Letters and Packets whatsoever'. Queen Anne's postal monopoly explicitly applied to letters 'sent to and from all and every the Parts and Places of Great Britain and Ireland, North America, the West Indies, and other her Majesty's Dominions'.[12] The postal act of 1711 remained the basic postal law of England and its colonies until well after the American revolution. Although applicable in the American colonies, the postal monopoly law was often evaded by colonists.

Postal service in eighteenth-century England and America was far different from what we think of as postal service in the twenty-first. It was not merely a difference in degree, but a difference in kind. The original idea of postal service is suggested by the phrase 'sending post or with speed'. To 'send post' was to transport by means of a series of posts, or relay stations, located every 10 to 15 miles along a 'post road'. Post houses for a 'horse post' stabled horses for riders carrying letters between towns. Letters were conveyed either by 'through post', that is, by means of a single rider who obtained fresh horses at each station, or by 'standing post', that is, by a series of riders each of whom handed the mail to a subsequent rider at the next station. A 'foot post' was similar in concept but relied upon walking messengers. The essence of postal service was extraordinary speed, hence to 'send post' was virtually synonymous with to send 'with speed'.

Much like the pony express in the western United States a century or two later, the function of a 'postal service' – that is, a conveyance service provided by a system of posts – was to provide transportation for letters that was more rapid and reliable than possible for general freight. The hoped-for rate of travel was about seven miles an hour in the summer and five in the winter. By its nature a postal system was an inter-city service. Letters and packets were transported from a public facility such as an inn, coffeehouse, or dedicated post office in one town to a similar facility in another town. In these uncertain times, postage was paid not by the sender in advance but by the addressee upon collection at the destination post office. There was no local collection or delivery service within a city or town.

As is evident from the 1635 proclamation, the term 'letter' originally referred to a message recorded by hand, usually, because of the high cost of paper, on a single scrap of paper just large enough for the message it contained. Envelopes, a French innovation, were not introduced in the United States until the mid-1800s. For privacy and protection, letters were originally folded and sealed with wax. Given the space limitations of a horseman's saddlebags, postage rates naturally depended on the number of sheets of paper sent. A correspondence containing a single sheet was called a 'single letter'. A correspondence extending to two sheets of paper – that is, two letters or a single letter with an enclosure (such as a deed or certificate) – was called a 'double letter'. Three sheets constituted a 'triple letter'. Since it was difficult to seal more than three sheets of paper with wax, a correspondence of several sheets or several correspondences sent at the same time to the same addressee (a common occurrence in times of infrequent sailings) were tied with twine into a bundle or 'packet'. This seventeenth-century terminology was used to specify postage rates in the United States until 1863; it is used to describe the postal monopoly to this day.

3. DEVELOPMENT OF US MONOPOLY STATUTES, 1775–1782

3.1 Early Postal Monopoly Laws, 1775–1845

Early American postal laws were derived from English precedents but soon assumed a more democratic and peculiarly American flavor. In the new Republic, facilitating distribution of newspapers became a primary goal of the national post office while surveillance of the citizenry was of little concern. Although the American post office was not used to raise general government revenues, high postage rates on letters generated substantial subsidies for low newspaper rates and, later, a national system of mail stagecoach services. With regard to the postal monopoly, the English proscription against the establishment of private postal systems was retained and extended to other forms of staged transportation, such as stagecoaches and packet boats, but the United States abandoned English rules prohibiting carriage of letters by individuals.

The American post office originated, naturally enough, in distrust of the British Post Office as a conduit for rebellious sentiments. In 1775, the Second Continental Congress established its own post office. On July 4, 1776, Congress declared independence from England and, in 1778, established a new government under the Articles of Confederation. The Articles vested the Congress with the 'sole and exclusive right [of] . . . establishing and regulating post offices'.[13]

When the revolution was secure, the Continental Congress reorganized the post office with the comprehensive but poorly drafted Ordinance of October 18, 1782. The 1782 ordinance included a postal monopoly provision modeled on that of the British postal act of 1711. Like the British act, it granted to the post office a monopoly as follows:

> no other person whatsoever, shall have the receiving, taking up, ordering, despatching, sending post or with speed, carrying and delivering of any *letters, packets or other despatches* from any place within these United States for hire, reward, or other profit or advantage for receiving, carrying or delivering such letters or packets respectively . . .[14]

The addition of the term 'despatches' (that is, dispatches) appears to signify nothing more than preoccupation with the recent war; 'despatches' referred to letters of an official or military nature.

The Articles of Confederation proved unequal to the task of unifying the colonies and was replaced by the current federal Constitution in 1789. The Constitution authorized the Congress to establish 'post offices and post roads',[15] but unlike the Articles, did not grant Congress the sole and exclusive power to do so. In its first three sessions, Congress continued in effect the Ordinance of 1782.

The first substantive postal law enacted by the new government was adopted in 1792.[16] In 1794, Congress replaced the 1792 law with a more mature version.[17] The postal law was refined again in 1799. In the 1799 act, the postal monopoly provision read as follows:

> That if any person, other than the Postmaster General, or his deputies . . . *shall be concerned in setting up or maintaining any foot or horse post*, stage wagon, or other stage carriage, on any established post road, or from one post town to another post town on any road adjacent or parallel to an established post road, or any packet boat or other vessel, to ply regularly from one place to another between which a regular communication by water shall be established by the United

> States, *and shall receive any letter or packet, other than newspapers, magazines, or pamphlets*, and carry the same by such foot or horse post, stage wagon, or other stage carriage, packet boat, or vessel . . . shall forfeit, for every such offence, the sum of 50 dollars.[18]

The 1799 act retains the phrase 'letters and packets' to define the basic scope of the monopoly. However, the statute as a whole indicates that the meaning of these terms was continuing to evolve. In specifying postage rates, the 1799 act refers to a 'letter composed of a single sheet' instead of the term 'single letter'. This phrasing suggests that 'letter', used alone, could refer to an entire written communication, and not just to a single sheet. On the other hand, the statute also states that a packet must contain 'four distinct letters' in order to qualify for quadruple postage, apparently using 'letter' in the sense of a single sheet of paper. In short, the term 'letter' is used in both old and new senses.

The 1799 act also reflected a subtle but fundamental change from the scope of activities proscribed under former British law. The British law prohibited both the carriage of letters or packets by individual persons for hire and the setting up of private postal systems, a concept later extended to common carriers. Since 1794, the American law has repeated the second prohibition ('setting up or maintaining any foot or horse post, [etc.]') but not the first. Hence, it was lawful in the United States for a private individual to carry letters for someone else even if he could not set up a postal system to compete with the government post office. As Postmaster General Return Meigs observed in 1822, with the introduction of steamboats more persons traveled by water than by land because of the 'greater economy and convenience' and 'most of the passengers are charged with letters' since 'there is no law prohibiting passengers from carrying letters'.[19]

In 1825, Congress repealed prior postal laws and enacted the first general codification of the postal laws. The monopoly provision of the 1825 act prohibited only the transmission of *letters*, suggesting, perhaps, a congressional understanding that the term 'letters' encompassed what used to be called 'packets'.[20] Although the 1825 act repeated the prohibition against carriage of letters by common carriers, it eliminated the prohibition against 'setting up' posts found in the 1792 act. Perhaps this omission was inadvertent, for in 1827 the prohibition against setting up competitive posts was reenacted. Moreover, the 1827 act referred again to a monopoly over the carriage of 'letters and packets'.[21]

3.2 Cheap Postage and Suppression of Private Expresses, 1845

The concept of a 'postal service' as a fast inter-city transport system operating by means of a series of relay stations remained essentially unchanged from 1635 to the mid-1830s. The Industrial Revolution, however, precipitated a 'transportation revolution' which fundamentally altered the concept of a post office. The steamboat was introduced in America in 1807 by Robert Fulton; the steam railroad by Peter Cooper in 1830. As these two new means of transportation became widespread, it was suddenly possible to transport large quantities of passengers and freight at the highest speed attainable. The essential characteristic of the pre-industrial post office, extraordinarily fast transportation of small quantities of letters and documents, was rendered obsolete along lines of travel where steam-powered vehicles were available. Any entrepreneur could board a railroad or steamboat with letters in his baggage and transport them between cities as fast as the post office. In fact, many did so. It was common for newspapers and other businesses to hire private messengers to convey time-sensitive information. In the late 1830s, regular 'private express' companies were organized as the railroads and steamship lines developed into usable transportation systems. Private expresses operated first in the Boston area and on the routes between Boston, New York, and Washington.[22]

At first, the Post Office resisted implications of the new technology. In 1836, the Post Office started its own express mail service, making improved use of stage coaches and riders. By 1839, however, it was clear that there was no practical alternative to reliance upon railroads, and express mail was discontinued. The Post Office also launched prosecutions against private express companies under the traditional postal monopoly laws. These failed because the courts concluded that conveyance of letters by railroad passengers was not prohibited by a monopoly over the establishment of horse and foot posts.[23]

The Post Office then turned to Congress. Postmaster General Charles A. Wickliffe urged increased penalties against private express companies and postal control of railroad schedules. He also advised Congress to resist the popular demand for substantially reduced postage rates – inspired by the 'cheap postage' reforms adopted in England in 1840 – because this would jeopardize the policy of financial self-sufficiency that had guided the Post Office since the first days of the Republic. Wickliffe also claimed that the monopoly over the transmission of 'packets' already gave the Post Office a monopoly over the carriage of newspapers and miscellaneous printed matter. He wrote, 'The words "packets" or "letters" are not used in this connexion as synonymous. Packets, more properly, may be defined to mean printed matter, such as newspapers, prices current, slips, &c'.[24]

Congress responded with the postal act of 1845. The centerpiece of this act was a sharp reduction in postage rates. The act also added a new provision that prohibited inter-city transportation of letters by private express to supplement existing prohibitions against private postal systems. The 1845 act introduced a separate rate status for circulars and miscellaneous printed matter (there were no mail 'classes' at this time) and included such items in the postal monopoly. The key private express provision read as follows:

> *it shall not be lawful for any person or persons to establish any private express or expresses* for the conveyance, nor in any manner to cause to be conveyed, or provide for the conveyance or transportation by regular trips, or at stated periods or intervals, from one city, town, or other place, to any other city, town, or place in the United States, between and from and to which cities, towns, or other places the United States mail is regularly transported, under the authority of the Post Office Department, of *any letters, packets, or packages of letters, or other matter properly transmittable in the United States mail, except newspapers, pamphlets, magazines and periodicals* . . .[25]

The phrases 'mailable matter' and 'matter properly transmittable in the United States mail' were specifically defined in the act to include, in addition to letters, newspapers, magazines and pamphlets, and 'all other written or printed matter whereof each copy or number shall not exceed eight ounces in weight'. The practical effect of the 1845 monopoly was to add miscellaneous written and printed matter weighing eight ounces or less to the traditional monopoly over the carriage of 'letters and packets'.

3.3 Extension of the Monopoly to Local Services and the Postal Code of 1872

Until the Civil War, the Post Office remained essentially a contracting office for inter-city transportation services. Delivery of local, intra-city letters was pioneered by private companies such as Boyd's Despatch in New York City and Blood's Despatch in Philadelphia. One authority has counted 147 private local postal companies.[26] The 'locals' introduced adhesive postage stamps at least as early as 1841. The Post Office did not introduce stamps until 1847 and did not require their use until 1851. Efforts by the Post Office to suppress the locals failed when, in 1860, a federal court ruled that the postal monopoly pertained only to the transportation of letters over 'post roads' between post offices and did not prohibit the delivery of letters within a single postal district.[27]

In 1861, Congress overturned this judicial decision by an obscurely worded, undebated rider to an appropriations bill that extended the postal monopoly to 'all post routes which have been, or may hereafter be, established in any town or city by the Postmaster General'.[28] As it turned out, this amendment was the key to the postal monopoly for the next 150 years as local delivery, rather than inter-city transport, gradually took over as the central function of the Post Office and later the Postal Service. In 1861, however, the Post Office did not provide local delivery services except by messengers who were paid separately by the addressee if mail delivery was desired. It was the postal act of 1863[29] that enlarged the mission of the Post Office by providing for 'free city delivery' in major cities, that is, delivery without charge to the addressee.

The 1863 act also introduced another concept that would become important in future discussion of the postal monopoly. It divided the mail into three 'classes' and defined letter postage by weight step instead of the number of sheets of paper. Only at this point did the original meaning of the key term 'letter' (a single sheet of paper) lose practical significance as far as postal rates were concerned.

While the 1863 postal act was still under consideration by Congress, the Post Office set in motion the events that led to the postal code of 1872. Postmaster General Montgomery Blair proposed a comprehensive bill to 'revise and codify' the postal laws, the first codification since 1825.[30] Congress did not enact the proposed code, but in 1866 it established a commission to codify all of the laws of the United States. In 1869, this commission produced a few specimen titles, including a new postal code which strongly resembled the legislation proposed by the Post Office in 1863.[31] The specimen postal title was enacted into law with minor revisions as the postal code of 1872.

Although congressional sponsors of the 1872 act portrayed their bill as essentially a codification of prior law, the new law in fact made fundamental but apparently unnoticed revisions in the scope of the monopoly. Most significantly, the 1872 act reverted to the phrase 'letters and packets' to define the scope of mail within the monopoly, thus eliminating the 1845 phrase 'other matter properly transmittable in the United States mail'. In the 1872 code, the private express provision read as follows:

> *That no person shall establish any private express for the conveyance of letters or packets*, or in any manner cause or provide for the conveyance of the same by regular trips or at stated periods, over any post-route which is or may be established by law, or from any city, town or place to any other city, town or place between which the mail is regularly carried.[32]

Reversion to the phrase 'letters and packets' to define the scope of the postal monopoly and the definition of first class mail as wholly or partially written documents left unclear the status of certain documents used in commerce and generally referred to as 'commercial papers' rather than letters. There was considerable debate about this matter.

In the summer of 1881, Postmaster General Thomas James asked Attorney General Wayne MacVeagh to rule upon the status of such items under the postal monopoly:

> I have the honor to request that you inform me whether . . . it is a violation of [the postal monopoly law] for an express company to carry for hire, regularly, in sealed or unsealed envelopes, *written matter which is by law subject to letter postage when sent by mail, such as manuscript for publication, deeds, transcripts of records, insurance policies, and other written or partly written documents used by insurance and other companies in the transaction of their business.*
>
> In other words, *will you define the limits of the monopoly of the Post Office Department in the carriage of first class matter*, that is, matter which is by law subject, when sent in the mail, to letter postage, and also the exact meaning of the words '*letter or packet*' as used in the sections of the Revised Statutes referred to. Questions involving these points are constantly presented to this Department for decision, and I greatly desire your decision thereon[33]

MacVeagh replied that such commercial documents were not within the *letter* monopoly and that the term 'letter' extended no further than common usage:

> *In my opinion, it is no violation of [the postal monopoly law] for an express company to transport the documents mentioned in yours of 15th instant.*, viz., manuscripts for publication, deeds, transcripts of record, insurance policies, &c.
>
> It is prohibited, and an offence, to carry 'letters or packets.' *What is a letter I can make no plainer than it is made by the idea which common usage attaches to that term.* From the connection in which it is used, I have no doubt that 'packets' means a package of letters.[34]

The statutory provisions defining the postal monopoly have not changed materially since the postal code of 1872. The 1872 act was reenacted in the 1874 Revised Statutes, a general codification of US law.[35] The penal postal monopoly provisions were incorporated into the Criminal Code of 1909.[36] Other than minor stylistic revisions, the 1909 code made only one significant change to the main postal monopoly provisions, adding an exemption for letters of the carrier. The postal monopoly portions of the 1909 code were reenacted without significant change as part of the Criminal Code of 1948.[37] From 1872 to 2006, the only significant changes in the legal measures defining the scope of the postal monopoly are found in administrative rulings issued by the Attorney General, the Post Office Department, and the Postal Service. While the Postal Accountability and Enhancement Act of 2006 did not change the core concepts of the statutory monopoly, it made several significant revisions.

Today, the most important remnant of the pre-industrial postal monopoly law is found in section 1694 of the criminal code. As noted, the pre-industrial postal monopoly banned establishment of foot posts, horse posts, and other staged transportation services to transmit letters and packets, a prohibition that was later extended to carriage of letters by common carriers established for other purposes. Section 1694 provided:

> Whoever, having charge or control of any conveyance operating by land, air, or water, which regularly performs trips at stated periods on any post route, or from one place to another between which the mail is regularly carried, carries, otherwise than in the mail, any letters or packets, except such as relate to some part of the cargo of such conveyance, or to the current business of the carrier, or to some article carried at the same time by the same conveyance, shall, except as otherwise provided by law, be fined under this title.[38]

The most significant of the private express provisions adopted in 1845 is now found in subsection 1896(a) of the criminal code:

> (a) Whoever establishes any private express for the conveyance of letters or packets, or in any manner causes or provides for the conveyance of the same by regular trips or at stated periods over any post route which is or may be established by law, or from any city, town, or place to any other city, town, or place, between which the mail is regularly carried, shall be fined not more than $500 or imprisoned not more than six months, or both.[39]

4. DEVELOPMENT OF ADMINISTRATIVE INTERPRETATION

4.1 The Post Office versus the Railroads (1890s)

While the postal monopoly statute remained relatively fixed after 1872, interpretation of the statute evolved under pressure of events. Relations between the Post Office and the railroads were contentious ever since the earliest railroads gave rise to the development of private expresses. By the 1890s, large railroads were coalescing into great national systems of roads with interlocking directorates and cross-stock ownership. Railroads represented a different order of organizational complexity from that employed in earlier commercial and manufacturing activities. They depended upon the smooth integration of a host of smaller and simpler companies.[40] Railroad operations therefore generated a constant flow of documents between companies with closely related activities. A railroad train typically included not only cars belonging to the railroad company that owned the locomotive and the tracks but also freight cars operated by express companies, freight cars owned by other railroads, and passenger cars operated by companies such as Pullman. A railroad company might operate trains over not only its own tracks but also tracks belonging to other companies. Railroads were also closely integrated with other types of companies. Telegraph companies used railroad rights of way for their lines and provided services for both the railroad and general public, often using joint employees and sharing both costs and profits. Similarly, hotels and restaurants were built along railroad rights of way and were integrated with, or alternatives to, dining and sleeping car services.

The Post Office had traditionally acquiesced in the railroads' carriage of letters and documents relating to these interrelated operations. But beginning in about 1896, the Post Office decided that railroad transmission of such documents violated its monopoly. The Post Office declared that a railroad violated the postal monopoly if it transported its own mail to or from other companies or transported another company's mail in connection with joint services provided with the railroad. Further, the Post Office held that a railroad could not send mail by special messenger over the lines of another railroad.

To apply these new rulings, the Post Office had to decide whether various documents unique to railroad operations were to be considered 'letters and packets'. On January 7, 1897, the Assistant Attorney General for the Post Office, John L. Thomas, advised that 'car tracers' and 'junction reports' were 'letters'. These documents were standard forms listing movements of railroad cars; they were completed in writing but unsigned and addressed impersonally to a position such as 'car accountant' at a given station. Using exhibits such as shown in Figure 15.1 (the deletions of printed matter were proposed by

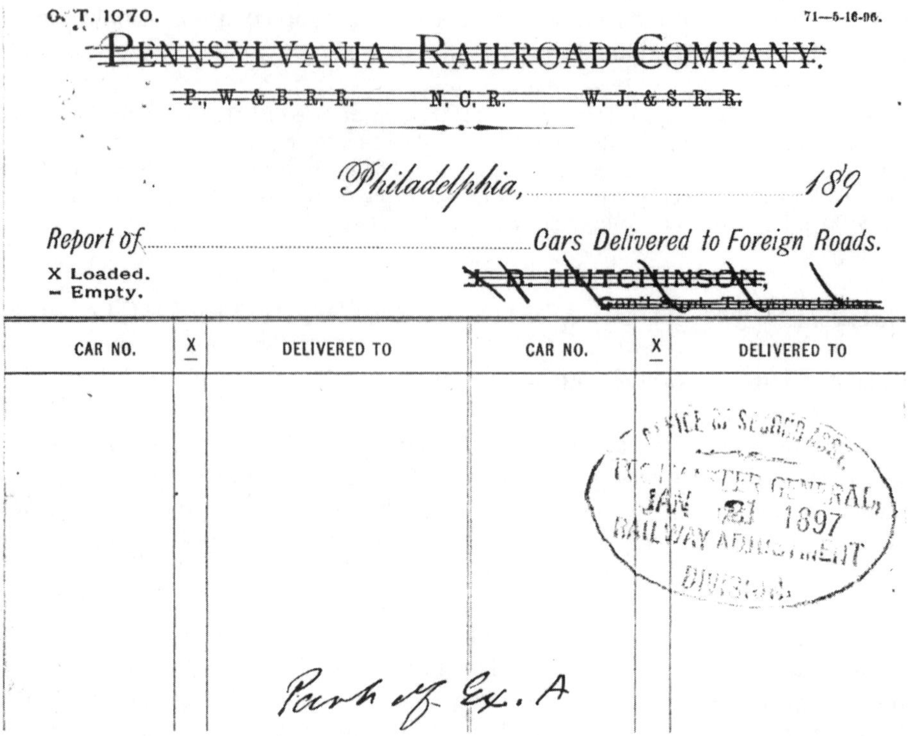

O. T. 1070. 71—5-16-96.

~~PENNSYLVANIA RAILROAD COMPANY.~~

~~P., W. & B. R. R.~~ ~~N. C. R.~~ ~~W. J. & S. R. R.~~

Philadelphia, 189

Report of .... Cars Delivered to Foreign Roads.

X Loaded.
– Empty.

~~J. R. HUTCHINSON,~~
~~Gen'l Agt. Transportation.~~

CAR NO.	X	DELIVERED TO	CAR NO.	X	DELIVERED TO

JAN 21 1897

Part of Ex. A

Figure 15.1 *Railroad 'car tracer' form reviewed by J.L. Thomas*

the railroad), Thomas reasoned that to constitute a letter a document 'must be wholly or partly in writing and there must be a sender and an addressee'. Thomas dealt with the absence of a sender's name by noting 'some *person* made out the reports and tracers, and that person, whether known or unknown, must be held to be the sender' (emphasis original). In regard to the impersonal address by title and station, Thomas stated: 'this, in my opinion, is sufficiently explicit to make the inclosure a matter for personal attention of the person holding the position of car accountant of the road at the point designated, and so far as he is concerned such inclosure has the characteristics of a personal correspondence and is therefore a letter'.[41]

In applying the postal monopoly to railroad mail, the Post Office for the first time employed an administrative definition of the term 'letter' that was not rooted in the statutory distinction between letters and other types of documents. Rather than asking, for example, whether a particular type of document was more like the traditional concept of a letter or more like the traditional concept of a commercial paper, the Post Office based its approach upon an abstract definition of 'letter' and asked whether the mail in question could fit within that definition. In effect, Thomas held that a 'letter' was any communication wholly or partly in writing that was composed for the attention of an identifiable person or office.

A month after Thomas's opinion on car tracers, the Post Office published a pamphlet reprinting a selection of postal monopoly rulings relating to application of the monopoly to railroad mail.[42] Most of the rulings purporting to limit the right of a railroad to carry mail related to its business or to use special messengers were later reversed or limited by the Attorney General, the courts, or the Post Office itself.[43] As noted above, Congress amended the postal monopoly law in 1909 to make explicit what the Attorney General had already declared, that a railroad (or any other company) could transport its own letters. Nonetheless, Thomas's approach to defining the term 'letter' initiated a new, more flexible administrative approach to defining it for purposes of postal monopoly. The pamphlet on railroad mail remained the standard summary of the Post Office's position on the postal monopoly for the next decade. In 1901, the Second Assistant Postmaster General cited this pamphlet as authority for the proposition that 'tissue copies' of waybills were considered to be 'letters',[44] even though waybills were undoubtedly within the traditional concept of commercial papers relied upon by Attorney General MacVeagh in 1881.

4.2 Opinions of Post Office Solicitor Lamar (1910s)

In 1913, William H. Lamar was appointed Assistant Attorney General for the Post Office Department, a title that was changed to Solicitor in 1914. Lamar was 54 at the time of his appointment, a veteran of the Spanish American War and the Justice Department and the son-in-law of a US Supreme Court Justice. In early 1916, Lamar issued a series of opinions which substantially expanded upon the postal monopoly approach adopted in the railroad mail cases.

On March 10, 1916, Lamar considered the lawfulness of a messenger system established for the carriage of 'fire insurance policies, bills of debits and credits, and other insurance data' between insurance companies, agents, brokers, and a common clearing house called the Chicago Board of Underwriters. The clearing house and insurance agents were all located within a single office building. Lamar ruled first that the corridors of a public building served by letter carriers were 'postal routes'. He then considered whether the documents in question were 'letters', quoting with approval a dictionary definition ('a written message, usually on paper, folded up and sealed, sent by one person to another') and brief discussions of the term 'letter' culled from three federal cases. The first case dealt with postal fraud and discussed the meaning of 'letter' in a context wholly different from the postal monopoly.[45] The second case concerned the mailability of obscene 'letters'; it not only bore no relation to the postal monopoly but suffered from the added defect of having been overruled.[46] The third case was an 1851 Supreme Court opinion holding that an order for goods was 'clearly mailable matter' and thus within the postal monopoly law of 1845.[47] The principle that Lamar derived from these sources was that 'a letter is a message in writing'. On this basis, Lamar seems to have reasoned that all writings could be deemed 'letters' and that therefore the monopoly included all first class matter:

> Insurance policies as documents and bills, receipts, etc., as such, are acceptable in the mails and acceptable only as first-class matter. If deposited for handling by the Postal Service they become 'letters,' and when they are handled by private concerns or parties they are none the less so within the meaning of [the postal monopoly law].[48]

On May 5, 1916, Lamar went beyond first class mail and addressed wholly printed matter. He held that the postal monopoly also forbade a railroad from transporting printed circulars that were being distributed to members of a railroad union. Lamar concedes that circulars were third class rather than first class matter, but states,

> While for some purposes a distinction is observed between 'letters' and 'circulars,' for example, the act of March 3, 1879 (20 Stat. 260), placing *written* letters in matter of the first-class and 'circulars' in the third-class as 'miscellaneous printed matter,' yet as respects the postal monopoly the term 'letters' has a broader signification and embraces 'circulars'.[49]

To support this ruling, Lamar cites, in addition to the sources noted above, phrases from post-1872 laws which refer to circulars as 'printed letters' which can be posted at third class rates.

Notwithstanding this broad rationale, when later questioned by Congress about the status of third class matter under the postal monopoly, the Post Office fell back on the dubious argument that the term 'packet' could be interpreted to include not only multi-sheet letters but also pamphlets, magazines, newspapers and the like. In 1919, the chairman of the House postal committee asked Postmaster General John Koons directly, 'Does [the postal monopoly] include any of the mailable matter now mailable as third-class matter, such as letters and circulars?'. In a reply drafted by Lamar, Koons wrote, 'This Department has not attempted to assert a monopoly in the carriage of mail matter other than that of the first class, included unquestionably in the phrase "letters and packets" '.[50] Koons, however, continues 'there is a species of third class matter, however, the status of which with respect to the "private express" statute is not so clearly settled as would be desirable; that is to say, pamphlets, magazines, newspapers and the like'. Koons suggests that such documents might be considered 'packets'. He acknowledges, however, that nine years earlier, a federal court held that 'packet', as used in the postal monopoly law, referred to a packet of letters,[51] but he suggests that the court's finding might be considered mere 'obiter dicta', that is, general observations not intended to have legal effect. Koons's suggestion, notwithstanding, it seems that no one else since 1919 has questioned the proposition that, as the court concluded, in the postal monopoly law the word 'packet' is merely an old-fashioned term for a multi-sheet letter.

Lamar left the Post Office Solicitor's post in June 1921 after seven years of service. Between June 1921 and November 1951, postal solicitors issued approximately 166 opinions dealing with the postal monopoly. Most claim a monopoly over the carriage of various items; some disclaim a monopoly. Almost all are devoid of legal citations. Disregarding a handful of opinions dealing with the scope of exceptions to the monopoly and mere repetitions of the postal monopoly statutes, the Lamar opinions comprise the basic body of legal reasoning presented by Post Office solicitors in support of an enlarged administrative interpretation of the postal monopoly after 1916.

4.3 Postal Monopoly Regulations of the Postal Service (1974–2006)

The Postal Reorganization Act of 1970 abolished the Post Office Department and established the US Postal Service as an independent federal agency. In 1974, the Postal Service adopted comprehensive postal monopoly regulations that substantially revised the previous administrative definition of 'letter'.[52] The new definition was 'a message directed to a specific person or address and recorded in or on a physical object'. A 'message' is defined as 'any information or intelligence that can be recorded' where 'recorded' is explained as follows:

> Methods by which messages are recorded on tangible objects include, but are not limited to, the use of written or printed characters, drawing, holes, or orientations of magnetic particles in a manner having a predetermined significance.[53]

This definition apparently included within the postal monopoly all physical communications of a textual nature, whether recorded by means of writing, printing, images, or electromagnetic process. In response to criticism that the proposed definition of 'letter' incorrectly extended the monopoly to commercial papers long held to be outside the monopoly, the Postal Service cited the authority of 'original general definitions':

> [Checks and other commercial papers] were declared not to be letters on the theory that they are evidence of rights of the holder rather than written messages. Such a theory is inconsistent with *the original general definitions of 'letter'* because such documents are in fact messages, conveying information of several kinds.[54]

Similarly, the Postal Service responded to objections to the inclusion of newspapers in the definition of 'letter' by explaining 'newspapers and periodicals also meet the tests in past guidelines for determining what are letters . . . an exclusion of newspapers and periodicals seems of doubtful validity'.[55]

Nonetheless, the Postal Service mitigated opposition to its new definition of 'letter' including provisions in the regulations which 'suspended' the postal monopoly. These suspensions created administrative exceptions from the postal monopoly for newspapers, magazines, and checks (when sent between banks). As statutory authority for these suspensions, the Postal Service cited a statutory provision, then section 601(b) of title 39, which originated in an 1864 postal act.[56] It is at least open to question, however, whether this provision was ever intended by Congress to confer authority to suspend the postal monopoly.[57] Nonetheless, suspensions were part and parcel of the Postal Service's new administrative definition of the 'letter' monopoly. The suspension power allowed the Postal Service to maintain a broad definition of the monopoly because it could be used to deflate the efforts of anyone petitioning Congress to review the monopoly statute. Whenever protests against the monopoly were gaining ground in Congress, the Postal Service would adopt a narrowly drawn suspension that was sufficiently inclusive to satisfy most of the agitators.

This most notable example of this strategic use of suspension authority was the development of a suspension for urgent letters. In the mid-1970s – in a virtual replay of the rise of the private express companies in the 1840s – small 'courier' companies such as DHL, Federal Express, Gelco, and Purolator began to offer especially rapid transmission services for 'time-sensitive' documents such as checks, bills of lading, engineering drawings, and so forth. When the Postal Service claimed that such activities were violating the postal monopoly, these companies and their far larger customers made a strong case to Congress to reconsider the monopoly statutes. The Senate committee approved a bill to revise the monopoly and the House committee was nearing the same decision, when the Postal Service adopted a new suspension for 'urgent letters'.[58] Additional suspensions were added for data-processing materials (under certain circumstances) and international remail, among other things.[59]

The only major federal case to consider the meaning of the key term 'letters and packets' since 1970, indeed since 1872, upheld the Postal Service's 1974 administrative definition of 'letter'. In the *ACTMU* case,[60] decided in 1979, a divided D.C. Circuit Court of Appeals held that printed advertisements were within the postal monopoly over 'letters and packets'. The court's judgment was based substantially upon the 1974 Postal Service regulations and the 1916 opinions of Solicitor Lamar. Although the *ACTMU* case relied heavily on historical analysis, the court was uninformed about key elements of the history of the postal monopoly law, including the 1881 opinion by Attorney General McVeagh and the 1919 Post Office Department letter to Congress resting a claim of monopoly over third class matter on an expansive definition of 'packet'. No court has ever considered the Postal Service's claimed authority to suspend the postal monopoly.

5. POSTAL ACCOUNTABILITY AND ENHANCEMENT ACT, 2006

The Postal Accountability and Enhancement Act of 2006 (PAEA) modified the scope of the statutory monopoly in certain respects and, perhaps more importantly, made significant changes in its administration.

Substantively, the PAEA added two new exceptions to the postal monopoly. The act exempts from the postal monopoly both (i) letters that weigh 12.5 ounces or more and (ii) letters for which the amount paid for private carriage is at least six times the current charge for the first ounce of a single-piece first class letter (that is, meeting either condition is sufficient to escape the postal monopoly). The PAEA provided a statutory basis for private carriage of letters in circumstances in which the Postal Service purportedly suspended the postal monopoly by administrative regulation.[61]

In terms of administration, the PAEA apparently repealed the authority of the Postal Service to issue regulations to define the scope of its monopoly.[62] The PAEA changed the scope of the Postal Service's rulemaking authority from 'to adopt, amend, and repeal such rules and regulations as it deems necessary *to accomplish the objectives of this title*' to 'to adopt, amend, and repeal such rules and regulations, not inconsistent with this title, *as may be necessary in the execution of its functions under this title* and such other functions as may be assigned to the Postal Service under provisions of law outside of this title'.[63] Since the main provisions of the postal monopoly law appear in title 18 of the United States Code, their definition or administration does not appear to be 'functions under this title', that is, title 39. The only significant postal monopoly provision appearing in title 39 is section 601, but authority to administer this provision was explicitly vested in the Postal Regulatory Commission.[64] Moreover, the PAEA added a provision that explicitly forbids the Postal Service from establishing any rule or regulation 'the effect of which is to preclude competition or establish the terms of competition unless the Postal Service demonstrates that the regulation does not create an unfair competitive advantage for itself or any entity funded (in whole or in part) by the Postal Service'.[65] This ban would seem to include postal monopoly regulations. Finally, the PAEA explicitly repealed the statutory provision upon which the Postal Service relied as its authority to suspend postal monopoly.[66]

Given the substantial role of administrative interpretation in the history of the postal monopoly law since 1872, these changes could have an important effect on the practical implications of the postal monopoly law, but these implications have yet to be clarified. Neither the Postal Regulatory Commission nor the courts have yet had occasion to address postal monopoly provisions of the PAEA.

6. SUMMARY AND CONCLUSIONS

The English postal monopoly originated in the political turmoil of seventeenth-century England and represented the first attempt by government to exert control over the mass communications systems of society. To this day, the postal monopoly law bears traces of this original purpose in its prohibition against private carriage of 'letters and packets'. Later English monarchs took further advantage of the postal monopoly to raise general revenue by taxing communications. It was precisely such uses of governmental authority that prompted the Americans to revolt at the end of the eighteenth century. With the benefit of three centuries of hindsight, one can plausibly question the wisdom of ever transplanting the English postal monopoly law to American soil.

As it turned out, however, the new American democracy retained the concept of a postal monopoly but fundamentally changed its purpose and the role of the national post office. In the hands of early American legislators, the national post office was used neither to spy on the people nor raise general revenues, but rather became a public service for 'spreading the news', as historian Richard John (1986) has put it. In this new world, the postal monopoly allowed high prices on letters to underwrite low prices on newspapers. At the same time, English rules prohibiting carriage of letters by individuals were abandoned and the monopoly pared back to a rule against the establishment of private 'postal' systems. Thc new postal paradigm lasted for about half a century. Then, between the 1840s and the 1870s, the national post office and postal monopoly law evolved again under the transforming and pervasive influences of the Industrial Revolution. In a series of ad hoc steps, Congress added intra-city delivery to the Post Office's original mission of inter-city transmission and extended the postal monopoly law to prevent private provision of both private inter-city express services and local intra-city penny posts. In 1872, Congress sorted out and codified this piecemeal collage of postal laws for the first time since 1825 and the last time until 1960. The postal monopoly statutes, last debated by Congress in 1845, assumed essentially their current form in the postal code of 1872.

Since 1872, in the absence of further guidance from Congress, the Attorney General, the Post Office Department, the Postal Service, and the federal courts have struggled, successively and intermittently, to adapt the nineteenth-century postal monopoly laws to changing circumstances by promulgating increasingly elaborate administrative 'interpretations'. Since the postal world of the early twenty-first century bears almost no resemblance to the postal world of the late nineteenth century, it is unsurprising that one may reasonably question whether the postal monopoly regulations of today are entirely congruent with the intent of Congress 135 years ago. Yet, however understandable this may be, given the constitutional primacy of Congress, it is not acceptable that the administration of law has been allowed to drift so far from its statutory moorings.

In the Postal Accountability and Enhancement Act of 2006, Congress has created a timely and long overdue opportunity to bring clarity and logic to the American concept of the postal monopoly. Congress has codified the liberal portions of past administrative rulings (the 'suspensions') and repealed (apparently) the authority of the now business-like Postal Service to issue further regulations defining its own monopoly. At the same time, Congress has given the independent Postal Regulatory Commission new authority to adopt clarifying regulations as needed. More fundamentally, Congress has directed the Postal Regulatory Commission to prepare a comprehensive study of the history and future need for the postal monopoly and submit a report by December 2008.

NOTES

1. The best historical review of the US postal monopoly as governmental policy is G.L. Priest, 'The history of the postal monopoly in the United States' (1975). Priest's article focuses upon motivations underlying monopoly legislation but does not offer detailed analysis of specific provisions of the monopoly or describe the evolution of administrative implementation after 1872. The best general historical review of the legal concepts of the monopoly is J.F. Johnston Jr., 'The United States postal monopoly' (1968). See also Craig and Alvis (1977) and Donnici et al. (1976).
2. This report is required by the Postal Accountability and Enhancement Act, Pub. L. No. 109–435, § 702, 120 Stat. 3198, 3243 ('a comprehensive history of the monopoly on the delivery of mail'). The history of the postal monopoly is only part of the Commission's study. The Postal Regulatory Commission has retained George Mason University to assist in the preparation of this report. The author is assisting George Mason University in this project. The views expressed in this chapter are the personal views of the author only and should not be construed to represent the views of Postal Regulatory Commission or George Mason University. Moreover, it should be noted that the history of the postal monopoly is complex and in some cases controversial; the views of the author expressed in this chapter reflect his present understanding and could be modified by further research.
3. 18 U.S.C. §§ 1693–99 (2000 & Supp. V 2006).
4. 39 U.S.C. §§ 601–06 (2000 & Supp. V 2006) and Postal Accountability and Enhancement Act, Pub. L. No. 109–435, § 503(a), 120 Stat. 3198, 3234, amending 39 U.S.C. § 601.
5. 39 C.F.R. Parts 310 and 320 (2007).
6. Postal Reorganization Act of 1970, P.L. 91–375, 84 Stat. 727.
7. Proclamation of July 31, 1635, Patent Roll (Chancery) 11 Car I, Pt 30, No. 11 (emphasis added).
8. Post Office Act of 1660, 12 Charles II, c. 35 (1660) (emphasis added).
9. See generally, Robinson (1948 [1970], 48–55).
10. Woolsey (1894 [1969], 9).
11. Fuller (1972 [1980], 18–19).
12. Post Office Act of 1711, 9 Anne, c. 10 (1711).
13. Articles of Confederation, art. IX.
14. Ordinance of October 18, 1782, 23 J. Cont. Cong. 670 (emphasis added).
15. Constitution, Art. I, sec. 8.
16. Act of February 20, 1792, ch 7, §14, 1 Stat. 232, 236.
17. Act of March 8, 1794, ch. 23, § 14, 1 Stat. 354, 360.
18. Act of March 2, 1799, ch. 43, § 12, 1 Stat. 733, 735 (emphasis added).
19. 'Compensation to Deputies and Mail Agents – Effect of Steamboats on the Revenue of Post Office' (February 1822) in *American State Papers: Post Office* 92.
20. Act of March 3, 1825, ch. 64, § 19, 4 Stat. 102, 107.
21. Act of March 2, 1827, ch. 61, § 3, 4 Stat. 238.
22. The effects of the transportation revolution on postal service and the US economy generally were widespread and fundamental. See generally, Taylor (1951 [1977]) and Harlow (1934 [1976]).
23. See, for example, *United States v. Thompson*, 28 F.Cas. 97 (D. Mass. 1846); *United States v. Adams*, 24 F.Cas. 761 (S.D.N.Y. Nov. 1844); *United States v. Kimball*, 26 F.Cas. 732 (D. Mass. April 1844).
24. *Report of the Postmaster General in relation to the establishment of a private express between New York and New Orleans*, S. Doc. No. 66, 28th Cong., 2d Sess., at 3 (January 21, 1845). In arguing that 'packet' was used broadly in the postal monopoly provision, Wickliffe was likely relying upon an 1843 opinion by Attorney General Nelson which declared that the term 'packet' included 'newspapers, magazines, or pamphlets', 4 Ops AG 276 (1843).

25. Act of March 3, 1845, ch. 43, § 9, 2 Stat. 732, 735, (emphasis added).
26. Perry, (1966, 1).
27. *United States v. Kochersperger*, 26 F.Cas. 803 (E.D. Pa. 1860).
28. Act of March 2, 1861, ch. 73, § 4, 12 Stat. 204, 205.
29. Act of March 3, 1863, ch. 71, 12 Stat. 701.
30. House Comm. on the Post Office and Post Roads, 37th Cong., 2d Sess., 'The Post Office Department, Prepared by the Post Office Department for the Committee on the Post Office and Post Roads' (Comm. Print 1863).
31. 'Report of the Commissioners to Revise the Statutes of the United States', H.R. Misc. Doc. 31, 40th Cong., 3d Sess. (1869).
32. Act of June 8, 1872, ch. 335, § 228, 17 Stat. 283, 331 (emphasis added).
33. Letter from T.L. James, Postmaster General, to W. MacVeagh, Attorney General, 15 June 1881, in National Archives (POD), Entry 2 (emphasis added).
34. Letter from W. MacVeagh, Attorney General, to T.L. James, Postmaster General, 29 June 1881, in National Archives (POD), Entry 136, Box 1, Case 9 (emphasis added).
35. The provisions corresponding to current 18 U.S.C. § 1696(a) and (b) were R.S. §§ 3982 and 3984, 18 Stat. 770, respectively.
36. Act of March 4, 1909, ch. 321, 35 Stat. 1088. The provisions corresponding to current 18 U.S.C. § 1696(a) and (b) were then sections 181 and 183, 35 Stat. 1123–24, respectively.
37. Act of June 25, 1948, ch. 654, 62 Stat. 683. Section 1696 appears at 62 Stat. 777.
38. 18 U.S.C. § 1694 (2000 & Supp. V 2006).
39. 18 U.S.C. § 1696(a) (2000 & Supp. V 2006).
40. Chandler (1977, 171–87).
41. Post Office Department, 'Orders and Decisions relative to Railroad Mail Matter compiled by the Second Assistant Postmaster General', 6 February 1897 at 11.
42. Post Office Department, 'Orders and Decisions relative to Railroad Mail Matter compiled by the Second Assistant Postmaster General', 6 February 1897.
43. Although Thomas's approach to defining the term 'letter' initiated a practice using a flexible administrative definition for the purposes of defining the postal monopoly, most of the rulings purporting to limit the right of a railroad to carry mail related to its business or to use special messengers were later reversed or limited by the Attorney General, the courts, or the Post Office itself. Compare 3 AAG POD 132 (June 3, 1895) (Op. No. 1107) (letter to railroad) and 3 AAG POD 140 (June 26, 1896) (Op. No. 1111) ('carrying by railroads of their own letters') with 21 Ops AG 394 (Aug. 12, 1896) (railroad may transport its own mail but not mail of connecting lines). Compare 2 AAG POD 877 (Op. No. 956) (1890) (telegraph company mail); 3 AAG POD 140 (Op. No. 1111) (1896) (hotel company mail) with *United States v. Eire Railroad Co.*, 235 U.S. 513 (1915) (railroad may transport telegraph company mail with whom railroad has joint venture). See 3 AAG POD 146 (1896) (railroad may not regularly send mail by its messenger over another line), reversed by 6 Ops Sol POD 293 (1915) (public utility may regularly deliver invoices by its employees to customers).
44. Letter from the Second Assistant Postmaster General to J.D.B. DeBox, Assistant General Counsel, Nashville, Chattanooga & St. Louis Ry., dated July 13, 1901, in National Archives (POD), Entry 136, Case 61.
45. *United States v. Denicke*, 35 F.407 (C.C.S.D. Ga. 1888).
46. *United States v. Gaylord*, 17 F.438 (C.C.S.D. Ill., 1883). Gaylord held that an obscene 'letter' was within the scope of a postal law provision that made obscene 'writings' nonmailable, but the Supreme Court upheld another line of cases holding the opposite. *United States v. Chase*, 135 U.S. 255 (1890). *Gaylord* was thus overruled *sub silentio*.
47. *United States. v. Bromley*, 53 U.S. (12 How.) 88 (1851).
48. 6 Op. Sol. P.O.D. 373, 380–81 (1916).
49. 6 Op. Sol. P.O.D. 397, 398 (1916). Original emphasis.
50. Letter from Acting Postmaster General J.C. Koons to Halver Steenerson, chairman, House Comm. on Post Office and Post Roads, dated August 18, 1919.
51. *Williams v. Wells Fargo & Co. Express*, 177 F. 352 (8th Cir. 1910).
52. The first notice of proposed rulemaking was published on June 29, 1973. 38 Fed. Reg. 17512 (1973). A revised version of proposed regulations was the subject of a second notice of proposed rulemaking issued on January 30, 1974. 39 Fed. Reg. 3968 (1974). The regulations were adopted in a third notice on September 13, 1974. 39 Fed. Reg. 33209 (1974).
53. 39 Fed. Reg. 33209, 33211 (1974) (§ 310.1(a)).
54. 38 Fed. Reg. at 17513 (emphasis added).
55. 39 Fed. Reg. 3969.
56. Act of March 25, 1864, ch. 40, 13 Stat. 37, codified at 39 U.S.C. § 601(b).

57. See Priest (1975, 79–80).
58. 44 Fed. Reg. 61178 (September 11, 1979), codified at 39 C.F.R. 320.6 (2006) ('suspension for extremely urgent letters'). See generally, *Postal Service Amendments of 1978: Hearings Before the Subcommittee on Energy, Nuclear Proliferation, and Federal Services of the Senate Committee on Governmental Affairs*, 95th Cong, 2d Sess. (1978); S Rep No 95–1191, 95th Cong., 2d Sess. (1978); *Private Express Statutes: Hearings Before the Subcommittee on Postal Operations and Services of the House Committee on Post Office and Civil Service*, 96th Cong., 1st Sess. (1979).
59. The suspensions are set out in 39 C.F.R. 320 (2006). International remail is mail which is prepared in one country and transported to a second country for tender to the national post office. The mail may be destined for addresses in the country where it is posted or in a third country.
60. *Associated Third Class Mail Users v. U.S. Postal Service*, 440 F.Supp. 1211 (D.D.C. 1977), *aff'd* 600 F.2d 824 (1979), *cert. den.* 444 U.S. 837 (1979).
61. Postal Accountability and Enhancement Act, Pub. L. No. 109–435, § 503(a), 120 Stat. 3198, 3234, adding 39 U.S.C. § 601(b). The grandfather provision refers to 'such carriage is within the scope of services described by regulations of the United States Postal Service . . . that purport to permit private carriage by suspension of the operation of [former 39 U.S.C. § 601(a)]'.
62. See Federal Trade Commission (2007), 'Accounting for Laws That Apply Differently to the United States Postal Service and Its Private Competitors' 16 ('The PAEA also repealed the administrative authority for the USPS to issue regulations to define the scope of the monopoly').
63. See 39 U.S.C. § 401(2) (2000) and Postal Accountability and Enhancement Act, Pub. L. No. 109–435, § 504, 120 Stat. 3198, 3235, amending 39 U.S.C. § 401(2) (emphasis added).
64. Postal Accountability and Enhancement Act, Pub. L. No. 109–435, § 503(a), 120 Stat. 3198, 3234, adding 39 U.S.C. § 601(c) (2000).
65. Postal Accountability and Enhancement Act, Pub. L. No. 109–435, § 403, 120 Stat. 3198, 3226, adding 39 U.S.C. § 404a(a)(1).
66. Postal Accountability and Enhancement Act, Pub. L. No. 109–435, § 503(a), 120 Stat. 3198, 3234, repealing 39 U.S.C. § 601(b) (2000).

BIBLIOGRAPHY

Benjamin, Maynard H. (1997), *The History of Envelopes*, N.p.: Envelope Manufacturers Association.

Chandler, Alfred D., Jr. (1977), *The Visible Hand: The Managerial Revolution in American Business*, Cambridge, MA: Harvard University Press.

Craig, Roger P. and William T. Alvis (1977), 'The postal monopoly: two hundred years of covering commercial as well as personal messages', *University of San Francisco Law Review*, **12** (fall): 57–87.

Donnici, Peter J., Larry L. Hillblom, L. Patrick Lupo and Mary Beth Collins (1976), 'The recent expansion of the postal monopoly to include commercial information: can it be justified?', *University of San Francisco Law Review* **11** (fall): 243–74.

Fuller, Wayne E. (1972), *The American Mail: Enlarger of the Common Life*, Chicago, IL: University of Chicago Press; reprint, Chicago: University of Chicago Press, 1980.

Harlow, Alvin F. (1934), *Old Way Bills: The Romance of the Express Companies*, New York: D. Appleton-Century; reprint, New York: Arno Press, 1976.

John, Richard R. (1986), 'Private mail delivery in the United States during the nineteenth century: a sketch', *Business and Economic History*, 2nd ser., **15**: 131–43.

Johnston, Joseph F., Jr. (1968), 'The United States postal monopoly', *The Business Lawyer* **23** (January): 379–405.

Perry, Elliot (1966), *Byways of Philately*, Federalsburg, MD: J.W. Stowell Printing.

Priest, George L. (1975), 'The history of the postal monopoly in the United States', *Journal of Law and Economics* **18** (1): 33–80.

Robinson, Howard (1948), *The British Post Office: A History*, Princeton, NJ: Princeton University Press; reprint, Westport, CT: Greenwood Press, 1970.

Scheele, Carl H. (1970), *A Short History of the Mail Service*, Washington, DC: Smithsonian Institution Press.

Taylor, George Rogers (1951), *The Transportation Revolution, 1815–1860*, Vol. 4 of *The Economic History of the United States*, edited by Henry David', Harold Faulkner, Louis Hacker, Curtis Nettels and Fred Shannon, New York: Rinehart; reprint, Armonk, NY: M.E. Sharpe, 1977.

United Kingdom, The Post Office. (n.d.), *The Birth of the Postal Service*, Post Office Green Paper No. 15, London: HMSO.

United States, Federal Trade Commission (2007), 'Accounting for Laws That Apply Differently to the United States Postal Service and Its Private Competitors' 16 (December), http://www.ftc.gov/os/2008/01/080116postal.pdf, accessed 1 March 2008.

United States, Post Office Department (1897), *Orders and Decisions relative to Railroad Mail Matter compiled by the Second Assistant Postmaster General*, February 6 (pamphlet).

United States, Post Office Department (1905, 1908, 1928), *Official Opinions of the Assistant Attorneys-General for the Post Office Department*, Vols 1–5, Washington, DC: Government Printing Office.

United States, Post Office Department (1928, 1929, 1936, 1952), *Official Opinions of the Solicitor for the Post Office Department*, Vols 6–9, Washington, DC: Government Printing Office.

Woolsey, Mary E. (1894), *The Early History of the Colonial Post-Office*, Rhode Island Historical Society; reprint, New York: Philatelic Literature Review, 1969.

16. Competition, wages and politics in the delivery sector: the case of postal minimum wages in Germany

Alex Kalevi Dieke[†] and Ralf Wojtek[‡]

1. INTRODUCTION

Since 1998 – the year gradual liberalization was introduced in Germany – several hundred operators have entered the German market for letter delivery to compete with the incumbent Deutsche Post AG (DPAG). Virtually all of these operators provide end-to-end delivery and many of them operate at a local or regional level. In total, they deliver about 10 percent of all letters posted in Germany today (2007), up from less than 4 percent in 2003.

With the recent growth of competitive mail delivery, a controversial political debate about working conditions at the entrants has emerged in Germany. Since winter 2006/07, labor unions, socialist and social democrat parties, and incumbent Deutsche Post have strongly argued in favor of sector-specific minimum wages, and such minimum wages were introduced in December 2007. The possibility of sector-specific minimum wages arises in Germany because there is no general minimum wage law, and wages are traditionally agreed between trade unions and employers' associations. Concerns about working conditions during postal reform are not particular to Germany. Indeed, similar political concerns can be seen in a number of other European countries, and aspects of employment policy have been introduced into the Third Postal Directive that was adopted in early 2008.[1] In this directive, the European legislator stipulates that on member state level 'the granting of authorizations may, where appropriate, be made subject to or impose an obligation to respect working conditions laid down by national legislation' (Art. 9, 2nd paragraph, 5th indent). Therefore, the issue of working conditions is likely to be on the agenda of other European countries, too, during the implementation of the Third Postal Directive.

In Germany, effective from January 1, 2008, and simultaneously with the complete liberalization of the mail market, the government issued a Decree declaring the minimum wage agreed between the union Vereinte Dienstleistungsgewerkschaft, or ver.di as it is commonly known, and the employers' association of postal services (AGV Postdienste) binding on all providers of mail services. AGV Postdienste is dominated by the incumbent, Deutsche Post. The agreed wages are closely related to those paid by Deutsche Post.

† WIK Wissenschaftliches Institut für Infrastruktur und Kommunikationsdienste.
‡ Heuking Kühn Lüer Wojtek, Hamburg, Germany.

The objective of this chapter is to discuss the reasons that led to the introduction of the sector-specific minimum wage in Germany, and the (preliminary) impact of the minimum wage on the mail market. The chapter is organized as follows: Section 2 summarizes the development of competition in the German mail market before minimum wages were introduced, assembles the empirical findings that are available on wages in the postal and delivery sector, and discusses the difference in wages paid by the incumbent Deutsche Post and the entrants. Section 3 reviews the political process that led to the introduction of minimum wages and Section 4 describes the state of litigation. Section 5 deals with competition law aspects and Section 6 goes on to discuss the market impact of sector-specific minimum wages on the costs of competitive operators, the first reactions of entrants to the new minimum wage, and the likely effect on competition in the market. Based on this experience, Section 7 concludes by suggesting possible lessons that the recent developments in the German market might offer for other countries.

2. COMPETITION AND WAGES IN THE GERMAN MAIL MARKET

In the German market for delivery of letters, competition developed to a considerable extent even before full liberalization: The market share of Deutsche Post AG in terms of total (licensed) letter volume was 96.3 percent in 2003 and 91.4 percent in 2006 and was estimated to be 89.6 percent for 2007 by the regulator (Bundesnetzagentur, 2007, p. 23). Light letters and direct mail weighing less than 50 grams were under the monopoly until the end of 2007, and this segment accounts for most of the total letter volume. Consequently, only very few entrants have focused on delivering heavy letters. What was more important for the development of competition was the explicit liberalization of value-added services, combined with legal definitions that required relatively little value to be added on top of the standard universal service product (for example, guaranteed overnight delivery, or day-certain delivery).[2]

Most of the competitors[3] operate at a local or regional level, and many of these firms were established by local publishers that traditionally provide morning delivery of newspapers to their subscription customers. In the last two or three years – along with overall growth of competitor volumes – the market has witnessed massive consolidation: many of the smaller local operators have been acquired by two groups that have established themselves as the leading operators in the market, second to Deutsche Post AG. There are approximately 700 competitors active in the market. Together they hold a market share of approximately 10 percent. The two largest competitors are PIN Group – which is owned by several German publishers – and TNT Post Deutschland, a subsidiary of the Dutch incumbent TNT Post. Exact revenue information is available from neither, but various press articles report that each of them had a turnover of approximately €200–350 million in 2007, with PIN Group having somewhat larger operations than TNT Post. In autumn 2007, both groups reported making deliveries – either themselves or through local partners – in a substantial part of Germany (approximately 75–90 percent of all addresses) and aiming at full nationwide coverage in the short term. These plans have been revised due to the introduction of the minimum wage (see Section 6, below).

2.1 Deutsche Post AG

Deutsche Post AG, the German incumbent, has substantially restructured its operations and business strategy following privatization (since 1995). With respect to the letter business, the first major change was a complete re-engineering of the sorting processes, sorting center locations, and transportation infrastructure (following its transformation plan, *Briefkonzept 2000*). A second strategic change was the introduction of outsourcing, for example, of retail outlets (the former post offices) and transportation services.[4] A third key element of Deutsche Post's strategy to become more efficient was the introduction of new collective wage agreements (CWAs) in 2001/02 that substantially reduced wages for new personnel.

It is widely recognized that incumbents, before deregulation and in the early days of deregulation, usually pay their employees a 'wage premium'.[5] That is, they pay wages higher than what would be paid in a fully competitive labor market. For example, Wachter et al. (2001, pp. 21f.) estimated the wage premium for United States Postal Service (USPS) employees (the mark-up over wages for similar jobs in competitive, non-postal industries) as being from 20 to 35 percent for different types of labor. For the German letter market, Dieke and Zauner (2007), in a survey conducted for the German regulator Bundesnetzagentur, find indications of a similar wage premium (see Table 16.1).

Table 16.1 summarizes the working conditions (hourly wages, weekly working hours, and annual vacation permit) offered by three employers, or groups of employers. The second column of the table relates to workers at Deutsche Post's letter operations, and the values are averages for different types of labor, for example, delivery postmen/women, sorting staff and drivers.[6] The values are taken from the CWA that is applicable to workers who joined Deutsche Post later than August 2003. Information on working conditions offered by competitors (last column) is from a survey of the 100 largest licensed operators in the German letter market. By contrast, the information for subcontractors represents best estimates of Dieke and Zauner, based on CWAs for industries to which subcontractors typically belong and interviews with subcontractors of Deutsche Post AG and relevant associations.

In 2000 and 2002, Deutsche Post reached an agreement with the unions that lower wages could be paid to staff who joined the firm after a cut-off date.[7] According to these 'new CWAs', wages for new labor (hired after the cut-off date) are 30 to 40 percent lower than those applicable to old labor. For example, a newcomer delivery postman/woman at Deutsche Post may earn €10.14 per hour while his/her incumbent colleague makes €16.40 per hour. Consequently, the wage premium between workers at Deutsche Post, on the one hand, and workers employed by competitors or subcontractors on the other, is in fact higher than Table 16.1 suggests. As no information is available from DPAG on the share of its staff that receives high or low wage levels, it is difficult to state the exact value of the wage premium paid by the incumbent.

From what is available, however, it seems clear that average wages at Deutsche Post are at least 40 percent higher than those paid for similar jobs with competitors (in March 2007). Moreover, Deutsche Post pays the same wages throughout Germany while geographic differences are very common in most other industries. This means that the wage premium over local competitive wages will be even higher in low-wage (typically high-unemployment) regions, but the difference will be less in high-wage (typically lower-unemployment) regions.

Table 16.1 Working conditions in the German letter market: DPAG, subcontractors to DPAG, and competitors (WIK survey, March 2007)

	Deutsche Post AG (new CWA)	Subcontractors of Deutsche Post AG	Competitors
Average wage per hour (€)	11.40	8.00	8.44
Average working hours per week	38.5	43.0	38.8
Average vacation entitlement per year (days)	28.0	28.0	22.9

Source: Dieke and Zauner (2007, p. 34).

In addition to internal measures to enhance efficiency, Deutsche Post has, since the beginning of the millennium, increasingly outsourced some of its letter operations in order to reduce its cost base and to gain flexibility. There was massive outsourcing related to transportation and transformation of post offices into retail outlets operated by agents. In contrast to the parcel business, however, no delivery functions have been outsourced. In the 10-year period from 1997 to 2006, outsourcing is estimated to be equivalent to staff reductions of 20,000 to 25,000 full-time jobs in total (Dieke and Zauner 2007, p. 14). The subcontractors pay wages that are broadly comparable to those paid by competitors in the letters market, and significantly lower than those of Deutsche Post AG (see Table 16.1).

2.2 Competitors

Since the introduction of competition to the letter market in 1998, the German regulator has provided annual employment statistics for the entrants. The number of employees has increased gradually to 48,000 persons in 2006, compared to an employment of approximately 150,000 persons in Deutsche Post's letter business (Bundesnetzagentur, 2007, pp. 40f.). The majority of persons employed by competitors are part-timers. However, the regulator has not published information on wages in the postal sector before 2008.

Wages paid by competitors to Deutsche Post were first investigated in summer/autumn 2006 in a study (that was reported in the press to be) commissioned by ver.di, the largest union for the services sector in Germany (Input Consulting, 2006). The study – based on a survey of competitors, analysis of openings published by job centers, and interviews with unions and workers' councils – found average hourly wages to be €7.00 in Western Germany and €5.90 in Eastern Germany.[8] The validity of these results, however, was limited because only 55 out of approximately 1,000 firms surveyed participated in the survey; and the majority of these firms were small or very small competitors with annual revenues of less than €0.5 million. The study results were used by proponents of a postal minimum wage to claim a common practice of exploitation of labor and 'wage dumping' in the liberalized postal market. At this time, ver.di was calling for a general minimum wage (for all sectors) of €7.50 per hour.

In early 2007, the postal regulator Bundesnetzagentur asked WIK to conduct a more comprehensive survey of working conditions at the largest 100 competitors (by revenue), as well as an analysis of those at DPAG and subcontractors that work for the incumbent.[9]

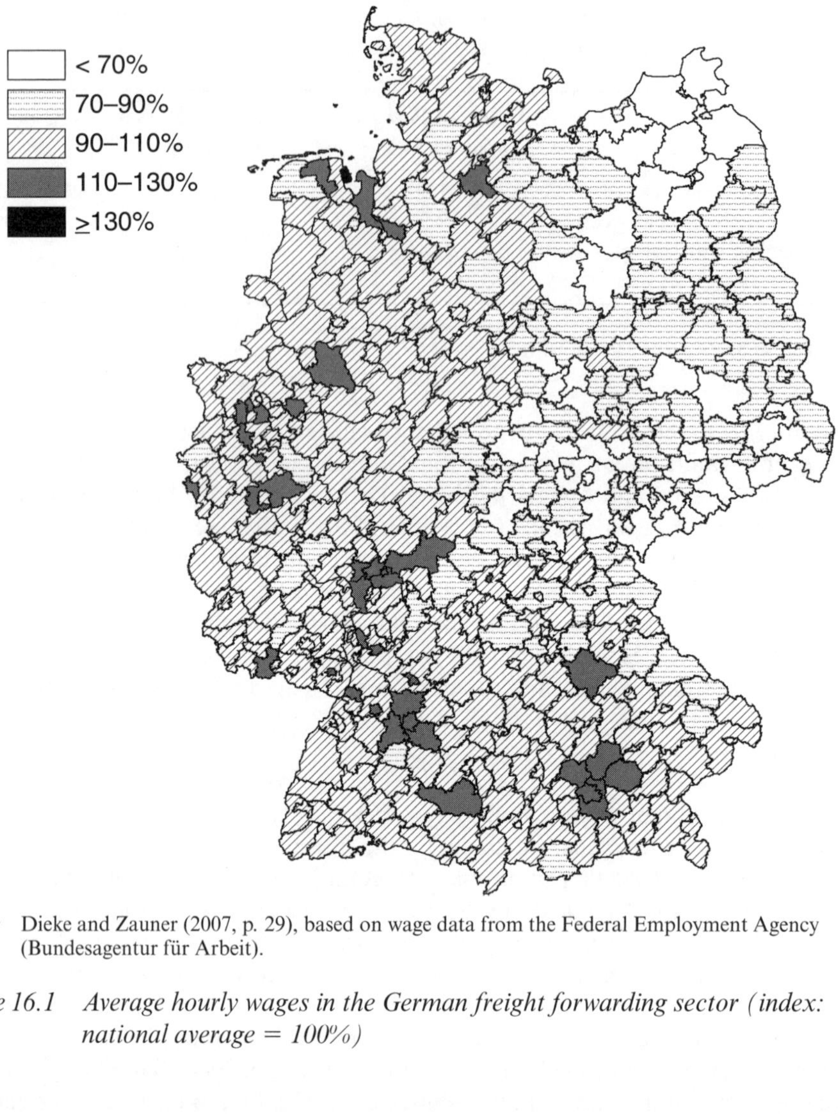

Source: Dieke and Zauner (2007, p. 29), based on wage data from the Federal Employment Agency (Bundesagentur für Arbeit).

Figure 16.1 Average hourly wages in the German freight forwarding sector (index: national average = 100%)

The study found wages paid by competitors to be €8.44 on average for all types of labor (see Table 16.1) and €7.94 for delivery staff. Out of 100 firms in the original survey, 38 responded. These 38 firms account for 94 percent of total revenues in the letters market (including Deutsche Post), and the 37 responding competitors account for 45 percent of the total revenues of all competitors.

The survey further noted that Deutsche Post pays uniform national wages while there are significant regional differences between wages paid by private competitors. The survey's response rate did not allow determination of wage levels for competitors by separate geographic regions. However, the study showed that significant geographic wage differences exist in many other industries in Germany, including, for example, printing, retail selling, distance selling, freight forwarding, and data processing. As an example,

Table 16.2 Average hourly wages paid by DPAG and competitors (€) (Bundesnetzagentur survey, summer/autumn 2007)

	Deutsche Post AG	Competitors		
		Average	East	West
Sorters	11.34	7.68	6.11	8.10
Drivers	11.99	7.73	6.23	8.08
Delivery postmen/women	12.13	7.28	6.18	7.71
Administrative clerks	16.01	10.97	9.23	11.24
All employees	13.04	7.79	6.38	8.23

Source: Bundesnetzagentur (2008, p. 5).

Figure 16.1 illustrates regional differences between wages paid in the freight forwarding business, a highly competitive industry. Average wages for each of the 440 counties and independent municipalities in Germany (*Landkreise und kreisfreie Städte*) are shown as a percentage of the national average. Analysis of other industries shows clearly that there are significant wage differences between regions in Germany and that wages are generally higher in urban metropolitan areas and in Western Germany than in rural areas and in the East.[10] Compared to competitive environments, the study concludes that the uniform wages paid by Deutsche Post are unusual but can be explained by the firm's history as a government entity (there is a tradition of uniform wages in federal government entities in Germany).

In response to the controversial political discussion in 2007, the regulator undertook a mandatory survey of wages paid by all – approximately 1,500 – licensed postal operators. This survey was launched in late June 2007, and results became available in early 2008 (Bundesnetzagentur, 2008). Following some delay due to litigation over the regulator's competence to request this information, almost all operators (94 percent) finally contributed to the survey. According to Bundesnetzagentur, those operators that did not respond could not be contacted by the regulator at all, and most likely no longer exist or do not provide any services under their license.

This latest survey confirmed earlier findings that average wages paid by competitors in the postal market are somewhat higher than those reported by the first study (€5.90 East/€7.00 West), but are significantly below the median wage of all German workers. The results also demonstrate the existence of a significant wage premium included in Deutsche Post's wage levels (see Table 16.2).

At the same time, more granular data on wages paid in different regions became available from this survey: while competitors paid €7.79 in the nation on average, the average wage was only €6.05 in Brandenburg (in Eastern Germany at the Polish border) – the state with the lowest average wage, but €10.27 in Saarland (in Western Germany on the borders of France and Luxembourg). For nine of 11 Western German states, the average wage was above the national average, but it was below average in all five Eastern states (Bundesnetzagentur, 2008, p. 7). The regional differences between wages paid for delivery postmen/women in the German states are further illustrated in Figure 16.2 below (see Section 6).

3. THE POLITICAL HISTORY OF POSTAL MINIMUM WAGES IN GERMANY

Since the beginning of postal liberalization, politics in Germany (as elsewhere) has been concerned about postal wages. Addressing these concerns, the 1998 Postal Act stipulates that 'a license shall be denied when . . . facts warrant the assumption that the applicant fails to a not inconsiderable extent to meet the basic working conditions common in the licensed sector'.[11] In the absence of a clear legal interpretation of this stipulation, the regulator has, until recently, implemented this legal requirement by monitoring that all licensees abide by general labor legislation and contribute to the public social security systems.

An intense political debate about postal wages and liberalization in Germany started in autumn 2006, when ver.di published the first study on wages paid by competitors in the postal market. A coalition of postal workers' unions, Deutsche Post AG, and socialist and social democrat parties were afraid of the negative social effects of wage competition in the sector and argued that protection was needed to further the interests of workers in the postal sector. Several policy options were proposed during this debate as potential 'remedies'. The study commissioned by ver.di listed the following options: (i) withdrawing or delaying full liberalization; (ii) more rigorous license conditions, or a more restrictive application of current license conditions (see citation from the Postal Act in the paragraph above); (iii) collective wage agreements between unions and competitors in the mail markets; (iv) a general minimum wage for all sectors; and (v) a specific minimum wage for the postal sector.

Deutsche Post has explicitly contributed to this debate. A press release in March 2007 cautiously suggested holding up both liberalization and minimum wages:

> In order to secure jobs in Germany in the future, further steps toward the liberalization of the mail market must be taken reasonably and with a sense of responsibility. 'We are concerned about the political framework for the full opening of Germany's mail market,' said Klaus Zumwinkel [CEO of Deutsche Post]. The current situation, where there is no agreement on a harmonized liberalization throughout Europe and where nothing stands in the way of competitors pursuing a strategy of wage dumping, runs contrary to the practice of fair competition. (Deutsche Post World Net, 2007)

During 2007, the regulator came under political pressure to implement the 'social' license conditions more rigidly. The debate – and the demand for minimum wages – became more intense simultaneously with the decision to liberalize the mail market completely. The incumbent and many politicians held the view that Bundesnetzagentur should interpret 'the basic working conditions common in the licensed sector' (§ 6 Postal Act) to be the wages paid by market-dominant Deutsche Post, and that the regulator should consequently withdraw licenses from firms that pay lower wages than Deutsche Post (reported, for instance, by El-Sharif, 2007). There is, however, substantial doubt as to how the requirements of the Postal Act should be interpreted: a legal study prepared for the regulator in early 2007 concluded that the relevant benchmark for 'common' or 'usual' wages in a deregulated industry could not be derived from the wages paid by the incumbent. Instead, the benchmark would need to consider the working conditions offered by companies that compete with delivery firms for job seekers on local labor markets (Säcker,

2007). In contrast, a legal study presented by a foundation related to the Social Democratic Party (SPD) argues that 'common' working conditions could not mean anything but the conditions offered to the majority of workers in the sector, that is, those offered by Deutsche Post which accounts for 90 percent of the mail market (Blanke, 2007).

After a period of controversial debate within the government coalition (consisting of the conservative Christian Democratic Union (CDU) and the SPD), the coalition agreed on a compromise in late August 2007. Reportedly, it was agreed to end discussions about delaying the date of full liberalization (31 December 2007) but, in return, to impose a sector-specific minimum wage. It was agreed that this minimum wage would be introduced by extending the 'Employee Assignment Law' (*Arbeitnehmer-Entsendegesetz*) to the postal sector. Originally, this law was introduced to impose conditions agreed between social partners in Germany on foreign workers who work in Germany on a temporary basis, for example, on construction sites or in cleaning services. Thereby, domestic workers should be protected from wage competition by foreigners who are 'assigned' to work in Germany temporarily. Where a CWA exists in a sector – and applies to the majority of employees in this sector – the contracting parties can request the government to make such CWA mandatory for all firms operating in the same sector (including foreign firms).

Under the Employee Assignment Law, only CWAs agreed by associations of employers are eligible, not agreements between individual employers and unions. Deutsche Post AG has individual CWAs with several unions. Only a few days after the political compromise, Deutsche Post AG established an employers' association (Arbeitgeberverband Postdienste e.V.) that consisted, next to Deutsche Post, of several of its subsidiaries, but no competitor was a member of the association. Later on, leading competitors PIN Group and TNT Post reported that they had not even been contacted and asked to join the association. In early September 2007 (September 4, 2007), the association reportedly entered into a CWA on minimum wages for the postal sector with ver.di, and requested from the government that this agreement be made mandatory for the sector. The minimum wages agreed in the CWA were €9.80 for delivery postmen/women in Western Germany, €9.00 for delivery postmen/women in the East, and €8.40 (West) or €8.00 (East) for other workers.

Since these wages are close to, but lower than wages agreed in existing CWAs of Deutsche Post with ver.di, the minimum wage agreement has no economic impact on the incumbent or on its employees. Rather, the minimum wage agreement – once declared binding – has an impact only on competitors of the incumbent (and possibly on some of its subcontractors, provided that they are predominantly active in the mail delivery business). Thus, there is the interesting situation that an employers' association which is dominated by the incumbent and does not include a single competitor negotiated a minimum wage agreement, which affects only third parties, the competitors of the incumbent. It has been suggested, therefore, that a CWA which does not apply to the negotiating party itself but only to its competitors cannot be considered as representative of the industry (Thüsing, 2008, p. 25).

This CWA at first referred to all firms that deliver letters no matter how few, and even if this is not their main business. It was then found that this definition includes many firms that hold licenses and sometimes deliver letters, but whose principal activity is something different, for example, morning delivery of newspapers. Since newspaper delivery firms employ a large number of persons, it was highly questionable whether the employers' association founded by Deutsche Post would account for the majority of sector employment. Therefore, this agreement, which may be termed the 'Postal CWA', was changed to apply solely to firms that predominantly provide delivery of letters.

When the competitors were faced with the possibility of the Postal CWA being declared binding, they themselves formed an Employers' Association (AGV New Delivery Services). At the same time, employees mainly coming from the competitor PIN Group started to form their own Union of New Delivery Service Workers (New Union). Although the New Union quickly gained acceptance among the employees of the competitors, it was quickly dubbed a 'bogus union' by ver.di and the incumbent. In December 2007 the new employers' association AGV New Delivery Services and the New Union entered into their own CWA. According to this CWA, the 'Competitors' CWA', wages for all postal employees in Eastern Germany are set at €6.50 per hour and in the West at €7.50 per hour. While these amounts are less than the wages set by the Postal CWA they constitute a significant increase in the actual minimum wages paid by competitors (before the Competitors' CWA was concluded) both in Eastern and Western Germany (approximately 20 percent in Eastern Germany and approximately 8 percent in Western Germany).

On 21 December 2007, Parliament adopted a law extending the scope of the Employee Assignment Law to include mail delivery. In amending the law, in the preface to this amendment, the legislator refers to the conceived danger of 'wage dumping', the influx of foreign workers following liberalization of the postal market, and the lack of union agreements applying to competitors. On 28 December 2007, the government issued a decree declaring the minimum wage agreement concluded by ver.di and AGV Postdienste binding on all companies that predominantly offer mail services and their employees.[12]

4. STATE OF LITIGATION

Immediately upon the passing of the government regulation on postal minimum wages several parties, including PIN, TNT and the association of couriers, brought a lawsuit against the German government with the request that the government decree be declared null and void. The main arguments brought forward by the plaintiffs were based on a defense of their constitutional rights. In particular, it was alleged that the decree violates the rights of competitors and the New Union to conclude a CWA of their own. It was claimed that the Postal CWA was not representative of the industry and could not, therefore, be extended by government decree to competitors. The economic impact of the Postal CWA was addressed as well. It would lead to an average increase in labor costs of 20 to 40 percent, thus making it impossible for competitors to offer nationwide mail services. The cost increase could not be absorbed by competitors acting outside metropolitan or other high-wage areas; these companies would have to be closed down. According to the plaintiffs' allegation the Decree violated their constitutional right to exercise their profession.

The government argued that the plaintiffs had no standing to sue directly against a government decree. According to the government, the mandatory minimum wage was necessary in order to avoid wage dumping. It was argued that companies that rely on wage dumping would not be worth it to survive in a liberalized market. The government took the position that the Postal CWA was negotiated by parties representing more than 50 percent of all employees in the postal business and that it is, therefore, truly representative of the working conditions in the entire industry.

On March 7, 2008 the administrative court of Berlin (VG Berlin), after an eight-hour hearing, rendered a judgment declaring the decree null and void. In its judgment the court relied mainly on the argument that the government has no power to issue a decree which declares minimum wages mandatory even on those companies which are already party to another CWA. In addition to this argument, the court indicated that it had certain doubts regarding the reasonableness of declaring the Postal CWA mandatory without having due regard to the economic impact on competitors. The government immediately appealed the decision. It is likely that the appeal will take several months to be decided by the Superior Administrative Court.

In the meantime, the legal situation is unclear. According to the decision of VG Berlin, the decree is null and void, and no company can be obligated to pay the minimum wages decreed by the government on the basis of the Postal CWA. On the other hand, if VG Berlin is overturned by the Superior Court or even later by the Supreme Administrative Court, the decree might be considered valid *ab initio.* Usually it takes at least two to three years to obtain a final judgment from the Supreme Administrative Court. This means that for a period of at least two years neither competitors nor their employees can be certain of the actual applicable wage. As long as the risk of an adverse ruling cannot be ruled out, companies may have to allow for reserves on their balance sheets for additional payments on wages and social security. Given this uncertainty – and the economic burden of the potential liability – competitors may have to make a decision on continuation or withdrawal based on economic conditions in place before the final judgment is rendered. If they are forced to withdraw from the market, they may console themselves with the possibility of claiming damages later if the Supreme Administrative Court upholds the judgment of first instance.

5. COMPETITION LAW ASPECTS

In December 2007, before the law and the decree were enacted, the German Association of International Express Companies (BIEK) filed a competition complaint before the European Commission arguing that the agreement on minimum wages between AGV Postdienste and ver.di constituted a scheme to obstruct competition. Just recently, TNT was reported to have filed a competition complaint based on Article 86 of the European Treaty against the German government, claiming that the decree on minimum wages leads to an unfair infringement on competition (Article 81) and violates the freedom to establish business throughout the European Union (Article 43) by raising rivals' costs.

Generally, according to European jurisprudence and literature, CWAs are considered to be beyond the reach of competition rules. Although CWAs do have an impact on competition, it would be impossible for the parties to labor agreements to improve the working conditions of their constituents if such agreements were to be measured by competition standards. Therefore, the European Court of Justice (ECJ) has ruled that a labor agreement, which has been negotiated in a dialogue between the parties and has developed as the result of wage negotiations is not prohibited by competition rules.[13] On the other hand, in the same judgment the Court also stated that an agreement which goes beyond the objective of improving labor conditions of the constituents represented by the parties may indeed collide with competition rules (Büdenbender, 2000, pp. 44ff.). This statement may be taken as an indication that a labor agreement, which extends to companies and persons, who were not party to it or who were not even represented by either party, may indeed be subject to competition rules. In particular, the fact that competitors were explicitly excluded from the negotiation process could lead to the conclusion that the Postal CWA is not to be considered as a typical labor agreement, which would be outside the scope of competition rules.

In addition, the fact that the government allowed the Postal CWA – and only it – to become mandatory might be considered as granting an exclusive right (to Deutsche Post) within the meaning of Article 86 of the EU Treaty, whose reasonableness would have to be measured against competition rules. If only Deutsche Post is entitled to have wages declared mandatory by virtue of its dominant position and the number of employees resulting from its market share, one may indeed consider this as a special right of the incumbent.

6. IMPACT OF MINIMUM WAGES ON THE MAIL MARKET

In March 2008 (as this chapter is being written), only two months have elapsed since the minimum wage for the postal sector became effective. Moreover, after the recent decision by the Berlin administrative court, it is not certain that the minimum wage will ultimately become effective at all. Consequently, it is too early for a mature assessment of the practical impact of the minimum wage on the market. However, this section attempts a preliminary assessment of the impact of the minimum wage, assuming it will be held applicable. To this end, the section will (i) discuss the increase in competitors' labor costs that result from the minimum wage; (ii) assess the resulting impact on the total costs of competitors; and (iii) review the competitors' initial reactions to the minimum wage.

Figure 16.2 illustrates the average wages paid by competitors before the conclusion of Competitors' CWA to their delivery postmen/women in the 16 German states, according to the recent survey conducted by German regulator. The figure also indicates the minimum wage (€9.80 West / €9.00 East) introduced in December 2007 for delivery staff. The gap between average wage levels in a state and the minimum wage then indicates the resulting average increase of labor cost for the operators in this state. Based on this data, the minimum wage causes an increase of labor cost for delivery staff by at least 30 percent on average, and by at least 7 to 58 percent in the different states.[14] It is obvious that such a massive increase in factor prices would have a significant impact on the overall profitability of the competitors and their overall ability to continue in the market.

If the share of labor cost in total cost of the competitors were 70 percent, the minimum wage would result in an increase of competitors' total cost by at least 22 percent.[15] The negative impact on competitors will be greater, the lower the current wages paid by these operators. If the regional wage levels are inversely related to regional unemployment, then the negative effect on competitors will be particularly high in areas with low current wage levels and high unemployment. Moreover, increasing labor costs affect competitors' cost of delivery strongly because the productivity of their labor (in delivery) is less than 30 percent of the average productivity of Deutsche Post delivery staff: While

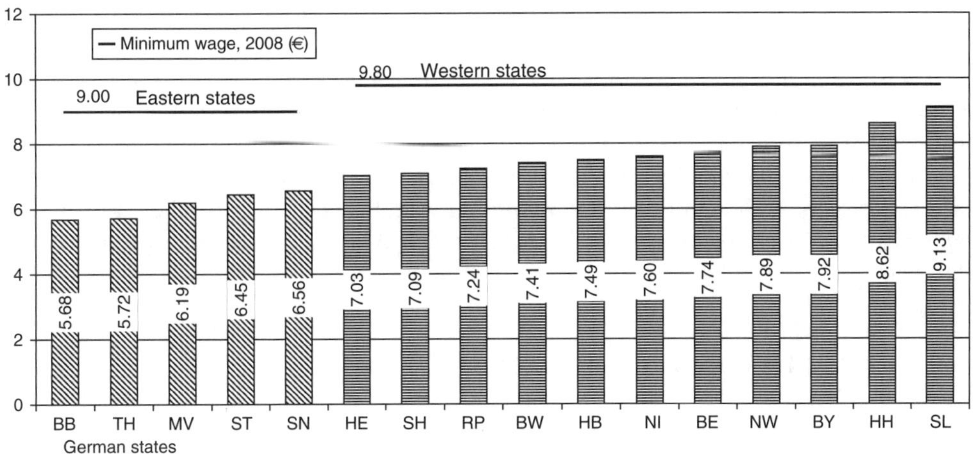

Note: Abbreviations of German states: BB Brandenburg, BE Berlin, BW Baden-Württemberg, BY Bavaria, HB Bremen, HE Hesse, HH Hamburg, MV Mecklenburg-Vorpommern, NI Lower Saxony, NW North Rhine-Westphalia, RP Rhineland-Palatinate, SH Schleswig-Holstein, SL Saarland, SN Saxony, ST Saxony-Anhalt, TH Thuringia. Eastern states are shown in diagonal cross-hatching, and Western states shaded in horizontal cross-hatching.

Source: Quander (2008).

Figure 16.2 Minimum wage and average wages paid by competitors to delivery postmen/women (on state level)

postmen/women employed by competitors typically deliver 30 to 40 letters per hour, those employed by Deutsche Post are estimated to deliver 137 letters per hour.[16] Consequently, competitors can incur much higher unit cost in delivery per letter even at significantly lower wage levels.

The first reactions of the two large competitors to the minimum wage give rise to serious concerns about the future development of competition in the German letters market.

Even before the minimum wage became effective – but in the wake of its announcement – the main shareholder of PIN Group, publishing firm Axel Springer, announced its withdrawal from the Group by selling its interest. In December 2007, Springer refused to provide funds needed to avoid bankruptcy of PIN Group. PIN Group is now managed by an insolvency administrator and according to press reports, 39 of approximately 120 companies that belong to PIN Group filed insolvency applications in January 2007. Between December and mid-March, PIN Group is reported to have laid off about 3,000 employees, and 4,000 more will lose their job by the end of March (Welt Online, 2008). While there is a chance that PIN Group's troubles may also be due in part to business expansion in an overly optimistic manner, it is clear that the threat of a cost increase of 20 percent would frustrate investors in any business and even more so if the firm is already in a difficult situation. At present, PIN Group pays the mandatory minimum wage, but payment is made out of social security funds, since PIN Group itself is insolvent. If the minimum wage is to stay, it seems rather unlikely that PIN Group will be able to maintain operations with close-to-nationwide coverage in the medium term. Nonetheless, there is little doubt that the more profitable companies of the Group will stay in the market.

TNT Post, in its annual report for 2007, has published financial results for its German mail unit. It reported a loss of €31 million on revenues of €233 million. Following publication of this report, TNT Post has announced that it is seriously considering withdrawing from the German mail market if the minimum wage is maintained (Sheen, 2008). As a first reaction to the imposition of minimum wages, TNT Post cancelled a project to expand its services to the 13,500 German branch offices of its joint venture partner, Hermes.

7. CONCLUSIONS

Although experience with the minimum wage for the postal sector in Germany is very recent (January to March 2008), there are strong indications that this minimum wage – if it is to stay – will severely harm the prospects of competition in the German letters market. The introduction of the minimum wage was followed by a wave of bankruptcies, and it was blamed by the insolvent operators as the reason for this turmoil. PIN Group alone laid off about 7,000 employees in the first quarter of 2008. It is uncertain whether either of the two leading competitors – PIN Group and TNT Post – will stay in the market.

While first experience with *this* minimum wage in Germany is clearly negative, it is not so clear that this effect is a necessary result of introducing minimum wages as such. Today, Germany is one of the few European countries that does not have a general minimum wage. In this respect, persistent high unemployment (at rates close to 10 percent over the last 15 years) does not suggest that German labor market policies have been particularly successful. This chapter offers no conclusion as regards the merits of general minimum wage laws.

This chapter strongly suggests that sector-specific minimum wages are detrimental, in particular if the sector is dominated by an incumbent. In such a case it is always likely that the rules of the game will be set in accordance with the interests of the incumbent itself and the union that has most of its constituents as employees of the incumbent. If a sector-specific minimum wage is considered at all, the interests of competitors should be given proper representation within the negotiation process.

In determining the 'sector' of sector-specific wages, consideration should be given to the similarity between postal delivery services and similar delivery services or services using similar skills. After all, why is delivery of parcels or newspapers so different from delivery of letters that one would want to impose minimum wages on one activity but not the other? German experience shows that, on top of the effect on competition, imposing sector-specific rather than general minimum wages is very difficult from an administrative standpoint. The situation may become even more complicated if 'non-postal' authorities (the customs police) have to enforce the minimum wage and assess whether or not an undertaking's 'primary activity' is delivery of addressed letters, newspapers, or something else.

The more 'specific' the wage regulation, the greater is the invitation to market participants to avoid such regulation by using business schemes which are outside the scope of the wage regulation. For example, there is already a discernible trend towards outsourcing mail delivery to companies whose main business is in the area of transportation or newspaper delivery. Here again, the incumbent is setting the pace. In March 2008, Deutsche Post announced the beginning of a pilot cooperation with a publishing house for delivery of unaddressed mail. The chairman of the regulatory authority, Matthias Kurth, suggested that competitors should be 'creative' in order to be able to cope with the minimum wage. All of this seems to indicate that a postal sector-specific minimum wage is more detrimental than beneficial to the industry as such.

Finally, comparing wage premiums paid by different incumbents and analyzing the reasons underlying such differences offer promising subjects for future research.[17] It appears that labor relations of postal incumbents and the effect of liberalization on these relations differ from country to country, and this warrants further research.

NOTES

1. Directive 97/67/EC as amended by Directives 2002/39/EC and 2008/6/EC. The term 'Third Postal Directive' refers to the original directive as amended in 2008.
2. Licences granted for delivery of these value-added services were referred to as 'D-licences'.
3. In this chapter, the term, 'competitor' means 'competitor to Deutsche Post' and is used synonymously with 'new entrant'.
4. A more comprehensive presentation of the strategic re-engineering of Deutsche Post during the 1990s can be found in Maschke (2002, pp. 308ff). In particular, Maschke explains how Deutsche Post has managed to overcome opposition from trade unions by making operational changes, staff downsizing and outsourcing 'socially compatible'. The most important element of this approach was that Deutsche Post committed itself to refraining from mandatory redundancies.
5. Such a wage premium may even be negative. For example, inflexible public sector legislation may prevent an incumbent from paying competitive wages. Where incumbents pay uniform wages, wage premiums can certainly be negative in urban high-wage areas. In these circumstances, incumbents find it hard to hire qualified and motivated personnel. PwC (2006) suggests that Polish Post may be in this situation (p. 57).
6. The average wage of €11.40 was calculated from wages determined by the new CWA for different types of labor, weighted by the share of each class of labor in total employment of DPAG's letter operations.
7. The cut-off dates for the new CWA were 1.1.2001 and 1.9.2003 for two different types of labor. See Dieke and Zauner (2007, pp. 8f.).
8. In the statistics presented in the chapter, the terms 'East' or 'Eastern Germany' refer to the five states that joined the Federal Republic of Germany at the re-unification in 1990, that is, the territory of the formerly communist German Democratic Republic (but not Eastern Berlin). 'West' or 'Western Germany' refers to the territory of the Federal Republic of Germany before 1990 (and Eastern Berlin). The reason for adding East Berlin to the 'West' in the statistics we present is that no separate data on postal wages are available for the former two parts of Berlin.
9. The results are published (in German) in Dieke and Zauner (2007).
10. Graphs for other industries look very similar to Figure 16.1 (for freight forwarding). See appendices of Dieke and Zauner (2007).
11. § 6 Postal Act (quoted from translated version available on ministry website, www.bmwi.bund.de).
12. About the same time the value of Deutsche Post's shares surged and the former chairman of Deutsche Post sold his stock options, reportedly realizing a gain of some €4 million.
13. See ECJ judgment of 21 September 1999, C-67/96 'Albany' and Aicher and Schuhmacher (2007).
14. The values (30 percent on average, 7 to 58 percent in the 16 states) show how much higher the minimum wage was compared to the average wage level before the introduction of the minimum wage. Only if the wage level were completely uniform in a state, would this percentage equal the increase in average labor cost. But in practice, the competitors will have paid some employees more than the minimum wage even before the minimum wage law, and will continue to do. Consequently, average wages will be higher than the minimum wages. Therefore, the real average increase in labor costs will be more than 30 percent, depending on the heterogeneity of current wages.
15. The authors are not aware of published research on cost analysis for entrants to the postal market. For incumbents with small volumes – comparable to those of entrants in Germany – Cohen et al. suggest that

delivery alone will account for more than half of total costs (2006, pp. 6 and 14). In this perspective, 70 percent appears as a reasonable estimate of the share of labor in total entrant cost.

16. These productivities were stated by TNT Post at the Berlin administrative court. See Verwaltungsgericht Berlin (2008, pp. 4f.).
17. Some evidence and very interesting ideas on the reasons that may explain different wage premiums for different incumbents are suggested by Bickerton (2006).

REFERENCES

Aicher, J. and F. Schuhmacher (2007), 'Art. 81 Rn. 27', in E. Grabitz and M. Hilf, *Das Recht der Europäischen Union*, Munich: C.H. Beck.

Bickerton, G. (2006), 'Postal deregulation and its impact on postal workers: a Canadian union perspective', in M.A. Crew and P.R. Kleindorfer (eds), *Liberalization of the Postal and Delivery Sector*, Cheltenham, UK and Northampton, MA, USA: Edward Elgar, pp. 203–16.

Blanke, T. (2007), 'Wettbewerb, Prekarität und Sozialschutz. Die sozialen Lizenzanforderungen nach § 6 Abs.3 S.1 Nr.3 PostG', Rechtsgutachten im Auftrag der Friedrich-Ebert-Stiftung (Legal expert opinion prepared by Friedrich-Ebert-Stiftung), Berlin/Bonn.

Büdenbender, U. (2000), 'Anmerkung zum Urteil des EuGH in Sachen Albany International BV ./. Stichting Bedrijfspensioenfonds Textielindustrie', in ZIP 34, pp. 44ff.

Bundesnetzagentur (2007), 'Tätigkeitsbericht 2006/2007', Bonn, December.

Bundesnetzagentur (2008), 'Arbeitsbedingungen im lizenzierten Bereich. Endergebnis der Auskunftsanordnung gemäß § 45 PostG vom 22, Berlin/Bonn, Juni 2007' (Working conditions in the licensed area. Final results of the request for information under § 45 post G issued on 22 June 2007), February 2008.

Cohen, R., M. Robinson, R. Sheehy, J. Waller, S. Xenakis, G. Scarfiglieri and V. Visco Comandini (2006), 'The role of scale economies in the cost behavior of posts', in A. Dieke and A. Niederprüm (eds), *Regulating Postal Markets: Harmonised versus Country-specific Approaches*, WIK proceeding no. 11, Rheinbreitbach.

Deutsche Post World Net (2007), 'Deutsche Post World Net with solid 2006 annual results', Press release, Bonn, 20 March.

Dieke, A. and M. Zauner (2007), 'Arbeitsbedingungen im Briefmarkt', WIK Discussion Paper no. 295, Bad Honnef.

El-Sharif, Y. (2007), 'Postgesetz könnte Briefträgern helfen', *Tagespiegel*, 22 November.

Input Consulting (2006), 'Liberalisierung und Prekarisierung. Beschäftigungsbedingungen bei den neuen Briefdienstleistern in Deutschland', Study for German trade union Vereinte Dienstleistungsgewerk schaft (ver.di), Stuttgart, December.

Maschke, W. (2002), 'Transformation at Deutsche Post World Net: using the example of socially compatible workforce adjustment', in M.A. Crew and P.R. Kleindorfer (eds), *Postal and Delivery Services: Delivering on Competition*, Boston, MA: Kluwer Academic, pp. 303–19.

PricewaterhouseCoopers (PwC) (2006), 'The impact on universal service of the full market accomplishment of the postal internal market in 2009', Study for the European Commission, DG Internal Market, May.

Quander, P. (2008), 'Marktbeobachtungen', Presentation at PostLiberal conference, Hanover, 19 February.

Säcker, F.J. (2007), 'Soziale Schutzstandards im Postregulierungsrecht', Rechtsgutachten erstattet der Bundesnetzagentur für Elektrizität, Gas, Telekommunikation, Post und Eisenbahnen (Legal expert opinion prepared for Bundesnetzagentur für Elektrizität, Gas, Telekommunikation, Post und Eisenbahnen – a German government authority), Berlin.

Sheen, M. (2008), 'TNT in threat to quit Germany', *Financial Times*, 18 February.

Thüsing, G. (2008), 'Legitimation und Repräsentation als Voraussetzung der Regelungszuständigkeit – Voraussetzungen der Branchenerstreckung eines drittgerichteten Tarifvertrags nach § 1 Abs. 3a AEntG', Study prepared for TNT Post Deutschland.

Verwaltungsgericht Berlin (2008), 'Judgment of 7 March 2008', PIN Mail AG ./. Bundesrepublik Deutschland (VG 4 A 439.07).

Wachter, M.L., B.T. Hirsch and J.W. Gillula (2001), 'Difficulties of deregulation when wage costs are the major cost', in M.A. Crew and P.R. Kleindorfer (eds), *Future Directions in Postal Reform*, Boston, MA: Kluwer Academic, pp. 115–37.

Welt Online (2008), 'Pin Group verhandelt mit drei Investoren über Übernahme', 4 March, www.welt.de/welt_print/article1754239/Pin_Group_verhandelt_mit_drei_Investoren_ueber_Uebernahme.html, accessed 27 March 2008.

17. Liberalization and market performance: towards higher efficiency in Sweden*

Peter Andersson[†]

1. INTRODUCTION

Sweden was the first country in the world to truly liberalize its postal market. The statutory monopoly given to the state Post Office in 1888 was removed on 1 January 1993. In 1994, the Post Office was turned into a public company, Sweden Post (Posten AB), completely owned by the state. A new Postal Act and a Postal Ordinance replaced the old monopoly proclamation and the Post and Telecom Agency, the new regulatory authority, was established. The government signed a contract with Sweden Post which included the provision of universal services without any support from the state.

Thus, Sweden represents an interesting benchmark for postal liberalization as the reforms took place 15 years before those in most other European Union (EU) countries. Why did Sweden's reform precede that of other EU countries? What were the objectives of liberalization and have they been fulfilled? How did Sweden Post respond and to what extent has it been challenged by entrants? What has happened to the performance of the market: prices, productivity, quality, innovation and efficiency? What has happened to universal services? Can we learn anything from the Swedish experience about the design of the regulatory framework for a modern, competitive postal market?

Section 2 will give the background to the reforms in 1993–94 and an explanation why reform occurred in Sweden long before it did in other countries. Section 3 presents the new entrants and their strategies and how Sweden Post responded. In Section 4, the effects on market performance are presented and Section 5 concludes with some lessons of general interest from the first 'full-scale' test of a liberalized postal market.

2. MARKET REFORM IN SWEDEN

2.1 Background to Postal Liberalization

Liberalization of the postal market took place in a time of changing basic conditions in the market. In the 1980s, fax and later the Internet and communication by e-mail emerged as substitutes to postal services. On the other hand, the total demand for communication increased rapidly. Postal companies began to shift from providing overnight distribution

† Linköping University.

of time-sensitive messages to mass communication and goods from businesses and the public sector to households. Large shipments of identical letters, 'bulk mail', increased significantly. Production has been subject to rapid technological change. Automatic sorting machines have been introduced, and sorting of mail has turned from manual, labor-intensive work at night time to industrial high-tech production. New information technology (IT) enabled senders to pre-sort bulk mail according to postal code.

Liberalization of Swedish postal services first appeared on the agenda in 1988 when a Government Commission[1] began a study of the possibility of reforming the telephone, railway and postal sectors. Reforming the postal sector was not primarily in response to its changing conditions. Rather, it was justified by concerns for the efficiency of public authorities in general, related to a long period of low growth in the Swedish economy, which coincided with the EU starting its reform work for the internal market.

At the same time, the Post Office's regional and social responsibilities (only later renamed 'universal services') remained an important objective. The Government Commission recommended business as usual for postal services: only with surpluses from profitable areas could the Post Office continue to provide nationwide services. It was given some more independence from political decisions: limited by a price cap, it was allowed to decide on postage rates and use revenues to finance some of its investments. Further liberalization was rejected.

In May 1991, the world's first true challenger to an incumbent Post Office appeared. CityMail started delivery of pre-sorted bulk mail in central Stockholm. It claimed that its activities were not within the services protected by the Post Office's monopoly. The Post Office responded by reporting CityMail to the public prosecutor, but in 1992 before any decision was taken, CityMail declared bankruptcy.

The Swedish financial sector was liberalized by the Social Democrats in the 1980s. Subsequently in 1991, a non-socialist government was elected and with economic growth featuring as a top priority. It wanted to create incentives for competition in the economy and reform state enterprises. However, for the postal sector, the issue of social and regional responsibilities had to be solved before regulatory reform could be carried out.[2] When CityMail announced that it would re-enter the business in 1993, the government suddenly reversed its opinion. In only a few days, it submitted a bill to parliament and the night before Christmas it was decided to remove the 1888 monopoly proclamation from 1 January 1993.

2.2 Full Liberalization in 1993–94

As a result of the rapid decision, there was no new legal framework to replace the old. Neither the preconditions nor the effects of market reform were analyzed. Not until 14 months later were the new Postal Act and a Postal Ordinance introduced. At the same time, the Post Office became a public company, 100 percent state owned. The Swedish National Post and Telecom Agency (PTS) became the regulatory authority for the sector, and later for all electronic communications and IT. Sweden Post signed a contract with the state that contained, among other things, the conditions for the provision of universal services. Later, this was included in Sweden Post's license conditions.

The Postal Act has been revised three times. In 1997 the scope of the universal service was extended and all operators were required to obtain a license from PTS. In the second revision in 1998, price regulation was reformed and legislation adjusted to the new EU Directive from 1997. The third revision of 1 July 1999 concerned the regulation and conditions for access to the postal infrastructure. In 2004, a new Government Commission[3] analyzed the market and evaluated the reforms. It proposed new adjustments in order to enhance the competitive conditions, but as of 2008 no new bill has been presented; policy and legislation from the 1990s remains in place. Postal policy since 1998 is contained in the Postal Act:[4]

> There should be a postal service throughout the country, meaning that everyone must be able to send and receive items of mail weighing a maximum of 20 kg. Postal services shall be of good quality and it should be possible to have such postal items conveyed at reasonable prices. For single-piece mail, prices should also be uniform.

2.3 Why Market Reform so Early?

The changing conditions of the postal sector were important preconditions for liberalization, not dissimilar to other European countries, but Sweden differed in its institutional settings. First, a vague construction of the monopoly from 1888 opened a possible loophole for an entrepreneur to establish a new company. Sweden did not have a well-defined reserved area; the monopoly was related to sealed hand-written letters. With CityMail on the market, regulatory reform became urgent. Second, the Post Office was a 'public enterprise', not a public authority. This particular organizational form for some state activities already gave the Post Office greater independence than it would have as a public authority and the step to become a public company was therefore smaller. Its business-oriented management saw new commercial opportunities and preferred to trade monopoly protection for letters for freedom to expand internationally and into the financial and IT sectors.

Moreover, Sweden was at the time unusually reform friendly. Both a Social Democratic and a non-socialist government were concerned with persistent low growth and promoted reforms in order to stimulate competition and make public enterprises more business oriented. This resembles the pro-competitive agenda in the EU as part of the Lisbon strategy in the 2000s. It coincided with the expansionary ambitions not only from the Post Office but equally the Telephone Office and the national electricity producer Vattenfall. Of the three only the last became truly successful on the international market. It is almost paradoxical that a company protected by a statutory monopoly wants it removed. Whereas other European monopolists defended their rights, Sweden Post Office acted in favor of deregulation. Swedish politicians could not resist the combined pressure from the Post Office promising to maintain universal services and the desire to rescue the unexpected new entrant, CityMail.

In economic analysis, it is often assumed that liberalization takes place because the monopolist is X-inefficient and needs competitive pressure and/or uses market power to charge too high prices. None of these rationalizations was important when Sweden reformed its postal sector. In fact, there was no explicit objective at all, and the Commission that prepared the Postal Act did so when the monopoly was already removed. Postal policy still lacks any other objective than to preserve universal services (see the quotation above).[5]

3. MARKET RESPONSE TO LIBERALIZATION

3.1 Entrants and Their Strategies

CityMail was established by a Swedish businessman, Bror-Anders Månsson, with a remarkable career, good connections in other businesses and sufficient funds to finance the start-up. He was the only entrepreneur to understand that market conditions changed as well as to discover the ambiguous monopoly proclamation and design an establishment strategy long before any entry models were presented.

At the time, Sweden Post Office did not offer any discounts for pre-sorted mail. CityMail concentrated only on bulk mail, so collection and sorting costs were completely avoided. By delivering only in areas with a dense population (first only central Stockholm, later the entire Stockholm region as well as the second and third most populated cities in Sweden) CityMail could quickly obtain a critical mass of recipients.

It is still contested whether delivery is less expensive in large cities in Sweden than in rural areas. CityMail claims high delivery costs in cities due to congestion. Most likely, delivery by car to residential areas in small and medium-sized cities is the least expensive. An entrant such as CityMail cannot perfectly cherry-pick low-cost and/or high-income routes and customers, but has to target some sufficiently large areas with the same first digits in the postal code. This means that it acquires a mix of more- and less-profitable areas, but aims at a high concentration and low transportation costs.

Moreover, CityMail competes by delivering only second class mail. By doing so, it can deliver to each address only every third day and its postmen can serve three routes instead of one as for Sweden Post. In the early years CityMail delivered every second day, but it has found that every third day is an even more efficient business model for second class mail. All postmen in Sweden belong to the same union, so it is impossible to negotiate lower wages for a new operator. Instead, CityMail competes with higher productivity and initially value-added services that Sweden Post did not offer. The incumbent has the advantage of economies of scope, because it delivers first class mail every day and can bring other classes only at the incremental cost, and it has strong economies of scale.

It has taken a long time for CityMail to obtain sufficient volumes to match the cost advantages of Sweden Post. The company became bankrupt in 1992 and again in 1995 but was able to return with new capital raised by its original founder. The company did not become profitable until it had been in business more than 10 years. It was later owned by British Consignia and thereafter by Norwegian Post. In 2008 it delivers to 43 percent of Swedish households and plans to expand in new regions to cover 60 percent of all recipients in 2009.[6] It deals with 12 percent of all bulk mail in Sweden.[7]

Another and completely different form of entry occurred mainly in 1996–98 by small local firms delivering only intra-city mail from local businesses and public authorities. Some also have households as customers, issue their own stamps and have letterboxes in the streets. Most of them exited the market rapidly, but around 30 have become profitable and remain in business. They are typically in cities with 5,000–75,000 inhabitants. They are usually self-owned without advanced technology and compete with low costs and offer faster distribution. Some firms have tried to combine their small flows of mail with newspaper delivery or courier services without success. Other local operators have tried to

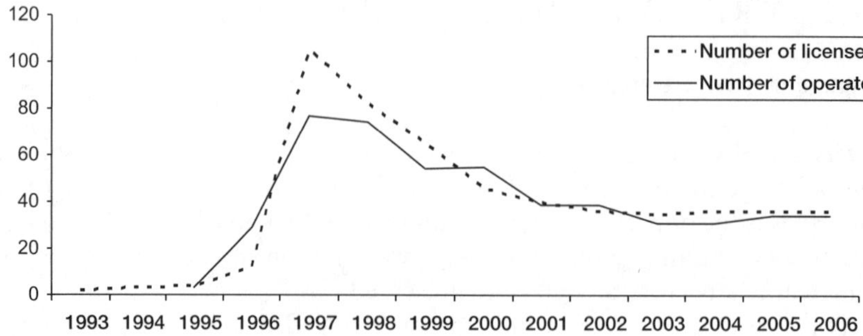

Source: SIKA (2007).

Figure 17.1 Number of licensees and active postal firms, 1993–2006

create regional networks in order to expand the number of addressees. With a few exceptions this has also failed due to uneven mail flows.[8]

In addition to a daily delivery from Sweden Post, another 43 percent of households get mail from CityMail every third day and less than 1 percent from a local operator. The market structure has been transformed from a monopoly to a dominant firm and fringe competitors (Figure 17.1).

3.2 Responses by the Incumbent

As already mentioned, the Post Office argued in favor of liberalization. Nevertheless, it responded harshly when CityMail entered the market and both legal and market competition began. The Post Office reported CityMail to the public prosecutor for infringing the legal monopoly. It also renegotiated contracts with key clients as well as offered favorable prices for customers choosing it for all its distribution until such exclusivity clauses were prohibited by the Competition Authority.

In 1996 when CityMail expanded to new areas, Sweden Post reacted with zonal pricing: different price levels for different regions in the country. This resulted in a long legal conflict with the Competition Authority that ended in the Supreme Court two years later. There, Sweden Post was able to prove lower delivery costs and allowed to charge lower prices for bulk mail in a zone covering the 19 largest cities. Earlier versions of zonal prices were refused, and Sweden Post was found to have abused its dominant position. By suggesting these prices at the time of CityMail's expansion, it intended to force the competitor out of the market, according to the verdict. Sweden Post paid an undisclosed sum in damages. Since then, most legal conflicts have ended, until recently when Sweden Post wanted to extend its zone in response to the planned expansion by CityMail.

Sweden Post's letter business has been profitable ever since market reform in 1993. In the 1990s, profits were around 1 billion SEK per year. Subsequently, there was no separate division for letters, although Sweden Post has declared that profits have been declining but remained positive for letters. In the 2000s, Sweden Post made losses. This was due to the unprofitable network of post offices, later losses in Svensk Kassaservice, IT investments and adjustment costs. In 2006 the situation improved, and in 2007 Sweden Post made a large profit and contributed a record yield to the state.[9]

Table 17.1 Volumes (million addressed items) and market shares (%), 1996–2006

	1996	1997	1998	1999	2000	2001	2002	2003	2004	2005	2006
Total volume	3,421	3,385	3,446	3,425	3,429	3,337	3,307	3,267	3,258	3,215	3,210
Sweden Post	98.2	96.4	95.6	94.2	95.3	94.4	93.7	93.0	91.9	91.8	91.1
CityMail	1.5	1.6	4.4	4.7	4.3	5.2	5.8	6.6	7.7	7.9	8.6
Other operators	0.3	0.6	0.6	0.4	0.4	0.4	0.4	0.4	0.3	0.3	0.3

Note: Volume statistics are missing for other operators before 1996.

Source: See www.pts.se.

Table 17.1 shows that CityMail slowly gained market share and that postal volumes peaked around the year 2000, but declined very slowly thereafter. In addition to delivered addressed mail, the number of unaddressed items has skyrocketed, rising from 1.5 billion in 1995 to over 3.5 billion in 2007.[10]

Local operators have not become a significant threat to Sweden Post. But why do these local operators, with prices 25–40 percent lower than Sweden Post, not win the entire local market? Explanations are lack of trust in new operators as well as insufficient marketing from the new entrants and costs for senders to separate the local mail from the rest. Also, large firms might well receive larger discounts if they give large contracts to a single-market player, and this can only be applicable to Sweden Post or CityMail.[11] Why did entry cease after 2001? About 30 small local firms have indeed been successful and are profitable. Rational entrepreneurs in other small cities would probably be able to enter the market successfully, particularly as there are now other operators to learn from. The conditions for starting business are better than in 1997, since now access to the postal infrastructure is regulated. If postal consumers are rational, the explanation must be high switching costs, a risk premium for choosing alternative providers, or insufficient information about the alternatives.

4. MARKET PERFORMANCE: TOWARDS HIGHER EFFICIENCY

Sweden has among the highest volume of mail per capita in Europe (WIK, 2004). Not only has the demand for postal services reached a peak (Table 17.1), but also the composition of mail is changing. Overnight mail (first class) volumes are falling in relation to second and third class mail, and single-piece mail compared to bulk mail. Table 17.2 shows the market shares for different products in 2003.[12]

The impact of liberalization on volumes is weak compared to other shifts in demand trends. Substitution and the slow GDP growth in the early 2000s explain the overall volume decline. Liberalization had a modest effect on reducing the decline in overall demand for postal services, because it has held down price increases. More importantly,

Table 17.2 The composition of mail products (volumes) in 2003

Bulk mail	%	Single-piece mail	%
Total of which:	73	Total of which:	23
third class (ADR)	33	first class	80
second class	28	second class	20
first class	21		
magazines	18		

Source: PTS (2004).

it has contributed to increasing the market share for bulk mail because of lower prices (see next subsection).

4.1 Prices

Table 17.3 shows the change in prices for mail between 1991 and 2006. The starting year is 1991, because Sweden Post had already started to respond to the competition from CityMail before liberalization was completed. In all comparisons, only Sweden Post's prices are shown. For delivery in Stockholm, Göteborg and the Skåne regions and on the island of Gotland, CityMail is an alternative. Its prices are always negotiated, so direct comparisons are impossible. The prices are supposed to be lower than the list prices of Sweden Post.

Prices have changed substantially: by 1992 third class letters had been temporarily abolished and there was only second class mail with various kinds of discounts depending on the type of mail preparation. The discount for pre-sorting was about 10 percent. Sweden Post offered contracts with 'exclusivity clauses' with a better price for those who used only Sweden Post (and not CityMail for Stockholm delivery) until there were complaints from the Competition Authority. It can be noted that the profitability of Sweden Post increased in 1992–94, despite the competition from CityMail. Sweden Post introduced bulk mail and a new third class in 1995. Subsequently, prices for such products fell. In 1998, the zonal pricing with a discounted price for the largest cities reduced those relative prices even more. The relative price for single-piece mail increased sharply in 1997, since when, only minor adjustments to relative prices have been made.

Large customers' ability to negotiate better prices has increased with competition. Such contracts are business secrets. The discount in contracts can be assumed to be 5–10 percent for unsorted mail and 15–30 percent for sorted mail – the discount varies between customers.

Table 17.3 shows that the price structure has changed dramatically, making second class mail, pre-sorted mail, delivery in large cities and heavy letters relatively more inexpensive. The real price is up to 50 percent lower than in 1991 for certain products, contract discounts unaccounted for. Value-added tax (VAT) was imposed on single-piece mail in the mid-1990s. If the VAT is included, the increase in real price is 78 percent for first class and 68 percent for second class single-piece mail.

Previously undisclosed information from Sweden Post shows that the nominal average price for single-piece mail rose by 80 percent (including VAT) between 1990 and 2004. In

Table 17.3 Change in real price 1991–2006 for selected products (excl. VAT) (%)

	20 gram		50 gram	
	List price	Negotiated price	List price	Negotiated price
Third class				
Unsorted	+49	+42	+49	+42
Pre-sorted	+37	+10	+34	+10
Pre-sorted, large town delivery	+17	−6	+17	–6
Second class bulk mail				
Not sorted	+16	+5	−37	−40
Pre-sorted	−9	−27	−48	−58
Pre-sorted, large town delivery	−22	−37	−55	−64
First class bulk mail				
Not sorted	+34	+28	−22	−26
Pre-sorted	+22	−2	−31	−45
Pre-sorted, large town delivery	+9	−13	−36	−49
First class, single letter	+43 (+78)		+43 (+78)	
Second class, single letter	+35 (+68)		+35 (+68)	
First class local delivery (min. 250)	+10		+12	

Note: Large town delivery is delivery to the 19 largest cities in Sweden, for which Sweden Post has been able to prove lower delivery costs than to the rest of the country. CPI has been used for calculation of real prices. Negotiated price assume a 5% discount on first class and 25% discount on second class mail. Figures in brackets are inclusive of 25% VAT, which was imposed on single-piece mail in two steps 1994 and 1996.

Source: PTS database, Sweden Post, Statistics Sweden, own calculations.

Table 17.4 Cumulative change in Sweden Post's volumes, revenues and prices, 1990–2004 (%)

	Single-piece mail	Bulk mail	All letters
Volume	−41	−5	−16
Revenue (nominal)	+6	+18	+13
CPI deflated price	+34	−8	+1

Source: Sweden Post in Cohen et al. (2006).

the same period, bulk-mail prices rose by 24 percent and the weighted average of all prices by 35 percent. Nominal revenues for single-piece mail are about 6 percent higher (a sharp decline from a peak in 1998 when revenues were 27 percent higher than in 1990), for bulk mail, 18 percent higher, and for all products, 13 percent higher. The accumulated change on volumes, revenues and real prices for Sweden Post between 1990 and 2004, according to this study, is displayed in Table 17.4. The fact that the price level for mail rose at only 1 percent more than inflation supports the effects of competition. It could be expected that such a labor-intensive industry would have increasing relative prices over time.

Despite the price increases for single-piece mail, the postage in Sweden is currently near the average for European countries. Such comparisons are difficult because products differ; VAT levels and exchange rates vary considerably. A comparison of the cheapest single-piece product (but the upper weight limit differs between countries) shows that Sweden is in twelfth place of the 27 EU states even with its high VAT.[13] Only four European countries have a VAT on the postage.

4.2 Quality of Service

In many respects, quality of services in Sweden was already high before liberalization, but the Post Office was a production- rather than customer-oriented organization. A shift towards being a more consumer-friendly organization is an intangible but important effect of market reform, together with the newcomers' focus on their customers. According to PTS's (1998) first survey after liberalization, postal consumers found that the operators' quality was high and that they were willing to adjust to consumer demands more than before liberalization. The improvements were most significant for the largest customers. PTS (2003) summarized in its evaluation of the first nine years that the quality of service was in line with what is demanded. PTS (2006b) reported that 37 percent of consumers found postal services good value, and 37 percent not good value. The same survey also asked whether people were satisfied with the delivery of postal services: 68 percent were very satisfied, 25 percent were quite satisfied and only 3 percent were dissatisfied. Such qualitative information may reflect the change in response to consumers more than price, reliability or productivity data.

Sweden is Europe's fourth-largest country but has a small population. The services to sparsely populated areas remain at the same level as in the 1980s. Sweden Post provides services to the entire nation on a commercial basis and without compensation. Rural areas in Sweden are served by its 'rural postmen'. There are 2,500 routes and 730,000 households (of about 4.5 million) served by such workers. They function like a 'mobile post office' and not only collect and deliver letters and parcels but provide financial services and some other services not related to the postal sector. Accessibility in the most remote locations has improved since liberalization. The number of households without service five days a week was about 1,550 in 1990, in 1996 it was 1,209 and in 2005 it was down to 1,118.[14]

Reliability is high and Sweden is at the top internationally concerning overnight delivery according to an international comparison (WIK, 2004). Since 1999, the share of overnight single-piece mail arriving the next day has been stable between 95 and 96 percent. Before that, Sweden Post had its own system for measuring reliability and the figures were at the same level, with the exception of 1996–97, when the introduction of the new national network and automatic sorting temporarily led to lower reliability, about 90 percent.

The number of access points declined slowly until 2001 when Sweden Post completely redesigned its network of service points. The traditional post office was closed down completely. It was replaced by business centers with postal services primarily targeted at the needs of businesses, mostly in areas where such activities were dense. However, private persons can send letters and parcels at business centers.

For ordinary households, a new network of partner offices became the most common type of service point. Such offices provide services for sending and collecting letters and

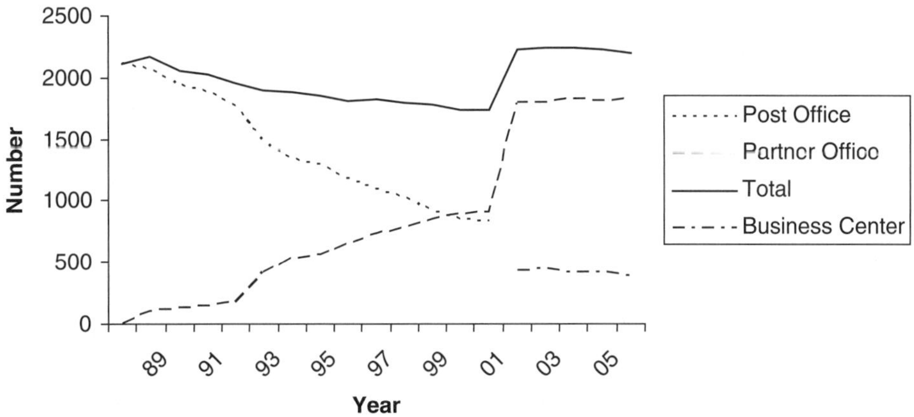

Note: Because of changes in service levels, the numbers are not completely comparable. Some 189 of the partner offices (in remote locations) provide a limited range of services.

Source: SIKA (2007).

Figure 17.2 The number of service points, Sweden Post, 1989–2006

parcels, including track and trace of parcels and stamp sales, that is, all those postal services traditionally provided by a post office. These partners are usually grocery stores, gasoline stations, kiosks and so on. Such partners have longer opening hours, even on weekends, and are located in central shopping areas where people pursue other activities. The network of post offices before 2002 was on average open 42 hours per week. Today's partner offices are on average open 77 hours per week. For most consumers, the accessibility to a service point has improved since the beginning of liberalization. This shows among other things in the average time a parcel remains at the access point before being collected. Before the reform, Sweden Post estimates this time to be 11–13 days. Today it is 3.2 days. The average number of times that a household visited a post office in 2001 was 1.8 per year. The type of grocery stores where today's services are offered are on average visited 1.6 times per week.[15]

The total number of service points increased in the reform by 39 percent between 2001 and 2005 (Figure 17.2). In sparsely populated areas, the number fell by 26 percent and in rural areas outside cities by 15 percent, whereas in cities the number increased by 15 percent.[16] In addition to these service points, another 2,030 shops have contracts with Sweden Post to sell stamps. They are franchise-takers and sell a complete set of stamps at their nominal value.[17] Selling of stamps is unregulated in Sweden, so any shop can buy stamps and resell them. A few add a margin to the nominal stamp value, but many offer them at the nominal value as a service to their customers. For collection of letters, there are 1.8 times more letter boxes in the streets per 1,000 inhabitants, compared to the EU average.[18]

4.3 Innovation, Employment and Productivity

It is often assumed that liberalization will result in more innovation in an underdeveloped industry. Indeed, there has been a lot of innovation in the postal sector in the past 15 years.

However, at least in Sweden, not much of it can directly be attributed to liberalization. But one can assume that liberalization drove the market players to implement new innovations earlier in order to remain competitive or even try to create entry barriers. CityMail made the organizational innovation, which is the most apparent result of liberalization. By only delivering second class mail, it tripled its postmen's productivity and by only delivering bulk mail, it paid its customers for preparing the mail with a discount that Sweden Post did not offer at that time. It also led the process towards customer orientation.

The effect on employment and productivity depends largely on the situation before liberalization. Even before liberalization, Sweden Post Office was considered to be relatively efficient as a postal monopolist. One study (Cohen et al. 2006) reveals that Sweden was number 11 among 21 countries in productivity in the early 1990s. However, the Swedish figures are based on the total number of those employed by Sweden Post Office. If only the number of those employed in the letter division are counted and figures recalculated, Sweden ends up in second place, which would support the alleged efficiency of the Post Office.

It is clear that employment in the postal sector has been reduced since liberalization started. In 1991, about 3,000 million addressed and 1,300 million unaddressed items were delivered with a total of 34,400 employed in the letter division. In 1999, 3,500 million addressed and 2,000 million unaddressed items were delivered with 24,500 employed.[19] Sweden Post's labor costs were 60 percent of total costs in 1995 and down to 50 percent in 2002.[20] However, the reduction in employment in the letter business can be partly explained by outsourcing and pre-sorting by customers.

The reduction in Sweden Post is partly counteracted by employment in new firms. CityMail employs about 1,300 people and the remaining operators a few more. The total employment in enterprises in the postal sector went down from 42,800 in 1995 to 32,200 in 2006.[21] Sweden is among the EU countries that reduced employment in the postal sector the most in recent years; in many countries it increased in the same period.[22]

There are indications that there existed a wage premium in Sweden's postal sector before liberalization. The average income for employees in the postal sector in relation to the private sector in general has fallen by about 20 percent since 1993; the decline occurred during the first years after liberalization.[23] This can be explained by monopoly rents transferred to postal workers before competition was introduced. Alternative explanations are, however, a change in the composition of age and education among the employees and an increased share of part-time employees. An international comparison of labor costs show that Sweden has a middle ranking among European countries with the UK and France at the top.[24]

According to the study by ITPS (2004), there was a once-and-for-all increase in Sweden Post's productivity shortly after liberalization. It increased by about 20 percent due to a reorganization of the postmen's shifts. Between 1995 and 2000, there was another 10 percent increase in productivity, making a total of 32 percent. Since 2001, productivity has fallen because of the decline in volumes and lost economies of scale.

It is puzzling, however, why the introduction of a completely new national network and automatic sorting machines in 1996–97 or the increased share of pre-sorting by customers are not more visible in productivity. Moreover, rising volumes can contribute to the increase in productivity in the 1990s, if there were unutilized economies of scale.

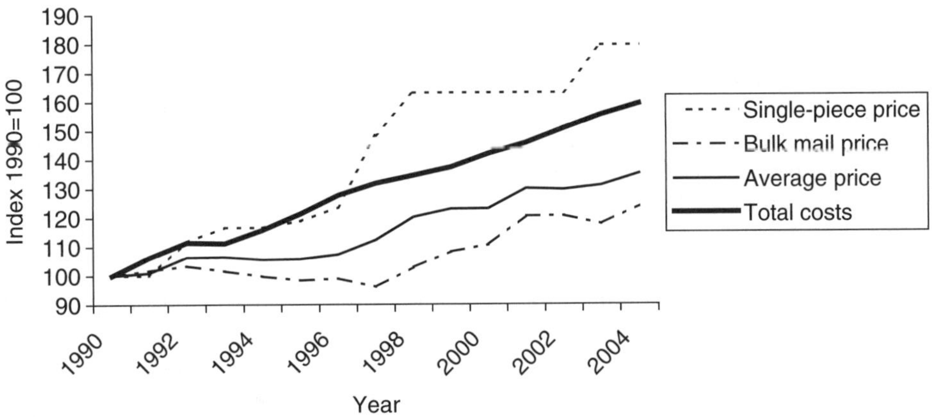

Source: Sweden Post, presented in Cohen et al. (2006, appendix).

Figure 17.3 The development of prices and input costs for Sweden Post, 1990–2004

Cohen et al. (2006) have also estimated the increase in productivity. The average nominal price level of Sweden Post increased by 35 percent, but input costs increased by 60 percent, thus, the gain in productivity must explain why prices have risen significantly less than costs (Figure 17.3). If the nominal prices instead of CPI are 'deflated' with the increase in input costs, a measure of productivity change is obtained. Nominal prices for Sweden Post's mail increased 17 percent less than total input costs.

4.4 Diseconomies of Scope: Financial Services

Along with some other countries around the world, the Post Office in Sweden has also provided other services than mail delivery. The Post Office started its own bank in the nineteenth century, which in the 1970s merged with a private bank and is today known as Nordea, one of the four large banks in Sweden with the state owning 20 percent. The Post Office owned the postal giro between 1929 and 2002, when it was sold. It was mostly used for payments for small businesses and households: traditionally, post offices have been used for making over-the-counter payments, and until the 1980s, this was the most common way to pay bills in Sweden. Later, sending bills with a payment order to the bank became common and today the Internet accounts for 59 percent and payments via mail, 32 percent (down from 79 percent in 1999). The share of payments made directly over the counter is less than 1 percent.[25]

Thus, the traditional network of post offices provided two types of services, financial and postal. These then became independent of each other, and in the 1980s, with fewer payments made, the network was starting to become unprofitable and made losses equal to the surplus in the letter division.

In 2001, Sweden Post carried out the aforementioned reform of the network of post offices. The reform in 2001 meant that financial services were moved into a separate subsidiary of Sweden Post, Svensk Kassaservice. Since then, that company has run a smaller network of offices for payments, usually in the former locations of post offices. Sweden Post receives a subsidy, but not sufficient to cover the losses.

This reform became unpopular in Sweden. People had difficulty finding where to make payments on the rare occasions they needed to. Older people unfamiliar with the Internet found themselves having to travel long distances to get to those locations. Despite the improvements of accessibility to postal services at partner offices, postal services were not to be found in the usual places.

For some time Sweden Post became very unpopular and its well-known trademark depreciated in value. It had failed in directing people to the new locations for postal services; it acquired a bad reputation for closing down the network of post offices that few people used and for the unprofitable financial services that they did not want to provide. Swedish Quality Index, which surveys people's trust in many different organizations and institutions, placed Sweden Post at the bottom of the list for households' and number 26 of 29 for companies' ranking in 2006. Not until 2008, do the surveys indicate that Sweden Post is again rapidly increasing in popularity. However, the recent unpopularity of Sweden Post cannot be blamed on liberalization as it occurred over 10 years after the reforms.

It is illustrative that a much-needed reform of services that were both unprofitable and no longer related to postal services failed, and other countries planning a similar separation must design a better alternative. A plan for the separation from Sweden Post is being drawn up and public procurement of those services is a possibility; the reform will take place within the next few years.[26]

4.5 Summary of Effects on Market Performance: Welfare and Efficiency

The overall economic effects of liberalization are positive but relatively modest. Market reform is no panacea for achieving efficiency in the postal sector, let alone for driving growth in GDP. Nevertheless, the market has developed in the right direction. Sweden Post Office was a relatively efficient postal operator with a modern management prior to liberalization, so the scope for improvement was less than elsewhere. The major effects have been on prices and productivity. Prices were too uniform and have been adjusted towards costs. A competitive entrant introduced new products and services and stimulated the productivity of the former monopolist. More items are delivered by fewer people. Innovation has come early. Quality of service was already high but particularly in the business segment, the operators have become more customer oriented. At the same time, the universal service obligation (USO) has been maintained for 15 years without external support. Necessary but transitorily unpopular reforms of the post office network have been carried out.

Welfare is measured by the change in the sum of consumers' and producers' surplus. To quantify such change, much data are required that are not available. It is clear that senders of bulk mail, today around three-quarters of all mail, have gained substantially. Prices are much lower. Quality of service is better. There are more consumer-adapted products and two providers for many recipients. Senders of single-piece mail have retained the high quality but on the other hand have to pay much higher prices. It is difficult to conclude that this has outweighed the improvements in the bulk-mail segment and thus, the sum of consumers' and producers' welfare is higher as a result of the reforms.

The outcome is sometimes regarded as redistribution from households and small businesses to the large mailers. It should be recalled, however, that the information distributed by bulk mail to households is often something they require. Most is communication from companies of which they are customers, or essential public information: bank statements, invoices, membership information, catalogues and so on. If there is competition in the rest of the economy, households gain indirectly as customers of the firms that can economize on the postage.

The positive effects on market performance can to a large extent be attributed to the existence of CityMail. It has resulted both in higher internal efficiency of Sweden Post and market efficiency. Sweden Post acknowledges the importance of a visible competitor. When a postman from CityMail stood face to face with one from Sweden Post in the elevator, the potential threat of competition became a reality, and this led to actual improvements. However, it is difficult to find any significant contribution to efficiency from the local operators; this is often rather an example of inefficient entry. The relative success of liberalization in Sweden is not the result of a well-designed reform. Rather, the reforms were not thoroughly prepared, there were no clear objectives and no overall postal policy has been developed.

5. LESSONS FOR DESIGNING A REGULATORY FRAMEWORK FOR A MODERN, COMPETITIVE POSTAL MARKET

With this in mind, what can be learned from market reform in Sweden? It is desirable to create a 'level playing field'. However, it is inevitable that a state monopolist has advantages and disadvantages compared to entrants. Regulation cannot do away with this background and start a market from scratch. The Post Office prefers to underline the burden of the USO. Management's intentions to reform the organization may be limited for reasons of politics, culture or a union's resistance when it gets exposed to competition. On the other hand, the state monopolist has advantages: it is not only running a business, often it owns or controls the postal infrastructure and is simultaneously the regulator of the market itself. It has one of the best-known trademarks, benefits from scale economies and the advantage of serving the whole country with all products.

Swedish experience shows that it requires significant financial strength for an entrant to establish a permanent threat to the incumbent. If the incumbent is relatively efficient, it requires organizational innovations to meet its cost advantages; the labor market in Sweden prevents wage competition unless the firm is self-owned. It is crucial to obtain sufficient volumes quickly in order to get economies of scale, and reduce risk and vulnerability.

The following list summarizes the lessons from liberalization in Sweden:

1. *Create equal financial treatment* In Sweden, VAT was imposed on postage in the mid-1990s. This was required in order to equalize the competitive conditions. It resulted in a sharp increase in postage rates, but this was mitigated by it being part of a general tax reform and by the issuing of discounted stamps for households. Whether to impose VAT is a question for tax policy; it is important that competitive conditions

are the same for all operators. Other issues, not present in Sweden, may concern pension payments, equal tax regulation for state and private operators, price of fuel for transportation and so on.

2. *A regulator* Initially there was little experience available from other countries or sectors and the Swedish regulator PTS had to develop its own competence. Today, most countries have a postal regulator, and it is crucial that it has sufficient competence, integrity and power. It should be able to carry out economic analysis, and have a mandate to obtain necessary information from the incumbent, which has not always been the case in Sweden. Theory predicts that it can be captured by the incumbent, but in Sweden, PTS has rather promoted the interests of other competitors.[27]

   Some administrative issues of common interest must be resolved. PTS has established a unit for incorrectly addressed letters, financed by a fee from the operators. A common address file for all Swedes and companies reduces transaction costs both for operators and for individuals. In this case, the operators themselves run a jointly owned address file company, originally created by CityMail. A license requirement can protect consumers against uncommitted operators and if the fee is low, trigger entry by being a mark of quality.

3. *USO can be provided after liberalization* Swedish experience shows that the USO can continue to be provided even after 15 years of liberalization in a large and sparsely populated country with declining demand. The evidence from Sweden supports several USO studies, that the financial burden is relatively small, even if country-specific factors make generalizations difficult. Because there is no accurate calculation of the financial burden of the USO in Sweden, it appears better to liberalize first, and later ascertain any services that for commercial reasons no operator is willing to provide. Then, those services can be subject to tender or paid for by a fee imposed on all operators.

4. *Equal access to the postal infrastructure* Major problems during the first years after liberalization concerned the control of the post-code system, entrants' access to door codes and letterboxes in apartments, the right to put postboxes along the streets, handling of and payment for forwarding of mail given to the wrong operator and access to central address files. It seems that the incumbent created unwarranted obstacles for entrants, one important example being the price of and conditions for access to its post office boxes. These problems have now been resolved by a combination of amendments to the Postal Act and voluntary agreements.

5. *Access to the network of the USO provider* The commercial decisions of the operators determine the level of upstream access to their network that will be offered to clients, since such access has never been regulated in Sweden. When CityMail entered the market in 1991, the Post Office had no discount for pre-sorted mail. As a consequence of entry and the response by the incumbent, access for customers with pre-sorted bulk mail has since been made available.

   Few new entrants can offer nationwide delivery from the start. Just as, for example, telephone companies transfer calls to other operators according to regulated conditions, it should be possible to forward mail likewise. New operators in Sweden can always pay Sweden Post the regular postage for such mail. Then, however, they will make a loss on each letter. If they provide worksharing, they should get a regulated non-discriminatory price from Sweden Post that represents cost savings for the larger firm.[28] The Government Commission in 2005 proposed that access regulation be introduced in the Postal Act in a similar way as is already the case for telephone services. Access regulation would probably stimulate further competition.

Regulating other operators' access to the network of the incumbent is probably a better alternative than price regulation. Bulk-mail prices are not regulated but there is a price cap on single-piece mail in order to limit the market power of Sweden Post. This may be necessary as a temporary protection for consumers, but over time it rather interferes with competition. Today, the 20-gram letter is in fact underpriced because of the price cap, which would be an abuse of dominant position if not caused by regulation itself. This may deter entry into the single-piece mail market, because this is the base product that operators that do not specialize in bulk mail would want to offer. A price cap on one market can over time force Sweden Post to cross-subsidize single-piece mail with revenues from bulk mail, making both submarkets less efficient. However, PTS defends the current price cap in order to protect consumers and competitors.[29]

6. *A careful design of policy and the role for involved stakeholders* As mentioned above, Sweden lacks an overall postal policy. This is a problem, not least for the regulator, which has no benchmark against which to monitor the market.

Competition policy has not worked well for newly liberalized markets and is slow to implement. The legal processes can take years, and entrants can fail in the meantime. At least temporarily, there is a need for sector regulation. The distribution of power between the regulator and the Competition Authority must also be made clear.

Finally, as long as the Post is owned by the state, the goals for state ownership must be made clear. In Sweden, the state has been criticized for being an inactive owner with vague objectives.[30] There is also a risk of confusion when the state both regulates a market and owns the largest company. Separation of power within government is necessary, but in Sweden, these issues have long been dealt with in the same ministry. A better solution would be, for example, to have the Ministry of Industry deal with regulatory issues, and the Ministry of Finance with ownership, but there is still a risk that ownership issues would dominate. Privatization of Sweden Post has never been on the agenda, not even on that of the current non-socialist government which is selling other state-owned companies.

NOTES

* The author's research on the postal sector in Sweden has been financed by Söderbergska stiftelserna.

1. SOU (1990:27).
2. Government Bill 1991/92:100.
3. SOU (2005:5).
4. SFS (1993:1654).
5. A new Government Commission in 2005 suggested a much more comprehensive goal: 'Access shall be available to a broad supply of postal services at prices and a quality corresponding to customers' demands . . . An important means of achieving this will be to create the preconditions for effective competition between several actors, without distortions and unwarranted restrictions. The Government shall guarantee that everyone has access to universal postal service of high quality and at reasonable prices' (SOU, 2005:5).
6. CityMail.

7. PTS (2007a).
8. Andersson (2001).
9. Sweden Post Annual Reports.
10. SIKA (2007).
11. Andersson (2001).
12. Such figures are usually not available in Sweden but the operators presented them to PTS as a basis for the analysis of the Government Commission during 2004. The bulk-mail share has increased even more since 2003.
13. See http://www.freefairpost.com/pdf/FFPI_quarterly_news_18.pdf.
14. PTS (2006a).
15. Internal figures from Sweden Post.
16. Survey by the Swedish National Rural Development Agency.
17. Internal figures from Sweden Post.
18. ITPS (2004).
19. Sweden Post, Annual Reports 1990–2000. After 1999, Sweden Post has no letter division and the number of employees related to letters is unknown.
20. SOU (2005:4).
21. SIKA (2007).
22. SOU (2005:4, p. 433).
23. SOU (2005:4, p. 435). Two different statistical sources are used and they produce similar results.
24. Ibid.
25. PTS (2007b).
26. As proposed by Andersson (2004) and SOU (2005:5).
27. Andersson (2004).
28. Advances in technology may in fact make upstream access more complicated. Mail is already processed in the early stages of production, for example bar codes are attached and sorting is carried out down to the order of delivery. Thus, the ability for other operators to prepare mail in a way that reduces downstream costs for the incumbent is reduced.
29. Special statement to the report from the Government Commission (SOU, 2005:5).
30. Andersson (2004), SOU (2005:4 and 2005:5).

REFERENCES

Andersson, P. (2001), *Deregulation and the Internet – New Challenges to Postal Services in Sweden*, Linköping studies in Arts and Science no. 228, Linköping University (diss.).

Andersson, P. (2004), *Tio år efter postmarknadens avreglering: effekter och reformförslag*, Swedish Competition Authority, April.

Cohen, R., P. Jonsson, M. Robinson, S. Selander, J. Waller and S. Xenakis (2006), 'The impact of competitive entry into the Swedish postal market', paper presented at Rutger's University annual conference on Postal and Delivery Services, Bern, Switzerland, June 3.

Government Bill 1991/92:100, *Budgetpropositionen*.

ITPS (Institutet för tillväxtpolitiska studier: Institute for Growth Policy Studies) (2004), *Samhällsekonomisk analys av effekterna av liberaliseringen av postarknaden – underlag och överväganden för Post- och kassaserviceutredningen*, Falkenhall B: och Kolmodin A, Swedish Institute for Growth Policy Studies.

PTS (Post och Telestyrelsen: Post and Telecom Agency) (1998), *Pris- och serviceutveckling för stora brevsändningar under 1990-talet – en fallstudie*, PTS report 1998-06-11, Stockholn.

PTS (2003), *Nio år med postlagstiftningen – en utvärdering*, PTS report, Stockholm.

PTS (2004), *Den svenska postmarknaden – en beskrivning och övergripande analys*, PTS report, Stockholm.

PTS (2006a), *Service och konkurrens 2006*, PTS report, Stockholm.

PTS (2006b), *Undersökning av befolkningens post- och kassavanor 2006*, PTS report, Stockholm.

PTS (2007a), *Service och konkurrens 2007*, PTS report, Stockholm.

PTS (2007b), *Undersökning av befolkningens post- och kassavanor 2007*, PTS report, Stockholm.

PTS database of postal prices. Communication from PTS, PTS report, Stockholm.

SFS (Svensk författningssamling: Swedish law) (1993:1654).

SIKA (Statens institut for kommunikations analys: Swedish Institute for Transport and Communications Analysis) (2007), *Postverksamhet 2006* report, Stockholm.
SOU (Statens Offentliga Utredningar: Government Public Inquiry) (1990:27), *Post och tele – affärsverk med regionalt och socialt ansvar*.
SOU (2005:4), *Liberalisering, regler och marknader*.
SOU (2005:5), *Postmarknad i förändring*.
Sweden Post Office/Sweden Post Annual Reports 1990–2007.
WIK (2004), *Main Developments in the European Postal Sector*, WIK-Consult, Bad Honnef, Germany. http://www.freefairpost.com/pdf/FFPI_quarterly_news_18.pdf.

18. The French postal market in the wake of the Postal Law of 2005*

Catherine Gallet-Rybak,[†] Cécile Moreno,[†] Daniel Nadal[†] and Joëlle Toledano[†]

1. INTRODUCTION

The objective of this chapter is to provide an overview of the French postal sector, three years after the approval of the Postal Law in May 2005. It is based on publicly available information and notes some of the problems encountered by postal market participants, to the extent that these have been referred to ARCEP (Autorité de Régulation des Communications Électroniques et des Postes) for decision. In the process, it will also provide some perspective on the specifics of the new regulatory framework in France. It is based in part on the results of the 2006 Annual Review of the postal market conducted by ARCEP. This review covered both regulated/licensed operators as well as operators in markets not subject to regulation, such as parcels, express mail, unaddressed advertising mail and mail preparation.[1]

Section 2 reviews the principal missions of ARCEP, as determined by the legislative framework put into place in 2005. Section 3 examines the market situation in 2006, beginning with an overview of market results. Section 4 analyses some of the market dynamics related to entry. Section 5 considers regulatory issues relating to the opening of the market to competition, as these have come before ARCEP in its role as postal regulator. The point of departure will be to convey the elements of the business models of selected licensed operators in order to describe thereafter some of the obstacles they have encountered and, on the other hand, also to describe several important issues that have developed smoothly and have not given rise to frictions or interventions by ARCEP. Section 6 concludes with a preliminary assessment of the opening of the French postal market to competition. The objective is to understand the current dynamic of this continuing process in upstream markets as well as in the market for delivery services for letter mail, which will be fully opened to competition as of 1 January 2011.

† ARCEP, Autorité de Régulation des Communications Électroniques et des Postes.

2. THE NATIONAL LEGISLATIVE FRAMEWORK

2.1 ARCEP's Role and Responsibilities

The scope of postal regulation in France covers activities associated with postal services comprising collection, processing, transportation and delivery of postal items that are ultimately delivered as part of regular postal routes. Excluded from this regulation are, for example, the following: unaddressed advertising mail, intra-city courier, and express transport services.

The new French Postal Law[2] of 20 May 2005 (hereafter cited as the 'Postal Law') profoundly transformed the regulatory framework applicable to the French postal sector and to the French national postal operator, La Poste. Besides enacting the European judicial framework, the Postal Law covers notably the organization of the market for postal activities and setting up the regulation of this market through the creation of ARCEP. The Legislature charged the former telecommunications regulatory authority ART (Autorité de Régulation des Télécommunications) with the additional responsibility to oversee the opening and operation of the postal market, as well as with the financing and safeguarding of universal service. The Postal Law also recast the legal framework for the financial services of La Poste, with the creation of the Postal Bank (Banque Postale), which is not covered by postal regulation. Finally, accessibility constraints on postal counters and collection points throughout the French territory were defined in the Postal Law, and La Poste was given the responsibility for ensuring this and financing of same. While these responsibilities are technically not covered by postal regulation, there is some interaction of these accessibility constraints with the Universal Service Obligation (USO), as discussed further below.

The Postal Law reorganized the statutory and regulatory governance of the postal sector, with two major sections in its text. The first concerned the 'principles governing postal and electronic communications' (hereinafter cited as CPCE), which regroups the applicable rules for postal services in general, and for universal postal service in particular. The CPCE also spells out regulatory procedures and, notably, the role of ARCEP. A second major section of the Postal Law revises the earlier Postal Law of 1990[3] relating to the governance and operations of the public enterprise La Poste (and which are not directly of concern to ARCEP).

The 2005 Postal Law establishes the following responsibilities for ARCEP in overseeing the opening and operations of the postal market: in providing licenses to exercise postal activities; in issuing public notices on tariffs and on the quality of universal service; and in approving tariffs for the reserved sector (expected to remain at a limit of 50 grams until the beginning of 2011, in line with the Third Postal Directive of the European Union). ARCEP's multiple roles and responsibilities are shown in Figure 18.1.

In 2006, numerous publications appeared, among which a decree and an order[4] spelling out the conditions under which ARCEP would license operators offering letter-mail service[5], as well as a decree and several regulatory orders relative to the postal universal service. Concerning the scope of the network of post offices, the Postal Law is the foundation for a formalization of mandatory territorial coverage of counter services. This formalization spells out the terms of accessibility of contact points (counter services and

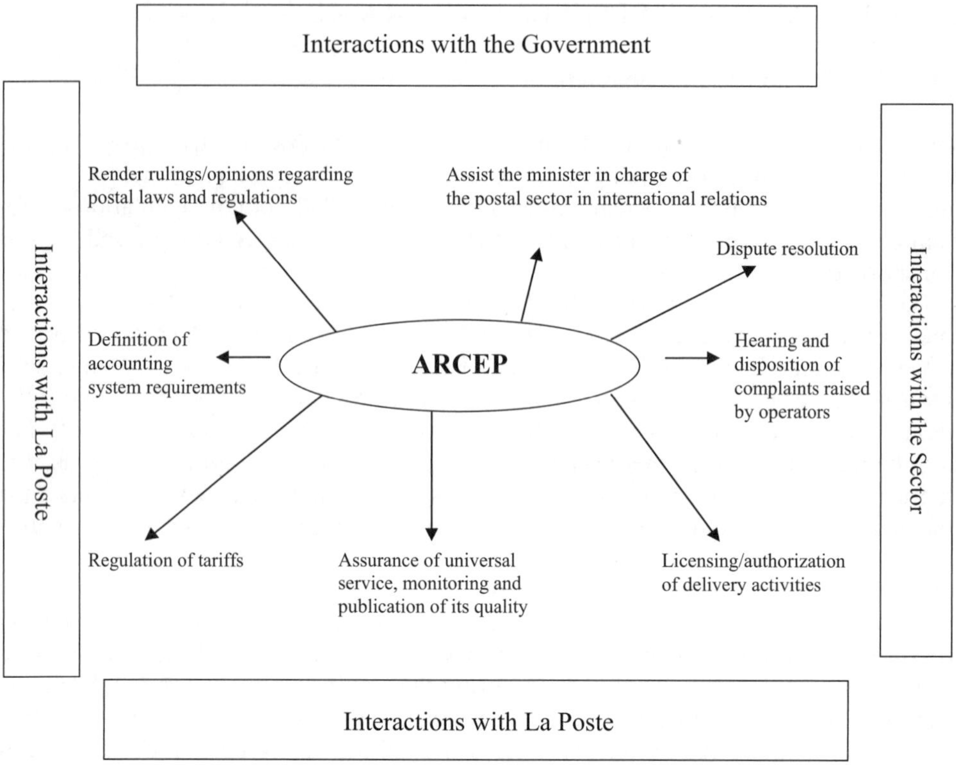

Figure 18.1 ARCEP's missions

collection points), and is presently larger in scope than would be implied by La Poste's USO, as explained by Senator P. Herisson (2007, p. 31):

> The recent Decree No 2007-29 of 5 January 2007 concerning universal postal service specifies the obligation of postal presence in terms of the accessibility of universal service in the following terms: at least 99% of the national population and at least 95% of the population in each Department should be no greater than 10 kilometers distant from a point of contact and communities with more than 10,000 inhabitants should have at least one point of contact for each 20,000 inhabitants. These constraints imply 7,500 points of sale in France. The requirement to provide adequate territorial coverage, which is the responsibility of La Poste as part of its public service mission, will complement this minimal required coverage. The 2005 Postal Law cited above foresees, thus, that 90% of the population will be situated no greater than 5 kilometers and 20 minutes away from a point of contact to La Poste: the added territorial presence thus required corresponds to a public service, which is to be recognized and appropriately assured through legal and financial planning.

The current scope of the postal network, which comprises nearly 17,000 points of contact (counter services of various sorts), satisfies thus the obligation in the Postal Law concerning the most binding constraint on postal presence linked to territorial coverage. This obligation, which goes beyond the requirements of the USO, is covered in part by public compensation via a national postal fund.

2.2 Definition and Regulation of Universal Postal Service

The Postal Law (Article L.2) designated La Poste as the universal service provider (USP). In France, 'universal postal service' corresponds to a set of obligations for La Poste, aimed at guaranteeing the provision of a number of services for everyone, and providing for the control of its quality by ARCEP. The characteristics of universal service and the USO were specified in the Decree of 5 January 2007. These include: (i) the development of a 'catalog' of designated universal postal services, subject to the approval of ARCEP and the minister in charge of postal sector;[6] (ii) specification of service quality objectives by ministerial order; (iii) transparency of the rules governing the provision of universal services and of the standards of quality adopted to measure these; and (iv) the obligation for a uniform tariff for single-piece mail.

ARCEP monitors the conditions associated with the financing of the universal service. In particular, the Postal Law charges ARCEP (Article L.5-2 8°) with recommending to the minister in charge of the postal sector all measures necessary for guaranteeing the provision of universal service, to the extent that financing by La Poste does not appear feasible under equitable conditions. The possibility of a compensation fund is also foreseen in Article L.2-2 of the Postal Law, which would follow staged procedures starting with a request by La Poste, followed by an opinion by ARCEP and a decision by the government. This mechanism would not be automatically activated upon market opening. Indeed, the effects of competition are often progressive and not necessarily destabilizing.

The reserved sector of La Poste currently encompasses mail items of less than 50 grams and whose price is less than 2.5 times the base tariff for single-piece letters (which sets an upper limit of €1.35 at present rates). ARCEP regulates the tariffs for the universal service offerings of La Poste, defining in particular the basic framework underlying these tariffs and overseeing their periodic adjustment every few years.

3. OVERVIEW OF THE FRENCH POSTAL MARKET[7] AS OF 2006

As shown in Table 18.1, the revenue of all operators involved in the delivery of addressed mail items in France and for export was in excess of €14.5 billion in 2006. The letter-mail market is the most important component of this revenue (amounting to €8.4 billion), more than half of total revenues. In 2006, the average unit price for letter mail was €0.51.

Although unaddressed mail accounted for almost half of total volumes, it generated only 4 percent of total revenues. The distribution of such mail is clearly a low value-added service, with average prices of about €0.04 per item. Its distribution requires neither collection, nor daily delivery rounds, and it is not considered a posted mail item; this market is unregulated. In contrast to the unaddressed mail, revenues in the parcel-post market ('ordinary' parcels and express parcels together) represent about 24 percent of the total revenues, but only 2 percent of total market volumes. In fact, the average price of a parcel shipment is among the highest price of any category of mail items, with an average price of €4.4 for an ordinary parcel and €7 for an express parcel.

Let us now consider the volumes of mail delivered (see Table 18.2). In terms of volume, domestic letter mail and unaddressed advertising mail are clearly the two largest streams

Table 18.1 Revenues for postal activities and related item-delivery markets (€ m, excluding VAT)

	2005	2006	Change (%)
*Addressed items delivered in France**			
Items of correspondence	8,470	8,435	−0.4
Registered letters and parcels	1,302	1,382	6.1
Parcels	3,464	3,698	–
Of which 'ordinary' parcels	1,464	1,598	9.1
Of which express light parcels	2,000	2,100	–
Paid press delivery**	492	484	−1.7
Total addressed items delivered in France	13,728	13,999	2.0
*Addressed outgoing international items***			
Items of correspondence	500	422	−15.5
'Ordinary' parcels	74	85	14.6
Press	31	29	−6.2
Total addressed items exported	605	536	−11.4
Unaddressed items			
Total unaddressed advertising	630	658	4.5

Notes:
* Estimated revenues for domestic and incoming international. Incoming international items are included in the figures for letter mail, items delivered against signature (registered items), parcels, newspapers and unaddressed advertising mail.
** Does not include revenues associated with press portage. Portage applies to the distribution of unaddressed periodicals to a defined list of recipients/addressees, in contrast to periodicals with an address affixed to them. Portage is not considered a postal activity. Totals may not sum due to rounding.

Source: ARCEP, Observatoire des activités postales, Enquêtes annuelles (Summary of Postal Activities, Annual Surveys), 2005 and 2006.

of mail items. Supported by double-digit growth in e-commerce, the market for light parcels (those weighing less than 30 kilograms) turned out to be one of the most dynamic markets in the postal sector. It represented in 2006 nearly 700 million parcels distributed in France, more than half of which were 'ordinary' parcels. Incoming international traffic represented only 2 percent of total volume in 2006, not including express mail. Notwithstanding a decrease of 2.8 percent, the distribution of subscriptions to periodicals constituted the third largest market by volume, with 2.7 billion newspapers and magazines distributed via postal operators or non-postal home delivery.

3.1 The Letter Mail Market in France

In 2006, 83.5 percent of letter mail was delivered under the postal monopoly: mail items of 50 grams or less. In 2005, the reserved sector, which was more extensive (items up to 100 grams), accounted for 92 percent of total letter mail delivered. The revenues from the reserved sector represented 73.5 percent of total letter-mail revenues in 2006, compared with 83 percent a year earlier when the reserved area was larger. The relative size

Table 18.2 Postal activities and related item-delivery markets (volumes, millions of items)

	2005	2006	Change (%)
*Addressed items delivered in France**			
Items of correspondence	16,806	16,540	−1.6
Registered letters and parcels	276	279	1.1
Parcels	638	665	–
Of which 'ordinary' parcels	358	365	2.0
Of which express light parcels	280	300	–
Paid press delivery**	2,789	2,710	−2.8
Total addressed items delivered in France	20,509	20,194	−1.5
*Addressed outgoing international items***			
Items of correspondence	523	480	−8.1
'Ordinary' parcels	7	8	18.0
Press	28	27	−2.8
Total addressed items exported	558	516	−7.5
Unaddressed items			
Total unaddressed advertising	18,570	18,568	0.0

Notes:
* Estimated volumes for domestic and incoming international. Incoming international items are included in the figures for letter mail, items delivered against signature (registered items), parcels, newspapers and unaddressed advertising mail.
** Includes volumes associated with press portage. Totals may not sum due to rounding.

Source: ARCEP, Observatoire des activités postales, Enquêtes annuelles (Summary of Postal Activities, Annual Surveys), 2005 and 2006.

of the reserved sector compared to the competitive sector is summarized in Tables 18.3 and 18.4.

Bulk mail versus single-piece mail

As shown in Table 18.5, nearly 58 percent of letter mail delivered in 2006 originated with business mailers as bulk mail, which is to say as mailings with volumes greater than 400 pieces, of the same type and tendered by the same mailer. A substantial part of this bulk mail (60 percent) was processed by mail preparation companies. These companies undertake preparation, sortation and postage/permit evidencing and tendering of the mail they collect into the distribution network of La Poste or another postal delivery provider. The mail preparation market is defined by pricing practices and technical conditions set by La Poste. The Postal Law foresees the possibility of *ex post* intervention by the regulator through the power to resolve disputes that arise between the USP and bulk mailers as well as mail preparation companies.

From Table 18.5, we note that of the total letter mail in 2006, 35 percent was tendered as bulk mail by mail preparation companies, while 23 percent was tendered as bulk mail directly by mailers to some delivery service provider. The remaining 42 percent of the letter mail was tendered as single-piece mail, 23 percent from business mailers and 19

Table 18.3 The reserved sector versus the competitive sector

	2005	2006	Change (%)
Revenues (€m, VAT excluded)			
Reserved area	7,013	6,201	n.s.
Competitive area	1,457	2,234	n.s.
Total revenues for items of correspondence	8,470	8,435	−0.4
Volume (in millions of items)			
Reserved area	15,429	13,804	n.s.
Competitive area	1,377	2,736	n.s.
Total volumes for items of correspondence	16,806	16,540	−1.6

Source: ARCEP, Observatoire des activités postales, Enquêtes annuelles (Summary of Postal Activities, Annual Surveys), 2006.

Table 18.4 Share of total letter market mail deliveries accounted for by the reserved sector versus the competitive sector (domestic and import) (%)

	Volume		Revenue	
	2005	2006	2005	2006
Reserved area*	91.8	83.5	82.8	73.5
Competitive area	8.2	16.5	17.2	26.5
Total items of correspondence	100	100	100	100

Note: * In 2005, the reserve sector encompassed items weighing less than 100g and in 2006 items less than 50g.

Source: ARCEP, Observatoire des activités postales, Enquêtes annuelles (Summary of Postal Activities, Annual Surveys), 2006.

percent from households and small businesses. In total, 81 percent of letter mail originated with business mailers. Two-thirds of the total letter mail was addressed to households, the remaining third to business. Household to household mail represented only 3 percent of the total.[8]

Letter mail and direct mail[9]

As shown in Table 18.6, direct mail represented 29.5 percent of total letter mail delivered in 2006, while revenues from direct mail represented only 19.5 percent of total letter-mail revenues. For the same quality of service, direct mail is in fact priced at some 20 percent [10] below that of other mail items including, in particular, transactional mail from banks and utility companies.

Table 18.7 shows the share of advertising mail as a fraction of total business-originating mail. At present, direct mail represents a bit more than half of business mail. This share increased slightly by 1.7 percent in 2006, reflecting a decrease of 300 million in the total volumes of bulk mail together with a slight increase in the volume of direct mail.

Table 18.5 *Shares of bulk and single-piece letter mail domestic and incoming international (millions of items)*

	2005*	2006	Change (%)
Industrial traffic (bulk >400 items)	9,873	9,571	−3.1
Unprepared industrial traffic from bulk customers	4,598	3,820	−16.9
Prepared industrial traffic	5,275	5,751	9.0
Single-piece traffic dropped off at the distribution operators	6,933	6,968	0.5
Single-piece business mail	3,673	3,824	4.1
Single-piece residential and small business mail	3,260	3,144	−3.6
Total items of correspondence delivered in France	16,806	16,540	−1.6

Note: * 2005 pro forma traffic including financial services items from La Poste. Totals may not sum due to rounding.

Source: ARCEP, Observatoire des activités postales, Enquêtes annuelles (Summary of Postal Activities, Annual Surveys), 2005 and 2006.

Table 18.6 *Direct mail revenues and volumes in relation to total letter mail*

	2005	2006	Change (%)
Revenues (€ m VAT excluded)			
Items of correspondence, direct mail excluded	6,732	6,788	0.8
Direct mail	1,738	1,647	−5.2
Total items of correspondence	8,470	8,435	−0.4
Volumes			
Millions of items			
Items of correspondence, direct mail excluded	11,950	11,668	−2.4
Direct mail	4,856	4,871	0.3
Total items of correspondence	16,806	16,540	−1.6

Note: Totals may not sum due to rounding.

Source: ARCEP, Observatoire des activités postales, Enquêtes annuelle (Summary of Postal Activities, Annual Surveys), 2006.

Table 18.7 *Direct mail volumes as a fraction of total business-originating mail*

Millions of items	2005	2006	Change (%)
Industrial traffic	9,873	9,571	–3.1
Direct mail	4,856	4,871	0.3
Share of direct mail in industrial traffic (%)	49.2	50.9	1.7

Source: ARCEP, Observatoire des activités postales, Enquêtes annuelles (Summary of Postal Activities, Annual Surveys), 2005 and 2006.

Table 18.8 *Revenues and volumes for outgoing international mail*

	2005	2006	Change (%)
Revenue (€ m, excluding VAT)			
Items of correspondence	500	422	−15.5
Press	31	29	−6.2
Parcels	74	85	14.6
Total revenues for outgoing international	605	536	−11.4
Volume (millions of items)			
Items of correspondence	523	480	−8.1
Press	28	27	−2.8
Parcels	7	8	18.0
Total volumes for outgoing international	558	516	−7.5

Note: Totals may not sum due to rounding.

Source: ARCEP, Observatoire des activités postales, Enquêtes annuelles (Summary of Postal Activities, Annual Surveys), 2005 and 2006.

3.2 Courier and other International Mail: Outgoing

The French market for outgoing international mail in 2006 generated €536 million on a volume of 516 million mail items. This market represented 4 percent of the internal market (not including express and unaddressed mail) in terms of revenues and nearly 3 percent in terms of volumes. Outgoing international letter mail is completely open to competition at all weight levels. It is, however, subject to licensure requirements by ARCEP. The operators are for the most part affiliates of other European postal operators (Belgian Post, Deutsche Post Global Mail, Royal Mail, Spring, and Swiss Post). IMX was the only independent operator engaged in international mail in France at the end of 2006. We see in Table 18.8 that outgoing international volumes decreased by 7.5 percent and corresponding revenues by 11.4 percent between 2005 and 2006. The decrease in volumes follows that observed in the decrease in overall letter mail in France in 2005, with a decrease of 2 percent in this total between 2004 and 2005.

4. MARKET DYNAMICS: END-TO-END COMPETITION AND THE DEVELOPMENT OF UPSTREAM ACTIVITIES

4.1 Licensed Operators

Regulatory requirements concerning licensing of postal operators

The procedure for licensing foreseen in Articles L.3 and L.5-1 of the CPCE of the Postal Law was completed in 2006 by a decree[11] and an order.[12] The nature of the activities for which licensing is required is appreciably more restrained in France than in certain other European countries such as Germany and the United Kingdom. In France, it concerns activities related to delivery and outgoing international mail. No regulatory framework has ever been implemented for sectors such as parcel delivery, express mail, or mail preparation and consolidation activities. On the other hand, as liberalization of delivery of addressed mail (both letter mail and advertising) takes shape, it will be important to follow the evolution of the market and to manage carefully the obligations imposed on licensed operators, in particular to ensure their reliability.

The licensing procedure is not intended to present an obstacle to market entry, and the number of licensed operators is accordingly not limited *ex ante*. The objective is to put into place an accessible procedure for the greatest number of entrants, while providing ARCEP sufficient information (through, for example, the collection of appropriate statistics) to ensure its mission to control and, if needed, to sanction inappropriate conduct, thereby protecting consumers of postal services. Licensing procedures therefore create a framework of mutual rights and obligations for operators participating in delivery markets for letter mail domestically and internationally. Several licensed operators have emphasized that ARCEP licensure provides a signal of competence and reliability for their customers.

Licensure is valid for a period of 10 years; it is renewable. It is specific to the named licensed party and is not transferable. The licensing decision is subject to satisfaction of a number of legal and regulatory conditions,[13] technical and financial capacity to implement the service, measures and tools to guarantee performance, reliability and quality of the postal service and financial viability.

The market for outgoing international mail being now open to competition, services for outgoing international mail are the object of a simplified licensing system, namely: in the absence of a response from ARCEP to the contrary, at the end of two months, the application for a license is considered approved.

The principal obligations of licensed operators are the following:

1. employees assigned to delivery functions must carry a professional identification and a distinctive insignia identifying themselves as postal service providers, in order to ensure the tranquility of private premises to which they have access;
2. standard operating procedures must be established to ensure the proper accomplishment of ensigned delivery routes;
3. operational procedures must be established to guarantee the confidentiality of mail, the integrity of its contents, the protection of personal data, and the respect for the privacy of users of postal services;
4. the activities proposed must be accompanied by a management system to correct problems identified, and any provider handling mail items must be able to be identified by an indicia on the items handled; and
5. postal operators must make available to their customers information on their commercial offering and they must establish a procedure for managing complaints which is simple, transparent and free.

ARCEP monitors the fulfillment of these obligations, reinforcing this through information and through its powers to sanction violations. In case of violation, ARCEP can withdraw a license.

Obtaining a license gives, notably, the right of access to private letterboxes and other resources of the historical operator La Poste, which are indispensable to new operators in the exercise of their postal activities (access to the postcode directory, as well as information collected by La Poste on change of address, a redirection service for addressee change of address, and a delivery service for access to post office boxes in post offices[14]).

Level of licensed market activity to date

To date, ARCEP has approved 20 postal licenses. Of these, 12 are for service providers for domestic mail for delivery of letter mail weighing more than 50 grams (one of these 12 licenses is for La Poste to deliver to this segment of the market); nine are for outgoing international mail to the rest of the world (one of these nine is for La Poste's international mail).[15] These operators could have a limited geographic coverage (for example, a single city), in which case we shall refer to them as 'local operators' in what follows. In contrast, Adrexo announced from the start its intention to provide national coverage.

In 2006, the domestic market for delivery of letter mail in excess of 50 grams represented 2.7 billion items and €2.2 billion in revenue. As in other postal markets, the part of the French market that is effectively contestable is smaller than the entire market open to competition. In practice, market opening primarily affects advertising mail, and less so business transaction mail. In the addressed advertising mail market, only business mailings delivered in urban areas is seriously in play. What this implies is a theoretically contestable market amounting to about 500 to 700 million euros per annum (about 25 percent of the overall market for letter-mail delivery).

What is the level of activity of these licensed operators in the market and what significant trends does one observe? The delivery of letter mail by operators other than La Poste remains marginal and not competitive (in 2006, 140,000 mail items in excess of 50 grams were distributed by local operators and 25 million items by Adrexo, as part of its network for delivery of unaddressed advertising mail). In contrast, the smaller market for outgoing international mail is more mature and dynamic.

Interestingly, the enactment of the Third Postal Directive, and the ultimate date of 2011 for full liberalization, seems to have given rise to a sudden pause in new licensing activity. For example, several operators (in the parcel and express mail segments) interested in obtaining a license to begin delivery activities of addressed mail seem now to prefer to await the full opening of the market before proceeding.

Local and niche operators

Operators proposing services limited to a local area differentiate themselves from La Poste through various value-added services, such as time-definite delivery. These are small niche operators employing between one and 50 people. Some of these are messenger services, wishing to extend their activities to handling postal items, following the example of Fox Messenger. Others, like Althus and Solgeco 26, are providing service to small and medium-sized enterprises (SMEs), delivering themselves a part of the mail they collect and tendering the remainder to La Poste. The logic of their respective business models is quite diverse and is tied to their originating activity and to the demands of their local clients.

The total revenue of these local operators, including all their activities from preparation of mail to consolidation, postage evidencing, collection, and tendering, amounted to approximately €3.1 million in 2006. Their tariffs are some 10 to 15 percent lower than those of La Poste. Within the framework of their licensed activities, these operators distribute from 50 to 1,500 items per day, with an average weight between 51 and 200 grams.

Althus initially proposed to potential business customers a service to optimize their general mailing expenses. Althus identified market needs for outsourced mailing activities and developed specific solutions aimed at business mailers and professionals. This company, after its creation in October 2000 in Chambery, underwent significant growth, including setting up offices in Annecy in January 2005 and opening of the Solgeco 26 franchise in Valence.

Fox Messenger also identified unmet market needs of certain customers in the town of Pau (independent professionals, SMEs and banking agencies) and proposed to them mail collection services, pick-up services for their post office boxes, mail delivery and an urban messenger service.

LET Services was created in 1994 and operates in the region of Alsace-Lorraine. This company has diverse activities related notably to the handling and delivery of business mail to other businesses, and especially to banking establishments. Their activities include postage/permit evidencing for third parties, mail preparation for small mailings (from 100 to 3,000 exemplars), inter-site shuttles for document exchanges, bagging, and an urban messenger service. However, the company also provides outsourced services such as transport, delivery and management of archives and storage and supply of printed matter. LET Services has also responded to various specific local demands, including developing a daily delivery service for medications for pharmaceutical wholesalers, and automotive spare parts for a network of automotive repair shops. LET was licensed in 2007 in order to be able to complete the palette of mail services it can propose to potential customers.

In 2006, the first two licensed local operators, Althus and Fox Messenger, delivered less than 150,000 mail items (>50 grams) in the framework of their license. In 2007, the 10 licensed local operators delivered together approximately 1 billion mail items.

In summary, these messenger services, small parcel delivery organizations and service providers specializing in the management of business mail, including at times mail preparation, were already well established in the local economy when they decided to enter the >50 grams addressed mail market. Doing so completes their mail product portfolio for their business customers. These customers can then find among the most advanced operators the full range of mail services. These operators would, of course, tender mail weighing less than 50 grams to La Poste (at least until full market opening in 2011). The delivery of letter mail in the >50 grams category constitutes simply a complement to their other local activities; it is not sold as a separate autonomous service. These operators are exploring the possibility of completing these activities of collection and tendering and of posting of mail, but they claim that in general this complementary delivery activity is not currently profitable. At the moment, therefore, these local operators are not developing dedicated networks for delivery of letter mail. To the extent that they do any delivery, their delivery network is the same as that which is used for collection and deposit of mail.

The case of Adrexo

In 2006, ARCEP approved the first postal license for the enterprise Adrexo which had as its ambition to 'become the first French private postal operator'. Adrexo is a delivery service provider of unaddressed printed matter (8.2 billion items were distributed by Adrexo in 2007) with a nationwide network. Adrexo utilizes its national delivery network for unaddressed mail to distribute a lower volume of addressed mail (the product is called 'Combimail') and it has set up in the principal metropolitan areas a dedicated delivery network for addressed mail (the product 'Adrexomail'). However, with the announcement that full market opening would take place on 1 January 2011, the deployment of the latter network for addressed mail was frozen. The initial objective was to attain 50 percent coverage of the territory as of the date of full market opening projected to occur in 2009. Indeed, Adrexo announced in February 2008 that it would no longer operate its dedicated delivery network within the next few months because of 'the report of full liberalization as of 1 January 2011, as well as the continuing uncertainties and disappointments suffered in Europe by private companies operating in the addressed delivery market'.[16]

At first glance, Adrexo's announced strategy resembles that of CityMail in Sweden (Toledano, 2004 and Andersson, Ch. 17, this volume) or that of Sandd or Selekt Mail in the Netherlands. Upon entry into the letter-mail markets, these companies bet on beating the historic operators through a low-cost business model. They did not propose a daily delivery schedule and their geographic coverage was tied to the density of the population of their respective countries (coverage of 45 percent for CityMail and national coverage in the Netherlands). Their objective has been to offer a less costly alternative for the delivery of non-urgent business mail. Their aim was to capture a market share of 5–10 percent. In 2007, CityMail delivered 275 million mail items and Sandd 400 million, corresponding, respectively, to revenues of 70 and 80 million euros.

It is interesting to compare the Adrexo experience with the above examples in mind. In 2006, the volume of letter mail delivered by Adrexo, using its national network for unaddressed printed matter, was approximately 25 million pieces, with resulting revenues of €16 million. Adrexo uses this same network, for example, to deliver the annual 'yellow pages'. Adrexo had opened several dedicated delivery networks for addressed mail in the dense zones outside Paris, serving some 17.6 percent of the accessible mail boxes with approximately 900 employees dedicated to addressed mail delivery and undertaken through 3,900 routes. In 2007, the revenue resulting from this dedicated delivery network for addressed mail was essentially fueled by trial runs by customers and operated at a loss amounting to €18 million. This explains, in part, the February 2008 announcement by Adrexo that it will cease its activity in this domain. It seems clear that Adrexo has not been able to develop a profitable, dedicated network for addressed mail delivery, with sufficient coverage and volumes to allow it to grow revenues and achieve economies of scale. Whether it will be able to do so after 2011 and full market opening remains to be seen.

Outgoing international mail: a market where competition has developed

Several European national postal operators (Belgium, the Netherlands, Germany, Switzerland), through affiliates or direct operating divisions, as well as the company IMX France and La Poste, have postal licenses to transport addressed letter mail from France to the rest of the world. The market share of La Poste in this market is 80–85 percent. As shown in Tables 18.1 and 18.2, this market represents a revenue of €536 million on a volume of 516 million mail items (letter mail, newspapers and ordinary parcels). The market has been liberalized since the end of the 1990s.

The first entry by a foreign operator into the French international mail market occurred in 1995 with the company Mailfast, which later became a subsidiary of TNT and today is known as Spring. The company IMX France, created in 1989, is the only privately owned French company involved in international mail that is recognized by the Universal Postal Union (UPU). IMX France offers outgoing international mail services from

France to the rest of the world, selecting from its own services, as well as those of other service providers, the best tariffs and the best conditions for transport and delivery. IMX also operates as an extraterritorial point of exchange for the Belgian and German postal operators, and IMX has obtained from these two the right to use their postal indicia.

The product offerings of La Poste and the affiliates of the national postal operators from Germany, Switzerland, as well as the Dutch and UK affiliate companies operating as part of the company G3worldwide Mail NV, all contribute to handling various parts of the French outgoing international mail. They offer generally value-added services, including mail preparation, file management, subscription management, storage and bonding, registration, customs clearance, and management of undelivered items and returns. They attempt to capture upstream mail destined for their own territory, while also offering services for other parts of the world.

The Belgian La Poste is also present in France, operating directly from its national base and without a separate affiliate in France. It offers collection, sortation and tendering services for outgoing international mail (letter mail, parcels and registered mail services) from France to Belgium and the rest of the world, supported by its own domestic and international network.

To date, the large operators involved with international mail, with the exception of IMX and its affiliate Press'tissimo, which operates locally in the Paris region, have not attempted to extend their operations to activities in the domestic mail market in France.

4.2 The Market for Mail Preparation

Historical background

Mail preparation encompasses all mail preparation activities for bulk mail prior to tendering of such mail to a postal operator for final delivery. Mail preparation began to develop at the end of the nineteenth century in speeding up the delivery of newspapers. It was extended to other sectors with the advent of direct mail and mail-order sales in the 1960s. The major strikes in 1975 reinforced this evolution, as mail preparation permitted the load on mail sorting centers and made them less vulnerable to the strike.

The system which developed during this period was based on a tri-partite relation in which the mailer paid La Poste postage at full tariff rates, while La Poste, in return, remunerated the customer or the provider of the mail preparation service for their work in preparing and pre-sorting the mail. The growth in mail preparation in France accompanied the growth of business mail, mainly for the benefit of small and medium-sized mail preparation companies.

Relations between mail preparation providers and the historic operator changed over time with the improvements in postal sorting productivity made possible by new generations of mail processing technology. La Poste demanded improved quality and at lower prices from these mail preparation providers. As a consequence, these organizations had to modernize their production methods and the sorting and addressing technologies they used.

During these past years, the product portfolio offered by La Poste to business mailers has also evolved in significant ways. New product offerings are now based on net tariffs, which is to say tariffs which exclude payments for specific types of work in preparing the mail. As a consequence, this new tariff structure has led to the establishment of direct relations between La Poste and business mailers. Under this new approach to tariffs, mail preparation activities accomplished by the mailer or a third party are now remunerated based more closely on the actual level of the preparatory work accomplished prior to tendering the mail to La Poste, providing greater transparency to mailers on the costs of mail preparation.[17]

Network access: regulation and dispute resolution

Defined by tariff practices and technical conditions of La Poste, upstream access to the postal delivery network is not regulated *ex ante*. The Postal Law foresees the possibility of *ex post* intervention by the regulator in its power to hear disputes (as specified in Articles L.2-1 and L.5-4 of the Postal Law) between the USP and bulk mailers as well as mail preparation operators. To date, ARCEP has rendered only a single decision within this framework, and that on a technical subject. The company Office France Marketing (OFM, a mail preparation company created in 1986 and belonging to the group ROUTEX) brought to ARCEP a request to hear a dispute in April 2007. The dispute concerned a decision by La Poste to move an integrated postal control center located on the premises of OFM to a facility operated by La Poste. ARCEP rejected OFM's demand to require that La Poste reverse its decision to move the operations of the integrated postal control center to premises controlled by La Poste. However, in its decision, ARCEP asked La Poste to modify and clarify conditions in its mail preparation agreements concerning locational and security constraints imposed by La Poste for receipt of mail by mail preparation companies. OFM appealed this decision. In February 2008, the Court of Appeal of Paris upheld ARCEP's ruling.

Structure and state of play in the French mail preparation market

Today, the French mail preparation market for business mail generates approximately €1 billion per annum. More than 7 billion mail items were workshared in France in 2006. Among these, 3.8 billion were direct marketing items and 1.9 billion were transactions mail, according to ARCEP's statistics on postal activities. Some 200 enterprises of a variety of different types participate in this market.[18]

In 2007, the consultancy company Basic undertook a study (Basic, 2007) commissioned by ARCEP, which allows one to identify the contours of the French mail preparation market and to show how it is structured, in particular in terms of its relations with the postal operator, with an eye to the consequences of full market opening.

The three traditional businesses in the mail preparation market are concerned with direct marketing mail, transactional mail, and newspapers/periodicals. While these traditional areas have constituted for mail preparation professionals a reasonable structure to understand the historical reality of mail preparation activities, this segmentation has become somewhat dated given the evolution of postal technology, value chains and the strategies of the actors involved. A segmentation in terms of strategic profiles seems, however, to provide a schematic better adapted to the realities of the market. Basic provides such a segmentation, based on a detailed analysis of the financial and social data of the 200 companies present in the sector from 2001 to 2005 as well as the nature of their governance structure. Besides mail preparation organizations supporting newspaper periodical distribution, which is a group unto itself, five profiles can be distinguished in the French mail preparation market: (i) affiliates of incumbents; (ii) independents; (iii) SMEs;

Table 18.9 Overview of mail preparation providers by strategic segment (%)

	Affiliates of large mailers	Affiliates of incumbent POs	Independents	SMEs	Integrated communication companies
Change in revenue between 2001 and 2005	7.0	11	5.0	2.0	6.0
Average annual profitability 2001–05	3.7	−0.4	5.7	5.7	4.7
Change in profitability between 2001 and 2005	−3.7	−2.4	−0.6	−1.9	5.6
Average annual investment level, 2001–05	17.5	9.6	7.7	6.4	8.8
Average debt level as a percentage of equity, 2001–05	247.0	118.0	110.0	160.0	290.0
Change in debt level between 2001 and 2005	−20.0	−9.0	−18.0	47.0	−50.0

(iv) subsidiaries of integrated communication companies; and (v) affiliates of large mailers.

This segmentation exhibits the diversity of existing mail preparation providers, with the affiliates of other national postal operators (incumbents in their own markets) playing a dominant role in the structure of the sector. The independents, which are the target providers for new entrants in the delivery sector, have managed to achieve reasonable economic results. The other groups of mail preparation providers have posted mixed results, with certain of the SME providers encountering significant financial problems. The details are worth noting here (Table 18.9).

Concerning the affiliates of incumbents, although they number only six, they represent some 17 percent of the total revenue of the sector, the third highest of the five segments noted. Their mail preparation affiliates, in effect, provide them a foundation for acquiring a customer base. In other words, these affiliates are playing a role as a point of entry into the market for the national postal operators.

In terms of revenue, the independents represent 32 percent of the mail preparation market. They are distinguished by the quality of their services and by their commercial relations. They are currently the likely acquisition target of operators who are now planning on entering the market, given their healthy economic status based on profitability[19] (of 5.7 percent) and productivity[20] (of 1.39 percent) steadily ahead of other mail preparation providers. These independents, however, exhibited relatively weak investment levels[21] (namely 7.7 percent) compared to the other profiles of mail preparation firms, which may jeopardize their capacity to co-invest in projects with their customers.

The SME mail preparation providers, defined in Basic as the set of companies realizing less than €4 million in revenues, is quite a heterogeneous group representing some 23 percent of the total mail preparation market. Over the course of the last few years, the revenue of these companies experienced the weakest rate of growth (2 percent per annum) within the five strategic segments identified above, their growth being essentially defined by growth in their standard products for their existing customer base. This rate of growth, however, hides significant disparities across this group. Many companies experienced declining revenues (42 percent of the total) and others, in contrast, experienced significant growth in both revenue and profits (some 58 percent of the total).

The mail preparation providers that are subdivisions of integrated communication providers correspond to enterprises that developed mail preparation services as part of an overall portfolio of communication products. Representing 15 percent of the revenue of the mail preparation market, this group is highly concentrated, with seven leading companies garnering more than 90 percent of the total revenues for this group. The profitability of these companies has risen strongly from 2001 to 2005 and (at 4.7 percent) is above the average of the group as a whole. Similarly, their revenue has shown healthy growth (6 percent per annum between 2001 and 2005). These companies are, however, highly leveraged (with an average debt level of 290 percent of their equity), though they have been reducing their indebtedness over the period in question (with a reduction in their debt structures of some 50 percent over the period from 2001 to 2005). The highly leveraged structure of these companies is reflected in part by their levels of investment (8.8 percent), which is slightly above average for all mail preparation companies.

Finally, mail preparation affiliates established by large mailers were developed to respond to the needs of the direct mail sector (*Vente par Correspondence*) and the financial services sector. It represents today only 7 percent of the mail preparation market, but the revenue in this group has continued to grow at an annual rate of 7 percent, representing above-average performance for all mail preparation organizations. Small in number, these companies still have to demonstrate their capacity to develop outside the protective dependence of their mother companies.

The future of the mail preparation market in France

According to Basic (2007), the mail preparation market is likely to follow the trends observed over the course of recent years in both qualitative and quantitative terms. Basic also concludes that the trends reported here are likely to be reinforced by the announced full market opening of the sector in 2011. Dematerialization of transactions mail (also known as electronic substitution) has been rapid and continuing, confirming various projections that have been made in this regard. However, electronic substitution in direct marketing remains relatively weak. The withdrawal of Adrexo, announced in February 2008, from the delivery market will consolidate the central place occupied by La Poste in the definition of product offers by mail preparation providers to their customers. Indeed, ARCEP will not intervene in the definition of service offerings by La Poste except *ex post* in the case of a formal dispute being lodged with ARCEP. Restructuring and consolidation activity in the mail preparation sector are also not likely to modify either this basic scenario or the mail preparation products offered in the market. Further growth based on the respective competencies of each of these strategic segments can be expected to continue for the more dynamic actors in each segment.

5. REGULATION OF THE LICENSED MARKET IN THE WAKE OF THE POSTAL LAW

As seen above, competition in the outgoing international mail market is well developed. Because of this, established international operators have not submitted any major requests for regulatory action or decision. On the other hand, operators delivering letter mail have brought to the attention of the regulator two principal obstacles hampering their development: (i) multiple post marks on mail items (when more than one postal provider has handled the item); and (ii) access to mail boxes, especially in multi-apartment buildings. We review each of these cases separately.

5.1 Multiple Post Marks on Mail Items

Background

At the end of 2006, La Poste notified ARCEP that it had found in its network some undeliverable mail items (items that could not be delivered because of missing, incomplete or incorrect addressing) carrying a double post mark, its own and that of Adrexo. La Poste complained that this represented an abuse of its brand. The items in question had been put together by mail preparation organizations that had utilized envelopes and plastic films already pre-imprinted with a postal permit (that is, postage evidencing) indicia of La Poste. These items were tendered to Adrexo for delivery and they carried the note 'delivered by Adrexo' (*distribué par Adrexo*) without masking the postal permit information of La Poste.

Not long thereafter, Adrexo also contacted ARCEP complaining that La Poste was requiring Adrexo to mask the Adrexo trademark (by an opaque strip or by blacking out) before La Poste would accept items from Adrexo's clients destined for zones that Adrexo did not serve. Adrexo claimed that this requirement to eliminate multiple post markings, created a barrier to entry. In fact, applying opaque stripping or blacking out of a trademark are costly, which take time and which, in addition, are broadly rejected by originating customers, who are quite attached to the aesthetic appearance of the advertising material they send as addressed mail.

In a market in which La Poste was the sole delivery organization, the pre-printing of postal permits, which is at the origin of the multiple post mark issue, did not pose any particular problem. When advertising campaigns require annual printing runs, the mail preparation provider can pre-print in advance film strips or large quantities of envelopes in order to rationalize costs and also to save time. However, if the advertiser changes its distributor in the course of the year, it will have to sell off unused stock of film or envelopes with the pre-printed postal permit information. Similarly, when an advertiser decides, for the same campaign, to use Adrexo for part of the delivery of its mailing, the question of costs tied to separating the mail by address, and the adjustments and setups of machines to prepare the mailing, naturally arise.

The mailer is supposed to trade off the costs associated with a change in operator, so-called 'switching costs', and the savings in postage it would realize in switching to an alternative operator. The larger the volume of mail tendered to the alternative operator for delivery (where volume depends, *inter alia*, on the geographic coverage offered by the alternative), the greater the potential savings in postage available to compensate for these switching costs.

All of this points to the fact that the case of double post marks on mail items is an irritant both for La Poste, complaining of abuse of its brand, as well as for alternative operators, in this case Adrexo, constrained to reprocess mail items carrying a double marking. Finally, multiple post marking is a source of confusion for customers.

ARCEP's position

Per Article L.5-2 1° of the Postal Law, ARCEP is charged with monitoring the compliance of licensees with their legislative and regulatory obligations. And, in France, marking of mail items is an obligation of licensed operators (Article 3 of the order of 3 May 2006). In view of these facts, double marking is clearly not illegal, but it presumes reasonable practices of the operators permitting readability of the mail items by users. International experience shows that it takes time to achieve a market outcome in which stocks and contents of pre-imprints have been sold off and where advertisers no longer are committed to using films or pre-printed envelopes. This experience also allows additional perspective on two idiosyncrasies of the French market.

First, consider the alternative operators Sandd and Selekt Mail in the Netherlands. They prepare the mail themselves without recourse to third-party mail preparation providers, as mail preparation is an important part of their overall business. In contrast, given the numerous mail preparation providers in France for business mail, Adrexo did not choose to vertically integrate upstream to achieve a full-service mail preparation operation.

An additional issue is that countries like France that require visible marking of licensed operators handling mail are nowadays few in number. The United Kingdom, for example, has also implemented a regulation that each licensed operator must print on all the mail items it handles a 3-digit identification code, while such an obligation does not exist in Germany, the Netherlands or in Sweden. International experience shows that in the long run, once workable competition is established, the market adapts and solutions emerge. Thus residual cases of mail items imprinted with a double post mark can be expected to gradually die out. In effect, for an equivalent service, the savings in postage realized by advertisers by using alternative operators should be sufficient to compensate the additional costs associated with the development of reconfigurable films and the separation of addressing files according to final delivery operator.

During the transition phase, ARCEP has issued an opinion that it would consider it inappropriate for La Poste to systematically block the distribution of mail items carrying a double mark. However, this practice will only be residual and transitory. Delivery operators and mail preparation providers will need to sensitize large mailers to the practices that will facilitate the emergence of competition, among which would be an explicit identification on mail as to which operator had responsibility for its delivery.

5.2. Access to Mail Boxes

Background of the problem

More and more apartment buildings have opted for permanent and secure access control. Thus, 120,000 apartment buildings of a total of a million in France are now equipped with a system of controlled access, whereas this number was only 5,000 in the year 2000. At the same time, lifestyles have been such that various service providers are being called on to enter these buildings at the demand of residents, more and more frequently, in order to provide their services. This includes notably the delivery of mail, delivery of merchandise and personal services.

Since 2004–05, postal operators have been pointing out the difficulties of accessing letterboxes in residential apartment buildings that have opted for permanent locked access. New entrants in the market have been complaining of discrimination relative to La Poste, which is equipped to enter all of these buildings, notably if these are equipped with a 'VIGIK' access control system.[22]

Access stems based on keys or building codes have existed for some time. Generally, a 'PTT key' permitted La Poste to access mail boxes in multi-unit buildings. The broader availability of this easily reproducible key gave rise to the development of access control systems that were more secure. The system VIGIK, created by La Poste, for example, provided a technical solution to the needs of residents and operators, but its utilization in a postal market in the process of being opened to competition has raised several questions (for example, it is not easy to add or suppress the registration of an operator, the system itself having been conceived when La Poste was the sole delivery operator). The system is quite secure and operates on a rechargeable badge principle. Operators are allowed access if their enterprise has been approved by the building beforehand and if they have pre-registered their badge with VIGIK Central prior to the start of their route. The badge is not usable without this pre-registration, and the registration itself only lasts for a single day, but it does provide access to all buildings equipped with VIGIK.

Buildings with VIGIK have to be equipped with an electronic lock, which allows access only to those service providers whose 'service identification code' has been registered beforehand with the electronic lock. Thus, at the moment when a building installs this system of access control, it decides for which service providers it wishes to permit access, as well as the days and times when access will be permitted. Note, however, that it is likely to be complicated for a new entrant to be registered in the electronic lock systems of every building. It has to find the manager of the building, contact him, get a decision made, and then effect the registration. The registration of the service identification code of this provider also typically requires the intervention of a professional technician, whose bill for services (per door in the building complex) would be about €50.

Thus, this access system has created a strong and stable protective barrier for existing service providers. Thereby for La Poste the market has bypassed some of these difficulties with the invention of the practice of 'native access'. In the factory, the manufacturer registers in the registration control centers (which are installed on the premises of service providers so that they can re-register their badges) and on the electronic locks (which will be installed on site at the building using these), the service identification code of La Poste. In fact, La Poste therefore has automatic access to the set of buildings equipped with VIGIK, which is not the case for its licensed competitors, notwithstanding the requirements of Article L.5-10 of the Postal Law requiring equal access.

The public consultation on the access problem

In 2006, ARCEP initiated a work group prior to the public consultation of 2007 and brought together several interested stakeholders concerned with the problem of access to individual mail boxes. Besides the delivery operators who were directly concerned (including licensed operators as well as newspaper and parcel distributors), real estate professionals participated as well. This work group permitted an inquiry and examination of the complexity of the questions raised which bordered on the law of property, competition law and postal regulation. On this occasion, it was also underlined that the rules of governance and operation for the VIGIK system exhibited notable differences in relation to the received law of standards and certification. In particular, it was noted that VIGIK is a brand name and not a technical standard. Moreover, the supervisory board for the management of the brand name VIGIK gave effective control of this brand to La Poste, who maintained a veto right and material control of VIGIK.

In November 2007, ARCEP therefore launched a public consultation in order to develop and share an analysis of this situation, to gather a broad set of points of view and to surface potential solutions. The responses to this consultation highlighted the necessity to accommodate several key elements:

1. Concerns for security and tranquility of residents wishing to maintain control of the conditions of access to buildings where they live.
2. The rules of competition between several categories of operators. For example, between postal operators who deliver only addressed mail, postal operators who also deliver unaddressed advertising mail, and other operators who deliver only unaddressed advertising mail.
3. Equal access for postal operators to mail boxes, as well as newspaper and periodical delivery services, under the conditions inscribed in the Postal Law, which is the only subject on which ARCEP could legitimately intervene.

A short-term solution and open questions

The debate aroused by the public consultation created propitious conditions for setting up a short-term solution permitting immediate access to all licensed postal operators. This solution permits them, using established identification procedures, that is to say sharing the same service identification code in the VIGIK system, to access mail boxes located in buildings equipped with this system of access control. The consultation also underscored the necessity of implementing a new governance system for VIGIK, based on fair and transparent procedures and permitting the emergence of sustainable solutions.

Finally, the public consultation permitted stakeholders to raise other questions that are not within the scope of competence of ARCEP, such as access to emergency services and improving the flexibility of access control systems (for example, to facilitate the addition or suppression of service providers for entry to a building).

5.3 Access to Technical Infrastructure

In contrast to the above issues, the question of access by alternative operators to the technical infrastructure controlled by La Poste (address codes and so on) has not given rise to difficulties. Access agreements are based on negotiated tariff arrangements between La Poste and alternative licensed operators. For example, Adrexo and La Poste have signed several agreements, without the intervention of ARCEP, concerning access of Adrexo to post boxes, address codes and other technical infrastructure controlled by La Poste.

Indeed, access to such infrastructure is in compliance with the requirements of Article L.3-1 of the Postal Law, licensed operators are to be provided access 'under transparent and non-discriminatory conditions', subject to technical constraints and tariffs laid out in negotiated contracts to this end with the USP, and using resources, owned or controlled by the USP, which are indispensable to carrying out their postal activities. The resources in question comprise national address codes and the matched correspondence between these codes and geographic information on streets and addresses, information collected by La Poste on address changes, and a capability or a distribution service (to allow alternative operators access) to mail boxes located in post offices. In addition, in the case of a dispute concerning access agreements between La Poste and a licensed operator, ARCEP can be asked to intervene by either party.

Thus, in the future, alternative operators, on request, can expect to have access to post office boxes located in post offices, as well as information on changes of address, maintained by La Poste. In particular, while the related questions of access and address codes have remained points of tension in many countries, the French Postal Law has provided a framework that has resolved these issues sufficiently clearly in law to allow regulation and public consultation to find solutions in practice.

5.4 Ongoing Regulatory Issues

Other subjects of typically national character are raised in recurring fashion by licensed operators. They reflect the present state of the market, and the dominant role played by La Poste in this market. Some issues of recent interest have included:

1. What is the legal standing of registered mail items delivered by licensed operators relative to registered mail items delivered by La Poste?
2. In relations with public agencies and organizations, consideration of official filing dates and deadlines often requires the use of mail, with the posted date on a mail item being taken as proof of timely compliance. In this regard, what is the value accorded to a posted date by an operator licensed by ARCEP?
3. Public agencies have inquired as to the possibility of receiving cost estimates for delivery of items weighing more than 50 grams, in the context of public tender offers. Several technical and practical questions arise here, notably the possible allotment of national market tenders to geographic zones or on the basis of distinctions between mailings within the reserved sector and the competitive sector, which might necessitate launching distinct tenders for the different allotments.
4. The issue of VAT exists in France, but it is not the principal barrier to entry. La Poste is exempt from VAT but is subject to a wage tax. The fiscal characteristics of the French system imply that this subject is less critical than in other European countries. Moreover, with the monopoly limited to 50 grams, it is essentially heavier addressed advertising mail that is the concern. In this area, most mailers of these items can recover any VAT expenses they incur with other licensed operators than La Poste. This is in contrast to mailers of transactions mail, such as banks and insurers, for example, who cannot recover VAT expenses.

6. CONCLUSIONS

Three years after the approval of the Postal Law, this overview of the French postal markets and our analysis of two important elements of these markets, those for licensed operators and for mail preparation, lead to several conclusions.

Competition in the delivery of addressed mail weighing more than 50 grams is still marginal. La Poste has a 99 percent market share of letter mail in France. This observation clearly underlines the question as to the existence of a viable economic model for this mail delivery. Local operators who have done the best are those who have diversified their offering to provide 'one-stop shopping'. Given the present opening of the market, delivery of addressed mail remains a complementary activity, not a primary activity, for alternative operators. The example of Adrexo reinforces this hypothesis. In any case, the market for outgoing international mail is more competitive, since alternative operators have obtained about a 10 percent market share here.

The principal obstacles encountered by licensed operators had not been identified in the beginning and they are rather specifically French. The problems of access to individual mail boxes located in multi-apartment buildings have hampered the development of competition. Following a public consultation conducted by ARCEP, a solution allowing access for all licensed operators, on equal terms, has been identified.

Generally, licensed operators in France have not vertically integrated. There are a few exceptions to this general rule. For example, Alternative Post, which began as a mail preparation company, now delivers addressed mail in greater Lyon; and IMX-France owns a shop to produce micro-film records for periodicals and newspapers it delivers.

Representing more than a billion euros in revenues, the French mail preparation market is the second largest such market (behind the United States) in the world. The dynamic of this market is particularly uncertain at present, with the various actors following very different trajectories. The group Diffusion Plus achieved a revenue of close to €100 million in 2007, an increase of 25 percent over its 2004 revenue. In contrast, other mail preparation companies, such as Mecanic Routage in 2006, saw themselves constrained to sell or merge their activities.

What lessons might one draw from this preliminary assessment?

International experience shows that both time and practice are required in order for competition to develop in the postal sector. Implementing a dedicated delivery network for addressed mail requires investment and specific competencies which new entrants may not have in the requisite measure. The beginnings of CityMail were difficult in Sweden (Toledano, 2004). Without getting into the current debate, competition has taken time in Germany to take root and many of the actors present in the second half of the 1990s have disappeared today. Sandd and Selekt Mail took several years before the liberalization of Direct Mail in the Netherlands to be significant players there. Against this perspective, the recent history of Adrexo resembles that of other operators in other countries in the past.

On perspectives which the French market offers, these will necessarily stimulate debates before the implementation of the Third Postal Directive. Indeed, besides the progressive opening of the market for all postal activities, the postal policy for the European Union, in contrast to the telecommunications sector, has been limited to general principles. The choice of regulatory instruments and market governance has been largely left to the national level from the very beginning. Just to touch on a few major subjects:

- since the beginning of the European Community harmonization process, the limits of monopoly in the postal directives have been set as allowable maxima;
- the definition of universal service presents elastic contours and it has been, in fact, interpreted differently at the country level across Europe;
- the form of licensing and procedures for implementing price regulation are not detailed; and
- nor are conditions of network access.

Altogether, the precedents for the Third Postal Directive do not dictate unique and harmonized regulatory procedures for its implementation. Therefore, it will be the country-by-country debate on the institutions and governance for achieving the full liberalization of postal markets, the main objective of this Directive, that will have to inform and shape this process as we go forward. The beginning stages of the French approach to this process have been described here. The further course of this evolution will no doubt be the result of the continuing interaction of political and market forces that are at work in this sector.

NOTES

* Prepared for the 16th Conference on Postal and Delivery Economics, May 28–31, 2008 Albufeira, Algarve, Portugal. It reflects the views of the authors only and not necessarily those of ARCEP.

1. In France, the upstream market covers preparation, sortation, postage and tendering of the mail collected into the distribution network of La Poste or another postal delivery provider. In the United States, these activities are often referred to collectively as 'worksharing'.
2. 'Loi N° 2005-516 du 20 mai 2005 relative à la régulation des activités postales', (Law N° 2005-516 of 20 May 2005 relative to the regulation of postal activities), posted in the *Journal Officiel de la République Française*, 21 May 2005.
3. 'Loi N° 90-568 du 2 juillet 1990 relative à l'organisation du service public de La Poste et à France Télécom', (Law N° 90-568 of 2 July 1990 relative to the organization of public service of La Poste and of France Telecom), posted in the *Journal Officiel de la République Française*, 8 July 1990.
4. '*Decret*' (decree) and '*Arrêté*' (order) are both part of secondary legislation taken by the government to apply specific parts of the law. A decree is a regulatory rule taken by the President of the Republic or the Prime Minister in their exercise of their respective functions. An order in the present context is a regulatory rule emanating from a minister; an order can also be issued by an administrative authority such as a prefect or a mayor.
5. 'Décret N° 2006-507 du 3 mai 2006 relatif à la régulation des activités postales et modifiant le code des postes et des communications électroniques publié', (Decree N° 2006-507 of 3 May 2006 relative to the regulation of postal activities and modifying the published code on postal and electronic communications), posted in the *Journal Officiel de la République Française*, 5 May 2006.
6. In France, ministerial portfolios can change with governments. At present, the minister in charge of postal matters is the Secretary of State for Enterprises and International Commerce, who is attached to the Ministry for Economics, Finance and Employment.
7. The scope of the ARCEP markets observatory exceeds postal items in the strict sense of the term as these exclude express items and unaddressed advertising. Mail preparation, as an intermediate activity, is not included but is studied separately in Section 3.2, below.
8. Le Courrier en Chiffres – Données 2006, Groupe La Poste, Paris, p. 4.
9. In France, it is possible for the sender to personalize the content of direct mail items. In addition, La Poste has developed some extra services in the D + 4 to D + 7 range that are less expensive for addressed advertising mail.
10. The 20 percent figure is an estimate based on comparison of the baseline tariffs Tem'Post MD4 and Tem'Post G4 (pre-sorted to the postal code and mechanized) for items of less than 35 grams.
11. Décret N° 2006-507 (see n. 5, above).
12. 'Arrêté du 3 mai 2006, pris en application de l'article R. 1-2-6 du code des postes et des communications électroniques relatif aux obligations des prestataires de services de services postaux titulaires d'une autorisation' (Order of 3 May 2006, implementing article R.1-2-6 of the code of postal and electronic

communications concerning the obligations of service providers of postal services requiring licensure), posted in the *Journal Officiel de la République Française*, 5 May 2006.

13. Article R. 1-2-6 du Décret N° 2006-507 du 3 mai 2006 relatif à la régulation des activités postales (see n. 5, above).
14. Article L3-1 of Law N° 2005-516 of May 2005 on regulation of postal activities (see n. 2, above).
15. La Poste has a single license for all of its activities outside the reserved area (domestic and international), so the total number of licensees is indeed 20.
16. The official release is in SPIR, *Résultats annuels 2007*, 20 February 2008, which states in part that the deployment of the Adrexo addressed delivery network would be stopped because of the '*report de la libéralisation totale au 1er janvier 2011, des incertitudes qui subsistent et des déconvenues subies en Europe par des groupes privés sur le marché de la distribution adressée*'.
17. For additional details on mail preparation tariffs in France and elsewhere, see Crew and Kleindorfer (Ch. 3, this volume).
18. More than 700 companies are listed in the census conducted by INSEE (the French agency responsible for registering corporate entities), but Selced, the trade association of companies in logistics and direct mail, claims that only 200 companies are active in the mail preparation sector in France.
19. Profitability is defined as EBITA (earnings before interest taxes and amortization) as a percentage of sales.
20. Productivity here means labor productivity, defined as the ratio of value-added to total labor costs.
21. Investment level is defined as the ratio of current depreciation to value added.
22. The VIGIK system is an electronic identification system developed by La Poste to control access to multi-unit buildings. A more detailed description of it is given below. See also http://www.vigik.com/.

REFERENCES

Basic (2007), 'Etude relative à l'activité de routage en France' (Study concerning mail preparation activity in France), ARCEP, Paris.

Herisson, Pierre (2007), Rapport n° 193 (2006–2007) fait au nom de la Commission des Affaires Économiques sur sa proposition de résolution présentée en application de l'article 73bis du Règlement sur la proposition de directive du Parlement Européen et du Conseil modifiant la directive 97/67/CE en ce qui concerne l'achèvement du marché intérieur des services postaux de la Communauté, déposé le 31 janvier 2007 au Sénat, Paris.

Toledano, Joëlle (2004), 'La Suède, laboratoire de la regulation postale' in J. Toledano (ed.), *Economie postale, Les Fondements*, Paris: Economica, pp. 235–62.

19. United Kingdom postal services regulation

Richard Eccles[†]

1. INTRODUCTION

In the United Kingdom (UK), postal services markets were fully liberalized with effect from 1 January 2006 under the Postal Services Act 2000. This is subject to a requirement on all postal operators to hold a license granted by the Postal Services Commission ('Postcomm'). Licenses are required for all operators transporting letter mail items weighing less than 350 grams for a price of less than £1.[1] These thresholds reflect the original reservable area thresholds under the EC Directive 97/67 on the internal market for postal services (the 'Postal Directive'). Postcomm's policy is to grant licenses to all operators subject only to compliance with certain essential requirements. A more relaxed legal regime applies for the grant of licenses outside the reduced reservable area under the second EU Postal Services Directive, Directive 2002/39/EC (50 grams or 2.5 times the fastest standard tariff, 65 pence in the UK). The universal services provider, Royal Mail, is also required to hold a license and indeed Royal Mail's license is the principal measure by which Royal Mail is regulated. Postcomm has granted 19 long-term licenses to other postal operators.[2]

The primary statutory objective of the regulator, Postcomm, under the Postal Services Act 2000, is to ensure the provision of the universal service.[3] Moreover, the universal service must be provided at affordable prices and at a geographically uniform tariff throughout the UK.[4] The promotion of effective competition between postal operators is an additional, but secondary objective of Postcomm,[5] being expressly subject to the primary duty of ensuring the provision of the universal postal service. Further, the objective of promoting effective competition is itself subordinated to furthering the interests of postal service users.[6]

The Postal Services Act 2000, as amended by the Postal Services (EC Directive) Regulations 2002 (SI 2002 No. 3050), provides for an exemption from the basic requirement to hold a license to provide postal services for any postal service which is both outside the scope of the universal postal service in the UK and not substantially similar to such service (sections 7(1A) and 7A(1)).[7]

Where licenses are requested for the provision of a postal service, in respect of mail items weighing less than 50 grams and which are conveyed for a price per item of less than 65 pence, and which no person other than the universal service provider (Royal Mail) is authorized to provide, Postcomm will grant such license only if the grant of a license and the grant of other similar licenses of this nature will not endanger the ability of Royal Mail as the universal service provider to provide basic postal services, and also on the

† Bird & Bird, London.

basis that the license must contain provisions to safeguard the universal service and ensure compliance with specified essential requirements (regarding confidentiality, security, privacy and environmental and regional planning issues) (section 12B(2), (5) and (6)). Where a license is requested for the provision of a postal service in respect of mail items which are within the 50 grams and 65 pence thresholds and which another person other than the universal service provider is already authorized to provide, and also where a license is requested for a postal service in respect of mail items which equal to or exceed such weight or price thresholds, Postcomm will grant a license subject to such provisions being included in the license to safeguard provision of the universal service and to fulfill such essential requirements (section 12B(3), (4) and (5)).

Despite the legal liberalization, less than 1 percent of end-to-end deliveries of addressed mail volumes are handled by other, new entrant postal operators, as opposed to Royal Mail.[8] Further, the volume of mail delivered end-to-end by competitors to Royal Mail was down 10 percent in 2006/07 compared with the previous year. By contrast, significant levels of competition have taken effect upstream by means of downstream access to Royal Mail's postal network, whereby mail is collected and sorted by a competing operator and fed into Royal Mail's network for final delivery. These downstream access volumes are increasing rapidly; Royal Mail made 2.4 billion access deliveries in 2006/07 compared to 1.2 billion in the previous year, and the volume of access mail delivered by Royal Mail has increased from 12 percent of its total operational volume in 2006/07 to 20 percent in the nine months from April to December 2007.[9] The overall size of the letters mail market increased over a period of several years until 2006/07, when it fell by 2 percent.

This chapter is structured as follows. Section 2 mentions the various types of activities that constitute criminal offences in relation to postal services under the Postal Services Act. Section 3 explains the main competition regulatory obligations on, respectively, new licensed operators and the universal service provider, that is, Royal Mail (including the scope of the universal service obligation), and reviews the leading regulatory decisions of Postcomm in respect of Royal Mail. Section 4 explains the retail price controls on Royal Mail and Postcomm's rejection of Royal Mail's proposed introduction of retail zonal pricing. Section 5 explains the license regime governing Royal Mail's provision of downstream access to its postal network and the standard and zonal agreements offered by Royal Mail for such access. Section 6 draws some conclusions regarding the need to bring forward the implementation into UK law of the 2008 EU Postal Directive (Directive 2008/6/EC) to counterbalance the effects of full liberalization (UK postal markets having been fully liberalized since 2006), the need to bring the pricing controls on Royal Mail in line with the EU Postal Service Directive (Directive 97/67/EC as amended), and the case for relying on competition law rather than *ex ante* regulatory controls in a fully liberalized postal services market.

2. OFFENCES IN CONNECTION WITH POSTAL SERVICES

The Postal Services Act creates various offences in connection with postal services, updating and superseding previous legislation.[10] These offences, which the Act also gives Postcomm the power to investigate, are the conveyance of letters without a license (section

6(2)); interference with mail by postal operators (section 83); interference with mail generally (section 84); sending prohibited items by post (section 85); affixing advertisements on certain letterboxes (section 86); certain misleading statements (in particular in relation to letterboxes) (section 87); and obstruction of business of the universal service provider (section 88). The Act gives Postcomm the power to investigate these offences and in this connection to request information and to exercise powers of enforcement of search and seizure.[11]

3. REGULATORY OBLIGATIONS

3.1 New Licensed Operators

The standard license granted by Postcomm to operators other than Royal Mail is for a 10-year period, whereby 10-years notice of termination can be given as from 25 March 2016. Under such standard licenses, the licensee is required to provide information about its performance in reaching its contract targets (and about any complaints it has received) in each financial year. The licensee is required to furnish Postcomm with such information as Postcomm may require for the purpose of the performance of Postcomm's statutory functions. A license fee is payable where the licensee's turnover from licensed postal services (excluding access payments to Royal Mail or any other licensed postal operator) exceeds £10 million.

In addition, all licensed postal operators are required by their license to comply with a mail integrity code and a common operational procedures code. The mail integrity code contains rules on security of the mail handled and on procedures for minimizing exposure of mail to the risk of loss, theft, damage or interference, together with other provisions on staff recruitment, training and disciplinary procedures. The common operational procedures code is designed to manage inter-operator issues in a multi-operator environment. These procedures ensure shared responsibility for dealing with re-posted mail (forwarded mail and mail marked 'gone away' or 'return to sender'), misposted mail (mail put in the wrong collection box or bag) and miscollected mail, so as to deal with the fact that most misdirected mail will need to be extracted from Royal Mail's system to be transferred to the intended licensed operator to be returned to the sender. For this purpose, the code also contains provisions requiring the use of mail identification codes to enable operators to identify mail intended for another operator and to reroute it accordingly.

3.2 The Universal Service Provider – Royal Mail

Royal Mail is required to provide the universal service at affordable and uniform (standardized) prices. This is subject to a right to agree prices with individual customers provided it does not unduly discriminate between them.[12] In addition to being required to provide the universal service at a geographically uniform tariff, Royal Mail is required by its license not to reduce the nature or scope of its regulated services without Postcomm's consent. These are onerous obligations and it is therefore of great importance to determine which services are or are not within the scope of the universal service obligation.

The universal postal service was not properly defined in the Act. It is defined by the Act only in a negative manner, in that certain characteristics are to be disregarded concerning the question of whether the service is dissimilar to the universal postal service, in particular the following: the service in question not complying with the statutory definition of the universal service; providing a service to only certain persons within a class of persons or, as regards three-day delivery services, collection at a specified place, delivery at a specified time, recorded delivery or special postage payment arrangements.

The scope of Royal Mail's universal service obligation was particularized for the first time in Royal Mail's modified license as from March 2006, following on from decisions adopted by Postcomm in June 2004 on the universal postal service and in June 2005 on the universal service for bulk mailers. Royal Mail's license obligation to provide the universal service covers the following:

1. priority and non-priority mail services (first and second class postal services) for letters and packets;
2. the bulk-mail element of the universal service through Mailsort 1400 and Cleanmail, first and second class in each case (Mailsort 1400 covers mail of all formats up to 2 kilograms in weight and pre-sorted according to the location of Royal Mail's 1400 delivery offices, while Cleanmail is an 'entry level' bulk-mail product typically used by smaller businesses which does not require the use of sorting machines);
3. a non-priority parcel service for parcels;
4. a secure service (that is for registered and insured items); and
5. international outbound airmail and surface mail.

Postcomm's decision expressly excluded from the universal service Royal Mail's economy mail service ('Mailsort 3'), a worksharing scheme involving three-day delivery, and also Royal Mail's specialized newspaper service ('Presstream'). Postcomm also expects Royal Mail to make clear in its published information on the services it provides, which services are provided on the universal service basis and which are not.

As a result of Postcomm's 2004 and 2005 decisions on the universal service and the 2006 modification of Royal Mail's license, Royal Mail's bulk-mail products other than Mailsort 1400 and Cleanmail and also Royal Mail's specialized newspaper delivery service, Presstream, are outside the scope of the universal service. Further, the provision of downstream access is outside the scope of the universal service as regards the provision of access to other postal operators (as opposed to access to direct access bulk-mail customers). However, Postcomm's June 2005 decision indicates that the bulk-mail products which are not expressly universal service products, and also downstream access products, fall within the scope of the universal service even though they do not form part of the universal service.

The scope of service required in the provision of the universal postal service is stipulated in section 4 of the Postal Services Act.[13] This requires that at least one delivery of letters and parcels (collectively, 'postal packets') must be made every working day to the home or premises of every individual or other person in the United Kingdom, and at least one collection of postal packets must be made every working day from each access point (that is, post boxes or other facilities provided by Royal Mail for the receipt of letters or postal packets into its network). Postcomm can allow derogations in respect of exceptional geographical conditions or other circumstances but has not done so.[14] Further, such postal services (including the incidental services of receiving, collecting, sorting and delivering postal packets) must be provided at affordable prices and in accordance with a uniform tariff throughout the UK, and a registered post service must also be provided at such prices.[15] However, these provisions are without prejudice to the rights of the universal service provider to include individual agreements with customers as to prices.[16] Royal Mail is required by its license to achieve quality of service standards for various groupings of universal service products, namely retail first class, retail second class, bulk first class, bulk second class, bulk third class, standard parcels, European international delivery, and Special Delivery (next day).[17] The license conditions require Royal Mail to achieve specified performance rates for the target delivery dates. The user is entitled to automatic compensation if Royal Mail's performance falls short by more than a specified margin, and Postcomm can commence an investigation if the performance falls short of the required standard by a further margin. Letters should be properly delivered by the end of the first, third, or seventh working day for first class, second class, and international or third class services respectively, in each case after the day of collection or receipt by Royal Mail.

When Royal Mail fails to meet the required performance standards, compensation schemes apply to determine the amount of automatic compensation to which users are eligible on proof of delayed delivery. These schemes are adopted under the Postal Services Act 2000 and include principally Royal Mail's Retail Scheme and Bulk Mail Scheme.

Royal Mail's license includes the following competition-related obligations on Royal Mail:

1. to negotiate access to its network at prices based on a reasonable allocation of costs and without unduly discriminating between users,[18] or on the basis of an access code to be agreed with Postcomm;[19]
2. avoidance of any unfair commercial advantage in favor of any Royal Mail business or any other party in connection with the grant of network access;[20]
3. to grant no more favourable terms to Royal Mail's own business or related persons for access to its postal facilities than those on which the facilities are made available to other persons;[21]
4. not to disclose any information obtained through provision of network access to any other business of Royal Mail Group;[22]
5. avoidance of undue discrimination or undue preference between persons or classes of persons;[23]
6. avoidance of excessive or predatory pricing;[24]
7. transparency of pricing of postal services by means of the submission to Postcomm and Postwatch (the Consumer Council for Postal Services) of details of the tariffs, including discounts and credit facilities, for the provision of postal services;[25]
8. to provide Postcomm with copies of merger control notifications and informal submissions made to the European Commission or the Office of Fair Trading;[26]
9. employment of a competition compliance officer to facilitate compliance with the competition regulatory obligations under the license;[27]
10. accounting separation as regards individual types of licensed services, other universal postal services and individual types of postal services outside the universal service, and non-postal services, respectively;[28] and

11. not to reduce the scope of its regulated services or to offer less favourable terms to users (as compared with the position in March 2006) without Postcomm's approval.[29]

The price controls on Royal Mail are reviewed later in this chapter.[30]

Royal Mail is also subject to quality of performance obligations imposed pursuant to its license. These quality obligations are reinforced by compensation schemes for business users, involving 1 percent reduction in postal charges for each 1 percent that Royal Mail falls below the national target (up to 5 percent) and a retail compensation scheme to compensate customers for domestic first class mail not delivered within three days. In addition, Postcomm can impose a financial penalty on Royal Mail if it considers that Royal Mail has not used all reasonable endeavors to achieve the service targets. For this purpose Postcomm would take into account the representations by Postwatch, the postal services consumer protection body.

The requirements on Royal Mail not to engage in predatory pricing or to impose any terms or conditions which are unduly preferential or discriminatory for or against any person or class of persons, parallel the corresponding requirements under the rules against abuse of dominant position under EC and UK competition law (Article 82 of the EC Treaty and Chapter 2 of the Competition Act 1998, respectively). Taking account of this, Condition 11(3) and (4) of Royal Mail's license require that questions as to whether or not any conduct of Royal Mail may infringe Condition 11(2) of its license shall be interpreted and determined consistently with the treatment of corresponding questions arising under EC and UK competition law as to whether or not the relevant type of conduct would be regarded as an abuse of dominant position.

The license obligations on Royal Mail not to show any undue discrimination or preference for or against any person or categories of persons have to some extent been clarified by means of an investigation carried out by Postcomm in late 2004 and concluded by means of a decision of 20 January 2005 adopting certain commitments of Royal Mail: Investigation into Royal Mail Catalogue and Advertising Mail Promotion Scheme.[31] The investigation concerned a trial promotion undertaken by Royal Mail with 12 catalogue mailing customers during July and August 2003, with the aim of verifying whether it was feasible to launch a wider catalogue and advertising market promotion to grow the overall catalogue mailing market. This raises the issue of whether the granting of discounts to customers by reference to their incremental mailings as opposed to the absolute volume of their mailings, can constitute undue preference or discrimination, in so far as it could result in different prices (after discount) being applied to customers mailing equal volumes. Postcomm questioned whether such a policy could ever be implemented by a company with the dominance of Royal Mail in a way that is acceptable in practice, but did not reach any conclusion, stating rather that it would be disproportionate to prohibit Royal Mail from seeking to introduce schemes intended to develop incremental mailing. In the present case, Postcomm considered that the evidence indicated that growing the postal market was not the only aim of the promotions and that Royal Mail had not taken adequate safeguards to ensure that in practice account handlers applied the available discounts only to incremental mailings, as opposed to using the discounts to grant incentives to customers to switch mailings from a competitor of Royal Mail.

In order to close the case, Royal Mail provided assurances to the effect that any new promotions launched by Royal Mail would first be subject to a promotion approval process involving regulatory and competition law approval at a senior level and that Royal Mail would proactively involve its Compliance Officer in this process. The Compliance Officer is required to be appointed under Condition 13 of Royal Mail's license for purposes of facilitating compliance by Royal Mail with the competition regulatory provisions of the license.

Some further indication of Postcomm's approach to the interpretation of the non-discrimination requirement in Condition 11 of Royal Mail's license was given in its case closure decision on Business Mail Secure,[32] concerning a discount scheme offered by Royal Mail on its Business Mail Secure (BMS) service. Postcomm concluded that there was insufficient evidence on costs and customer behavior for any conclusion as to whether BMS might be unduly discriminatory or unduly restrictive against any class of customer and concluded that there was no evidence to suggest that BMS was predatory. However, Postcomm considered that there was nonetheless the possibility of undue restriction and/or discrimination resulting from the structure of BMS discounts and the terms and conditions of the service. Postcomm considered that a customer could commit to a high-volume mailing to qualify for the maximum BMS discount, but then subsequently post a lower volume (which would not qualify for the maximum discount). Postcomm also considered that a customer might pay different prices for equivalent mailings where equivalent costs have been incurred. As a result, Postcomm recommended that it would be fairer for BMS discounts to be offered on a per-mailing basis, rather than on an annual basis, subject to a customer posting a minimum of 200,000 items per year. Postcomm also recommended that Royal Mail should monitor the number of letters conveyed for each customer, on a monthly or quarterly basis, in order to enable Royal Mail to take remedial action if it appeared that volume forecasts were not being met for particular customers.

4. RETAIL PRICE CONTROLS ON THE UNIVERSAL SERVICE PROVIDER

The current price controls under Royal Mail's license apply during the 2006–10 period, after which the current controls could be renewed or new price controls could be introduced reflecting a further pricing review to be carried out by Postcomm.

The previous price controls which applied from 1 April 2003 to 31 March 2006 involved inflation-based price controls by means of a 'tariff basket' approach that allowed an overall price increase equal to the increase in the retail price index (RPI) less 1 percent, provided that Royal Mail was allowed to re-balance tariffs by raising the price on any individual product in any one year by up to 2.5 percent more than this overall allowable price change.

The current price control provision, Condition 21 of Royal Mail's license, contains complex formulae for Royal Mail's retail pricing comprising a variety of specified factors. It is important to note that the pricing provisions contain no reference to the prices being *geared* or *oriented* to costs as required by the relevant provision of the EU Postal Services Directive 97/67 and the further amending Directive 2008/6/EC, respectively.

As has already been mentioned, Royal Mail is required to apply affordable prices and a uniform tariff in setting its prices for postal services within the scope of the universal service obligation. These obligations are contained in both section 4(1)(b) of the Postal Services Act 2000 and Conditions 2(3) and 21(17) of Royal Mail's license.

Royal Mail's license contains further provisions limiting the extent to which Royal Mail can change the criteria for setting its prices, including the following: first, the proposed pricing structure following a price adjustment must be more cost-reflective than the existing pricing structure; second, the change must not be introduced in such a way as to lead to unreasonable changes for postal users; and third, the change must be revenue neutral.[33]

The price control provisions of Royal Mail's license apply to all regulated services, not just to services within the scope of the universal service obligation, and therefore cover a wider range of services than the universal postal service; for example, the price controls are applied to bulk-mail services which are outside the scope of the universal service, as well as those bulk-mail services which are within the universal service.

As regards bulk-mail services which are outside the universal service obligation, Royal Mail has applied for, but Postcomm has declined, approval for retail zonal pricing.[34] The introduction of such zonal pricing, that is, geographically de-averaged prices, would take into account the differential costs of delivery of bulk-mail items to different parts of the country. Postcomm stated in its decision that it is not opposed to the principle of non-geographically uniform tariffs, but rejected this specific form of retail zonal pricing proposed by Royal Mail, on the grounds that it would involve unreasonable changes to users contrary to Condition 21(19)(c) of Royal Mail's license and would involve discriminatory pricing contrary to Condition 11(2) of the license. Postcomm's reasons can be summarized by reference to the criteria of unreasonable changes to users, and price discrimination, respectively.

On the criterion of unreasonable changes to users, Postcomm decided as follows. First, Royal Mail was considered not to have attempted to share with its customers the burden of the non-price changes required to implement what would be a complex pricing structure and to have failed to consider an adequate mitigation scheme for the most-affected users. Second, Royal Mail had not yet made available sufficiently approved information on its prices to customers so that they can take account of the substantial complexity of the proposed retail zonal prices, as compared with the existing uniform pricing structure, which Postcomm believed resulted in a lack of transparency. Third, Postcomm considered that the proposed manner of introducing retail zonal pricing would impose unreasonable additional costs on users, which it considered would mainly be for the benefit of Royal Mail in the application of its revenue protection procedures. Fourth, since Royal Mail already operates a zonal pricing system for network access prices, Postcomm considered that the introduction of a different zonal pricing structure for retail products would cause distortions to competition which would also involve unreasonable changes to users.

On the issue of price discrimination, Postcomm decided the following. First, Postcomm considered that the introduction of the proposed five-zone retailing pricing structure was not adequately supported by Royal Mail's underlying cost data and would therefore be likely to be discriminatory. Second, Postcomm considered that the proposal would seriously distort the margins available between Royal Mail's access and retail prices. Postcomm considered that in the existing situation in which competitors generally competed with Royal Mail's uniform retail price by using its standard uniform access price, the introduction of retail zonal pricing would distort competition, while competition would also be distorted if Royal Mail were to set zonal retail prices on a different basis from the zonal access prices which it also offers.

On the latter point, Postcomm considered that having two inconsistent zonal pricing structures, one for retail and one for access services, would distort competition by artificially boosting upstream competition in some parts of the market and foreclosing upstream competition in other areas. However, as noted in Postcomm's decision, Royal Mail's license specifically includes provisions for it to introduce zonal pricing for price-controlled products outside the universal service, with Postcomm's approval.[35] Since Postcomm expressed itself to be generally supportive of pricing structures that are more reflective of costs, the possibility is left open for Royal Mail to introduce a suitable retail zonal pricing application which is consistent in competition terms with the zonal prices which it offers for network access.

Royal Mail is required by its license to take steps to ensure transparency of its prices. Royal Mail is required by Condition 7 of its license, not to offer discounts to customers without submitting to Postcomm and Postwatch details of the tariffs including discounts and credit facilities under which it offers to provide the relevant postal services. In November 2003, Postcomm served a provisional enforcement order on Royal Mail for breaching this condition in respect of offers to provide postal services for catalogue mailings at a discount, which offers had not been notified to Postcomm.[36] Royal Mail provided an undertaking in lieu of confirmation of the provisional order, confirming that it would in future provide the required tariff and discount details to Postcomm and Postwatch prior to offering such tariffs or discounts to users and that it would publish the terms of such new tariffs on its website.[37] Royal Mail further undertook not to offer any contractual arrangements for the conveyance of letters or postal packets other than on such tariffs (including discounts and credit facilities) which have been so notified and published.

5. ACCESS TO ROYAL MAIL'S POSTAL NETWORK

Royal Mail provides downstream access services in respect of its mail conveyance and delivery network, whereby mail consolidators and competing postal operators, and also some direct access bulk-mail customers, enter their mail into Royal Mail's postal network downstream. The entry point is typically at a delivery office or sorting office for downstream conveyance and delivery by Royal Mail. Royal Mail is required by its license (Condition 9) to provide such access services. It must either adopt a code for the grant of access to other postal operators to its network or negotiate the grant of access with other operators with a view to agreeing terms for such access. Such terms must be on prices that are based on a reasonable allocation of costs and must not unduly discriminate between persons having access to Royal Mail's postal facilities. In the event that negotiations fail to lead to agreement, either of the parties can appeal to Postcomm to issue a direction to Royal Mail concerning the terms of access.

The license also imposes price controls on Royal Mail for the grant of access. The Postal Services Act is silent on the cost–price relationship for access prices to Royal Mail's postal facilities. Such access price controls are left to Postcomm to implement by means of the conditions of Royal Mail's license. Such specific price controls are contained in Condition 21(5) of the license, and stipulate that prices for access services (as defined in the license) be set by reference to a margin between the corresponding retail and access services, known as the 'headroom margin'. The primary objective of Postcomm's policy in controlling Royal Mail's access prices is to avoid a 'margin squeeze' between Royal Mail's access prices and the corresponding retail prices. The drafting of the license and, in particular, the formula for calculating the headroom margin is based on maintaining a price differential as between the prices for the relevant retail and access services that existed on 31 March 2006, the date immediately before the current license conditions took effect following Postcomm's 2006 price control review. It is notable that this 'headroom margin' approach to price control has no reference to the costs of service provision and therefore appears to be out of line with the EU law requirement under the EU Postal Services Directive 97/67 (as amended).[38]

Royal Mail offers a National Condition 9 Access Agreement setting out detailed standard terms on which an access user can enter mail into Royal Mail's mailstream. The mail handed over by the access user must comply with the national geographic posting profile requirements, whereby each posting made by the access user must include items for delivery to 31 postcode areas defined as 'mandatory' and must also hand over mailing items for delivery to a minimum of 60 postcode areas (subject to a tolerance of 15 percent). Based on this defined geographic profile of the mail handed over, the prices charged for access are geographically uniform, that is, the access user pays the same price for each mail item handed over, regardless of its destination within the UK.

The Condition 9 Access Agreement contains detailed requirements for the mail in respect of which access is to be granted. The access user must hand over mail items of a minimum volume or value on a daily, weekly or monthly basis and must hand over the mail items during a specified 'access slot', a defined 30-minute period on a working day, at a specified inward mail center. The mail must be pre-sorted and marked with a return address and an indicium as specified in the Access Agreement. The mail can be sorted to either inward mail center or delivery office selections, subject to differences in the respective downstream access prices. The access customer is also required to observe specified forecasting requirements. The access customer must pre-sort and present the mail in accordance with the Access Agreement and according to one of the relevant Royal Mail access services.[39] All such services are for delivery on the working day following the date on which the access customer hands over the mail to Royal Mail.[40]

The National Condition 9 Access Agreement is based on the original downstream access agreement which was negotiated by Royal Mail in late 2003 with UK Mail, which served as a precedent for subsequent access agreements. This agreement was reached voluntarily, though against the background of a notice that had been issued by Postcomm at an earlier stage, of a proposed direction on downstream access by UK Mail to Royal Mail's postal facilities (in May 2003) in the event of failure of either party to agree terms. The conclusion of the access agreement avoided the need for a confirmed direction from Postcomm. A key feature of the agreement with UK Mail and of the subsequent National Condition 9 Access Agreement is that the access customer benefits from geographically averaged access prices, but only on condition that it gives Royal Mail a typical national 'fall-to-earth' of mail to deliver, in other words an average price for an average mail profile. A corollary of this approach would seem to be that if an access customer required Royal Mail to deliver mail in only expensive-to-deliver areas, then it would have to pay more than the basic access price per mail item specified in the Access Agreement. At the time the original Access Agreement was negotiated, Postcomm acknowledged the possibility of a different price or price structure being introduced in respect of mail being deposited by Royal Mail by access users whose requirements were irregular or infrequent and which therefore gave rise to different processing costs to Royal Mail.

As a result, Royal Mail also offers, as an alternative to the National Condition 9 Access Agreement, Zonal Access Agreements. Such Zonal Access Agreements provide variable access prices by reference to five price zones into which each of the 10,500 postcode sectors in the UK are allocated, based on criteria of delivery point density and delivered volume. Each posting is priced on the basis of the number of items for delivery in each zone. Such agreements allow for geographically variable prices by reference to the geographical profile of the specific posting. Access users under Zonal Access Agreements have to meet additional presentation requirements so as to identify the zone to which each mail item is to be delivered.[41]

Both National and Zonal Access Agreements are also offered by Royal Mail in a further variation, the Access Agency Agreement, whereby a licensed postal operator seeks access, as agent for the customer sending the relevant mail items. An advantage of this is that the postal operator seeking access avoids a charge of value-added tax (VAT) on the downstream element of the postal service provided by Royal Mail because the downstream postal service is charged by Royal Mail to the licensed operator's sending customer, through the agency of the operator. This means that the licensed operator is only required to charge VAT on the upstream service that it provides to its customers. Royal Mail is exempt from charging VAT on its postal services, as the incumbent universal service provider. The Access Agency Agreement assists licensed operators in achieving, as far as possible, equal VAT treatment to Royal Mail.[42]

The introduction by Royal Mail of its first geographically de-averaged or 'zonal' prices for network access gave rise to complaints by three other postal operators[43] which resulted in a Postcomm investigation and eventual decision to the effect that Royal Mail was in contravention of Condition 10(2) of its license. This condition requires it to act in a manner best calculated to ensure that it does not obtain an unfair commercial advantage in connection with the provision of access to its postal facilities.[44] This decision by Postcomm was based on its findings of structural shortcomings in Royal Mail's operations, rather than in the substantive features of the zonal price offer. These shortcomings found by Postcomm centered on the lack of any physical separation, at the relevant time, of Royal Mail's Retail and Wholesale teams or of any separation of data systems, accounts, and security systems, and also a lack of separation of Royal Mail's Wholesale team from its Regulatory Affairs department. The Wholesale team was based within the Regulatory Affairs department of Royal Mail until December 2005. This blurring of functions was combined with the absence of a clear, contemporaneous written policy to ensure avoidance of unfair commercial advantage to Royal Mail in connection with the provision of downstream access and the absence of an effective staff transfer policy to prevent staff from transferring at short notice between the Retail and Wholesale teams. Further, Royal Mail was found to have failed to have developed any clear policy to deal with possible misuse of confidential information obtained as a result of giving downstream access to its postal facilities in connection with such staff transfer. Postcomm also considered that Royal Mail had been in contravention of Condition 13(1) of its license as a result of its failure to ensure that its Compliance Officer reviewed its procedures for compliance with Condition 10.

Postcomm originally imposed a fine of £2.16 million on Royal Mail, but although this was reduced to £1 million as a result of Royal Mail's representations,[45] this penalty was cancelled by the High Court as a result of an appeal by Royal Mail.[46] Royal Mail successfully argued that Postcomm's application of the penalty was unlawful because Postcomm had failed to follow its published policy on financial penalties when the fine was set and had not given reasons for departing from that policy. Postcomm was required to publish a policy statement concerning the imposition of penalties and the determination of their amount under section 31(1) of the Postal Services Act. In the context of the present case, Postcomm found that its policy on financial penalties was too difficult to apply in a rational and consistent manner and therefore abandoned the starting-point element of the policy. Instead it took a different approach to setting the penalty, of what was 'necessary and proportionate to publicly mark the breach and deter other contraventions'. The Court held that there had to be very good reason for a public authority to fail to follow its published policy. A discovery that a published policy failed to achieve what had been intended was not in itself sufficient reason to justify departing from the policy. Accordingly the penalty on Royal Mail was quashed.

6. CONCLUSIONS

At the time of writing, competition regulation of postal services in the UK, and of Royal Mail in particular, is at a critical phase. Competition has developed rapidly by means of downstream access even though (as at the start of 2008) less than 1 percent of end-to-end postal service deliveries are provided by Royal Mail. Postcomm is carrying out two important reviews of postal services at present: it is conducting its Strategic Review, 'The Postal Market 2010 and Beyond' which was launched in May 2006 and on which it published its 'Emerging Themes' paper in August 2007; and it is also currently carrying out a consultation in respect of access services in relation to Royal Mail's postal network.[47] In addition, in December 2007 a panel of three prominent citizens was convened by government to carry out an independent review of the UK postal services market and to report to the government.

Postal services have been fully liberalized in the UK since 1 January 2006, well ahead of the required time scale under the amended EU Postal Services Directive 97/67. Under the 2008 amendment to the Postal Directive (Directive 2008/6/EC), member states are not required to liberalize their postal sectors fully until 1 January 2011 (and for some member states, 1 January 2013). The 2008 Directive contains a number of provisions designed to counterbalance the effects of full liberalization on the position of the incumbent universal service provider and to safeguard the provision of the universal service under economically stable conditions. Since full liberalization already exists in the UK postal sector, there is a strong case for bringing forward the implementation into UK law of the provisions in the 2008 Directive as soon as possible.

Royal Mail can claim to be over-regulated under its present license, in that too many operational decisions require regulatory approval of, or at least, pre-notification to or consultation with, Postcomm. These obligations affect the competitive position of Royal Mail by constraining its ability to take and implement operational decisions under normal commercial conditions, given that such requirements do not apply to other licensed postal services providers.

As a minimum, it may be appropriate to limit the scope of the uniform tariff obligation on Royal Mail so as to apply basically to single-piece mail items only, in accordance with the 2008 Directive. This would achieve consistency with the provisions of the Directive. Moreover, by reference to the provisions of Royal Mail's license on pricing, further provision could be made to bring the regulatory controls on the universal service provider, Royal Mail, more in line with the Directive. First, the basis of price controls on its retail services should be revised so as to clearly provide for coverage of the fully allocated costs of service provision in accordance with Articles 12 and 14 of the Postal Directive.

With regard to the setting of tariffs for the provision of access (downstream) to Royal Mail's postal services network, the EU Postal Directive already establishes that the central regulatory requirement for universal service providers is to treat consolidators or competitors in the same way as direct customers of the universal service provider in granting access. By contrast, the combined retail and access price controls that currently apply in the UK, through the headroom margin in Royal Mail's license Condition 21(5), along with a uniform tariff obligation, limit Royal Mail's flexibility in taking steps to protect its position by adjusting its prices in the face of competition. The headroom margin requirement under Royal Mail's license is based on the policy objective of avoiding a 'margin squeeze' by Royal Mail. However, margin squeezes are in all other sectors subject to competition law rather than a sector-specific regulatory requirement.

In any event, in a fully liberalized postal services market, there is a strong case for relying increasingly upon competition law rather than specific *ex ante* regulatory controls on the incumbent. It remains to be seen what the outcome of Postcomm's current Strategy Review and Access Review will be and to what extent the current license controls on Royal Mail will be liberalized as from the implementation of Postcomm's next Royal Mail price review in 2010.

NOTES

1. That is, a license from Postcomm is not required if the postal items transported by a delivery company meet either one of two criteria: either the postal items weigh 350 grams or more or the postal items are conveyed for a charge equal to or exceeding £1.
2. As of 31 March 2008.
3. Section 3.
4. Section 4(1) (b).
5. Section 5.
6. Section 5(1) states: Subject to section 3 [Postcomm] shall exercise its functions in the manner which it considers is best calculated to further the interests of users of postal services, where appropriate by promoting effective competition between postal operators.
7. Under a separate Regulation (SI 2002 No. 200), the Postal Services Act has been amended so as to remove the requirement for a license in respect of the collection of letters for the provision of outbound international postal services from the UK. Also outbound postal services themselves are, and already were, excluded from the licensing requirement.
8. Postcomm's Strategy Review, 'The Postal Market 2010 and Beyond, Emerging Themes', August 2007, section D XI.
9. See www.psc.gov.uk/about-the-mail-market.html.
10. Post Office Acts of 1953 and 1969.
11. Sections 47–49.
12. Section 4(1) of the Postal Services Act 2000 and Royal Mail's license (Schedule 2, Condition 2).

13. Also Condition 2(4) of Royal Mail's license.
14. Section 4(1) (a).
15. Section 4(1) (b) and (c).
16. Section 4(2) (b).
17. Condition 4(2) (a).
18. Condition 9 Part 1.
19. Condition 9 Part 2.
20. Condition 10(2).
21. Condition 10(5).
22. Condition 10(3).
23. Condition 11(2)(a).
24. Condition 11(2)(b).
25. Condition 7.
26. Condition 12.
27. Condition 13.
28. Condition 15.
29. Condition 21(1) – (4).
30. See Section 4 below.
31. Postcomm Decision dated 20 January 2005.
32. Business Mail Secure, final report of the Postal Services Commission, August 2007.
33. Condition 21(20) and (21).
34. Royal Mail's Retail Zonal Pricing Application for Non-Universal Service Bulk Mail Products, Postcomm's decision January 2008; Determination indicating dissatisfaction with application to introduce zonal pricing, Postcomm, December 2007.
35. Condition 21(18) and (19).
36. Provisional enforcement order by Postcomm under section 23 of the Postal Services Act 2000, 25 November 2003.
37. It may be noted that the requirement that such tariff details be so submitted in advance of their application is an extension of the actual requirement in the license, which does not refer to the time factor.
38. See Ch. 14, this volume.
39. These services are: Access 1400, Access 120 Letter, Access 120 Large Letter A3 Package & Packet, Access 120 Optical Character Recognition, Access 120 Customer Bar Code (CBC), Access 700 CBC and Access Walksort.
40. See Postcomm, Access Review, A Consultation Document, January 2008, Chapter 3.
41. Ibid., paragraph 3.21.
42. Ibid., paragraphs 3.22–3.24.
43. The complainants were UK Mail, TPG and Express Ltd.
44. A Complaint about Royal Mail's Offer of Zonal Downstream Access: Report and Decision of the Postal Services Commission, February 2006.
45. A Complaint about Royal Mail's offer of Zonal Downstream Access: Second Report and Decision of the Postal Services Commission, July 2006, and Final Report and Decision of the Postal Services Commission, September 2006.
46. *Royal Mail Group plc v Postal Services Commission* [2007] EWHC 1205, judgment by the High Court, Queen's Bench Division, 25 May 2007. The appeal by Royal Mail was brought under section 36(1)(b) of the Postal Services Act 2000.
47. Postcomm, Access Review, A Consultation Document, January 2008.

20. The diverse characteristics of postal reforms in Asia: privatization, corporatization and liberalization*

Shoji Maruyama† **and Shinichi Sano**†

1. INTRODUCTION

In the European Union (EU), recent parliamentary approval of the Third Postal Directive (published officially on February 28, 2008) requires the complete elimination of exclusive rights or reserved areas for the designated postal operators in 2011 or 2013 at the latest. Partly in anticipation of the implementation of the new Directive, European postal operators have undertaken significant restructuring initiatives, including in some cases privatization of the public postal operator through initial public offering (IPO). Continued commercialization and corporatization of their activities has been the strategy chosen by postal operators to counter the contraction of ordinary mail volume and the competitive threats posed by entrants. Postal reforms similar to those in the EU, that is, liberalization of the postal market and privatization of the former state-owned postal operator, have also been implemented in Asia, though these have tended to occur under country- rather than region-oriented backgrounds, since there is less political and economic movement toward transnational integration than in Europe. Despite such environmental differences, however, the traditional mission of maintaining the universal service obligation (USO) continues to be imposed on the incumbent operators.

For example, in Japan, the newly established postal operator, Japan Post Service Co., Ltd., created as a result of postal privatization on October 1, 2007, will continue to face virtually the same USO as the former public corporation. Nevertheless, the regulatory authority in Japan recently proposed a new entry-promoting policy including the introduction of an access regime in the correspondence delivery market. This proposal will be evaluated in the light of its impact on the ability of Japan Post Service Co. to preserve the current USO. For similar reasons, in China, where the former China Post Bureau was partly restructured into a public corporation, China Post Group, liberalization discussions concerning new entry have been restricted to the value-added domestic and international express mail business. It is noteworthy that in many countries in Asia where the transformation of the traditional public postal operator has been a major policy objective, market liberalization has been rarely observed. Instead, countries have opted to preserve the USO by relying on funds for the incumbent drawn from the reserved area.

† Japan Post Service Co., Ltd.

In this chapter, we shall provide an overview of postal structural reforms and postal market liberalizations in major Asian countries and territories based on reports published in recent years. The chapter also presents some comparative results based on cross-sectional comparison with postal operators in developed countries in Europe (former EU15), North America (the United States and Canada), and Oceania (Australia and New Zealand). We shall also discuss future prospects for postal reform in Asia in the light of reform initiatives undertaken and their potential impact on preserving universal services and the USO. The organization of this chapter is as follows. Section 2 summarizes the economic trends and characteristics of major Asian countries and then presents a comparative analysis based on economic indicators regarding national postal operators and their postal markets. Section 3 covers the privatization and/or corporatization of major postal operators. Section 4 discusses recent initiatives on market liberalization, focusing on some specific countries in Asia. Section 5 concludes with a discussion of the implications of these developments, including the preservation of the USO in each country.

2. ECONOMIC EXPANSION AND POSTAL MARKETS IN ASIA

2.1 Economic Characteristics of Asia

The Asian economy, which successfully overcame the foreign currency crisis caused by the sharp decline of the Thai baht in the late 1990s, has achieved relatively high economic growth at the beginning of the twenty-first century. Among the major countries in Asia, China and India have been growing at an annual rate of about 10 percent during these years, while also contributing to world economic growth and expansion of trade by absorbing intermediate and consumer goods from Japan, Southeast Asia, and other regions. These flows of international trade were effectively reinforced by China's accession to the World Trade Organization (WTO) in 2001 and India's continuing open economic policy from 1991.

In this chapter, we shall focus on 12 countries and territories in Asia – Japan, China, Hong Kong, Taiwan, South Korea, Singapore, Thailand, Indonesia, Malaysia, the Philippines, Vietnam, and India – to analyze the economies and postal services in the region.[1] A comparison of annual economic growth rates for 1986 and 2006 by country or territory reflect (i) a slowdown of growth rates in Japan, South Korea, and Taiwan, (ii) continuous high growth in China, and (iii) upturns in the growth rates of the Southeast Asian countries (see Figure 20.1).

As a result of high economic growth, the national wealth or nominal GDP per capita in major Asian countries and territories has also improved. As a result, income disparity within this region has diminished during these twenty years with more countries being categorized as high income (see Figure 20.2). While in 1986 only Japan was categorized as a high-income country with more than US$10,000 GDP per capita, in 2006, five countries qualified for this category. The number of low-income countries with less than US$1,000, on the other hand, decreased from six to two within this timeframe.

In Asia, when high economic growth and the improvement of living standards are achieved, active political movement to expand internal trade volume by lowering tariff and non-tariff barriers through free trade agreements (FTAs) is observed.[2] Unlike in

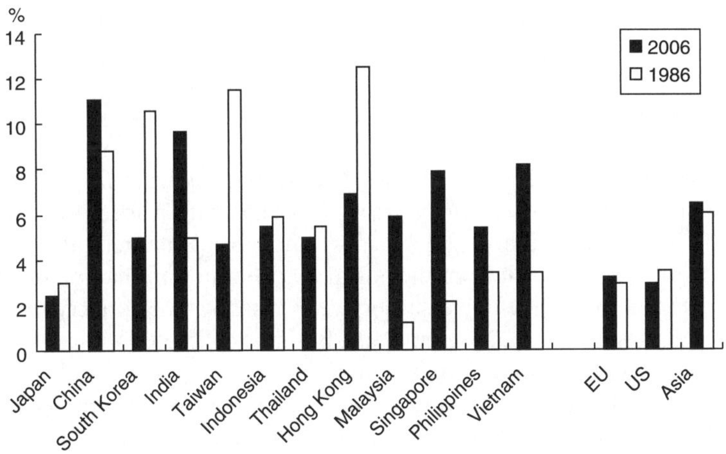

Note: Countries and territories are ordered by the amount of nominal GDP in US dollars.

Source: IMF statistics.

Figure 20.1 Trends of economic growth rates in major Asian countries

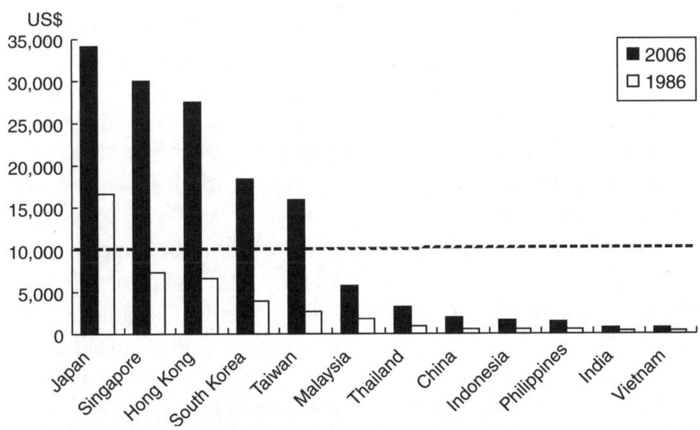

Note: Countries and territories are ordered by the amount of GDP per capita in 2006.

Figure 20.2 Distribution of GDP per capita in major Asian countries

Europe, where since 1952 membership in the EU has expanded to 27 countries from the original six members of the European Coal and Steel Community (ECSC), the political movement toward a regional economic bloc is limited in Asia. Although regional cooperation in Asia has been achieved – in the form not only of the Association of Southeast Asian Nations (ASEAN), but also ASEAN plus three (ASEAN, Japan, China and South Korea) and Asia-Pacific Economic Cooperation, APEC (including the US, Canada, Australia, New Zealand and Russia) – achieving economic and political integration equivalent to the EU is seen as a challenging task due to the still significant differences in national income standards and complicated non-economic factors of a religious, cultural and historical nature (Nakajima, 2006).

2.2 Fundamentals in the Asian Postal Market

There are significant differences among major Asian countries in terms of geographical features such as population and territory areas, as well as with respect to key economic indicators. This implies that the postal business and postal markets also have major differences. Such differences result from the postal service tradition that incumbent postal operators are required to provide universal service throughout the country to which they belong. In this subsection, we shall present some business characteristics and market features of the postal services in major Asian countries.

In the study of developing countries in Latin America by Ansón et al. (2006), postal volume per capita, which decides the postal market structure, was explained by such variables as macroeconomics, communications, geography, and income levels. They showed that the GDP per capita and volume of mail per capita showed statistically insignificant correlations for low-income countries, and positive relations for middle-income countries. Cohen et al. (1997) conducted a comparative analysis targeting major postal operators in North America, Europe, Oceania and Japan using some fundamental macroeconomic and postal information. A model to regress labor productivity – the ratio between postal volumes weighted by business activities and invested workforce – on (i) postal volumes per capita, and (ii) postal wage premiums (that is, the excess of wages above those in the private sector) found that each explanatory variable positively impacted on the level of productivity, and that about 60 percent of labor productivity could be explained by these two variables. These two studies show that postal volume per capita has a significant role in determining the cost structure of postal operators and also that it could be explained by country-specific macroeconomic factors.

Figure 20.3 depicts the relationship between postal volumes per capita and nominal GDP per capita while distinguishing the 12 Asian postal operators from 19 operators in the developed countries in the EU15, the United States, Canada, Australia and New Zealand. Figure 20.4 shows the relationship between postal volumes per postal worker as a proxy for labor productivity and postal volumes per capita. The numerical information in these figures for the year 2005 has been transformed into natural logarithms, and was derived from the Universal Postal Union (UPU) postal statistics and annual reports of postal operators.

Due to the lack of degree of freedom or the number of observations (n = 12) and the significant differences in business coverage among Asian postal markets, it was not possible to obtain relevant results through econometric estimation using the restricted cross-sectional information. The postal characteristics in the 12 Asian markets, therefore, are analyzed by comparison with other markets in the developed countries in Europe, North America and Oceania. According to Figures 20.3 and 20.4, wide variances can be observed among the Asian postal markets compared with those among industrialized countries. The relationship between postal and economic variables in each figure shows that there is a statistically significant positive correlation between both variables (coefficients of correlation of 0.96 in both cases) in Asian markets, and that the coefficients of correlation would be slightly decreased when postal markets in other

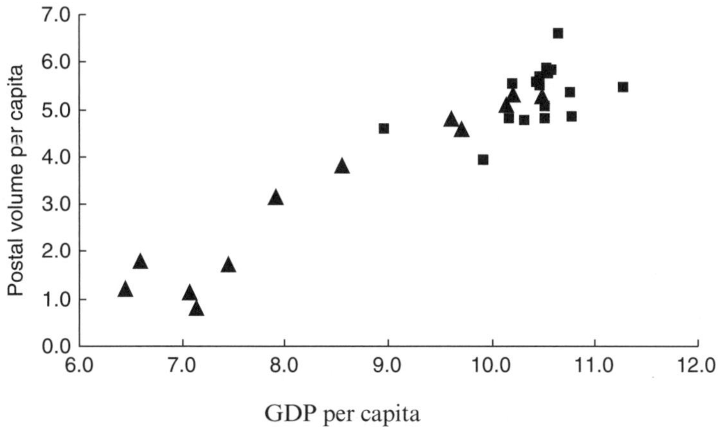

▲:POs in Asia ■:POs in developed countries in EU, North America, Oceania

Figure 20.3 Relationship between volume per capita and GDP per capita

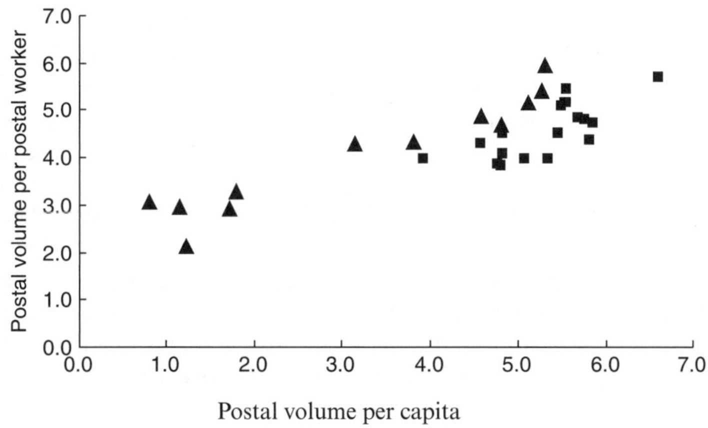

▲:POs in Asia ■:POs in developed countries in EU, North America, Oceania

Figure 20.4 Relationship between volume per worker and volume per capita

developed countries are included, although a positive correlation would still be preserved.

By analyzing postal demand structure in the Asian market, it can be seen how alternative communication methods – notably the electronic exchange of information over the Internet – have affected postal demand in recent years. It is widely understood and observed that new electronic methods using the Internet have substituted for communication by physical mail in developed countries to a significant degree, a trend that has caused the continuous decline of ordinary postal items in spite of economic expansion.[3] In contrast, Ansón et al. (2006) showed that in developing countries, information technologies (ITs) including the Internet could be viewed as supplemental communication

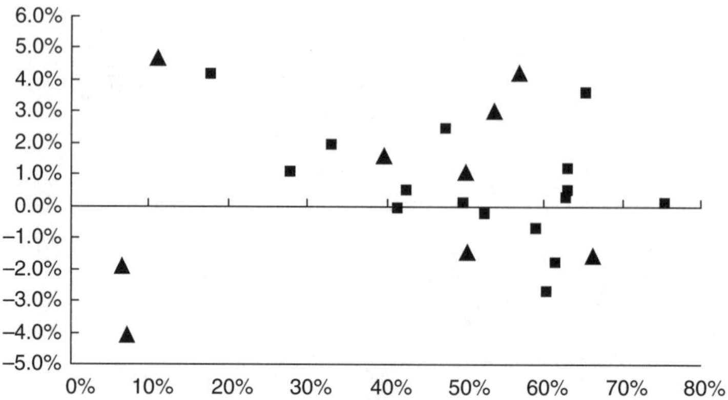

Note: X-axis: Internet coverage, Y-axis: 5-year total change in postal volumes

▲:POs in Asia ■:POs in developed countries in EU, North America, Oceania

Figure 20.5 Relationship between volume change and internet penetration

methods and that substitution between these two forms of communication was not observed statistically. These analyses imply that the postal demand structure differs according to the market environment and macroeconomic conditions.

Figure 20.5 depicts the relationship between the growth rates in the volume of ordinary postal items in the last five years and Internet coverage in 2005 in the postal markets of Asia and other industrialized areas. Only five of nine data points in the Asian market are shown due to lack of data. A slightly negative correlation between the relevant variables could be observed (coefficient of correlation: −0.45), while an indefinite relationship is apparent among Asian postal markets. In Asia, there are countries with widespread Internet use and a high rate of increase in postal volume and countries with comparatively low Internet coverage and a decreasing volume of postal items coexist in the current market conditions. This mixed relationship between mail and the Internet in Asia implies that the postal demand structure in this region cannot simply be explained by electronic substitution and that further analysis regarding national competitive and regulatory environments is required to better understand the characteristics of the market.

2.3 Universal Service Obligation and Postal Reform

According to Article 1 of the Universal Postal Convention adopted at the 1999 Beijing Congress, member countries shall ensure that all users/customers enjoy a right to universal service involving the permanent provision of quality basic postal services at all points in their territory, at affordable prices. The national regulatory authorities responsible for postal services have obliged their postal operators to fulfill the country-specific USOs based on the relevant stipulation.

A postal USO can be defined and analyzed as composed of three components: (i) the scope of products under the USO, (ii) service quality as indicated by accessibility of postal facilities, delivery frequency, doorstep delivery, and other aspects, and (iii) price constraints set on USO products in the form of measures such as uniform pricing, price-cap regulations (PCRs) and break-even rules (Ambrosini et al. 2006). Such a categorization of the USO is useful for comparing the obligations imposed on different postal operators; however, this methodology cannot easily be applied to Asian postal markets, since a transnational framework for defining the USO in country-specific terms (such as the EU postal directives) does not exist in Asia. Without such an overall legal framework, definition of the USO in this region is unclear.

The USO characteristics of the 12 Asian postal markets targeted in this chapter can be broadly summarized in terms of three components (UPU, 2006): (i) product coverage (ordinary letters including postcards and standard parcels), (ii) service quality (adequate service provision throughout the country or territory), and (iii) price regulation (affordable postal rates or uniform postal rates).

In addition to these common provisions, there are additional national requirements. For example, the postal operator in China is required to provide free service for soldiers stationed at borders. While parcel products in Japan were exempted from the USO together with a recent postal reform in 2007, the maximum weight for USO letters was kept at four kilograms, compared with two kilograms in Malaysia, the same as the USO standards in the EU postal directive.

The postal USO, which has effectively satisfied postal users' demands for communications, is now facing a new type of challenge in the form of postal reform. Postal reform was formally categorized as a sequence of five phases in Campbell (2002): corporatization, liberalization, deregulation, re-regulation and internationalization. At the initial stage of reform, postal operators were assumed to continue to generate sufficient revenue from postal and other activities to maintain universal service (ibid., p. 412). This assumption, however, does not necessarily guarantee the postal market for every country and in every timeframe.

In the next sections, we shall present two significant trends of postal reform in Asian markets – (i) corporatization/privatization of postal operators and (ii) liberalization of postal markets – from the viewpoint of the possibility of maintaining the USO after reforms. In addition to describing the progress of reforms among postal customers, competitors, regulators and postal operators, two additional issues will be discussed. One possible problem is whether a postal operator after privatization has incentives to streamline unprofitable businesses imposed as part of the USO such as single-letter delivery to remote areas, since commercialized operators will definitely be required to make constant and stable profits to distribute to lenders and shareholders. The other problem is the risk of inducing 'cream-skimming' entry after market liberalization, assuming continuation of USO restrictions on the postal operator, especially the uniform postal rate throughout the country. Such entry behavior will directly affect the revenue and cost structure of a postal operator and its ability to subsidize the unprofitable business through the profitable one. If the government's priority for public policy is to preserve the universal service or USO as one of the traditional features of the postal business, it is then absolutely necessary to design appropriate postal reforms that enable public objectives and operational outcomes to be balanced after implementing the reforms.

3. POSTAL REFORM IN ASIA I: CORPORATIZATION AND PRIVATIZATION

3.1 Overview: Corporatization and Privatization

Postal operators in Asian countries are, in general, aiming to achieve management efficiency and business expansion by transforming former government-run administrations into corporatized or privatized entities. The process of corporatization and privatization, however, has different characteristics by country and territory, and the details of transformation have not been sufficiently clarified in previous studies in the postal field. We can extend earlier analysis concerning management reform of postal operators by applying the analytical framework shown in Yamashige (2007), which emphasizes two dimensions for the managerial reform of public business: ownership and objectives of management. 'Ownership' is determined by which entities lose financial worth when the relevant business loses money. The business would be categorized as 'government owned', therefore, if the government assumes the entire burden of liability in the case of bankruptcy. 'Objectives' is determined by the ultimate goal of management and may be described as falling between the pursuit of financial profits and public interests. The objectives of business would be categorized as 'private' if the management goal is the accumulation of profits. Within this framework, categories and possible directions of postal management reform are shown in Figure 20.6.

Transforming a government postal institution such as a ministry or other government agency into a state-owned enterprise (SOE) or ordinary stock company fully owned by the government will not cause any changes to ownership, although efficient and transparent management through the introduction of governors and board members from outside the company can be expected. Establishing a government-owned postal company, or 'corporatization', is sometimes regarded as 'privatization in the broad sense' since actual ownership changes are not realized.

A public finance initiative (PFI) is a more aggressive type of reform which relies upon pursuit of private profits under government ownership. In PFI, the right to manage a public business is leased to a private sector company, and business restructuring is accomplished by exploiting private funds and management know-how. PFI can be categorized as BOT (build–operate–transfer), where management is ultimately returned to the government, and BOO (build–own–operate), where management is kept permanently in the private sector. In Asian postal markets, BOT-style PFI was applied in the Philippines' postal reform in 2006.[4]

Reform measures such as IPO management buy-out (MBO), and trade sale (bulk selling) can be categorized as 'privatization in the narrow sense', on the grounds that they are accompanied by changes in ownership and can be expected to achieve effective corporate governance through private ownership. In postal services, IPO can be observed not only in Germany and the Netherlands in Europe, but also in Singapore and Malaysia in Asia, where privatization has proceeded gradually by diminishing the government's share of ownership to certain levels after an IPO. While MBO has never been implemented around the world as a postal reform, with the exception of discussions in the UK about employee shareholding of Royal Mail Group plc (*The Times*, March 5, 2006), the trade sale of a public postal operator to a private company was conducted in Argentina in 1997,

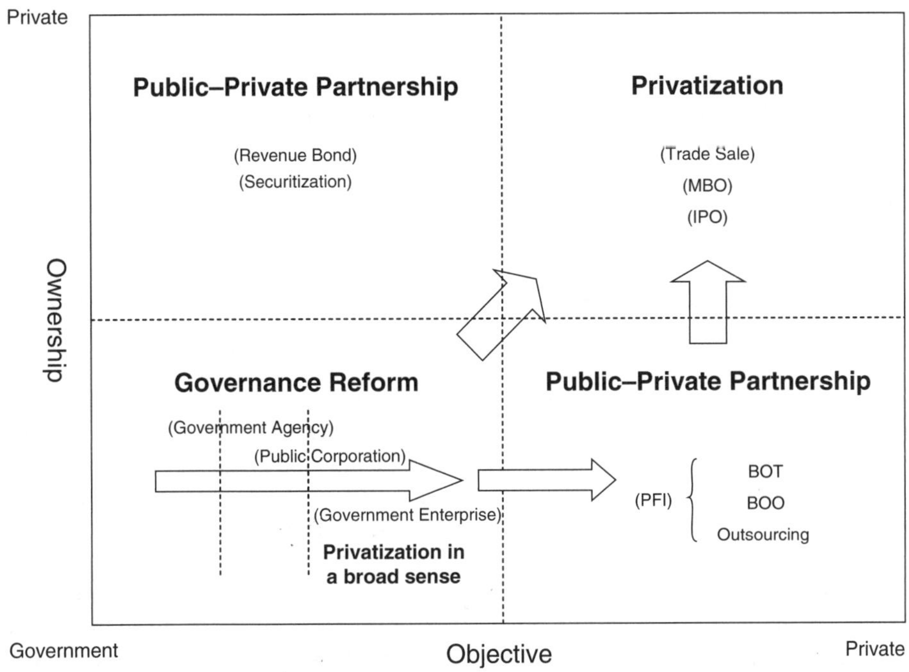

Source: Modified by authors from Yamashige (2007).

Figure 20.6 Matrix of postal reform regarding operational structure

although the privatized postal operator was re-nationalized in 2003 after it went bankrupt (Dow Jones Newswire, November 19, 2003).

Corporatization and privatization in public utility industries such as postal services should be pursued while maintaining a balance with the sustainability of the USO. Regardless of ownership structure, privatization will make the relevant operator a more profit-oriented entity, likely to be accompanied by management incentives to slash operational costs by raising the price of monopolistic products, streamlining unprofitable business, and degrading service quality. The following possibilities should also be taken into consideration.

The minimum standards of products and services provided by a postal operator are determined by the USO. The USO may restrict the ability of the operator to restructure its products and quality of service. If the operator faces an extensive USO, the management flexibility may be insufficient. If the postal service is deemed an important public service, then it may be that any deterioration of service would be considered socially unacceptable and only quality improvements can be expected after reform. If some products and services are provided in a competitive market, service quality degradation may drive away customers. Since the postal service is traditionally assumed to provide uniform service quality throughout the country, service degradation only in certain areas could raise the transaction costs for postal users as they seek to confirm the level of service quality at specific destinations.

The effects of postal reform and the restructuring of a postal operator on universal services are thus heavily influenced by the restrictions of the USO. The degree of social requirements for postal services and the competitive environment will be likely to cause different market outcomes. We shall investigate the relations between postal reform and the USO in depth, focusing on postal operators' reforms in Asia.

3.2 Postal Privatization and USO in Japan

In Japan, the former Ministry of Posts and Telecommunications (MPT) was transformed into the Postal Service Agency (PSA) in 2001 at the same time as ministerial reform, and then incorporated as the Japan Post Corporation in 2003. Although this public corporation was operating according to a management plan set by the regulatory authority for a period extending to March 2007, privatization bills for Japan Post were continuously debated during the 2005 session of the Diet, and finally enacted by both Houses in October 2005. Japan Post was privatized by being transformed into a wholly government-owned stock holding company, Japan Post Holding Co., Ltd, on October 1, 2007.[5] This transformation may be categorized as privatization in a broad sense, as shown in Figure 20.6. Japan's postal service is a significant presence in the country's financial, banking, and insurance sectors, and these financial services overwhelm mail delivery services in terms of revenue and assets. Due to such an asymmetrical financial structure, Kisugi (2007 p. 61) characterizes Japan's postal reform as 'the privatization of compelling postal savings and postal insurance as a financial institution market mechanism rather than the privatization of mail delivery'.

The privatization of Japan's mail business resulted in the establishment of two stock companies: Japan Post Service Co., Ltd, which handles sorting, transportation and delivery of mail and parcel items and has a net capital of JPY 20 billion, and Japan Post Network Co., Ltd, which handles acceptance of mail and parcel items at post office counters and has a similar amount of net capital. Initially, the parent company will hold all the stocks for these two postal subsidiaries as well as the stock of two other financial business units: Japan Post Bank and Japan Post Insurance.

One of the characteristics of Japan's postal reform and privatization is that the postal USO redesign was conducted along with the postal reform. Japan's postal USOs before and after the 2007 reform are shown in Table 20.1. Two changes in the USO are especially significant: exemption of parcels from the USO and simplification of procedures for changes in rates.[6]

After the 2007 postal reform, parcel products – ordinary parcels and booklet parcels – must be provided under the freight business law and regulated by the Ministry of Land, Infrastructure and Transport, rather than under the Postal Law administered by the Ministry of Internal Affairs and Communications (MIC). This modification was introduced to level the playing field with competitive operators that have delivered small package products for thirty years. It was assumed that a nationwide competitive market will guarantee universal package delivery even in remote and rural areas. Postal operators have provided parcel services strategically, not only because parcel handlings have the characteristics of scope economies with mail handlings (Wada et al., 1997), but also because demand for this product has benefited from rapidly growing electronic commerce via the Internet and mobile phones.

Table 20.1 Japan's postal USO before and after privatization

Operator	Japan Post Corporation 日本郵政公社 JAPAN POST ——→	Japan Post Service Co., Ltd JP POST 日本郵便
Management style	Public corporation	Stock company (Japan Post HD 100%)
Period	April 1, 2003 – September 30, 2007	October 1, 2007–
Product coverage	– Postal items (1st, 2nd, 3rd, 4th class, international, domestic parcels) – Special delivery (e.g. registered)	– Postal items (1st, 2nd, 3rd, 4th class, international) – Special delivery (e.g. registered)
Quality of service	– Nationwide network of post offices, collection boxes – 6 days a week, once a day delivery – Delivery within 3 days	– Nationwide network of collection boxes – 6 days a week, once a day delivery – Delivery within 3 days
Rate regulation	– Approval for ordinary, special and international postal items (less than JPY 80 for the standard letter) – Notification for parcel postal items	– Notification for postal and parcel items (less than JPY 80 for the standard letter) – Approval for 3rd and 4th class

Source: Postal Law and the relevant provisions.

The procedure for rate regulation was also changed by the 2007 reform. Prior to postal reform, MIC approval was required for rate changes of ordinary postal products. After reform, only notification to the ministry is required for postal rate changes, with the exception of third class mail (for example, designated newspapers and magazines approved by the postal service) and fourth class mail (for example, designated educational and Braille mail items), which are guaranteed under the Local and Social Contribution Fund as a public policy and for which approval of rate changes is required. Meanwhile, however, other significant restrictions regarding prices were unchanged by the reform. These may be summarized as follows: (i) the postal rate at the minimum weight category for formatted mail items shall be no more than the current rate (JPY 80) under an ordinance of the ministry, (ii) the postal rate for first class (formatted and unformatted mail) and second class (postcard) mail shall not vary by the demographical characteristics of the destination, and (iii) the ministry retains authority to require the postal operator to change rates if necessary (*ex post* regulation). These regulations, therefore, are not aimed at giving the postal operator sufficient management flexibility in terms of pricing behavior.

Thus, Japan Post Service Co., Ltd. is expected to continue as the virtual equivalent of a public postal service just as it was before postal reform, even though the management structure has been transformed from a public corporation to a privatized company. In addition to this requirement, stocks for Japan Post Service Co. and Japan Post Network Co. will not be authorized to be held by any entity other than the holding company, Japan Post Holding Co. (Japan Postal Services Company Law). According to the Postal Privatization Law, up to two-thirds of the stock of the holding company will be sold by the government as soon as possible before 2017, indicating that the management of postal and network business will be governed indirectly by private capital.

3.3 Postal Corporatization and Privatization in Asia

In China, the China Postal Group Corporation was established as a public corporation with registered capital of RMB 80 billion after it was separated from the former State Post Bureau in November 2006. The postal savings bank was incorporated as a subsidiary of the Group. This was the most significant postal reform since the establishment of the Ministry of Posts and Telecommunications in 1949 and the establishment of the State Post Bureau in 1998 (which split off the telecommunications business from the postal services).

The recent reform had been debated at the State Council, China's cabinet, since 2005. The State Council confirmed that the postal service was an important public service and the postal network was a major communication infrastructure. To improve service quality, the reform required the separation of administrative functions from entrepreneurial functions, the strengthening of governmental supervision, the guaranteeing of general and special services, and assured postal security (People's Daily Online, July 21, 2005). Prior to reform, postal services lost money, and government subsidies were required for several years after 1999. The former postal administration had net financial losses of RMB 1.1 billion in 2004 and RMB 400 million in 2005 (*Shanghai Daily*, December 19, 2005; Shanghai Daily.com, February 23, 2006). Improvements in profitability are expected from reform, although the financial statements were not officially published in annual reports.[7]

The USO in the Chinese postal market obliges the postal operator to provide a wide range of public services, not only to guarantee the basic communication right of citizens but also to maintain the stability of the regime and promote national solidarity (China State Post Bureau Annual Report, 2005). Ensuring the USO is emphasized under the public management structure.

The postal operators in Singapore and Malaysia were both transformed into stock companies from governmental organizations in the early 1990s and listed on national stock exchanges through IPOs. While these countries' postal services are strongly privatization oriented from the viewpoint of ownership and management depicted in Figure 20.6, the objectives of privatization reflect the different motivations in each country's economic and industrial policy.

Singapore Post (SingPost) was established in 1992 as a stock company and full subsidiary of Singapore Telecom, which was owned by the Singapore government. For Singapore Telecom, the sale of SingPost's stock was part of a strategy of divesting non-core business in order to focus on its core telecommunications business (Yahoo! Asia News, December 12, 2005). The postal market in Singapore, as discussed below, was fully liberalized on April 1, 2007, allowing the postal operator 15 years, which drove SingPost to diversify its business structure during that period. After 2003, SingPost introduced financial services such as lending and insurance within its retail division, a separate unit from the mail and logistics division. The USO in Singapore was expected to be provided by a privatized postal company, which has successfully diversified its financial foundation as a result of postal reforms.

Postal privatization in Malaysia was originally planned together with the listing of 24 other utilities and public services on the stock exchange, including sectors such as ports, iron manufacturing, banking and tourism promotion. Pos Malaysia became an incorporated entity in 1992 and was granted business freedom. In 2001, the Malaysian government decided to sell all shares of Pos Malaysia to the private investment holding company Phileo Allied, while holding 32 percent of Phileo ownership. Phileo changed its corporate name to Pos Malaysia & Services Holdings Bhd, or PSH, in 2002. Khazanah Nasional Berhad, the investment holding arm of the Malaysian government with stakes in more than 40 companies, now holds 32 percent of PSH ownership. This type of national investment fund is called a 'Sovereign Wealth Fund' (SWF) and contributes to the improvement of national asset value by strategic long-term holding of stocks for companies around the world. Pos Malaysia, which has been listed on the Malaysia Stock Exchange since 2007, has restructured into four business units: Pos Mel (mailing), Pos Laju (courier), Pos Niaga (network) and Pos Logistik (logistics). Restructuring has enabled the postal operator to explore and adapt new business opportunities beyond traditional mail services including the provision of the USO (Pos Malaysia website).

In other Asian countries as well corporatization and privatization of postal businesses have been implemented, although each country is at a different stage of reform. In late 2005, the Thai government announced a plan to establish a 'super-holding' company to supervise more than twenty state enterprises, including postal, telecom, railway and energy businesses, aiming to boost enterprises' efficiency (Thai News Service, November 8, 2005). In Korea, where little progress has been observed in postal reform in terms of modifying the business structure of Korea Post as a government institution, a plan for comprehensive reform of governmental organization, including privatization of the postal service by 2012, was published on January 16, 2008, by a preparatory governmental committee led by the newly elected president (*Nikkei Newspaper*, January 17, 2008).

4. POSTAL REFORM IN ASIA II: LIBERALIZATION

4.1 Overview: Liberalization

There has been little progress in postal market liberalization in Asian countries, with a few exceptions where improvement in service quality was expected through competitive pressure as a result of policies promoting entry. In most countries in Asia, a broad reserved area is assigned to a designated postal operator regardless of management structure. These circumstances are closely related to the limited political support for a uniform service market within Asia similar to that in the EU, as described in Section 2. The Second EU Postal Directive (2002/39/EC, Recital 7) stipulates that actions must be taken to 'speed up liberalization in areas such as postal services, the stated aim being to achieve a fully operational market'. Liberalization, however, can be crucial in Asia for attaining market maturity through economic expansion and globalization. Robert Campbell describes market liberalization as being more sensitive to price, market, and customer issues for the shareholders and management and as contributing to the efficient use of resources and the creation of price and market sensitivity (Campbell, 2002). While a postal operator in a monopolistic environment can set its rate without worrying about cost inefficiency, under competitive market conditions, the rate will be pressured to be cost oriented, assuming an efficient operation.

Market liberalization will have substantial effects on the provision of the USO, since it may invite market penetration by entrants into profitable business areas which the postal operator uses to subsidize the unprofitable USO business. For the USO, the effect of liberalization could be more severe than the effects of privatization or transformation, which could be lessened by achieving successful business expansion or efficient management. The need for a public policy to preserve the USO, such as a universal service fund (USF), state aid, pay-or-play mechanism and other measures, should therefore be carefully investigated and discussed. Refocusing the USO on small customers may be another policy option when liberalization policy is introduced to a monopolistic postal market (Crew and Kleindorfer, 2006c; Oxera, 2007). We shall survey market liberalization in Asia from the viewpoint of the impacts on the USO and ensuring universal service.

4.2 Market Liberalization in Japan

In Japan, the Postal Law that was enacted in 1947 and amended in 2007 has stipulated the monopolistic handling of 'correspondence items' by Japan Post Service Co., Ltd. The Correspondence Delivery Law that was enacted in 2003 paved the way to enabling private operators to deliver correspondence items under certain business restrictions. This was followed by consecutive proposals by the MIC in 2006 and 2007 to promote new entry into this business. The purpose of introducing private correspondence delivery companies is 'to enhance public welfare by starting correspondence delivery while ensuring universal and fair service provisions and providing more options for customers [Correspondence Delivery Law]'. The MIC expected that the private delivery would enhance convenience for customers by introducing a competition principle to the universal service provided by the postal operator (MIC, 2007).

In Japan, 'correspondence item' refers to a document that expresses the sender's will to a specific person or provides notification of a fact (Postal Law). Non-correspondence, therefore, includes envelopes containing leaflets, credit cards, gift coupons, periodicals, magazines and catalogues, which may be delivered by freight operators as 'freight items' rather than postal items without being regulated under the Postal Law.[8] On the other hand, no operators have applied for the nationwide 'general' category license for correspondence delivery, since (possibly) the requirements for this business – such as uniform rates, collection and delivery on more than six days a week, delivery within three days and universal installation of collection boxes – seemed too restrictive for potential operators to enter the new business.

This outcome caused the MIC to reconsider the effectiveness of the correspondence delivery regulations and organize a 'study group concerning the redesign of the postal and correspondence business' in 2007, soon after completion of the work of a previous study group concerning reserved areas and competition policy in 2006. According to the interim report issued on November 26, 2007, the MIC's new proposals to promote entry into the correspondence business can be summarized as follows:

1. permission for correspondence delivery by cooperation with multiple operators, including access to the postal operator's network by entrants; and
2. reduction in thresholds of weights and rates for 'special' correspondence delivery business from four kilograms or JPY 1,000.

Although the 2003 policy allowing entry of private enterprise was initially limited to prevent severe damage to the provision of the USO by the public postal operator, additional deregulation is now being persistently pursued, motivated by the fact that there have been no entries into the general correspondence delivery business. The interim report by the MIC study group suggests the necessity of investigating possible policies to ensure the USO, in addition to policies specific to Japan's postal market, that is, the regulations on correspondence delivery. Policy options such as a USF composed of contributions from relevant operators and tax exemptions or state aid have not, however, been vigorously investigated. Japan's postal market has so far ensured the USO by applying a relatively restrictive policy toward the correspondence delivery business while accepting entry into the non-correspondence market with few regulations. The two recent policy proposals to promote the correspondence business have the possibility of seriously influencing the sustainability of the USO in the long run. The policy redesign should be applied while taking into consideration the developing competition environment in non-correspondence business.

4.3 Market Liberalization in Asia

In Singapore, while collection and delivery of printed papers and parcels, including magazines and advertising brochures, have been provided under a competitive environment since the 1970s and express letter services have been liberalized since 1995, basic mail services, which include the collection and delivery of letters and postcards, were exclusively provided by SingPost until the end of March 2007. This monopoly license with a term of 15 years was granted to SingPost in 1992, when the postal company was established as a subsidiary of Singapore Telecom. On April 1, 2007, after conducting a series of public consultations, the government decided to fully open the basic mail service when the effective term of the license expired.[9] After the full market opening, postal operators will be categorized into the following two types according to the licenses granted by the regulatory authority, IDA (Infocomm Development Authority):

1. *Public Postal Licensees (PPLs)* A service that complies with the USO, including provision of island-wide letter collection and delivery services, maintaining a minimum number of post boxes and post offices for customers' easy access.[10] Currently the only licensee is Singapore Post, with a license term of 15 years.
2. *Postal services operators (PSOs)* The service that the operator provides is determined flexibly, and the license has a term of 10 years.

The introduction of a full market opening policy in Singapore was accompanied by government expectations that competition would create jobs, generate cost savings and improve service quality (Channel News Asia, February 5, 2007). The government was also expecting that the average growth rate of mail volume, 2 percent per year, would continue in the near future and that liberalization of the postal market would produce spillover benefits for the growing printed paper business.[11] From the competitors' point of view, the liberalization policy was welcomed since there could be opportunities to provide slower services at lower rates and services that enable big companies to use Singapore as a hub for sending out internationally bound invoices (*Straits Times*, February 7, 2007).

An evaluation of the effect of the full liberalization on the USO in Singapore is still difficult, with little public information on the competitive environment available so far. It is likely that there will be no designations of a PPL operator other than SingPost, since the obligation to provide universal service is too restrictive for new entrants. The effect will be to keep the incumbent operator as a sole universal service provider (USP). Setting 15 years as a preparation period before full liberalization has been effective for the incumbent, since it was possible for it to implement efficient management in order to face severe competition in the future.

Other than in Japan and Singapore, there has been little significant liberalization policy observed in the mail markets in Asian countries apart from in the Philippines, where mail delivery is fully opened to new entrants under the license scheme.

In China, the monopolistic delivery of basic letters and postcards by a postal operator remained unchanged by the postal reform that transformed the management structure. In contrast, there have been continuous debates among the government, domestic private operators and international express operators concerning deregulation in the domestic and international express mail market. Although the critical point of debate was whether to grant exclusive rights to deliver express parcels weighing less than 150 grams to the state-owned China Post (*Financial Times*, October 5, 2006), public information regarding the outcome of this draft of the new Postal Law is still unavailable. Substantial economic and trade growth in China has generated urgent demand for high-value products such as domestic intra-city, domestic inter-city, and international Express Mail Service (EMS). High demand has caused high incentives for operators to enter the market, even while there is a continuous decline in the volume of ordinary letters delivered by the postal operator.

In Korea, the incumbent postal operator has been granted a reserved area to handle and deliver correspondence items – documents and other items depicted by letters, signs, and marks for communication – with the exceptions to the monopoly being in-house documents, notes attached to consignments, foreign trade-related information and other items (the Presidential Ordinance and relevant provisions of the Postal Law). In Malaysia, Indonesia and Thailand, where delivery of mail weighing more than two kilograms is already liberalized, the postal operators can maintain their practical monopolies in the handling of letters because of the relative predominance of lightweight letters and postcards in the postal demand structure.

5. CONCLUSIONS

As we have presented the backgrounds and procedures of postal reforms in Japan, China, Singapore, Malaysia and other countries in this chapter, the progressive management reforms of postal operators and the slow movement toward market liberalization among countries and territories can be noted as characteristics of Asian postal services. While postal services in Asian countries and territories was formerly provided by public entities, most postal operators in this area have undergone transformational reforms of their management structure by corporatization and/or privatization. Generally, these reforms have the common characteristic that postal restructuring was implemented mainly as part of a series of structural reforms of governmental or public administrational systems. Postal operators that have moved toward privatization of ownership and adopted objectives for management have expanded their businesses by moving into new areas such as retail services, exploiting network facilities, and adding to domestic and global logistics by acquisitions. In contrast, postal market liberalization policy in Asia has seen slight progress among countries and territories in the area, where the incumbent's monopoly over delivery of basic letters with small weights has been mostly retained. Traditional postal policy to ensure the USO by funding it from profits earned in reserved areas has been applied in Asia in spite of significant reforms of the management and governance structures of postal operators.

To obtain a perspective on the future of Asian postal markets, possible changes in market conditions in this region should be considered. Asian postal markets could benefit from increases in GDP per capita and income standards through high economic growth. Economic prosperity could bring growth in postal volume per capita and improvements in postal productivity. If such favorable economic conditions and market maturity develop in the future, they may present possible opportunities for potential entrants, which will enhance entry incentives and competitive pressures. For the regulatory authority, therefore, prudent policy design will involve promoting new entry while balancing conflicts among postal users, competitors, and the incumbent operator. Deliberate market evaluations regarding the soundness of the management of the USP and competitive developments will be essential to preserve the postal USO as a minimum service standard while sustaining continuous and reasonable profits for postal operators in the competitive market.

NOTES

* The contents of this chapter are solely the personal views of the authors and do not represent official opinions of Japan Post Service Co., Ltd.

1. International Monetary Fund statistics show that the nominal GDP for these countries and territories in 2006 in US dollar terms is about 80 percent of that in the US and 70 percent of that in the EU. Hong Kong will be regarded as a 'territory' in this chapter while taking the independent category of Hong Kong (Post) in the UPU postal statistics into consideration, although this area is technically a Special Administrative Region of China.
2. ASEAN, which was formed in 1967 and currently comprises 10 member countries, is moving toward removing a tariff barrier between the original five member countries in 2010, and is committed to concluding FTAs with China, India and Japan, respectively, from 2010 to 2012.
3. Examples of electronic substitutions can be observed in the United States, where first class mail volume has already been affected by the Internet and other electronic communications (US Postal Service Annual Report, 2006) and Germany, where the market for mail communication contracted by about 3 percent as a result of substitution by electronic communication media (Deutsche Post World Net Annual Report).
4. In the Philippines, the government leased the postal operator to a Japanese IT firm for seven years from 2006, with a contract for the IT company to enhance operational efficiency, modernize post offices and turn the post over to the government upon the expiration of the lease contract (*Philippine Daily Inquirer*, March 21, 2006).
5. See Campbell and Porges (Ch. 21, this volume) for the legal frameworks of Japan's postal privatization.
6. The USO regarding over-the-counter business at post offices was also changed as follows: the Post Service Company has been obliged to consign counter business such as the acceptance of mail and parcels, and sales of postal and government stamps, to the Post Network Company (Law regarding the consignment of over-the-counter postal business). Special policy consideration is paid to the assurance of postal services at the post office counter, especially in remote areas.
7. Future reform plans of the China Post Group, such as privatization, have not been published yet. An IPO of China Postal Savings Bank, the mainland's fifth-largest bank in the range of two to three billion US dollars, has allegedly been consulting with investment bankers (Reuters, March 3, 2006; May 8, 2007).

8. Such delivery business of non-correspondence items or 'private mail' by freight operators could expand rapidly in these years while making use of economies of scope in the delivery of small packages, which has a 30-year business development history (Maruyama, 2006).
9. IDA press release on February 5, 2007, 'Singapore's Postal Sector to Fully Liberalise'.
10. SingPost will be given the right to hold the full set of letterbox master door keys after full liberalization, which will enable it to access locked letterboxes that are installed in apartment blocks. The prices, terms and conditions for other postal operators to access the delivery network of SingPost will be regulated by the regulatory authority (IDA, 2007; *Straits Times*, February 7, 2007).
11. Statement by the Minister for Information, Communication and the Arts, February 5, 2007.

REFERENCES

Ambrosini, X., F. Boldron and B. Roy (2006), 'Universal service obligations in the postal sector: economic learnings from cross-country comparisons', in Crew and Kleindorfer (eds) (2006a), pp. 23–38.

Ansón, J., R. Cuadra, A. Linhares, G. Ronderos and J. Toledano (2006), 'First steps towards new postal economics models for developing countries: learning from the Latin American experiences', in Crew and Kleindorfer (eds) (2006b), pp. 217–36.

Campbell, R., (2002), *The Politics of Postal Transformation – Modernizing Postal Systems in the Electronic and Global World*, Kingston, Ont: McGill-Queen's University Press.

Cohen, R., E. Chu, W. Ferguson and S. Xenakis (1997), 'A cross-sectional comparison and analysis of productivity for 21 national postal administrations', in M.A. Crew and P.R. Kleindorfer (eds), *Managing Change in the Postal and Delivery Industries*, Boston, MA: Kluwer Academic, pp. 83–109.

Crew, M.A. and P.R. Kleindorfer (eds) (2006a), *Progress toward Liberalization of the Postal and Delivery Sector,* New York: Springer

Crew, M.A. and P.R. Kleindorfer (2006c), 'Approaches to the USO under entry', in Crew and Kleindorfer (eds) (2006b) pp. 1–18.

Crew, M.A. and P.R. Kleindorfer (eds) (2006b), *Liberalization of the Postal and Delivery Sector*, Cheltenham, UK and Northampton, MA, USA: Edward Elgar.

Kisugi, S. (2007), 'Legal theory of regulations on public utility business and liberalization', in J. Fujiwara and M. Yajima (eds), *Market Liberalization and Public Utility Business*, Tokyo: Hakuto-Shobo Publishing (in Japanese), pp. 58–83.

Maruyama, S. (2006), 'Competition structure and future postal reform in Japan', in Crew and Kleindorfer (eds) (2006a), pp. 369–84.

Ministry of Internal Affairs and Communications (MIC) (2007), 'Interim Report: the Study Group Concerning the Redesigning of Postal and Correspondence Business' (in Japanese), Tokyo.

Nakajima, S. (2006), 'Current status and future perspectives in the East Asia community', in R. Kiyono and S. Nakajima (eds), *Economic Growth in Eastern Asia and Relations among Japan, US and the EU*, Tokyo: Koyo Shobo. (in Japanese), pp. 59–86.

Oxera Consulting, Ltd (2007), 'Funding Universal Service Obligations in the Postal Sector', a study prepared for La Post, De Poste–La Poste, Hellenic Post, Poste Italiane, P&T Luxembourg, Correos, Magyar Post, Cyprus Post and Poczta Polska http://www.oxera.com, accessed 1 February 2007.

Universal Postal Union (UPU) (2006), 'Status and structures of postal administrations', UPU website, http://www.upu.int/status/en/index.shtml, accessed 31 January 2008.

Wada, T., C. Tsunoda and J. Nemoto (1997), 'Empirical analysis of economies of scale, economies of scope, and cost subadditivity in Japanese mail service', Institute for Posts and Telecommunications Policy (IPTP) discussion paper series Tokyo.

Yamashige, S. (2007), 'Restructuring in transportation network business', in S. Yamashige and Daiwa Institute of Research (eds), *Japan's Transportation Network*, Tokyo: Chuokeizai-Sha (in Japanese), pp. 48–57.

21. How much postal reform in Japanese postal privatization?*

James I. Campbell Jr.[†] **and Amelia Porges**[‡]

1. INTRODUCTION

On 1 October 2007, the curtain came down on over 130 years of postal banking and insurance in Japan, as Japan Post Public Corporation was dissolved and its functions devolved to successor postal and financial corporations at the outset of a 10-year privatization process. Former Prime Minister Junichiro Koizumi, the strong-minded reform politician who had pushed through the decision to privatize, was there with corporate chiefs and other political leaders to cut the ribbon at the launch ceremony for the new Japan Post Group.

The privatization process thus launched was not, and is not, focused on revitalizing postal delivery services, for the overall stakes have always been much larger. Koizumi's key objective as prime minister was to achieve fiscal and political reform by unlocking the billions of dollars in banking and insurance assets held by the postal system and cutting off the flow of these assets into government spending. Postal reform as such was an afterthought. Enactment of the postal privatization package took many years of political struggle, a legislative stalemate, a snap election campaign focused on postal privatization, and a landslide victory for Koizumi after he campaigned against the recalcitrant within his own party. The political compromises he made along the way have influenced the design of privatization and will affect all of the Japan Post Group entities on a continuing basis.

Japan Post Bank, Japan's largest bank, and Japan Post Insurance, its largest insurance company, will continue to be financially intertwined with Japan's two regulated postal organizations, Japan Post Service and Japan Post Network, under the umbrella of their joint owner, Japan Post Holdings. Moreover, all of these organizations are expected to enhance their profitability by entering new business areas, such as international express mail, express parcel delivery, and logistics in the case of the new postal delivery company. It is not clear whether or how the government will prevent cross-subsidization between regulated activities and these new areas or cross-subsidization of new activities by the assets accumulated under public ownership.

Japan's postal reform package thus differs significantly from postal reform in other industrialized countries. Indeed, key elements in those reforms are not present in the Japanese scheme at all. Structural compromises in the Japanese approach also raise

† George Mason University.
‡ Sidley Austin LLP.

significant issues for postal policy, for fair competition in physical delivery and financial services in Japan, and for the government bodies that will supervise the package's implementation in years to come.

This chapter discusses the privatization package and its implementation in comparative perspective, combining analysis of postal regulatory issues and of the legal and policy background in Japan. It follows up on and updates the earlier study by Porges and Leong (2006).

2. POSTAL LAW AND DELIVERY SERVICES IN JAPAN

While the Japanese post office was established in 1871, the current Postal Law of Japan dates from 1947.[1] The 1947 law established the national post office, Japan Postal Services, as a department of the Ministry of Communications, providing five classes of letter mail plus parcel post.[2] By 1973, the fourth and fifth classes of mail had been consolidated.[3] This service mandate remained unchanged until the privatization laws of 2005.

In 2002, the Japan Post Law[4] transformed Japan Postal Services into Japan Post Public Corporation (Japan Post), a public corporation staffed by civil servants and specifically authorized to provide both the letter post and parcel post services regulated by the Postal Law. The same organization also provided postal banking services and postal life insurance services, activities which wound up holding a quarter of personal financial assets in Japan (Porges and Leong, 2006).

Although Japan Post was a separate public corporation, the Japan Post Law and the Postal Law gave the Ministry of Internal Affairs and Communications (MIC) broad authority to direct the provision of postal services. The MIC closely supervised postal operations, approving Japan Post's Postal Regulations and Operations Manual, approving changes in postage rates and determining matters such as maximum size of postal parcels, standards for ordinary mail, or methods of mail collection and delivery; the MIC could exempt charities from postage, exempt areas from nationwide delivery standards and provide for 'matters necessary to carry out this law other than those provided for in this law'.[5]

Japan also modified the postal monopoly in 2002. The Postal Law gave Japan Post a monopoly for the carriage of 'correspondence', defined as 'writings that express the intentions of the sender, or notify facts, to a specified recipient'.[6] In 2002, the Diet enacted a new Correspondence Delivery Law[7] permitting licensed private operators to deliver 'correspondence' as an exception to the postal monopoly set out in the Postal Law. The new law provided licenses for two types of correspondence delivery services: (i) general correspondence delivery with nationwide six-day-a-week collection and delivery, meeting service standards set by the MIC and charging MIC-regulated uniform rates, and (ii) special correspondence delivery of large-size or heavyweight correspondence, correspondence delivered within three hours, or correspondence for which the delivery fee exceeds ¥1,000 ($9.95).[8]

The general correspondence delivery license was an empty promise. A licensee would have to duplicate the facilities of Japan Post and submit to MIC controls similar to those imposed on Japan Post. Since 2002, no company has applied for such a license. It has even been legally impossible to offer general correspondence delivery through a group of providers or in collaboration with Japan Post. The special correspondence delivery license is more feasible, but it is still restrictive compared to other industrialized countries. The licensee must submit a business plan to the MIC, demonstrate its capacity to do business, comply with any conditions that the MIC attaches to the license, submit reports to the MIC, and accept such inspections as the MIC requires. As of March 2008, there were 253 special correspondence delivery licensees of which only 13 operated nationwide.[9] Parcel delivery companies have also competed in delivering non-monopoly items to individual customers, including catalogs, unaddressed direct mail, and parcels (Maruyama, 2006).

Letter mail in Japan has been declining absolutely since FY 2001, when it peaked at 26.7 billion items. Per capita use of letter post (178 items per year in 2005) is well below levels in other large industrialized countries such as the United States (714), the United Kingdom (334), France (291), and Germany (218), although comparable to the European Union (EU) as a whole (197) (Japan Post, 2005). By FY 2006, mail volume had declined to 24.7 billion items due to electronic diversion and competition from domestic delivery providers, and it was predicted to continue (Japan Post, 2007). Japan Post Holdings predicts that this decline will continue (Japan Post Holdings, 2007a). In recent years, Japan Post has made up some of the decrease in letter-post volume through efforts to recapture its share of the parcels market. (Mizutani and Uranishi, 2003).

International letter post is small and declining more rapidly than domestic mail overall. Outbound international mail, 75.7 million items in FY 2006, is only 0.3 percent of domestic mail volume. Inbound international mail is about three times as much as outbound. In FY 2006, letter-post items were about 86 percent of outbound international mail, parcels were 2 percent, and International Express Mail Service (EMS) was 12 percent. Outbound international letter post peaked in FY 1991 at 125 million items and has been declining ever since, due in part to the activities of the international express companies. In FY 2006, outbound international letter post amounted to only 64 million items, 51 percent of the 1991 level. In the last decade, Japan Post's most successful international product has been International EMS. International EMS began in 1982 and reached 10 million items in FY 2006 (Japan Post, 2007).

The Japanese market is also served by large parcel companies that offer nationwide door-to-door services for parcels, luggage, and other goods. Yamato Transport started this *takkyubin* service in the 1970s and remains the market leader. Other major companies include Sagawa Express and Nippon Express (Nittsu). The international express companies DHL and TNT began service in Japan in the 1970s, and were later joined by the two other major global express operators, FedEx and United Parcel Service. The parcel and express companies are all regulated under domestic trucking statutes.

3. POSTAL PRIVATIZATION: THE CONTINUING STORY

The postal privatization package of 2005 was composed of six laws[10] that provided for actions to take place during and before a 10-year transition period starting on 1 October 2007 and made consequential amendments to existing law. The Postal Privatization Law establishes the basic structure, procedures, and goals of the process, and provides for incorporation of the new Japan Post Bank Corporation and Japan Post Insurance

Corporation. Four special laws charter other entities to succeed Japan Post and specify their objectives and business scope: the Japan Post Holdings Corporation Law, the Japan Post Service Corporation Law, the Japan Post Network Corporation Law, and the Law on the Independent Administrative Entity (a government corporation which will manage legacy postal savings and life insurance assets and liabilities). Finally, the Law on Adjustments amends the Postal Law and other existing laws referencing Japan Post to reflect changes in organizational structures and Japan Post's dissolution.

On 23 January 2006, the MIC incorporated Japan Post Holdings as a shell corporation to begin the process. The government owns all of the stock of Japan Post Holdings and is required to list and sell off up to two-thirds of these shares as soon as possible during the transition period. On 1 October 2007, Japan Post was dissolved and its operations, assets, liabilities, and employees were split among (i) Japan Post Holdings, the parent company; (ii) Japan Post Holdings' subsidiaries Japan Post Bank, Japan Post Insurance, Japan Post Services and Japan Post Network, and (iii) the Independent Administrative Entity.

Japan Post Holdings will initially hold all stock in its four subsidiaries. Japan Post Bank and Japan Post Insurance will be created under normal company law. They will not have government guarantees for their deposits or policies and will be required to pay taxes, pay into client security funds, and comply with applicable financial regulations and standards for capital adequacy.[11] During the transition period, Japan Post Holdings is required to list their shares and sell them all. As for the two postal subsidiaries, Japan Post Service inherits the postal monopoly from Japan Post, and Japan Post Network provides counter services for the other Japan Post Group companies. Japan Post Service and Japan Post Network are 'special companies' (*tokushu gaisha*) created by statute, not under normal company law. Although Japan Post Holdings' statutory charter requires it to hold all of the shares of Japan Post Service and Japan Post Network, as noted above up to two-thirds of the shares of the parent company are to be sold to the public during the transition period.[12]

The Postal Privatization Law set out basic principles designed to cement into place the Koizumi reform program for the postal-financial complex. It endorsed 'fair and free competition' and the need to 'ensure equal conditions for competition with business operators that carry on the same type of service as the services of the new corporations' – regardless of whether those services are financial or postal in nature. It also endorsed the idea that leaving to the private sector as much as possible those matters it can do will contribute to achieving a freer and more vital economy and society.

To keep implementation on track, the Postal Privatization Law created a five-member Postal Privatization Committee (PPC), appointed by the prime minister and reporting to a cabinet-level Postal Privatization Headquarters overseeing privatization. The law also required Japan Post Holdings, working with Japan Post, to submit a Basic Plan (issued on 25 January 2006) and a detailed Implementation Plan (issued on 27 April 2007), setting out the division of assets, business projections and business plans for the successor entities (MIC, 2007c).

After passage of the privatization laws, Koizumi appointed Heizo Takenaka, the economist who had led Koizumi's postal legislation effort, as the MIC Minister and Minister for Postal Privatization. He also appointed as PPC chairman Naoki Tanaka, a think-tank economist who had been deeply engaged on financial and postal reform since 2001. To forestall later slippage, Takenaka had Japan Post Holdings issue the Framework of the Implementation Plan on 31 July 2006 (Japan Post Holdings, 2006), and the Koizumi administration chose the leadership of the successor entities (Takenaka, 2006, pp. 239–41). The PPC must report on privatization at three-year intervals and has stated that it intends to issue interim reports as well. The PPC must also deliberate and issue opinions on applications by Japan Post or its successor entities for licenses to enter into new lines of business and on applications for MIC approval of its business plans. In June 2007, the PPC issued its evaluation of Japan Post Holdings' implementation plan.[13]

4. POSTAL REFORM IN JAPAN IN PERSPECTIVE

The EU, the United States, Australia, and New Zealand have all enacted major postal reform legislation in the last dozen years. Each has taken its own path to postal reform, but for all the basic public policy issues have been essentially the same. In each jurisdiction, the post office is regarded as important both as a key element of the communications infrastructure and as a large employer. As in most countries, before practical alternatives to the postal service existed, government tolerated inefficiency, which yielded the political bonus of extra jobs, and encouraged services which were popular with voters even if not cost-justified.

At the end of the twentieth century, conditions changed, and all were confronted with the same basic question: given the decline in the postal letter business and increasing competition from other delivery services, how can the national post office be equipped for commercial survival and avoid a future of increasing public subsidies? All four jurisdictions have concluded that postal reform must include four elements: (i) conversion of the post office into a more commercial organization; (ii) repeal of the postal monopoly after a reasonable transition; (iii) definition of universal service; and (iv) creation of an independent regulator to discharge specific government functions (if any). In this section we consider how the postal elements of the Japanese privatization package compare with the trend in these four.

4.1 Commercialization of the Post Office

To adapt to changing, and increasingly competitive, markets, governments have concluded that the post office must be structured more like other commercial undertakings. In most cases, the first step is to reorganize the post office as a corporation subject to normal company law. Although governments initially own all shares of the resulting entity, increasingly governments are concluding that ownership must be transferred to private shareholders as well. In addition, commercialization implies that, except for specifically defined rights and obligations, the national post office will, on the one hand, have the same freedom to manage its activities as a private company and, on the other, be subject to the same commercial rules as a private company, including rules to ensure fair competition in the marketplace.

In the EU, corporatization of the public postal operator has become the rule rather than the exception, and privatization appears likely to follow. Nineteen of the 27 EU member states have reorganized their public postal operators under normal company law.

Six EU public postal operators are at least partially privatized as well, with all of the shares of TNT (the Netherlands public postal operator) and a majority of the shares of Deutsche Post (Germany) in private hands (WIK 2006, p. 43).

In the United States, the Postal Service remains a government agency, but it was insulated from political control by the Postal Reorganization Act of 1970. The Postal Accountability and Enhancement Act of 2006 further separated operational from political and regulatory controls.

In New Zealand and Australia, the public postal operator has long been corporatized, although still government owned. New Zealand's post office department was transformed into a corporation under the companies act in 1987 and is in fact operated very much as a private corporation. Australia Post became a government corporation in 1994.[14]

Japan moved only part way down this path and then stopped. In 2002 Japan Post was re-established as a government corporation with separate accounting, but it was not subject to company law, continued to be staffed by civil servants, and remained closely supervised by the MIC. The statutes that establish Japan Post Holdings, Japan Post Service, and Japan Post Network, and define their scope and governance, also endow the government with continuing control or a veto. The MIC had veto power over the original articles of incorporation of these companies. Since Japan Post Holdings holds all of the shares of Japan Post Service and Japan Post Network, and the government is required to hold at least one-third of Japan Post Holdings forever, the Postal Privatization Law effectively ensures that the government will have veto power over changes in these articles or other key corporate decisions. The MIC and the prime minister (whose office includes the Financial Services Agency, Japan's financial services regulator) jointly established the Basic Plan of succession which was the blueprint for the Implementation Plan, and their approval was also required for the Implementation Plan.[15]

The MIC will continue to exercise more direct supervisory authority as well. It has the right to approve the social contribution services plan (which funds certain deficit services of Japan Post Service); the company's annual business plan; any change in its articles of incorporation; any transfer of important assets; and Japan Post Service's postal regulations and Management Guidelines. The MIC will also have the power to order changes needed to enforce the law. While the MIC will no longer have discretionary authority to approve rates for letters and cards (other than the standard 25-gram letter), it gains new authority to approve Japan Post Service's subcontracts as well as its entry into new businesses. The MIC will receive the accounts of Japan Post Service, will supervise its compliance with the law, and may order inspections and reports as it deems necessary.[16] It has comparable supervisory authority over Japan Post Network.[17] In short, the independence of the national post office remains largely a formality.

The plan also leaves important parameters undefined for some make-or-break issues affecting any potential competitor, service consumers, and the extent of efficiency benefits to the Japanese economy. Consider a basic problem presented by postal reform in all industrialized countries: the proper allocation and future use of the assets amassed by the postal administration using public funds during the period before reform. Issues of this nature led to long-standing contention regarding Deutsche Post's purchase of DHL with funds from sales of legacy real estate and other legacy assets. Although the European Commission approved Deutsche Post's purchase of DHL without addressing this contention directly, it imposed several conditions on the operation of Deutsche Post to ensure fair competition.[18] The United States has gone further. A recent postal reform law requires the Treasury and the Postal Regulatory Commission (PRC) to develop an independent and impartial plan to divide the assets of the Postal Service between a fund for market dominant products and a fund for competitive products, and prohibits the Postal Service from subsidizing competitive products with revenues from market-dominant products.[19]

The Postal Privatization Law calls on the government to take measures, including imposing limitations on the successor entities, to ensure 'equal conditions for competition' with private businesses in the same service areas (Articles 2–3, 8). Although the law provides for an independent Appraisal Committee to value the assets (Article 165), the law provides no clear standard for fair division of assets.

Japan Post Service or Japan Post Network could also potentially draw directly or indirectly on the vast pool of assets represented by the shares of Japan Post Bank and Japan Post Insurance. A hint appears in the Implementation Plan Framework of July 2006, which, in a discussion of the assets of Japan Post Service, states that 'Although its net assets are projected to be ¥200 billion, Japan Post Service will be a wholly-owned subsidiary of Japan Post Holdings, and *since Japan Post Holdings will have sufficient net assets, after privatization an increase in capital should be possible*' (Japan Post Holdings, 2006, p. 18, emphasis added). The implication is that Japan Post Holdings will dip into the financial resources it has as owner of the financial subsidiaries, if Japan Post Service needs more capital to compete more effectively.

Moreover, the Implementation Plan contemplates that initially 99 percent of the operating income of Japan Post Network will come from fees for counter services paid by Japan Post Bank and Japan Post Insurance (both of which will also have independent sales offices) and fees from Japan Post Service (Japan Post Holdings, 2007b, p. 83). These fees are to be provided for under long-term contracts concluded when the successor entities separate on 1 October 2007. The fees provide an obvious and non-transparent opportunity for cross-subsidization and questionable transfer pricing.

The PPC's comments on the Implementation Plan point to all of these issues. The PPC stresses generally that 'safeguarding equal conditions of competition is essential' (PPC, 2007, p. 2). It urges the MIC and the Financial Services Agency to keep certain specific issues in mind when considering whether to approve the Implementation Plan and supervising the successor entities. The PPC notes that the division of public assets acquired with government funds is a critical issue for these enterprises and that it must be fair; the PPC states that consistent and rigorous accounting and disclosure is necessary before and after the division of assets (ibid., p. 3). Moreover, the PPC urges that because the circumstances are abnormal, the regulators must verify market prices, require cost accounting, and ensure that the long-term contracts with Japan Post Network are at arm's-length prices, both immediately and on a continuing basis (ibid., p. 4).

Any uncertainty regarding the disposition of the two financial entities will cloud the entire privatization process. The Implementation Plan now calls for the listing and sale of shares in the financial subsidiaries and the parent Japan Post Holdings at the same time, in FY 2010 if possible (Japan Post Holdings, 2007b, p. 6). Since roughly 91 percent of Japan Post Holdings' value consists of its shareholdings in the two financial firms, if Japan Post Holdings' shares are sold first, buyers' evaluation of their potential gains from the sale of Japan Post Bank and Japan Post Insurance will determine the market value of

Japan Post Holdings' shares. Unless the financial entities are sold first, the uncertain valuation of future sales of the financial entities will likely complicate the sale of Japan Post Holdings' stock.

Even after the financial entities have been sold and Japan Post Holdings reverts to the role of holding company for Japan Post Network and Japan Post Service, it may be difficult to offer shares of Japan Post Holdings given the extent of government control over the management of Japan Post Holdings, Japan Post Service, and Japan Post Network under their organic statutes and the Postal Law. Wise investors may be reluctant to purchase shares in a commercial venture when they will have little or no power to determine its commercial success.

4.2 Definition of Universal Service

A clear definition of the postal operator's 'universal service obligation' or USO is another key element for privatization. The concept of an explicit USO is a recent development in postal law, resulting from the increased emphasis on commercialization and competition. If the public postal operator is to be given commercial freedom, it must be allowed to decide for itself which business opportunities and markets to pursue. At the same time, to satisfy voters dependent on traditional postal services, government must define specifically which postal services it will continue to guarantee to all citizens, either by imposing requirements on the public postal operator or by regulating the delivery services market generally.

The EU Postal Directive, for instance, requires member states to adopt measures to ensure a broad level of universal service. National definitions of the USO are typically quite detailed. In many cases, the USO applies to letters, direct mail, newspapers and periodicals and similar items weighing up to 2 kilograms and to parcels weighing up to 20 kilograms. The USO also specifies access (number or density of post offices, postal agencies, and public collection boxes), quality of service (number of collections and deliveries per week and percentage of mail to be delivered within given timeframes for different classes of service) and users' rights (procedures and remedies for complaints by mailers and addressees) (WIK, 2004, pp. 34–44). Australia fixes its USO by regulation, and limits it essentially to monopoly services.[20] New Zealand sets out its USO through a Deed of Understanding between the government as owner and New Zealand Post, providing for service quality, access and uniform maximum fees.[21] In the United States, the Postal Regulatory Commission is now developing for Congress a proposal for a modern definition of the USO.[22]

In Japan, since 1 October 2007, universal postal service has been provided by Japan Post Service (which also inherits the postal monopoly) based on a mandate in Article 1 of the Postal Law to 'promote public welfare by provision of postal services at the lowest possible charges, on a nation-wide scale and in a manner fair to all'. The range of universal services includes the four classes of domestic mail (in accordance with size and weight limitations specified by the Postal Law), plus international mail (ordinary, small packet and EMS), and certain types of special handling mail such as registered mail. Parcels are outside the USO. Mail collection must include nationwide provision of mailboxes and post offices. Postage rates must be uniform nationwide and for mail under 25 grams must not exceed ¥80 (about US$0.75). In general, delivery must be provided at least daily from Monday to Saturday, within three days from dispatch, to each household nationwide. These standards derive partly from direct requirements in the Postal Law and partly from the legal requirement that the MIC must approve postal service management guidelines (*Yūbin gyōmu kanri kitei*) drawn up by Japan Post Holding and applied as from 1 October 2007 (MIC, 2007b, and 2007d).

The Japanese USO thus falls somewhere between a pre-modernization general statement of mission for a governmental department and a post-modernization definition of specific public service obligations for a commercial entity. If the MIC is considered the ultimate manager of the national post office, then the definition of universal service does not provide external guidance to the sector, as it should in a modern postal law; rather the USO remains a set of internal instructions issued to a postal operator by superiors in the ministry. There is no clear distinction between what postal management must do as a public servant and what it may do as a commercial enterprise. There is no definite way to calculate the cost of the public service that the USO requires.

In this connection as well, the PPC's recent comments on the Implementation Plan point to an important issue for the future of privatization. Noting that package services are no longer within the USO, the PPC argues that equality of competitive conditions between Japan Post Service and its private competitors will increase the convenience and utility of the system for Japanese consumers. The PPC urges that when the MIC considers an application from Japan Post Service for a license to enter any of the new business areas listed in the Implementation Plan – such as new direct mail products, domestic third-party logistics or the international freight business – the MIC require transparent and public separation of income from USO postal services and other services, in order to avoid improper cross-subsidization (PPC, 2007, p. 3).

4.3 Repeal of the Postal Monopoly

Industrialized countries generally recognize that the objective of making the public postal operator more efficient and competitive implies repeal of the postal monopoly. The postal monopoly, or 'reserved area', invites poor service and induces inefficiency by insulating the public postal operator from choices of customers and the threat of competition.

In the EU, the Postal Directive of 1997 committed member states to a program of 'gradual and controlled liberalisation of the market'. Member states were authorized to continue postal monopolies but only to 'the extent necessary to ensure the maintenance of universal service'.[23] Sweden, Finland, the United Kingdom, and Germany have already repealed their reserved areas. Overall more than half of the letter-post service in the EU is now offered without monopoly protection. In February 2008, EU amended the Postal Directive to require repeal of most postal monopoly laws by 1 January 2011 and all by 1 January 2013.[24]

Outside the EU, New Zealand repealed its postal monopoly in 1998.[25] Australia retains a postal monopoly but has adopted numerous exemptions, including intra-corporate mail and letters priced at more than four times the price of a basic postage stamp.[26] In the United States, a recent law requires the PRC to review the history and future of the postal monopoly and report to Congress by 2008.[27]

In Japan, as noted above, the 2002 Correspondence Delivery Law provided that private companies could be licensed to provide postal services within the postal monopoly area but made conditions so stringent that no private company has ever applied for a license. In 2005–06, the MIC established a 'Study Group on the Reserved Area and Competition Policies in Postal Services' to review the Correspondence Delivery Law, but in June 2006, the Study Group recommended only minor changes, citing the need to protect universal postal service.[28]

In February 2007, the MIC again set up a 'Study Group on Re-examining the Postal and Correspondence Delivery System'. This group is scheduled to report in 2008 with proposals to modify the postal monopoly. The group is examining both the system in Japan and postal liberalization in other countries. The future of the postal monopoly might be in doubt. The same political forces that prevented earlier liberalization remain, though as of 2008, the immediate uncertainties about execution of the October 2007 privatization have been resolved.[29]

4.4 Independent Regulation

Transformation of a public postal operator into a more commercial and competitive organization also requires an independent regulator. In modern postal laws, there are typically two related objectives to regulation: (i) to ensure the fairness and quality of universal service and (ii) to prevent the public postal operator from competing unfairly against private companies.

To ensure good-quality universal service, the regulator controls the prices and services of the public postal operator and perhaps other providers of universal services. Regulation may also involve ordering or contracting for universal services in areas not adequately served. To prevent unfair competition, the regulator controls 'cross-subsidy' by the public postal operator, that is, using revenues earned in markets where the public postal operator has a monopoly or market-dominant position to underwrite costs incurred in competitive markets. Cross-subsidy is considered unfair to both the competing operator's and to the public postal operator's customers in non-competitive markets. A commercially minded public postal operator – whether organized as a government ministry, independent agency, or normal corporation – cannot be entrusted with regulating itself. Hence, the regulator must be institutionally independent of these stakeholders.

The EU Postal Directive provides that 'Each Member State shall designate one or more national regulatory authorities for the postal sector that are legally separate from and operationally independent of the postal operators'.[30] In some cases, the Commission has gone so far as to initiate infringement procedures against member states to ensure the independence of the regulator. For example, in 2001, the Commission condemned France for failing to establish 'any institutional arrangement ensuring, thanks to a proper separation of duties, that the tasks of economic and financial monitoring, on the one hand, and of supervision of La Poste, on the other, are carried out completely independently one of the other'.[31]

Other industrialized countries have adopted different strategies for regulation of the post office. Australia assigns regulation of the public postal operator to the Australian Competition and Consumer Commission (ACCC), whose first job is enforcement of the competition laws. The ACCC is responsible for (i) overseeing prices of Australia Post's reserved services; (ii) resolving disputes about the terms and conditions for Australia Post's bulk-mail services; and (iii) monitoring for cross-subsidy between reserved and non-reserved services. Significantly, the ACCC may also require Australia Post to keep necessary records. In 2004, government strengthened these regulatory powers in response to complaints about unfair competitive practices.[32] In the United States, the PRC is structurally independent from both government and the Postal Service and exercises substantial supervisory authority over postal practices.[33]

In Japan, there is no independent and permanent regulator for postal services equivalent to those established in most other industrialized countries. The only institutionally independent entities that will provide oversight of the postal services provided by Japan Post Holdings, Japan Post Service and Japan Post Network are the Postal Privatization Commission and the Japanese Fair Trade Commission (JFTC). The PPC has demonstrated itself to be knowledgeable and attentive to market competition issues, yet as an advisory committee, its ability to act will depend entirely on the priority that the prime minister places on postal privatization. Moreover, the PPC is only temporary. The Postal Privatization Law created it, and the cabinet-level Postal Privatization Headquarters to which it reports, only for the duration of the transition to privatization, and both organizations will cease to exist in October 2017. By that time, the two financial entities, Japan Post Bank and Japan Post Insurance, will have been privatized and will be subject to the normal regulation applicable to like banks and insurance companies. But the statutory scheme does not contemplate any complete privatization of Japan Post Service and Japan Post Network or true separation from government, and as of October 2017, there will be no organization charged with ensuring that the postal entities compete fairly and that their activities benefit the public.

The JFTC might help fill this gap. It is the enforcer of Japan's Anti-Monopoly Law and other competition laws, and these laws apply fully to all of the successor entities.[34] Amendments to the Anti-Monopoly Law in April 2005, with increases in staff and resources, have substantially increased the JFTC's ability to vigorously enforce the laws and to apply competition policy to new areas. On 21 July 2006, the JFTC issued a lengthy report on competition issues raised by postal privatization.[35] The report examined the economics of the postal business and the competition policy problems posed by growing competition between Japan Post and private operators. The report discusses in detail the implications of laws and judicial decisions from the EU and other postal reform countries. The report also identifies examples of Japanese governmental intervention in favor of Japan Post, including vehicular traffic regulations, access to change of address databases, and customs procedures. In broad terms, the report concludes that the concept of 'equal footing' is critical to the success of postal privatization and that the JFTC should maintain a watchful eye over the process. In the end, however, the capacity of the JFTC to control Japan Post Holdings and its ministry without an explicit legal mandate is unproven.

In addition, the MIC will supervise the postal entities on a continuing basis under the postal laws and the Postal Privatization Law. For instance, since 1 October 2007, parcel service has no longer been regulated under the Postal Law and is excluded from the scope of regulated mail; only letter post is still regulated.[36] Thus, in theory, Japan Post Service's parcel delivery operations are on an equal footing with domestic parcel companies, and both are regulated by the trucking laws. The Japan Post Service's authorizing statute permits Japan Post Service to provide 'postal delivery service provided under the provisions in the Postal Law',[37] but requires MIC approval before Japan Post Service can provide any 'other services'.[38] As the PPC has observed, the MIC can attach conditions to this approval so as to require transparent accounting and separation of USO and non-USO services. But the MIC is not an independent regulator. As the agency with jurisdiction responsible for supervising Japan Post Holdings, Japan Post Service and Japan Post Network, it has a stake in their success and cannot be truly impartial.

In short, although there exists some level of independent scrutiny of the national postal operator in Japan, no institution wields the independent legal authority of postal regulators in the EU, the United States, and other industrialized countries.

5. CONCLUSION

Japan's postal privatization package has embarked upon privatization, but only for the financial entities that were the principal targets of Koizumi and his fiscal reformers. The package opens a new era in fiscal and political reform – but not (yet) for postal services. The postal successors to Japan Post are not truly corporatized, are not commercial entities operating separately from government, and are not on any credible path toward true privatization. The vast assets of the postal banking and insurance companies are not effectively separated from the operation of the national post office; there is no clear, independent definition of universal service; and there is no plan (yet) to phase out the postal monopoly. Most fundamentally, there is no prospect for truly independent regulation of the public postal operator unless the authority of the PPC can be strengthened and made permanent or the JFTC can exercise broad regulatory authority without benefit of a specific regulatory mandate. While 'postal privatization' began formally in Japan in October 2007, modern postal reform still needs to be addressed.

NOTES

* Views expressed in this article are solely the personal views of the authors.

1. Postal Law (*Yūbin hō*), Law No. 165 of December 12, 1947.
2. Postal Law at § 16.
3. See Japan Ministry of Posts and Telecommunications, *Postal Law and Regulations of Japan*, Postal Law § 16 (1973).
4. Japan Post Law (*Nihon Yūbin Kōsha Hō*), Law No. 97 of 2002.
5. Postal Law (before entry into force of 2005 amendment) §§ 17(4) (postal parcels); 19–2 and 20 (charities); 32(1) (postage methods); 56 (collection boxes); 75–2 (postage rates, publication of accounts); 75–3 (Postal Agreement); 75–4 (public disclosure of rates, etc.); 75–5 (order changes in rates); 75–6 (Operations Manual, delivery standards); and 75–9 (general supervisory authority).
6. Ibid., Art. 5(2).
7. Law Concerning Correspondence Delivery by Private Sector Operators, Law No. 99 of 2002.
8. Yen–dollar exchange rates are as of 17 March 2008 (US$1.00 = JP¥ 96.88).
9. Ibid. at Arts. 2(7) (minimum charges); 31 (capacity to do business); 34 (conditions); and 36 (reports and inspections); data on licensees from MIC (2007).
10. Laws No. 97 to 102 of 2005, respectively.
11. Time deposits and life insurance contracts entered into before 1 October 2007 still retain government guarantees, but have been transferred to the Independent Administrative Entity.
12. Japan Post Holdings Corporation Law, Law No. 98 of 2005, Art. 5.
13. PPC opinions at http://www.yuseimineika.go.jp/iinkai/iken.html, including opinion of 12 April 2006 (agreeing to authorization by the MIC of Japan Post's investment with ANA in a new cargo airline, JP Express Co., Ltd.); two opinions of 5 July 2006 (on implementing regulations for the Postal Privatization

Law); opinion of 8 June 2007 (on Japan Post Holdings' April 2007 Implementation Plan); opinions of 5 July, 6 September and 10 September 2007 (on Cabinet Orders and ministerial orders implementing the Postal Privatization Law); opinion of 5 November 2007 (on freeing business operations of Japan Post Bank and Japan Post Insurance); opinion of 23 January 2008 (approving entry into advertising-related businesses by Japan Post Services); and opinions of 22 February 2008 (approving offerings of credit cards and mortgage loans by Japan Post Bank and offerings of variable annuities by Japan Post Insurance; approving entry by Japan Post Service into new businesses in parcel delivery, gasoline retailing and auto repair).The PPC can and does ask for public comment and can demand documents, explanations, and other cooperation from all governmental officials and agencies, including the postal successor companies and private persons.

14. In the United States, the Postal Service is established as a federal agency which is independent of government because ultimate management authority is vested in nine governors appointed by the President for fixed 7-year terms. Although the US Postal Service has not been corporatized, an official review of the future institutional form of the Postal Service is to be completed by 2011.
15. See Postal Privatization Law Arts. 36 (incorporation); 70(2) (articles of Japan Post Service); 161 (Basic Plan); and 163 (Implementation Plan); Japan Post Holdings Law Art. 11 (changes in articles).
16. Postal Law, as amended effective 1 October 2007, Arts. 67 (scope of accounts to be published); 68 (Postal Regulations); 70 (Management Guidelines); 71 (authority to order 'changes to postal charges, Postal Regulations, or Postal Service Management Guidelines if such orders are determined as necessary for the enforcement of this law'); 73 (subcontracts); 75 (Ministerial Ordinance); Japan Post Service Law Arts. 3 (entry into non-traditional businesses; 4 (social services); 7 (business plan); 8 (transfer of assets); 9 (charge in articles); 10 (financial statements); 11 (form of public accounts); 12 (supervision); and 13 (reports and inspection).
17. Japan Post Network Law Art. 6 (social services); 9 (business plan); 10 (transfer of assets); 11 (charge in articles); 12 (financial statements); 13 (supervision); and 14 (reports and inspection).
18. European Commission, Case No IV/M.1168 – DHL / Deutsche Post (26 June 1998).
19. Postal Accountability and Enhancement Act, Pub. L. 109-435, § 401, adding 39 U.S.C. 2011 (2007).
20. Australia, Australia Postal Corporation (Performance Standards) Regulation 1998, as amended. The universal service obligation placed on Australia Post is relatively light compared to that of other post offices.
21. According to this document, NZ Post promises, *inter alia*: (i) to provide a 6-day-per-week delivery service to more than 95 percent of delivery points; (ii) to maintain the stamp price below NZ$0.45 (US$0.31); (iii) not to introduce a rural service fee; and (iv) to maintain a specified number of post offices (some operated by NZ Post and some franchised to others). The government has authorized that NZ Post shall be the sole designated postal operator representative at the Universal Postal Union for five years.
22. See Postal Accountability and Enhancement Act, Pub. L. 109-435, § 702. This provision requires the Commission to conduct a two-year study of the history and future of universal service and the postal monopoly in the United States and to recommend appropriate changes. Its report is to be submitted to Congress and the President not later than December 21, 2008.
23. European Union, Directive 1997/67/EC, Recital 8 and § 7.
24. Directive 2008/6/EC of the European Parliament and of the Council of 20 February 2008 amending Directive 97/67/EC with regard to the full accomplishment of the internal market of Community postal services, OJ L 52, 27 February 2008, p.3.
25. Postal Services Act 1998, New Zealand.
26. Australian Postal Corporation Act 1989.
27. Postal Accountability and Enhancement Act, P.L. 109–435, §702.
28. Ministry of Internal Affairs and Communications, 'Information and Communications in Japan', (White Paper 2006, pp. 60–61).
29. MIC press release, ' "Yūbin – Shinshōbin Seido no Minaoshi ni Kansuru Chōsa Kenkyūkai" no Kaisai' (Convening of Investigation and Study Group on Reexamining the Postal and Correspondence Delivery System), February 2, 2007, text at http://www.soumu.go.jp/s-news/2007/070206_2.html; all documents and minutes for this study group are available at http://www.soumu.go.jp/yusei/seido_minaoshi/index.html.
30. European Union, Directive 1997/67/EC, OJ L15, 21 January 1998, p. 14, § 22.
31. European Union, Commission, Decision 2002/344/EC of 23 October 2001, OJ L 120, 7 May 2002, p. 19, para. 29. The activities to be monitored involved setting volume thresholds and tariffs for pre-sorted mail.
32. Australia, Postal Services Legislation Amendment Act 2004, No. 69 (2004).
33. New Zealand, Postal Services Act 1998, as amended. The New Zealand postal law essentially treats the postal services market as an ordinary business regulated in the same manner as other commercial activities. The postal law imposes consumer protection obligations on delivery services conveying letters. The only special supervision of the public postal operator is found in disclosure regulations imposed on the public postal operator which are designed to deter anticompetitive behavior. In particular, New Zealand Post is required to disclose the number of bulk-mail contracts at each discount level and the justification

for such discounts. Periodic strengthening of disclosure requirements imposed on New Zealand Post since 1990 suggests that the government initially underestimated the competitive problems posed by deregulation. New Zealand, Postal Services Act 1998, as amended, § 61.

34. Act on Prohibition of Private Monopolization and Maintenance of Fair Trade (Law No. 54 of 1947).
35. Concerning the Postal Business and Competition Policy Issues Related to Implementation of the Postal Privatization Law: Responding to Anti-Competitive Acts that Utilize the Monopoly Area (July 21, 2006). This report drew in part from Singham (2006).
36. Article 16 of the Postal Law prior to amendment by the Postal Privatization Law. After amendment, the mail classification provision of the Postal Law, renumbered as Article 14, provides, 'Postal items shall consist of 1st, 2nd, 3rd and 4th Class Mail'. There is no reference to parcels in the entire revised Postal Law.
37. Postal Delivery Corporation Law § 3(1). In addition, Japan Post Service is authorized to provide 'sales of stamps as delegated by the government' and 'services pertaining to' postal services and sale of stamps.
38. Postal Delivery Corporation Law § 3(3); in this connection, the MIC is specifically required to 'take care not to cause any unreasonable harm to the profits of business operators that carry on the same type of service'. Postal Privatization Law § 77. Postal Privatization Law § 74(1) gave Japan Post Service a six-month grace period to allow it to obtain the trucking license from the Ministry of Land, Infrastructure, and Transport (MLIT) that is required for delivery of parcels.

BIBLIOGRAPHY

Iijima, Isao (2006), Koizumi Kantei Hiroku (Secret Memoir of the Koizumi Cabinet), Tokyo: Nihon Keizai Shimbun Shuppansha.

Japan Post (2005), Statistics on Japan Post (FY 2005).

Japan Post (2007), Postal Services in Japan 2006, http://www.japanpost.jp/en/group/past/2007/pdf/jp/all.pdf, accessed 15 June 2008.

Japan Post Holdings (2006), 'Nihon Yūsei Kōsha no gyōmu tō no shōkei ni kansuru jisshi keikaku no kokkaku' (Framework of the Implementation Plan for Succession to the Business etc. of Japan Post), 31 July, http://www.yuseimineika.go.jp/iinkai/dai6/sirou1.pdf, accessed 15 June 2008.

Japan Post Holdings (2007a), 'Nihon Yūsei Kōsha no gyōmu tō no shōkei ni kansuru jisshi keikaku (Gaiyō)' (Implementation Plan for Succession to the Business etc. of Japan Post (Overview)), 27 April, http://www.japanpost. jp/privatization/pdf/070910_01.pdf, accessed 15 June 2008.

Japan Post Holdings (2007b), 'Shōkeigaisha ga okonau gyōmu no un'ei no naiyō oyobi mitōshi' (Substance and forecast for operation of businesses to be carried out by the successor companies) ('Implementation Plan'), 27 April, http://www.japanpost.jp/privatization/pdf/070910-02.pdf, accessed 15 June 2008.

Maruyama, Shoji (2006), 'Competition structure and future postal reform in Japan: in comparison with international liberalization', in M.A. Crew and P.R. Kleindorfer (eds), Progress Toward Liberalization of the Postal and Delivery Sector, New York: Springer, pp. 369–84.

Ministry of Internal Affairs and Communications (MIC) (2007a), 'Shinshōbin seidō to jigyō no genjō ni tsuite' (Present situation of correspondence delivery system and operations), document distributed to February 21, 2007 session of MIC Study Group on Reexamining the Postal and Correspondence Delivery System (Yūbin – Shinshōbin seidō no Minaoshi ni Kansuru Chōsakenkyūkai), http://www.soumu.go.jp/yusei/seido_minaoshi/070221_1_si4.pdf, accessed 15 June 2008.

Ministry of Internal Affairs and Communications (MIC) (2007b), 'Nihon no Yūbin no Yunibaasaru Saabisu' (Japan's Postal Universal Service), document provided by MIC to 12 April 2007 meeting of MIC Investigation and Study Group on Reexamining the Postal and Correspondence Mail System, text, http://www.soumu.go.jp/yusei/seido_minaoshi/pdf/070412_1_si3.pdf, accessed 15 June 2008.

Ministry of Internal Affairs and Communications (MIC) (2007c), Collected privatization implementation documents, http://www.soumu.go.jp/yusei/mineika/index.html, accessed 15 June 2008.

Ministry of Internal Affairs and Communications (MIC) (2007d), 'Yūbin yakkan oyobi Yūbin gyomu kitei no ninka' (Approval of postal guidelines and postal business regulations), 8 August, http://www.soumu.go.jp/s-news/2007/070808_3.html, accessed 15 June 2008.

Ministry of Internal Affairs and Communications (MIC) (2008), List of licensed correspondence delivery providers, http://www.soumu.go.jp/yusei/pdf/tokutei_g.pdf, accessed 15 June 2008.

Mizutani, F. and S. Uranishi (2003), 'The post office vs. parcel delivery companies: competition effects on costs and productivity', Journal of Regulatory Economics, **23**, 299–319.

Porges, Amelia and Joy M. Leong (2006), 'The privatization of Japan Post: ensuring both a viable post and a level playing field', in M.A. Crew and P.R. Kleindorfer (eds), *Progress Toward Liberalization of the Postal and Delivery Sector*, edited by New York: Springer, pp. 385–400.

Postal Privatization Committee (PPC) (2007), 'Nihon Yūsei Kosha no gyōmu tō no keizoku ni kansuru jisshi keikaku ni taisuru Yūsei Mineika Iinkai no iken ni tsuite (iken)' (Opinion of the PPC regarding the Implementation Plan concerning succession to the businesses of Japan Post), 8 June.

Singham, Shanker A. (2006), 'Competition and regulatory issues in network industries: case study lessons for Japanese telecoms and postal sectors', JFTC Competition Research Policy Center discussion paper, Japanese Fair Trade Commission March.

Takenaka, Heizō (2006), Kōzo kaikaku no shinjitsu: Takenaka Heizō Daijin Nisshi (The Reality of Structural Reform: The Ministerial Logbook of Heizō Takenaka), Tokyo: Nihon Keizai Shimbun Shuppansha.

WIK-Consult (2004), 'Main Developments in the European Postal Sector', study for the European Commission, July, http://ec.europa.eu/internal_market/post/studies_en.htm.

WIK-Consult (2005), 'The Evolution of the Regulatory Model for the European Postal Services', Study for the European Commission, July, http://ec.europa.eu/internal_market/post/studies_en.htm, accessed 15 June 2008.

WIK-Consult (2006), 'Main Developments in the Postal Sector (2004–2006)' Study for the European Commission, May, http://ec.europa.eu/internal_market/post/studies_en.htm, accessed 15 June 2008.

22. Postal reform in Australia

Chris Paterson[†]

1. INTRODUCTION

For almost twenty years the postal system within Australia has undergone a process of continual reform. The need for this reform has been underlined by the emergence of an increasingly dynamic postal landscape. Until the early 1990s, changes in Australian mail volumes correlated highly with fluctuations in the level of domestic economic activity. In subsequent years, electronic substitution, mail rationalization, and consolidation have challenged this traditional relationship. In addition, the wider mail market is now exposed to significant growth in online fulfillment services and increasing acceptance and penetration of direct mail. These factors have created new challenges and opportunities while also redefining the industry's main players. Against this backdrop, Australia Post has transformed itself through a mix of competition, opportunity, and regulation to become, by international standards, one of the best-performing postal organizations.

Reform within Australia has, however, been tempered by an acknowledgment of the real difficulties in reconciling the commercial and social responsibilities of the nation's postal operator, Australia Post. Under Section 27 of the Australian Postal Corporation Act, Australia Post is required to deliver standard-sized letters to all but the most remote parts of Australia even if the costs of delivery exceed revenue. This relatively onerous requirement in honoring its universal service obligation (USO) represents a distinct point of difference when contrasting the Australian case to most other postal authorities in the developed world. Similarities may, however, be drawn with Canada and Sweden. In the case of the former, an exclusive privilege under Section 14 of the Canada Post Corporation Act is granted to the corporation for 'collecting, transmitting and delivering letters to the addressee thereof within Canada'.[1] In the Swedish case the national postal regulator has required Sweden Post to provide universal postal service as a condition of its license.[2] Certainly other European countries such as the UK, Germany and France have vastly greater population densities than Australia. So, too, do countries with greater land masses, such as the United States, by virtue of a significantly larger population base despite the similarities to Australia's geographic scale. Such considerations have therefore weighed heavily in the reform of the domestic postal industry, especially with respect to the application of uniform tariffs for reserved service mail.

This chapter proceeds with Section 2 defining the core business activities of the national postal operator in addition to highlighting a number of key performance indicators and business scale measures. A chronology of the reforms that have taken place within the

† Diversified Specifics.

Australian postal industry since 1975 when the Australian Postal Commission (hereafter referred to as Australia Post) became the operator of the national postal service is presented in Section 3. This timeline illustrates the importance placed on balancing delivery service obligations with commercial accountability which has resulted in the unique set of reforms that have emerged within Australia. This process has given rise to a changing mix in both the reserved service categories and the extent to which worksharing is now encouraged. Economic welfare outcomes are dealt with in Section 4 by assessing the price, efficiency, and service standards realized by the postal reform process. The conclusion in Section 5 then reaffirms some comparative successes of the Australia Post model and acknowledges the difficulties associated with altering the status quo as relates particularly to downstream access levels.

2. A SNAPSHOT OF AUSTRALIA POST

Since the commencement of the postal reform process, Australia Post has established itself as one of the nation's most successful major companies. Today, Australia Post's core business activities include the provision of: letter services; parcels and logistics services; inbound and outbound international mail services; retail services; financial services; and other ancillary services (including joint ventures). Since corporatization, Australia Post has invested heavily in mail collection, processing, and delivery activities. Australia Post's retail network underpins the nation's postal infrastructure and enables it to meet its commercial and social obligations. A number of Australia Post's key performance indicators and business scale measures are presented in Table 22.1.

The figures in the table illustrate that the existing competitive and regulatory mix within Australia appears to have yielded positive results despite a large land mass and relatively small population which, when combined, manifest themselves into a comparatively onerous USO. Such obligations have also tended to take on greater importance in recent times as the profits from the services reserved to Australia Post have diminished relative to the non-reserved categories (see Figure 22.1). The widening of this interval illustrates a propensity for Australia Post to operate in an increasingly competitive space by virtue of its entry into new markets not covered by its mandated monopoly.

In the reserved segments, Australia Post has also become increasingly susceptible to competitive pressures in recent times. Factors that traditionally governed fluctuations in the diminishing reserved segment have undergone a fundamental change over the greater part of the last decade. Historic small-letter volume data dating back to 1976 strongly correlate with the level of non-farm economic activity.[3] However, the strength of this correlation began to wane at the turn of the century as the impact of electronic substitution, in the form of Internet and phone-based alternatives to the traditional mail item, began to emerge. Figure 22.2 illustrates this divergence as the typical consumer was faced with a broadening set of choices when engaging in a bill payment activity.

It is not unreasonable to expect this trend to continue at an increasing rate as small-letter rationalization and consolidation on the bill presentment side of a transaction accompanies the sustained growth in substitutive practices already evident in the realm of bill payments. That is, although there is no empirical evidence to suggest that the consumer has accepted an online relationship with the biller, there do appear to be trends

Table 22.1 Australia Post 2006/07, some statistical highlights

Highlights	Statistics
Performance indicators	
Revenue (AU$ million)	4,711.1
Profit after income tax (AU$ million)	400.7
Ordinary dividend (AU$ million)	297
Domestic standard letter delivery performance (%)[1]	96.3
Estimated economic contribution (AU$ billion)[2]	2.36
Scale measures	
Total mail volumes (million)	5,516
Delivery points (million)	10.3
Direct employees	34,732
Total postal outlets	4,449
Rural & remote location postal outlets	2,553

Notes:
1 96.3% of domestic standard letters delivered by Australia Post were either on time or early (in contrast to an equivalent 95.6% in the preceding year).
2 As a contribution to the Australian economy via payments for goods and services (AU$2.08 billion), and capital assets combined with business acquisitions (AU$283.7 million) (Australian Postal Corporation, 2007), p. 43.

Source: Australian Postal Corporation (2007, pp. 8, 20, 43–5).

emerging which indicate that consolidative practices by the major mailers will provide an eventual downside to bill presentment standard letter volumes.[4] These trends have significant ramifications for the future of workshared small-letter volumes and for the funding of the USO given the changing mail mix that has occurred within the reserved letter segment at Australia Post in recent times.[5] Figure 22.3 provides an illustration of how workshared (PreSort Barcoded) small-letter volumes constitute a majority of 54 percent share, in 2006/07, of total (reserved) small-letter volumes in contrast to an equivalent figure of 37 percent in 1995/96.

Should the downward pressures exerted by substitution on the bill payments side of a transaction be replicated by increases in consolidation and rationalization on the bill presentment side of a transaction, then it is not unreasonable to expect an eventual decline in both standard letter segments. Regular upward readjustments to nominal price therefore become essential in determining the extent to which Australia Post can subsidize an already onerous USO and ensure the effective achievement of mandated social responsibilities in the face of such trends.

3. THE REFORM TIMELINE

The term 'postal reform' has been defined as 'taking steps that will ultimately allow and require the post office to operate more like a private company in a commercial environment more like a normal competitive market', (Campbell, 2002, p. 40.). Fundamental to the dis-

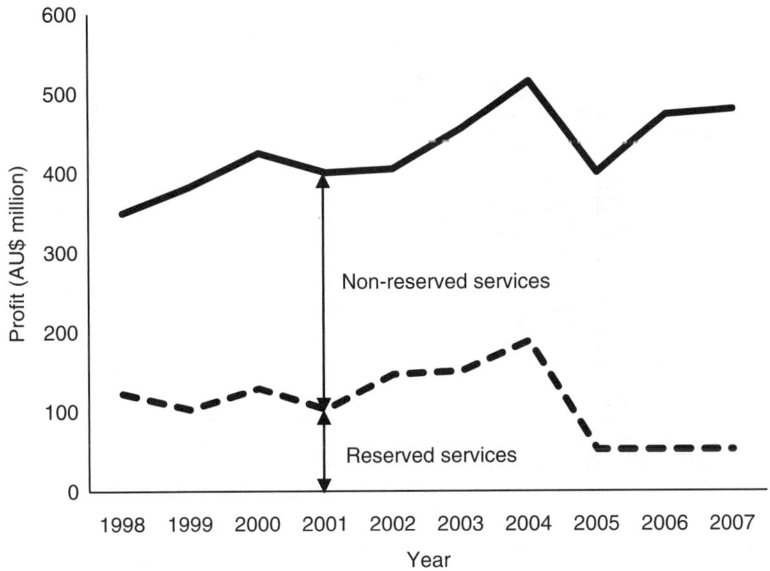

Note: Profit before interest, income from joint ventures and tax. Data pertaining to the years 2005–2007 is given by the Australian Equivalents to International Financial Reporting Standards (A-IFRS). Alternatively, data prior to and inclusive of 2004 is a function of accounting standards applicable to these periods (AGAAP).

Source: Australian Postal Corporation (2007, p. 44).

Figure 22.1 Australia Post Reserved vs Non-Reserved Profits

cussion on improvements to postal services within Australia is an understanding of the reform process that the current structures and scope of operations have evolved from as this provides an insight into the cultural, geographical, and psychological influences pertinent to the region. To this extent, it was under the Australian Postal Services Act of 1975 that the Australian Postal Commission (trading as Australia Post) became the operator of Australia's national postal service. The transformation into its own unique entity occurred when, on July 1 of that year, the Postmaster General's Department was divided into two bodies, forming also the Australian Telecommunications Commission (then known as Telecom Australia and later re-branded Telstra). The first stage in postal reform within Australia, however, took place in 1989 when corporatization occurred.[6] Typically this initial step in the reform process occurs for three primary reasons: (i) to reduce political interference; (ii) to facilitate budgetary accountability; and (iii) to increase transparency. In 1989, the Australian Postal Corporation Act established Australia Post as a government business enterprise.

The 1989 Act specified that the principal function of Australia Post is to supply postal services within Australia and between Australia and other countries.[7] It is governed by a board of directors and operates as a commercial business enterprise. The 1989 reforms meant that the Commonwealth government retained ownership of Australia Post and received dividends, taxes, and customs duties from the firm similar to that of a private

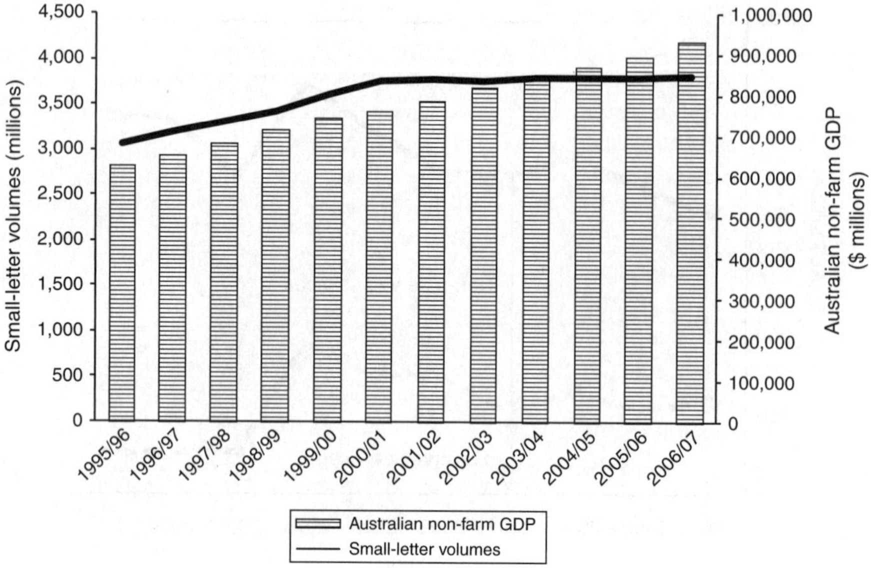

Sources: Small-letter volumes: Australia Post; Australian Non-farm GDP Cat. No. 5206.0 Table 6 Gross Value Added by Industry, Australia, Chain volume measures, Australian Bureau of Statistics.

Figure 22.2 Australian Non-farm GDP vs. small letter volumes

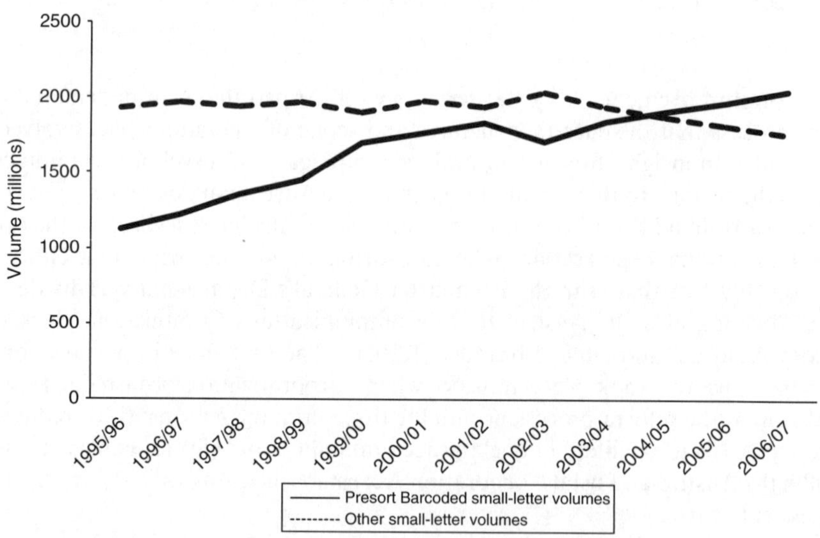

Source: Diversified Specifics, (2007, Chart 2.1.1. p.15); data provided by Australia Post.

Figure 22.3 PreSort Barcoded small-letter volumes vs. other small-letter volumes, 1995/96–2006/07 (financial year)

company. Shareholder responsibilities became part of the government's ministerial responsibility (at present jointly attributable to the Minister for Communications, Information Technology and the Arts, and the Minister for Finance and Administration). Therefore, effectively ministers ultimately wield both governmental and commercial authority over Australia Post.[8]

Following corporatization, in 1992, the Australian government referred public and private mail services, courier services, and parcel services (including electronic services) within Australia to an Industry Commission for inquiry. The terms of reference specified that the Commission should report on institutional, regulatory or other arrangements subject to influence by governments in Australia that inhibit efficient resource use and advise on courses of action that could remove such inhibitions and facilitate improved efficiency.[9]

In response, the Industry Commission recommended that the Commonwealth government consider replacing its objective of providing the letter service at a uniform charge for standard letters with a maximum affordable charge for standard letters capped at the existing basic postal rate (BPR). Moreover, if the maximum charge objective were accepted, the Commission then recommended that the reserved services protection no longer be afforded to Australia Post from 1 January 1995.[10] The rationale behind the suggested reforms was that increased competition would result in a broadening of choice for consumers and would encourage Australia Post to look towards more efficient processes. Opportunities for cross-subsidization between reserved and non-reserved services would be eliminated, and emerging technologies and alternative supply chains could develop. The Commission's report acknowledged that 'under a deregulated market letter prices would vary' and that 'it would not be possible to meet the objective of a uniform rate of postage for standard letters'.[11]

However, while the Commonwealth government agreed to the reforms in principle, it did not implement them to the extent to which the Industry Commission had suggested. Rather, in the Australian Postal Corporation Amendment Act of October 1994 (Commonwealth of Australia, 1994), Australia Post's monopoly was only somewhat reduced with the weight of a mail item reserved cut from 500 to 250 grams. In addition, the minimum competitors could charge was also reduced from 10 to four times the basic letter rate, that is, to AU$1.80 (from AU$4.50). Australia Post, under the amended Act, was authorized to provide any postal or non-postal service; however, this freedom was constrained by continuation of its USO or community service obligation (CSO) as it is known in Australia. Australia Post is required to deliver letters within an area defined to be reasonably accessible to all citizens of Australia on an equitable basis, by residential or commercial location. In addition, delivery performance standards were imposed to reflect the social, industrial and commercial needs of the Australian community.[12]

Reform was back on the agenda in February of 1998 when the Australian government requested that the National Competition Council (NCC) advise on practical courses of action to improve competition, efficiency and consumer welfare in the postal services sector.[13] The NCC deemed that Australia Post's performance reflected a lack of competition in postal services. A key recommendation, however, related to the onerous nature of the USO within Australia. The Council recommended retaining the USO because there was 'no feasible alternative to delivering on the social benefits'.[14] With this in mind, the

1998 NCC review recommended the retention of the uniform BPR for non-bulk standard-size letters.[15] When it came to business customers the recommendation was that Australia Post be allowed to offer discounts with the maximum allowable rate capped to the uniform BPR applicable to the standard-size letter. At the same time, the Council recommended the opening up of business mail to competition. For household mail, the Council recommended retention of the monopoly but a reduction in the minimum competitor price for household letters from four to two times the standard letter rate.[16]

The NCC's recommended deregulation of all business mail was subsequently rejected by the Australian government in preference to a reduction in Australia Post's reserved service obligations. Indeed, a Bill was proposed in 2000 that sought to convert Australia Post from a statutory corporation into a public company (wholly owned by the Commonwealth). When this Bill was withdrawn due to the reservations about last-mile delivery issues, a 2003 Bill replaced it, again, with an underpinning rationale of driving improvements in the delivery of Australia Post services.

Recent reforms have also emanated from the Australian Competition and Consumer Commission (ACCC). The Trade Practices Act and the Australian Postal Corporation Act grant the ACCC three key regulation responsibilities as relates to postal services in Australia. These responsibilities include: (i) evaluating any proposed price changes relating to Australia Post's reserved services; (ii) conducting inquiries into Australia Post's supply of bulk mail services when disputes arise over the terms and conditions, and (iii) assessing the extent of cross-subsidy between Australia Post's reserved and non-reserved services. The existence of this independent postal sector regulator can be regarded as the second stage in postal reform occurring within Australia as the ACCC's role is to curtail any 'unfair competition' against private companies and ensure the fairness and quality of universal service.

The Postal Services Legislation Amendment Act of 2004 amended the Australian Postal Corporation Act to grant the ACCC record keeping rule (RKR) powers which require Australia Post to maintain records relevant to any of the ACCC's regulatory roles. As noted above, in most recent years the ACCC has reported on cross-subsidy issues in response to complaints that Australia Post was engaging in such practices to improve its competitive position. The objective of the regulator in this instance is to ensure that Australia Post is not taxing users from its reserved service (that is, letters) to then subsidize the users of its non-reserved services (that is, parcels). If this were the case, then Australia Post would have an unfair advantage over the other players in the non-reserved segment. As illustrated in Figure 22.1, the revenue received from Australia Post's reserved services has been decreasing over time relative to that generated by the non-reserved category.[17] These trends emphasize Australia Post's expansion into new areas that possess synergies with existing elements of the postal system. In addition, the scope of mail items under reserved service have, over time, through the aforementioned reforms been scaled back. Exclusions to the reserved service include the delivery of (among others): newspapers; magazines; letters weighing more than 250 grams; letters to an office of Australia Post where it is then lodged for delivery under a bulk interconnection service; the carriage of a letter from an office of the individual or organization sending the letter to another office of that individual or organization; and letters to the provider of an aggregation service, for the purposes of aggregation in order to use a bulk interconnection service.[18] Therefore, the majority of Australia Post's revenue and profit now emanates from activities undertaken in fully and partially competitive markets.[19] In March 2007, the ACCC's second cross-subsidy investigation concluded that 'the regulatory accounts do not provide evidence of cross-subsidy from Australia Post's reserved services to the non-reserved services'.[20]

4. OUTCOMES OF POSTAL REFORM IN AUSTRALIA

Assessing the effectiveness of the competitive and regulatory mix that has evolved over almost twenty years since the date of corporatization, must be undertaken in light of the outcomes generated for the differing stakeholders that comprise the Australian postal industry. The fundamental elements that dictate economic welfare provide the structure employed within this section to facilitate such a discussion. These elements include price, efficiency and service quality outcomes.

4.1 Price

The quasi-fixed pricing system under which Australia Post operates minimizes any transaction costs that may arise due to regular changes in nominal price.[21] When the BPR increased in 2003 from 45 to 50 cents, this represented the first price increase on a standard small-letter item in 11 years.[22] Such a lag provides incentives for Australia Post to improve its cost base and productivity outcomes so as to garner sustainable short-term improvements to its bottom line, at least until nominal price again changes. Australia's BPR ranks as one of the lowest when considering letter prices internationally among developed countries.[23] Given the length of time that nominal price has been fixed in Australia, the real price of small letters therefore has trended downward.

In regard to workshared ('PreSort Barcoded') volumes, regulatory pricing outcomes have tended to be more restrictive, and the 2003 BPR increase reflected the ACCC's general pricing view that the average price for 'Other' small-letter volumes could increase, yet the average for PreSort Barcoded letter volumes (bulk letters) should not.[24] Indeed, the price of PreSort Barcoded letter volumes has not increased since 1992.[25] This approach is significant given the increasing importance of workshared letters within the small-letter category at Australia Post, illustrated in Figure 22.3. This service is offered at a discount to the BPR that is intended to reflect the avoided average transport costs otherwise incurred by Australia Post. Private firms are therefore permitted to interconnect with Australia Post by tendering PreSort Barcoded letter volumes downstream.

Australia Post's PreSort Barcoded prices, in the main, therefore reflect a combination of: the estimate of upstream processing cost savings accumulated prior to lodgement; factor (labor and capital) efficiency initiatives undertaken by Australia Post; legislative requirements governing reserved service products given that PreSort Barcoded letters are a significant subset, and commercial imperatives. Apart from a general understanding that the BPR will be fixed for periods of approximately five years, a formal structure for price regulation, such as a CPI-X price determination, is not evident in Australia and there is no evidence to suggest a change in this approach in the foreseeable future.

4.2 Efficiency

In terms of labor productivity, Australia Post has engaged in significant technological investments that have stimulated total factor productivity of operations to increase by 3.5 percent per annum.[26] Such investments, mainly taking place in the realm of mail processing, have included successive evolutions of Optical Character Readers (through to Multi Line Optical Character Readers). The 1995 introduction of FuturePost itself represented a five-year $500 million investment in plant and equipment. For Australia Post this marked a concentrated period that focused on automation in the processing and delivery of mail via a combination of technological improvements, mail processing network centralizations and a proliferation in the utilization of barcoding. As a result, between 1993 and 2003, Australia Post's cumulative labor productivity growth was more than double that of the Australian economy (that is, Australia Post: 62 percent; Australian economy: 26 percent).[27] In essence, labor was substituted for capital and, as a consequence, labor productivity levels have tended to exceed equivalent outcomes attributable to other international postal authorities.[28]

4.3 Service Performance

Australia Post has specified various criteria in the postal industry that dictate their own service performance objectives. These include providing fast, frequent, and reliable mail delivery service performance; providing dispersed and convenient access to postal services throughout Australia; and resolving customer complaints.[29] Of these criteria, delivery service performance is a crucial element of Australia Post's legislative requirements.[30] In terms of letter delivery service, Australia Post is required to attain a 94 percent on-time delivery of all domestic non-bulk-letter volumes. In 2006/07, they exceeded this figure by delivering 96.3 percent of domestic letters either on time or early (in contrast to an equivalent 95.6 percent in the preceding year).[31] It is therefore unlikely that providing private companies with access to the Australian postal industry downstream would improve delivery service performance, given the historically high standards set by Australia Post. Should the delivery performance standards continue to remain high and prevent moves towards mandated competition in delivery, then it also appears unlikely that a complex schedule of downstream access prices will develop in Australia as has resulted in some European countries where FMO is underway.

5. CONCLUSION

The Australia Post model delivers its commercial and social responsibilities effectively through its efforts to provide: a reasonable price that is low by world standards, incentives for labor and capital efficiency gains, high levels of delivery service performance, and substantial rates of return to the Australian community via its dividend and tax payments. The reform process, thus far, has been successful in maintaining postal service across a very large land mass at a high standard while substantially reducing the scope of the postal monopoly.

The light-handed regulatory approach may partly explain these successes. That is, in capping the BPR, Australia Post is motivated to achieve ongoing cost efficiencies to maximize its return over the period when nominal price remains fixed. However, with the changing competitive landscape in Australia now characterized by increasing forces of substitution, rationalization, consolidation and fulfillment, intervention will most likely take the form of increasingly regular upward movements in the BPR to ensure that the aforementioned high levels of social and commercial performance standards are maintained. The corporate structure at Australia Post, with a board of four to eight directors, also has appeared to effectively mimic the accountabilities of private enterprise. In doing so, executive compensation is commensurate with the private sector and this ensures that those who are capable and qualified, as determined by the labor market, have their hands on the levers of policy at Australia Post.

When assessing legislative changes to the competitive landscape, it should be noted that the benefits of increased competition will largely accrue to the business sector. Access upstream has manifested itself through statutory interconnection in the PreSort Barcoded segment of Australia Post's reserved service. By reducing the monopoly in this manner, larger business customers have been empowered with increased flexibility and discounted prices.

Downstream competition, however, has not evolved to the same extent as elsewhere. This is partly a result of the onerous USO in Australia arising from its land mass and population characteristics. Countries characterized by relatively more extreme last-mile delivery costs, such as Australia, must engage in greater tariff rebalancing to recover margins. A corollary of this is the difficulty of introducing downstream competition, with associated political and social ramifications resulting from the increased pressure on the national postal carrier's ability to underwrite its USO. That is, some degree of restriction on downstream competition is a quid pro quo for the USO. The more demanding the USO, the more difficult it becomes to achieve full market opening. The existing high level of delivery service performance achieved by Australia Post also raises questions as to the possible improvements that increased competition might yield in this area.

NOTES

1. Consolidated Statutes of Canada (1985), c. C-10, 1980-81-82-83, c. 54, s. 14, subject to the exclusions outlined in Section 15.
2. Sweden, Postal Services Act, as amended, section 5b.
3. Diversified Specifics (2002).
4. Telstra (the dominant player in Australia's telecommunications industry) recently announced a major bill consolidation strategy labelled 'The Telstra single bill'. The key elements of this offering involved the consolidation of multiple bills relating to different Telstra services into a single bill at the expense of individual monthly statements. The movement to a single bill for Telstra customers was automatic, with multiple service users having to 'opt in' if they wished to retain their current billing arrangements.
5. The 'PreSort Barcoded small-letter' segment consists of bulk (300+) lodgements of (i) Business transactional letter volumes such as bills, statements, share notices and letters advising customers of price increases, policy changes, etc; and (ii) Direct mail including promotional letters, brochures and other addressed promotional material that satisfies the relevant small letter category size and weight requirements; the dominant product category is PreSort transactional letters. As defined in Diversified Specifics, (2007, p. 8, footnote 4).
6. The first stage in postal reform is generally regarded as corporatization, with successive stages taking the form of: independent regulatory supervision; market liberalization; and then privatization.
7. Section 14, p. 7, Australian Postal Corporation Act 1989, Act No. 64 of 1989 as amended, as prepared on 26 September 2007 taking into account amendments up to Act No. 156 of 2007.

8. As noted and discussed in Campbell (2002, p. 43) citing the Australia Post Act (Australian Postal Corporation Act 1989), Sections 22-24, 33, 49, 73, 79, and 83. Noting Australia Post is authorized to borrow money from the government 'on such terms as the Minister for Finance determines in writing', Section 60.
9. See Terms of Reference, Industry Commission (1992).
10. Industry Commission (1992, p. xviii).
11. For further discussion on this matter, see Recommendation 17 of Industry Commission (1992, p. xviii).
12. Australian Postal Corporation Act 1989, as amended in Sections 3, 16–19, 27.
13. Terms of Reference, National Competition Council (1998, Section 2, p. 5).
14. Ibid., p. 137.
15. Ibid., p. 141.
16. Ibid., p. 230.
17. Ibid., p. 66.
18. For reserved service coverage and exclusions, see Sections 29 and 30 of the Australian Postal Corporation Act 1989, Act No. 64 of 1989 as amended, as prepared on 26 September 2007 taking into account amendments up to Act No. 156 of 2007, Prepared by the Office of Legislative Drafting and Publishing, Attorney General's Department, Canberra.
19. Australian Postal Corporation (2007 p. 45).
20. ACCC (2007, p. 2).
21. Transaction costs in this sense are complexities and administration difficulties that would otherwise arise if nominal price was set on a rolling basis based upon short-run marginal costs.
22. The BPR is directly applicable to the 'Other small-letter' segment which consists of full rate business mail, cheque payments and other consumer correspondence that satisfy the relevant small-letter category size and weight requirements; the major products categories are Ordinary Letters and Clean Mail. As defined in Diversified Specifics, (2007, p. 8 footnote 3).
23. Australia Post's BPR of 50 cents is among the lowest of all OECD countries when considering relative postage stamp prices adjusted for exchange rate differences. For further detail on such relative comparisons, see, Australian Postal Corporation, (2007, p. 14).
24. ACCC (2002b, p. 13).
25. At the time of writing, March 2008, Australia Post have lodged a draft notification with the ACCC for a 10 percent increase in the nominal BPR in addition to a general rise in the PreSort segment. The total extent of the price rises is estimated by Australia Post to be 8 percent (Australian Postal Corporation, 2008).
26. This evidence pertains to the 1992–2002 period, and is reported in Meyrick and Associates (2002). Also ACCC (2002a, p. 7), where Australia Post claims that productivity growth between 1991 and 2001 has been twice the national average.
27. Lee, (2004, p. 30).
28. In 2003, Australia Post's labor costs were 49.5% of total costs (down from 62.1% in 1993). This compares to equivalent figures at the time of: UK 57.3%, Canada 63.5% and USA 78.9% (Lee, 2004, p. 30).
29. Lee, (2004, p. 31).
30. Australian Postal Corporation Act 1989, as amended in Section 27.
31. Australian Postal Corporation (2007, p. 15).

REFERENCES

ACCC (Australian Competition and Consumer Commission) (2002a), 'Australia Post Corporation Ltd: Draft Pricing Notification', May.

ACCC (Australian Competition and Consumer Commission) (2002b), 'Australian Postal Corporation Price Notification Decision', October.

ACCC (Australian Competition and Consumer Commission) (2007), 'Assessing Cross-Subsidy in Australia Post 2005–06', March.

Australian Postal Corporation (2007), 'Australia Post Annual Report 2006/07', October 17.

Australian Postal Corporation (2008), 'Australia Post Seeks Increase in Letter Rates', February 15, Corporate Media Release.

Australian Postal Corporation Act 1989, Act No. 64 of 1989 as amended, as prepared on 26 September 2007 taking into account amendments up to Act No. 156 of 2007, Prepared by the Office of Legislative Drafting and Publishing, Attorney General's Department, Canberra.

Campbell, J.I. (2002), 'Modern postal reform laws: a comparative survey', in M.A. Crew and P.R. Klendorfer (eds), *Postal and Delivery Services: Pricing, Productivity, Regulation and Strategy*, Boston, MA: Kluwer Academic, pp. 39–58.
Commonwealth of Australia (1994), 'Australian Postal Corporation Amendment Act 1994', no. 142, as an Act to amend the Australian Postal Corporation Act 1989 and Part VIIA of the Crimes Act 1914.
Consolidated Statutes of Canada (1985), 'Canada Post Corporation Act', R.S.C. 1985, c. C-10.
Diversified Specifics (2002), 'Executive Summary: Small Letter Volume Analysis', report produced on behalf of Australia Post.
Diversified Specifics (2007), 'Domestic Small Letter Segment Volume Demand: Public Document', December, report produced on behalf of Australia Post.
Industry Commission (1992), 'Mail, Courier and Parcel Services', Report No. 28, 30 October.
Lee, G. (2004), 'Towards effective competition in postal services: The Australia Post model', Discussion Paper, presented at the ACCC Regulatory Conference, July.
Meyrick and Associates (2002), 'Australia Post: Past and Forecast Productivity Growth', August.
National Competition Council (NCC) (1998), 'Review of the Australian Postal Corporation Act'.

23. Postal reform in developing countries: challenges and choices

Juan B. Ianni[†]

1. INTRODUCTION

Little research has been conducted on why postal reform and modernization in developing countries has lagged behind similar initiatives undertaken in the industrialized world. However, this lack of progress has serious implications both for these countries and for the postal world at large. First, the low productivity of universal service providers (USPs) in developing countries means that governments must direct large subsidies to these operators. Scarce resources must be diverted from critical areas such as health, education, and so on to support what should be a commercially self-sustaining activity. Thus, primarily through taxes and the purchase of value-added services, consumers must pay relatively high prices for less than desired quality. Consumers also willingly pay private operators five or six times the USP's basic tariffs in order to obtain acceptable service levels (Ansón et al., 2006).

Through the Universal Postal Union's (UPU's) Quality of Service Fund, industrialized countries are investing a significant level of resources to improve quality of service in developing countries and maintain the integrity and competitiveness of the international mail network. These efforts have met with some success, but to fully exploit such gains, USPs in developing countries must achieve a much higher level of operational and financial performance. Furthermore, as the UPU moves towards a cost-based terminal dues system, developing country USPs must bring costs and prices into alignment or risk negative compensation flows with higher-priced industrialized countries (Evsen and Roy, 2000).

Furthermore, while the growth of digital communications is exponentially larger than that of the postal industry, the postal network in many developing countries still remains the best means for nationwide distribution of information, goods, funds, and government services. Finally, while it must be admitted that little analytic research has been done to demonstrate the synergistic relationship between postal development and economic growth, it would appear intuitive that inefficient postal services cause delays in the transmission of information, goods, and most importantly in cash flows. This is demonstrated in developing countries where bill payers typically spend inordinate amounts of time paying utility and other bills in person (Walsh, 2001).

Improving postal performance in developing countries through postal reform not only benefits the citizens of those countries but also improves the integrity and competitiveness of the international mail system as a whole. This chapter first considers the comparative

[†] Postal Policy Expert, Nashville, USA.

pace of postal reform in industrialized and developing countries (Section 2) and the specific challenges to postal reform in the developing world (Section 3). It then suggests some strategies to overcome these challenges (Section 4) and provides examples of developing countries that have successfully implemented these strategies (Section 5). Section 6 concludes.

2. REFORM IN INDUSTRIALIZED AND DEVELOPING COUNTRIES

By adhering to the UPU Acts, governments are obliged to provide universal postal services to all of their citizens. While the specific level of this service is defined nationally, there is general consensus that the primary goal of postal reform is to ensure that citizens receive an adequate level of universal services at the lowest possible cost to both the government and consumers. Liberalization of postal markets (where portions of these markets have been reserved to USPs), better regulation, USP rehabilitation and commercialization, and increased market production have further been identified as the most-effective strategies for achieving this goal.

Within industrialized countries, there has been continuing progress on postal reform. Through its postal directives and ongoing negotiations, the European Union (EU) has lowered the reserved area for universal services from 350 to 50 grams with full liberalization (subject to the continued maintenance of universal service) scheduled for 2011. Several markets (the United Kingdom, Finland, Sweden) have entirely eliminated the reserved area and some USPs (Germany, Malta, the Netherlands) have been privatized and run as fully commercialized businesses. At the same time, the EU has defined precise quality standards and monitoring systems for universal service and developed cost-based international remuneration systems. The United States passed the Postal Accountability and Enhancement Act based on market segmentation into dominant and competitive product areas and established inflation-indexed tariff increases. Japan has started a serious discussion of postal reform, and Australia and New Zealand continue to move forward on reform initiatives already several decades old.

The pace of postal reform in the developing world, particularly among least developed countries, has been far slower. There is no regional initiative in the developing world comparable to the EU's drive to increase competition in the market while maintaining universal service. In fact, in many developing countries, government-supported USP's continue to have a *de jure* monopoly over large segments of the postal market even though *de facto* competition has reduced their market share to minority status. Furthermore, over 45 percent of countries with GDPs under US$5,000 per capita have operating revenues lower than operating expenses (Kenny, 2006) and continue to lose market share in spite of significant government subsidies. Per capita mail volumes, at least those captured within the UPU's *Postal Statistics*, are so significantly skewed towards more industrialized countries[1] that it is easy to question whether such markets are part of the same industry. This disparity is further shown in the varying rates of productivity for USPs in different national income strata (Figure 23.1).

These differences can also be noted on a regional basis, particularly in terms of one of the faster-growing segments of the postal market, parcels (Table 23.1).

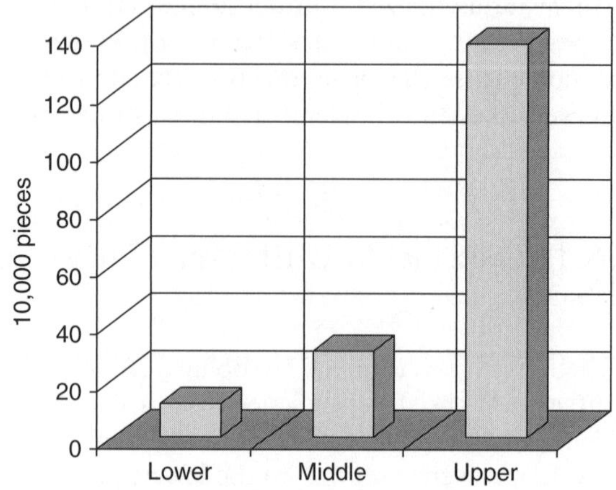

Figure 23.1 *Letter-class mail processed per employee*

Table 23.1 *Letter post (per capita) and parcels (per 1,000 inhabitants) in various regions*

Region	Letter-post/capita	Parcels/1,000 inhabitants
Africa	3.0	6
Latin America/Caribbean	18.9	283
Asia and Pacific	12.5	80
Europe and CIS	37.3	140
Arab countries	4.9	5
Industrialized countries	403	6,375

Source: UPU.

A much higher level of competition exists in postal markets of the Latin American region, where the USP is frequently a minority player among hundreds of postal operators, than in Africa, where a single USP normally dominates a much smaller market. This appears to be driven not by the relative strengths of regulatory frameworks but instead by the existence of sufficient market volume to warrant competition in Latin America. Commercialization of USPs in the developing world has been limited, primarily due to the low level of private investment. In those cases where significant private investment has been made (for example, Argentina) it has achieved only limited success.

3. POSTAL REFORM CHALLENGES IN DEVELOPING COUNTRIES

Numerous challenges impede postal reform in developing countries. The most significant is low letter-class volumes when these should form the foundation for the rest of the postal market. Of the 158 USPs reporting per capita mail volumes in the UPU's *Postal Statistics*

(2006), 75 (47 percent) report figures of less than 10 pieces annually; 41 (26 percent) report less than 1 letter per year, bringing into question whether such service can truly be called universal let alone financially viable. Moreover, most of this volume is concentrated in a very small populace and geographic portion (large cities) of the market. Such low volumes limit economies of scale and profitability and lower investment and development opportunities. While UPU figures cover only the USP's volumes, they are indicative of overall market size and represent the segment of the market used to finance universal service if a reserved area has been established for the USP.

There has been an ongoing and healthy debate concerning the reasons for low postal volumes in developing countries and the impact of this result on postal costs. One view holds that postal volumes are very closely tied to GDP levels. As a network industry, postal unit costs will necessarily be higher for lower volumes, even when factors such as lower labor costs, limited delivery, and reduced quality of service are factored in (Cohen et al. 2004; Kenny, 2006). According to this view, the unit costs for universal service mail for lower-volume markets (less than 10 pieces per capita) could be as high as US$0.60 per letter without delivery to the door and US$0.76 per letter with such delivery. 'The point is clear that letter delivery becomes considerably more expensive in low-volume environments, not merely because of rising costs of home delivery, but also because the other fixed costs of the network are divided up amongst far fewer stamp purchases' (Kenny, 2006, p. 80). In very low-volume scenarios (less than one piece per capita), if prices were raised to match such costs, universal service mail would simply become a low-priced version of courier mail without any value-added benefits. This is precisely what has occurred in many low-volume markets where consumers are resorting to private couriers for basic services.

A counter-view has been expressed that postal volumes in developing countries are driven by different factors from those in industrialized countries, particularly when a differentiation between lower- and middle-income countries is made: 'Low-income countries are thus very far from a postal economic model exclusively relying on economies of scale at delivery' (Ansón et al., 2006, p. 219). In this view, literacy levels, demographics, and national communication patterns are more important than levels of economic development in determining postal volumes in low-income countries. The main inhibitors to postal growth, thus, are not economic (low incomes, lack of mail-intensive industries, and so on) but rather the low level of access to mail services; in other words, 'build it and they will come'. However, it has not been demonstrated that increasing access to mail services in low-volume mail markets significantly increases postal traffic. Furthermore, this same view makes an argument for strong monopolies as a means of increasing volumes and efficiency for a single operator. There seems to a tension between this and the earlier statement that low-volume markets are very far from relying exclusively on economies of scale in delivery.

The outcome of this debate has strong implications for the postal reform agendas and strategies in developing countries that will be discussed below. Here, it is enough to note that in any network industry, regardless of the factors *producing* demand, greater volumes will provide more opportunities for economies of scale, increased quality, and decreased unit costs.

Many postal markets in developing countries are also highly fragmented, with numerous operators competing for low volumes. In Peru, more than 450 private operators are licensed to provide postal services, while in Colombia there are over 200 licensed 'specialized operators' offering what are essentially basic postal services with value-added options. In these countries, as in many others, there are also a significant number (perhaps as high as 1,000 in some countries) of 'informal' operators (including utilities delivering their own bills, transportation companies, and even individual travelers).[2] Many operators offer services without any license or regulation. Such fragmentation arises from two major causes, weak regulation and the inability of the USP (or any other operator) to capture dominant market share. Some postal liberalization economists argue that market fragmentation should drive down postal prices. However, this has not been demonstrated in practice and there are strong counter-arguments for what is termed a 'destructive level of competition' with too many operators processing too little volume while duplicating each other's delivery networks. Fragmented markets with many 'niche' and temporary players also lead to widely varying levels of quality, as evidenced by the high percentage of value-added services (for example, registration) purchased in developing countries.

A lack of comprehensive knowledge of postal markets also inhibits postal development and reform in developing countries. Comprehensive postal market studies have been completed in only a handful of developing countries (Colombia, Honduras, Jordan, and so on) because such studies are extremely costly and time-consuming. Not knowing the actual *demand* for or the precise *cost* of universal services means it is defined strictly in terms of supply (access to postal services, levels of quality, and affordable prices) without regard to actual demand or cost. As a result, over time, universal service becomes increasingly more expensive and USPs a greater financial burden for the government. The long-term result can be the 'vicious cycle' of poor quality, low volumes, weak finances, and inadequate investment, regardless of the degree of formal liberalization undertaken.

Governments in developing countries are also challenged by the need to improve performance in a wide range of non-postal public services and infrastructures. Furthermore, because of the rapid advance of digital communications in some developing countries, the postal sector is sometimes seen as a 'legacy' or 'sunset' industry whose reform is not essential. As a result, with some noteworthy exceptions, the postal sector does not receive the ongoing policy attention and resources needed to implement sustainable reform.

Finally, while it is beyond the scope of this chapter to discuss the myriad economic, demographic, and infrastructure challenges confronting the postal sector in the developing world, the one factor that outweighs all others is the lack of adequate address systems:

> Unlike planned urban areas in developed countries, streets and properties (in both rural and urban areas) in most African cities are poorly named and numbered. Streets and parcels are often characterized by a lack of physical address, a poor sign and name-posting, absence of or very poor numbering systems, and a duality of 'official' and 'popular' naming practice. (United Nations Economic and Social Council, 2005, p. 23)

Even in middle-income countries such as Costa Rica, the absence of an adequate addressing system has an impact on mail volumes: per capita mail volume stands at 6.1 whereas in countries at a similar level of economic development (with better addressing systems) averages range from 14 to 35 pieces annually.

4. POSTAL REFORM STRATEGIES FOR DEVELOPING COUNTRIES

4.1 Develop Relevant Universal Service Definitions and Financing Methods

The first strategy recommended is to develop relevant universal service obligations and prices that reflect the actual demand for and cost of such services. Too often, such definitions use a 'shotgun' approach, mandating unnecessary levels of service and artificially low prices. Postal reformers must do a better job in explaining to constituents that businesses and government typically generate 85–90 percent of all mail; therefore, setting prices below costs provides an indirect subsidy to large mailers (Walsh, 2002). For the famous 'man in the street', who in all likelihood mails less than one letter per year, a significant increase in price or decrease in frequency of delivery has little practical or financial impact.

The cost of universal service is normally defined as the loss that this service incurs, regardless of whether a net avoided cost or other methodology is used. Therefore, in principle, if the service 'breaks even' financially, no financing method is required. The methods used to finance this loss should be based on the national postal market. In a market that is highly competitive and/or has very low volumes, it makes no sense to maintain a reserved area that is unenforceable and economically unjustified. Instead, private operators should be 'taxed' through licensing fees for not having to serve unprofitable portions of the market. While universal service funds generally have not been applied successfully in the industrialized world (the EU), they have had some limited success in the developing world, for example in Colombia (Houpis et al., 2005). If direct government subsidies are used instead of or in combination with a universal service fund, they should be directly linked to a precise estimation of the service's cost (and the government's willingness to support losses) and phased out over time.

4.2 Improve Quality of Service

An additional strategy is to focus on improving quality of service in the postal market. In low-volume markets, quality is frequently a more important element in raising postal output than price. As an example, letter volumes in Trinidad and Tobago grew by 156 percent and customer satisfaction by 32 percent between 1998 and 2004 despite two significant tariff increases (Guislain, 2004; World Bank 2007). The growth in letter volumes was driven fundamentally by increases during the same period in on-time delivery performance from 50 to 85 percent. Improving quality of service means first establishing regulations that define acceptable quality for universal service and then ensuring that all operators offering such services meet these standards.

4.3 Increase Private Sector Participation

Increased private sector participation in USPs is most effective when it is targeted at specific areas of achievable improvement. The postal reforms in both Guatemala and Trinidad and Tobago (see below) were based on a strategy of first improving the USPs' quality of service, volumes, and revenues through management contracts then increasing private sector participation through a longer-term concession or public equity sale. There are numerous other mechanisms for achieving such increases, including management contracts, concessions, strategic partnerships, joint ventures, subsidiaries, and franchising of postal outlets. In fact, the mechanism used is less important than a clear definition of what can be accomplished by private sector participation.

4.4 Commercialize USPs

Commercialization of USPs transforms them from subsidized government agencies into self-sufficient businesses. Developing countries have used many different strategies to achieve this goal. In Guatemala, Trinidad and Tobago and more recently Armenia, external expertise and resources have been enlisted to increase efficiency in preparation for further private sector participation. In Brazil and Tanzania, internal restructuring and incorporating value-added services maximized performance. This has allowed the USP to take advantage of its ubiquitous network and unique location at the core of three critical business flows: information, goods, and funds. While these examples used different models, one constant can be noted, namely the use of quantitative performance targets, indicators and measurement systems to improve performance and accountability.

4.5 Develop Policy Statements to Sustain Reform

National postal sector policies are a key element in reaching sustainable reform. They are concise but comprehensive documents providing a very high-level 'Vision' of what the postal sector should look like over the next 5–10 years and how to get there.[3] A sector policy also serves the important function of establishing a priority and sequence among what may be conflicting reform goals. Examples might be the desire to extend universal service coverage while simultaneously reducing its costs or the drive to increase private sector investment in the USP while simultaneously liberalizing the postal market. While postal sector policies are sometimes developed *after* new postal laws and regulations have been enacted (Tanzania), it is generally advisable to have the policy document available first so that it guides development of the legal and regulatory framework.

Successful postal sector policies require support from a wide range of government and stakeholder constituencies (including public and private operators, individual and business mailers, employee organizations, legislators, non-governmental organizations, and so on). This is particularly important when policy changes, such as the imposition of a new licensing regime and fees, directly impact on commercial interests. Fortunately, several institutions including the UPU and the World Bank as well as individual postal consultancies are promoting best-practice approaches for developing postal sector policies.

4.6 Reserved Areas versus Competition

In determining how to ensure sustainable postal reform, one of the thorniest issues is whether a reserved area or increased competition is the more effective strategy, or whether they should be used in combination with other mechanisms such as a universal service fund. The phased approach for introducing competition being used by the EU is, in effect, a compromise. However for countries with very low postal volumes and *de facto* market liberalization, the more pertinent question is, does a reserved area provide any real benefit? In most low-volume markets, reserving a significant portion or even all of the postal market to a single postal operator does not generate sufficient volumes and profits to cover the losses incurred by the universal service obligation (USO), particularly if this obligation has been overextended to respond to political, social, or geographic needs.

Furthermore, as numerous postal markets demonstrate, the mere existence of a legal reservation covering some portion of the mail does not guarantee observance of this monopoly. In fact, once *de facto* liberalization has occurred, consumers (particularly businesses) will not use a designated operator if it does not meet their mailing needs. Instead, they will opt for more-efficient operators (assuming they exist), whether or not these are functioning legally. Reserved areas, like subsidies and universal service funds, are *mechanisms* for funding the losses incurred through the provision of universal service. However, if the specific postal items and weights, acceptable levels of service, and affordable prices, included within this service are not clearly defined, it will be impossible to accurately determine USO costs. If costs are not known, then it will be similarly impossible to determine whether a reserved area is economically justified. In the absence of such information, it does not seem justifiable to try to enforce a monopoly.

In some developing countries, the USP also does not have the processing and delivery capacity to handle the volumes that theoretically would result from enforcing a reserved area. This is demonstrated by the fact that there are other providers in the market. Therefore, the government has to decide whether the level of investment needed to build such capacity would result in better universal service at a lower cost to the government. While it must be admitted that *de jure* or *de facto* liberalization does not appear to generate significant new postal volumes in developing countries, this should not be interpreted as a rationale for imposing or enforcing reserved areas where they are not economically justified or enforceable.

5. EXAMPLES OF SUCCESSFUL POSTAL REFORM

The examples below illustrate how some developing countries have used the strategies described above to implement successful postal reform. These are not meant to be exhaustive case studies, or reform 'models', but rather a general indication of how reform challenges and inhibitors can be overcome using the strategies described above. The focus on the USP reflects its role as the government's agent in fulfilling the universal service obligation.

5.1 Trinidad and Tobago: Building the Postal Market through Better Quality of Service

Before reform, postal market performance steadily declined in Trinidad and Tobago. Annual per capita mail volume stood at 12.6 pieces, well below the average of 26 pieces for countries at the equivalent level of economic development. Overall mail volume dropped 20 percent between 1995 and 1999 despite significant GDP growth; the USP incurred chronic financial losses (UPU, 2006). Quality of service within the market was extremely poor and only 50 percent of the population expressed any level of confidence in the USP. In 1999 and with World Bank support in the form of an US$11.4 million loan, the government determined to increase private sector participation to improve USP performance. A strong policy and regulatory framework were enacted first to establish a foundation for this strategy: the Postal Act of 1999 established a corporation, Trinidad and Tobago Post (TT Post) with more management autonomy and increased commercial flexibility. The reserved area for letters was maintained to provide time for the public operator to develop commercial strength before subjecting it to greater competition and the market for parcels and courier (express) mail was liberalized. Regulation of the postal sector would be in the hands of an independent Public Utilities Commission.

Private sector participation was increased through a five-year (1999–2004) management contract ('Delegated Management Agreement': DMA) with Transend Worldwide Limited, the consulting subsidiary of New Zealand's public operator. The contract obligated Transend to manage TT Post in line with international best practices; management fees were based on annual quality of service (coverage, on time delivery, customer satisfaction) and revenue targets (total revenue and profit). Perhaps most importantly, achievement of these targets was measured on an ongoing basis by independent third parties using quantitative performance indicators.

The positive impact of the DMA on TT Post's performance was exceptional: postal volumes between 1998 and 2002 grew by 165 percent. In terms of productivity, items processed per employee grew by more than 400 percent and revenue per employee by more than 200 percent, despite a 39 percent reduction in staffing. At the same time, productivity, as measured by dwellings per letter carrier increased by 46 percent. Revenue grew by almost 72 percent from 1998 to 2002. Similar gains were achieved in terms of quality of service: on time mail delivery increased from 50 to 81 percent for D + 1 (delivery one day after posting) target mail and 92 percent for D + 2 (delivery two days after posting) mail. This was extraordinary considering that delivery area coverage was nearly doubled during the same period. Furthermore, despite two tariff increases, customer satisfaction increased from a base of 50 percent to a high of 82 percent, demonstrating once again that, in lower-volume markets, the availability of postal services with high quality is more important to customers than price. The annual per capita mail volume grew to 38 pieces at the end of the DMA, exceeding the figure of 26 for countries with equivalent GDPs.

There were two areas where the postal reform in Trinidad and Tobago did not live up to expectations. The first was the continuing loss of revenue suffered by the USP. To a great extent, this was due to the attempt to significantly increase universal coverage and quality while simultaneously trying to cut its costs, indicating a need to prioritize and sequence reform goals. The second was the failure to move directly from the management contract to a concession or other means of further increasing private sector participation (the management contract was extended for two years). However, the government recently determined to establish TT Post as a state-owned limited liability company, and is considering selling shares to the public (World Bank, 2007).

5.2 Guatemala: USP Commercialization through Progressive Privatization

During the years preceding the establishment of a management contract for postal services in Guatemala in 1998, per capita mail annual volume stood at 2.09 pieces, below the average of 5.5 pieces for countries at Guatemala's GDP level. An estimated 250 private, unlicensed operators charged fees that were 50 to 100 times those of the public operator, but still had 90 percent of the market for basic services. The USP was overstaffed, in an extremely weak financial position, provided poor quality, and was heavily subsidized; financial losses were approximately US$23,110,056 for 1995–97.

During the second half of the 1990s, the World Bank supported the Guatemala government's establishment of a two-phased project for postal reform: first, a short-term management contract to improve operator performance and profitability; and second, a long-term concession to increase private sector participation and reduce the government's direct involvement in public postal services. World Bank support was predicted on three clear goals: ensuring an acceptable level of universal services; reducing the government deficit associated with these services; and increasing private sector participation in the postal sector.

Over the full five years of the management contract (1999–2003) and the first two years of the concession, a steady improvement could be seen. The newly established USP, Correo de Guatemala, S.A., handled nearly 80 percent more universal service mail. During the first three years of the contract, the operating deficit was reduced by roughly 28 percent of the deficit for the previous three years (World Bank, 2003). During the first two years of the concession (2004–05), the USP began to show modest profitability while paying concession fees to the government. Total staffing was reduced from 2,300 to 990 at the start of the management contract and has remained well below that number despite improved processing and delivery times. Universal coverage, in terms of number of post offices, average area covered by a post office, and number of inhabitants per post office remained fairly steady from 1999 to 2005 and the price for a 20-gram letter has remained stable at approximately 3 US cents. Annual per capita mail volume grew to its highest point (3.14 pieces) in 2006 (UPU, 2006). Less progress has been made on establishing a strong regulatory framework for the postal sector, probably due to the absence of a comprehensive postal sector policy.

5.3 Brazil: Reform without Privatization and Limited Liberalization

Brazil is a middle-income country whose successful postal reform is often cited as a model for other developing countries. Unlike reforms in the EU and in many developing countries, Brazil's postal reform was based less on liberalization and more on utilizing the postal network a means of advancing economic and social goals. Furthermore, there appears to be no impetus to change the USP's institutional format and Empresa Brasileira de Correios e Telégrafos (ECT – 'Correios') remains part of the government.

With regard to the postal sector, Brazil has traditionally taken a path distinct from its regional counterparts. Most postal sectors in the Latin American region have been nearly totally liberalized, either through specific legislation (Argentina) or by *de facto* market domination by numerous licensed and unlicensed operators. By contrast, Brazil has reserved all letters and postcards, and telegrams for the USP. Parcels, printed papers, and courier (express) mail are open to competition. The Ministry of Communications supervises the postal sector, but since no postal operators other than ECT are recognized, regulation consists of monitoring ECT's fulfillment of the USO. ECT's monopoly and its own profitability provide sufficient financing for universal service (the basic charge for a 20-gram letter is 34 US cents). The government also made significant investments in

ECT's modernization and provided it with a high level of organizational autonomy and commercial autonomy.

The government and ECT also expanded and strengthened the postal network to 'universalize' its reach to underserved areas of the country. Between 1999 and 2005, 1,268 postal outlets were added to the USP's network (over 50 percent of the total 12,448 post offices are run by non-postal staff). Delivery methods such as neighborhood 'delivery cluster boxes' and mobile post offices for rural areas were utilized to lower costs; at-home delivery mail stands at 80 percent, an exceptional level for a large country with many isolated regions. Service and access levels were also adjusted to reflect actual demand, ranging from a high of five days a week in urban areas (more than 50,000 inhabitants) to weekly in rural areas (less than 500 inhabitants) served by mobile units.

ECT has taken full advantage of this support and commercialized its activities by focusing its marketing efforts on major businesses while simultaneously providing a reliable product for individual mailers. As a result, it has been recognized in public surveys as having the highest level (90 percent) of credibility among all public and private institutions (including religious and educational institutions) in Brazil (Siciliano, 2006). It also has been able to consistently maintain profitability and pay a portion of its proceeds into the Public Treasury without subsidies from the State (UPU, 2007).

The new role of the postal network in strengthening economic growth and social cohesion was demonstrated by the decision to offer banking services through postal retail outlets. In 2001, ECT formed a partnership with Banco Bradesco, the largest private sector bank in Brazil, to offer basic banking products ('Banco Postal'). Under the terms of the agreement, Bradesco provides equipment and training and ECT fixed infrastructure and personnel. The goal of offering financial services (including small loans) through postal outlets was to increase access to formal financial services where these were not available, and increase national savings levels (World Resources Institute, 2008). By 2005, Banco Postal's services were available through 5,522 postal outlets, holding 4.5 million current accounts. In 2002, 1,750 Brazilian municipalities were identified as having no banking services; by 2005, Banco Postal was operating in 96 percent of these principalities. Nearly 60 percent of its customers were small savers earning less than US$80 per month, approximately one-third had secured loans (Ivatury, 2007).

Postal reformers also utilized the postal network as a potential channel for increasing international exports from Brazil and expanding public access to Internet services. In order to fully exploit the congruence of critical business flows (information, goods, and funds), ECT also offers a full range of logistics and value-added services. From a social cohesion standpoint, ECT's network is used to distribute textbooks, medicines, as a voting center during elections, and to achieve bi-directional communication between the government and citizens. In many ways, Brazil's use of ECT's network for economic and social purposes achieves many of the goals described in calls for a broader understanding of universal postal service to include other public and service sectors (Kenny, 2006, pp. 85–7).

Does this mean that limiting competition in the postal market and making large investments in the USP to improve its ability to provide economic and social benefits should be the reform model for all developing countries? Before answering this question, one must consider some unique attributes of the Brazilian postal market.

First, Brazil produces large letter-class volumes (averaging around 50 pieces per person annually) compared with other countries at a comparable level of development (ranging from 9.1 to 25 pieces). This figure, combined with a large population, mail-intensive economic sectors (the service segment is 65 percent of national GDP), and strong advertising and marketing industries, produces sufficient volumes to economically justify a reserved area. It would be economically impossible to achieve the same benefits in a low-volume postal market. Furthermore, because of ECT's traditional level of efficiency, *de facto* competition for letter mail has been extremely limited. Next, Brazil's high level of literacy (nearly 90 percent) and the existence of 257 cities with more than 100,000 inhabitants concentrate volumes and provide savings that can be used to financially cover more-costly service areas. In fact, at 82 percent, Brazil's level of urbanization is reflected in its percentage of home delivery (80 percent) and the concentration of postal volumes (83 percent) in just 20 percent of its states. Brazil also has relatively efficient transportation systems and, perhaps most importantly, a strong addressing system (46 million addresses). Large volumes and good addressing systems have allowed ECT to utilize advanced and less-costly mail processing processes and maintain high quality of service levels.

In other words, Brazil's postal market resembles and functions much like one in an industrialized country. Postal reformers in most developing countries face much bleaker prospects including scarce development resources, large USP deficits, chronically poor service, small markets, and significant levels of unregulated competition. This is not to say that Brazil's postal reform does not provide many useful lessons for other developing countries, but rather that these must be scaled and adapted to local realities. As an example, the addition of non-postal products and services to the existing postal portfolio (for example, banking services) succeeded here because of the high degree of public confidence in ECT. Without such confidence levels, it would be important to start with the more basic task of improving postal efficiency and dependability (as was done for example, in Trinidad and Tobago, Guatemala and Tanzania).

5.4 Tanzania: Regulatory Reform and Accountability

Tanzania's postal reform faced formidable challenges. Tanzania is one of the poorest countries in the world (estimated GDP per capita of US$1,100 purchasing power parity in 2007) with 70 percent of its population living in rural areas inaccessible during much of the year. Annual per capita mail volumes have typically been less than one piece per person, with nearly all traffic located in a few large cities. There is virtually no addressing infrastructure or home delivery for basic mail services. As is typically seen in least developed countries, the postal market is dominated by business-generated mail (over 80 percent of mail flows). Informal providers such as transportation companies and individual travelers serve a large portion of the postal market. The performance of the USP prior to reform was extremely poor: mail volumes were decreasing and quality of service was neither measured nor controlled (Lohmeyer and Ianni, 2002).

With support from the World Bank, the government implemented a postal reform program in the early 1990s based on three strategies: develop a strong regulatory environment for the postal sector; commercialize the USP's operations and finances; and increase its accountability through a performance contract.

Regulatory reform provided a series of new postal laws and regulations passed in 1993 (updated in 2005) that first separated posts and telecommunications and then created separate policy, regulatory, and operational responsibility for the postal sector. Universal service was defined precisely and the reserved areas set at 500 grams (instead of all letters and postcards), providing some scope for future liberalization. The parcel and courier markets were completely liberalized. Regulations were developed concerning pricing and service quality for universal service mail, and licensing procedures and standards established for competitive market segments. In 2003, the government codified its commitment to ongoing postal reform in a National Postal Policy.

In the ensuing years, competition has grown in the courier and parcel markets. The regulator's website today indicates that licenses have been issued to 47 international, regional and national couriers; in 2001 only two licenses had been issued (Guislain, 2004). While coverage, in terms of numbers and location of post offices has remained relatively constant and quality has improved, after initially increasing, postal volumes have flattened and per capita letter-mail volume remains below one piece per person.

Postal reform provided the newly established USP (Tanzania Posts Corporation: TPC) with more commercial autonomy, but also significantly increased its accountability. A performance contract specifying USP performance targets in five areas – quality of service, security, profitability, volume growth, and customer satisfaction – was established for TPC and signed by all major government stakeholders. As with the management contract in Trinidad and Tobago, performance was quantitatively measured by independent, non-postal entities. Financial incentives and penalties for meeting or missing targets were set for TPC management and its board of directors, although it is not clear whether these have ever been invoked.

TPC reduced operational costs by adjusting the existing network, increased contracting out of postal functions, and staff reductions (nearly 45 percent through attrition). Transportation companies have contracts with TPC for delivery and collection of mail in remote areas. Some basic postal functions in rural areas have even been contracted out to local headmasters and teachers. TPC commercialized internally by dividing the business into three profit centers: mail, counters, and express (courier) mail. While quality of service has improved to 85 percent for next-day delivery, it does not appear that further gains can be achieved without significant new investments. TPC has managed to keep operating costs (before taxes and dividends paid to the government) below revenues from 2000 to 2006 and has essentially been self-financing. However, this required significant tariff increases and service-level adjustments to reflect actual demand and costs, and the introduction of a two-tiered pricing system based on speed (*economy* and *priority*).

Tanzania's case demonstrates that formidable challenges can be overcome if postal reform goals and strategies are based on the realities of the national economy and local postal market. By law, TPC is required to generate revenues to cover its costs. Current tariffs for a 20-gram letter are US$0.20 (economy) and US$0.36 (priority). By fixing the principle that TPC revenues must cover costs, postal reformers ensured that universal service levels would be adjusted to accurately reflect actual demand and cost. By sequencing goals correctly (first regulatory reform, then USP rehabilitation with limited but targeted private sector participation), this reform also increased long-term sustainability.

5.5 Azerbaijan: Adding Value to the Universal Postal Service Network

The reform of the postal sector in Azerbaijan was initiated only recently. However, it is worth reviewing now due to the unique strategy being used to implement reform, namely, to rehabilitate the universal service network and utilize it as a means of improving national access to the formal financial sector. During the second half of the 1990s, Azerbaijan launched an economic recovery program that yielded exceptional results, including annual GDP growth of over 30 percent in some years. However, most of the growth was in the oil-related sector and as of 2001, approximately 50 percent of the population still lived in poverty (World Bank, 2004). The prevalence of shallow financial markets and a lack of access to financial services and credit were identified as key elements restricting growth beyond the oil sector. Bill presentment and low collection rates (at best 30–40 percent) in rural areas were cited as a particular problem. The average population served by bank branches in Baku is approximately 39,000 and about 71,000 in urban centers outside of Baku; financial services were essentially unavailable in rural areas (in 2003 there were less than 100 bank branches outside Baku). However, compared to these figures, the average population served by the USP (Azerpost, S.E.) post offices was 4,998, with 90 percent of these offices located in rural areas.

Therefore, in 2005 the government established a 'Financial Services Development' project with World Bank support of US$12.25 million to strengthen, expand, and modernize postal financial services. In addition to providing wider and deeper access to basic financial services, the FSD project is designed to strengthen the basic postal infrastructure and management systems and extend modern communication services (telephones, fax, e-mail, Internet) along with e-government and e-commerce applications through the postal network. Strengthening Azerbaijan's ability to receive and distribute remittances from overseas through the postal network was a major goal, as this cash flow represents a major source of foreign direct investment.

Despite having a strong regulatory framework for universal services and a booming economy, Azerbaijan's postal sector performance is below expectations. The annual per capita mail volume of 1.3 pieces is well below the average of 8–15 pieces for countries in its GDP range. While increasing access to financial services, the FSD is also designed to increase demand for basic postal services by increasing Azerpost's range of financial product offerings. These would include both existing services (bill payments, delivering salaries, pensions, and other social payments) and new financial products (domestic and international fund transfers, time limited and permanent deposits; sale of smart cards, payments, collections, and issuance of government documents and permits, and so on).

FSD is an opportunity to improve sector performance and to add significant value to the USP network. Azerpost has the advantage of currently being a major distributor of pensions and other governmental financial instruments and therefore is familiar with basic financial transactions. The Financial Services Development Project also provides a unique opportunity to demonstrate that the postal services can be merged with the financial services to provide significant benefits for economic growth and wealth distribution. The project is now in its early implementation phase and is awaiting legislative action that would provide Azerpost with the authority it needs to expand its portfolio of financial products.

6. CONCLUSION

Achieving sustainable reform in developing countries is challenging, but as the examples above show, it can be achieved. Reform was successful in these cases because it was based on goals and strategies scaled and adapted to the national economy, regulatory environment, and postal market. There is no 'magic bullet' or single set of strategies that will accomplish all of these goals in a given country. However, the role of the UPU, the World Bank, and others in developing a set of 'best-practice' options is key to increasing the number of reform success stories. These organizations can also take the lead in developing a better understanding of where the postal service fits within the overall communications revolution, particularly for those countries where access to communications is critical to growth but development resources are scarce.

NOTES

1. Average annual letters posted for GDP capita (purchasing power parity) segments: < US$ 1,000 = 0.9 pieces; US$1,000–US$5,000 = 4.6 pieces; and >US$5,000 = 98.4 pieces (Kenny 2006, p. 81).
2. While the infrastructure requirements for telecommunications and other communications options impose high market entry barriers, a 'bicycle and a basket' are all that are required to start a postal business.
3. Excellent examples of postal sector policies recently developed for Jordan, Tanzania, and Trinidad and Tobago can be found at: www.moict.go.jo, www.tcra.go.tz and www.ttdraftsectorpolicy.org.

REFERENCES

Ansón, J., R. Cuadra, A. Lindares, G. Ronderos and J. Toledano (2006), 'First steps towards new postal economics models for developing countries: learning from the Latin American experience', in M.A. Crew and P.R. Kleindorfer (eds), *Liberalization of the Postal and Delivery Sector*, Cheltenham, UK and Northampton, MA, USA: Edward Elgar, pp. 217–36.

Cohen, R., M. Robinson, G. Scarfiglieri, R. Sheehy, V. Visco Comandini, J. Waller and S. Xenakis (2004), 'The Role of Scale Economies in the Cost Behavior of Posts', WIK, 8th Königswinter Seminar, Bad Honnef, 16–18 February.

Evsen, Hattice and Bernard Roy (2000), 'Elements on the economy of postal operators in developing countries', paper presented at CRRI–Rutgers 8th Conference on Postal and Delivery Economics, Vancouver, June 7–10.

Guislain, P. (2004), *The Postal Sector in Transition and Developing Countries: Contributions to a Reform Agenda*, Washington, DC: World Bank Group.

Houpis, G., A. Lara and M. Williams (2005), 'Estimating the net cost of the USO: a case study of Colombia', paper presented at CRRI–Rutgers' 13th Conference on Postal and Delivery Economics, Antwerp, June 1–4.

Ivatury, Gautam (2007), 'Brazil's Banking Correspondents, Consultative Group to Assist the Poor (CGAP)', www.microfinancegateway.org, accessed 20 March 2008.

Kenny, Charles (2006), 'Questioning the monopoly-supported postal USO in developing countries', in M.A. Crew and P.R. Kleindorfer (eds), *Progress toward Liberalization of the Postal and Delivery Sector*, New York: Springer, pp. 75–87.

Lohmeyer, Jurgen and Juan B. Ianni (2002), *The Postal Industry in an Internet Age*, 2nd edn, Bern/Washington, DC: Universal Postal Union/World Bank Group.

Siciliano, Paulo (2006), 'El Desarrollo de la Red Postal y la Consecución de los Objetivos del Milenio – ECT Correios do Brasil', presentation to the UPU Council of Administration, Universal Postal Union, Bern, March.

United Nations Economic and Social Council: Economic Commission for Africa (2005), 'Geographical Data as National Asset: Benefits of National Situs Addressing System for Africa: An extended summary', Addis Ababa, 23–25 April.

Universal Postal Union (UPU) (2006), *Postal Statistics*, Bern.

Universal Postal Union (UPU) (2007), *Status and Structures of Postal Administrations*, Bern.

Walsh, Tim (2001), *Delivering Economic Development: Postal Infrastructure and Sectoral Reform in Developing Countries*, London: Consignia plc.
Walsh, Tim (2002), 'Exit, voice and postal performance in developing countries', in M.A. Crew and P.R. Kleindorfer (eds), *Postal and Delivery Services: Delivering on Competition*, Boston, MA: Kluwer Academic, pp. 265–76.
World Bank (2003), 'Implementation Completion Report (ICR) on a Loan of US$13.0 million to the Government of Guatemala for Private Participation in Infrastructure: Technical Assistance Loan (PPI-TAL)', Washington, DC: World Bank Group.
World Bank (2004), 'Project Appraisal Document (PAD) Proposed Credit to the Azerbaijan Republic for a Financial Services Development Project', Washington, DC: World Bank Group.
World Bank (2007), 'Implementation Completion and Results Report (ICR) (Trinidad and Tobago)', Washington, DC: World Bank Group.
World Resources Institute (2008), 'Banco Postal', www.nextbillion.net, 15 April.

24. India Post: an agenda for restructuring and commercialization*

V. Ranganathan†

1. INTRODUCTION

'You can think of India Post as an old fashioned network trapped in the bricks and mortars of a dying mail service; or you can think of it as an extraordinary human network that facilitates incredible access to virtually all Indians', according to Mieko Nishimizu (2002), Vice President, South Asia Region of the World Bank. Both sides of this duality are evident in this brief survey of the current status and prospects for the reform of India Post.

To understand India Post, one must begin by placing India itself in perspective. India is the seventh largest country in the world, having an area of about 3.3 million square kilometers. If one superimposes the map of India over that of Europe, India stretches from the Atlantic shore of France in the west to Ukraine in the east and from the Arctic islands of Scandinavia in the north to parts of North Africa in the south. India's population of 1.1 billion people is about one and a half times the population of all of Europe, but 25 percent of its people live on less than one US dollar per day. Yet India Post manages to provide access to all persons living in this vast region, including those who have nebulous addresses.

India Post is the largest postal network in the world with 155,699 post offices (March 2006). Ninety percent of post offices are located in rural areas. On average, a post office serves an area of 21.2 sq km and a population of 6,623 persons. In addition, through the Post Office Savings Bank, India Post administers 162 million savings accounts with an average value of about US$700 per account.[1] India Post also handles 96 million money orders, averaging US$18 each. It employs 250,714 persons full time and another 298,571 persons on a part-time basis. Postal revenues cover only 84 percent of total expenditure, leaving a deficit of around US$0.3 billion on revenue of US$1.56 billion (July 2006).

Nonetheless, India Post's annual mail volume of 6.7 billion in 2005/06 is tiny when compared with the 200 billion items transported by the United States Postal Service. Moreover, total mail volume in 2005/06 represented a decline of 7.36 million/from the previous year, exacerbating India Post's plight of too many post offices with too little mail. With competition from the Internet and from courier services, decline has become chronic. Postage and stamps account for 43 percent of total revenue. Other sources include revenue from the Savings Bank (44 percent), sale of money orders (6.4 percent), and miscellaneous receipts and recoveries for services (6.5 percent). The Ministry of

† RBI Chair Professor, Indian Institute of Management, Bangalore.

Table 24.1 Cost and profitability of postal services, 2003–04

Sl. no.	Service	Average cost	Average revenue	Deficit/ surplus (+)
1	Postcard	6.89	0.50	6.39
2	Printed postcard	6.92	6.00	0.92
3	Competition postcard	4.80	10.00	+5.20
4	Letter card	7.02	2.50	4.50
5	Letter	7.96	10.04	+2.00
6	Registered newspaper	9.34	0.39	9.00
7	Registered newspaper – bundle	15.89	0.79	15.00
8	Book post – book patterns	11.35	7.27	4.00
9	Book post – printed book	19.06	4.37	14.69
10	Book post – other periodicals	18.07	9.44	8.63
11	Acknowledgement	6.18	3.00	3.18
12	Parcel	80.94	57.17	23.77
13	Registration	32.90	17.00	16.00
14	Speed post	44.54	36.08	8.46
15	Value payable post	21.09	4.07	17.02
16	Insurance	42.78	53.21	+10.43
17	Money order	53.20	27.39	25.81
18	Telegraphic money order	68.35	29.39	39.16
19	Postal order	21.42	2.18	19.24
20	International mail	23.71	35.56	11.85

Note: The cost figures are based on allocation, which is itself based on revenue share. Since most of the costs are fixed and sunk costs, the surplus/deficit figures have to be understood with this proviso.

Source: India Post (2007).

Finance has given India Post a large indirect subsidy by asking them to carry out the Savings Bank function as an agency activity, for which India Post will be paid separately by the ministry based on the number of accounts.

Of the postage and stamps revenue, about 51 percent is derived from commercial products of the Postal Service, including Speed Post, Business Post, Express Post and Retail Post. Retail Post is a service whereby India Post acts as a collection agent for other utilities and collects a service charge. Most of India Post's mail-related services do not cover costs (see Table 24.1). Within the mail service, only foreign mail, competition postcard, and letter categories yield revenues which exceed costs. In the non-mail service, only insurance does so. However, with about 76 percent of the total expenditure arising out of salaries, which are fixed costs, and without a calculation of incremental costs for various types of services, India Post is handicapped in being unable to determine the margin of contribution or assess the relative profitability of its various services. That being the case, the figures of surplus or deficit for each service are at best arbitrary.

On the whole, the picture of India Post is that of a donkey carrying a large load of overweight items. India Post looks on helplessly as its value-added services are being poached by the private couriers, who offer almost the same reliability but at a significantly lower cost. The couriers are able to do so due to flexible pricing, flexible schedules to suit

Table 24.2 India Post operating revenue and expenditure (US$ million)

	%	2005–06	2006–07
Revenue	100*	1,306	1,560
Mail	21.0	271	
Commercial mail	22.0	286	
Money order	6.4	83.5	
Savings bank	44.0	580.6	
Miscellaneous	6.5	85	
Expenditure		1,607	1,860
Deficit		301	300

Note: * Number is rounded.

Source: India Post (2007).

customers' needs, and use of part-time staff with market-based, if exploitative, wages. While India Post struggles to do an honest bit of service for the citizenry, it is simultaneously bearing the burden of 'officers' who are completely out of touch with competition and bereft of the knowledge and skills needed to act in the changing competitive marketplace. Yet these postal officers earnestly seek to preserve the existing organization and even to enter into new remunerative areas which will give them extra contribution margins to cover the huge deficit (Ranganathan, 2005).

In this chapter, Section 2 addresses the dilemmas that India Post faces in balancing its commercial and social obligations. Section 3 outlines near-term strategies and opportunities for entering new areas and strengthening the financial position of India Post. Section 4 summarizes certain restructuring issues. Section 5 offers some conclusions.

2. DILEMMAS FOR THE INDIAN POSTAL SERVICE

India Post must discharge an enormous universal service obligation (USO), transmitting mail from one corner of the country to the other at affordable rates, attending to the mailing needs of the army, and carrying books and articles at subsidized prices. While the bulk of its work is in the social sector, that is, in carrying ordinary mail, the major part of India Post's revenues comes from its banking operations (see Table 24.2). While services such as Speed Post, Media Post, Business Post, and Express Post have registered profits and revenue increases, revenues from personal mail and greeting cards are in deficit and are declining.

Overall, India Post incurs an annual deficit of approximately US$300 million (Rs 12.1 billion). While it is doing a good job in the social sector – letters in general are delivered within a week – it is not performing well in competitive market sectors such as courier, logistics post, and so on. Although India Post does not have specific figures for its competitive segments, the general feeling in India Post itself is that they are losing market share progressively. In many cases, even government departments, including the Reserve Bank of India, choose to send their value-added mail, including reports, through private couriers! India Post's reply to this is that the private sector is able to offer unofficial inducements both to private airlines to give preference to their shipments and to decision makers in government departments, a contention hard to prove. What is visible, however, is the lower rates of private couriers to customers in competitive segments and the higher rates in monopoly segments, a pricing flexibility that India Post is unable to match. In order to reduce the deficit and gain autonomy – flexibility in pricing and incentives to employees who carry more load and earn more revenue for the organization – India Post is diversifying into new areas such as international money transfer, mutual funds, and so on. In some cases, as in money transfer, India Post is trying to leverage one of its existing strengths, namely, its extensive distribution network. In other areas, as in mutual funds, India Post is entering unknown territory, where its employees have no skill or expertise.

Although banking yields 44 percent of total revenue, India Post provides this service merely as an agent of the Ministry of Finance. The banking revenues (that is, from deposits) of the postal department go directly to the Ministry of Finance and all savings account balances are transferred to the State Bank. Since the Indian government bears the entire deficit arising out of higher interest rate paid to Post Office Savings Bank customers, there is very little motivation for the postal department to make organizational innovations in this segment, which provides a vital financial support to the post office. Perversely, since the payment from the government is based on number of accounts, the compensation system leads to artificial splitting of accounts, on the one hand, and to direct control exercised by the Ministry of Finance over the postal department, on the other.

Government directly influences the operation of the postal services, as well, with unfortunate results. Government fixes tariffs for various postal articles, but due to bureaucratic delays, revision of postal tariffs fails to keep pace with the increase in operating costs. Lack of budgetary autonomy impedes India Post's entry into new services and management of its investments. Despite subsidies given by the government, low postal rates have starved the system of resources for development and led to a loss in quality of the service. Management has no merit-based incentives and hence is unmotivated, while a unionized labor force is inefficient with consequent high costs. While it is likely that private control would make it more difficult to achieve the social obligations of postal service, the current situation shows that governmental control is hindering efficient operation. A solution balancing the two extremes has to be found.

3. IMMEDIATE STRATEGIES AND NEW AREAS

The most important core strengths of India Post are the last-mile connectivity to an exceedingly large group of potential consumers and the immense data resources that it possesses (it knows the addresses of most citizens!). Building on these strengths, there are several new areas which India Post is currently exploring (Sarma, 2002). In expansion and diversification, however, India Post should generally be guided by the following strategies (Bell, 2002):

1. Make maximum use of the unique benefits of 'the last mile' especially in rural areas.
2. Use the wealth of postal data to foster several new services as extensions of existing services. In non-metropolitan towns most savings seem to be kept in postal savings

accounts. Finance companies are entering into contracts with India Post to access this financial goldmine and market their financial services. India Post is investigating how to convert this advantage into an opportunity, not just, as presently, by performing agency services for others to profit from but also to enter into this market itself and gain larger margins.

3. Reduce unit cost of delivery of service in rural areas by adopting the emerging indigenous wireless technologies.
4. Tap the incremental demand of postal services arising from increasing rural income.
5. Collaborate with private sector companies where possible to exploit new areas.

Overall, there appears to be significant potential for India Post to enter new areas as part of the strategy to exploit its core strengths. New areas could include financial services, information access, e-government, e-commerce, pension and insurance products, and microfinance. This section considers the details for several of these potential areas.

3.1 Financial Services and Intermediation

The underlying theme should be 'collaborate rather than compete' as India Post develops relationships with other financial intermediaries and institutions. India Post brings to such relationships an outstanding distribution channel suitable for a variety of financial and non-financial products and information. Partner institutions would offer strengths in products, processes, and technology. Potential partners (and India Post is already allied with some of them) include commercial banks, rural finance institutions, pension funds, insurance companies, capital market intermediaries, stock brokers, and mutual funds (Kochar, 2002). If the existing infrastructure and capacities of India Post can be leveraged suitably, this strategy could bring significant improvements in the financial state of the postal service.

With electronic interconnection, post office banks will be able to provide a new range of financial services. India Post will be able to offer 'anytime/anywhere' banking to new segments of society. Popular saving services like recurring deposits, daily savings, and term deposits can be exploited. To make them more attractive, doorstep collection is required. The postman/woman, in the course of his/her daily route, can be used for this purpose. Such schemes are already being exploited by institutions like KBSLAB (Krishna Bhima Samruddhi Local Area Bank) in Karnataka and Andhra Pradesh, states in southern India. KBSLAB has saving deposits of Rs 10 million with over 4,000 depositors and outstanding loans of Rs 30 million. Using postmen/women as delivery agents for banking services has several advantages. They have a good understanding of the area. They have a good rapport with the local citizens. They go to almost all villages in the area everyday. And they are already known and respected. Unlike in some countries, the security of the postman/woman is not an issue, for he or she is unlikely to be robbed. In India, the postman/woman is not perceived as a disciplining representative of government, but rather as a service agent.

Extension of India Post into micro-finance also appears feasible provided certain basic tenets are followed (Thomas, 2002; Mahajan 2002). Loan origination, appraisal, documentation, lending and collection must follow a fixed schedule. To have better control the same person should do the appraisal, disbursement, and collection. Postmen/women can do the loan disbursement and repayment collection without much training, but some initial training will be needed with respect to the initial appraisal. Since they are employed only part-time in rural areas, the main concern is whether they will have the time to provide such services in addition to their regular job.

Pension and insurance products constitute another significant opportunity. India Post currently provides the facility of disbursing the Provident Fund[2] to retiring defense personnel, but several unexploited domains, such as insurance, are also coming within its ambit. Indeed, in several countries, the public postal operator already offers insurance services. At present India Post also provides life insurance coverage to clients, based upon their interest and choice. It has already done business for a sum assured of US$1.4 billion, and the portfolio looks promising for the future.

3.2 Information Access

Several countries, including some in the South Asia region, are well advanced in establishing Internet access through post offices. The South African public information terminal is a good example. Customers are provided access to the Internet and free e-mail accounts. In this manner they are given better access to information and quicker communications. The main problem lies in the initial amount of capital investment which must be funded by government. Another potential problem is that poorly motivated postal employees may not provide adequate maintenance for the system.

India Post is already offering an innovative rural service, using the rural postal network to provide a mobile public call office facility at the doorstep of consumers. This service uses wireless in local loop technology. It can do more. For instance, it can partner with initiatives such as the '*e-choupal*'[3] operated by ITC, a giant Indian agri-business firm and network of Internet kiosks in Tamil Nadu, a state in the southeastern region of India.

E-choupal is basically a program to allow farmers to get real-time information about agricultural markets despite their distance from the *mandis* (wholesale marketing yards). *E-choupal* has established computers and Internet access in key rural areas where the farmers can directly negotiate the sale of their produce with wholesale buyers, eliminating the need for market middlemen. The personal computers and Internet access at these centers enable farmers to obtain information on *mandi* prices and good farming practices and to place orders for agricultural inputs such as seeds and fertilizers. These services help farmers improve the quality of produce and realize a better price. In the village, the *e-choupal* kiosk is run by a *sanchalak*, a trained farmer who is initiated in Internet service provision by ITC. The computer housed in a farmer's house is linked to the Internet via phone lines or VSAT connection and serves an average of 600 farmers in 10 surrounding villages within about a 5 kilometer radius. In the Tamil Nadu experiments, in addition to agricultural services, the Internet kiosks also act like an Internet café, providing e-mail and web surfing, and crucially, tele-medical facilities and e-governance.

Due to the *e-choupal* services, farmers have seen a rise in their income levels because of increased yields, improvement in quality of output, and a fall in transaction costs. Even small farmers have gained. Now the *e-choupal* needs to be generalized and scaled up, so that it does not serve the interest of just one buyer of agri-business, but the interests of many producer farmers. Such a scaling up is possible for India Post.

3.3 E-government

If the post offices are connected via computers – for which India Post has made budget provisions recently – there is the potential to utilize the system to help expand e-government services. E-government has proved to be valuable in promoting transparency and vigilance among citizens and in reducing corruption. The post office, with its increasingly interconnected network, can be instrumental in this effort. The program can succeed through public–private partnerships (PPPs) and extensive training of the postal staff.

One of the significant e-government projects in India is the Bhumi project that is computerizing land records in Karnataka, a state in southern India. Through this initiative, farmers can get official records of their lands fairly easily and are released from the clutches of the village middlemen. Working closely with the banks, the project enables farmers to get loans instantly using their land as collateral while also helping banks by ensuring that the same collateral is not offered to multiple banks. The local village office of India Post can act as the Internet kiosk for the farmer to obtain the land records from the Revenue Department.

3.4 E-business and E-commerce

Participating in e-business and e-commerce can revolutionize the way the post offices are doing their current business. E-business has several applications that can be classified under two main headings: enhancement of *existing* services and introduction of *new* services (Jain, 2002).

If connected via Internet or Intranet, post offices will be able to offer a range of new or enhanced communication services. The list begins with e-mail and hybrid mail services. Hybrid mail is essentially a service in which e-mail is printed and delivered by India Post as a hard copy. Although this service is already in operation, at present India Post sees it as a failure, due to the high cost of the service (25 cents a page, compared to the same charge a private/Internet café levies for half an hour of surfing) and incomplete provision of infrastructure, for example, absence of printers and last-mile connectivity of personal computers to servers which are located far away. Similarly, money orders are also sent electronically. Here, India Post is experiencing teething problems in quickly distributing the large amounts of cash to the village postman/woman and maintaining the inventory levels of cash at the last-mile post office. Access to electronic networks will also permit real-time tracking of postal parcels, a feature that will enhance customer satisfaction and increase the popularity of parcel post. With its unique infrastructure and economies of scale, an electronically capable India Post will also be able to utilize its infrastructure to provide access and delivery for other couriers, leveraging the scope of its network. At the same time, India Post will be able to provide a range of e-government services, including: caste certification; marriage, birth, and death registration; and vehicle registration.

4. RESTRUCTURING OF INDIA POST

The driving force in any postal reform effort should be to unlock and utilize the immense financial assets of the postal system, which is usually conceived of as a large network of post offices and delivery systems. Apart from the basic job of collection and distribution of posts, however, India Post also provides the service of savings bank.

Reeling under deficits, surplus staff in rural areas, and a general employment freeze, India Post is undergoing a crisis of labor shortages in cities where the volume of work has increased hugely. The Supreme Court rejected a demand by India Post requiring multi-store apartment builders to provide mail boxes for all occupants on the ground floor. As a result, the postman/woman has to deliver the mail to every floor at every office. It perforce had to resort to outsourcing some of its delivery. The experience has not been good. The excessive workload in large cities has led to huge masses of mail articles being simply dumped, both by departmental staff and by outsource agents. This crisis has prompted a soul searching within India Post where PPPs and franchising are being looked at as serious options. So far, franchising activities other than delivery (which India Post holds dear to its heart) have been tried, but there are no takers. The private sector is only interested in delivery. Many existing post offices could be converted to a franchisee mode over time if labor is willing.

In order to satisfy the demands of the USO, India Post is expected to increase the scope of its activities, especially in the rural areas. However, since India Post already has too many offices with too little mail, and since many offices in rural areas are manned by part-time staff, it stands to reason that future expansion should be accomplished here on a franchisee basis. But this requires financial viability at the rural post office level, which is where the Internet kiosk model promises some potential.

The post offices throughout the country form the network backbone of the India Post. The transfer of mail and parcels between these post offices forms a natural monopoly because of the existence of economies of scale. On the other hand, the delivery of mail, parcels and money orders is an area where competition can be encouraged by having private sector franchisees. At the same time, economies of scope could also be exploited by making the post office area multifunctional. Accordingly, distribution of the mail should be open to private courier services. Competition arising from the private sector will lead to professionalism, innovation, and a more progressive attitude in the working staff. However, in order to allow competition, the labor union needs to be persuaded. It is also possible to visualize the delivery department of India Post and its authorized private sector franchisees as a PPP. Once the delivery department is given sufficient autonomy to make its own decisions in a decentralized manner, based on considerations of profitability, it should be allowed to form its own policy regarding the distribution of mail to the people. An autonomous delivery department should make its own decisions regarding the usage of its manpower, transport resources, interaction with other private firms, and new programs for profit. The inter-post office transfer of mail and articles which forms part of the natural monopoly could be subjected to a regulated price, and the delivery segments could be classified into two groups, namely, USO products and market products. The USO products, such as ordinary mail, would be delivered at government-specified prices, with government providing the required subsidy. The remaining market products, such as Speed Post, could be left to the competitive market.

The next step is to decide how to integrate the banking and e-services functions. The banking and services departments, including insurance, could be located in the same post office as the network and delivery departments, but with a separate set of accounts and preferably treated as a separate profit center. Alternatively, the banking and insurance departments could be privatized and allowed to become independent ventures. A third possibility is that they could work under the aegis of government and be considered as an extended USO function. Since India has a huge rural sector, the postal banking services should preferably stay in the public sector.

5. CONCLUSION

India Post presents an interesting mixture of issues. It is a public service providing socially necessary, low-priced services; at the same time, it is an inefficient operator, unable to compete in the commercial sector. Without its banking and insurance operations, India Post's deficit would increase from US$300 million to more than US$850 million. Both the government and India Post are deeply conscious of the deficit, and India Post is making efforts to enter new commercial areas as well as delegating responsibility to regional heads to readjust their labor portfolios. However, a number of obstacles stand in the way of improving India Post's efficiency. Both management and staff are firmly opposed to privatization. Thus, although restructuring and partial privatization in the form of franchising and PPPs are options worthy of exploration, unless the incentives facing labor and management are changed significantly, little progress will be made. India Post is a case where reform has great potential. Transforming this potential into actual effective reform remains a major challenge.

NOTES

* With research assistance from Gangopadhyaya, winter intern. Valuable inputs from Ms Meera Datta, Chief Postmaster General, Karnataka and Ms B.P. Sridevi, Director, India Post.

1. All monetary figures are expressed in US dollars. The exchange rate used for conversion is 1 US dollar equals 40 Indian rupees.
2. The Provident Fund is a statutory savings fund created for employees who do not receive a pension. Part of the saving is contributed by the employee and part is contributed by the employer. The delivery of the Provident Fund is outsourced to post offices because of the higher cost of delivery by the government itself!
3. '*Choupal*' metaphorically refers to a mat where all farmers sit and learn to browse through the Internet to ascertain prices in various markets.

REFERENCES

Bell, Simon (2002), 'Transforming a Postal Infrastructure to Deliver Modern Information and Financial Services', Report and Recommendation, India Post 2010: Conference on harnessing the outreach infrastructure of India's Postal Network, 12 and 13 November, New Delhi.

India Post (2007), *Annual Report 2007*, New Delhi.

Jain, Rajesh (2002), 'E-Business Applications for India Post', Report and Recommendation, India Post 2010: Conference on harnessing the outreach infrastructure of India's Postal Network, 12 and 13 November, New Delhi.

Kochar, Chanda (2002), 'Financial Intermediation: Access and Expansion', Report and Recommendation, India Post 2010: Conference on harnessing the outreach infrastructure of India's Postal Network, 12 and 13 November, New Delhi.

Mahajan, Vijay (2002), 'Using the India Post Network for Micro Finance Services', Report and Recommendation, India Post 2010: Conference on harnessing the outreach infrastructure of India's Postal Network, 12 and 13 November, New Delhi.

Nishimizu, Meiko (2002), 'Inaugural address', Conference on harnessing the outreach infrastructure of India's Postal Network, 12 and 13 November, New Delhi.
Ranganathan, V. (2005), 'The challenges of reform for the Indian postal services', *Economic and Political Weekly*, 17 September, 4121–5.
Sarma, E.A.S. (2002), 'Postal Reforms in the India Context', Report and Recommendation, India Post 2010: Conference on harnessing the outreach infrastructure of India's Postal Network, 12 and 13 November, New Delhi.
Thomas, Susan (2002), 'A Role for India Post in Agricultural Markets', Report and Recommendation, India Post 2010: Conference on harnessing the outreach infrastructure of India's Postal Network, 12 and 13 November, New Delhi.

25. Postal reform in Israel*

Avi Azuz,[†] Udi Nisan[‡] and Eli Sagi[§]

1. INTRODUCTION

Over the past two decades the Israeli postal market has undergone wide-ranging reform. The process began with the establishment of the Israeli Postal Authority (IPA) in 1987 and culminated in 2006–07 with the creation of the Israeli Postal Company (IPC), the opening of the bulk-mail market to competition, the introduction of a new set of tariffs (in November 2007) and the granting of a new license to the IPC (in January 2008), thus creating a regulatory framework and introducing additional flexibility in the introduction of new products.

The reform in the Israeli postal sector has been part of an economy-wide process, which started in the mid-1980s. From the early days of the Israeli statehood until that time, its economy was characterized by heavy government involvement in almost all dimensions of economic activities. The economy consequently created a huge budget deficit (reaching almost 15 percent of GDP in the early 1980s) and experienced an accelerating inflation that culminated at 10–15 percent per month! A dramatic, very successful, Stabilization Plan was applied that eliminated almost completely the problem of inflation. As part of this plan, the government began withdrawing from its excessive involvement in the economy, and the reform process accelerated.

The purpose of this chapter is to describe the reform process in the postal industry and the debates that accompanied it, with emphasis on the unique traits of the Israeli market.

In Section 2, we provide a snapshot characterization of the postal sector with a focus on attributes that tend to be Israeli specific. This section also follows the timeline of the reform process with emphasis on the unusual criterion of the gradual opening of the bulk-mail submarket to competition. Section 3 is devoted to the role of pricing in the reform process. The government, which recognized the fundamental role of pricing in the introduction of competition, appointed a committee of experts (the Sagi Committee[1]) to recommend a new set of tariffs for the universal service provider (USP). In addition, we discuss the imminent tension between the need to preserve the USO and thus secure the financial viability of its sole provider (that is, the IPC) on the one hand and the wish to create a pro-competition environment on the other. As well as the issue of preventing cross-subsidization, two controversial core pricing issues will be raised: access to local distribution centers (LDCs) and price flexibility. Section 4 will present a view of the future in an attempt to evaluate the course of future developments. In particular, the Israeli

† Ministry of Communication.
‡ Government Companies Authority.
§ Berglas School of Economics, Tel Aviv University.

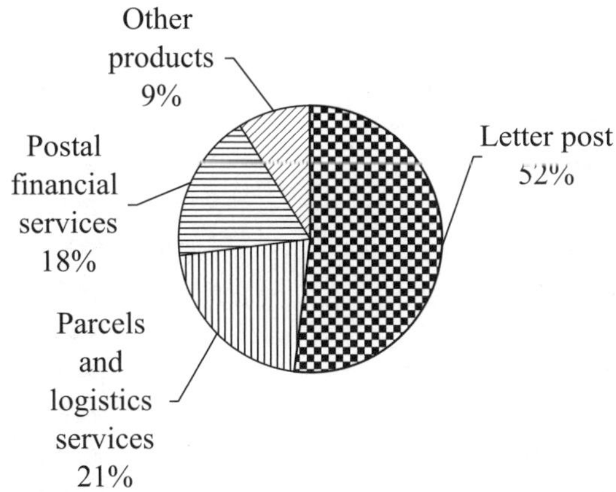

Source: Universal Postal Union (UPU) data.

Figure 25.1 IPA sources of income, 2006 (% of total)

government is considering the privatization of the IPC and the transformation of the Postal Bank into a commercial bank.

2. BACKGROUND

Israel can be classified as a small to medium-sized economy with a population of 7.2 million (as of October 2007) consisting of approximately 2 million households, and a GDP of $184 billion ($26,500 per capita in 2006).[2] Its postal industry generates annual revenues of some $800 million[3] (2006) from the delivery of some 710 million postal items (about 100 per inhabitant). The dominant firm in the market is the government-owned IPC, since it is the only USP and operates in every submarket.

The IPC employs approximately 6,500 people, of whom 2,000 are subcontracted. About 40 percent of the IPC's workforce are postmen/women and about one-third man the postal counters. The company has a network of 679 branches, of which 60 percent are franchises. In 2006, IPC revenues totaled $430 million. Figure 25.1 shows that letters accounted for about half of the revenues and the Postal Bank, which utilizes the nationwide network of postal branches, accounted for another 20 percent. International comparison puts Israel in a rather low position regarding the use of postal services and in a high position regarding certain density indicators, such as the number of inhabitants per postal employee and per postal branch and its tariffs are considerably lower than those in many comparable countries (see Figures 25.2 and 25.3).

2.1 Timeline

Postal services in Israel (Box 25.1) were originally provided by a branch of the government – the Ministry of Postal Services (the name was later changed to the Ministry of Communication – MOC). During the 1950s, several taxi companies were granted

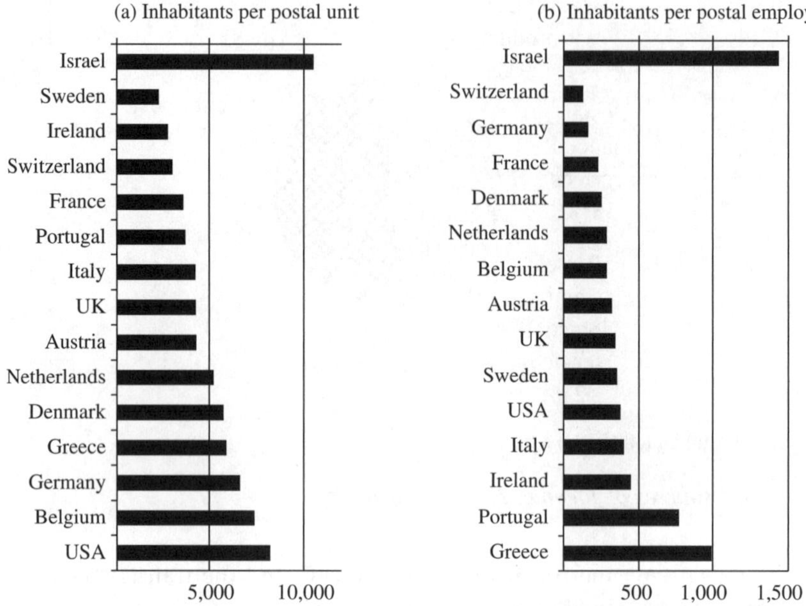

Source: IPC Statistical Yearbook 2006.

Figure 25.2 Number of inhabitants per postal unit/employee

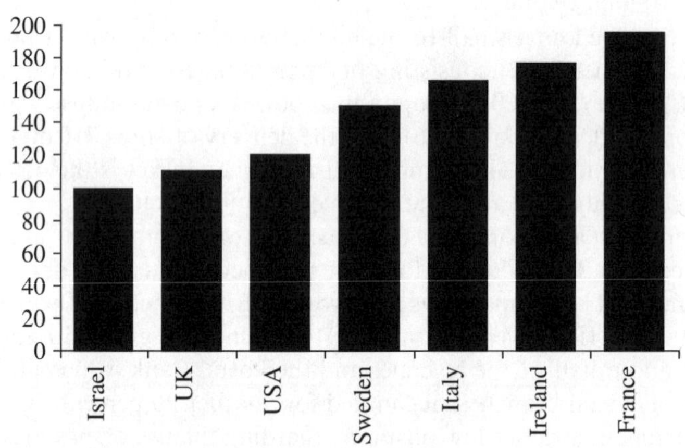

Source: IPC Statistical Yearbook 2006.

Figure 25.3 Price of regular mail item, international comparison 2006 (Israel=100)

authorization to carry goods on their routes; other than that the market was controlled by the government. In general, postal services were conservative in nature and did not keep up with technological innovations and changing market conditions. The Herzog Committee (1973) was appointed to address these issues and recommended that postal services be separated from telecom services and that the responsibility for postal service be transferred from the MOC to an independent authority. Some 11 years after the Herzog Committee presented its recommendations, the responsibility for providing postal services was transferred to the IPA, which was controlled by the MOC. During the 1970s, the MOC authorized limited competition in the domestic courier services and allowed a few transportation companies to use their vehicles for this purpose.

BOX 25.1 THE DEVELOPMENT OF THE POSTAL MARKET IN ISRAEL: TIMELINE

1948	Establishment of the State of Israel Establishment of the Ministry of Postal Services Telecom and postal services are nationalized
1971	Name changed to the Ministry of Communication
1973	Herzog Committee
1976	Authorization to provide postal services Small number of companies (mainly taxi companies) are granted authorization to provide courier services
1986	IPA law creates monopoly on all letters weighing less than 500 grams
1987	Establishment of the IPA MOC becomes the regulator of the postal market*
1999	Brodet Committee
2001	First (unauthorized) competitor in the bulk-mail segment (using a permit for courier services)
2003	Segment for mail priced above 4.5 times the 'basic stamp' (including international mail and registered mail) is opened to competition McKinsey Report
2006	Partial opening of the bulk-mail market to competition Establishment of the IPC Sagi Committee Report
2007	Full opening of the bulk-mail market to competition Granting of license to the IPC

Note: * Telecom activities were separated from the MOC in 1984, from which point the MOC became only the regulator of the telecom market.

The IPA Law (1986) defined the reserved mail market as including all mail items weighing less than 500 grams, thus opening up the way for courier services to provide delivery for items weighing more than that. In fact, courier companies started delivering items of all weights – the MOC did not react and the entire courier market was de facto opened up to competition.

The Brodet Committee (1999) was appointed by the Minister of Communication and the Minister of Finance with the objectives, among others, of recommending an optimal market structure and set of tariffs and ways to introduce competition and expand the scope of postal services. The committee made the following recommendations: the full opening of the Israeli postal market to competition; the transformation of the IPA into a government-owned company; and separating the company into a mail delivery company and a postal branch company. Under considerable political pressure, the report was not in fact adopted by the government. Nevertheless, it was the catalyst for many of the measures later implemented by the government in the postal market.

In March 2001, a private company began providing mail delivery services to large bulk-mail customers. The company's defiant act, encouraged by the recommendations of the Brodet Report, relied on an old and questionable authorization to provide postal services granted to it in 1978 by the Minister of Communication. The government ordered the company to cease all mail delivery activities and as a result the company appealed to the Supreme Court. The legal debate lasted for several years and in the meanwhile a status quo was maintained: the company continued its activity without expanding its volume.

The Brodet Committee influenced the postal liberalization process even though its recommendations were not formally adopted. First, the report instigated the introduction of competition in the delivery of all mail items priced higher than 4.5 times the 'basic stamp' (in January 2003). Second, in March 2003, the government commissioned another report, from McKinsey & Co. consulting company, to design a 'road map' for the optimal method of opening the postal market to competition. In accordance with the McKinsey Report, the government decided to liberalize the market in four steps: first, to transform the IPA into a government-owned company; second, to open the postal market to competition; third, to create a new set of tariffs; and fourth, to modify regulatory practices. As a result, a committee of experts (the Sagi Committee) was appointed in November 2004 to recommend a new set of tariffs for IPC services.

In March 2006, the IPA was transformed into the IPC and in September of that same year the Sagi Report on setting new tariffs was submitted. The report was adopted six months later and the tariffs came into effect 13 months later, in November 2007. On January 3, 2008, following a drafting process of over two years, a license to the IPC was finally granted. The license determined the regulatory framework in which the company operates in terms of the definition of universal service and the relationship between the regulator and the Company. Moreover, the license defined a framework for the addition of new and even non-postal services.

Today, the bulk-mail segment is entirely open to competition and in accordance with the recommendations of the McKinsey Report, the non-bulk-mail segment will be opened to competition in July 2009.

2.2 Universal Service Obligation (USO)

Israel is a small country in geographical terms with an area of 22 thousand square kilometers. About half of the territory is unpopulated (the Negev desert in the southern part of the country). More than half of its 7.2 million inhabitants live in the two metropolitan areas of Tel Aviv[4] and Haifa, which account for only 11 percent of the country's total area. So, from a delivery network point of view it is a rather small and dense country.

As mentioned, postal services in Israel were provided by the government during the 1948–87 period, and following that by the IPA until 2006. During this period, postal services were provided without a legally binding USO definition. Since it was both the service provider and the regulator, the government did not feel compelled to guarantee quality of

Table 25.1 USO definitions in Israel – selected items

Item	Definition
Location of delivery	Residence/office
Exceptions for location of delivery	LDC for a given list. Distance between an LDC and a served household must not exceed 500 meters
Mail collection	At least once a day and no less than 5 times a week
Postal branches	To be open at least 5 days a week
Mailboxes	New mailboxes will be deployed such the distance between a mailbox and a served household does not exceed 1,500 meters
Delivery of regular domestic mail (up to 2 kg) and domestic registered mail	87 % – within 2 business days 96 % – within 3 business days 100 % – within 4 business days
Delivery of a domestic package (up to 20 kg)	50 % – within 3 business days 87 % – within 4 business days 96 % – within 5 business days 100 % – within 7 business days

service through laws and regulations. Nonetheless, according to the McKinsey Report (2003) and Einhorn and Spiegel (2006), the quality of postal service in Israel was on a par with that in other developed countries.

Only during the process of transforming the IPA into the IPC did the need arise for a proper legal definition of a USO. The General License for the Israeli Postal Company Ltd. for the provision of postal services, monetary services on behalf of the subsidiary company, and additional services, was granted, following lengthy public debate, on January 3, 2008. The license finally provided a guarantee of the provision and quality of specific postal services in Israel (Table 25.1).

The terms of the license take into account the financial volatility of the IPA during the 2001–04 period and public sector labor agreements. Consequently, the definition of USO reflects the current level of service with the following exceptions: the frequency of mail distribution is reduced from six days to five; postal branches are permitted to be open only five days a week;[5] and the IPC is allowed to continue operating the existing LDCs[6] (under some restrictions) although the deployment of new ones is subject to a set of rules appended to the license.

2.3 Local Distribution Centers

Mail delivery in Israel, as in other countries, is not necessarily to the recipient's home/office address. Other methods, which are usually aimed at solving logistical difficulties, include mobile post offices, rented PO boxes and delivery to a postal branch. Israel employs yet another, and rather unique, method: local distribution centers. LDCs were originally created in order to provide adequate service to localities with no street names, challenging topography or low population density. In these areas, mail recipients must collect their mail at an LDC (which can sometimes be more than 500 meters from their home) rather than receiving it at their own address.

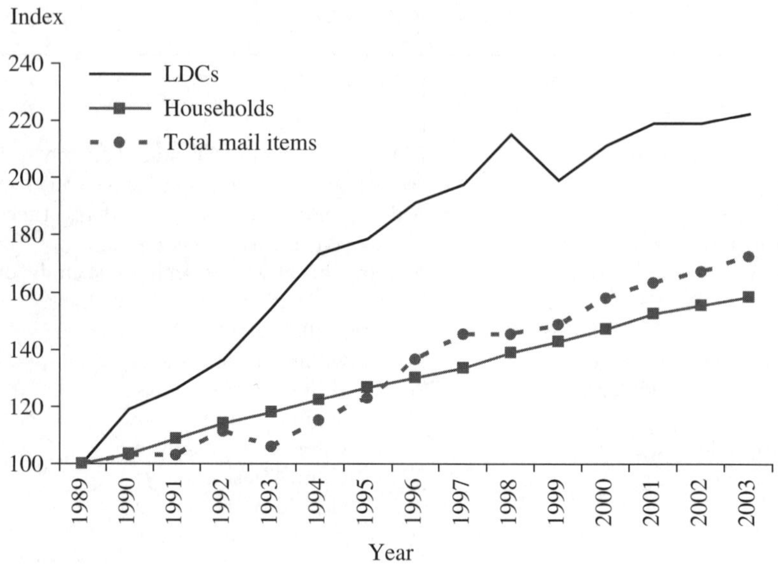

Source: IPA Statistical Yearbooks 1989–2004.

Figure 25.4 Growth of local distribution centers (indices, 1989=100)

A typical LDC is a concrete structure about 4 square meters in size. The structure contains a grid of 450 metal mailboxes. The structure has one locked entrance for the use of the mailman/woman, while each customer has access to his/her own locked mailbox from the outside. The IPC has deployed these structures in city centers or in shopping malls and usually clusters a few structures together, thus creating an LDC with more than 1,000 mailboxes. Another type of LDC is a grid of mailboxes installed in an outward-facing wall of a postal branch, with access for the mailman/woman from the inside and customer access from the outside.

The use of this delivery method has expanded significantly during the 1990s, as is evident from Figure 25.4. One reason for this was the influx of about one million immigrants from the former USSR during the 1990s, which increased Israel's population by nearly 20 percent.[7] In order to meet this challenge, the IPA relaxed the criteria for opening new LDCs and expanded their deployment throughout the country.

Currently, as much as 16 percent of mail items handled by the IPC are delivered to LDCs. There is wide support for this method among the municipalities. They consider LDCs to be a way of communicating with their constituency (through billboards put up next to them) and of encouraging local small businesses (by forcing the IPC to locate the LDCs in business centers and shopping malls). The general public (that is, the mail recipients) are not part of this decision-making process and are not even consulted on the matter.

The future of LDCs has become a prominent issue at this stage of the reform. Two main questions arise in this respect. First, does this phenomenon conform to universal service, or is it a lower-quality service that should not be extended beyond its current level? Second, if this practice continues, should new entrants be allowed to access this infrastructure? If so, under what terms and what are the resulting pricing implications? This question is of great importance as this delivery method is substantially cheaper than regular delivery (to the recipient's home/office address).

As to the first question, the license which was issued to IPC permits distribution of mail in LDCs. However, regarding additional LDCs in the future, after considerable debate, the MOC set strict criteria for opening a new LDC, which is then still subject to MOC approval.

The second question was dealt with in detail by the Sagi Committee. The Committee concluded that the centers should be accessible to all interested permit holders, subject to access fees, the structure of which was also recommended by the Committee. As for the IPC's own tariffs, the Committee set up differential tariffs for mail items delivered to LDCs versus full address delivery (see Section 3 below for details).

2.4 Opening of the Bulk-mail Segment to Competition

McKinsey's 'road map' recommended gradual opening of the bulk-mail segment to competition, as had been done in a number of countries. However, the criteria to be used in this process were rather unusual. Rather than the commonly-used criteria of weight or price or other criteria such as distance, sending size and volume, the report suggested that consumer type be used as the criterion. The McKinsey Report suggested opening the bulk-mail segment to competition in three stages. During the first stage, which was to last two years, all bulk-mail customers (with the exception of the government and its agencies, banks, insurance companies and health maintenance organizations (HMOs) would be permitted to use the services of competitors. During the second stage, which would also last two years, all customers would be free to choose their mail service provider. The main justification for this unusual criterion was the fact that most items being delivered in the bulk-mail segment are within the low-weight, low-price bracket, which means that such a constraint would not be effective. In the third stage, the limits on volume for bulk mail would be further relaxed, thus opening all business mail (which accounts for 70 percent of total mail volume) to competition.

3. TARIFFS AS A KEY FACTOR IN THE REFORM[8]

Among its other tasks, the Sagi Committee was instructed to design a set of tariffs that would reflect the costs of the various postal services and would achieve the seemingly conflicting goals of the reform: on the one hand, to promote the development of competition and overall economic efficiency, and on the other, to ensure both the provision of universal service in the future and the financial stability of the IPC, currently (and for the foreseeable future) the only USP provider. The Committee began its work in November 2004 and submitted its final report in September 2006. The report was adopted in full by the Minister of Communication and the Minister of Finance in March 2007, despite objections raised (primarily from the IPC). Bylaws were enacted and the new tariffs went into effect as of November 1, 2007.

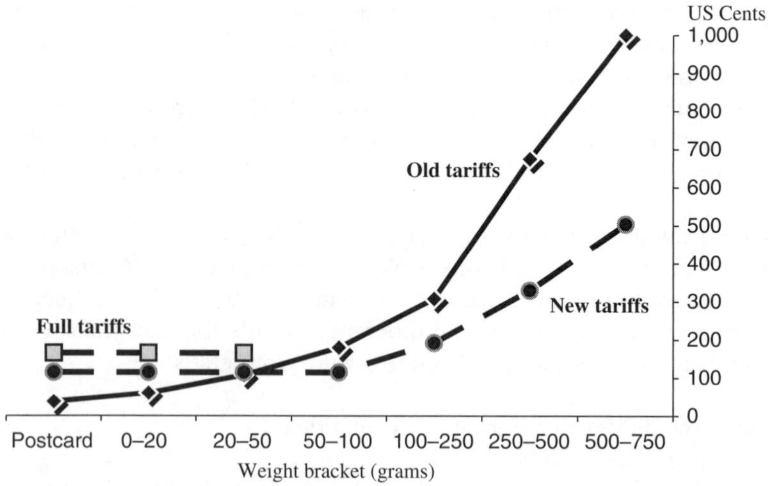

Source: Sagi Committee Report.

Figure 25.5 Tariffs for outgoing single-piece mail to the USA (US cents)

3.1 Costing Methodology and Principles

The committee was fortunate to have at its disposal very detailed datasets on both the 'aggregate' and 'high-resolution service-specific' levels. The aggregate data included: recent financial reports;[9] pro-forma forecasts;[10] and forecast loss of market share.[11] The high-resolution service-specific data included a very detailed matrix of cost elements for each service; a matrix of postmen's/women's time allocation per activity; and a vector of the standardized time input by tellers per postal counter activity.[12] Tariffs were calculated based on the high-resolution data, with adjustments viewed by the Committee to be appropriate, including a 'normative' rate of return on working capital per service.[13] The resulting tariffs were combined with the forecast volume of each service in order to obtain a predicted financial report that would make it possible to assess the effect of the tariffs on the IPC's financial stability. In designing the set of tariffs, the Committee had in mind to encourage competition, primarily by adopting a cost-based approach, and to promote efficiency, primarily by identifying and eliminating existing distortions.

3.2 Pro-competition Pricing

The datasets available to the Committee made it possible to estimate the cost for each service using the inputs specific to that service along the chain of value. A great deal of effort was devoted to avoiding cross-subsidization, especially between single-piece and bulk mail and across weight brackets. An important means for achieving this was to allocate fixed costs to all services, including those open to competition.[14]

For example, consider international outgoing mail. As can be seen in Figure 25.5 the new tariffs, which are cost based plus a profit margin, were significantly higher than the old ones (however, the old tariffs for items in the high-weight brackets were much higher than cost).[15]

Most international outgoing mail items are in the lowest weight brackets (less than 100 grams). Clearly, the old tariffs in this segment of the market, which was fully opened to competition a few years ago (January 2003), were not conducive to promoting competition.

3.3 Efficiency Pricing

The Committee identified a large number of distorting elements in the old tariff system which reduced efficiency in all its various forms: X-efficiency, business efficiency and economy-wide efficiency. In the bulk-mail segment, a system of volume discounts on the old tariffs, which reflected shipment size (monthly aggregated volume per weight bracket), yielded a list of some 80 different tariffs, with very little relation to cost. This led to unjustified and inefficient consolidation arbitrage activity, which had become a common practice and, among other things, resulted in too many weight brackets for bulk mail, especially at the lower end of the scale. This caused the excessive need for the public to visit postal counters, thus wasting their time and imposing extra costs on the IPC. Reducing the number of weight brackets at the lower end of the scale is also efficient in the sense that it is cost based. The Committee concluded that operational cost differences among these brackets were too low to justify different tariffs. As a matter of fact, the conclusion that the weight of a postal item is an insignificant cost factor is as old as the Queen Victoria Penny Black itself. Crew and Kleindorfer (1991, p. 3) quote from the 1837 pamphlet written by Sir Rowland Hill, the founding father of modern postal services, who concluded, based on a cost analysis, that 'the expenses of . . . delivery are not affected by the weight of each letter'.

In the case of single-piece mail, the number of brackets was reduced from six to four (in the range of 0–500 grams), and in particular, the lightest-weight bracket, which accounts for the vast majority of volume in this category, was widened from 0–20 to 0–50 grams. Another part of the effort to reduce the importance of the weight factor in pricing and to improve overall efficiency was the recommendation to introduce size-based pricing in the next phase of the reform. This is similar to the 'pricing-in-proportion' (PiP) regime that was recently adopted by Royal Mail in Britain and is being introduced by New Zealand Mail in March 2008).[16]

The existence of numerous, and rather arbitrary, categories of volume discounts was another of the main sources of inefficiency in the bulk-mail segment. Two-thirds of these were eliminated in the new set of tariffs. Under the new regime, discounts are based on only one factor: the cumulative monetary value of a customer's shipments in each three-month period.

3.4 Tariff Flexibility

In the new era of competition, the IPC clearly needs some freedom of action in order to stay competitive, and price flexibility is a key means in this context. The international postal liberalization process has leaned more towards allowing USPs to exercise price flexibility, for example, through price-cap regulation, rather than imposing rigid price regimes that unduly restrict the flexibility of the USP. The rationale has been the desire to finance the USO and to ensure the financial stability of incumbent USPs. This approach has recently been reinforced in the European case, as the EU approaches the next stage of full market opening (FMO) in 2011–13. The PwC report recommends that 'Price flexibility for business products should be encouraged . . . at least for bulk mail'.[17] This is in spite of the potential counter-competitive effect it may have, as the report itself indicates: 'Price flexibility may raise concern over the exercise of predatory pricing by the USP against entrants'.[18] This is, however, a common approach. British and French national regulatory authorities (NRAs) impose limitations on the pricing practices of incumbent USPs as long as they enjoy a dominant market position, although they are allowed some flexibility relative to generic tariffs, subject to non-discrimination requirements in the treatment of their customers versus their competitors.

The pricing regime prescribed by the Sagi Committee is more rigid than in the British and French cases. All tariffs under regulation will change over time strictly according to an adjustment formula, which allows a uniform cross-service annual reduction of tariffs at a predetermined rate of 1.5 percent. This rate is based on a 'normative' cost-efficiency factor.[19] This reduction was part of a 'safety-net' granted to the IPC by the government.[20] In particular, the use of single-piece tariffs to make up for the effect of the loss in the IPC market share in other segments (mainly bulk mail) was disallowed. Not only are tariffs rigid, they are also, required to be transparent (and posted publicly), geographically uniform and non-discriminatory, in accordance with the pricing principles stated above.

One of the implications of the fixed tariff approach adopted is that the IPC may have difficulties bidding for public tenders. A few large-mail senders, such as public authorities, banks and telecommunication corporations, account for the vast majority of bulk-mail items. Since the market is now open to competition, they have begun to select their mail delivery providers by means of tenders. The IPC is at a disadvantage in this situation. Another implication of this policy is that the IPC, unlike its competitors, cannot offer all varieties of bundled services (for example, printing and delivery, as described below), which their competitors can. Moreover, the IPC's tariffs for all regulated services are required to be publicized, transparent, geographically uniform and non-discriminating among customers. To some extent, these asymmetries leave its hands tied in a competitive market, as is claimed by the IPC.

3.5 The Viability of the IPC

Apparently, the conflict between the position of the Sagi Committee and the more-prevalent view of allowing greater pricing flexibility to the USP (for example, in the EU as reflected in the PwC report cited above) reflects the unavoidable tension between the two objectives. The Sagi Committee, while being well aware of the prevalent approach and its rationale, took the opposite position based on a number of arguments, the most important of which focused on the financial viability of the IPC.

According to the Committee's evaluation, the IPC is financially viable in a fairly robust way, a conclusion that was arrived at using the Committee's computational model. According to the baseline scenario forecast, which assumes a gradual loss of market share in competitive segments that will reach 33 percent by 2010,[21] the IPC will remain profitable. Sensitivity analyses for worst-case scenarios suggest that the IPC will remain 'in the black' even if its share in these segments drops to 50 percent.

In fact, the authors expect the IPC's financial results to exceed those in the simulations (under each of the scenarios). Moreover, the profits forecast by the model assume a rate of cost reduction of 1.5 percent[22] (the 'normative efficiency factor'), on which the tariff reduction was based. The potential for cost streamlining certainly goes far beyond that, especially under a business-minded management. For example, unit labor costs could be reduced through the following measures: moving from six to five delivery days per week, as permitted by the IPC's license (the model's computations were based on six delivery days which existed until 2007); optimizing the use of physical capital (in particular, relocation of head offices, operation and sorting centers which are currently located on expensive real-estate); outsourcing (transportation, some delivery activities, franchising of postal agencies); and delivery subcontractors. This is not an exhaustive list, but merely indicates some of the potential efficiency-promoting measures that were not included in the simulations/models underlying the tariff recommendations. In particular, for any given market share, the IPC's profit potential should exceed the estimates of the model.

The model did assume that new products, especially non-postal services offered at postal counters, would generate further income. However, the magnitude of these additional revenues may have been underestimated in the model. Efficiency at postal counters can be enhanced by various measures, such as the use of stamp-vending machines, which will allow the enhancement of non-postal services (such as financial services, certain insurance products, submission of legal documents or tax forms)[23] offered at the counters. New products in non-competitive markets are not subject to price regulation and can be priced in a much less restrictive manner.

These initial assessments may nonetheless prove to be wrong and IPC loss of market share may turn out to be much more rapid and pervasive. However, there are several safeguards that guarantee the IPC's financial stability. Thus, if the IPC loses its monopolistic position in any of the segments (that is, falling below 50 percent of total items delivered), regulations would be lifted and the company would be granted full price flexibility. Even if it loses 'only' 40 percent of a certain segment, the regulator may consider granting some degree of price flexibility, as has been recommended by the Committee. In addition to the above arguments, it should be noted that the current tariff regime will be in force for only a limited period (until mid-2010), following which it will be subject to revision. If a serious threat to the stability of the IPC evolves during this period, the revision of tariffs will take that into account. To the extent that competition does develop, the IPC will, by definition, lose some business. In the case of a rapid deterioration during the next couple of years, the regulator will have the ability to intervene and to provide an emergency remedy, such as allowing price flexibility or relaxing one or other of the USO constraints. In conclusion, price flexibility *per se*, as important as it is, is just one type of business flexibility and it was the Committee's view that there is plenty of scope for effective business strategy beyond pricing.

3.6 The Likelihood of Competition

The rigid approach recommended by the Committee is indeed pro-competition biased. However, the market environment is asymmetric to begin with in favor of the IPC. In particular, it has been the (almost) sole operator for 60 years and enjoys the advantage of being the well-known and respected incumbent.[24] Therefore, some counter-asymmetric measures are justified, such as a rigid pricing regime, in order to achieve balance and to create a conducive environment for the development of competition.

In view of the limited size of the Israeli market, the best chances lie in the bulk-mail submarket, where 'downstream' segment (distribution) dominates. In addition, entrants can follow the example of the first competitor in this segment, who introduced a new type of service (a combination of upstream service and downstream hybrid access) through a joint venture between a carrier and a technologically advanced printing house. Their service provides 'one-stop shopping' to the customer who has to supply only the content of the mail and a list of addressees in digital format. The delivery firm takes care of printing the letters, sorting them by zip code and even the postman's/woman's route, and delivering them to LDCs or delivery centers. The price they charge covers the whole package.

There are two other main factors that will encourage the development of competition. The first is the USO, which will almost by definition encourage competition in the sense that new entrants are not subject to it. This allows them to cherry-pick the lucrative niches, such as high-density regions, business and commercial centers and LDCs (see below) where delivery costs are low. The latest entrant into the Israeli bulk-mail market, which began operating in 2007, has won a tender issued by Israel's largest landline telephone company. The tender involves the delivery of part of the company's mail (mostly invoices) in several high-density districts.[25] The second factor in the case of Israel is the relatively high cost of labor to the IPC, especially of postmen/women. These workers' contracts reflect public sector labor agreements, which are not binding on new entrants.

The Committee regarded the monitoring and regulating of possible predatory behavior by the IPC, which may attempt to fend off potential entrants, to be a difficult task. This could lead to a result in which no significant competition develops and it may be impossible to ascertain whether this should be attributed to the small size of the Israeli market or to the pricing practices of the IPC. These considerations, and the overall financial health of the IPC, led the Committee to conclude that in the Israeli case the approach of encouraging competition, with some (manageable) risk to the IPC's financial stability, was preferable to the approach that emphasizes the viability of the incumbent USP at the cost of reduced competition in the postal market.

3.7 Local Distribution Centers – Access and Pricing

LDCs, described above, tend to be an Israeli phenomenon. To the best of our knowledge, to the extent that in other countries similar methods of delivering mail exist, they account for much less than the Israeli fraction of (16 percent) of mail items. The use of this method has expanded significantly in Israel since the 1990s. The cost of LDCs is much lower than full delivery due to the elimination of the need for the postman/woman to 'walk the delivery route'. The cost saving is evident from the tariffs set for the two methods of delivery (see Table 25.2): 26 cents for regular delivery and less than half that for LDC. The 14-cent difference is accounted for by the cost of the 'postman's walk'.[26]

The Assets Agreement between the Ministry of Finance and the IPC recognizes the latter as the owner of the LDCs. This status raises the question of whether licensed new entrants have the right of access and if so, under what terms. Given the relatively low cost of this delivery method, entrants have an obvious interest in having the option of accessing the LDCs. The IPC, however, has most stringently refused, claiming that as the owner

Table 25.2 Tariffs by segment and delivery method (US cents per unit)*

Segment/delivery method	New	Old
Single piece	39 (0–50 gr)	38 (0–20 gr)
Bulk mail		
Average	24 (0–30 gr)	23 (0–15 gr)
To addressee	26	
To LDC	12	
Access fee to LDC	3	

Note: * According to an exchange rate of 4 NIS per USD.

Source: Sagi Committee Report.

of the LDCs it is not obligated to let others, especially their competitors, enter its property. Also, it argues, since these structures are unmanned, under free access of competitors, it would not be able to guarantee the safety of the contents of the mail boxes, including mail distributed by their own postmen/women. Finally, the IPC has claimed that if competitors are allowed access to LDCs, it will encourage the creation of firms specializing in delivering bulk-mail items to LDCs only. Such cherry-picking practices might trigger or accelerate a detrimental 'graveyard spiral' phenomenon.

The Committee's position on this issue has been very clear in stating that the denial of access to USP infrastructure, particularly a component that produces such significant reductions in cost, is inconsistent with the notion of opening the market to competition and goes against worldwide practices in this area.[27]

If IPC tariffs were identical for the delivery to LDCs and directly to the recipient's address, while entrants would be prevented from accessing LDCs, a de facto cross-subsidy would be created. Entrants would have to bear the full and higher cost of delivery to a recipient's address while the IPC would be charging a tariff based on an average of the cost of delivery to the recipient's address in high-density areas and the cheaper cost of LDC delivery in low-density areas. On the other hand, making LDCs available to entrants (as recommended by the Committee) while leaving the IPC with one tariff for both delivery methods, would mean that their price for LDC-addressed items would be 'artificially' higher than that of their competitors.

The solution offered by the Committee, which involves differential tariffs for the two methods of delivery, solves both difficulties. What facilitates the application of this approach is the fact that there exists a one-to-one correspondence between the type of delivery and the zip code. Thus, each LDC has its own zip code and each zip code refers to just one of the two types of delivery.[28] This price differential applies to bulk mail only since it cannot be expected that single-piece mailers will know what category their mail item belongs to. Thus, tariffs for single-piece mail will remain the same for both types of delivery.

Entrants will be charged an access fee in order to deliver to an LDC, which reflects the cost of the structure's maintenance and a return on the capital invested by the owner (the IPC). The Committee further recommended that if an entrant is denied access to an LDC, then the IPC will have to make the delivery itself for a charge equal to the fixed access fee, which will certainly be less than the cost to be incurred by the IPC. This was meant primarily as a disincentive for such unilateral action to be taken. Any bilateral agreement regarding the terms of access (including access fee) is obviously an acceptable, preferred, solution.

The IPC has so far stood fast in refusing to allow access to LDCs. The MOC has held a hearing on the issue and received the comments of all relevant parties. None of the competitors, apart from one, expressed interest in taking advantage of this option. The access to LDCs involves a number of operational difficulties, which were not yet fully resolved by mid-2008. As things stand now, it appears that few entrants will take advantage of the option of using the LDCs on their own. Others will prefer to hand over the mail addressed to LDCs to the IPC for a bilaterally negotiated fee that will probably fall somewhere between the IPC's tariff of 26 cents and the access fee of 3 cents.

4. LOOKING TO THE FUTURE

As described above, the process of opening up the postal market to competition has been largely completed during the last three years. This has involved the creation of a new structure of cost-based tariffs and the revamping of postal regulation through the approval of the IPC license. Two further 'reforms' are currently being considered by decision makers, which we describe under the headings 'market developments' and 'changes in the IPC's ownership structure'.

4.1 Continuing Market Developments

During 2006 to mid-2007 the market was characterized by tariffs uncertainty while waiting for the submission of the Sagi Committee Report and then for the ministers decision regarding its adoption. The IPC has taken advantage of this uncertainty in an attempt to retain its larger customers. This situation has to some extent slowed the development of competition and only at the end of 2007, when the new tariffs went into effect, did the rules of the game become clear. In January 2008, the IPC's license went into effect, thus allowing it to expand the services it offers. Recently, competition began to expand and a number of contracts between delivery companies and large bulk-mail senders were signed which provide an indication of things to come. One of the dominant companies in the printing industry signed agreements with a number of large companies to provide services that include the distribution of mail. How all of this will develop is yet to be seen.

The regulators are keeping a close eye on the development of competition in order to determine whether the IPC's claims regarding the new tariffs are justified. They also wish to ensure that competition does not develop at a pace that will threaten the provision of universal service. The evidence so far does not indicate that this is the case, although it is clearly too early to make an informed judgment. The lack of progress in hearings concerned with competitors' access to the LDCs has compromised the ability of competitors to provide nationwide service and has therefore hampered the development of competition in the area of bulk mail.

Despite the establishment of new tariffs and the revision of the IPC license, a number of tariff issues remain to be dealt with by the government in the near future. The Sagi

Committee has recommended that the transition to pricing by size be considered (similar to the PiP system used in Britain), which will more correctly reflect cost. The regulator has to prepare the grounds for the implementation of appropriate tariffs by setting the physical standardization of mailboxes and issue relevant directives.

According to the original plan for opening the postal market to competition, the next stage will involve the expansion of the definition of bulk mail through a reduction in the threshold volume level for mail items to be defined as such. The goal is to introduce competition into commercial mail of smaller volumes. Finally, according to the original plan, the possibility is to be considered of fully opening up single-piece mail to competition, although according to the conventional wisdom this will only be accomplished on paper and will not actually lead to the entry of new competitors.

4.2 Changes in the IPC's Ownership Structure

As part of the government's economic policy during the last 20 years to privatize government corporations, with emphasis on sectors in which there is a potential for competition, the government has twice decided during the last three years to privatize the IPC. The first decision was a general one that presented a plan which included the creation of a postal corporation, the opening of the market to competition, the revision of regulations and, in the final stage, the privatization of the company. The second decision involved a general plan for privatization. In the first stage of the plan, up to 49 percent of the company's shares would be issued on the Israeli local stock exchange. The second stage would involve the sale of the controlling stake. The Government Companies Authority (GCA, the governmental body that is responsible for the privatization of government companies in the Ministry of Finance), in coordination with the MOC, is drawing up a privatization plan. According to the plan, the first stage, which includes the issue of shares to the public, will be implemented in 2009 and, a year later, the controlling shares will also be sold. In parallel, talks will begin with the company's employees to guarantee their rights during this process.

As part of the standard privatization process, there are a number of significant issues that must be dealt with: regulation, services to the government, land rights, workers' rights, security issues and others. These processes are liable to be lengthy ones even in the case of a standard privatization. In the case of the IPC, some of the issues have been dealt with during the past three years in the context of the creation of the Company: land rights, workers' rights (still ongoing), the issuing of a new license and the adoption of the new set of tariffs. There remain two main areas to deal with. The first is workers' rights, including the final resolution of the IPC's pension obligations to its workers. The second is the determination of tariffs for financial services that the IPC provides through the Postal Bank.[29] In addition, prior to privatization, a decision will be made regarding the appropriate 'safety net' to ensure the continuation of universal service, taking into account the development of competition up until the date for privatization and as part of the negotiations with the workers.

One of the central issues in the discussions of the privatization process is related to the Postal Bank rather than the IPC itself. In contrast to a regular bank, the Postal Bank has two main functions: collection of payments on behalf of government bodies and various firms (primarily for services to the public) and their clearance and the management of demand deposits (without overdraft facilities) for, among others, low-income individuals or individuals who are unable to open an account at a commercial bank. The Postal Bank serves as a clearing house for payments totaling some $50 billion annually, which is equivalent to more than one-quarter of GNP. Another important characteristic of the Postal Bank is its broad geographic distribution in the form of about 700 branches. This is similar to the total number of branches of the four largest banks, which account for the vast majority of banking sector activity. There are clearly a number of competitive and other issues to be sorted out in determining the appropriate structure of the Postal Bank as part of a privatized IPC. Discussions on this point continue.

While there are many hurdles yet to overcome in the privatization process, it is important to see this as a further natural step of the postal reform process that has been described in this chapter. Indeed, providing the basic incentives for efficiency and innovation associated with a privatized commercial undertaking is viewed by both the IPC and its competitors as a reasonable next step in the reform process, assuming that issues of the USO, labor contracts and financial services can be worked out satisfactorily. In our view, given the progress to date in resolving tariff and safety-net issues, and the prospects of competition now unfolding, the process of preparing for privatization should be relatively brief and there is a high probability that the first stage of the plan mentioned above (that is, the issue of shares to the public or some other method of privatization to be decided on by the government) will indeed take place in 2009.

In summary, postal reform in Israel has gained significant momentum in recent years following the opening of the market to competition, the revamping of the tariff structure and the clear definition of the IPC's rights and obligations in its new license. This process continues and is likely to lead to a new and important stage with the privatization of the corporation, which is expected during the next two years. At the same time, the provision of additional services, such as the sale of insurance at postal branches and the provision of additional advisory services, is expected to generate a major change in the definition of a postal branch. The transformation of the Postal Bank into a commercial bank could constitute an additional stage in the changing role of the neighborhood post office in which one only buys stamps and sends letters. Much remains to be done, but the process is clearly proceeding.

NOTES

* The views expressed in this chapter, are the authors' own and do not represent the institutions of their affiliations.
1. The Committee for the Determination and Updating of Israeli Postal Corporation Tariffs. All three authors of this chapter served on the Committee.
2. In purchasing power parity terms, Central Bureau of Statistics, 2007.
3. Estimates of the Ministry of Communication.
4. Statistical Abstract of Israel 2007-No.58, Central Bureau of Statistics, http://gis.cbs.gov.il/shnaton58/density2007.pdf.
5. On the condition that some postal branches will remain open as backup on Fridays.
6. On LDCs – see detailed discussion below.
7. Half of which occurred in just two years.
8. This section deals primarily with bulk-mail tariffs, which was one of the last two sectors to be opened up to competition. The competition in this sector constitutes one of the major threats to the IPC's financial stability.

9. IPC.
10. Israeli Government Companies Authority.
11. McKinsey Report.
12. IPC.
13. The normative rate of return was calculated using the WACC (weighted average cost of capital) method.
14. The fully-allocated cost method, rather than the long-run incremental cost accounting method, was applied to all services.
15. Even then, the new tariffs for the low-weight bracket do not fully reflect cost. Charging for full cost immediately on the introduction of the new tariffs would have raised the price for the low-weight bracket for single-piece mail almost threefold. Thus, on social welfare grounds, the committee saw fit to refrain from such a sharp jump and recommended a more moderate rise for the period until 2010.
16. For details, go to the Royal Mail site at www.pricinginproportion.co.uk or the Postcomm site at http://www.psc.gov.uk/royal-mail-standards-and-prices/pricing-in-proportion.html. See also New Zealand Post website http://www.nzpost.co.nz/Cultures/en-NZ/AboutUs/PricingInProportion/.
17. PricewaterhouseCooper, 'The Impact on Universal Service of Full Market Accomplishment of the Postal Internal Market in 2009', Final Report submitted to the European Commission, May 2009, p. 194.
18. Ibid.
19. However, during the negotiations between the IPC and the MOC over its license and the implementation of the new tariff regime, the 'efficiency factor' was cut to only 0.5 percent.
20. This is difficult to understand since one would have expected the IPC to do the opposite in order to facilitate its ability to compete in the bulk-mail segments.
21. In the bulk-mail segment. Similar losses of market share were assumed for other competitive segments.
22. See note 20.
23. The government is now considering whether to grant the Postal Bank a commercial bank license (see discussion below).
24. During the Committee's hearings, entrants estimate that this is equivalent to a 10 percent price advantage.
25. Details of the volume and geographic coverage of the tender are not public knowledge.
26. The price gap also reflects a (small) difference in the return on capital.
27. The arguments regarding the possible difficulties in maintaining the security of mailbox contents were dismissed since there are simple, rather cheap, technical solutions available.
28. One should not expect any behavioral changes (by mailers) as a result of this price differential. Mail senders will probably not change the division of their mail between the two methods as a result of this price difference.
29. The Sagi Committee avoided the pricing of these services.

REFERENCES

Brodet Committee (1999), 'Analysis of the Postal Sector', Final Report, August, Jerusalem, Israel (in Hebrew).

Crew, Michael A. and Paul R. Kleindorfer (1991), 'Ronald Hill's contribution as an economist', in Crew and Kleindorfer (eds), *Competition and Innovation in Postal Services*, Boston, MA: Kluwer Academic, p. 3.

Einhorn, Talia and Yossi Spiegel (2006), 'Structural changes in the postal sector in Israel', *Economic Quarterly*, March, 116–65 (in Hebrew).

McKinsey & Co. (2003), 'Defining a Deregulation Strategy for the Israeli Postal Industry', study commissioned by the Israeli government.

PricewaterhouseCoopers (PwC) (2006), 'The Impact on Universal Service of the Full Market Accomplishment of the Postal Internal Market in 2009', study commissioned by the European Commission, Final Report submitted May.

Sagi Committee (2006), 'The Israeli Postal Company's Tariffs Setting and Updating Committee's Report', Final Report, September, Jerusalem, Israel (in Hebrew).

Index